Desmond Stewart spent the first twenty-four years of his life in England, culminating in his classical education at Oxford. He then spent many years in the Middle East where he acquired sufficient experience and knowledge to inspire a series of novels, translations from Arabic literature and factual accounts of the region he knows well.

Published in 1972, *The Middle East: Temple of Janus* received wide critical acclaim and his biography of Theodor Herzl, the founder of modern political Zionism, received special attention when it was first published in 1974.

He now lives in Norfolk, but spends much of his time in Cairo.

D0985996

Theodor Herzl

Artist and Politician

Desmond Stewart

Quartet Books

London Melbourne New York

Published by Quartet Books Limited 1981
A member of the Namara Group
27 Goodge Street, London W1P 1FD

First published in Great Britain by
Hamish Hamilton Limited, London, 1974

Grateful acknowledgment is made to the following for the use of
their copyright material:
The Herzl Press
Excerpts from *The Complete Diaries of Theodor Herzl*, ed. by
Raphael Patai, trans. by Harry Zohn, five volumes, New York,
1960
The Soncino Press, Ltd
Extracts from *The Pentateuch and Haftorahs; Hebrew Text, English
Translation and Commentary*, Dr. J. H. Hertz, London, 1960

ISBN 0 7043 3352 X

Manufactured in the U.S.A.

CONTENTS

MAPS & DIAGRAMS

FOREWORD

The ambition to write a new biography of Theodor Herzl came to me in 1970. I had then completed *The Temple of Janus*, a history of the Middle East from the opening of the Suez Canal to the present day. Of the major figures who affected my chosen century and region—from Khedive Ismail and Sultan Abdul Hamid to Atatürk and Nasser—Herzl seemed intrinsically the most interesting and the most mysterious. The man who had linked the Western notion of the state to Jewish messianic dreams was in himself as vague as a stained-glass ikon. This book is therefore an attempt, not to contribute to the polemics for or against the political movement with which he is identified, but to discover the human being who lived from 1860 to 1904 and who combined the qualities of dreamer and man of action to a unique degree.

A new biography, like a new map, must in some sense be a critique of its predecessors. But it would have been far harder to write my book without the previously published studies of Leon Kellner, Jacob de Haas, Josef Patai, Alex Bein, Josef Fraenkel and Israel Cohen. To my forerunners, dead or living, I therefore express my thanks, even if, in my text, I disagree with their dates, interpretations or conclusions. I acknowledge my further debts by cities. In Budapest Mr. George Makai not only gave me valuable clues to sources but extended to me the hospitality of his apartment. Mrs. Agi Scott and Dr. Alexander Scheiber of the Orthodox Jewish Seminary on different occasions escorted me to many of the buildings associated with Herzl's boyhood. In Vienna I was assisted in my research by Dr. I. Balic of the Österreichische Nationalbibliothek, by Mr. David Alpern of the Israelitische Kultusgemeinde Wien and by Dr. Fiegl, Oberarchivrat of the Amt der Niederösterreichischen Landesregierung. In Reichenau an der Rax, Herr Hans Spitzer of the Standesamt aided my inquiries into the circumstances of Herzl's marriage while Herr Michael Waissnix and his sister combined hospitality in their *Schloss* with detailed information about the Thalhof and Rudolfsvilla, the latter being the site of the Herzl wedding. Professor Heinrich Schnitzler (whom I thank for the photograph of Arthur Schnitzler, his father) and Mrs. Theresa Nickl helped me understand the Herzl-Naschauer milieu by supplementing the invaluable information already available in their edition of the correspondence between Arthur Schnitzler and Olga Waissnix; Mrs. Nickl's help in working out the intricate family relationships of the family into which Herzl married was invaluable. In Paris Count Eric Nemes helped me to understand the Habsburg background to Herzl's youth. From Spain Mme. Maxa Nordau wrote most helpfully about her memories of Herzl's children and their relationship with their family. In London I had the moving experience of attending divine service in the West London Synagogue with Asher and Renee Winegarten and of then welcoming the Sabbath in their house. Mr. Mark Braham wrote me over a hundred letters on points connected with Jewish life while Mr. Bruno Marmorstein, former Chairman of the Board of Governors, Jews' College, kindly consented to read chapters of my typescript. Dr. Margaret Clarke put at my disposal her perception of problems and her wide knowledge as to how to solve them; her skill as a translator was of great assistance in the interpretation of one or two of Herzl's early letters. Professor Walter Laqueur recommended certain texts which I might otherwise have ignored. Mr. Gerald Abrahams corresponded with me about *halacha*, the Jewish traditional law. Mr. N. M. Brilliant allowed me to read an unpublished paper on "Early British Zionism" by S. Sarna. The staff of the British Museum and the London Library showed their usual courtesy in helping my inquiries; to the British Museum I owe the map of the East African region proposed for Jewish settlement and gratefully acknowledge the permission of the Trustees to publish it. To the Soncino Press I am grateful for permission to quote from Dr. J. H. Hertz's edition of *The Pentateuch and Haftorahs* and to Mr. Alan Neame I extend similar gratitude for his permission, and that of his British publisher, Hodder & Stoughton Ltd., to quote from his book *The Happening at Lourdes*, which he was kind enough to dedicate to me. From Clifton College the Reverend David Stancliffe, Mr. Jock Crawford and Mr. Albert Polack corresponded with me about the education of Herzl's son, Hans. From Oxford Dr. Albert Hourani sent me bibliographical advice while from Jerusalem Dr. Alex Bein and Dr. Michael Heymann, Dr. Bein's successor as director of the Central Zionist Archives, kindly replied to what may have seemed niggling questions. In Nicosia Dr. Ebert of the Goethe Institute went to great trouble in obtaining for my use works published in Germany. In Cairo Dr. Abul Inayn allowed me access to the files of *The Egyptian Gazette* while Mr. Ibrahim Ghali discussed with me the papers of his late uncle, Butros Pasha Ghali, Foreign Minister at the time of Herzl's Egyptian visit. In Ottawa my brother

Dr. T. H. M. Stewart, in association with his colleague Dr. Jules Eli Harris, advised me on the interpretation of Herzl's medical history. In New York, where Miss Jean Sulzberger helped me with advice and books, my publishers—in particular my editor, Miss Lisa Drew, and her assistant, Mr. Ray Waitkins—won my renewed gratitude for the patience with which they endured a difficult manuscript and the deftness with which they edited it for publication. To Miss Clara Godson belongs the credit for obtaining most of the photographs. I must thank Dr. Raphael Patai and Mr. Harry Zohn for allowing me to use extracts from their admirably complete edition of Herzl's Diary. Dr. André Ungar, Rabbi of Temple Emanuel, Westwood, N.J., corresponded with me about the Budapest of Herzl's day and allowed me to quote from an article in *Contemporary Judaism*. From the University of California, Los Angeles, Professor Peter Loewenberg aided my research into Herzl's psychological structure. While thanking those named and hoping that unnamed creditors will accept my general thanks, I absolve each one from any involvement in a point of view which is mine alone.

CENTRAL EUROPE in 1880

The Habsburg Empire
Military Frontier
Occupied 1878

Vistula

POLAND

RUSSIA

Vistula

• Cracow

G A L I C I A

• Lvov
(Lemberg)

Chernovitsi •

BUKOVINA

Tisza

Debreczen •

• BUDAPEST

Cluj (Klausenburg) •

N G A R Y

T R A N S Y L V A N I A

Szeged •

Maros

B A N A T

R U M A N I A

Belgrade

N I A   S E R B I A

Danube

O T T O M A N

• Sarajevo

SANJAK OF
NOVI BAZAR

E M P I R E

MONTE-
NEGRO

0   50   100   200
                    miles

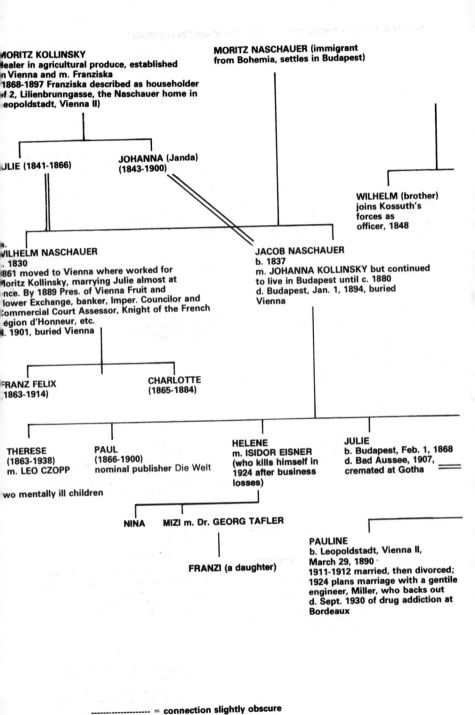

MORITZ KOLLINSKY
Dealer in agricultural produce, established
in Vienna and m. Franziska
(1868-1897 Franziska described as householder
of 2, Lilienbrunngasse, the Naschauer home in
Leopoldstadt, Vienna II)

**MORITZ NASCHAUER (immigrant
from Bohemia, settles in Budapest)**

JULIE (1841-1866)

**JOHANNA (Janda)
(1843-1900)**

**WILHELM (brother)
joins Kossuth's
forces as
officer, 1848**

WILHELM NASCHAUER
b. 1830
1861 moved to Vienna where worked for
Moritz Kollinsky, marrying Julie almost at
once. By 1889 Pres. of Vienna Fruit and
Flower Exchange, banker, Imper. Councilor and
Commercial Court Assessor, Knight of the French
Légion d'Honneur, etc.
d. 1901, buried Vienna

JACOB NASCHAUER
b. 1837
m. JOHANNA KOLLINSKY but continued
to live in Budapest until c. 1880
d. Budapest, Jan. 1, 1894, buried
Vienna

**FRANZ FELIX
(1863-1914)**

**CHARLOTTE
(1865-1884)**

**THERESE
(1863-1938)
m. LEO CZOPP**

**PAUL
(1866-1900)**
nominal publisher Die Welt

**HELENE
m. ISIDOR EISNER
(who kills himself in
1924 after business
losses)**

JULIE
b. Budapest, Feb. 1, 1868
d. Bad Aussee, 1907,
cremated at Gotha

two mentally ill children

NINA   **MIZI m. Dr. GEORG TAFLER**

FRANZI (a daughter)

PAULINE
b. Leopoldstadt, Vienna II,
March 29, 1890
1911-1912 married, then divorced;
1924 plans marriage with a gentile
engineer, Miller, who backs out
d. Sept. 1930 of drug addiction at
Bordeaux

----------------- = connection slightly obscure

THEODOR HERZL'S ANCESTORS, CONNECTIONS AND DESCENDANTS

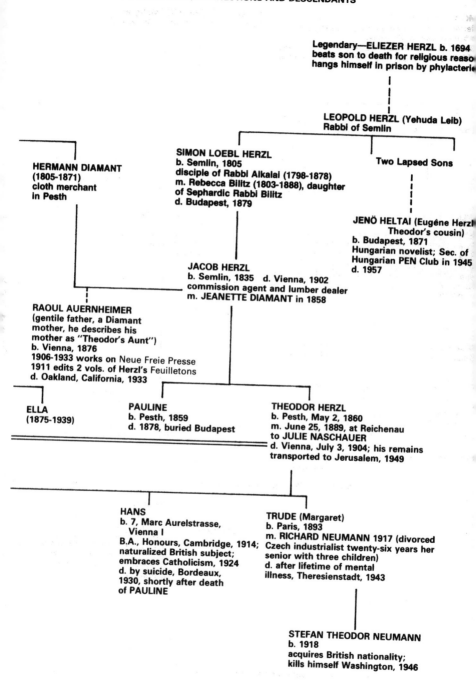

Legendary—ELIEZER HERZL b. 1694
beats son to death for religious reaso[n]
hangs himself in prison by phylacterie[s]

LEOPOLD HERZL (Yehuda Leib)
Rabbi of Semlin

HERMANN DIAMANT
(1805-1871)
cloth merchant
in Pesth

SIMON LOEBL HERZL
b. Semlin, 1805
disciple of Rabbi Alkalai (1798-1878)
m. Rebecca Bilitz (1803-1888), daughter
of Sephardic Rabbi Bilitz
d. Budapest, 1879

Two Lapsed Sons

JENÖ HELTAI (Eugéne Herzl[,]
Theodor's cousin)
b. Budapest, 1871
Hungarian novelist; Sec. of
Hungarian PEN Club in 1945
d. 1957

JACOB HERZL
b. Semlin, 1835   d. Vienna, 1902
commission agent and lumber dealer
m. JEANETTE DIAMANT in 1858

RAOUL AUERNHEIMER
(gentile father, a Diamant
mother, he describes his
mother as "Theodor's Aunt")
b. Vienna, 1876
1906-1933 works on Neue Freie Presse
1911 edits 2 vols. of Herzl's Feuilletons
d. Oakland, California, 1933

ELLA
(1875-1939)

PAULINE
b. Pesth, 1859
d. 1878, buried Budapest

THEODOR HERZL
b. Pesth, May 2, 1860
m. June 25, 1889, at Reichenau
to JULIE NASCHAUER
d. Vienna, July 3, 1904; his remains
transported to Jerusalem, 1949

HANS
b. 7, Marc Aurelstrasse,
Vienna I
B.A., Honours, Cambridge, 1914;
naturalized British subject;
embraces Catholicism, 1924
d. by suicide, Bordeaux,
1930, shortly after death
of PAULINE

TRUDE (Margaret)
b. Paris, 1893
m. RICHARD NEUMANN 1917 (divorced
Czech industrialist twenty-six years her
senior with three children)
d. after lifetime of mental
illness, Theresienstadt, 1943

STEFAN THEODOR NEUMANN
b. 1918
acquires British nationality;
kills himself Washington, 1946

THEODOR HERZL

PART ONE

The
President of Wir

1860–78

"I was born in Budapest, in a house next to the synagogue . . ."[1]

CHAPTER 1

The mountains that form Europe's icy hub diminish as they roll east from Switzerland until, at Buda, they form a series of leafy hills. A fortified palace, a church with roof tiles bright as a Fair Isle sweater, the cloisters of the Fisherman's Bastion alike look down on water. For here the Danube, central Europe's mightiest river, abruptly turns south on its long journey to the sea. Across the water (more often the color of iron filings than violets) starts the continent's largest plain: 37,000 square miles of earth, flat and shimmering as a giant lake. Bounded by the Danube and spreading uncorseted into the plain lies Pesth, in its nineteenth-century spelling. Its builders used the flat terrain for a grid of stately boulevards and transversing streets, their component houses built in a style of neo-classical munificence. As in Manhattan, that other geometric city, Pesth's bold streets reflected confidence. In 1859 the city was growing rich. Into its flat roofscape a Viennese architect, Ludwig Forster, introduced a flamboyant addition: a synagogue costing the equivalent of sixty thousand gold sovereigns and rising in a style described as Moorish-Gothic.[2] Forster's design reconciled bizarre extremes. The red brick façade with Romanesque doorways and great rose window stood firm as a railway entrance. On either side of the main door minaret-like towers supported two giant copper balls, each topped by a small kingly corona, its stamen an upward-thrusting spike. Inside, the synagogue recalled some late Roman bath, though its focus, a baldachinoed niche set in a structure resembling a Christian reredos, was for the Ark of the Law. The men worshiped in pews similar to those in Protestant churches; on each side two galleries, one above the other, were reserved for the women. A Hungarian rabbi has described the temple as the product of a community too rich to be modest; another rabbi, born in Hungary but become American, has written of "a veritable ocean liner in praise of God."[3]

The synagogue faced a thoroughfare devoted to tobacco, a product of the Ottoman Balkans to the south. Depending on whether you spoke German or Hungarian, the street was known as Tabakgasse or Dohány-utca. Visitors to the new synagogue saw, joined to the left of its façade, an urban mansion typical of nineteenth-century Pesth: a solid island, in the Roman usage of the term, whose three stories gave on to an inner courtyard. In one of its apartments, furnished in the heavy style then fashionable, a child was conceived in the year that the synagogue first opened its doors. Here, too, on May 2, 1860, Jeanette Herzl presented her husband Jacob with his first son and second child. Hungary was a country whose people knew many languages, as so few studied theirs. The boy's Hungarian name was Tivadar, but to his family he would be known as Dori, short for the German version, Wolf Theodor.

An astrologer, predicting the structure of a life yet to be lived, takes the place and hour of his subject's first breath as the pegging of the human tapestry. But the nineteenth century, a rationalist age, thought that astrology and torture had been abolished for good. No tea-table magician was called to predict the likely character of this "gift of God" (as Theodor means in Greek). If he had, he would have diagnosed the child as an undiluted Taurus, possessed of solidity of purpose, a conservative cast of mind and an attachment to earth, shown either in love of gardens or a devotion to some particular land.

The place in which he was born, and the date of his birth, pegged the environmental loom through which hereditary factors, then enemies, friends and accidents, were to shuttle like the planets in an astrologer's chart. Pesth was an appropriate birthplace for one of the most remarkable men of his age and the instigator of the most hazardous venture of the century to follow. Events of symbolic importance coincided with his birth.

Pesth had informally constituted one city with ancient, hilly Buda since the construction of a suspension bridge across the Danube in the 1840s. Ferry steamers, which crossed between Buda and Pesth "every hour, starting as the clock strikes,"[4] helped the de facto union. The bridge (which still stands) was built according to the designs of William Tierney Clark, whose London masterpiece was the first Hammersmith Bridge.[5] To bridge the Danube cost ten times more than to build the synagogue and won its designer "a golden snuff-box, set with brilliants," presented by the Archduke Karl on behalf of the Habsburg Emperor in Vienna. Tierney Clark's 410-yard structure was a product of the early industrial revolution; classical balance and engineering innovation still went together. The great coiled cables, strong enough to resist massed ice and the tumultuous steps of invading and retreating armies, were balanced by a pair of metal lions frowning at either end.

The iron bridge linked banks more opposed in character than any to be found in Britain. Buda, the west-bank town, occupied the site of settlements going back to neolithic, then Celtic times. This bank of the Danube had been open to the Romans, who left remains of a palace built by Hadrian and an arena where the frontier army was entertained. The danger to Buda always came from the east, across the indefensible plain, the route of the Huns and then of the Magyar horsemen, who arrived in the tenth century to establish the first Hungarian state, temporarily destroyed by the Mongols in 1241. Buda's Matthias Church, started by King Bela IV in the thirteenth century, had been completed in time for its conversion to a mosque by Suliman the Magnificent in 1541. The Ottomans maintained Buda as their regional capital until 1686, when the Austrians won it back for the faith of Christ. During their occupation the Turks uncovered a nexus of thermal springs and built baths which continued to be used by the citizenry after the Turks departed. The Matthias Church was turned back to its original purpose. In the nineteenth century its pillars were painted in gaudy patterns that could inspire a maker of exotic sweets. Buda was the administrative center of Habsburg rule.

Pesth, the commercial and industrial city on the other bank, was described in a thirteenth-century document as a very rich Teutonic township. In the late eighteenth century the Habsburgs gave it the largest barrack and artillery depot in Europe and possibly the world, the Neugebäude. But Pesth's first challenge was not military. A flood in 1838 did so much damage that it would be remembered into the succeeding century. Pointing hands on marble plaques still recorded the levels reached by the waters. When eventually a new street was driven into the Jewish quarter, breaking the previously continuous line of synagogue, the Herzl birthplace and other houses, it was named after the baron who had used his private boat to rescue citizens.

The city rebuilt in the wake of the flood fostered a social life modeled on that of Western Europe and very different from that of the Ottoman past. The British influence went further than the span of the suspension bridge. Two shipwrights based on Venice, Andrews and Pritchard, had established the steamship line linking the Hungarian capital to Vienna, 163 miles northwest. The river journey from Vienna took only thirteen hours; the journey back against the current took twice as long, so that travelers in this direction usually preferred the train. A station façade was therefore embellished with statues to Stephenson and Watt, pioneers of steam. On a more social level, the National Casino imitated the clubs of Pall Mall. Permanent members and temporary (for it opened its doors to visitors with the right credentials) mounted an ornate staircase to rooms where the London *Times* and the *Edinburgh Review* were laid out for reading, as well as the chief newspapers of Vienna, Berlin and Paris. Middle-class Hungarians or Jews were not, however, included in the welcome. Hungary was an aristocratic society.

The union of Buda with Pesth was to be formalized in 1872, a generation after the bridge suspended a road between them. The world would take another generation to notice an astonishing aspect of the double city—its expansion.[6] Its growth in population was as spectacular as the explosion of births in twentieth-century Asia; it was less regarded, however, since the nineteenth century was a period of general European growth. The colonizing powers of the Atlantic seaboard, England, France, Holland, Portugal and Spain, controlled the destinies of more than half the world. In rhythm with the growth of their overseas empires, the populations of London and Paris more than tripled during the century's first nine decades. Since London and Paris controlled so much overseas territory, their surplus citizens could migrate to whatever part of the globe pleased them most. The Habsburgs' domains were, by contrast, confined to Europe and during the same ninety years Budapest's population multiplied more than eightfold. The expansion over the whole century was even greater. The two towns had entered the nineteenth century with a total population of just under 55,000; united Budapest would enter the twentieth century with more than 700,000. In this dramatic expansion Budapest's one rival was Berlin, the Prussian city to the north. In both cities the change was in more than numbers. It showed also in the quality of life. As late as 1871—the year when Berlin became the capital of a grandiose new German empire—its sanitary conditions were reputedly the worst of any city in Europe; Budapest was also a byword for disease. Yet through planned urbanization, the upstart capitals of central Europe by the end of the century were to rival London and Paris for hygiene, efficiency and public education. Thus Budapest and Berlin not only stood where Catholic and Protestant Europe confronted the East, in the shape of the empires of Czar and Sultan; they also straddled two different modes of living: the unhygienic squalor of the past and the new civilization that owed more to physician, engineer and statistician than to priest or King.

Thus the Pesth which welcomed in Dori Herzl its latest inhabitant was outwardly as bustling and as modern as any new city in America. There were some close parallels. Just as stockades or trading posts became Indianapolis and St. Louis, so a rustic township in central Europe equipped itself with the things of modern civilization, from hotels like the Königin von England and Erherzog Stephan to botanical gardens, hospitals and jails. The first underground railway on the European continent was to be built (though not for another generation) in Budapest.

But important differences offset the resemblances. American cities, populated by European settlers and their African slaves, were built on unplowed soil. The previous tenants had been North American nomads, their mores and traditions so alien that they were hardly more to the intruders than figures in folklore. The modern cities of Budapest and Berlin sucked their population from a cultivated landscape where peasantry and landlords were possessed by ancient and stubborn ideas. The people of Hungary, no less than the Americans, had a sense of frontier. But a different sense. To the newcomer in Indianapolis or St. Louis, the frontier was geographic space, to be bridged by railway and riverboat, to be policed by sheriff. The only ideas in the prairie air were new ideas brought from Europe, washed clean of superstition. To the citizens of Pesth the frontier was more menacing. To the south the Ottoman empire was within a short river journey: the expanding empire of the Czar lay just beyond the Carpathians. Both empires had affected Hungary for ill.

Another frontier, between past and present, zigzagged through the heart of the city. Visitors would compare Pesth's new-built streets with Piccadilly or the rue de Rivoli, only to catch their breath at dramatic contrasts, at splendor overtaken by rustic simplicity. One visitor noticed "magnificent equipages, glittering with liveried hussars behind the carriages, encountering a troop of wild horses caught from the Puszta, or a herd of faun-colored, long-horned oxen, with savage herdsmen in sheepskins." To the east of the Botanic Gardens, the Städtische Theater for plays in German and another for plays in Hungarian, beyond the university and its fifteen hundred students, across the Puszta, or plain, with its tall yellow sunflowers, soared the mountains of Transylvania, the most easterly province of the Habsburg empire. Hungarians disputed this great Alpine horseshoe with "outland" Germans and Romanians (who possess it today); but few disputed the existence of the vampire. Malign creatures were whispered to lodge by day like blood-gorged bugs in the carapaces of their coffins, then roam the nocturnal woods in search of the red ichor which kept them, if not immortal, then undead. The fogs of such sanguinary myths eddied but a few hours' journey from the National Casino and the gaslit cafes with their music and wine.

But uncouthness could be found nearer to hand than in Transylvania. The plain (where alone the Magyars were in a commanding majority) lacked the small resident gentry described in the novels of Jane Austen, the class that had brought urban values to the English countryside. Hungarian landlords lived in feudal detachment from the peasants when they did not live far from them in Buda or Paris. This involved more than a lack of social polish. The countryside was poor and its people sick. The death rate was higher than in any other European country except Czarist Russia.

The London firm of John Murray produced, with other guidebooks, regular editions of a *Handbook for Travellers in Southern Germany*. The editions of 1858 and 1863, which immediately preceded and followed Dori's birth, included Hungary under this title. Readers hardy enough to contemplate a holiday in those parts were given stern advice. "A medicine-chest, or at least a supply of quinine and calomel pills, will be taken by every person, when informed of the dangerous fevers, agues, etcetera, bred in the pestilential marshes at the mouth of the Danube." Those who visited the smaller towns could expect scant comfort.

> The Hungarian inns, i.e. such as one meets with out of Pest and the other great towns, are on the whole the worst I have found in Europe. They are generally of one story, planted in the midst of a courtyard ankle-deep in mud, with an arcade running round them; broken steps and uneven pavements lead up to them. Landlord and waiter are seldom at hand to receive a traveller when he presents himself; the attendance is slow and bad; but these are trifles. I am not over nice, but I must confess the public dining-room, with its tobacco fumes, dogs, the practice of spitting to excess, and not unfrequently the horrid smell of garlic, and, what is worse, the total absence of all attempt to purify the apartment, filled me with disgust. But you are no better off in the bed-rooms: they are equally bespitten, and as seldom cleaned. The spider nestles for ever in the corners, and his tapestry is the only drapery which adorns the bare walls. As for the beds, I shudder to think of them. With all the discomforts of Germany, they have this in common, that they are usually filthy. The sheets are sewn on to the coverlid, and how often they serve it is impossible to say. You must specially *order* clean sheets, and your desire will then be complied with.

The horrid smell of garlic, supposedly a shield against vampires encouraged most British travelers to take to the river. But even there all was not nice. The Hungarians "almost surpass the Americans in the filthy habit of spitting, which is not always confined to the deck."

The backward Hungary of May 1860 was neither an independent country nor yet an equal partner in a plural state. It was a recently reconquered province of a stagnant empire. But on Magyars of all classes the century's strongest force imposed a sense of unity. "Nationalism was the enthusiasm, almost the superstition of the times."[7] Nationalism linked the cattle drivers of the plain, the peasants, the landlords to the minority of townsmen; barely a tenth of Hungarians lived in towns with more than ten thousand inhabitants. This nationalism was a different force from the impulse that had powered the century's first revolts against the Turks. The Serbs under Kara George, the Greeks under their bishops had fought a theocratic empire in the interests of a different theology. The Serbs and Greeks were Christians revolting against Islamic rule, and each Christian group had its particular way of worshiping Christ. Hungary enjoyed no such religious unity. Just under half its population were Roman Catholics. As for the rest, Protestants, split between the Lutheran and Calvinist persuasion, counted for just over a fifth, as did the Orthodox, split in their case into those in union with Rome and those in schism. Hungarian Jews were around a twentieth of the population. Those who felt themselves Hungarian were linked by a sense of historic and linguistic identity and by a desire to resist. The resistance was directed against two forces. In combating the German-speaking regime of the Habsburgs, Hungarian nationalism was generously liberal. In combating the national feelings of the Slavs and other minorities in their midst, the Hungarians were as illiberal as other nationalists have always been.

In 1848 and immediately after a new French revolution against the Bourbons, this Hungarian sense of identity had exploded into a national revolt under the inspired leadership of Lajos Kossuth. On March 3, 1848, Kossuth demanded parliamentary government for Hungary and constitutional government for the rest of the Habsburg empire. Kossuth's demand set off a chain of revolts in Austria itself, where Metternich was overthrown, and in Italy. The movement for Hungarian independence was defeated by two forces: a hasty alliance between Austria and Russia, and by the resistance to Kossuth's ideas of Czechs, Romanians and Serbs inside the Hungarian portion of the empire. The Austrians reimposed their rule while Kossuth fled to forty-five years of exile in Turkey, England, America and Italy. During his brief rule Kossuth had endeavored to win the Jews of Hungary to the Magyar cause by decreeing their emancipation. This, along with Hungarian freedom, had been temporarily reversed by the triumphant Habsburgs.

Thus in the year of Herzl's birth Hungary was outwardly quiescent. The year hung indeed at a pivotal point in modern European history. Seventy years earlier the French Revolution had declared the rights of man. "Men are born and remain free and equal in rights. Social distinctions can be founded on public utility alone." At that time the third principle of the Declaration of the Rights of Man had seemed no less generous. "The principle of all sovereignty resides essentially in the nation. No body and no individual can exercise authority, if it does not take its origin from the nation." Yet this doctrine was to lead to national mania. Seventy years later Europe would enter its furnace. The exaltation of the national group as the source of all good would have reached its frightening if logical conclusion.

Theodor Herzl was to live and die between the liberal and the national idea. A dramatic event in the week of his birth lit up these contradictory forces. On May 5, 1860, Giuseppe Garibaldi, liberal and nationalist in equal parts, embarked from Genoa with two ships and some eleven hundred volunteers. Once the ships were outside Sardinian waters, the men were solemnly presented with uniform shirts. Their color—scarlet—no more symbolized social revolution than the same color did when used for British possessions on the map of the world. Red symbolized the blood men were ready to spill for the nationalist ideal. When Garibaldi's men landed in Sicily six days later they defeated men whose uniforms symbolized an older conception of the state: that men were subjects of a ruler appointed by God.

CHAPTER 2

On May 10, 1860, the infant Theodor played the central role in a rite older than the invention of the alphabet or the use of metal. Circumcision, though not in the strict sense a sacrament,[1] made him physically a Jew; in essence he was one already through being the son of a Jewish mother, though he would not reach the fullness of conscious commitment until his bar mitzvah thirteen years later. In a sterner, more theological sense he would only deserve the title of Jew when he served God by the fulfillment of the commandments.[2]

Among the well-wishers who thronged the Herzl house were two men with traditional titles and special functions. The *sandek* was the equivalent of a Christian godfather, the word being derived from the late Greek *synteknos* and so testifying to a time when Judaism formed an accepted element in Hellenistic culture, its scriptures translated into Greek, its doctrines attracting pagans unsatisfied by the riotous theology of Mt. Olympus. The *mohel*, the second functionary, was the circumciser. His office must have deterred many would-be converts throughout the centuries.

The ceremony, which was introduced with a prayer from Jacob Herzl, had three traditional stages, each with its Hebrew name. The first was called *Milah*. In this the baby was placed on a pillow on his *sandek*'s knee; the *mohel* removed the child's lower garments and showed his godfather how to hold his legs. He then seized the foreskin between the thumb and index finger of his left hand and pulled it forward from the glans, immediately in front of which he placed a pronged metal shield. The *mohel* then took his knife and, with one clean sweep, cut off the foreskin. In the second stage, or *Peri'ah*, the *mohel* seized the inner lining of the foreskin, which still covered the glans, with the trimmed thumbnail and index finger of each hand and tore it so he could roll it gently back over the glans, exposing this completely. The third stage (which was to be modified for hygienic reasons in the twentieth century) was known as *Meẓiẓah*, a term for sucking the blood from the wound. The *mohel* took some wine in his mouth and applied his lips to the wound. After exerting suction he then expelled the mixture of blood and wine into a mug not unlike those used as christening gifts. This procedure, repeated several times, completed the operation, except for the control of the bleeding and the dressing of the wound.*

The rite—so much more ancient than Christian baptism—was practiced in the Middle East long before it was adopted by the Hebrew patriarchs or codified by the later Jewish priests. To this day it is practiced by all Muslims and in Egypt by the native Christians, or Copts. Since the foreskin is a perishable part, primitive graves can provide no evidence as to the origins of the rite, though so radical an interference with nature must have had one first practitioner in one first place. Reliefs in tombs surrounding the Vth Dynasty pyramids at Sakkara nevertheless confirm that Egyptians were circumcised at least a thousand years before the advent of the patriarchs.

The earliest mention of circumcision in the Bible occurs a third of the way through Genesis, the first of the five books that constitute the Pentateuch. However, despite the priority of Genesis in the biblical canon, its dating and authorship are a matter of dispute. Orthodox Jews believe that, along with the other four books of the Pentateuch, it forms part of the Torah (or Teaching) revealed to Moses. Other scholars argue that it was written down by priests after the Exile, who correlated traditions and legends of varying authority and date.†

In the Genesis account God approaches Abram, a ninety-nine-year-old nomad from Mesopotamia, with a proposal for a solemn bargain. Under it the deity proposes to raise nations from the seed of the old man; Abram's issue, like Banquo's, will be kings hereafter; Canaan, in which Abram was at the time a tolerated transient, would become the land of his descendants in perpetuity.

For these advantages God sets his terms:

---

* This account is based on the article on Circumcision contributed by Aaron Friedenwald, a Baltimore physician, to Vol. IV of the 1903 edition of the Jewish Encyclopaedia.

† Abram Leon Sachar, for example, in his much reprinted *History of the Jews:* "Patient puzzling over the earlier historical books of the Bible has made it plain that they were the compilation of a number of hands, written in different periods for different purposes."

This is My covenant, which ye shall keep, between Me and you and thy seed after thee: every male among you shall be circumcised. And ye shall be circumcised in the flesh of your foreskin; and it shall be a token of a covenant betwixt Me and you. And he that is eight days old shall be circumcised among you, every male throughout your generations, he that is born in thy house, or bought with money of any foreigner, that is not of thy seed. He that is born in thy house, and he that is bought with thy money, must needs be circumcised; and My covenant shall be in your flesh for an everlasting covenant. And the uncircumcised male who is not circumcised in the flesh of his foreskin, that soul shall be cut off from his people; he hath broken My convenant.[3]

The Genesis account shows that circumcision had a different meaning to the Hebrews than to others who practiced it. It was not a tribal badge, since nudity had long since been abandoned; nor was it an ordeal for adolescent braves; still less was it ordained for the hygienic advantages that recommend it to modern physicians. It was a physical mark of a spiritual commitment.

Two passages which come later in the Bible nevertheless hint more ancient implications. One involves the individual experience of the greatest Hebrew teacher; the other a collective experience connected with the conquest of Canaan.

When Moses left Midian, on his way back to Egypt after serving his gentile father-in-law, he had evidently not yet conformed to the Abrahamic covenant. For "it came to pass on the way at the lodging-place, that the Lord met him, and sought to kill him. Then Zipporah took a flint and cut off the foreskin of her son, and cast it at his feet; and she said: 'Surely a bridegroom of blood art thou to me.' So He let him alone. Then she said: 'A bridegroom of blood in regard to the circumcision.'"[4]

This account has suggested to some that the early Hebrews, like other primitive circumcisers, may have regarded the rite as the prelude to marriage. Two explanations have been advanced for such a view of circumcision. According to one, the operation was thought to facilitate sexual intercourse, while according to the other, masculine blood was a propitiary offering to the dark forces of generation. To his early worshipers the god's appearance as a pillar (of cloud by day and of fire by night) was in keeping with this aspect of his powers.

The account of group circumcision occurs in the book of Joshua. Ten days after the Hebrew invaders cross the Jordan on their way to Jericho, God instructs Joshua, Moses' successor: "Make thee knives of flint and circumcise again the children of Israel the second time."[5]

An explanation is offered for this somewhat surprising command.

The circumcised Hebrews of the Exodus had died off, while the new generation brought up in the deserts of Sinai and Moab had failed to maintain the custom. But only the circumcised could possess the land.

The reference to knives of flint (an echo of the earlier action by Zipporah) indicates the immense antiquity of circumcision. The Hebrew invasion of Canaan is usually dated between 1220 and 1200 B.C. The historical Joshua lived well inside the Iron Age: a century earlier a dagger of imported iron had been buried with Tutankhamun.[6] The use of knives of flint, antedating copper as well as iron, is an archaism of the kind common in most religious traditions.

The Joshua account has, as penultimate incident, a sentence with the ring of agonizing truth. "When the circumcising of the whole nation was over, they stayed to rest in the camp till they were well again." When adults are circumcised in unhygienic surroundings, infection and suffering are easy concomitants. Joshua's tribesmen had nothing more sophisticated with which to dress their wounds than the burned rags and ashes still being applied by Arabian tribesmen when Charles Doughty visited them in the nineteenth century. The biblical command to circumcise male children on the eighth day shows a characteristic concern with lessening pain. Performed in the cloudy dawn of life, the operation avoids agony inevitable after adolescence. The nineteenth century had meanwhile introduced its own refinements. The Herzl parents probably used a dressing first popularized in north Germany. It consisted of one part dilute sulphuric acid, three parts of alcohol, two parts of honey and six parts of vinegar.[7]

At the end of the account God makes a comment on this mass circumcision which has puzzled commentators. "This day have I rolled away the reproach of Egypt from off you."‡

The Hebrews sojourning in Egypt were either uncircumcised because they entered the country in that condition or because the practice had been forbidden them by the Egyptian authorities. At first this would not have mattered, as the children of Israel were clients of their fellow Asiatics, the Hyksos. When the XVIIIth Dynasty mustered the strength to expel these foreign kings, the Hebrews were

---

‡ Dr. J. H. Hertz in his commentary on the version of the Pentateuch generally used in Anglo-Saxon synagogues writes: "Possibly the Egyptians had forbidden it to them, since they reserved the rite for the priests and the aristocracy. Others suggest that the omission of the practice in the wilderness signified God's rejection of that generation, since circumcision was the sign of the covenant between Him and Israel (Gen. XVII, 10F). The Egyptians may have taunted them with this. The present circumcision, therefore, signifying their restoration to His favour and the renewal of the covenant, removed the stigma together with the Egyptians' taunt." *Pentateuch and Haftorahs*, London: Soncino Press 5720-1960, p. 1010.

not only put to forced labor but mocked for not conforming to the Nilotic practice of circumcision. The verse implies that the Hebrews now invading Canaan (where except among the Philistines circumcision was the rule) were not to be mocked again for the same cause. It is therefore ironic that, more than a thousand years later, young Jews who took part in pagan athletics (always practiced in total nudity) were mocked on opposite grounds. So much so that some embarrassed Jewish wrestlers persuaded surgeons to give them back the simulacrum of a foreskin. A writer in the Jewish Encyclopaedia has coined the term "epispasm" to describe this operation. (Only the adjective "epispastic" occurs in the Oxford English Dictionary.) Its connotation, of drawing out with blisters, suggests that the process was painful. It was also condemned by rabbinical opinion. The book of Jubilees, probably composed at the end of the second century B.C., adverts to the practice: "Whosoever is uncircumcised belongs to 'the sons of Belial,' to 'the children of doom and eternal perdition'; for all the angels of the Presence and of the Glorification have been so from the day of their creation, and God's anger will be kindled against the children of the Covenant *if they make the members of their body appear like those of the Gentiles,* and they will be expelled and exterminated from the earth."[8]

A child like Theodor whose parents had him circumcised on the eighth day was thus involuntarily committed to a history that had wandered from the age of flint, through triumphs and defeats, to the age of railways and the daily press. Membership in a minority hurts and stimulates in direct proportion to its alienation from the majority. In becoming different in his body from the Hungarians whose foreheads were sprinkled in the name of the Holy Trinity Benyamin Ze-ev[9] (as Dori was named in Hebrew) was committed to a minority with stern commitments. For circumcision was only the first requirement of a covenant that required much more. To the gentiles (the latinate translation of *ha-Goyim,* the Hebrew phrase for "the nations") circumcision conferred on the new baby a mysterious status. He was doomed to be regarded, perhaps with respect, perhaps with hatred, but always as in some sense other. And the spirit behind the Jewish law had intended no less than this. All its ceremonies, rituals and obervances were designed to remind the Jew that God "in His wisdom saw fit to set aside one people as the chosen vehicle for the ultimate attainment of the unity of all peoples, which He has revealed as the aim and purpose of all human development."[10]

The doctrine of the Chosen People* can easily be misunderstood:

---

* The doctrine finds a classical exposition in the *Book of the Kusari,* a dialogue by the thirteenth-century Spanish Jew Yehudah Halevi.

gentiles may see in it proof of Jewish arrogance and Jews may find in it cause for self-satisfaction. It is a knife-edge doctrine.

The scriptures and the rabbis who have expounded them make plain that the election was one of pain and anguish. If the Jews were picked out of mankind, it was for a service, and a service wherein backsliding was severely punished and wherein success was often but another name for martyrdom. Even in the comparatively tolerant society of Hellenistic Alexandria, the Jews had been resented because of their refusal to partake in the feasts of the pagan gods. Non-participation in group activities, not the later accusations of usury or financial domination, was the first charge thrown at this dedicated people. When paganism gave way to Christianity, and when Christendom became a crusading society, persecuting those who denied its doctrines, the Jews led an increasingly separate existence. Their separation was the result of their obedience to a Law that through innumerable minutiae of requirement and restriction maintained their dedication to a special function. To the religious Jew this service was a delight. "The very law which the uninstructed slanders as 'a burden, a yoke, and a snare,' this very law with its 'petty restrictions' is the treasure which brings most happiness to Jews. 'The Lord wished to bring happiness unto Israel, wherefore He gave him many precepts and laws.' "[11]

If the law were denied, if the doctrine were given a secular interpretation, there could be dangerous results. In the Jewish case, the sense of election could be used to buttress the normal human tendency to glorify one's own group over others. If the doctrine were taken over by other peoples and used against latter-day extensions of the enemy tribes of the Old Testament, the result could be racial doctrines of the most pernicious kind.

Whatever his approach to religion might turn out to be, circumcision enrolled the sleeping baby in the European minority with the deepest pride, the longest and most painful past and the most uncertain future.

The pride and the pains endured for its sake were old. What was new in Herzl's circumcision was that the future it shadowed could be ambiguous. Until the middle of the eighteenth century the Jewish situation was hard but clear. Part of the hardship came from the hostility of gentiles; part from the requirements of a highly complex law. For the covenant, it must be repeated, was no collective winning of a lottery ticket. It was felt as a group involvement in the sternest of tasks: that of keeping alive the knowledge of the One God in a world He had created but which had often refused to know Him. There was an awe-inspiring balance of blessings and curses attached to the teaching of Moses:

> And all the peoples of the earth shall see that the name of the LORD is called upon thee; and they shall be afraid of thee. And the LORD will make thee over-abundant for good, in the fruit of thy body, and in the fruit of thy cattle, and in the fruit of thy land, in the land which the LORD swore unto thy fathers to give thee. The LORD will open unto thee His good treasure the heaven to give the rain of thy land in its season, and to bless all the work of thy hand; and thou shalt lend unto many nations, but thou shalt not borrow. And the LORD will make thee the head, and not the tail; and thou shalt be above only, and thou shalt not be beneath; *if thou shalt hearken unto the commandments of the* LORD *thy God, which I command thee this day, to observe and to do them; and shalt not turn aside from any of the words which I command you this day, to the right hand, or to the left, to go after other gods to serve them* [author's italics].[12]

The words in italics show the condition for spiritual primacy among the nations. The curses on the Hebrews who did not obey every detail of the Mosaic Law occupy twice as much space but may be briefly summarized. Among the first consequences would be physical disease and infertility. But after madness, blindness and distraction of mind would come oppression at the hand of others: "The LORD will cause thee to be smitten before thine enemies; thou shalt go out one way against them, and shalt flee seven ways before them; and thou shalt be a horror to all the kingdoms of the earth."

The conclusion would be a siege at the hands of "a nation of fierce countenance, that shall not regard the person of the old, nor show favour to the young." This people would besiege the descendants of Abraham in all of their cities. Cannibalism, vigorously described, would be the recourse of the besieged and as a climax the Lord would scatter those whom he had previously delighted in rewarding "among all peoples, from one end of the earth even unto the other end of the earth."[13]

With the Roman capture of Jerusalem in A.D. 70, and the failure of a second-century revolt under Bar Kokhba, the Jews had experienced in full the plight prophesied for them. Dispersed throughout Europe and the Mediterranean, they had lived apart, determined never again to invite the punishment of God. The wall round the ghetto had been built by two sets of hands. On the one hand by the nations to whom the Jews had become a horror, on the other by the Jews, determined to live out in minutest detail the way ordained for them by their prophets, and above all by Moses. A saying of Shemaiah, a contemporary of Herod the Great, succinctly expresses their attitude to life in this world. "Love work and hate mastery, and make not thyself known to the government."[14]

The ghetto was thus a place of seclusion and places of seclusion easily arouse suspicion or scorn. A nunnery could mean a brothel in Elizabethan slang†; modern usage employs "ghetto" for a slum where those belonging to a religious or racial minority live worse lives than others. The Jewish ghetto deserves this careless connotation in part. But to see it only so would be to see it incompletely. The ghetto was also a fortress with some of the functions of a monastery: a place of refuge where men dedicated to concerns differing from those of everyday society studied the Torah and strove to live not only by its precepts but in the spirit of charity which underlay them. Their seclusion from a world that countenanced slavery, torture, persecution and crusades was no bad thing. Just as Christian convents lit rushlights from the Hellenistic world for barbaric Europe, so the Jewish ghetto preserved a unique form of monotheism long after the people of Israel had suffered the scattering foretold by Moses. Jewish thinkers had come to see in this diaspora not only a punishment for their sins but part of the inscrutable providence of God.

The bastions of the ghetto had crumbled in the lifetime of Theodor's grandparents; the last nineteenth-century ghetto, that of Rome, would cease to exist a few years after he was born.

The system of legal seclusion had not been practiced in England since the return of the Jews under Oliver Cromwell, or in North America, where the Jews had been formally emancipated ever since the 1787 Constitution stipulated that no religious test should be required for those taking public office. The forces that destroyed the ghetto in continental Europe, like those that constructed it, came from inside as well as out. The French Revolution's Declaration of the Rights of Man had removed any philosophical basis for segregation and by 1831 Judaism was officially recognized in France, along with Christianity, as a subsidized state religion. The Jews of Holland had been emancipated as early as 1796 along with those of what was to be Belgium. In the German states emancipation was achieved by a seesaw process, revolutionary movements establishing it and reactionary movements impeding it till its explicit establishment in the 1871 constitution of the German empire. The gentile movement to emancipate the Jews sprang from the current of ideas, part gener-

---

† Hamlet's "Get thee to a nunnery!" is a taunt inspired by his conviction that Ophelia was letting herself be used as a sexual pawn by Polonius and the King.

ous, part skeptical, which culminated in the French Revolution. On the generous side were such warm spirits as Gotthold Ephraim Lessing, who crowned a lifetime of theological freethinking with his blank-verse drama, *Nathan the Wise.* (In it Lessing argued that noble characters can be found inside all religious faiths and therefore no form of religious exclusiveness has a basis in reason.) On the skeptical side were those who had begun to doubt all variants of the religious faith that had originated in the Semitic East.

While the ghetto's outer walls were thus assailed by gentile cannon, Jewish sappers were undermining its fortifications from within. Without and within the forces were strong. The humanitarian spirit of the age would abolish slavery, tolerated for so many centuries by religious people; its skepticism would produce the spectacle of a Bishop of Paris abjuring his faith before the revolutionary Convention. Inside the crowded, insalubrious ghetto similar tendencies were at work. While English deists and French encyclopedists questioned the teachings of the Church, Jews, and particularly those in Germany, rejected their age-old faith altogether or tried to adapt it to prevailing modes. Moses Mendelssohn, the original of Lessing's Nathan, strove to maintain a balance between Jewish participation in general society with the conservation of Jewish values. But Jews invited late to the banquet of European civilization found it easy to overindulge. The culture of Germany was temptingly accessible to modernizing Jews. In the switch from Yiddish to German they need make no greater linguistic effort than a Neapolitan who cultivated Florentine Italian. Mendelssohn himself was not only a writer of originality but a German stylist. A swift result of the interaction between a more tolerant Europe and a more questioning synagogue was the growth of what came to be known as Reform Judaism. "Instead of Jewish law being the perpetual standard of reference in every activity and feeling of the Jew, as it had generally been up till then, the Jewish law had to justify itself before the bar of European civilisation—at least in the eyes of those Jews to whom the entrance into European society was a paramount ideal to be achieved. And they were the vast majority of Western Jews." This quotation comes from the introduction to a modern edition of a major work by a German rabbi, Samson Raphael Hirsch, who saw in this quest for cultural assimilation one more instance of Jewish backsliding. The ghetto had symbolized the determination of Jews to remain a separate, holy people, as cut off from the lures of gentile culture as nuns from marriage or monks from the market place. The compromise between Judaism and gentile values that came with the destruction of the ghetto seemed to Hirsch a new example of the spirit that had led the Hebrews of the Exodus to worship a statue of Hathor or the Jews of the Hellenistic period to take part in the public games and to deny their physical circumcision. It must have the same dire result.

But despite Hirsch's warnings, his editor continues, the movement of Reform, which had originated in Germany, spread like wildfire across the whole continent of Europe and thence to America.

> As the so-called Reform Rabbis recognised neither Bible nor Talmud, nor any other Jewish religious source, as a binding authority, there was hardly any Jewish institution, however fundamental, which at one time or other was not made the target of their attack. Thus the covenant of Abraham was attacked by Abraham Geiger, the founder of Reform Judaism, and ridiculed by his disciple Emile J. Hirsch. The Sabbath was transferred to Sunday by Samuel Holdheim, another Reform luminary. Yom Kippur was called by the New York Reformer J. M. Weiss valueless, gloomy, and one of the last remnants of our outworn institutions in the Jewish faith. Belief in the immortality of the soul was compared by the already quoted famous Reform preacher Emile Hirsch with drugs and anaesthetics. Tishah be'Av, the supreme day of mourning for our lost State and Temple, was made a day of dancing and rejoicing.[15]

Jews, monolithic to their enemies and mysterious to the uninterested, were in fact torn in a manner characteristic of all Western religions in the nineteenth century. On the one hand were those who wished at all costs to come to terms with a liberal age; on the other those who believed that in a stormy sea the only guide was a fixed star. The parents of Theodor Herzl were as conscious of the storm as other Jews. Like others assimilated to German culture they had one of two choices: either to break with the synagogue altogether or to conform to some of its rules while breaking others. Unlike two of his uncles, "Jacob Herzl did not dissolve his bonds with Judaism—but he did not draw them very close, either. Custom and upbringing had made him a Jew, and he remained one."[16] He was a businessman, and not an intellectual. Jacob Herzl would continue to value the simple beauty of the eve of Sabbath, when, the dining table transformed to an altar of domestic piety, his wife would light the two candles while, head covered, he blessed first the wine, then the loaves of bread under their fair white napkin. Yet Jacob doubted many of the things his father had believed and knew that his son was likely to doubt more. In circumcising Theodor on the eighth day he adhered to a custom his son would put in doubt. In adhering to such aspects of the Jewish tradition, Jacob Herzl was no different from his Christian contemporaries who celebrated Christmas without being convinced of the

Virgin Birth or who gave their children Easter eggs without believing in the Resurrection. Such ceremonies were, in the words of one nine-teenth-century Jew, pious family souvenirs; their abandonment would make life drabber. And not only drabber. They would involve betrayal. The Jewish situation had elements lacking in the Christian. The last catacombs had been abandoned in the early fourth century; the ghetto was an experience still remembered by prospering Hungarian Jews. They had grown up under laws imposed on them by gentiles, forbidding this or commanding that. If they moved a short distance across the Carpathians they could enter an empire where Jews were still largely confined to one area, the Pale of Settlement.‡ To break, therefore, with a tradition maintained at the cost of suffering would seem, unless the break were made from deep conviction, an act of treachery to an immemorial and compelling past.

‡ The Pale comprised twenty-five provinces of Czarist Russia (in Poland, Lithuania, White Russia, the Ukraine, the Crimea and Bessarabia) where Jews were allowed to live. The system dated from a decree of Catherine II in 1791. Professional men with a high school diploma or big businessmen were allowed to reside outside the Pale. The Pale was legally abolished in March 1917, though it had been abolished in effect two years earlier.

CHAPTER 3

Ignorant of his commitments, the child slowly surfaced to conscious existence as a dependent, demanding ego. His first months were those of hot Hungarian summer and long, warm autumn. The blurred brightness of day, the lamplit shadows of night focused into shapes, the people who attended his cradle. We could have guessed that the three figures who first became known inmates of his world must have been unusual, since their influence contributed so much to the creation of an unusual man. But we have no need to guess. External sources confirm that his parents were remarkable; from the boy himself we will learn the lasting impact of his sister.

The prime shape to impose itself, the object to which he reached first, was naturally his mother, Jeanette. Jeanette Herzl was the anxious guardian of his childhood, the guide whose judgments would remain unchallenged in a storm of conflicts, the trusted respondent and refuge in the stress of his most active years and the one person for whom on his last bed he would struggle to postpone death. If all this love concealed a secret doubt, a disguised hatred, it would only complete the portrait of her power.

What did she look like? The hagiography of memory quarrels with photography.

> Those who had known her in her girlhood carried to the end of their days the recollection of her striking beauty. The thick, jet-black hair, the lofty forehead balancing the straight lines of her nose, the little mouth which in repose looked serious to the point of bitterness, but which would liven suddenly into wit and mockery and brilliance—all these made up a highly individual appearance. In

her little world she was definitely a personality, and she knew it. But she was equally known for other qualities: for goodness of heart and sincerity.[1]

A surviving studio portrait suggests other qualities. It confirms the luxuriant hair, the dark recessed eyes under the proud brow; but it shows a mouth not so much small as domineering and fretful, the mouth of someone to whom reality has not proved what she had expected or bargained for but whose chin shows the determination to get what she requires against all opponents. A loop of fox fur, an edging of more fur to her sleeve, dark clothes: an island of white—the small, spoiled hand of one who probably labored little and who had much time to brood on those dear to her, those whom she must control. Nearly forty years later a fervent admirer of her son was to describe a "mother proud with the reserve of noble breeding."[2] Her demeanor owed less to noble breeding than to the spiritual toughness shown by her maternal grandmother: widowed early she had supported her children by door-to-door peddling. This detail, which hints the dramatic improvement in Jewish fortunes, is one of the few that survive of Jeanette's family. For the biographer who extols her beauty tells us that "of the ancestry of this interesting woman we know even less than her husband's."[3] This need not surprise. From the time of the Crusades (when Jewish symbiosis with Christians degenerated into separate subjection) until the eighteenth century, the Jews who left record of themselves belonged to two basic categories, exemplary rabbis or outstanding apostates. Inside the ghetto distinction was won only by piety and learning.* There were no "good familes" in the gentile sense. A man's ancestry availed him little. A *mamzer*—the derogatory term for a child born of adultery or incest—traditionally took precedence over a high priest, if the former were learned in Torah and the latter ignorant.

The Jews who won fame by leaving the ghetto and submitting to baptism were either accepted into the Christian religious life, so leaving no heirs, or received by marriage into Christian families, so merging in the mass of gentile society. Jews who adhered to the faith of their fathers suffered disabilities that made impossible for them the kinds of achievement that ennobled gentiles. This situation had begun to change in the eighteenth century, particularly in the German states to the north of Austria. Court Jews, the favorites of kinglets eager for money, acquired considerable fortunes and dressed like Christians. Their wealth was precarious, since it aroused envy, or involved debts,

---

* One exception is Glückel of Hameln, 1646–1724, who after being widowed wrote her memoirs in vivid Yiddish.

which a trumped-up prosecution could dispel by the creditor's disgrace or death. But this wealth, while it was undisturbed, could help the less favored Jews in the ghettos; it also led to the emergence of a Jewish aristocracy, based on money. Mayer Amschel Rothschild started one famous dynasty when he abandoned his previous occupation of dealing in antique coins to become the financial agent to the landgrave of Hesse-Cassel during the convulsions that followed the French Revolution. But inside the Habsburg domains, from which both of Herzl's parents derived, such opportunities only arose much later. As recently as 1781 it had been forbidden by Austrian law for more than one Jewish male in a family to marry. This attempt to restrict Jewish increase was only one timber in a fabric of restrictive law. What was still disallowed is shown by the need for the liberal Emperor Josef II to enact a special law in October 1781 permitting Jews, for the first time, to learn and practice crafts, to study the arts and sciences in Austrian colleges and universities and to engage in farming, albeit with minor restrictions. A further decree of November the same year was yet more illustrative of the limitations in law and attitude previously existing. Jews were now proclaimed to be fellow human beings and excesses against them were discountenanced. They were allowed to carry arms. The body tax was abolished. Yet even these concessions were too radical to survive in their first application. Josef repented them on his deathbed and his successor, Franz II, had them canceled. Franz II reigned from the year of the French revolutionary Terror until 1835, when Jeanette's father was already thirty.

Gabriel Hersch, or Hermann Diamant as he was known in German, was born and brought up in Pesth, a *tabula rasa* city of new men and new possibilities. There was something of the *tabula rasa* to Diamant's cheerful self. He was a man without myths, witty, shrewd at making money, a self-confessed skeptic in matters of religion. Many of the Diamants were baptized or married Christians. Like most Budapest Jews he felt linked neither to the Magyar nationality struggling to life after centuries of alien domination, nor to the Jewish past, but to the culture of the German states. Germany was the country of the *Aufklärung*, or Enlightenment, which had given the Diamants the standards by which they lived. Love for German culture did not mean that they supported the Habsburg dynasty when, under Metternich, it represented clerical reaction. Wilhelm Diamant, Hermann's brother, fought with the Hungarian national movement in 1849 against the armies of the Habsburgs and their Slav allies. He did not enlist because of conversion to Magyar values but because liberalism at this time was a feature of European nationalism. The political

philosophy of Kossuth, whose short-lived parliament had passed a bill
emancipating the Jews, resembled that of Garibaldi and Mazzini. But,
with the fall of Metternich, Vienna had become the symbol of a plural
society in which all men of civilized standards could use their talents.
In Habsburg Budapest Hermann Diamant had started a clothing business which made him rich. The triumph of local nationalisms, whether
Magyar, Romanian or Slav, could produce an intolerant atmosphere
as bad for business as for individual rights.

Her father's values impressed Jeanette for life. She managed and
furnished her house, dressed and conducted herself in a manner that
would have found echoes in any middle-class home in Vienna, Hamburg or Berlin. German culture was for her, as for her father, a faith
to live by. "The Jewish world, not alien to her, did not find expression
through her," Alex Bein has written. Instead, "there was not a day on
which she did not dip into German literature, especially the classic."
Naturally "her conscious efforts were all directed toward implanting
the German cultural heritage in her children." These efforts succeeded.

Jeanette allowed the Jewish holy days to interrupt her bluestocking
program out of loyalty to her husband. Jacob Herzl had been raised
in a very different atmosphere and it maintained some hold on him. It
did so in the person of his father, Simon Loebl Herzl, who had
never broken with the practices of Judaism and who had never uprooted himself from Semlin,† the small frontier town in which, for
more than a century, the Herzls had lived. Improved communications
made it possible for the old man to pay frequent visits to his son in
Pesth. Theodor learned about Semlin both from his father, who had
been born there, and from his grandfather, who returned to it after
his visits. The town and its people formed a strong contrast to the city
and citizens of Pesth.

Semlin lay on the south bank of the Danube in the Military Frontier, an area belonging to the Habsburg crown until 1881 and having
as its distinctive landmarks high wooden towers with clappers and
beacons piled ready to give warning if the Turks should return. To the
north, across the Danube, lay the European empire graced in Theodor's early years by Milan and Venice as well as Prague, Budapest and
Vienna. To the south sprawled the semi-oriental empire of the Sultan,
stretching physically into Africa and Asia and spiritually into the
Arabian Nights. In the early eighteenth century the Herzls had come
south from Bohemia, following the advancing Austrians as far south
as Belgrade and then retreating with them to Semlin, which became

† Semlin was known as Zimony in Hungarian.

the chief customs post and quarantine station for those moving upriver from the Balkans. The Herzls lived two lives there. Physically, they were identified with the Austrians, speaking German and educating their children in the local schools, serving in the militia and acting as military suppliers to the imperial forces. Spiritually, along with some thirty other Jewish families, they looked inward on the synagogue. Simon Loebl Herzl had been the son of the rabbi and had had two brothers. These two, Theodor's great-uncles, had found the atmosphere claustrophobic and had abandoned Semlin and Judaism in one bold move. Simon Loebl Herzl had remained faithful to town and faith. He took pride in blowing the shofar, or ram's horn, at New Year and in leading the small congregation in the Kol Nidre (an annual prayer annulling rash vows between God and man), which ushered in the Day of Atonement (Yom Kippur). He transferred the devotion he had felt for his father to the town's new rabbi, Yehudah Alkalai, a man strikingly different from Jeanette Herzl's Germanic heroes.

Alkalai[4] was himself the son of a rabbi, his father having served in Sarajevo, the largely Turkish town farther south that was to be the tinderbox for the First World War. Alkalai had been born there in 1798, a decisive year for the Ottoman empire, whose subject he was. In the summer General Napoleon Bonaparte landed a French army in Egypt and defeated the mameluke barons who controlled the country in the Turkish interest. The French irruption into Egypt awoke that country from a sleep of centuries; it also heralded a period in which the vast Ottoman domains were to be assailed by European ideas as well as armies. Yehudah spent his boyhood in Jerusalem, where there was a small Jewish community. His travels opened his eyes to the weakness of the Ottoman empire.

Thanks to his grandfather on the frontier, Theodor had an early awareness of the strange, anachronistic empire to the south. In their prime, the Ottomans had ruled the strongest, best-organized state in Europe. But their prime was long past and their empire's peculiar constitution made it fissiparous. Unlike European nation states, the Ottoman empire was an assembly of "millets," or religious groups, protected by and owing allegiance to the Sultan, who represented the dominant, Islamic element in the state. It was tolerant in matters of religion. Christians practiced their various forms of cult under their own church leaders; Jews were equally free to worship as they wished. But once any of these groups tried to secede from the empire there was bound to be Turkish resistance. Alkalai had witnessed the first breakaway attempts of such nations as the Serbs, then the Greeks, to be followed by Romanians and Bulgars. Secession was practicable for these peoples, as they formed compact majorities in regions at the edge of the empire. It was not easy for the Armenians, since they were scattered throughout Anatolia, hardly forming a majority in a single province. For the Jews it was not a practicable prospect at all. In Palestine itself they formed a tiny minority and elsewhere were only found in large numbers in Smyrna and Salonika, where they had found refuge after their persecution in Spain. For any inclined to day-dream about a return to Palestine there was a historical warning in the career of a seventeenth-century Smyrna-born Jew, Sabbatai Zevi. Zevi had proclaimed himself the Messiah and had been rumored as intending to conquer Palestine with an army recruited in Arabia. To many simple Jews the false Messiah had proved a Pied Piper of disaster. After wild upheavals and a crazy attempt to depose the Sultan, Zevi had embraced Islam and been jailed in an Albanian fort. The sufferings of his followers became a cautionary tale to Ottoman Jews, most of whom repaid the Turks for giving them refuge by proving loyal and useful subjects. In fact, until the Enlightenment made Germany attractive, the Jews had generally sided with the Turks against the Austrians, chief champions of Christendom.‡

But by the time Yehudah Alkalai and Theodor's grandfather came to manhood, the Ottoman empire exerted less pull on Jewish affections. Alkalai had sensed the change in possibilities. When he was twenty-seven, he was appointed rabbi to Semlin. Living in the flyblown frontier town, with the decaying Ottoman empire on one side and the new nation states of Europe on the other, Alkalai began to argue that the Jews too should strive for a national home of their own. The only proviso he made, in accord with the Talmudic tradition, was that they should avoid a trial of force. He proposed instead that they should buy Palestine through a joint-stock company, similar to the steamship trust that had opened the Danube to navigation. Just as the patriarch Jacob had bought a parcel of ground at Shechem, so little by little the Jews should acquire land until they had constructed a nation on its own soil which would enjoy a tributary status under the Sultan. The rabbi expressed these ideas in a book, *A Lot for the Lord* (*Goral la-Adonai*), published in Vienna three years before Theodor's

‡ At some cost to themselves. Their support for the Turks in Hungary give rise to the incident known as the Purim of Buda. In 1684 an Austrian army besieging Buda had been driven off by the combined efforts of Turks and Jews. Reports of this reached Italy just as the Jews were celebrating Purim. The ignorant thought they were celebrating a Christian reverse and a pogrom was only averted by the intervention of Italian and German soldiers in the service of the Doge of Venice. When Buda was finally freed, disabilities were imposed on the Jews.[5]

birth. Alkalai wrote of the pain he felt that Hebrew had gone out of use. "Because of this our people was divided into seventy peoples; our own language was replaced by the seventy languages of the lands of exile."

Simon Loebl Herzl, who spoke of Alkalai's ideas on his visits to Pesth, was exceptional in taking them seriously. To orthodox Jews they seemed to contravene the traditional teaching that the Exile was ordained by God and would end only with the coming of the Messiah. It was not for mortal man to prod Providence into action.[*] To the liberal merchants and bankers of Pesth, Alkalai's proposals seemed the uncouth and superstitious products of a world they had left behind. But the rabbi was to practice what he preached. He migrated to Jerusalem in 1874, when Theodor was fourteen, and died there four years later.

The Herzl parents would listen to Simon Loebl's enthusiasms with the politeness due from the young to the old. Jacob's business interests were involved with the Habsburg economy while Jeanette's holy tongue was that of Lessing and Goethe. But if their parents had chosen Vienna as their lodestar, not Jerusalem, Theodor and his sister were still uncommitted. At least with half an ear they took in the dreams inspired in their grandfather by his friend and rabbi. Alkalai's proposals seeped into that well of the mind wherein to forget is also to store.

Apart from the link with Semlin, the remoter origins of the Herzl family were mist-enshrouded. Where there is mist there is often magic. In a society on a rising tide, where old moorings rot and new destinations glitter, people still seek for the embellishing family connection. In England Benjamin Disraeli's claim that his family derived from Spain passed into the early biographies. To ambitious Jews an origin in Spain matched the appeal of Norman blood to Englishmen or *Mayflower* transit to North Americans. The Disraelis in cold fact reached London from the Middle East by way of Italy.

The Herzls maintained a similar family myth. Dori imbibed it from his mother and when he grew up imparted it to a disciple[6]: "Theodor Herzl on the paternal side had a great-grandfather, Lobel, who though an orthodox rabbi, even in his day experienced the bitterness

[*] Simeon Singer, a British rabbi who was later converted to ideas similar to Alkalai's, recognized the difficulty in any political movement to regain Palestine in an address entitled "Jews in Their Relation to Other Races," delivered at South Place Institute, London, on March 9, 1890: "Two oaths, says a doctor in the Talmud, God imposes on Israel. First, that they shall not seek the restoration of their land by means of violence, and next, that they will not rebel against the nations among whom they dwell. That is to say, it is not to physical force but to the growth of moral influence that we are to look for the restoration of our ideals."

of assimilation. For of his three sons, only one, Simon Low Herzl, Theodor's grandfather, remained loyal to Judaism. Lobel was a Spanish Jew who was forced in Spain to accept Christianity. To escape the Inquisition he migrated and as a Marrano, re-Judaised in Constantinople." This story (with other versions) has a vagueness that makes it suspect. No evidence for the Spanish connection has yet been produced. This Lobel Herzl, the grandfather of Jacob Herzl, was a contemporary of Napoleon. The major attack on the Jews of Spain—with the enforced choice between conversion or exile—had taken place at the end of the fifteenth century, after the peninsula's reconquest by the Catholic kings. The Holy Inquisition thereafter periodically sought out secret Jews, or Marranos, from the descendants of the converts. This hunt was not discontinued until the end of the eighteenth century, when the Inquisition was abolished. The story represents a conflation of the generations, if it is not a fairy tale. But the derivation from Spain appealed to Jeanette Herzl as much as it had appealed to the Disraelis. Spanish Jews, she told her son, who never forgot it, were of the tribe of Benjamin, and therefore of royal blood.[7] For her son's Hebrew name the Herzls chose the same name—Benjamin—that Mrs. Disraeli had chosen. Jacob Herzl's kingly descent could compensate for provincial birth and less developed culture.

Jacob Herzl transmitted more to his son than a handful of myths and a Germanic family name.†

His solid head, his square-cut beard were forms on which Theodor would improve; but Jacob's mouth was that of a businessman, practical and aware of limits, not sensitive and ambitious. The physical legacy had spiritual codicils. Jacob's finicky attention to detail, his concern for neatness balanced Jeanette's stress on etiquette and social conformity. The balance extended to the relationship of husband and wife in this un-Bohemian family. The strong and forceful father seems at no time to have aroused hostility, or even resistance, in his son. To share authority with a self-willed wife, to have a son whose sensitivity owed much to a pampered mother, and never to engender an Oedipal situation was a remarkable achievement. Throughout Jacob's life, Dori revered and loved him, asking, we are told, his blessing on every undertaking. This acceptance of authority was another link with the other Benjamin. "The native tendency of the Jewish race," wrote the future Earl of Beaconsfield in a generalizing mood,[8] "is against the doctrine of the equality of man. They have also another

---

† Herzl is the affectionate diminutive of Herz, the German for "heart"; the equivalent in Hebrew is Leb. The variants of Leb—Lobel, Loeb, Low—were older forms of the family surname. The adoption of Herzl emphasized the conversion to German ideals.

characteristic—the faculty of acquisition. Thus it will be seen that all
the tendencies of the Jewish race are conservative. Their bias is to
religion, property, and natural aristocracy, and it should be the interest
of statesmen . . . that their energies and creative powers should be
enlisted in the cause of existing society." At acquisition Jacob Herzl
was no past master. But in other respects he conformed to the canons
of the "race" outlined by Disraeli.

The third member of the family triad was only one year older than
Dori. Pauline has been described as "the image of her mother," but
again, the photograph that should substantiate this claim does not.[9]
The natural expression suffers from the pose demanded by the Pesth
photographer: the rope of loosely plaited hair is too carefully casual,
the locket too neatly centered. But the hair is fair and the locket
is probably of no intrinsic value. Jeanette Herzl would have worn
some expensive jewel and her hair was raven-black. And though the
face's structure is similar, there are important differences. The expression of the mouth lacks bitterness or the power to mock. There is a
story that Rabbi Lobel Herzl had been an amateur of the Kabbalah,
the Jewish mystical tradition.[10] It gains one confirmation in the portrait of Pauline. Her spirituality was to be frozen before it could blur.
There is the space for lines of discontent from nose to mouth-end, but
it is not filled. Like a photograph on which the fixing agent has been
used too soon, this image would never be scored by experience. She
was the companion of Dori's boyhood, a less intense, more approach-
able version of his mother, yet an ally to the mother in focusing the
boy on home. A better student, as good a mind, she had no wish, or
time, to ignite the ambition to which her mother would have been the
ready bellows. She was a domestic Beatrice and as such set a standard
of innocence by which other women would be found deficient; as a
ghost-partner she would glimmer to her tormented brother. In his
published writings she was to appear repeatedly as an ideal of woman
without passion. In the secret life where fantasy fuses the tender feelings of childhood with the erotic pressures of adolescence she would
stand as a frustrating shade. The fusion would not take place. The
two sides would split. Unknowing *belle dame sans merci*, Pauline as
much as her mother were to form a male whose driving force would
search elsewhere than in love for its fulfillment. This was the price
for the reality behind the hagiographer's ikon: the mother and two
children walking through the center of Pesth and "making up an
extraordinarily beautiful picture."[11]

A picture of Dori, intended to be beautiful, shows him standing at
the first rung of life's ascending ladder.[12] After some preliminary

lessons at home, from a visiting tutor, Jeanette enrolled him in a preparatory school run by the Jewish community, the Pester Israel-itische Normalhauptschule. For the photograph she dressed him as a Habsburg version of Little Lord Fauntleroy. The child stands against a soft-bottomed chair, its back a tangle of ponderous carving. He seems a challenging little boy, his flat feet at "ten to two," his legs bulky in thick-cut trousers ending six inches above his shoes. Five ornamental buttons mark the pleats down the side. His mouth com-bines sensitivity with defiance. His eyes are watchful and aware. His left hand lies spatulate on a large book, doubtless a larder of the artist's earlier victims. He is a sturdy, large-browed child: one who could look after himself with the other children, getting by with a word rather than a blow.

Yet Frau Herzl took nothing for granted. She was one of those parents, odious to teachers, who fussily frequent their children's school. She was forever dropping in "to inquire about the progress and behaviour of her only son, the apple of her eye, over whom she watched zealously."[13]

So total and prying a devotion could be conjectured to have far-flung results, and conjecture will be proved correct. In the short term, too, it had an important issue.

Dori's least fancy was hallowed; his every remark was scried for omens. One such remark was inspired by the next shape, after rela-tions, to dominate a growing boy: his hero. Being selected, not im-posed by fate, a boy's heroes are sometimes more influential than his parents; they are also more revealing. Dori's first hero was "one of the foremost impresarios of his age," Ferdinand de Lesseps. The term "impresario," used by the poet John Pudney,[14] is apt. The man whose achievements dominated the first nine years of Theodor's life was a specialist in no particular science, still less that of engineering. Yet he was typical of the men who were transforming the nineteenth-century world. If de Lesseps lacked academic qualifications, he had genius and talent. His genius lay in sustaining a vision, his talent in the diplomatic arts which made the vision a reality. An inspired opportunist, he turned his acquaintance with an overweight prince (to whom, as French consul, he gave the macaroni forbidden by his father) to promptest use when the prince became, as Said Pasha, the ruler of Egypt. Taking the first ship to Alexandria, he won, against the wishes of the Sultan and the intrigues of the British, a concession to drive a navigable trench between Africa and Asia. This was the most radical interference with geography in human history and like other schoolboys all over Europe Theodor marveled as the heroic enterprise, now frustrated by lack of funds, now stymied by political opposition, struggled forward to the day in November 1869 when de Lesseps, standing beside the Empress of France on the Imperial yacht, led a procession of ships south from Port Said (the new town named after his dead benefactor) and into the Red Sea. The French ship was followed by others conveying the Habsburg Emperor, Franz-Josef, and the German Crown Prince.

The epic of the Suez Canal was told in regular installments by the German press as it was by the press of France and England. The grandiose nature of the achievement, the fame it brought the Frenchman who had inspired it delighted Dori's imagination. Doubtless he was not the only schoolboy to open his atlas in the hunt for new isthmuses to pierce for similar acclaim. The scraggy neck of land between North and South America was promising. "I intend to build a canal at Panama one day," Dori confided. "But tell no one. I don't want someone else stealing my idea."[15]

Other parents might have smiled at the whimsical remark; others have treasured it to tell their friends; Jeanette Herzl saw in her son's daydream a clue to his future. All over Europe schoolmasters were urging the inclusion of science in the education of children; in every Jewish community there was a breaking away from professions with which Jews had been identified in the past. It was hastily decided: instead of training to be a rabbi, merchant or banker, Dori would become a modern hero, an engineer.

CHAPTER 4

In deciding to make him an engineer, Dori's parents were ignoring the aspects of de Lesseps that their son admired. They acted in the same spirit as parents who put their son in the navy because of his fondness for a sailor suit. Such decisions, swiftly made, have protracted results. Theodor spent five years being trained in a curriculum with little appeal to his spirit. The Realschule, which he joined when he was ten, was a large, plain building not five minutes' walk from the Tabakgasse synagogue and home. It was a secondary school which emphasized the sciences and modern languages at the expense of Latin and Greek. The building would still be standing a hundred years later, in its entrance a bust of the liberal statesman who, among other acts of wisdom, completed in 1867 the emancipation of Habsburg Jews.*

Theodor joined the Realschule in the autumn of 1870, the close of a year that gave Germany the pride of place which France had known only twelve months before. Then the Empress of France had led the procession through the Suez Canal. The following year had totally undermined this French preeminence. As if to herald a revolution in power and the stirring to mastery of the German people which produced it, Richard Wagner's *Die Walküre* had been given its first performance on June 26. In the same year the elderly musician had married Cosima von Bülow; the daughter of Franz Liszt and a French mother, she yet believed with passion in the destiny of the German people. Hardly had the chords of the opera ceased to resound than

---

* Baron Jozsef Eotvos (1813–71); minister of cults and public instruction, he also wrote a novel inspired by Sir Walter Scott on the sixteenth-century Hungarian peasant war.

the French Assembly committed an act of folly worthy of music drama: it voted for war against Bismarck's Prussia. The French armies were routed as swiftly as in a play. The victory of Sedan, the personal surrender of the ailing Napoleon III intoxicated those who spoke German. It was a victory for diplomacy as much as arms. Although Prussia had defeated Austria a few years earlier, Bismarck's generous treatment of the south German state made Austrians as enthusiastic for the Prussian triumph as other Germans. For all Europe, from Queen Victoria in Windsor to the Herzls and Diamants in Pesth, the victory had moral implications. A new Protestant state had overcome an old, frivolous society, part skeptical, part papist. The discipline of Prussia, its serious attention to military tactics and engineering made it the custodian of an earnest future. Dori from this moment changes to Theodor: we see the Hungarian Tivadar no more. From now until the end of adolescence, his known heroes, the masks through which he would first articulate his thoughts, would be Germans by birth or baptism. The first was, and would remain, Prince Otto von Bismarck, "the man who stitched a torn Germany together with his iron needle in such a wonderful way that it no longer looked patched up."[1] This extraordinary exponent of limited war and limitless diplomacy had reached his triumphant zenith when on January 18, 1871, the Prussian king was crowned German Emperor in the Hall of Mirrors at Versailles. Suddenly Wagner seemed not so much a dreamer as a prophet. People took his ideas seriously, not only his music.

The proclamation of the German empire was more than a triumph: it was an act of historical revenge. There was an intended irony in the choice of place. In 1804, after the humiliating Prussian defeat at Jena, Napoleon had chosen Berlin as the place from which to announce his European hegemony. His Berlin Decrees, while directed against England, in effect proclaimed all Europe as a zone under French influence, if not control. Bismarck's triumph neatly reversed the situation under which German states had bowed to the will of France; it represented the emergence to flushed success of a movement of German nationalism long frustrated and impatient. Years later Theodor would look back on the events that coincided with his first term at the Realschule: "Do you know what went into the making of the German Empire? Dreams, songs, fantasies, and black-and-gold ribbons—and in short order. Bismarck merely shook the tree which the visionaries had planted."[2] He would come to the conclusion that while Napoleon, the victor of Jena, was greater than Bismarck, "his greatness was an inharmonious one."[3] These quotations are the adult reformulation of a childish hero worship, a period when black-and-gold ribbons, songs and fantasies had meant much to a boyish dreamer. He would throughout his life speak of Bismarck "with profound reverence and admiration."[4]

But though the exploits of the German superman dominated the Herzl breakfast table, Theodor was still only ten. He hurried out to class, not to drawing board or Reichstag. It is interesting to examine his marks—they have been preserved—for what they reveal. His best subjects that first year were Geography, History and German. He obtained high marks for Neatness and Conduct. His worst subjects were those most closely linked with his professed ambition: Mathematics, Geometry, Geometrical Drawing, Nature Studies and Penmanship. He won strikingly low marks for Religion. It is evident that thus early his efforts flagged for being misdirected. The Realschule emphasized the subjects where Theodor was naturally weak or temperamentally indifferent.[5]

To succeed as an engineer he would need to be good at the subjects that failed to interest him and in which he did badly. His talents were in the subjects that could be useful to an impresario or a writer. There was nothing remarkable in his interest in literature and fantasy —it was common among middle-class youths in German schools. His individuality showed in a practical approach to the fantastic. He preferred speculative writers about science to imaginative writers about the human psyche. He had been born at precisely the right moment to read the romances of Jules Verne when their pages were still fresh. *Five Weeks in a Balloon* had been published in 1862, *Voyage to the Center of the Earth* in 1864, *From the Earth to the Moon* in 1865 and *Twenty Thousand Leagues Under the Sea* in 1869, year of the Suez Canal. Verne's works were hastily translated into German, English and the other European languages. They had as their theme the extremities of terrestrial or extra-terrestrial travel. Yet Verne had studied law, not science; he had spent his youth writing librettos, a verse comedy and calculations for the stock exchange on which he gambled.

Theodor's bad marks in Religion (what would be called Scripture in Anglo-Saxon schools) are significant in the light of his future. Seen in the context of his time they are what might have been expected from a freethinking young contemporary of Marx and Darwin. Later, when he was committed to a cause with religious overtones, he was to produce, in an autobiographical sketch and in confidence to a disciple, three stories about his childhood attitude to religion. But as each made a polemical point, these important stories cannot be taken for literal truth. They may not even have been intended as such. "Some of his tongue in cheek statements have been taken too literally," one of his most devoted biographers warns us.[6] "The fine humour in Herzl's autobiography has not been generally appreciated." These stories, the humor and the point they make, will be discussed later. To illumine Theodor's adolescent approach to the scriptures we may turn to the record of a younger contemporary, also unequally torn between the heritage of Moses and Goethe. Jacob Wassermann's autobiographical *My Life as German and Jew* expresses an attitude to Jewish religious instruction that echoes what we know of Herzl's.[7] Wassermann was born in Fuerth, in Franconia, but later settled in Austria.

> Religion was a study, and not a pleasant one. A lesson taught soullessly by a soulless old man. Even today I sometimes see his evil, conceited face in my dreams. Curiously enough I have seldom heard of a kindly or lovable Jewish religious teacher; most of them are black zealots and half-ridiculous figures. Mine, like the rest, thrashed formulas into us, antiquated Hebrew prayers that we translated mechanically, without any actual knowledge of the language; what he taught was paltry, dead, mummified. Only from the reading of the Old Testament did we derive positive gain, but there, too, both the subject and its interpretation lacked true illumination. Events and characters were effective singly, unconnectedly, but the whole seemed rigid, frequently absurd, even inhuman, and was not ennobled by any loftier outlook. At times a ray broke through from the New Testament, like a gleam of light through a locked door, and curiosity blended with a vague dread . . .

Gleams of light came to Theodor from the Reformation rather than the New Testament. One of his earliest poems was concerned with Luther, the German nationalist and forerunner of Bismarck's *Kulturkampf* against the Catholic Church.† But Herzl would have recognized with some unease Wassermann's unfavorable contrast between his "modern synagogue, one of those quasi-Byzantine edifices to be found in most German cities, but whose upstart magnificence cannot disguise the fact that the faith has no power over the hearts of men" with the traditional *shuls:*

> tiny places of worship, often only little rooms in obscure, out-of-the-way alleys. There one could still see heads and figures such as Rembrandt drew, fanatic faces, ascetic eyes burning with the memory of unforgotten persecutions. On their lips the austere prayers,

† Entitled, *We Will Not Go to Canossa,* one verse contains the lines:
> Out of the long night,
> Through Luther's mighty power
> The German spirit has awaked.

appeal and malediction, grew real. Their bowed shoulders bespoke generations of humility and privation, they observed the venerable customs with the utmost faithfulness, with resolute devotion, and they retained their belief, though it was dulled, in the coming of the Messiah.[8]

A feature of Reform Judaism was its abandonment of "the doctrine that it is Jewish destiny to be miraculously transported by the Messiah to the Holy Land, there to have the entire levitical and temple apparatus recreated for him."[9] In his third year at the Realschule Theodor obtained a book of popular science by Aaron Bernstein, one of the founders of the Reform congregation in Berlin. In it "he read that the stream of electricity built a bridge over the entire world, that electricity was the real Messiah, and that its wonders would bring liberation to all nations and all enslaved human beings."[10] At first the idea seemed to blaspheme against what he had been taught in scripture classes. But within a short space of time he had accepted the notion as an interesting possibility.

Theodor's bar mitzvah took place on May 3, 1873: the day after his thirteenth birthday. His parents used the Christian term "Confirmation" on their engraved invitation cards.[11] The borrowing was apt. Both ceremonies had lost much of their earlier force. The child confirmed by his bishop wore his best clothes; he focused only fitfully on the occasion in Jerusalem when the bereaved disciples of Jesus "suddenly heard what sounded like a powerful wind from heaven, the noise of which filled the entire house in which they were sitting; and something appeared to them that seemed like tongues of fire; these separated and came to rest on the head of each of them."[12] Few Hungarian Catholics can have expected the miraculous graces of the first Pentecost, or the martyrdoms that followed. Nineteenth-century Jews were probably as vaguely focused on the drama of Sinai when Moses descended from the mountain bearing the tablets of the Law. In the Middle Ages, when the custom of bar mitzvah can first be traced, it marked the occasion when the young Jewish male made himself personally responsible for observing the 613 precepts of the Mosaic code. He then made a Talmudic address to his father's congregation while his rejoicing father blessed God for being freed from henceforth of responsibility for his offspring's actions. By the time of Theodor's Confirmation the Talmudic address had shrunk to the reading in Hebrew of a few verses of the Law. The accent was now on the afternoon festivities at home. And at home the Herzls had preoccupations. The union of Buda and Pesth the previous year had led to a boom only marred by a cholera epidemic. Jacob Herzl had invested his fortune in a venture connected with the timber that covered more than a quarter of Hungary: oak, fir, pine, alder and ash. By the spring of 1873 the boom was wilting and by the end of the year Jacob would have lost his capital.

But though there were similarities between the two modes of Confirmation, the religious predicament of a young Jew was sharper than that of the young Christian. A Christian who began to doubt first one doctrine, then another, need make no violent break, unless he was an iconoclast by inclination. He could practice as little or as much as he pleased of what was the good form of the majority; to doubt some articles of the Creed was only to join the conformist majority. The situation was different for Jews. The shawled votaries in Jacob Wassermann's *shuls* believed that they formed part of a "kingdom of priests, and a holy nation."[13] They welcomed the precepts of the Law in the same spirit in which Wordsworth had welcomed the discipline of the sonnet, comparing it to the vocation of a nun. Scrupulous obedience to the Law could open windows on vistas of spiritual beauty. The cost was not cheap and it was paid to the last farthing. An account of an orthodox Jewish peddler in a gentile environment illustrates this price in terms of detail.[14] "It meant praying in crowded railway trains, winding his phylacteries‡ round his left arm and on his forehead to the bewilderment or irritation of unsympathetic fellow-passengers. It meant living chiefly on dry bread and drinking black tea out of his own cup, with meat and fish and the good things of life utterly banned by the traditional law, even if he were flush."° Such orthodox Jews cared as little for the first night of *Die Walküre* as Christ had cared for the performances at the pagan theaters in Decapolis. But for the Herzl family, their fortune at the mercy of economic trends in the Habsburg empire, their emotions deeply involved in German culture, the laws were a burden, either to be rationalized away or bravely ignored. It was as hard for such Jews to assimilate the wearing of phylacteries to the Bismarckian ideal as it was for Bismarck to assimilate the Sermon on the Mount to *Realpolitik*. Burdens that are awkward weigh more tediously than those that are

‡ The custom of wearing phylacteries (in Aramaic *tephillin*, "attachments") derives from the commandment in Deuteronomy VI: 8, for the Hebrews to bind scriptural passages on the arm and head. These came to consist of two black boxes fastened to leather straps containing admonitory texts from the Pentateuch. Originally worn throughout the day (except on Sabbaths and holy days), they are now worn only during the morning prayer.

° The peddler is unable to eat "meat and fish and the good things of life"—not because all of them are prohibited, but because, traveling in gentile society, he cannot be sure that even permitted foods have been prepared in accordance with the dietary laws or that the utensils used for meat have not been used for milk, and vice versa.

heavy. It says much for the human acceptance of contradictions that both parties made the effort. In smart Berlin churches Prussians listened politely while admonished to love their enemies or turn the other cheek. Jews with boxes at the opera held bar mitzvah ceremonies in which their sons were supposed to stand in spirit with the 600,000 Israelites who heard the Law delivered from Sinai. Both exercises were easy for the majority, to whom hypocrisy is a pleasant part of everyday existence. They were harder for the sincere and for the probing.

The Herzls did not break with religion. Nor did they give it the place in their lives that it demanded. In fitting it into one slot of a complex urban life they were defeating the intentions of the post-Exilic priests who had codified the Mosaic Law. The priests had valued the elements in the Law that were awkward precisely because they made it impossible for the Jews to imitate the gentiles: instead, they would remind themselves and their sons of a supernatural destiny and charge.

The year following his bar mitzvah was important for the development of Theodor's personality. Along with the normal onset of adolescence, his father's eclipse, and frequent absences in efforts to restore his fortunes, encouraged Theodor's urge to be an individual. An original venture showed the powers of an organizer behind the diffidence of youth, the wish to write behind the daydreams of boyhood.

In what proved to be his last year at the Realschule, he founded, early in 1874, a literary society. It was recruited from his schoolfellows, boys of roughly the same age as himself, some of them his relations, one, a Diamant cousin, being the Secretary while Theodor was the President. Pauline and other girls of her age attended at least one of the meetings. Its membership was not restricted to Jews. Theodor's closest friend seems to have been a Hungarian, Gabor Borsanyi, since on a slip of paper dated January 26, 1874, they signed a compact of friendship and mutual aid to last until the end of the year. The society's name—Wir, or in English "We"—showed the normal exclusiveness of youthful groupings; but an air of precocious formality emphasized its elitist air. Its members had to address each other in the dignified German plural, as *Sie*, not the *Du* customary between relations, friends and comrades. The archives survive. They show that the members put in an amount of work almost inconceivable to later generations whose leisure hours are anesthetized by television. Something of the traditional Jewish devotion to learning was secularized in the lengthy fables, stories and essays read to other adolescents. One of Theodor's productions—significantly entitled *Obedience and Command*—required three sessions for its complete reading. Such pursuits left their pursuers with a lifelong feeling for literature, even if they did not become writers. In Theodor's case, it laid the foundations for a German style of euphonious elegance.

In founding his society, in writing on such different topics as Savonarola and "Oxygen," "Fashion" and Muhammad, he showed a grasp of reality strikingly different from when he had dreamed of building a canal or had idolized Luther and Bismarck. He was no longer a dreaming child. A child's daydreams need not mesh with the facts of his world. A physician's son may dream of becoming a clown, a girl with no voice of singing Norma. But with the onset of adolescence Theodor began to recognize the realities of his talents, temperament and position in society. He had no aptitude for science and in a short time he was to change schools. He recognized that a Luther or a Bismarck was an impossible target for imitation. Even if he decided to be baptized, he could hardly hope to play a major ecclesiastical or political role in German Europe. The German situation was the reverse of the British. The year that Theodor founded Wir Benjamin Disraeli became Prime Minister; in 1876 he would proclaim Queen Victoria as Empress of India. Yet no British Jew (including the Disraeli who wrote novels) had yet reached the top rank in literature, the major British art. While in German politics a Disraeli was still unthinkable, Jews were already attaining high positions in the German arts.

The young President of Wir had two new heroes: both of them were "German" poets. They appealed to him not only for their intrinsic merit but for the way in which they echoed his predicament, the sense in which each poet deserved inverted commas round the attribution "German."

Nikolaus Lenau—the pen-name of Franz Niembsch von Strehlenau —had been born in Hungary but wrote in German. Born in 1802, he belonged to the generation of European poets who responded to the early industrial revolution with a cosmic sadness. Expressed by both Goethe and Byron, this pessimism was raised into a philosophy by Giacomo Leopardi. Lenau was its Austrian spokesman. There was much in his ideas and feelings to captivate the adolescent Theodor. When he was thirty-five, Lenau had written an epic, *Savonarola*. This boldly proclaimed that liberation from political and intellectual tyranny was a precondition of Christianity. His liberal spirit had felt restive in an Austria still ruled by Metternich. In 1832 Lenau sailed to North America in search of Freedom and Peace. Instead of these

capitalized ideals he found an unromantic obsession with capital†
and he left his Ohio homestead after a year. Back in central Europe
he wrote love poems whose natural melancholy was increased by
their dedication to a forbidden object, Sophie von Löwenthal, the wife
of a friend.

But the stronger influence, because of closer affinities to himself,
was Heinrich Heine. Born to middle-class Jewish parents in Düs-
seldorf, Heine had died only four years before Theodor's birth. During
Heine's boyhood Napoleon's armies crashed into the jigsaw of statelets
that then constituted Germany. The French Revolution and the young
general who was its emissary severely jolted the age-old fabric of
German life, including its restrictions on Jews.

But Heine's life, like Herzl's, started with a misdirection when he
agreed to go into business with a rich uncle in Hamburg. The part-
nership failed and Heine took another false direction in deciding to
study law, first at Bonn, then at Göttingen university. Like Herzl at
the Realschule, he was far more interested in history and literature
than the subject of his specialization. At Göttingen he fought a pistol
duel with a student who had insulted him and used his six months'
suspension to explore Berlin, the capital of the only German state
admired by liberals. Its fashionable salons were as attractive to him as
those of the Faubourg St. Honoré to Marcel Proust seventy years
later. Once back in Göttingen, a few weeks before his graduation, in
a step that Herzl pondered intently. Heinrich Heine submitted to
baptism in the name of the Holy Trinity. His motives were practical.
He was already assimilated in "clothing, language and mode of life"[15]
to the German majority. In paying lip service to what he saw as the
dominant mythology, he was carrying his personal adaptation but one
stage further. He never repudiated his Jewish origins; indeed, critics
of his poetry have noticed affinities between his use of nature imagery
and that of the Hebrew poets, while his mordant prose manifested
"the withering scorn and ineradicable sense of justice common to the
leaders of the Jewish race."[16] But in metaphysics Heine was a cynic.
The moral earnestness that prompted his satire was devoted to this-
worldly ideals.

Heine's baptism may have facilitated his progress as poet, satirist
and producer of journalistic essays. His lyrics were put to music by
Schubert and Schumann; they seeped so completely into the German consciousness that when, a century later, his Jewish origins made

† Lenau characterized it, not entirely accurately, since America was by this time
independent, as "English dollar-lisping," or *englisches Talergelispel,* anticipating
similar comments on the Anglo-Saxons from, among others, Friedrich Heine and
Friedrich Nietzsche.

him unmentionable in German textbooks, his poems could be passed off with some credibility as anonymous folk songs. In his lifetime he was obnoxious to authority, not for his ancestry, but for his identification with the liberal (which then meant revolutionary) cause. Like other poets he was dogged with financial problems and disappointed in hopes of preferment. Although he was regarded as the leader of the Young Germany group of writers, he found his fatherland less and less to his taste. The middle-class revolution that in 1830 made Louis-Philippe King of France excited an exaggerated admiration. After moving to Paris in the following year, he applied for and received a subsidy from the French government on terms that made him to all intents and purposes a police informer. When he fell in love with a young saleswoman in a boot shop and despite her lack of education or taste made her his wife, the only link with Germany became a romanticized past.

To Herzl, the Jewish Hungarian, Lenau showed that someone born in Hungary could be a major German poet, Heine that a Jew could be. But the careers of both heroes carried troubling warnings. Lenau went mad in his early forties, then died in 1850 in a lunatic asylum. Heine's fate was yet more bitter. An incurable disease of the spine confined him for his last eight years to what he called "a mattress grave." The superficial Hellenism of his youth was withered by unbearable pain. His poetry grew deeper and more spiritual, but no positive belief consoled his deathbed. He lamented in one poem that no one would say the mourner's Kaddish for him, nor a Christian mass. He died in Paris in 1856 and was buried in Montmartre.

Jewish religious tradition has strongly affirmed that sin is punished in the here and now, not only in the hereafter. It would have been difficult for the young Herzl not to link Lenau's insanity with the adulterous inspiration of his *Neuere Gedichte* and Heine's mattress grave with his acceptance of baptism for reasons of social gain. Since his own life was to be involved with desires as frustrating as Lenau's and ambitions keener than Heine's, the death of his heroes cast a somber shade. A photographic study of Herzl aged fifteen shows a short-haired Narcissus with melancholy thoughts.

CHAPTER 5

In early February 1875, Theodor was removed from the Realschule, where his marks remained poor, and put under private teachers. Their task was to coach him in Latin and Greek for admission to the Evangelical Gymnasium, a high school with the traditional emphasis on classical studies. The Gymnasium was a solid yet elegant building attached to the city's main Protestant church.[1] It was a fortress of Germanic values.

Transplanted to this more congenial soil, Theodor no longer wilted. Within a year he was getting high marks amid companions who shared his literary tastes and background. A majority of them he remembered in later years as being Jewish.[2] So high a proportion was easily explained. The Jews formed the bulk of the still small Hungarian middle class, and many of them, like the Herzls, identified themselves with German culture. There were good reasons for them to feel closer to Protestants than to Catholics. Hungarian Protestants were, like the Jews, a minority, albeit a minority inside the ruling faith. More important, nineteenth-century Protestants in Europe were generally liberal while the leaders of the Catholic Church were not. In his *Syllabus of Errors*, published in 1864, Pope Pius IX had denounced the concept of toleration for non-Catholic religions; he had ended his *Syllabus* by declaring that "the pontiff neither can nor ought to be reconciled with progress, liberalism and modern civilization." Since Reform Jews believed in all three, they naturally felt more at home with the co-religionists of Luther and Bismarck than with those who owed obedience to this illiberal Pope. Pius had been declared infallible in 1870.

Though Theodor spoke Hungarian and would be able to write it correctly all his life,[3] he felt no great interest in Magyar culture. Yet since 1867 the Magyars had been equal partners with the Germans in what was renamed "the Dual Monarchy." In Hungary—described as the Realm of the Crown of St. Stephen—it was henceforth an offense to speak of the Habsburg monarch as Kaiser (or Emperor). Franz-Josef in Hungary was simply King. The Dual Monarchy seemed a useful formula. Its adoption was prompted by an Austrian need to shore up a fissiparous empire; and it was facilitated by the pro-Hungarian sympathies of the Empress Elizabeth. As a solution to the empire's gravest problem it was impermanent. Hungary's gain was made at the expense of the Czechs, Romanians and Slavs, who received no equivalent boost to their pride. Nor was the Kingdom of St. Stephen democratic, despite its separate Országgyülés, or parliament. An oligarchy ruled and exploited Hungary, its chief victims being the poor, not the religious minorities, whose condition had improved. Since 1867 the Jews suffered from no legal disabilities. What opposition to them existed derived largely from jealousy of their economic strength. Their importance, one later observer wrote, was "out of all proportion to their number, since they monopolize a large portion of the trade, are with the Germans the chief employers of labour, and control not only the finances but to a great extent the government and press of the country. Owing to the improvidence of the Hungarian landowners and the poverty of the peasants, the soil of the country is also gradually passing into their hands."[4] Yet although by the end of the century Jews were to form a fifth of Budapest's population, they would not experience, at least in Herzl's lifetime, the popular hatred felt for them in Vienna, where they were only one in ten. It was the vast Christian majority to whom Habsburg Hungary denied civil rights. The franchise, the least liberal in Europe, was confined to a mere 6 per cent of the population, being based upon property, taxation, professional or official position and ancestral privileges. Those not allowed the vote included all servants (in the most elastic interpretation of the term), apprenticed workmen and agricultural laborers.

Herzl's rejection of Hungarian culture, and ultimately of Hungary itself, was his response to a genuine dilemma. As the century aged, the nationality principle had grown increasingly sacrosanct among the respectable and the uncouth alike. "Where the sentiment of nationality exists in any force," wrote John Stuart Mill, "there is a prima facie case for uniting all the members of the nationality under the same government, and a government to themselves apart."[5] This liberal notion had penetrated the rambling empire of the Romanovs. In 1867—the same year that the Austrians had recognized the Magyar nationality—the Czar opened a great ethnic exhibition in St. Petersburg and addressed representatives of the Slav peoples in Eastern Europe as "my brother Slavs." The last universalist state in Europe had been the part of Italy ruled by the Pope: a poor advertisement. The withdrawal of the French garrison from Rome in 1870 enabled Italian nationalists to create a new Wir, or Noi—an Italian nation uniting the whole peninsula under a liberal king. Challenged for their identity, the Herzls and Diamants made a clear reply: they adhered to Germany, or its southern manifestation—a magnetic Vienna now dominated by liberal ideas. Budapest was thus a kind of exile and the Evangelical Gymnasium an outpost of Austria or better, Prussia.

✻ ✻ ✻

But however interested in ideas, however affected by politics, Theodor was an emotional as well as an intellectual being. His generous lips and liquid eyes balanced his supercilious brow. The sudden emergence of the power to love introduced a disturbing new element into his school days.

His contemporary and co-religionist, Sigmund Freud, basing theories of the human psyche on the study of patients from backgrounds very similar to Theodor's, was to argue that adolescence is normally accompanied by the direction of the libido toward members of the same sex. There are no traces of any such stage in Theodor's emotional development, at least as an adolescent.✻ Since his new school, like the first, was within a few minutes' walk of his parents' house, there was no need for him to live away from home. He was thus spared the barrack-like loneliness to which hothouse friendships are a desperate response. (*Young Törless*, Robert Musil's novel about the Austria of Franz-Josef, shows that such relationships flourished as painfully in central Europe as in England or France.) But a middle-class Jewish family imposed as tight restrictions as a school. His mother warned him against feminine lures and scrutinized his every moment with loving care; the community to which he belonged was omnipresent enough to make prudence essential. It was thus no easier for him to form relationships with girls of his own age than for boarders cooped up in school.

As a loving, not rebellious son, he adhered not only to the commands of his parents, but their values. As an adolescent he knew the

---

✻ Another psychoanalyst has found them later in Herzl's life: Professor Peter Loewenberg in *Theodor Herzl: A Psychoanalytic Study in Charismatic Political Leadership*, pp. 182–83, a work cited elsewhere in this book.

vast surge of subterranean wishes. There was a conflict. "As we grow older," Graham Greene has perceptively written,[6] "we are apt to forget the state of extreme sexual excitement in which we spent the years between sixteen and twenty." The trigger to excitement can be a glance, a touch; its explosion can be worked by a face seen once in the train, a photograph, a phantom created from the mind. The adolescent is unspecialized, seizing on fragmentary, fragile objects which can arouse a passion he remembers forever, though if they reappeared to him in adult life they might leave him unaroused. Byron looked back on a schoolboy friendship as the one pure affection of his existence. Herzl was to look back on an unrealized passion for a girl named Madeleine Kurz who is said to have died young. Herzl in later years repeatedly wrote that she had been his one real love. Reality or phantom, she was a step toward his later idealization of some members of her sex. "We need some poetry in life," he would write. "One should not change the lovely maidens into breadwinners like us. They ought to walk on meadows, to pick lilies or roses and to put them in their hair."[7]

If a young man's only feminine companion is a virtuous sister, idealization is an understandable reaction.† But it can be dangerous. While the dream object is established on a plinth, the real woman is jostled in the gutter. Women as a sex are unconsciously divided into contrasted tribes: mothers and sisters on the dexter, whores on the sinister side. The division is a bad preparation for marriage and a strong incentive to furtive adventures. But these are hard to accomplish in a city where the dreamer is well known. Instead, there is the stifling siesta, the blank night. The young man wakes tired and does not know why. He is surrounded by beloved, familiar faces—and would be anywhere else. In the swing to impurity he may buy his ticket to Bohemia or enlist in the *Légion*. Only later, as anonymous cities offer their trade, as general desire narrows to the particular, as the trigger gets worn through repetition, he is faced with the decisive choice: to capitulate to lust, or deny it sternly. Some capitulate. Willie Heath, innocent friend of the young Marcel Proust, is replaced by the butcher boys of Proust's later years, killing rats to excite him while the family furniture, even the photographs of his mother, are props. Byron becomes Don Juan. This is one way. The other is as radical. Lust is bound with a tourniquet. The man of power is born.

Sixteen, then seventeen, Theodor pushes on with his studies. He

---

† An interesting reverse equivalent is that of the Brontë household in isolated Yorkshire. There the one young male was a brother, Branwell, who reappears under various guises in the novels of his sisters.

spins his doom with his daydreams. His father goes away on business; the son stays at home. He begins to cultivate a sense of dress, the disdainful aloofness of the dandy. The still dreamy face half hides aggression. The warmth of the sensual mouth is checked by wary distrust. He is too narcissistic to have close friends; only allies or associates. "He was always shy," an acquaintance wrote later, when success had given him grounds for more confidence than he felt as a youth; "it was a torment for him to meet new people."[8] Shyness and hostility are linked. Shyness is the projection onto others of our own disdain. And we disdain because we lack confidence, because to have someone to despise balances our lack of strength. We, the worldwide members of Wir, despise the less cultured, the provincial, the dialect speakers. So when we enter a room, or sit to table with those of a different city, class or faith, we have behind our eyes a mental image of the strangers molded on ourselves. Because we are hostile, they will be hostile too. But because we are beginning to be equipped —we have studied French, English, the piano—we can brazen out the enmity of others with more than our beautiful clothes, with all the attributes of the dominant faction, which in the nineteenth century is the aristocracy. We are therefore willing to gamble our fortune on a card or fight a duel. We carry ourselves erect. We would be an aristocrat were we not already known for what we are. In another city we would not be known.

In this state of mind, or something like it, Theodor began, as thousands before and after him, to explore the sister-theme of death. "I have thought much of the purpose of human existence, the highest manifestation of life on earth."[9] Personal experience invades, still pompously veiled, the literary production of the schoolboy laboring toward a style. Youth is the time when extremes are savored. He swings between hedonism—"the aim of life was enjoyment and freedom from care"—and altruism—"the only possible aim of life was love for parents, for one's own, and for all human beings." But then to castrate the choice: a bleak knowledge of the "impotence of man." Death and annihilation are enigmas no Oedipus could solve.

The deaths that have scarred the twentieth century have largely been caused by injustice. The equivalent deaths of the nineteenth, the black lines prematurely ending chapters, were caused by disease. One dirt-borne killer, typhoid fever, boasted redoubtable victims: Prince Albert, the husband of Queen Victoria; Willie Heath, the innocent friend of Marcel Proust; Olga, the best-loved and cleverest of Lenin's sisters. Theodor's only sister must be added to them. In February 1878 Pauline Herzl caught the disease and within a few days was dead. This death, not the disappearance of the ghostly Madeleine, shattered boyhood.

The week of mourning prompted Theodor to a declaration of intent. The family were visited by their rabbi, Dr. Samuel Kohn. After the usual condolences, the rabbi questioned Theodor on his plans for the future. He would be taking his finals in June.

"I intend," he replied in German, "to be a writer."[10]

Neither the rabbi nor the family regarded writing as a secure profession. A compromise was agreed. Like Heine before him, Theodor would study law.

But not in Budapest.

For the crisis in the family's situation we have Theodor's terse account written hastily twenty years later. It was in English, a language whose nuances he never mastered, which explains the floating phrase at the beginning (it was he who was in the highest class at the Gymnasium, not Pauline): "While in the highest class in the Gymnasium, my only sister died, a girl of eighteen; my good mother became so melancholy with grief, that we removed to Vienna in the year 1878." Herzl's account conceals the strangest feature of the move, its speed. Alex Bein attributes this to Jeanette Herzl. "It was the mother who, crushed in spirit, found intolerable those surroundings—the home, the district, the city—which had once been filled with her daughter's presence. Within a week after Pauline's death the family moved to Vienna." Professor Bein, a previous biographer of Herzl, adds a fanciful description of Theodor's emotions.

> Left alone to his parents, he drew closer to them. He felt it incumbent upon him to mitigate their sense of loss by giving them a double mixture of love and tenderness and attention. The relationship between mother and son, which had always been tenderly intimate, acquired a new depth. His attitude toward his father, which had evolved from that of the child into that of the comrade, took on a new warmth. It was as if the three of them closed their ranks in order to hide the gap. These family bonds, which at certain moments might have seemed excessive in their strength, were resolved by death alone, the father passing away first, the mother last.[11]

Close-textured clichés surround the mystery with a protective hedge. In place of family arguments or discussion of plans for their new lodgings (and they were a prosperous family loaded with the cumbrous knickknacks of the day, not nomads), the fact of departure is presented as though grief normally makes people act in this manner. In fact, the precipitate move could only have been undertaken by an unusual mother. It was probably inspired by the feelings of two members of the family triangle, Jeanette and Theodor, against the silence of Jacob Herzl, who felt his daughter's loss most keenly. Jeanette seems not to have suffered the numbing helplessness, the wish to withdraw in silence amid mementos of the beloved that might be considered normal after so sudden an illness and so swift a death. Or if she felt these promptings, her urge to move and her ability to move outweighed them.

The decision to move becomes comprehensible when we concentrate on the place to which the move was made. Vienna symbolized the *Kultur* that had become a substitute for a religious faith. To Jeanette Herzl the beautiful mourning prayers of orthodox Judaism were as unavailing as they were to the young Jacob Wassermann after his mother's death: the duty of rising early every day for a year to say Kaddish at the synagogue almost made him hate her memory, though he had loved her dearly when she was alive.

Herzl's own motives were complex. It has been said that he guarded every keepsake of Pauline's as a sacred relic, that he would travel annually to Budapest on the anniversary of her death.[12] Yet though a study of his future Februaries fails to confirm this, there is no doubt of Pauline's all-important role in his emotional life. She had personified the femininity of which Madeleine Kurz was the projection. And now she personified death. He must have wanted to get away, not so much to avoid associations with the dead as to plunge into the city of life, the metropolis where the other extreme of his divided imagination, an urge to downward self-transcendence, could find play. Pauline had become death and the memory of beauty: she would haunt his writings, her name standing on the dedication page of his only important novel, her character providing the inspiration for the heroine. Budapest, which now held Pauline forever, thus stood for constraint. Vienna stood for freedom and life. Among the millions to whom the Herzls would be strangers, the creatures of erotic fancy must surely exist. As a student, no longer a schoolboy living at home, he could do what he had dreamed of doing, win admiration from larger groups than Wir and find replacements for Madeleine, if not Pauline. The departure from Budapest meant farewell to boyhood; the ascent to Vienna stood for ambition and desire. Both these were balanced in Theodor's nature by a melancholy deriving in part from his favorite writers, in part from his doubts about human existence. Perhaps in Vienna he would discover that life, surrounded as it was by "those eternal, insoluble riddles, death and annihilation," still had a purpose.[13]

PART TWO

The Young Knight
1878–84

If I become something better than an untalented scribbler
(my visitor, Mr. Doubt, decidedly doesn't think so) then I
shall mingle with people now and again as Baron von
Rittershausen, like that clever man Haroun al-Rashid, once
Caliph in Bagdad.[1]

CHAPTER 6

The Herzl parents rented an apartment in Leopoldstadt, the only part of Vienna on the left or east bank of the Danube, the side nearer to Budapest. It was a sprawling business district largely populated by Jews. Except for June, when he returned to Budapest to sit his school finals, Theodor spent the rest of 1878 absorbing, first Vienna, then after the autumn, the routine of a student in the faculty of law.

Vienna, the capital of the southern German empire, was a potent antidote to grief. The cosmopolitan city emphasized the more cheerful aspects of German culture. For the northern empire, 1878 was a year of great prestige: its Chancellor Bismarck presided over a gathering of statesmen planning how to shore up the Ottoman Sultan while distributing some of his outer provinces among themselves. But although Austria, with Britain, was a moving spirit behind the Congress of Berlin, and although the Habsburgs gained Bosnia and Herzegovina as directly administered territories while controlling the nominally independent Montenegro, the Viennese were more interested in living than ruling: their chief concern in 1878 was the creation of a capital to rival Paris.

Until just before Theodor's birth, the smallish inner city had been guarded by a colossal system of fortifications erected against the Turks. Now that the Turks were no longer a menace these had been pulled down and the vacant space had been turned into one of the world's most imposing boulevards, the two-mile Ringstrasse, which ran in a gigantic horseshoe around the old city with its cathedral dedicated to St. Stephen and its palace to the Habsburgs. The new

land at the disposal of the city fathers after the removal of the fortifications fetched such high prices that they could build lavishly, without incurring debt. The Ring, with an average width of fifty yards,
and planted with trees, became the spine to imposing vertebrae.
Theodor's first year some buildings still smelled of plaster while others, corseted in scaffolding, rang to the mason's hammer. The tall,
handsome young man, aware of his good looks yet still inexpert in the
art of using them, strode beneath innumerable male statues, perched
high on cornices or straining as giant caryatids to uphold doorways.
The city's heroic style, its particular blend of modernity and nostalgia,
marked him for life.

The modernity showed itself in new standards of hygiene, in an
ease of communication by rail that made Vienna the nodal point of
Europe, in the university where a school of law and economics, re-
formist, social-minded but non-Marxist, had affinities with the later
Fabianism of England. On another level, it showed in the collapse of
traditional restraints so that nocturnal Vienna offered excitement and
danger in a breath-taking potion.

The nostalgia was immediately apparent in the architecture. The
parliament building, dominated by its statue of Athena, had Hellenic
porticoes while the Rathaus, or municipal building, was fretted like a
Gothic fortress; the elegance of the Italian Renaissance lay suavely
on theaters and hotels. Spiritual signs matched the physical and these,
like the architecture, reflected a common European malaise at sudden
progress, a yearning to go back as well as forward. An age made by
engineers and businessmen dreamed of knights in armor. It was a
north European dream, peopling the Oxford Union with frescoes of
pallid knights, inspiring Disraeli to visit the lands of the Crusades,
turning the thoughts of Richard Wagner to Tannhäuser and Lohen-
grin.

Knighthood influenced Theodor Herzl in contrasted ways. As the
son of a Jewish father who had achieved a directorship in the Hun-
garia Bank but worked in Vienna as a stock-exchange agent, he saw
himself as the knight of a liberal and scientific future in which technology would transform the German empires and their neighbors, a
future in which the noble of every faith, or none, could, by conforming to one social standard, share in the ardors and rewards of power.
The social standard, the system of manners fit for a nineteenth-
century knight owed nothing to Talmud or Gospel; it found its style
in the brave swagger, the licentious elegance of student fraternities.
The imagery of knighthood was used on another less lofty level.
Simone de Beauvoir writes that modest women commonly "give a

nickname to the little boy's sex, speaking to him of it as a small person who is at once himself and other than himself."[2] Theodor called his own sex his "young candidate for Knighthood." There were enough contradictions in these roles to make his student days as mixed with peril and excitement as his student nights.

Yet outwardly, for much of his time, he maintained the stance of a dutiful, impeccable son. His Olympian conduct was nevertheless shot through by reminders that he was suspicious and therefore devious. His cousin Raoul Auernheimer* was two years old when the Herzls moved to Vienna. Theodor, then eighteen, frequently visited his family. Raoul, a writer, later recalled:

> He used to test me by placing a lump of sugar under the piano. I crawled after it, put it in my mouth and proudly stood up, banging my head against the rather unprepossessing underside of the piano. "That stupid boy," cried my cousin, joining my mother in the enjoyment of my unspeakable stupidity. But when, a week later, he repeated the experiment for the umpteenth time, something quite unexpected happened. I crawled under the piano and put the lump of sugar in my mouth, but instead of straightening up as expected, I crept, sucking away at the sugar, to the opposite side of the room, and only there did I carefully resume my vertical position, slowly and shyly looking upward.

After four years as a student Theodor played a further trick on his young cousin. Having offered to buy Raoul a penknife (and promoted for the offer to the style of uncle), he took him to a shop and showed him one knife encased in mother-of-pearl and another in horn. He told the six-year-old boy that the mother-of-pearl knife was the cheap one and the horn knife was the expensive. Which did he want? " 'This one,' said I, pointing to the mother of pearl knife. It was the more expensive one, however; my good uncle, who in his youth sometimes had too low an opinion of people in general, had simply wanted to put me to the test by switching prices."[3]

Vienna was similarly testing Theodor as to his future. In a city where success was a substitute for roots, he was to brood throughout his student days on how to win distinction. The faculty of law showed by its German title, *Facultät der Rechts- und Staatswissenschaften,* its close link with the state. Although its curriculum had been reformed in 1848 and now aimed to give the student more than the dry factual training hitherto usual, it was virtually a school for state servants. The first year was devoted to the study of Roman and

---

* Raoul Auernheimer, author of *Prince Metternich, Statesman and Lover* (1940), was the son of one of Jeanette's Diamant cousins by a Christian father.

German Law, the second to Canon Law, Austrian Civil Law and Criminal Law, the third to International Law, Political Economy and the Philosophy of Law. The fourth year was left a blank for the student's revision. Although Herzl was permanently influenced by Roman Law (thanks to a brilliant teacher from Thuringia, Gustav Demelius), he was not an outstanding student and did not take his degree in the minimal time.

His decision on leaving Budapest had been to be a writer. There were at least two ways, Vienna made clear, in which he could fulfill this ambition. He could be a journalist or a playwright.

Since the constitution of 1867, censorship had become less oppressive and the press had flourished. At the time of Herzl's arrival more than 250 newspapers were published in Austria. In the capital, the *Neue Freie Presse,* founded in 1864, was the best of more than a dozen daily newspapers with substantial circulations. Serious, closely printed and without photographic illustration, these papers had a voracious appetite for words. Most reserved a space at the bottom of their pages, ruled off from the rest by a line, for what were known as *feuilletons.* A *feuilleton* was a paddock of small print, running from page to page, in which a writer had anything up to five thousand words in which to display his wit, knowledge or sensitivity; he could do this through the medium of short stories, descriptions of places or comments on events of the day. A successful *feuilleton* would win its author fame as sparkling as the bubbles of champagne, and as short-lived. Theodor's copious productions as a schoolboy were a useful preparation for success in this popular form.

The theater was equally eager for plays that would appeal to the Viennese spirit. This was less serious than the Prussian, owing much to the cosmopolitan nature of Austrian society: until the loss of Milan and Venice to a united Italy, a large Italian community had brought grace while various Slav peoples continued their emotional addition. The Viennese spirit was less rational, or speculative, than the French, because the clash of nationalities produced a tension in which ideas could be dangerous. Viennese audiences most enjoyed the humorous, slightly risqué play or the operetta, where even music mocked itself. One of the buildings behind scaffolding in Herzl's days as a student was the imposing Burgtheater, a-building between 1874 and 1888. On the other side of the Ring from the Rathaus, this Renaissance edifice was to be stuck with statues personifying such qualities as *Heroismus* and *Egoismus,* its main entrance crowned with busts of Lessing, Goethe and Schiller. One evening Theodor and a friend sauntered past the structure hidden behind its screen. "You know," he remarked, "I'll be in there one day."

His ambition leaped further than words. In his first term he had already roughed out a complex scheme for a series of comedies. He chose a striking title: *Die Ritter vom Gemeinplatz*, or *The Knights of the Commonplace*.

The title was also significant, for Herzl lived in a tension between the commonplace world of every day—his parents' apartment, the grand piano of his cousins, the need to attend lectures, and to pay his fees—and the dreams inspired by an Imperial city. In 1878 this tension seemed to stretch against a sky untroubled by shapes more sinister than Athena or some allegoric male. Yet the liberal, progressive society in which Jews played a preponderant part could, if it closed its ears to waltz or aria, hear disquieting tremors.

The tremors were audible both north and south of the Alps. The economy that brought great rewards to some and starvation wages to others was not such as to foster a calm society. Five years earlier a German liberal statesman, Edward Lasker, had warned of the dangers of allowing the capital squeezed from a defeated France to be wasted in speculation rather than slowly digested for the needs of the state. Lasker was a Jew. So was Bethel Henry Strousberg, the ringleader in the sensational corruption denounced in Lasker's report. Sane observers saw that the preponderance of Jews in some financial scandals reflected Jewish preponderance in economic and industrial activities. For every Strousberg there were dozens of unnoticed Jews financing such pioneering activities as the construction of railways and the development of oil wells. But Wilhelm Marr, a Hamburg journalist, had exploited Lasker's disclosures in a pamphlet entitled *The Victory of Jewishness over Germanness*. The *Judenthum* and *Germanenthum* in Marr's title were vague, unwieldy bludgeons, hard to translate into another language. But Marr was the probable creator of another term— anti-Semitism—of which the world and Herzl would hear more.[4] Around such emotional ideas, so different from the idealism of Jeanette Herzl's Germanic heroes, reputations, as pamphleteers and demagogues, were also to be made in Vienna and other German towns.

CHAPTER 7

Vienna University was a place in which students heard lectures, studied and were examined; it was not a place where they ate or slept. A major part of the student's life was lived in the town. "In Vienna I studied law, took part in all the students' stupid farces . . ."[1] was how Herzl began his account in clumsy English; a biographer has amended the last phrase to read "the ridiculous pranks of the student body."[2] Farces or pranks, they had a seriousness characteristic of young Germans. The Oxford tradition of affixing chamber pots to spires would have seemed to them childish, the American custom of pantie raids unworthy of aspirant Casanovas. Continental students took part in politics a century before their Anglo-Saxon comrades. During Theodor's six years at Vienna students were to play an important role in undermining the liberal dream. Their characteristic sport—dueling—involved controlled violence very different from the accidental violence of English Rugby or American football. Extracurricular activities meant more to Herzl than set courses. He was never to shine in examinations and would rebuke a friend who pretended otherwise.

A liberal institution, the Akademische Lesehalle, still dominated, in 1878, the leisure of the more ambitious students. A cultural union with nearly a thousand members, it discountenanced affiliations with party or sect. The former president of Wir became an active member in its last thirty months of life. It was at the Lesehalle that Arthur Schnitzler (later a major playwright and novelist) first set eyes on Herzl. "I still remember the first time I saw you," he wrote later. "You were making a speech, and were being 'sharp'—so sharp! You were smiling ironically. If only I could speak and smile in that way, I thought to myself."[3] Schnitzler, like Herzl of Jewish origin, was attracted by the way in which Herzl's demeanor contradicted the traditional Jewish ideal. As debater Herzl disregarded the Talmudic teaching that to wound a man in public was as bad as shedding blood; his disdainful pride was a deliberate rejection of the rabbinical exaltation of humility as the highest virtue.* Schnitzler also admired the way Herzl dressed and tried to copy him. Yet in dress as in debate Herzl always seemed twenty paces in the lead. One attempt at sartorial competition was quickly punctured. Herzl, two years older than Schnitzler, allowed his dark eyes to rest on a newly purchased tie. "Till now," he said sadly, "I had considered you a Brummel."

Schnitzler was at this time an admirer rather than a friend. Theodor's two most intimate friends—they remained so until their untimely deaths within a year of each other and thereafter left no replacements—were Heinrich Kana and Oswald Boxer. Both men came from much poorer families than Herzl's. Kana's Romanian parents kept their self-respect in spite of poverty; three years older than Herzl, Heinrich had to support himself by tutoring the children of rich Jews. Boxer's father was a stock exchange tout, a speculator of the lowest water. Each young man represented a pole in Theodor's temperament. Kana was shy, unworldly and introspective, assertive only in the critical judgments he passed on a world he could not storm, though he, like Herzl, planned to write for it. Boxer had been born in Vienna the same year that Herzl had been born in Budapest. Physically he was tall and strong with a large head and lofty brow; his nose and far-gazing eyes betokened the pioneer. A man of fearless energy, he pretended to no more than talent. Like Kana he had subsisted through private tuition; his highest ambition was to succeed in journalism: slick, proficient, it did not matter so long as it paid.

Like his contemporary Sigmund Freud, Herzl in Vienna made close friends only among Jews. He shared with Kana and Boxer, not a Jewish faith, since all three were skeptics, but a Jewish predicament. Committed to a status none of them had asked for, which involved beliefs they did not accept, they could all three discuss from a shared position the ideas that struggled behind the Lesehalle's confident

---

* "Whoever causes by offensive words the face of his fellow-man to turn pale is almost guilty of shedding blood." Babylonian Talmud, B. Metsia 58b. The Gospel exaltation of the meek is constantly echoed by the rabbis. For example: "Who is a son of the World to Come? He who is humble, of lowly disposition, enters and leaves a room with bent form, and studies Torah constantly, without claiming any credit for himself." Sanh. 88b. The ideal is also supported by the Pentateuch. Cf. Numbers XII: 3, "Now Moses was the most humble of men, the humblest man on earth."

façade and which would lead to its collapse. To understand the young Herzl we must understand this clash of ideas.

As in Budapest, the major problem was one of identity. Asked in Hungary to declare themselves, the Herzls had chosen to be German since parochial nationalisms were potentially hostile while the Prussian state—the dominant German entity—was the logical continuation of the Enlightenment with its liberal ideals and its *Kulturkampf* against the power of the Church. But on Austrian soil, in German Vienna, *Deutschtum* (a more common form for what Wilhelm Marr had termed *Germanenthum*) seemed less inviting.

For a Jew in Austria to defend *Deutschtum*, as Herzl did, required either stubborness of soul or a long view of history.

Perhaps because it felt itself threatened by the clamant new nationalisms of Czechs and other Slavs, perhaps because the wounds of the Thirty Years' War and the Napoleonic occupation were still unhealed, *Deutschtum* had developed into a Pan-German nationalism different from anything to be found in France, England or America. Since the Reformation France and England had been clear-bounded states; the United States of America had lost no war since its foundation. Unquestioned frontiers, the lack of subordinate but seething nationalities made it easier for each country to relax. German nationalists, on the contrary, could look back on no settled state and no fixed boundaries. Instead they surveyed a humiliating history of division and overlordship by petty tyrants or destructive invaders; what unity had existed had done so under the grandiose label of the Holy Roman Empire. To the enlightened thinkers of the eighteenth century (Frau Herzl's mentors) the unity of German culture had either been enough or a good second best. But as German power developed with the defeat of France, so did a nationalism that found no precise territorial definition and therefore looked elsewhere. "Pan-Germanism was based on the idea that all persons who were of German race, blood, or descent, wherever they lived or to whatever state they belonged, owed their primary loyalty to Germany and should become citizens of the German state, their true homeland. They, and even their fathers and forefathers, might have grown up under 'foreign' skies or in 'alien' environments, but their fundamental inner 'reality' remained German."[4] Emancipated Jews and Germans were so closely linked that their ideas seemed to echo each other. Moses Hess, from the Jewish side, had made a very similar statement sixteen years earlier. Hess had started his intellectual life as one of the earliest Communists and an associate of Karl Marx, though unlike Marx he was never baptized. In 1848 his pro-German passion inspired him to set an anti-French poem to music. When he sent it to its German author, he received a snub.[5] By 1862, in *Rome and Jerusalem,* he was proposing a Jewish nationalism based on race. "Jews are not a religious group," he then wrote, "but a separate nation, a special race, and the modern Jew who denies this is not only an apostate, a religious renegade, but a traitor to his people, his tribe, his race." Hess's hatred for France had changed to love. "The French, the soldiers of progress, will break the gravestones, and the peoples will begin to rise from their graves. Just as Rome which since Innocent the Third has been the city of eternal sleep, is today being gradually resurrected as the city of eternal life by the stout hearted patriots who fight for Italian freedom, so Jerusalem too will awake." As Hess wrote (the days of Theodor's infancy) the French were at work in Egypt. Hess hoped to involve them in support of his dream. "France must, once she has built the Suez Canal, make it possible for the Jews to establish colonies on its shores, for without soil there is no national life." Theodor was not to glance at *Rome and Jerusalem* until he was thirty-eight nor read it properly until he was forty-one.[6] Nor did he read Wilhelm Marr's first book, *Der Judenspiegel,* published precisely the same year. In 1862 pamphlets pushing these racialist views among Jews or non-Jews were read by their authors and few else. The students of nineteenth-century Vienna, like their counterparts in twentieth-century America and Europe, followed culture heroes, men who symbolized in their persons the clash of ideas before these ideas were first examined and then expressed by politicians. In the summer that saw the Herzls installed in Vienna perhaps the most important quarrel of the century involved two such heroes: Friedrich Nietzsche, Germany's profoundest thinker, and Richard Wagner, certainly Germany's and possibly the century's greatest artist. Four years earlier Nietzsche had written that "all previous music seems stiff and uncertain when compared with Wagner's." He had extolled the German nationalism that inspired it. In 1878 he broke with his former idol. "To turn my back on Wagner," Nietzsche wrote, "was for me a piece of fate; to get to like anything else whatever afterwards was for me a triumph."[7]

His rejection did not mean reconciliation with the Christianity he had learned in his father's parsonage. Nietzsche's repudiation of Wagner started in aesthetics. "Wagner's art," he decided, "is absolutely the art of the age: an aesthetic age would have rejected it. The more subtle people amongst us actually do reject it even now. The coarsifying of everything aesthetic."[8] But this led him to ask what it was in the age that Wagner's art expressed. He answers: "That brutality and most delicate weakness which exist side by side, that running wild of natural instincts, and nervous hypersensitiveness, that thirst for emotion which arises from fatigue and the love of fatigue."⁹ Later, he would admit "I am just as much a child of my age as Wagner—i.e. I am a decadent. The only difference is that I recognise the fact, that I struggled against it."¹⁰

Parcel of the age against which he struggled, in advance of his time, was the conviction that race—not geography, climate or economics—constituted the decisive factor in history. In the Wagner household, where Nietzsche had been a courtier, it took the form of an exaltation of all things German with, as its natural corollary, the disparagement of other races. Wagner's second wife, Cosima, was the illegitimate daughter of Franz Liszt, a Hungarian, and his French mistress; among her ancestors there was at least one Jew. Yet racial bias affected her judgment even more than her husband's, inspiring her on one occasion to dismiss Sarah Bernhardt in *Tosca* as "an old she-ape."¹¹ As late as 1874 Nietzsche, then professor of classical philology in Basel, had pleased the Wagners by likening the German predicament—struggling for life against non-Germanic elements—with that of the ancient Greeks amid "a chaos of foreign forms and ideas—Semitic, Babylonian, Lydian and Egyptian."¹²

By 1878, the year of Nietzsche's revolt, Wagner was working on the plot of *Parsifal*. The anti-Christian and the parson's son in Nietzsche were alike repelled by Wagner's theme. The first revolted at symbols derived from Christian legend, such as the Holy Grail, while the second perceived the intellectual trickery by which a pagan mania was passed off as the Gospel. "If Wagner was a Christian, then Liszt was perhaps a Father of the Church!"¹³ Nietzsche explicitly rejected his former master's hatred of the Jews.† In his escape from Wagner Nietzsche turned south. "*Il faut méditerraniser la musique*,"¹⁴ he wrote, using French to say it. He praised Bizet for his dryness of atmosphere, his southern, tawny, sunburnt sensitivity; so different from Wagner. "This music is gay, but not in a French or German way. Its gaiety is African; fate hangs over it, its happiness is short, sudden, without reprieve."¹⁵

In a prophetic insight Nietzsche wrote: "I entertain the fear that the effects of Wagner's art will ultimately pour into that torrent which takes its rise on the other side of the mountains, and which knows how to flow even over the mountains."¹⁶ Nietzsche's con-

---

† Wagner's animus was against all non-Aryans, though this was a term to come into fashion later. Indeed, in *Parsifal*, the Moorish world overlooked by Monsalvat is more dangerous than Kundry, the Wandering Jewess whose only escape is annihilating death.

scious suggestion was that Wagner might end up an ally of the ultra-
montane, or extreme papal, party. A deeper prophecy lies buried in
the words: that from the German lands south of the Alps intolerance
would engulf all Germany; in Vienna, before Berlin or Frankfurt,
hatred of the Jews was to become a political force; Austria would
prove the nursery for those who saw history in racial terms.

Neither Wagner nor Nietzsche was a politician. Their quarrel has
a purity impossible in the bowl of compromise wherein statesmen
swim. In 1878 the issues involved had not entered Austrian politics.
Germanism was still a movement that Theodor Herzl, Heinrich Kana
and Oswald Boxer could accept; rich assimilated Jews indeed belonged to the German nationalist parties. But a politician who
preached something close to Wagnerism was already a brutal cloud
on the Viennese horizon. Georg von Schönerer[17] came from a background similar to that of the Herzls except that he was loosely Catholic while they were Jewish. Matthias Schönerer, his father, had risen
to wealth and nobility in a manner possible to Christian and Jew alike
in the post-Metternich Austria. He accepted the ideas that went with
Habsburg liberalism: humanism, Catholicism, tolerance, embodied
in a mixed society whose bond was obedience to the Emperor. Matthias Schönerer's chief work was the construction, between 1856 and
1860, of the Empress Elizabeth Railway, an enterprise financed by
the Rothschilds. Made a baron by Franz-Josef, he bought an estate
at Rosenau, inserted the "von" and assimilated himself to the country
nobility as deftly as many Jews to the urban plutocracy. His son
Georg (unlike Herzl) had a violent Oedipal reaction to his imposing
father. He rejected both liberalism and the Catholic Church. In so
doing he was destined to win applause, not only from nationalistic
students, but from the greatest anti-Semite of the coming age. "He
foresaw the inevitable downfall of the Austrian State," was the
comment of Adolf Hitler in *Mein Kampf*, "more clearly and accurately
than anyone else."[18] It would be as true to say that he worked for
this downfall. After election to the Austrian parliament in 1873, he
became the spokesman for the farmers, the group most implacably
hostile to the city and all it represented. He had convincing arguments against the ruling liberal coalition: its inability to deal with the
Slav nationalisms so threatening to German power, and its indifference to social problems. The same year that Herzl joined the Akademische Lesehalle, von Schönerer was elected an honorary member of
a very different student body, the Leseverein. The Lesehalle's greatest
president, a Jew, had taught that "in the temple of knowledge all
worshippers are equal."[19] The Leseverein taught that if Germans

could not be supreme in the Austrian empire it would be better for them to secede and adhere to Germany. The criterion for being German had not been formulated so as to exclude such devotees of German culture as the Herzls. But neither had it been formulated to include them. There was enough doubt to chill those who retained the eighteenth-century humanism of Lessing or who had veins filled with the same blood as Nathan the Wise. But in Theodor's case not enough to rule out personal distractions or to freeze ambition.

CHAPTER 8

In Budapest, Herzl had been inhibited by the proximity of his parents from meeting young women outside the family circle; his love affairs had been confined to daydreams. His chastity was enforced by prudence, not religious scruple. In his last year at the Budapest Gymnasium he had lumped Moses with Jesus and the Comte de Saint-Germain* in the category of "sly deceivers."[1] Thus disarmed from religious constraints, he arrived in a city whose young men were at least as dissipated as British soldiers. (In the British Army for the 1880s the infection rate for venereal diseases ran at 27,500 per 100,000 men per annum.[2]) The night life of Vienna was notorious throughout central Europe and its effects were not confined to the Austrian equivalent of "the lower ranks." To cite a tragic example: Crown Prince Rudolf, the only son of the Emperor Franz-Josef, was infected as a result of one of his countless amours in February 1886. Although the royal illness was passed off as catarrh of the bladder (caught, it was said, while lying on wet ground when out shooting) recent research has established that it was in fact gonorrhea and that the drugs recorded in the Court Pharmacy—the use of *Zincum sulphuricum* in particular—could have produced no cure. The Prince, it has been established, infected his wife, Crown Princess Stephanie of Belgium, who was not only rendered sterile by the disease but permanently alienated from her husband. His suicide pact at Mayerling may well have been the final result of this blighting mishap.[3]

The Viennese 1880s were not only half a century distant from the

---

* A mysterious eighteenth-century adventurer who claimed to have lived for two thousand years thanks to an elixir of his own invention.

discovery of penicillin; they were some decades from the general acceptance of terms and attitudes derived from psychoanalysis. Expressions such as "superego" or "sublimation" would have puzzled Herzl, while "id" and "libido" would have retained their Latin meanings of "that thing" and "lust."†

Invaluable as Freud's discoveries have proved, human beings enjoyed some advantages in living before they were made. Victorian worthies, the late Sir Maurice Bowra remarked,[4] could conduct irregularities behind a curtain of prudery without being embarrassed by a wide-awake public. Herzl was always candid. Coming to manhood when constraints were weakening but before each impulse of the flesh had been named and catalogued, he revealed much of himself and his basic nature. Not, of course, in public. Like most men he showed one face to the world, and another to intimate friends and his private self. The university saw the elegant, incisive intellectual admired by Arthur Schnitzler. A Youth Diary dating from 1882‡ and an intimate correspondence with Heinrich Kana which began still earlier reveal a self-doubting pessimist with underworld desires. To those who would see Herzl as he really was, who would discover the source of later achievements and torments, the candor and self-revelation of the correspondence and the Youth Diary offer illumination.[5]

Yet it is an illumination that has been little used. Some of his followers grew up when it was bad form to mention certain topics. Jacob de Haas, author of a biography in two volumes, is one example, having been born in London in 1872. The closest he comes to analyzing Herzl's emotional makeup is in a passage where he discusses him as a playwright. Herzl, de Haas proclaims, "detested the soil of sex problems, hated obscenity, and his farces lacked that 'double entendre' which, as everywhere else, brought most laughs on the German and Austrian stage. A cavalier in appearance, he was strangely indifferent to women; a clean, bourgeois mind and frugal habits kept him apart from the Bohemian circles of his profession. German sentimentalism toward places and things, extreme tenderness toward children, courtesy toward women, whatever their station, were characteristic of him."[6] He might have been describing Parsifal.°

---

† Five years older than Herzl, Sigmund Freud published his first work, *Studien über Hysterie*, in collaboration with Josef Breuer, in 1895; he published *Moses and Monotheism*, his last, in 1939. The general acceptance of his ideas can perhaps be dated to the 1920s when he contributed a substantial essay on psychoanalysis to the thirteenth edition of the Encyclopaedia Britannica. Pre-war editions had not mentioned the new science.

‡ See Appendix III.

° Hagiolatry played its part in charming the warts from the portrait given by de Haas. In his seven-hundred-word foreword he manages to invoke Kossuth, Garibaldi, Lincoln, Mazzini, Disraeli, "an Assyrian monarch" and the Messiah.

But later biographers have revealed no more, and this despite the meticulous neatness with which Herzl preserved the detritus of his past. Professor Alex Bein, born thirty-one years later than de Haas and until 1971 director of the Zionist Central Archives in Jerusalem, where the detritus is housed, merely refurbishes the de Haas portrait. "As a matter of fact, this 'blasé' man of the world was, in his heart of hearts, too much the sensitive spirit, the enthusiast and the moralist to permit himself to pluck whatever flowers happened to offer themselves to his senses."[7] An American psychoanalyst, Peter Loewenberg, was the first to advert to the unpublished correspondence with Kana and to examine the implications of the Youth Diary.† One letter is of such importance that it must be printed and annotated in full. It is important not only because it explodes the pious myths in which idolaters have attempted to bury Herzl but because of its grave implications for his medical history. The letter, dated June 8, 1880, was written from Vöslau, a thermal spa some nineteen miles from Vienna.

Dear Friend,

I am studying. Every day 10–15 sheets of canon law, plus a considerable amount out of Arndt.‡ I received your kind letter. But you have made a mistake. I did not want a syringe, but a ——— truss.**
I shall have to give myself into the hands of a speech-specialist because of my tongue-tiedness.†† I have put the ——— syringe on one side. Perhaps my next ++++‡‡ will be cured by means of sulphate of zinc.*** In one of the most high class ladies' fancy goods shops I got them to make a linen sheath for my penis, resorting to downright lies which I haven't enough ink to put down. Fortunately the seamstress was a young girl of seventeen summers, who cannot possibly know at that age what consequences unhappy love (unplatonic love naturally) can have.—True, she exerted all

† In *Theodor Herzl: A Psychoanalytic Study in Charismatic Political Leadership*, being part of *The Psychoanalytic Interpretation of History*, ed. Benjamin B. Wolman, New York: Basic Books, 1971.

‡ Karl Ludwig Arndt (1803–78), pupil of Savigny, was professor in Vienna in 1855. The works that Herzl would be studying for canon law: *Lehrbuch der Pandekten*, 1850–52; *Juristische Enzyklopädie und Methodologie*, 1843; *Gesammelte zivilistische Schriften*, 1873–74.

** Herzl omits the first part of the compound: possibly *"penis."* There is a play on *Spritze* (syringe) and *Schürze* (truss).

†† Because he cannot bring himself to speak plainly, both Kana and the seamstress make mistakes.

‡‡ The missing word is probably *der Tripper*, the German for gonorrhea.

*** "The local treatment of *Zincum sulfuricum* in the treatment of gonorrhea of the urethra was the standard treatment at the time—see I. Neumann, *Lehrbuch der venerischen Krankheiten und der Syphilis*, published by W. Fraumuller, Vienna, 1888." Professor Albert Wiedmann, director of the Second University Skin Hospital in Vienna, quoted by Judtmann, op. cit., p. 19.

her skill in order to satisfy me, but did not quite succeed. The said sheath is a little too tight for my penis, but I ask you: how is she to know that at seventeen? I can only get him in when he is being quite quiet, like a peaceful trouser-burgher. But that is extremely seldom, for bold German-Austrian as he is, in imitation of the great Paul Schulz, his fellow-truant from lectures,††† he rebels against my sheath regulation.‡‡‡ So I got them to make a second under-pants pocket for me, but, this time, my lies encountered some in-credulity. Surely she hasn't been inquiring somewhere! Or was it the strange shape that gave her ideas? You have very strange thoughts when you are seventeen.—However, this second apparatus also has its defects. It is true I can get the candidate for knight-hood into the linen shaft, but either he feels himself confined or he is now slipping out.—You see what erection dilemma fills my mind.*—Should I perhaps strip him of the whole hair shirt?—All right, but you must not forget, much dripping liquid† flows down. What would the washerwoman think?! Perhaps she would despise me. Should I risk it?

Yours‡

Theodor Herzl

Tell Russo and Fischer when you see them that I'll soon be writing to them.

This letter was written seven weeks before Herzl passed his first law examination and thus toward the end of his first period of stu-denthood: a phase in which, under the influence of Schopenhauer, he had doubted if life was anything but the swing between hope and despair, with despair the more rational of the two emotions. The frivolous tone of Herzl's letter to Kana is of the surface. The anxiety about infection was entirely justified. Professor Albert Wiedmann, director of the Second University Skin Hospital in Vienna, has stated that the methods available to medicine at the time Prince Rudolf fell sick "only rarely led to a complete cure of a venereal complaint of this nature."[8] If, as the text of the letter suggests, Herzl had caught gonorrhea, he was now afflicted with an ailment that even when it became chronic would be painful; it was an ailment that made mar-

---

††† Herzl invents the word *Conschwanzo* on the model of *commilito,* "fellow fighter." *Schwanz:* slang for "penis," but also for cutting lectures. Schulz must have been one of the militant German nationalists at the university who expressed his defiance of authority in absenteeism.

‡‡‡ *Zwangsverordnung. Schwanz* (tail) was also a characteristic in slang of the *Fuchs* (freshmen); which is the meaning of *Knappe,* applied a few lines further down to the penis. We may conjecture Schulz to have been a freshman, or near freshman.

* Erections of the penis are one side effect of gonorrhea.

† Hence the German name, *der Tripper.*

‡ *Ich grusse Dich.*

riage dangerous since it was easily transmitted and could in women cause yet acuter suffering than in men. Two independent bodies were to confirm that all was not well with his health. In 1880, the same year of this important letter, he applied to put in a year's voluntary service in the Austrian Army. (Military service in Hungary was compulsory for Hungarians; Herzl only acquired Austrian nationality in 1885.) At the age of twenty he was summoned before the Commission on Fitness for Military Service in Vienna. The Commission rejected him as "at present unfit for field service." Later in the year he repeated his request, this time with the 63rd Regiment of the Line, again in Vienna. Once more he was rejected as "unfit." The Army authorities preserved professional discretion and no further details have been published.[9] Almost the commonest cause for rejection of applicants for military service is the presence of a heart murmur; in the light of his later medical history, this would appear to be a likely cause for his rejection, even though there is no documented history of his having suffered from rheumatic fever.[10]

Two years later Herzl was in Pesth, staying at the Hotel de l'Europe. (This was one occasion when he was in Hungary for the anniversary of Pauline's death.) He wrote on March 5 to Kana, then taking his finals in Vienna, of the sweet melancholy evoked by every paving stone, well-known yet foreign.

> This is where my sister Pauline and my youth are buried, and I wept over both tombstones. But then the present took me in its arms and kissed me. And this young, spring-like present took the charming form of my sweet, darling cousin. She is sixteen and such a girl as you see only in your dreams. Were I four years older, I would marry her at once, and were I four years younger, I would fall in love with her . . . Anyway, it is a bad sign that I felt my fingers itching as if they wanted to explode in a poem. But I resisted. But just imagine a charming slender little Miss with brown hair and blue eyes and a charming mouth which I have, alas, kissed only once, when I arrived here. I would kiss all my centenarian aunts every day if it would give me the right to touch *her* lips with mine.[11]

This letter makes it clear that Herzl at this time was poor (he asked Kana to redeem a pawn ticket for him) and bitterly aware that his beautiful cousin would be married off to "some selected Jew, the possessor of a decent income."

A year later, in August, he was staying at Baden, some sixteen miles from Vienna; as its name suggests, it was a spa, possessing fifteen sulphur springs used for complaints of the bladder, among other

ailments. On writing paper which by now had THEODOR HERZL printed
on it, he wrote to Kana as *Mein lieber Jungel*

> Yesterday a misunderstanding worthy of high comedy. I was in
> Vöslau. There Frau Edith and her beautiful sister Clara play a
> ladylike game with a shabby little Jew who is at the same time an
> important writer: Joseph R. Ehrlich. This man, whom I met for the
> first time yesterday, is a most interesting character whom only a few
> people understand . . . The two ladies treated him with contempt
> [*en canaille* in the original] which any normal person would have
> discerned a long time ago. But he isn't normal, he's a genius, limited
> and witty, silly and splendid. He only lacks a gift for poetry to be a
> major poet. I don't want to continue my antitheses—though you
> would approve them if you knew him. I believe he can understand
> the most delicate nuances and is generous: yet he boasts that he
> found sixpence [*Zehnerl* in the original] and gave it to the waiter
> instead of keeping it. In his daydreams he no doubt encounters the
> goddesses of youth and beauty; yet he tells these ladies whom he
> hardly knows and to whom he looks up as patterns of aristocratic
> distinction—and who consider him a poor Polish Jew—that he dines
> off a slice of beef and a quart of wine. And he is thrilled with the
> slice of beef! Like someone for whom dinner is an exceptional lux-
> ury.
>   And now for the misunderstanding. Fräulein Clara presented her-
> self as a Major's wife, Clara von Rittershausen, me as Baron von
> Rittershausen, and "Eidlitz" as her unmarried sister. He fell for it,
> of course; it was like taking candy from a baby. Me, I complimented
> him on his (partly) excellent play. He seems incredibly naïve. (I
> spare you the clichés.) I only told him, Cato should resign at the
> end; that would be an expression of supreme wisdom. He replied:
> history demands that it should end the way he wrote it. He has
> never heard about the possibilities of poetic license.[12]

The rather tasteless joke made Herzl think of using the Rittershausen disguise in the same way as the Caliph of the Arabian Nights
had used the guise of a simple citizen. In part Herzl was prompted
by a delight in Germanic titles; but concealment could be useful for
erotic tastes which, if not as dangerous as those of his contemporary
Oscar Wilde, were open nevertheless to misunderstanding. He had
been twenty-two when he had fallen in love with his girl cousin of
sixteen. This liking for girls much younger than himself was to remain with him as he grew older. Among his own class his attachments
were kept more or less to the platonic level. In his last year as a
student he describes another encounter with a girl met at a soiree.[13]
A kiss on a shoulder, "where the seams of the lace-covering had

burst in a ravishing way, disclosing a dizzying neck and upper arm," led to a

formidable smack. A look in the mirror told me that I could not face the company with one red cheek, and so, to right the balance, I risked another kiss. Not only for the sake of balance: that lily-white, rosy-red girl's skin tasted royally! And a second slap made my face uniformly red, while the dance tune from the next room provided the musical background, aided by peals of laughter and the usual noise of after-supper jollity. As for us two, crime and punishment alternated. I was the culprit, she the avengeress, and gradually we found a rhythmic pleasure in this exchange of slaps and kisses. But it was strange how things progressed: the slaps grew weaker and the kisses stronger. Then, laughing, my slapping beauty threw herself into a rocking-chair while I stood in front holding its rounded legs in my hands. But she wished to rock and as I stood too close for her to kick off, she suddenly put her tiny feet on my trembling thighs and pushed and pushed . . . Can you see it, my friend? can you feel it? Two ridiculously small feet in blue silk, the soft leather on the black trousers of a not quite impotent gentleman. Palsambleu! Have I ever told you that I only love women who kick me? Of course, they must have feet like those which kicked me last night.

This liking for young girls was not to diminish but the age gap would grow. The next time he seriously fell in love was to be at the age of almost twenty-six with Magda, a child of thirteen. (In the interval, he tells us, he had become rough and tough; his heart, which loves love so much, has been cold and mute.) It is early January 1886 and he has eagerly been looking forward to a children's ball for the chance to see Magda. "I went towards her," he tells, not Kana, but his Diary,[14] "filled with longing. Such a little, big, beautiful lady she was, such a sweet one! I made to kiss her. Only her little blonde head—only that—was turned aside. I did not kiss her. Then she proceeded on my arm, like a little queen. I 'thee'd' and 'thou'd' her and she did the same to me . . ." He realizes that he is making a fool of himself, that his infatuation may be noticed. Yet jealousy surges when the girl, "her little dress still short, her sweet body undeveloped," is asked to waltz with boys of her own age, and she, "the premature coquette," agrees. In retaliation "I wanted to make her jealous and so flirted with the most lovely of the grown-up ladies." The incidents are recorded in the tones of Nabokov's Humbert Humbert; Magda's sly wink when at last he dares partner her recalls Lolita; and in both cases an interior realist is watching, weighing. In the cotillion there is a figure known as Ladies' Choice, Gentlemen's

Choice. "The sweet coquette makes as if she would rush towards me. Half way across, she stops short and dances with a little girl." He draws a bitter conclusion: when she grows up, she will do the same—only with another man. "In four years she will be treating me exactly as she wishes. And she will never love me. For her race loves only rich, vulgar stock-exchange louts—a vulgar tribe, but one which gets the finest women."

He goes home to lie awake; he is tempted to visit the ice rink where she skates.

Three days later he does so.

"Today I took the afternoon off. Straight to the skating-rink where I knew I should find my sweet, gracious, little one. There I stood like an old man at the ice-edge, gazing at rosy-cheeked youth as it glided past me. She noticed me, but was immediately off, vanished in the crowd." For half an hour he stared into the swiftly moving throng: jealous as Magda circles with a youth of fifteen. The pair recall Pyramus and Thisbe, or the Theodor of Budapest with Madeleine. He calls out "Fräulein Magda!" as she comes within range. She bows, gives a distant smile. After two hours she has had enough and unbuckles her skates. "I block the narrow path. She sees me from a distance, hesitates a moment, then comes determinedly towards me, intending to pass. I beg her to be kind. I promise never again to call her *Du;* only *Fräulein*. She nods ironically at our compact and leaves me standing."

The episode of Magda is one jump ahead of Herzl the student. But it shows the persistence of his interest in girls much younger than himself and illustrates his emotional problems. On the one hand and in part, he was what his idolaters have claimed him to be wholly: courteous, sentimental and fastidious. Yet the robust vigor of his psyche is attested by the quantity of his writings as a schoolboy and student, as well as by his thrustful arguments in Lesehalle or café. This vigor demanded physical expression. Vienna was a large and anonymous city compared with Budapest. Even so, the student with conspicuous good looks moved in restricted circles: relations, business associates of his father, other Jews. Attempts to translate emotions into actions would have been disastrous. His ambition was stronger than his lust; his prudence owed much to his membership in a minority. But to obtain one of these girls for his own seemed, in his student days, beyond his hopes. When twenty-two and in love with his cousin, he had written in a postscript: "Just imagine, if I had got the first prize, I would be somebody and could perhaps marry her." It was the same with Magda. "I need external success. A nest for this golden bird." Yet once caged, how long would such coquettes remain pubescent? "When she is fully developed, she will perhaps be just another marriageable daughter." He had foreseen Magda's betrayals; he could also foresee the vanishing of youthful slimness.

Only if his health recovered, only if he became successful, could he hope to marry. In the long interim he knew from experience how perilous it was to practice what James Boswell (an earlier sufferer)[15] had described with eighteenth-century relish as "venery." His forceful psyche was thus turned to diversionary outlets. The correspondence with Kana shows one of these. Herzl boasts (like Boswell, again, before him) of the size and erective power of his "young knight." This desire to impress a male confidant shows that the roots of Herzl's dandyism drank from the waters of Narcissus. If private love were denied (and what was dangerous for a student would have been catastrophic for a Doctor of Laws), the public passion of an audience —or even a crowd—must take its place. The desirability of becoming a writer, the need to win fame became evident and urgent. The first need for a writer was to read, voraciously. In the books he turned to he found posed the problems that had begun to shake Vienna.

CHAPTER 9

_____

_____

Theodor celebrated his twenty-first birthday on May 2, 1881. The transition to manhood is often a troubling occasion. In Herzl's case factors other than growing up cast their shadow. Two months earlier the Akademische Lesehalle had been dissolved. It was the victim of a violent harangue given by von Schönerer. The hero of the German nationalists had accused the institution of being a place where the young were polluted with liberal ideas.

The fact that "liberal" had become an insult showed the seismic change since 1878, the year that Herzl and his parents had migrated to Vienna. The liberal government which had sent its representatives to the Congress of Berlin no longer ruled. Many factors were involved in its collapse. While financial scandals had preoccupied the press, their own horrendous conditions increasingly angered the workers. The German-cultural approach of the liberals alienated the clamorous Slavs. In the new parliament of 1879, the liberals and their radical allies found themselves outnumbered. A colorless new Prime Minister, Count Taafe, was kept in power thanks to a clerical Right that had lost German support but maintained its powers thanks to an opportunist alliance with the more than a hundred Czech and Polish deputies. The Right was obsessed with a question of limited popular appeal—the restoration of Church control over the schools. The Slav demand for greater recognition of the linguistic and national rights of the minorities was even less popular with those (like Herzl) who felt themselves German.

The liberal collapse gave von Schönerer a pulpit from which, in the name of German nationalism, he could attack both poles of the new

Habsburg state. He assailed the Church for its support of the Imperial system; he assailed an oligarchy which represented the interests of capital for suppressing democracy. Many Germanizing Jews would have joined their applause to that of their Catholic or Protestant brothers. But for the first time a Viennese politician gave a baleful new twist to *Deutschtum*. The Jews, von Schönerer alleged, were enemies both of German national rights and the interests of the workers. Following a speech in which he contrasted the interests of landowners and productive workers on the one hand with, on the other, the "up-till-now privileged interests of mobile capital and the Semitic control over money and the word," his Viennese followers established an overtly anti-Semitic Society for the Defense of the Craftsman."[1] Von Schönerer did not approach the lowest layer of German society. (This was the later complaint of an otherwise respectful Hitler.) But he probably knew his demagogic business. He approached those who felt themselves most threatened. One hostile cardinal expressed the feelings of many German-speakers, and in particular country people, in asserting that the Habsburg system "offered status to the Jews without demanding nationality; they became the supranational people of the multinational state, the one folk which, in effect, stepped into the shoes of the earlier aristocracy." While the Jewish baron became a stock figure in political cartoons,[2] the lower middle classes envied Jewish success in industry and trade.

Jews had known reverses of fortune since the rise of the Pharaoh "who knew not Joseph." But in the more recent past when the Jews suffered setbacks in the Habsburg empire—such as the annulment of their formal emancipation after the Hungarian revolution—they could console themselves by looking north. Prussia, the nucleus of the German empire, had upheld the granting of constitutional rights to the member states of the German federation as early as 1815. The Prussian constitution of 1850, modeled on that of Belgium, guaranteed equality before the law, the rights of the individual and the freedom of religious organizations. Scientific inquiry was also unshackled by religious control.[3] Bismarck, the incarnation of Prussia, had shown the basic cast of his mind at the Congress of Berlin. Prince Gorchakov of Russia had argued that while it was natural that English, French, German or Austrian Jews should enjoy equality, this was because these Western Jews were different from those in Serbia, Romania and Russia, whom he described as "a pest to the indigenous peoples." Bismarck, who presided at the Congress, retorted: That may well be; but the nature of the Eastern Jew has been created by his condition:

the pitiful state of the Jews was perhaps to be traced precisely to the limitation of their political and civil rights.[4] Yet similar causes in Berlin had produced similar cases to those in Vienna. German Jews had supported Bismarck's *Kulturkampf* against the influence of the Catholic Church. Inevitably this made many Catholics hostile to the Jews. When in 1879 a Jewish-owned newspaper demanded a "front against Rome!," a Catholic paper countered by demanding a "front against the new Jerusalem."[5]*

Such attacks were not confined to Catholics angered by Jewish support for Bismarck's anti-clerical policies. Eugen Dühring was an intellectual known for his hatred for all forms of religion; he enjoyed a student reputation perhaps comparable to those of Sartre and Marcuse a century later. Blind, quarrelsome and arrogant, he now published a work entitled *The Jewish Question as a Question of Race, Morals and Civilization.* His thesis was revealed in his title. The Jews (who had been attacked in the past for their beliefs) were in reality dangerous, Dühring argued, because of their blood. Since a man's beliefs did not affect his race, conversion offered no solution; co-existence between Germans and this racial enemy was impossible; emancipation had been a perilous mistake. Dühring's book was to go into five editions during the next twenty years. It was echoed not only by innumerable pamphlets but by the *vox humana* of Adolf Stöcker, a court preacher whose Christian socialism derived directly from theories worked out by Roman Catholics and indirectly from the teachings of Ferdinand Lassalle, ironically enough a Jew. Stöcker was a member of the Prussian Diet, where he voted with the conservatives. The Diet was an excellent place from which to publicize bellicose ideas.

The anti-Semitic drift was resisted by leading Germans. The Crown Prince and Princess (a daughter of Queen Victoria and mother of the future Kaiser Wilhelm II) denounced anti-Semitism as a disgrace to Germany while leading thinkers, including the historian Mommsen, signed a manifesto that condemned the movement as being harmful to Germany as well as unjust to the Jews. But what halted a seemingly powerful current of opinion—which would not revive in Germany until the year following Herzl's death—was the spectacle of what such

---

* "The German people has at last opened its eyes. It sees that the true *Kulturkampf*, the true battle for civilisation, is the battle against domination by the Jewish spirit and by Jewish money. In all political movements it is Jews who play the most radical and revolutionary role, waging a fight to the finish against all that is left of legitimate, historical and Christian in the national life of the peoples." *Germania*, September 10, 1879.

ideas could do when they were allowed to infect the minds of simple
people. Two countries on the undeveloped fringe of capitalist Europe
—first Russia, then Hungary—were to provide instances of anti-Semitic
persecution that outraged Western Europe and America alike.

The same spring of 1881 which closed the Vienna Lesehalle opened
in Russia a carnival of bigotry without parallel in Europe since the
Inquisition. Slav nationalists who saw the Jews as alien joined those
who saw them as business rivals; intellects that borrowed their ideas
from Germany combined with minds still formed by superstition. A
tavern brawl in Elizabethgrad turned into an anti-Jewish riot. This
pattern was repeated in 167 towns and villages of western Russia.
Synagogues and houses were burned down, men killed, women raped.
A new word—pogrom—entered popular speech. But not everyone outside Russia condemned what it represented.

In Prague, then a provincial Austro-Hungarian city, a Roman
Catholic professor of Hebrew, Dr. August Rohling, fashioned a new
match, the self-igniting kind, for the dry timber of the Habsburg
backwoods. Publicly proclaiming that the Talmud required Jews to
work for the ruin of Christians, he implicitly condoned the pogroms
as acts of self-defense. One feature of his attack led swiftly to tragedy.
In his capacity of expert on Hebrew and things Jewish, Rohling offered in 1881 to depose on oath that the murder of Christians for
ritual purposes formed a secret part of Jewish religious discipline.
This charge, hardly more credible than the legend of Dracula, had its
roots in twelfth-century England. Shortly after Easter, 1144, the
mutilated body of a dead boy had been uncovered in a wood near
Norwich, a town with a wealthy Jewish community and a new cathedral. Instead of looking for a sex maniac (whose religious affiliation
would have had little bearing on the case) the superstitious mob
charged the Jews with killing the boy in mockery of Christ's passion.†
The idea may have been put into their heads by monks who needed
a tutelary saint for their cathedral, since its builder, Losinga, had not
been canonized. The charge was echoed in other English towns and
a century later Edward I bowed to the popular will and expelled all
Jews from his kingdom. This success was counterproductive to the
revenues of Norwich cathedral. The tomb of the popularly canonized
"St. William" drew fewer and fewer pilgrims as the banished Jews
shrank to figures in folklore; the shrine's annual takings could be
numbered in pence by the time of the Reformation. Rohling's attempt

---

† A rood screen in at least one Norfolk church still shows a youthful figure
stretched between pillars with his blood being collected in a chalice.

to refurbish this myth for the age of Darwin was immediately controverted by Christian as well as by Jewish scholars.‡ It was in any case a dying libel. New charges, unconnected with this particular myth, would arm twentieth-century fanatics. Yet Rohling's propaganda served to prove that any idea, however infantile, can serve as land mine for someone. The following April, when a Christian girl disappeared from the Hungarian village of Tisza Eszlar, people remembered the professor's revelations and promptly accused the Jews of planning to use her blood for Passover. Many Jews were jailed while in an epoch-making trial one boy was coached into giving false witness against his father.*

The shock waves from Russia—which in New York swung the retiring Emma Lazarus from scholarly belles-lettres to committed poetry†—do not seem to have affected Herzl. At least, not in Vienna and not in 1881. Instead, his knightly ideals prompted him, under the influence of Franz Staerk, a gentile friend, to apply for membership in Albia, a dueling fraternity or *Burschenschaft;* and this became a substitute for the Lesehalle in which he had spent so much of his first student years. The *Burschenschaften* had their origin in the Napoleonic Wars and their history reflected the development of German patriotism. Anti-French at the time of Napoleon, anti-Metternich at the time of that statesman's reactionary rule, they first stood for liberalism and then for German nationalism. In Austria, they grew stronger with each Habsburg defeat, embodying a nationalism that often saw in union with Germany the road to salvation. They are to

‡ Yet Rohling's charges were paralleled in Rome itself. Giuseppe Oreglia de San Stefano, S.J., contributed a number of articles on the same grisly theme to *La Civiltà Cattolica* between February 1881 and December 1882. "The practice of killing children for the Paschal Feast is now very rare in the more cultivated parts of Europe," he wrote in the issue of August 20, 1881, "more common in Eastern Europe, and common, all too common, in the East properly so called. [In the West, the Jews] now have other things to think of than to make their unleavened bread with Christian blood, occupied as they are in ruling almost like kings in finance and journalism . . ." By March 4, 1882, the priest was declaring: "Every practising Hebrew worthy of that name is obliged even now, in conscience, to use in food, in drink, in circumcision and in various other rites of his religious and civil life, the fresh or dried blood of a Christian child, under pain of infringing his laws and passing among his acquaintances for a bad Hebrew." The author, bound by the Jesuit vow of obedience to the Pope, does not seem to have been checked by Pope Leo XIII in his diffusion of charges as inflammatory as they were absurd.
* The trial, held at Nyiregyhaza from June 19 to August 3, 1882, finally discredited this form of anti-Semitism in Hungary. Brilliant counsel for the defense exposed the conspiracy; the public prosecutor withdrew the charge; the four judges, including one convinced anti-Semite, acquitted all of the accused.
† Emma Lazarus (1849–1887) wrote the poem later affixed to the Statue of Liberty, *The New Colossus,* after hearing of the sufferings of Jews in Czarist Russia.

be distinguished from the *Korps*, another type of student organization, which the government favored because it was non-political and devoted solely to dueling. They originally included Jews but at the time when Herzl joined Albia, the conservative *Burschenschaften* were beginning to exclude them. Albia was one of eight such conservative fraternities.‡ Albia had been founded in 1870 as Lipensia, changing its name to Albia in 1873. In 1877 it had combined with Gothia (founded in 1874) and taken the colors black, red and gold with a blue cap. Black, red and gold were the colors of German nationalism, as against the black and yellow of Austria.

Joining Albia involved Herzl in a strenuous program. He had to swill beer with other students, join with them in the choruses of bawdy, traditional songs, write articles for their paper and also devote four hours a day to the dueling activities which were the *Verbindung's* proper concern. Not having studied swordcraft in Budapest, he had to take special lessons from a fencing master.

At first sight it is puzzling to find the former president of Wir, the star of the Lesehalle, patronizing an activity that would find its defenders among extreme German nationalists and anti-Semites. (The Church had consistently attacked the practice for reasons equally valid for religious Jews.) It is also more usual for young men to progress from bodily to intellectual pursuits than the other way around. Much later in life Herzl would cite the wearing of a *Verbindung's* cap as a youthful folly.[6] Yet his motives for joining Albia sprang from impulses permanently powerful in his nature. His blue pillbox hat, worn to the front of his head at a jaunty angle, proclaimed his acceptance by the university's elite. Like many such elites, the membership of the *Burschenschaften* had contrasted qualities. On the one hand they exemplified aristocratic *sang-froid* and courage. (Albia alone accepted and fought seventy-five challenges in 1881.[7]) But they also lent themselves to mindless violence, becoming the shock troops of extremist politicians. "Drunken and brutal," Stefan Zweig writes, "the *Burschenschaften* attacked sometimes Jewish, sometimes Italian, sometimes Slav students." Some of the Jews who remained members voted in wary snobbery not to increase the Jewish percentage. Herzl's motives for belonging were different from theirs. Apart from assimilating himself to the student elite, he hoped, by acquitting himself well in gentile company, to show that the stereotype of a Jew as necessarily humble, stooped from study, meek, was in his case false. The readiness to fight a duel on a point of honor would prove one Jew's worthiness to be accepted socially. Partly from

‡ The seven others were: Alemannia, Brun, Germania, Akademische Libertas, Olympia, Silesia and Teutonia.

pride, partly from the nip of Nietzsche in the Austrian air, he was and would remain suspicious of pity and its stepson charity. Temperamentally he shrank from what Emma Lazarus called "the huddled masses" and "wretched refuse"°; to identify with them was unthinkable for his brand of knight. Something almost feminine in his quick, intuitive mind made it easy for him to accept, by projection of himself into his opponents' minds, their arguments. He had little use for rational dialectic as a reply to prejudice. Instead, he must make the young toughs of Vienna—the sons of rich families—exclaim: "but this man acts like a Prussian, not like a Jew!" His personality would naturally develop in later years, yet an incident dating from 1893 illustrates the attitudes that made him join Albia in 1881. A society to rebut anti-Semitic propaganda had been recently formed and he was asked by an Austrian equivalent of Emma Lazarus to help.† Herzl offered instead the suggestion that "half a dozen duels will do a great deal to improve the position of the Jews in society."[8] He would even fantasize about challenging the leading anti-Semites himself.

Each member of a *Burschenschaft* had a nom de combat. Herzl's was Tancred, the hero of Disraeli's novel, and the name of a twelfth-century king of Sicily. On May 11, 1881, without telling his parents he fought his obligatory student's duel. *Albiafuchs* Theodor Herzl fought *Alemanniafuchs* Karl Koch. Members of the two fraternities assembled in the clubhouse to watch. On Herzl's right stood his second, Franz Staerk, on his left, as testifying witness, stood his fellow law student, Hans Pischek. An outside umpire, vọn Strohbach of Teutonia, called for silence and initiated the contest. Both young men, heavily bandaged for protection, drew blood and the result was an amiable draw celebrated that evening by a drinking party.

But though he was fairly popular with his fellow duelists (fairly, since he never fought more than this one duel) he became aware of anti-Semitism, not in the gymnasium where he fenced, but in the university library where he read. He read so much that he was almost sure to encounter so prevalent an idea. From January to May 1882, for example, he enters no less than fifty books in his Youth Diary. This shaft let into the reading of his student days discloses an appetite voracious as a vacuum cleaner.

° *vide* concluding lines of *The New Colossus*, 1883:

> Give me your tired, your poor,
> Your huddled masses yearning to breathe free,
> The wretched refuse of your teeming shore . . .

† Regina Friedlander, widow of the founder of Vienna's leading newspaper, *Die Neue Freie Presse*, for which Herzl then worked.

Like other young men in other ages he read writers whose names would leap their century and place—Mark Twain, Balzac and Byron are three examples—and writers whose names now need to be rummaged for in literary companions. For example: January 19, 1882, two novels by Victor Cherbuliez, *Le comte Kostia* and *L'aventure de Ladislas Bolski*. He is regularly reading Wilhelm Jensen, Germany's most popular and prolific nineteenth-century novelist. But while Jensen had been his *literarischer Leibbursch‡* in his first year at Vienna, he now feels that Jensen is overproducing. (Jensen's production of over one hundred novels confirms Herzl's judgment.) His attitude to Dostoievsky has interest for the light it sheds on himself. *Crime and Punishment*, while admired as "a psychological novel of the first rank," has profoundly upset him. "It describes gruesomely, and with psychological truth, the sickness whose symptom is crime. But at the same time it is a book that disturbs. The feverish criminality of the hero makes the reader, if he's the least bit sensitive, physically sick. The talks between Raskolnikoff and the examining magistrate Porphyrius Petrovich, are magnificent. They play with one another like cat and mouse. What is remarkable is the cruel, voluptuous pleasure that the mouse itself takes in this." Herzl's reaction shows a characteristic fear of the id; it indicates the effort it cost him to control his inner passions lest they disturb his knightly calm.

Although for Jews as for Christians the nineteenth century was an age rich in theological writing, his reading list upholds his schoolboy indifference to religion. He no more reads Samson Raphael Hirsch than Cardinal Newman. Jewish writers do not figure among his heroes.

Yet on two succeeding days of February—the eighth and ninth—the Jewish question intrudes upon him. One of Jensen's many novels, *The Jews of Cologne*, shows a sympathy for medieval Jewry similar to that of Sir Walter Scott in *Ivanhoe*. Herzl noted:

> Often Jews give the pitiful impression of those descendants of ancient families that can do anything except work honestly with their own hands. But Jews were like that, are like that, only while the walls of ghetto intolerance shut in their bodies and minds; when the physical improvement of their race through cross-breeding with other races was forbidden to them. If intermarriage could take place unhindered—to the great advantage of the modern races as well as of the Jews—the psychological improvement would follow fast. The reason why the Jews have developed a different physique and mentality—strange and alas, even despised—is not because they

‡ A *Leibbursch* is a student attached in comradeship to a student junior to him, known as his *Leibfuchs*.

have maintained their specific "purity" (or "impurity," depending on your viewpoint) as they brought it from Asia; but because they seldom mixed with their peers in the families of other nations. The only way to solve the Jewish question is to promote a general improvement of the physical and metaphorical profile of the nation. The cross-breeding of the western races with the so-called oriental, on the basis of a common state religion—that is the great, the to-be-desired solution! Without the gloomy ghetto, fortress and force, whose influence endured long after its material walls had fallen,—like a tight ring that you still feel constricting your finger long after it's been painfully removed or cut—without the ghetto, which invisibly still limits the outlook of the lower-class Jews as well as many educated Jews too, without the evil ghetto of today and yesterday, that ring-finger on the hand of mankind which we know as Jewry, would not have developed, or misdeveloped, as it has. Just let that tortured finger move freely at last, uncompelled, uncrushed, and soon the pain of constriction will have vanished like a depressing memory; the furrow made by the tormenting ring will level up, and the finger will move freely, actively, industriously, with the others, for the good of humanity. At first the Jews had a great conceit of themselves as being the chosen ring-finger. But the ring gradually grew into the flesh and they rejoiced when it was taken away. But now they must struggle to catch up in all that lost development.[9]

The "ring" seems to represent the Law as well as the ghetto.

Next day Herzl opened Dühring's best-seller of the previous year, *The Jewish Question as a Question of Race, Morals and Civilization*. Bleakly it argued that for Jews to catch up, in Herzl's generous sense of the term, was impossible; the only catching-up they could do was in the sense of Fagin's pickpockets. Thus Jensen's portrayal of what may, with shame, be called Christian anti-Semitism was succeeded, as in some fairy-tale delirium, by the evocation of rationalized xenophobia; the updating in nineteenth-century terms of antique enmity. Hatred for Jews persists, Herzl notes; Dühring simply equips it with a new rationale. Ritual murder, accusations of poisoning wells or of starting plagues belong to a medieval world whose religious underpinning has collapsed. Yet how uninventive, despite the intervening centuries, the Jew-baiters are, how trite.

> They recognise, as does Herr Dühring, that religious attacks on the Jews no longer work. Now race must step forward! The faggots of the middle ages have become damp; they refuse to ignite. Modern fuel is needed for them to blaze jollily, for spluttering Jew-fat to send up its savory smell to the straight noses of Protestants, of those free-thinkers who replace the Dominicans who in the malodorous

middle ages superintended such matters. From fire to loot—or vice
versa—and Herr von Dühring and Company hunt for loot and find
it. One discovers "the national economy," another "public opinion."
Herr Dühring will soon be editing the great newspaper *Loyalty*.
Greed is the low, stinking motive of all movements against the Jews
who for centuries have wrought no change in this Christian morality. The only change—more sophistication, more erudition, more intelligence—though a rogue's intelligence it is. Yet despite new nursery tales against the modern Jews, one hopes for a brighter future
wherein humane, unimpassioned men will look back on contemporary anti-Jewish movements as educated men, even educated anti-
Semites, today look back on those of the middle ages.

As for Dühring's fervently promised "solution," Herzl denounces it
as no more than the rebuilding of the ghetto "coupled with a system-
atic dejudaising of the press and usury, both of which profitable concerns will come entirely into Christian-Germanic hands thanks to the
'mediatising of the financial princedoms.'" Yet Dühring has been led
by a play on words to a dull exposition of a poor expedient. "Mediatising" is hocus-pocus for old-fashioned robbery.

> And in any case, after you've *dejudaised* the courts, law, medicine,
> politics, after you get them out—what are the poor creatures to live
> on, if they can neither lend money, teach, heal, counsel, serve the
> state, write for the press, sell their books—or anything else? Will
> Dühring and his comrades in greed, having removed a dreaded
> competition, having added to their own wealth, having denied Jews
> the possession of morality, understanding, character, talent, will-
> power, but not a stomach, a digestive tract: will they feed them?
> Yet this Dühring is not only eager for loot. He is also a hypocrite, a
> rascal, a companion-piece to the God-mouthing Jesuit.

Dühring, peddling freedom, is a rascally freedom-Jesuit, an infamous
freedom-cleric. (Herzl's fury makes him almost incoherent.) "This
rogue—the teeth past which his villainies gush should be bashed in!—
turns up his eyes with odious mock-libertarian piety to say: To all
men, the most boundless freedom: but for the Jews, 'a law of exception': the new phrase for the medieval ghetto. For this man dares to
mouth the holy name of freedom . . ."[10]
One of the most violent passages Herzl ever wrote, it rings with the
accents of a lover scorned. But what adds the peculiarly Herzlian
touch is the acceptance of Herzl that the book is beautifully written
and contains valuable insights. "The obliquity of Jewish ethics and
the lack of moral earnestness in many—Dühring says in all—actions
of the Jews are pitilessly exposed and defined. We have a great deal

to learn from that." Herzl also confides to the Diary his admiration for Dühring's German style.

The following month Herzl revisited Pesth. Contact with Hungary, his physical removal from Vienna, revitalized his belief in German culture. Jensen, Dühring were back on their shelves; he was back in what by contrast with Vienna seemed a very provincial town. He wrote to Heinrich Kana: "During my absence Hungary has become still more Hungarian. A pity! So many of my friends, colleagues and fellow sufferers at the hands of our teacher of Hungarian have meanwhile ripened into perfect Hungarians. It is true they know no Hungarian, but they speak it with great perseverance, and he who was erstwhile Sonnenberg is now 'Muranyi' and Feigelstock calls himself 'Figalyi' . . . For my part I have taken great care to utter not one Hungarian syllable."[11]

CHAPTER 10

In the cold days of early 1883 Herzl had his one personal brush with the racial arrogance increasingly typical of nineteenth-century Europe. Compared with the humiliations being inflicted on Egyptians by the British or the Indo-Chinese by the French it had a gentlemanly resolution.

Yet insult cannot be weighed like cheese. What is not felt by one bruises another. A gnawing mouse can start an avalanche. Herzl's *amour-propre,* being linked to the need for self-respect and applause, being stronger than attachment to property or profit, was as sensitive as a photographic plate. The generation of Byron and Stendhal still cast its proud shadow on the students of the early 1880s.

The incident—composed of events unwinding between March 5 and April 3—is important for Herzl's development and it must be set in context. As this was Wagnerian, it was also complex.

On February 13, 1883, in a dank Venetian palazzo, Richard Wagner had died in the arms of Cosima. To music lovers who were German nationalists the loss was of a prophet whose last work, *Parsifal*, produced for the first time on July 26 the previous summer, embodied a message as well as a libretto. To music lovers who were not politically minded—such as the young American Gustav Kobbé, in Bayreuth to assess the opening performance for the New York *World*—the Master's final music drama seemed characterized by spiritual purity.[1] (Appropriately for this innocent view, the first performance in America would be on Christmas Eve, at New York's Metropolitan Opera House in 1903.) Wagner's creation of Kundry—in Kobbé's words "a sort of female Ahasuerus—a wandering Jewess"—seemed one of his most dramatic creations. And nothing more. "According to him [Wagner] she is condemned for laughing in the face of the Saviour as He was bearing the Cross. She seeks forgiveness by serving the Grail knights as messenger on her swift horse, but ever and anon she is driven by the curse hanging over her back to Klingsor (the sorcerer), who changes her to a beautiful woman and places her in his garden to lure the Knights of the Grail to destruction." German nationalists saw in the story of Monsalvat, the threatened castle of the knights, saw in Kundry, whose only words in the last act are *"Dienen, dienen"* ("to serve, to serve"), whose only benison is death (with no promise of resurrection), the mythic fulfillment of a doctrine their master had tirelessly expounded in prose. To a later age the doctrine seems less innocent, *"Dienen, dienen"* a grisly foreshadowing of the motto— *Arbeit Macht Frei* (Work Frees)—scrolled above the gateway of Auschwitz Camp. In *Religion and Art* Wagner gave the first hint—"it remains more than doubtful that Jesus himself was of Jewish stock"— of a notion that would be elaborated by his son-in-law Houston Stewart Chamberlain in a work revered by European racialists from its publication in 1898 until the death of Adolf Hitler in 1945.° In *Heroism*, written just before *Parsifal,* Wagner had credited Christ with the possession of a kind of superblood, both a miraculous antidote to racial decline and an agent of racial improvement. "Pride is a delicate virtue," Wagner then wrote, "suffering no compromise such as the mixing of blood." Wagner's hostility to Jews was so exaggerated as to suggest a secret admiration. Hatred became, in fact, a magnifying glass. "If a Jew or Jewess intermarries with the most extraneous races, a Jew will always be born." The superblood hardly seems to belong to Jesus.[2]

The mania had different results. While Nietzsche asked slyly if Wagner's father, Geyer, could not have been Jewish, one of the Master's disciples—a Jew—killed himself in despair at his ineradicable taint.

The death of Wagner—who to his disciples combined the powers of Shakespeare with those of Beethoven, but whom we may more soberly see as having combined the best and worst in one of the most creative periods in human history—encouraged pious hysteria among his admirers. These naturally included the members of Albia, whose German nationalism and manly preoccupations suited the fetid reli-

° Chamberlain's *Foundations of the Nineteenth Century* gets round the problem of Christ's racial origins by first stressing the divinity of Jesus to the exclusion of his manhood, and then arguing that a considerable element in the Jewish population of Palestine was in fact of Aryan origin. St. Paul's doctrine of grace is attributed in large part to the fact that Paul derived from Tarsus, a non-Jewish city.

giosity of Monsalvat. Parsifal, in Wagner's conception, was foolish as well as blond; destructive as well as therapeutic.

On March 5 the Union of German Students in Vienna held a *Trauerkommers*, or mourning celebration, in honor of the dead musician. Von Schönerer was among the four thousand students, university staff and parliamentary deputies who thronged the Sophienhalle. A gigantic flag in the black and red and gold of the German empire served as backcloth to speeches alternating with patriotic songs such as "Watch on the Rhine" and "Deutschland über Alles." Members of Albia attended, along with representatives of other fraternities. Among them was Hermann Bahr, three years younger than Herzl and an admirer of Herzl's nonchalant demeanor. As speaker after speaker plucked strings from the Wagnerian lute, Bahr forgot the Jew he knew (and with whom he would remain friends in later life) for the Wagnerian abstraction. Fired by stronger drink than Wagner would have allowed his knight, he launched into a highly emotional speech, underlining the political significance of Wagner's art, and finding in Kundry, fettered but awakening to join her sisters in neighboring lands, a symbol of the Jewish peril. Bahr's public acceptance of anti-Semitic German nationalism caused such a furor that the police rushed in to close the meeting. Von Schönerer seized the platform amid the fracas to denounce this interference with freedom of expression and to cry: *"Hoch unser Bismarck! Hoch Bismarck!"*[3]

Herzl had by this time become an inactive member of Albia[4]; like other Jewish members of the Vienna fraternities he sensed the increasingly hostile atmosphere in these right-wing clubs. He had not attended the *Kommers* in the Sophien Hall. But he read about it in the next day's papers. At this time he was in a mood of acute depression. Since he was only twenty-three and inexperienced, he had so far failed to win the love, so essential for him, of an audience of readers. In February 1882, he had entered a competition for the best *feuilleton* run by the *Wiener Allgemeine Zeitung* but had failed to secure an honorable mention, let alone a prize. A novel, *Hagenau*, lay unpublished in a drawer. (Its hero, Count Robert Schenk von Hagenau, has a middle-class friend-disciple who is Herzl thinly disguised.) A one-act comedy, *The Hirschkorn Case*, had been turned down by the Hofburgtheater, despite the efforts of a popular actor whom Herzl had enlisted as patron.[5]

Reading the press account, Herzl wrote a letter of intricate indignation to the fraternity's leadership. He had learned from the newspapers, he began, that a meeting to commemorate Richard Wagner, joined by members of the fraternity to which he had the honor of belonging as inactive member, had turned into an anti-Semitic demonstration. He had no intention of polemicizing over this retrogressive fashion of the day, but would point out that as a lover of freedom, even if he had not been a Jew (*selbst als Nicht-jude*), he must have opposed the movement with which his fraternity had become involved. Since there had been no clarification in the press to the effect that the fraternity disowned this involvement, and since silence could be taken for acquiescence—*Qui tacet, consentire videtur!* he added in Latin—and since he was marked by the disadvantage of Semitism—a term unknown when he had enrolled—he thought the most honorable course was for him to resign. For the last time he wrote "Tancred" beneath his signature.

Austrian students, like Anglo-Saxon, knew that no knight, or gentleman, willingly hurts another's feelings. No evidence suggests that the rowdy young members of Albia were deeply malicious. But they were human. Confronted with stark proof of their bad taste, hesitant on the frontier between justification and contrition, they chose, each aiding the other, to bluff it out, to conceal, with a further snub, or at least with cold formality, that they had accepted, under the impetus of emotion and drink, an attitude that could only wound a Jewish comrade. Herzl had written his letter on March 5. The Albia's governing body took almost a month to answer. In the interval some members urged that Tancred's action, in stating how badly they had behaved, deserved, not acceptance of his resignation, but dishonorable expulsion. Calmer counsels prevailed and the letter finally posted on April 3 was cold but not insulting. The Vienna Academic Fraternity Albia informed the law candidate, Theodor Herzl, that in accordance with a decision taken the day before, his name was removed from the fraternity's list of members, it being understood that he had eight days in which to return all relevant insignia. The curt letter was signed by E. Hoerne, student of law, and Rudolf Raabe, student of medicine.

Compared to other brutalities, Albia's participation in the *Kommers* and its consequent treatment of Herzl were not outstanding. But they were to have resounding and tragic results. The leading spirit in Albia, Paul von Portheim, proposed that while existing Jewish members should be retained, no new Jews should be recruited. Von Portheim was himself of Jewish extraction and the tension between fantasy and fact led him to commit suicide later that year. For Herzl, it was the first wedge in the tree trunk, presage for an eventually traumatic split in his feelings as a European.

Rejected for the military service whose comradeship he would have enjoyed—and if his own dissipations were the grounds, he will have known an echo of the obstinate guilt of the Albia leaders—rejected by editors and producers, he was now thrust forth from Monsalvat by his fellow knights.

The break with Albia had been decided after much hesitation, he told a friend, and had caused him pain.[6] In this situation naked success was the only insignia for revenge. Having surrendered his sword, he sharpened his pen. But for all the thousands of words written since the days of Wir, his style still combined the romantic with the pompous. For two years he had been working on a play called, significantly, *The Disillusioned.* It had brought him both beautiful and painful hours, he told Kana in a letter dated August 30. He had just finished the second act: "in good time, too, because I felt the approach of an evil guest called Mr. Doubt (*Herr von Zweifel*) who is a close-kinsman to the Devil (*Teufel*), through the rhyme."[7] He had reached this point in the play on alternate waves of strength and impotence; he was not to complete it.

The letter was written from Baden, the spa close to Vienna whose sulphur springs were particularly good for ailments of the bladder. Another letter to Kana of that summer is dated mysteriously "16, the Month of Affliction."[8] The letter gives no clue to the affliction. The envelope enclosed a money order for "sixty hard-earned *Speere*," which he asks Kana to pay to the dean in haste, presumably as the fee for his second law examination, which in the event he only just passed. He adds, though, the revealing statement: "Being an old gambler, I cannot resist risking my money once more on the green table. It is risky because my opponents are real Cossacks and I am a poor thing in comparison."

"The gambler," Peter Loewenberg has written,[9] "dares fate, forcing it to decide for or against him. He believes it his right to ask for special favor from fate. Good luck is the delivery of protection and the promise of continued blessings for future acts. Gambling is an attempt to force fate to do right by the gambler. In any casino gambling the odds of losing are slightly larger than the chance of winning. The gambler dares the gods to make a decision about him, hoping for their beneficence. If winning means the getting of needed supplies, loss is interpreted as ingratiation with the gods for the same purpose." The gambler, particularly if he has had a religious upbringing, has too a sense of uncleanness. We assess our meanness in charity or gifts and contrast it with our reckless generosity to the green baize tables. Then, having lost, we desire to escape with honor. We assume a stoic mask. We ape the exit of a disfigured knight.

Distress outlasted its month. As the leaves fell, the mood of nature mirrored his own. He was back in Vienna when he wrote, on November 27, 1883:

> Death and destruction: will it always be so? No success comes. Yet I need success. I am myself only when I am successful.
> There in my drawer lie my disappointed hopes. Nausea invades me at the work I have just completed, which has drunk of all my longings, hopes, struggles of a year, part of my youth, of my blood itself. I haven't even the wish to post it off. Why should I? Just to get it back with a printed slip. No sunbeam lights my path; I see no purpose before me; no flower blooms by the way . . .
> I will write no more, for even the blank page in front of me disgusts me; the very strokes of my pen nauseate me.
> No love in my heart. No longing in my soul. No hope. No joy.[10]

The mood was still with him at the moment of transition to his year of graduation. In a city of revelers he stayed at home. Alone, he turned to the mournful waters of Narcissus, his Diary.

> *New Year's Night, 1883–1884:*
> I do not spend it in company. I will not even sit up for the clock's twelfth stroke. But earlier will lie down for sleep, sleep that will carry me over the listlessness of an empty day in an empty life.
> All is empty! Heart of hope, brain of thought, pocket of money and life of poetry!
> In five weeks I shall be sitting for my doctorate in Roman Law— but I am no longer any good for study.

Yet the qualities he had inherited from Jeanette Herzl would carry him into 1884, through a visit to Paris in the spring and in late July recruitment to the Vienna bar as a judicial clerk.[11]

PART THREE

Lunging for Success
1884–94

All men, I believe, are at the start good, or as I term it, genuine . . . Then something happens, perhaps but the lapse of time, and they all become shams.[1]

CHAPTER 11

Herzl's legal studies, like Heine's before him, had afforded a pretext for a student's life, with its involvement in the flux of personalities and ideas. At the time the verbal combats of the Lesehalle, the fencing bouts of his Albia may have impressed him more deeply. But his formal education was under men of outstanding ability. Three at least were of a caliber to affect his permanent attitude to politics and the state. Lorenz von Stein, one of Hegel's most brilliant students, was professor of political science. As a young man he had planted himself in Paris, between 1840 and 1848, simply to study the movements of French socialism. After studying Saint-Simon, Fourier, Comte and Proudhon, he made the notion of state socialism a respectable part of the Viennese atmosphere. The brothers Carl and Anton Menger were two of von Stein's disciples. Carl, the discoverer of the law of marginal utility, lectured in particular to law students. His brother Anton taught that it was the duty of the state to intervene to make life tolerable for the lower classes and to give them justice. Like his master von Stein he was opposed to the violence implicit in Marxism. He argued that the social revolution could be accomplished by the state, and imposed through measures of law, not violence.[2]

While not immediately pressing to the ambitious young dandy who won his *Doktorat* in 1884, these ideas were on call in the creative deposit of his mind. His degree, more immediately, qualified him for a permanent post in the law service of the Austrian state; it guaranteed a secure if unexciting future should the talent believed in by his mother and himself prove an illusion. From August 4 until shortly before Christmas 1884 Herzl worked as a clerk in the *Landesgericht*, being concerned therein with criminal cases; four subsequent months spent working on commercial disputes in the *Handelsgericht* were followed by two months on civil cases under the *Landesgericht* where he had begun. Because his father had an ear complaint and went to Upper Austria in search of a cure, Herzl spent the June and July of 1885 working for the *Landesgericht* of Salzburg. His memories of semi-rural summer—his office in a tower invaded thrice daily by a carillon of bells—were gilded by retrospective happiness.[3] But at the time the glow came not from pleasure in his salaried employment, but from his first literary success. Halfway through his first year of legal practice an encouraging zephyr had puffed the sails of his intent, and made the year his last as a lawyer.

Early in 1885 he had decided to have another try at the *Wiener Allgemeine Zeitung's feuilleton* contest. The wounds of his first failure had healed. With new confidence he worked on a piece entitled "*Das Alltägliche*," or "The Everyday." In form a short story, it consciously satirized the conventional exaltation of the common round, the humble task; unconsciously it revealed the persistence of its author's distrust of others, the cause of his characteristic shyness on meeting strangers. The central character—hero would be too positive a word—is a mediocre official given to dreams. Since he can find in everyday things the fascination that others find in the extreme or the bizarre, a humble post and a cozy hearth complete his desires. He passes chaste, ennobling hours in the company of a fair-haired piano student. Without ever putting his love into words, he dreams of the day when he will have enough money to propose. Suddenly his calm routine is interrupted. He is visited by a school friend, Georg, who has tasted every experience and come to the conclusion that life is unprofitably stale. The bureaucrat, swept by pity for his friend's state of mind, cites his friendship with the blond student as proof that quotidian events need be neither ugly nor insipid. The blasé Georg is charmed by this everyday idyl and marries the fair student. The dreamer is left with the spectacle—of an everyday occurrence.

Heinrich Kana was the first person to whom Herzl showed his story. Kana, possessed of a skin too few, lacked cynicism as much as effective drive; but his qualities as a critic had established his moral authority with Oswald Boxer and Herzl alike. Kana read his friend's essay by the light of his window while Herzl, naturally apprehensive where his writings were concerned, sprawled on the day bed. Kana's judgment came in a fusillade of adjectives: "affected" . . . "insincere" . . . "false" . . . "sickly sweet."[4] But for the toil that had gone to its composition, Herzl would have destroyed his essay there and then.

Luckily, the second person to read it—the *feuilleton* editor—lacked Kana's severity. The cynicism which spoke the young man was more than balanced by the structural command which spoke the writer; when the young writer had experienced more widely he would say what he would find to say with elegance and punch. With compliments on its excellence in form and content he published *"Das Alltägliche"* in his issue of May 27. Herzl had, of course, seen his work in print before. As early as his days in Budapest he had contributed to the *Pester Lloyd*, while as a university student he had written for his fraternity magazine. But this time he was submitting a much worked-on essay to the most critical readers in the Habsburg world. Heartened by their acclaim he could now dismiss the strictures of his friend.

"You will assuredly have seen my *feuilleton* printed yesterday. With that frankness which you often construe as foolishness or arrogance, I must tell you that it pleases me very much today, and particularly today. I am so frank (or foolish or arrogant) with one man only—yourself. I hope, like the Georg of my tale, you can now perceive your error. You have earned the right, at least with me, for once to be wrong."

The Viennese consensus, as manifested by the *Wiener Allgemeine Zeitung*, dissolved his rancor over Kana's criticism and far outweighed the smallness of his fee. Kana, by contrast, possessed a sensibility that could not be assured of its rightness by applause; he was never to earn as much as Herzl nor to have behind him the unwearied support of well-to-do parents. Kana's criticisms of Herzl are the sole surviving evidence of a talent that was to slide beneath the waves of oblivion.

The publication of *"Das Alltägliche"*—which even Herzl confessed was *"ein wenig zu sentimentalisch"*—was psychologically of great importance. When a gambler throws more than he can afford to lose, and on a single number, and that number comes up, the gods themselves seem to signal. The success was not due merely to luck. The *feuilleton* form was to win Herzl a constantly increasing reputation in German-speaking Europe. His strong if mannered prose was to become a weapon apt for persuasion—if he should ever find a cause he wished to urge. His control of form, without which the paragraphs of an essay become a huddle of pillows, was to win him his first literary post; his talents as an observer of the worldly scene (inevitably unshown in this early work) later secured him a journalistic position hardly rivaled in the Europe of the 1890s. If as a writer *pur et simple* Herzl were ever to be revived—and stranger revivals have taken place—his revived fame would depend on his talents as an essayist: these same talents were to give his later Diaries their fascination.

Yet to the young man in his Salzburg turret—and to the less young Herzl in later, more metropolitan settings—an essayist's reputation was tantalizingly hard to savor. An essay could be imagined as being read in cafés, clubs and households; but its author was not present to see this happen. It did not represent the kind of success to charge batteries uncharged by personal love. The success of the playwright seemed much fuller and much more satisfying. The controller of human puppets paces in evening dress toward the footlights and the concluding applause. The young playwright could drink like an Olympian god the incense of today while tomorrow a pan-German reputation might spread to the rest of Europe too.

His happiness in Salzburg was thus dappled like sun through a vine. He was beginning to have a reputation in the capitals. The provincial chimes spoke of time slipping past. He had made a sortie into the world of letters, but a sortie masked in a faceless name.

In late July of 1885 Herzl showed the direction in which his ambition was moving.

Paul Lindau was a journalist and playwright twenty-one years his senior. He knew of Theodor thanks to a Berlin business friend of Jacob Herzl, Treitel by name. Lindau suddenly received a letter from Herzl suggesting that they collaborate on a play. Youth, the hasty generation in assault, was offering alliance to the established and therefore threatened. Lindau declined the alliance. But Herzl's Salzburg euphoria, the delightful illusion of a young, newly published writer that people will remember his work weeks after its appearance, lifted him happily over the rebuff. On August 5, a year and a day after he had begun it, he ended his legal career. He took with his briefcase a familiarity with judicial processes and diction that he would use, and the sense that no action in the great world could be complete unless it were clothed in legal dress.

All men modify their past; politicians frequently fabricate it. Years later, when he had become a politician, Herzl was to claim that he abandoned the law when he perceived that, as a Jew, he could never have hoped to be a judge.[5] To the Herzl of August 1885 there were more cogent reasons. "He wanted," Alex Bein has written, "success, standing, reputation, and he wanted them quickly."[6] Time, not religious affiliation, was the immediate obstacle. Even if he had been the gentile aristocrat of his daydreams, even if he had passed his examinations brilliantly and not merely adequately, he could not have hoped to occupy the highest position in a crowded profession before middle age. The law was a bureaucracy and promotion in most bureaucracies comes slowly. In the more profitable domain of private practice Jewish lawyers found the chief obstacle to their advance in the press of their fellows. But this was as delaying as bureaucracy. The acceptance of his *feuilleton* by a leading newspaper indicated that he could win fame as a writer more quickly than as a lawyer on either the official or unofficial ladder. His doting parents were ready to usurp the function of his doctorate, as cushion against financial stringency or postponed success.

The publication of his *feuilleton* had been a genuine confirmation of Herzl's bent. His consequent desertion of the law was swiftly followed by another success. Yet this time it was a goblin light luring him to the marshes of frustration and rage.

Immediately after he had closed his legal ledger, his parents financed a journey of recuperation. This took him by way of Munich and Heidelberg to the railway system of the Low Countries. In swift succession he visited Brussels, Bruges, Ostend, Antwerp, Leyden, making as he went the comments expected of the youthful traveler. The trip to Europe's western flatlands, the contemplation of oil paintings by the hundred were a rehearsal for the more important journey he planned for November: a visit to Berlin, the fountain at the windswept center of German culture whence Heine himself had first gulped the draughts of fame. Armed with the address of Treitel, his father's contact, he arrived in the Imperial German capital on November 20 and took a carriage to lodgings at 58, Unter den Linden, no mean address. In his luggage he carried three plays in manuscript. He now awaited, with what patience he could muster, the enthusiastic *Ja!* of some man of the theater to whom Treitel could provide the introduction.

At this moment the goblin light flared, and from the most unexpected quarter. The Star Theater, at the corner of New York's Broadway and Thirteenth Street, had invited the Dresden-born actor Friedrich Mitterwurzer (1844–97) to present a three-week season of plays calculated to exhibit his impassioned style of acting. On November 22, three days after Herzl's arrival in an indifferent Berlin, New York's German-language *Staats Zeitung* announced that Mitterwurzer would open his guest season the next day with *Tabarin*, a one-act play by Theodor Herzl. The play, one of the three in Herzl's Berlin luggage, had been inspired by a story of Catulle Mendès, the French

writer, and was set in the Paris of 1620. Its jester hero, played by the
actor-manager himself, discovers that his wife has been unfaithful and
in a melodramatic climax kills first her and then himself.

Tabarin, a one-night wonder, would not again be produced until
the season of 1895–96, when it was to receive nine performances at
the great Burgtheater in Vienna. But for the twenty-five-year-old
ex-lawyer this New World triumph seemed to beckon to the most
alluring fields. It would slowly become apparent that these fields
were sown with mines. Herzl's temperament, with its need for palpable success, and his membership in a minority that had found in
the theater an arena in which to excel encouraged him to expend
years of psychic effort on the production of theatrical *Stücke,* or
pieces, as he termed his plays. The success of *Tabarin* with a New
York audience echoed the success with his parents of his Panama
whimsey. Once again the result was a misdirection of effort. For although he had a feeling for the dramatic form, he was no more cut
out to be an Ibsen (and a reputation less than Ibsen's would not
content him) than to be a great engineer.

But in November 1885, in the flare of this success, the Berliners
around him seemed tediously staid. A letter he wrote to his parents
two days after the New York performance of *Tabarin* preserves his
mood. Although the written reviews would not arrive for a week or
more, the telegraph had proclaimed the fact of the play's production.
"Yesterday there was a *Grande Soirée* at Treitel's. Thirty or forty
hideous little Jews and Jewesses. No comforting sight."[7] Young writers are rarely patient and Herzl's impatience was steamed by angry
boilers. Although his outward manner was warmed by the glow from
Broadway, his inner, doubting self was rasped when not one Berlin
director, producer or actor showed the least interest in *Tabarin* itself,
its forerunner *The Hirschkorn Case* (which had now received an
amateur production in Vienna) nor its four-act successor, *Mother's
Little Boy.* He exploded in a letter to Kana on his sense of humiliation
at having to smile at those who would not accept his genius, at frequenting Philistines with the power to launch his play or exasperate
his spirits. Once again Kana survives as the critical mentor of Herzl's
moods. The moods are so typical that the comments deserve survival.

> What sort of humiliation, to frequent a few, ugly, unappetising
> men and show them a friendly face? Is that what you call rolling in
> the mire? Must they expiate the qualities you happen to dislike? In
> their own circle they are probably admirable people, good fathers,
> loyal friends, solid businessmen, literary Jews (*Literaturjuden*) or
> mothers-in-law, each with his or her place. You are therefore ex-

tremely inhuman, in believing, whether consciously or unconsciously, that if people displease you, you have the right to unrein
your feelings.

And you have no conceivable justification. Someone in the know
would here refer to the "Categorical Imperative." What kind of a
world would it be if everyone were allowed to make his subjective
sensibility the standard of his attitude to others?

But you are still worse, dear Theodor! At the risk of sounding
harsh, I must tell you that you are becoming presumptuous, no
more and no less. You presume all unwittingly. But if someone else,
who did not know you, as I do, for a basically simple, unpretentious
type, were to read your exaggerated superlatives, what would he
think? There goes a young man who has written a good play. To
have it produced, to win fame and success from it, is now his life's
purpose. Of course. But now he expects other people also to make
this play's production their life's purpose, to desist from all else and
concentrate on this. But if, as is their right, they refuse, if they show
interest only to his face, and then only in their accustomed manner,
or if their self-interest instead requires them to disappoint or hurt
him, this young man grows bitter, his view of the world is so distorted that while its evil aspects assume gigantic proportions, its
good aspects vanish. He only sees filth! filth! filth! and wishes to
vomit. From foolishness or excess of egoism? Not from foolishness,
since he has written a damn good play. So from excess of egoism.
Thirteen hundred million men inhabit the planet, each of them the
centre of his world. And here comes the thirteen hundred millionth
insisting that everyone else should cease to function.[8]

Though Herzl had a feeling for the dramatic and some talent for
dialogue, he was not to write plays that would be remembered either
for themselves or as the main achievements of his life. In no sense an
innovator, he had the bad luck to write in a period when the smooth
river of Austrian drama was changing course. He remained ten years
or so behind the avant-garde, manipulating drawing-room stereotypes
against a background of damask and chandeliers when the mood had
changed to realistic discussion of social problems. He was thus like
the playwrights who in the next century briefly continued to ask
"Tennis, anyone?" after *Look Back in Anger* had established a sterner
idiom in a bleaker setting. His contributions were peripheral to a
theater that has in any case weathered badly. Its chief dramatist,
Hermann Sudermann (1857–1928), has secured the gray approval of
some column inches in the standard reference books concerned with
the stage. Sudermann's best-known drama, *Die Heimat,* produced
in England and America under the title *Magda,* corsets "the new
woman" in the whalebone of the well-made play. Herzl's plays did

not even do this and are neither remembered in most reference books nor performed.

Later, when his dramatic impulse had found with much else, another outlet, Herzl himself veered between contrasted opinions as to the value of his "pieces." In a literary testament composed twelve years after the New York production of *Tabarin,* he was to write: "I think one ought to edit my theatrical pieces in a collection."⁹ But only one year later he devalued his dramatic works.

> A great many of my plays were performed in different theatres, some with great applause, others fell flat. Until this minute I cannot understand why some of my plays met with success, while others were hissed off the stage. However, this difference of the reception of my plays taught me to disregard altogether whether the public applauded or hissed my work. One's own conscience must be satisfied with one's work, all the rest is immaterial. I disown at present all my plays, even those which are still applauded at the Burgtheater [Imperial Court Theater in Vienna]. I don't care any longer for any of them.¹⁰

Posterity has upheld the second judgment. Only one shortish study devoted to Herzl as dramatist has appeared. Josef Fränkel, who primarily admired Herzl as creator of something other than plays, published it in Vienna thirty years after Herzl's death.¹¹ By then only two of Herzl's "pieces" were readily available in print,* the only way to find the texts of others would have been to advertise in booksellers' catalogues. Fränkel roundly accuses Herzl's co-religionists of being ungrateful for not keeping alive the dramatic works of one so intimately connected with their future. In Tel-Aviv bookshops one could find Hebrew translations of Conan Doyle, Edgar Wallace, of anti-Semites and even anti-Zionists, but not of Herzl.

Plays that do not survive turn the mind to metaphors from shipwreck. No lifeguard could revive a playwright who fails to carry the right equipment for survival. A dramatist can survive if he presents some perennial human problem with sufficient emotional or intellectual force. (The conflict, for example, between the laws of the state and the human conscience makes the *Antigone* of Sophocles relevant in most societies.) Or he nurtures human types so deeply, brings them so sharply to life, that a Hamlet or Cyrano de Bergerac leaps the barriers of dress and fashion to remain more alive than our next-door neighbor. Or like Oscar Wilde he decks a tawdry plot with lines of such brilliant wit that an Algernon and a Miss Prism become im-

* *The New Ghetto* and *The Fugitive.*

mortal. In an age of verse a dramatist may win pinions that help him to leap oblivion. But when a playwright lacks such equipment, as Herzl did, no audience, however grateful, can insufflate the kiss of life.

Only one of Herzl's plays—*The New Ghetto*—deserves to be called a tragedy. Otherwise, with the exception of *Solon in Lydia,* a conundrum play, and *Gretel,* a sentimental drama, Herzl's dramatic work consists of comedies: and for a comic writer Herzl lacked the one needful gift. He had, like his contemporary Georges Feydeau (1862–1921), a sense of situation; but he lacked the Frenchman's farcical speed, just as he lacked the mechanical brilliance that has preserved Goldoni. He was too much the son of his mother, whom a shrewd observer remembered as "stately, proud, virtuous . . . but entirely lacking in humor,"[12] to inject his creatures with that ichor without which wit is barren. Alex Bein admits with candor that "genuine humour, which provokes hearty and liberating laughter, and which calls, in the author, for the power to lift himself clear of his own life and the life of those around him, was denied him; he took himself too seriously."[13]

Nor are the plays bad enough to survive as period pieces in the way in which such melodramas as *Murder in the Red Barn* have survived. They spring from a mockable, overfurnished age; yet the decor is too feebly sketched, the dialogue is insufficiently grotesque to raise a sustained, unfriendly laugh.

Yet Herzl's plays are important as signposts on a mistaken road, and also as revelations of his character and preoccupations. The cynical manner in which they treat of love, on the level of flirtatiousness or sensuality, speak of the central emptiness in Herzl's life.[14] The titles of the fifteen plays he completed after *The Hirschkorn Case* show the concessions made by an essentially serious mind to popular taste. The dates of their composition and production show that though he sometimes had to wait for a production, he fared better than many playwrights who have had more to say and said it better. It is significant that the plays he wrote in collaboration with Hugo Wittmann, whose sense of humor was stronger than his own, were the most successful.

CHAPTER 12

H erzl was not the kind of dramatist who reveals his personal obsessions in his imagery, since his dialogue was never poetic or
close-textured. He revealed himself, or the things that worried him,
in his recurrent themes. Marriage in the Viennese mode is the most
outstanding. His own experiences with nubile young women and his
observations of how marriages were arranged in the society he knew
gave him a cynical outlook.

His infatuation for Magda, his foreknowledge of what the pubescent
coquette would so fast become had made January 1886 as bitter as its
skies. He cannot have foreseen, the cold afternoon when he had
watched the skaters in their furs, how quickly Magda would be replaced by the girl destined to embody, not only his personal experience of marriage, but his last attempt to love.

Julie Naschauer was eight years younger than Herzl. With the glowing health of the skating Magda, she had the Nordic good looks
that he most admired: her hair was as fair, her eyes as blue as those
of his imagined heroine in *"Das Alltägliche."* Herzl had known her
family since before he left Hungary, since the Naschauers, like the
Herzls, had moved to Vienna from Budapest. Julie, as well as her
brother and three sisters, had all been born in Hungary. But while the
Herzls had come to Budapest from Semlin in the south, the Naschauers
had come from the opposite direction, Julie's grandfather, Moritz
Naschauer, having been a native of Bohemia, the modern Czechoslo-
vakia. There were other similarities, other differences. Moritz Naschauer had lived and died, like Herzl's grandfather, in the strict Jewish tradition, which expressed itself in his case through devotion to

Jewish learning and philosophy rather than to an eccentric rabbi. Money meant less to Moritz than piety, though he acquired enough of the former to have his two sons educated in the modern manner.[1] The older brother, Wilhelm, moved to Vienna as early as 1861, when city records show him as a young man of thirty-one, working for the firm of Moritz Kollinsky and living in Leopoldstadt.[2] Almost immediately he married his employer's daughter, Julie Kollinsky, for a son, Franz Felix, was born in 1863, to be followed in 1865 by a daughter, Charlotte. (Neither seems to have married.) Jacob, who had remained in Budapest, as his brother's partner, married Johanna Kollinsky at around the same time. Julie was their fourth child, the others being Therese, Paul, Helene and Ella, the last being born in 1875 and dying unmarried in 1939. A mystery surrounds the two girls whom the brothers married. Moritz Kollinsky did not long survive the marriages while his widow, Franziska (described as "house-owner") lived until 1897, at the large house at Lilienbrunngasse that was the Naschauer home in Leopoldstadt. Nothing seems known of who the Kollinskys were, though the name is Polish. Whether Franziska was herself of Jewish maternal descent is not certain. If she was not, then according to *halacha*, or Jewish traditional law, neither Julie, the wife of Wilhelm, nor Johanna, the wife of Jacob, was Jewish either.[*] It is possible that Moritz Kollinsky urged on the double marriage of his daughters to the two Naschauer brothers as a bargain whereby the young men would have the advantages of money to offset any religious problems in the future when their own children became old enough to marry. In Wilhelm's case (whose children did not marry) the problem was not to arise.

The two brothers made the most of their opportunities. While Wilhelm remained in the Kollinsky house in Vienna, Jacob and Johanna stayed in Budapest until 1880, when they joined Wilhelm Naschauer in Vienna. The brothers founded an independent company under Wilhelm's name. It succeeded in a spectacular fashion. Their connections in both parts of the Dual Monarchy enabled them to profit from multitudinous projects: commissions for the Austrian Treasury, reclamation works connected with the control of the Danube, dealing in fruit and corn, and even the exploitation of a new fuel, oil,

---

[*] Although Franziska and Johanna are buried with their husbands but without religious inscriptions in the Jewish section of Vienna's Zentralfriedhofs,[2] the statement by Gerald Abrahams, leading writer on the Jewish religion, in *Jewish Chronicle*, 22, 1, 1971, that "the halacha is a sieve, though its reticulations are not the narrowest. It *excludes Herzl's descendants* [author's italics] it allows Spinoza . . ." must imply that Franziska Kollinsky, mother of Johanna, in turn mother of Julie, was in some way outside the congregation of Israel.

in the empire's eastern regions. Despite their wealth, they never developed those more refined ways of spending money that might have got them into the sixty-volume Biographical Dictionary of Austria, a work rich in Jewish names. Herzl saw them with frank, unsparing eyes as *nouveaux riches* whose way of life was contemptibly—if also enviably—different from that of the Herzls. Where the Herzls looked to Germany, the Naschauers looked, more materialistically, more superficially, to France. They were conspicuous at the opera; they larded their conversation with French phrases; they collected pictures and made no secret of the price. By 1889 Julie's uncle Wilhelm was a knight of the French Légion d'Honneur. They had buried any interest in religion with their Bohemian origins, carrying assimilation to gentile manners much further than the Herzls.† The children were not brought up to go to synagogue or observe the dietary laws.

Herzl began to frequent the Naschauers' when he was a student and after Jacob brought his family to Vienna. Julie had been at the age he found most attractive between 1880, when she was twelve, and the year he took his doctorate, when she was sixteen. But in those days he was a student worried about pawn tickets and his college fees; the difference of fortune between his family, modestly prosperous at best, and the Naschauers placed her among the forbidden fruits of a plutocratic paradise. It is doubtful whether even as a student he respected what Wilhelm and Jacob Naschauer represented; it is certain that he later despised them and their circle, as at least two of his major writings show.‡ But he was clear-sighted enough to see that their money could be extremely useful in less vulgar hands.

On February 28, 1886—the last day of the month which followed

---

† Jacob Naschauer's slow transformation *into his own father* is a curious consequence of hagiography. Leon Kellner's early account (1920) is unadorned: "Moritz Naschauer, who migrated as a young man to Hungary, and devoted more attention to the study of Jewish literature than to acquisition, gave his sons Wilhelm and Jakob (sic) 1837–1894 an exemplary education."[1] Dr. Alex Bein's first portrait of Julie's father (in his German *Biographie* of 1934) flatly contrasts Jacob Naschauer with his father Moritz: "Unlike his father who was more interested in Jewish literature and philosophy than in acquisition [*Erwerb*, as in Kellner's account], he was a typical example of every first generation of emancipated Jews, for whom emancipation made possible all kinds of swift financial ascent."[3] The English version of Dr. Bein's portrait (1957) transforms Naschauer's character as well as giving him a new first name. "Joseph Naschauer was the son of an immigrant from Bohemia. A man of wide culture, with special emphasis on Jewish philosophy and literature, Naschauer was also an exceptional business success."[4] From here it is another step to André Chouraqui's account (1970): "Herzl liked the man [Jacob Naschauer] for his wide culture, his intellectual courage and his knowledge in a field unknown to Theodor—Jewish culture and philosophy."[5]

‡ The Naschauer family circle are satirized in *The New Ghetto*, 1894, and *Altneuland*, 1902.

his passion for Magda—his Diary records a scene that shows the new
confidence of the published writer, the New York-performed playwright.[6]

> We were standing on the balcony. Jokingly, I asked her for a kiss.
> She refused—for one reason only: I might tell.
> "On my life, Julie, I won't."
> Then her rosy face evaded mine no longer. A kiss of such sweet-
> ness! Fresh, perfumed, yielding lips. I was quite moved when I
> stepped back into the room—in love.
> Unbelievable.

Julie conceded two more kisses three weeks later. On this occasion
prudence made them brief. Herr Naschauer—"my darling's unendur-
able papa!"—was conversing with two business friends in an adjoining
room. Herzl had not learned to smile on those he disliked, even when
they were the parents of his beloved. Although Julie implored him to
stay, he stumbled into the outside world; in its noisy solitude he would
retaste the triumph of her kisses. Contact with others was painful.
As he soiled his lips on a cigar, a glass, guilt stabbed him: he was
diluting his victory. But even as he perceived love's transitory nature,
he was consoled that he had won her love. She had drunk his second
kiss with *gourmandise.* In gentle parody of Naschauer conversation,
he used French.

That Julie so evidently liked him massaged his ego; he did not ask
himself too sharply if he reciprocated what she felt. "I am rather
touched," he wrote, "by this innocent little love. It is evident that she
likes me very much indeed." In a season of drought Julie's love was a
refreshing compliment: "a drop of sweetness in the bitter chalice of
dreary, unsuccessful ambition." His Diary, in its entry for May 10,
again stresses her infatuation for him. "A sweet word of love from that
dear little Juliette who, believing that I loved her, so loved me back—
that I must love her." On this occasion a friend had accompanied
Herzl to the Naschauer house. In the role of Herzl's envoy he had
discussed the relationship with Julie. She recognized, she confessed,
that the affair had no future. She was resolved not to be swept off her
feet by a man who could not afford her. What then, Herzl's friend
inquired, did the liaison give her?

"The present!"

Julie's rejoinder touched, rather than saddened, Herzl. He decided
it was kindest to inflict a small hurt at once than a deeper pain later.
He would break things off. But his resolution proved limper than he
wished. He took a first step ten days later. Julie had told him she

would be going to the Burgtheater on May 20. Herzl wavered. Logically the choice was between joining her at the play or staying at home. Instead he sat out the performance in a café across from the theater. At the end, when carriages were called, he contrived to pass hers, raising his top hat to her mournful nod. This was not all. He knew at which hotel the family would be supping. About eleven, he strolled into the dining room, greeting the others but pointedly ignoring her. "Her blue eyes grew steadily darker," he recorded. "She was genuinely hurt. Wasn't I, too? I did not look at her." Yet his emotions were still involved. If they had not been, he would not have waited in the banal café. A few days later, assailed by remorse, he explained what had prompted his cold behavior. She protested that such therapy, so far from curing the illness, made it worse. Another week and he stuck to his resolve. In response to a new invitation, he stayed away, sending neither apology nor excuse. It hurt him to persist, but persist he did. He wrote what he expected to be the epitaph on the affair and used the language that symbolized the abyss between the rich girl and the author still dependent on his middle-class father and mother.

"*C'est pourtant bien fini. F-i-n-i.*"

He then closed his Diary for a year.

It might have been better for both if the Diary had not reopened on their love. Herzl was no more brokenhearted by the rift with Julie in May than he had been by the break with Magda four months before. He had probably not loved Julie more; he had not scorned her family and its values less. Only two months after the final severance he was writing from France that "*Dieses Trouville ist ein Paradies.*"[7] The Channel resort, he continued to his parents, was assuredly the most enchanting place one could imagine. Its aristocratic elegance charmed one aspect of his soul while soft sand merging with sea delighted the central European to whom this new element was doubly attractive for being remote.

Jacob and Jeanette Herzl had rightly discerned that the antidote to their son's malaise was travel. The railway offered nineteenth-century Europeans movement certainly more pleasant, hardly less swift than modern airlines, since the trains ran with great punctuality for a much smaller traveling public. From the end of June until his return to Vienna in late August, Herzl was on the move through Western Europe, having reached France by way of the Tyrol and Switzerland. After a short stay in Paris he had moved to Normandy and the English Channel. The Victorian middle classes did not know the passion for the sun that would captivate their children's children.

In the 1880s the south of France was shuttered and bereft of foreigners during the summer months. Thus in choosing to recuperate from Julie in the Normandy of 1886 Herzl was choosing no secluded Arcadia; he was drowning his irritation in a sophisticated whirl. In visiting Dieppe, Rouen, Le Havre and particularly Trouville, he was also for the first time approaching the magnetic field of England. With a stronger fleet than those of the world combined, with its gold sovereign even more powerful than the armies of its Queen, its political theorists had much in common with Herzl's Viennese mentors. (Carl Menger had upheld Adam Smith in a much discussed essay in the *Neue Freie Presse*.) The island kingdom was to play a vital political role in Herzl's later existence. In 1886 he was already conscious of a power over the hazy horizon, a country of order and liberal beliefs.

Herzl's Norman holiday was passed in high spirits. Magda and Julie, worries about his health seem to have cast no cloud. He sent home, in brief messages, superficial impressions, indications of his physical moves. In so doing he obeyed his parents' very typical advice: he must write them postcards only, since his moods, impressions and ideas were the stuff of his serious writing, "which belongs, not to us, but to the world."[8]

His serious writing: here, alas, the sky was clouded. As he journeyed through what he called "a big piece of the world and a piece of the big world"[9] he carried with him two plays, one by an Englishman, the other by himself. Edward George Earle Lytton Bulwer-Lytton (1803–73), though remembered as a novelist, wrote a play with a name as short as his own was long: *Money*. Though written in 1840, this serious comedy continued to fascinate audiences at least until 1911, when it is recorded as having been produced for a Command Performance at London's Drury Lane. Herzl's play—*Seine Hoheit*, or *His Highness*—had been finished just before he set out on his travels. No sooner was it completed than he realized that his theme might too much resemble what he knew as *Bulwers Geld*. On many later occasions Herzl was to be troubled by a similar dread that he might be accused of plagiarizing other men's ideas. He was too intelligent to pretend, against the evidence, that what he had borrowed was his own. He must win—but on his own achievements. Thus when Kana, his severity unusually blunted by affection, had told his Romanian parents that Theodor had won the unanimous approval of his university examiners, Herzl had corrected him: he had, in truth, scraped home on a majority decision. So, too, the truth that *Tabarin* was taken from an idea of Catulle Mendès would trouble him when, in 1894, a new production of his first successful play was to be discussed with Burckhard, director of the Vienna Burgtheater. Now in the summer of 1886 he spent sleepless moments wondering if he had unwittingly purloined an idea from Bulwer-Lytton. After reading *Money* he was reassured to conclude that he and the Englishman had approached a similar target from different directions. For "His Highness" referred, not to a princeling or a duke, but to a potentate much more powerful: naked money. A commentator has summarized Herzl's attitude at this time as a conviction that money was power. It could purchase glory, honour and respect. It transformed petty traders into lords of society. He believed that it ruthlessly pervaded the world, tearing lovers apart, procuring marriages, breaking families into fragments, or inheritances. Loyalty, love, friendship, everyone and everything: you could buy them all with money.

The play had been written after his prediction that Magda would deteriorate into the spoiled wife of a stockbroker, when the difference in fortune between the Naschauers and the Herzls put Julie out of reach. The play could etch the mood, not exorcise it. The recurrent theme of money's power is not peculiar to Herzl. It is a leitmotiv in the work of Charles Dickens, another sensitive product of Victorian capitalism. To Dickens the rich bachelor is a deus ex machina; the miser could put things right if only he would disburse his gold. But Herzl's delineation of the power of money seems more mechanical since his characters, unlike those of Dickens, lack breathing life. They are puppets illustrating a theorem derived from a cold scrutiny of a more cynical metropolis.

Yet Vienna recognized the power of physical passion more openly than Dickensian London. And in the domain of Eros "His Highness" exerted his power most balefully. The ancient Latin tag—that marriage is a *consortium omnis vitae*—is rephrased by Dr. Ahlsdorf, the lawyer in Herzl's play, as a "consortium for the whole of life—a consortium for speculation."

Herzl's plot creaks to demonstrate that Ahlsdorf is right: except in regard to one person, the blond heroine Lucy. She has long believed that her mother, Thérèse, is as rich as she seems, that she flaunts her silk dresses and gives modish soirees as part of her duty to "good" society. Her mother, in fact, is up to her bustle in debt because of her pretense. Her credo is stark: without money she will not get on in society and without money Lucy will never find a husband. When Lucy learns the truth, she wants to start a new life and take a job. She decides to break with Franz Hellweg (the rich owner of a *Schloss*), whom her mother's pretensions have tricked and humiliated.

The faithful Josef Fränkel has preserved one scene (the tenth) from Act Three. It gives fairly, if in little, the flavor of Herzl's comic writing.[10]

LUCY   Mama?

THÉRÈSE   My child! Our friend Ahlsdorf has just told me that . . . that . . .

AHLSDORF   Out with it! Good news needs no preparation.

THÉRÈSE   . . . That an unexpected dispensation of fortune . . .

AHLSDORF   What long words you use! A hardheaded chap, one of your revered father's debtors, has at last resolved, Fräulein Lucy, to pay you what he owes.

LUCY   Really?

AHLSDORF   In fact, a larger sum.

THÉRÈSE   We . . . we find ourselves once more in better circumstances.

LUCY   Mama, it is not right for you to conspire against me with outsiders.

AHLSDORF   You don't believe us?

LUCY   Not one word. Herr Hellweg wants to donate us the money indirectly. Our sense of honour seems not worth outwitting, when it lets itself be outwitted so.

AHLSDORF   Your words touch my soul . . . The straight way is the best. Fräulein Lucy, I herewith frankly inform you that you have an inheritance in the offing.

LUCY   That I know to be untrue.

AHLSDORF   So? You forget that there is a man by the name of Ahlsdorf, who by handling the rights of others has acquired something of his own and who names you in his Will his plenary heir.

LUCY   Herr Ahlsdorf, I beg you not to mix in our affairs.

THÉRÈSE   Lucy!

AHLSDORF   Once more you touch my soul . . . I have deserved no better. Lucy, once you stretched your hand to me. I was too depraved to take it. Today, dear Lucy, I implore your small, brave hand. You cannot resist—you are my heir. You are a good match now. If you had studied Law, you would know that you cannot forbid me from naming you my heir . . . Understand?

FRANZ   (*at centre of stage*) Where's all this tending? I know not if Fräulein Lucy loves me. Yet if she loves me and does not trust that I never sought this wretched money—or if she be too arrogant to forget it herself—then will I on my way . . .

LUCY   (*trembling*) Franz!

FRANZ   (*on his knees before her*) Lucy!

AHLSDORF (*drawing Thérèse forward*) We see good things, Frau
Thérèse. Your stepson is inordinately rich.

THÉRÈSE (*laughing*) On that score I make you no reproach.

AHLSDORF And you are right. For as a thinker once intelligently
opined: Money alone does not make happy—one must also
have it.

Herzl returned to the theme of marriage a second time during his
estrangement from Julie. In January 1887 he wrote, in less than ten
days, a one-act play, *The Fugitive*. He wrote it, not to ease his heart,
but, as he hoped, to earn money for an Italian holiday. He had taken
his earlier play to Berlin and had not found a producer. Instead, he
had deepened his friendship with Arthur Levysohn, editor of the
Berliner Tageblatt. Levysohn commissioned him to write weekly (or
sometimes biweekly) articles about the cultural life of Vienna under
the heading *Journeys Round the Week*. These had made no great
impression on Berlin readers but Herzl had begun to develop severe
pains at the back of his head, physical concomitants of spiritual depression. A journey to Italy seemed a possible cure.

The theme of *The Fugitive* is as typical of Herzl the plot-maker
as the quoted scene is typical of Herzl the writer of dramatic dialogue.

Margarethe von Gerditz, the heroine, has abandoned her husband,
the foolish Hans. She wants neither a reconciliation with him (though
she loves him still) nor a divorce (since this would free him to destroy
some other woman). Margarethe lives in quiet and luxurious retirement with her companion, Adèle, on some income undisclosed. One
evening Adèle persuades her mistress to go to the theater. Margarethe
notices Adèle's impatience for her departure. And indeed, no sooner
has Margarethe left the apartment than Adèle goes upstairs to sum-
mon Rödiger, her lodger lover. While she is offstage, a man comes in,
hears a noise and hides himself in Adèle's bedroom. Adèle and
Rödiger return—but not to enjoy each other's company for long.
Margarethe has deliberately returned earlier than expected and
Rödiger has to escape. Margarethe, disappointed in her companion's
morals, searches for a lover and finds, concealed in Adèle's bedroom,
her own husband. Love reawakens through a fog of deceit: for Hans
claims he is fugitive from a vengeful husband. Margarethe plays the
piano, Hans kisses her hair, till a terrific clamor interrupts the reconciliation. Rödiger has heard the piano, has been told by the janitor
of a stranger's entrance, and enters in angry demand for an explanation. To protect her mistress, Adèle takes the blame. Rings are handed
back to the accompaniment of tears. But reconciliation all round is
achieved before the curtain falls. It leaves Margarethe once again in

possession of her fugitive, an abashed prisoner in a décor of bourgeois elegance with chandeliers. One sentence in the dialogue bears the stamp of experience: "Only to our intimates are we ruthless."[11]

Herzl rushed the play to Ernst Hartmann (1844–1911), a well-known actor at the Burgtheater. But Hartmann's reply was crushing: Herzl had talent, but should show more respect for life, should study it more deeply. The actor found the characters hardly more animated than waxworks from a theatrical museum.*[12] Herzl was enraged by Hartmann's comments. But his Italian excursion was not annulled. His father gave him two hundred guilders, and with this sum he could visit the sunlit peninsula as a privileged observer. But Herzl would naturally have preferred to travel on his earnings as a playwright. His father's gift was an irksome reminder of his dependence, of the fact that the career of *Schriftsteller* was still as hazardous as the rabbi in Budapest had said it would be.

The railway took him south by way of Venice, Pisa, Livorno and Rome to Naples and that blessed region where, in a good year, almond blossom glints in sun when Europe north of the Alps is gray and cold. In Capri he made the acquaintance of Sudermann the playwright and discussed a writer's problems with him.

In Herzl's case, these problems were about to achieve a temporary resolution. Italy helped. Herzl believed that this second jaunt—no more darkened by the sorrow of lost love than his Norman holiday—was the inspiration of his first true emergence in literary Vienna. The turning point came in the handful of days he spent at Amalfi. A surviving letter indicates his mood.

> With the youth of Amalfi I am *frère et cochon,* I the brother, they the swine. Like the ratcatcher of Hamelin, I wander round escorted by some fifty young rascals. They sing fishermen's songs in chorus while I beat time. The whole town of Amalfi has been in unbroken fiesta since my arrival. The frenzy of delight reaches its climax when for two *soldi* I scatter sweetmeats under the feet of the children. At once the ground heaves in a formless heap of mutually pushing and scuffling scamps, three or four deep.[13]

He wrote a *feuilleton* inspired by Amalfi and gave it the title "Emmelfey" in imitation of the way some English tourists pronounced

---

* The play was to be accepted for the Burgtheater on June 30, 1888, after winning the approval of Adolf Ritter von Sonnenthal, the grandson of a Berlin rabbi. Hartmann himself was chosen to play Hans von Gerditz, but possibly because of his lack of enthusiasm he instead directed the play when it was finally performed on May 4, 1889. *The Fugitive* was repeated annually for single performances at the Burgtheater until its last performance on February 17, 1898.

the Italian name. "Emmelfey" had a great success when the *Wiener Allgemeine Zeitung* printed it in its issue of March 25, 1887. So much so that when Herzl returned to Vienna, Baron Kolisch, who owned the newspaper, offered him the post of *feuilleton* editor.

The day before he started in his new post—an impressive one for a writer of only twenty-seven—he reopened the Diary, whose last entry had written off his affair with Julie.

> Since I wrote that last line, almost a year has passed. In the interim; *Seine Hoheit*, the trip to Trouville, then Berlin; *The Journey Round the Week*; and with all of that an increasing reputation, increasing nerves: the tedious concoction of feuilletons, the increased violence of the pain at the back of my head, the journey to Italy which I had envisaged as an escape, the return, again with no improvement. Now I am enrolled as feuilleton editor of the *Wiener Allgemeine Zeitung*. Tormorrow I begin my duties.

Herzl was not at them long. After a mere two months Baron Kolisch gave him notice of dismissal couched in cordial terms. A clue to the abrupt termination of Herzl's contract may lie in the collection of essays and journalistic pieces he published the same year. Its title —*News from Venus*—was misleading. The contents of the book were neither sensational nor erotic. But again and again a characteristic as basic as ambition and self-love obtrudes: a characteristic intertwined with these starker structures as morning glory on barbed wire: a penchant for dreaming. His first successful *feuilleton*—"*Das Alltägliche*"—was now reprinted. Significantly, it started with a dream. As a descriptive writer, Herzl's talents showed best with landscapes or seascapes which prompted him to reveries on the infinite, the boundless. Even when he lacked such inspiring backgrounds, when he was shut in the urban scenery he had known all his life, in sidewalk cafés, in dining rooms jungle-rich with silk hangings and cut glass, he was invisibly accompanied by aristocratic heroes or secondary selves. In one bitter essay he tells of a man who commits suicide because his wife prevents him dreaming. "My old habit, which has certainly been for me a source of sweetest pleasure, though also of much vexation, is the desire to dream. I have always found it a delight to lose the ground from beneath my feet, and to plunge into memory, or soar into the future."[14] This attitude colored his approach to love. Silken hangings, shaded lights, an atmosphere of luxury alone made love possible. "The décor is decisively important in that self-deception known as love."[15]

An aptitude for dreaming, when prompting to action, when empowering to push past the opposition of realists, could modify history. But in the newspaper office of 1887 it made for an absent-minded editor. Inefficiency, self-absorption, coupled perhaps with his tendency to overwrite, may have led to friction with his colleagues, then dismissal. Misconduct was certainly not involved. By this time his gaze was too firmly fixed on advancement for him to tolerate the dalliance described in the earlier letters to Heinrich Kana.

To set against the slap of misfortune he had, in July, the good news that *Seine Hoheit* had at last been accepted for production: by the Wallner Theater in Berlin. That New York had been followed by Berlin was a splendid omen. With his gambler's instinct Herzl thought of migrating to the authentic German capital. A newly founded theatrical magazine was looking for a manager. There was mention of a quarterly salary of 750 marks. But nothing was fixed. Then the same summer Oscar Blumenthal, a distinguished critic, resigned his position on the *Berliner Tageblatt*. But the hope that Herzl might succeed him again came to nothing. A third disappointment was the most tantalizing. Arthur Levysohn told him that the *Frankfurter Zeitung* needed a Paris correspondent: he would personally recommend Herzl for the position. Paris, the lodestar of the Naschauers, became his. He wrote excitedly to his parents:

"Heine was Paris correspondent. Then, after a literary general-pause, Lindau and Wittmann, too. Singer of the *Neue Freie Presse*, Blowitz of *The Times*, had almost the status of ambassadors. Levysohn began his big career as Paris correspondent of the *Kölnische Zeitung*."[16]

Though he was not to represent the *Frankfurter Zeitung*, Paris was established in his mind as the physical coefficient of Julie and success. And on September 7 his Diary records a triumph whose impact was the greater for coming in a season of disappointments.

> I have found my kind Julie again . . . my final love.
> She loved me all the time.
> I shall marry her. I have already told her so.

But there were giants to slay

> before I reach the sweet little princess. Today is a day of Job's messengers—and I have no job. Since July 15 I am no longer with the *Allgemeine*. The *Fremdenblatt* looks as if it will elude me. In that case I shall be once more a shipwrecked sailor thrust forth on the wild seas of Bohemia, unable to ask for Julie's hand . . . True, *Seine Hoheit* has been accepted by the Wallner Theater in Berlin. If it

flops, I shall find myself a beaten, broken, penniless man. Poorer than ever before, because my youthful courage has entirely vanished. Then I should have to say a final farewell to my beloved, for I don't wish her to forfeit her youth on my account. Perhaps I shall never succeed.

The recapture of Julie was a counterweight to the failure and partial success that in lonely rhythm had so far been his career. *Seine Hoheit* was not a flop. It was the kind of dappled victory most irritating to the ambitious. It was rejected by Adolf Ritter von Sonnenthal, co-director with Baron Forster of the Hofburgtheater. It was then produced at Prague in February 1888 and after that given its Berlin production. (That June von Sonnenthal made his amends when he accepted *The Fugitive*.) Yet Herzl was an established and mildly challenging writer. In May he had joined the Vienna Union of Journalists and the Writers' Concordia. His *Book of Folly*, dedicated to Dr. Arthur Levysohn, appeared later the same summer. It was a successor to *News from Venus* and was stuffed with epigrams that might at first sight suggest an affinity with Oscar Wilde. The affinity was one of the age, not one of temperament. Each man embodied his particular viewpoint in a style that linked surprise with the well-turned phrase. It was the style of the *fin de siècle*. No one writer used it exactly like another; yet all who used it shared an aversion for the earnest expressed in earnest terms. A few of Herzl's dicta indicate his particular concerns.

"Every work of art is a revelation—of power or impotence."

"Comedians understand no jokes."

"The shortest route to the director is by the back stairs. Whoever condemns it fears being met there."

"The public allows itself to be bored only by the famous."

"People congratulate on a success. How superfluous. Success itself is the unsurpassable joy."[17]

The loneliest love, it would be possible to say in similar spirit, is the love of success. And when success refused to come, or to come with the amplitude he sought, Herzl had no close friends on whom to call, no one with whom to use the punning, ironic language that made it possible to laugh at defeat or disease. Kana and Boxer were both in Berlin. While Boxer was succeeding as a journalist, Kana existed in a poverty uncushioned by parental help, unassuaged by even temporary success. He was poor, not because he was a Jew, but because he was a writer who could not readily market his wares. His predicament was not uncommon in the nineteenth century. James Thomson, who wrote *The City of Dreadful Night,* and Frederick Rolfe, who wrote *Hadrian VII,*

knew similar penury. Herzl offered Kana money. Kana not only refused it, but did so in painful terms. "I have lost belief in our friendship
this long time past," he wrote, "and that completely."[18] It was small
consolation that he had kept belief in Herzl's star. "Courage, toughness,
you have those in particular. You will, you *must*, get there."

Kana's plight roused Herzl's impotent sympathy. It made his own
conquest of a rich man's daughter a more valued triumph.

CHAPTER 13

E arly in 1889 Herzl asked Jacob Naschauer for Julie's hand in marriage and in so doing set in motion the great personal drama of his life. Agonizing and protracted, it was to be linked to the second, political drama of his life in the way that the reverse side of the moon is linked to the side we see. The two dramas were never to be equal. The second, with its thousands of actors, was to dwarf and conceal the first, with its small, domestic cast. The protagonists of the second drama were to have it in their power to obscure the first, vital though this had been for the emergence of their own political play. A characteristic of Herzl's second drama is the amplitude of its documentation, so that for those who bother to look, the outlines of his political plot are complete and for the most part clear. Yet where his marriage is concerned, the documents are eloquent by their taciturnity, the photographs by their absence.

Herzl may have put his emotions on paper as he decided to risk marriage. If so, the paper has not survived. Herzl was a cerebral man who wanted to be sure that he had fallen in love. He had repeatedly dreamed of discovering a successor to Madeleine Kurz, her life as brief as her surname. Now aged twenty-nine, he needed to set his emotions in harness if only to subdue the melancholy loneliness that was his dominant mood. He will have assumed his ability to prevail over Julie. However self-centered, he must have asked himself how the legacy of his student illness could affect his wife; but even the frankest diarists of his time rarely confided such problems to ink.

An enthusiastic letter of congratulation on his engagement arrived from Kana. Only the hungry can truly value bread. Kana in his Berlin

garret must have seen in his friend's engagement the achievement of
financial ease. Herzl himself was enough of a realist to value the economic independence marriage would bring. In nineteenth-century Europe—in this respect more backward than Islam—a woman's fortune,
including her dowry, passed under the control of the man she married.
The size of Julie's dowry can be inferred from Herzl's complaint,
eleven years later,[1] that all except twenty thousand guilders had been
consumed. Two hundred guilders had financed his Italian journey of
1887; one of his plays portrays a coal miner as earning one guilder and
twelve kreuzer for a twelve-hour day that began and ended with a
two-hour trudge.[2]

Yet it is doubtful if Herzl greeted the marriage with euphoria. He
was cynical, in the Viennese way, about pledges of eternal love. In his
recent *Book of Folly* he had written that "we always laugh at engagements on the stage because of the malicious joy innate in all of us."[3] It
is equally to be doubted if he believed that his flirtation with Julie
could mature into a lasting and satisfying love. Although marriage to
a rich man's daughter was a triumph for his pen, Julie had proved too
easy a catch for that inner self whose daydream had been confided to
his Diary: "Your strong arm snatches the resisting maiden, dismisses
her who yields . . . Queens will love you. But you will scorn them. You
will reject what offers itself and strive only for what is refused."[4]

As for Julie, her original attraction to Herzl had been largely physical; she had admitted as much by the greed of her kisses and her willingness to enjoy the present at a time when the affair seemed to have
no future. Yet she also admired the outstanding man of letters. Shallow
herself, she will have found little to complain of in her husband's
plays or books*; when they won applause, she could bask in it. She
will either not have sensed his deeper longings, or thought to control
them. At first she seems even to have pleased Jeanette Herzl, who
called her *die Kleine,* "the little one." But Julie already saw herself as
a great lady, as mistress of an independent household outdistancing
her unmarried sisters.

In 1889 Viennese Jews still largely lived in Leopoldstadt, the quarter
across the Danube Canal bridge. Jacob Naschauer was never to leave
it while Wilhelm only left it the year before he died. In this limited
world the Herzls and Naschauers were well known. It has been reported that the two Jacobs asked the Chief Rabbi, Moritz Güdemann,
to marry the young couple. The two fathers may have envisaged a
fashionable marriage in the city's chief synagogue. According to the

* At least those written before their marriage; she may have objected to carica-
tures of herself in his later writings.

same account (which is based on Güdemann's unpublished and un-obtainable Memoirs[5]) Güdemann seems to have at first agreed, and then pleaded family business outside Vienna as an excuse not to officiate. Güdemann, at this time in his mid-fifties, was one of two Chief Rabbis in Vienna; he was to become sole Chief Rabbi after the death of his colleague, Adolf Jellinek, in 1893. Born in Hanover, he had been elected rabbi of Berlin only to be turned down as too orthodox for that modernizing community. His whole experience had been German; he knew nothing of Hungary (the provenance of Jacob Herzl and Jacob Naschauer) with its different religious balance and different laws. His reasons for not officiating at the marriage may have been what they have been alleged; or they may have involved grave doubts as to whether Julie Naschauer, the daughter of Johanna and the grand-daughter of Franziska Kollinsky, was Jewish. His objections (if he had such) cannot have had to do with Theodor, whose status as a Jew was clear; nor can they have been based on the failure of both families to live completely Jewish lives, since such a failure was common, if not general.

In any case, no other rabbi has been named as having offered to take Güdemann's place. Nor was the marriage solemnized in a synagogue in Vienna or elsewhere. Instead, guests were bidden to a celebration in a Catholic mountain village some two hours by train from Vienna's Südbahnhof. The date was June 25, 1889.[6]

To the superstitious, neither year nor place were well omened. The year 1889 had begun with an almost Shakespearean instance of how good fortune can plummet in one night to crime and death. On the morning of January 30, Josef Count Hoyos, the hunting companion of Crown Prince Rudolf, found the Prince's body in the vaulted down-stairs bedroom of the Mayerling hunting lodge; beside it lay the still colder body of Baroness Marie Vetsera, not yet eighteen. The Mayer-ling tragedy had links with the place Jacob Naschauer chose for his daughter's wedding. Reichenau an der Rax, like Mayerling, was ap-proached by way of Baden, the spa in which Herzl had gambled as a student and to which he was often to return. Marie Vetsera's mother had a villa in Reichenau; the mansion to which the wedding guests were now bidden was named after Prince Rudolf.

It was probably the snob in Jacob Naschauer that decided him to take an apartment in the Rudolfsvilla for his daughter's marriage to a distinguished playwright. The mansion formed part of the property of the Waissnix family, prosperous peasants who had exploited the de-velopment of the railway to turn Reichenau into a spa on a small scale resembling Bath at the time of George IV. Emperor Franz-Josef was a

frequent visitor while his brother, Grand Duke Ludwig, owned a large
villa, Schloss Wartholz, in the village. Writers and artists joined cour-
tiers and social climbers as patrons of the resort. Two Waissnix brothers between them owned a hotel set in pleasure grounds, the Rudolfs-
bad (its specialty curative cold baths), and a large house, originally
known as Haus auf der Wag, suitable for letting. During the mid-1860s
this house had been rented entire for Prince Rudolf, his sisters and
their retinue. After they gave up their occupancy it was renamed in
honor of the Emperor's only son, Michael Waissnix becoming one of
his hunting and drinking companions. The Rudolfsvilla was divided
into substantial apartments, each consisting of some six rooms with a
private kitchen.[7]

If Reichenau's fashionable clientele attracted Jacob Naschauer, its
scenery appealed to the nature lover in Herzl. To him (as to Arthur
Schnitzler, who had an impassioned friendship with Olga Waissnix,
wife of one of the two brothers[8]) this last Alpine valley, its fields slop-
ing through woods on one side to the Schneeburg, on the other toward
the Raxalps, had scenic grandeur. It was a place for writing, walking,
repose, and all within a convenient distance of the capital. Whatever
his memories of the ceremony at the Rudolfsvilla, Herzl liked the
neighborhood; he was to revisit it on later occasions and choose
Edlach, a short walk from Reichenau itself, for his last desperate fight
to regain health.†

No photograph seems to have survived of the wedding reception
which mustered the Herzl, Kollinsky and Naschauer families over
champagne and Viennese cooking. It thus remains one of the few
opaque passages in Herzl's life.‡ But the entry in the registry of marriages kept at the Jewish community offices in Leopoldstadt gives the
hour of the celebration as 1 P.M. at Reichenau. This will have given
time for the marriage to have been performed by a rabbi or religious
teacher in Vienna, or if none such was forthcoming, in front of the
civil authorities; even in that case the rabbi at the Jewish community
in Leopoldstadt was required by law to enter it into the register
delivered to him by the state. The bride and groom and two necessary
witnesses will then have taken the railway on to Reichenau.

After the marriage, Theodor took Julie on a two-month tour by rail
of Switzerland and France. Julie was quickly pregnant. Early in 1890
Herzl was writing a *feuilleton* describing his joy at the arrival of the

† In another link with Mayerling: Count Hoyos also died at the Edlacherhof in
1899.
‡ An Appendix discusses the legal and religious complexities involving Herzl's
marriage.

son he was certain his first child would be. The essay was entitled "*Der Sohn.*" "This little one," he wrote, "has given me a tangible, sensuous love of life. For he is my son, my never-ending continuation, the guarantee that I shall forever inherit the earth, forever renewed as my son, my grandson, forever young, forever beautiful, forever strong."[9] The child born on March 29 proved to be a girl and was named Pauline after Herzl's dead sister. At this time the couple were living at 1, Stephanieplatz, just round the corner from the Herzl parents. By the following year, they had moved to 7, MarcAurelstrasse, a street of imposing apartment buildings in the inner town. Here the dream expressed in the *feuilleton* became a reality and a son was born to them on June 10, 1891. By the far older Jewish calendar he had been born on the fourth day of Sivan, 5651. Between the sixth and seventh of Sivan, Jews celebrated the festival of the Giving of the Law, a fleeting, symbol-less celebration "because it is not the week nor the month but the whole year that belongs to the Torah, and this is so because the Torah does not demand a symbol only, but life and conduct."[10] According to Torah, the child's life as a Jew should have started with his circumcision on the twelfth day of Sivan. But the Herzls decided not to circumcise him; nor was he given a Hebrew name. Instead, he was named Hans; a German form of John and without Jewish connotations, it was possibly a compliment to Julie's mother, Johanna Kollinsky.

Though fruitful, the marriage was unhappy. If the letters that passed between the members of this all too literate family had been preserved, it would be easier to be sure, not only what went wrong with the marriage, but how soon. But the relevant letters have disappeared.[11] In the consequent darkness, probably caused by the deliberate intervention of the actors in the second drama of Herzl's life, it is still possible to discern early unhappiness. In a famous passage Samuel Butler remarks that what the Italians call Death's daughter lays her cold hand most awfully on a man "during the first half-hour that he is alone with a woman whom he has married but never genuinely loved." Any honeymoon would have been a strain, so little did the serious husband and the frivolous wife have in common; the two months may have doomed their future. In the first year of his marriage Herzl worked on the libretto of an operetta, *Des Teufels Weib;* set to music by Adolf Müller, it was first performed on November 22, 1890, at the Theater an der Wien. The fantastic plot had little to do with the plot of his private drama; but the cover of the musical score was embellished with the picture of a devilish female.[12]

It bears a striking resemblance to portraits of Julie. Her cornflower eyes have been replaced by flames.*

There were causes for grievance on both sides. Even if Julie did not inspire *Des Teufels Weib,* she gave observers the impression of being *hysterisch,* which probably meant that she was emotional and possessive. She was extravagant, delighting in ostentation rather than the solid comfort that was Herzl's inheritance. Her husband's work threw him into contact with actresses whose virtue was easy and whose looks superior to her own. When she was pregnant she was jealous, even if Theodor gave her no cause. His plays—in which she found less to like after her marriage—did not earn enough to maintain her in the manner to which she had been spoiled. She probably demanded that she dip into her dowry even before he began to do likewise. If she suspected the secrets of his past, and how these could affect herself, a bitter new ingredient joined the devil's brew. This brew will have found a willing stirrer in Jeanette Herzl. She had long lived through her son and was reluctant to share him with a woman so unlike herself. Jeanette had been within a quick dash of her son during the first year of his married life; this may have been as harmful as the too long honeymoon. A pattern was cut in which Theodor would often slip away to lunch with his mother and father to escape the *Krach*—or din—at home. Even his upward move to MarcAurelstrasse did not place him out of reach of a quick cab. With a mother-in-law's understandable hypocrisy, Jeanette, despite her own indifference to religion, may have complained of Julie's capitulation to gentile values. The rift between the two women was to result in Julie's children siding impassionedly with her against a grandmother they learned to detest.[13]

* An additional, apparently unused stanza from the operetta may be more than an example of black humor. (It was found by Josef Fränkel in the Theater an der Wien and is reproduced in facsimile as an example of Herzl's handwriting on p. 38 of Theodor Herzl, *A Biography,* London: "Ararat" Publishing Society, 1946.) The following is a literal translation of what is by any standards mediocre verse:

> A quarrelsome female, a dreadful dragon,
> Becomes ill and the doctor examines her jaws.†
> Then he looks over his spectacles at the husband
> And whispers: "This is shocking, what I must tell:
> I believe there are tuberculous bacilli."
> The husband bears it with Roman fortitude.
> But what are his feelings when the next day
> He opens his newspaper: Ha! Koch has destroyed
> The strength of these bacilli. She will be saved for him.
> The man is a victim of Science.

† (*Rachen;* as in the English phrase "jaws of Hell," the Germans speak of *Rachen der Hölle.*)

Probably at all times Herzl found some solace in Pauline and Hans. But his love for his children was theoretical. He was never to be quite sure of their ages; while sentimentalizing about them—"Children are our greatest teachers"[14]—he proved ready to desert them at the least temptation.

It might have been better for his marriage if he had discussed it with a friend, rather than his mother. Just when he needed buoyant friendship he had depressing news from Kana. In the summer after the birth of Pauline his former critic wrote him a letter that showed a startling reversal of their roles. While Kana was morbid and desperate, Herzl was cast for an astringent role he found hard to play.

> Berlin. Kothenerstrasse 31,
> 9th August, 1890.

Dear kind Theodor,

You will have received my letter of yesterday. For me it was a ghastly day. I had promised Brahm an article which had to be in by six pm. The whole day I was unwell, and only kept myself on my feet by drinking a few cups of black coffee. Four o'clock came, then five, and I had not finished. Beads of sweat stood out on my brow, my hands began to tremble. At last I decided on an imperial stroke: sacrificing nothing less than the main theme, I finished and sent it off. Up till now he has not returned it. He will take it in the end. Then, in my eyes, he will be judged. It is the worst thing I have ever written him.

Why do I have anything to do with Brahm? Chiefly because I have no choice. The Berlin papers are as good as closed to me. Ehren-Levysohn, my former patron, could not even deign to ask me to send him something, without commitment. And I can't exist on what I earn with Mamroth and Mauthsen. So I was delighted when Brahm invited me to write on current affairs. So far as I know he is, apart from the literary transactions in which he is always involved, an honest man. [Kana used the Latin phrase *homo integer*.] If you know anything to the contrary, I beg you to tell me.

So far I have been unable to find an opening in family journals. Perhaps I'll succeed with the novella on which I'm working. Yet however desperate things get for me here, it has never occurred to me to return to Vienna. Whenever I hear of Vienna, then everything I must go through here seems bearable.[15]

Herzl recognized the chill of failure, since he had known it himself, if in more comfortable surroundings. His inability to solve Kana's problems, or put the friendship back on its old basis, made his Viennese apartment cold despite its warmth. (A portrait by the minor Austrian painter Max Kurzweil catches Herzl not only in the almost

insane frenzy of this period, but seated in a tavern, another place of
refuge from home. He is reading, staring-eyed, some bad news in the
press. His hair is as disheveled as his cravat.[16]) Early in February 1891,
when Julie was in the fifth month of her second pregnancy, he received the letter that seared him more than any other in his life. "My
dear, kind Theodor," it began, "your old friend bids you a last farewell
before he dies! I thank you for all your friendship and kindness. I wish
for you and all your dear ones all good fortune here below." Kana had
shot himself after ending the letter: "*Ich küsse Dich. Dein Heinrich.*"

The shock Kana's suicide caused him was shown by his response.
Julie's company was no consolation; her condition aroused no protective feeling. Four days after his friend's death Herzl took the train
south to Venice. The Adriatic city was bitterly cold. His grief mixed
with guilt drove him west to Milan. *Die Duse*—the great Italian actress
Eleonora Duse—was acting at the Teatro Filodrammatico and he
attended her performance. He passed the rest of the month touring
first the Italian then the French Riviera. He again indulged his fondness for gambling, seeking a sign. "A mania for gambling and a mania
for thrift," he wrote, "are only two facets of the selfsame passion."[17]
But no sign was given. Julie represented a security he unlovingly
loved, Kana a ghost whom he would never exorcise. He had returned
to Vienna to see her through the last weeks of pregnancy and the
birth of Hans.

The death of Kana had had an equally searing effect on Oswald
Boxer—an effect that was to deprive Herzl of his other friend. Boxer
showed what he described as his "great sense of abandonment and
loneliness" in a manner suited to his energetic temper. Perhaps because he kept his sights low, he had exploited his pen more shrewdly
than Kana. By his second year in Berlin he had been earning ten
thousand marks as a journalist. He was also active in good works,
frequenting Privy Councilor of Commerce Ludwig Goldberger, the
man who presided over the Berlin Central Committee for the resettlement in Brazil of Jewish emigrants from Russia. In 1890 Goldberger
had asked the thirty-year-old Boxer to visit Brazil and undertake in
person the selection and purchase of land from the government. Boxer
had hesitated. It is probable that Kana's desperate gesture helped him
make up his mind. In May 1891 he set out on what was to be a perilous task. Although his base would be São Paolo, a city with many
German settlers and some sense of hygiene, the country as a whole
was plagued with yellow fever.

If his marriage had had any warmth, the death of Kana and the
departure of Boxer might have drawn Herzl closer to Julie and her

children. Instead his double loss threw harsh light on the abyss between him and her. Rabbi Güdemann recorded that a few years
after he had been unable to marry Herzl, he had been called on by a
lawyer. The lawyer represented Herzl. He asked Güdemann to invite
Jacob Naschauer to call on him so that the rabbi could resolve a serious
family dispute. Güdemann refused. Naschauer should call on his own
initiative if he wanted the matter resolved. "I believe my attitude
helped Herzl," the rabbi wrote, "since by inviting his father-in-law
I might easily have stirred the spark of dissension into flame."[18] He
may have preserved from divorce an unhappy marriage. Julie may
have wanted the divorce as much as Herzl.

Less than two months after the birth of Hans, Herzl again left home.
This time the journey was more than an Italian holiday. He planned
to visit Spain by way of France and then go into North Africa.[19]
To Julie his departure may have seemed the first step toward a divorce, damaging though this would be for their two children, for
Herzl's finances and her own self-esteem. But Herzl's mind was more
taken up by grief for the dead Kana than concern for the living. He
took with him to Spain the idea for a novel, *Samuel Kohn*; it would
be based on his friend's short and tragic life. One completed passage
explored his hero's mood on the last evening before his fatal act. "One
evening he strolled along Unter den Linden, feeling superior to
everybody because of his imminent death. Mockingly he looked at the
officers of the guard, any one of whom he could take with him into
death. When the thought of doing something useful with his suicide
occurred to him, he became a commander. He walked in such a proud
and lordly manner that instinctively everyone got out of his way. This
placated him; he went home quietly and shot himself."[20] Herzl himself was probably as near to suicide at this moment as at any time in
his existence: or if not suicide, some desperate act.

CHAPTER 14

B ut Vienna and Julie receded; he listened to a sermon in the pale gray peace of Cologne cathedral; he passed five nights in the Paris of Toulouse-Lautrec and the Moulin Rouge. As he did so, he rediscovered solitude and the mood in which he could write. He finished several chapters of *Samuel Kohn*, then pushed it aside. The train took him farther away, farther south. In the mountainous border region between France and Spain he worked on four long essays, *The Start to a Spanish Journey*.[1] "In Tarbes, the Pyrenees capital," began the first, "I added a codicil to my Will. I forbade, in the categorical tones appropriate to the style of such documents, that my remains should be buried here, in the event that I be carried off by boredom. For I should rather live in Tarvis [a remote Tyrolean village] than be interred in Tarbes. Then to my surprise I awoke another morning and could continue my journey to Pierrefitte."[2] The euphonious balance of the prose, the confident egoism of the man who knows that his movements and ideas will interest his readers have as counterpoint the reference to death and burial, a theme seldom absent from Herzl's mind. The combination enchanted his readers and the essays inspired by the borderland between France and Spain had decisive results. In San Sebastian—"a melancholy place to stay, but beautiful, beautiful"— he was handed a cable from Vienna as he was preparing to leave for Madrid. It faced him with the choice between two kinds of future. For the *Neue Freie Presse* offered him the post of its Paris correspondent at a monthly salary of a thousand gold francs for a trial period of four months, with an additional eighty gold francs for each published essay. He must cable his answer by return.

The distinguished prose that had impressed the most respected newspaper in central Europe owed something to unfamiliar mountain scenery; it owed far more to his emotional relief in getting away from Julie and all that Vienna represented in terms of intrigue and theatrical hack work. The success of his writing secured him what he had always sought, but at an ironic price: the reharnessing of himself to Julie and his family, and the commitment of his pen to regular work. Any notion of a legal separation or divorce was ruled out; the ambassadorial status of his long-coveted position would require an ambassadress. And while it would be a joy to have his children within playing reach, he was clear-sighted enough to foresee the strain of living, even on his own terms now that he was financially secure, with a wife who would not grow less nagging as she grew older. As a writer he would no longer be free to continue journeying. North Africa,[3] the exciting fringe of civilization where the everyday would be a dream, would have to be abandoned. If he had gone, it is possible he would have stayed in a hotel, completing his novel and then returning. But something more Bohemian, more radical, was also possible. The Muslim world could have had on him the effect it had on Isabelle Eberhardt or Pierre Loti. Far from both mother and wife, he might have found there the cure that other Europeans at odds with their society found and would find. The torrid landscape which to Nietzsche had stood for health as against Wagner's sickness could have brought spiritual or physical release. His true desires, like those of Delacroix, might have revealed themselves in unfurtive strength in some casbah of Algiers or Tunis. He was only just past thirty. His penchant for the military virtues could conceivably have found in the Foreign Legion a *beau geste* to delete the remembrance of Vienna. (One of the best memoirs of life in the Legion, with a foreword by D. H. Lawrence, was to be written by Maurice Magnus, another Jewish misfit.[4]) Or with his powers of projecting himself into other men's positions—the same powers that in his recent essays made him see utility in Lourdes and had earlier enabled him to see style in Dühring—he might have espoused the Algerian cause as Wilfrid Blunt, the English poet, had espoused the Egyptian cause some years earlier. In the light of his future nothing is too extraordinary to be ruled out—if he had gone south. Instead, he cabled his acceptance and took the train north. The offer embodied too solid an ambition for him to spurn it. The two women in his brain, opposed though they were, alike urged acceptance: Jeanette, because she longed for her son's success, though she would never love Paris; Julie, because her husband's success could secure her what she had longed for all her life.

Yet the night before he left for Paris he scribbled on a scrap of paper: "I shall wear galoshes like a businessman."[5] For a man who had also written "Clothes always say something,"[6] galoshes said a lot. They said No to freedom and dreams, Yes to bourgeois conformity and controlled despair. Perhaps he rejected remote places because he had dreamed of them late and feebly. The theater had been his outlet for dreams, and it seemed closed. "The theater did not want to hear from me," he later wrote. "My self-confidence was bowed to the ground. I took the new job and truly believed that I would write for the stage no more."

He arrived in Paris on October 6, 1891. Premature snow was falling as he registered at the Hôtel de Hollande in the Rue de la Paix. The snow outlined the cornices, enhanced the perspectives, quietened the carriages, in a city entering one of its most brilliant decades. Its painters and poets, its impressionists and symbolists, held the eyes and ears of Europe; its appeals to grosser organs were as strong. Herzl knew the city's outline as a tourist; as correspondent he would have an unrivaled chance of painting whatever details he wished into his picture of the city. But the cold weather hinted a grim side to the Paris of pleasure. That winter France was to experience a series of industrial strikes, echoing the workers' demonstrations in Berlin and Vienna. The façades of Europe concealed ugly slums and these bred violent dreams.

Herzl's life was to have a similar rift between fair and foul. He was not a bachelor at the Hôtel de Hollande for long. In a few weeks Julie had packed what she needed for Paris and the family were reunited at another, more luxurious hotel in the Rue Drouot. From it they found, rented and moved to a large house in the Rue Monceau, near the park of that name and within a short walk of the Madeleine and the fashionable streets to which it was the hub. They set up house, not as lovers whose battles could fan the embers of attraction, but as wary partners in a consortium for life. Each made concessions. Julie conceded that Theodor, by his efforts, offered her a life in which she spent lavishly on clothes, theaters and entertaining. Herzl conceded that the impetuous egoism accepted in an artist was unacceptable in a correspondent. There were to be no public scenes, no shrieks followed by recourse to Jeanette Herzl, no tears followed by threats of departure. When he absented himself, it was on newspaper business; or in the summer vacation, when Paris closed down and the Herzl family moved back to Vienna; then he might secure, if he were lucky, a few weeks of therapy at Baden while Julie took the children to some more spectacular spa. The Herzl partners, like other rich Parisians, had servants and a carriage. A nursemaid, under Julie's eye, could take care of Pauline, still not two, and of Hans, whose first birthday would be celebrated the following year. The education of the children would not be a problem for some years; until tutors took over, servants could cushion the parents from the *Krach* of childhood. But when Pauline, never strong, fell ill in early 1893, Herzl took Hans, then nearly two, to sleep in his study for the night; he had a dread of infection. He also had legitimate cause for not sharing Julie's bedroom. During the summer of 1892 they had conceived their third and last child, Margaret Trude, who was born in Paris on May 20, 1893.

To most men in his position, the comfortable house in the Rue Monceau would have been a place of relief from the longhand world of the correspondent. Outwardly, his life was much as he had depicted it to his parents. The Herzl seen in public was an urbane figure, impressive for height and beard, courted by those he chose to frequent. But inwardly, at every reception, exhibition or performance, his mind was on the clock and the office where he must write out the copy to be telegraphed to his impatient editors, Bacher and Benedikt, in Vienna. After two years' experience he wrote cautionary words to a Budapest cousin who threatened to come to Paris. "A Paris correspondent must starve, sweat, freeze, work through the nights."

Finding little relief at home, Herzl spent longer hours on his job than it strictly required. He polished his dispatches till they became, sometimes, too elegant for their function. He cultivated artists and writers; he attended a cafe on Friday nights where intellectuals such as Max Nordau discussed the problems of the day. He followed unusual stories. He wrote of de Maupassant dying of syphilis in his asylum, wondering if he could not watch the insane genius from a spyhole. He followed the parliamentary debates in such detail, with such perception, that the book he based on them, *Palais Bourbon,* was a brilliant record of an epoch not usually remembered for its political life. He also had private griefs. His first year in Paris he wrote an obituary for Oswald Boxer. In January 1892 Boxer was on his way home after a six months' stint in Brazil. A one-day visit to Rio de Janeiro gave him yellow fever. On the twenty-sixth he was dead and the last close link with Herzl's student days had snapped. Herzl took refuge in Olympian detachment. "Life is not only a sorrow, but also a game over which the gods laugh in Homeric fashion. One must simply keep it at a proper distance."[7]

One problem hard to keep at a proper distance—particularly if the Olympian observer were a Jew—was the growing racial prejudice in the land of the Revolution. In Vienna the anti-Semitic movement had been initiated by two politicians, Georg von Schönerer and Karl Lueger. In France a perversely brilliant writer, Édouard-Adolphe Drumont (1844–1917), made anti-Semitism a potent force in the last fifteen years of the nineteenth century. His book *La France Juive* synthesized two different strands of thought. The notion of race, which played such an insistent role inside nineteenth-century heads, made it easy to postulate a conflict between Aryan and Semite. But how could the notion of a Semitic conspiracy convince when, at the time he was writing, there were less than eighty thousand Jews in the whole of France? Drumont gave the notion a new twist by linking it to a supposed plot by the Jews against Christian civilization. Drumont lifted his evidence for the danger from the writings of an honorary canon of Poitiers and Angoulême, the Abbé Chabauty. In a work entitled *Les Juifs nos Maîtres* (1882) the Abbé used two letters printed in a Jewish magazine of 1880 to "prove" that Jews living in fifteenth-century Constantinople had urged their co-religionists to go underground, to pretend to be Catholics, so as finally to turn the tables on the Christian majority and take over France. These two letters[8] laid the basis for a conspiratorial theory that would prove that such enemies of the Right as Marat (or anyone else) had in fact been crypto-Jews.

Although many French publishers must have suspected that such a book could draw support from a reservoir of popular resentment, the still dominant rationalist tradition made it difficult for Drumont to publish his book. He was helped by Alphonse Daudet (ironically, one of Herzl's closest French friends), who persuaded the firm of Marpon Flammarion to publish the inflammatory work.[9] When in its first week the book's sales hung fire, Daudet further intervened to secure a review in *Le Figaro* and this led first to a duel, then to one of those violent press battles that help a book's sales. Marpon Flammarion suddenly found that their list contained a best seller destined for a hundred editions.[10] Drumont's ideas particularly influenced those parts of France where Jews were either few or non-existent. The prejudice this unscrupulous polemicist had tapped was not so much religious bigotry (which usually yields to education) or xenophobia (which yields to experience) but fear. A section of French society that felt itself menaced discovered in "the Jew" a symbol for all it feared. Drumont's listeners included all those elements that had found in the Revolution not liberation but disaster. Members of the former aristocracy, conservative-minded peasants, much of the officer corps, above all the Church had resisted, and on the whole been worsted by, secularist forces.

Having discovered his audience, Drumont carried his battle onto the streets by launching, in 1892, a newspaper, *La Libre Parole*, whose mission was "to defend Catholic France against infidels, Republicans, Freemasons and Jews."[11] *La Libre Parole* was financed by one J. B. Gerin, who only two years earlier had edited a pro-Jewish newspaper, *Le National*. Drumont (who hung a crucifix in every office) happily sanctioned the fund-raising technique that consists of offering not to insult in return for money. Certain wealthy Jews, including Baron Robert Oppenheim, bought shares in the newspaper as a protection against attack. Yet Drumont ran *La Libre Parole* on more than prejudice and corruption. As a stylist he won admiration from many who did not accept his ideas; as an editor he knew how to exploit the energies of an unusually youthful group of assistants. The result was a forceful instrument for aggravating an existing split in the French soul. For to many of his contemporaries Drumont did not seem a pitiless demagogue attacking a powerless minority. To them, the Jews were a powerful element in a dominant faction; since the Rothschilds were known to have financial reserves many times greater[12] than the capital of the Bank of France, the Jews seemed to their foes to provide the sinews for the Third Republic. Although no less than Christians committed to belief in God, the Jews had become, for explicable reasons, associated with infidels (those who rejected the Christian revelation), Freemasons (who as a secret society were easily accused of having plotted the Revolution), and Republicans (who rejected the monarchical tradition of France). One Jewish writer, Hippolyte Prague, warned that outbursts of anti-Semitism, with other manifestations of violence, were largely prompted by "the discontent provoked everywhere by the legislative or governmental measures taken against religious denominations, in particular the expulsion of God from primary-school teaching."[13] But Prague was a farsighted exception. Most Jews saw no peril in being identified with the Revolution that had achieved their emancipation. In the spring of 1889—the year Prague issued his warning—special services were held in synagogues throughout France to commemorate the hundredth anniversary of the Revolution. Michael R. Marrus has collected an imposing series of quotations from Jewish writers lauding that event.[14] While Isidor Cahen described the Revolution as "our second law of Sinai," the historian Maurice Bloch equated 1789 with the fulfillment of Jewish prophecy: "The time of the Messiah had come with that new society which substituted for the old Trinity of the Church that other Trinity whose names can be read on all the walls: 'Liberty! Equality! Fraternity!'" Rabbi Kahn of Nîmes exalted the same event as "our flight from Egypt . . . our modern Passover."

These sentiments gratified Republicans; to those (and they were not few) who revered the memory of the Bourbons, who regarded Louis XVI and even Marie-Antoinette as martyrs, they will have helped to identify the Jews with the creators of the Terror.

From the vantage point of a succeeding century we can see that French Catholics and French Jews had more in common than they admitted. The displacement of Mary (a faithful servant of the Torah) by a harlot (arrayed as Reason) might well presage a revival of paganism and a destruction of moral sanctions perilous to both. But at the time mutual hostility shut out a wider view. In his account of Lourdes and its significance, Alan Neame has shown that the apparitions at the Grotto came as a much needed encouragement to the Catholics of France. It revived their spirits rather than their charity. While Eugène Sue's portrait of a Jesuit priest in *Le Juif Errant* was a mirror image of anti-Semitic portraits of Jews, and while Emile Zola wrote a book virtually demanding a suppression of all practices associated with Lourdes, the Catholics replied with increased venom. A parish priest, Abbé Cros, used *La Libre Parole* as ·a platform from which to announce "that all he asked was a Jew-skin mat beside his bed to trample on night and morning." Prejudice took more solid shapes than words. The same year as the Abbé's request

> the sculptor Raffl began work on the outdoor Stations of the Cross at Lourdes—fourteen gigantic groups consisting of 115 human figures each at least six feet high. Raffl's work was to some extent financed from the private fortune of the bishop of Tarbes, Mgr. Billère. The Romans are shown as sympathetically manly, but Judas, the Jewish nation, the Synagogue and Pharasaim are nightmarishly contorted in their hostility to the Saviour. Raffl fixed this image of infuriate Jewry in cast iron. A thick layer of paint and varnish adds morbid horror to the compunction these monuments inspire.[15]

Catholic fears—in their case, of anti-clerical moves by the government—were no less justified than Jewish. In 1899 the Prime Minister, Waldeck-Rousseau, began moving against the religious orders. In 1900 the Fathers of the Assumption were suppressed. The situation was to deteriorate further after the elections of 1902 when a new Prime Minister, Émile Combes, suppressed Church schools and sent their staffs into exile.

As a freethinker of Jewish origin, Herzl could easily have adopted a simple, secularist approach. In fact, his complex character made him as critical of Jews as of Catholics and ready to see good as well as evil in popular superstition. During his visit to the Pyrenees he had recognized the positive results of the apparitions and their episcopal supporter, the Bishop of Meaux; in his growing knowledge of French society he developed a somewhat disdainful attitude to French aristocracy and Jewish plutocracy alike.[16]

Yet in the early summer after Boxer's death three events placed a considerable strain on his Olympian detachment.

A new play, *Le Prince d'Aurec* by Henri Lavedan, prompted Herzl to write a long review. The play gave flesh to the themes of Drumont's diatribes. Herzl saw the play's two main characters as the Prince (the presumed inheritor of French traditions) and Baron Horn (a *nouveau riche* Jew). The aristocrat, so inferior to the Prussian ideal, seemed less well drawn than the parvenu Jew: *"einen Typus von unsagbarer Ergötzlichkeit,"* or "an extremely amusing type." In the eighteenth century each German princeling had his indispensable *Hofjude*. Lavedan had succeeded in creating an up-to-date version of the court Jew. "He no longer acquires excessive interest, no longer cheats, but instead is cheated." The modern *Hofjude* aims, not at money, but social promotion. Horn gives the Prince 400,000 francs, his wife another 300,000, so that the former will get him elected to his club, so that the latter will accept him as her lover. He is cheated by both. The Prince will not propose him for his club while the Princess rejects his advances out of contempt for him as a Jew, not out of loyalty to her husband. Herzl's only criticism of Lavedan's portrait was not that it did not make the parvenu sufficiently unpleasant. "Horn brags too little about his distinguished connections; when a Princess addresses him, he does not feel sufficiently honoured, does not stammer with sufficient joy. The insecurity of the Jew is not shown. Yet this, in real life, would be Horn's dominant characteristic. It would show itself in the abrupt interchange of arrogance and servility: though compassionate understanding accepts that the insecurity springs from long griefs, which are not yet over . . ."[17]

Immediately after writing his review Herzl for the first time set eyes on Édouard Drumont, then appearing in one of the numerous lawsuits prompted by his polemics. This first glimpse of a man with whom he was to maintain a curious relationship of mutual disdain and admiration (he first met him socially at the house of Alphonse Daudet[18]) was followed by an event that showed to what perilous ends Drumont's words could lead. *La Libre Parole* had been attacking French officers of Jewish origins from early in the year. Since the great majority of French Jews were German-speaking Ashkenazim from Alsace-Lorraine, it was easy to link prejudice against "Semites" with the more immediate dislike of Germans. The attacks led to a series of duels and in one of them, on June 24, a thirty-four-year-old captain in the Engineers, Armand Mayer, fell to the pistol of an anti-Jewish aristocrat. The duel, as a social form, had always appealed to Herzl, and would continue to do so. The premature death of the gifted young captain, the homage of a vast mourning crowd—the largest since the funeral of Gambetta a decade earlier—stimulated his imagination. He recorded the scene in impeccable prose sent over the wire to Vienna. A more conspicuous role was denied. In the aftermath he suddenly wrote to Arthur Schnitzler, congratulating him on a recent book. Schnitzler's novella was merely a pretext. The deeper prompting was the need for a friend, someone linked to his youth, someone to whom he could write about himself. His succeeding letters show self-disgust and a generous envy for Schnitzler's literary career. His own theatrical experience, he confided, had been pointless and unpleasant. "The pieces in which I believed, and into which I put true artistic effort, never saw the light of day. When, desperate, I manufactured something for the stage, I was produced—and despised. When I pause to reflect on my place in German literature—which I do but seldom—I am moved to laughter."[19] By comparison with Schnitzler's talents, then burgeoning like flowers in the summer garden, his own seemed paltry. He was a mere *Literat,* and as such *ein engherziger unduldsamer neidischer boshafter Tropf* (a narrowhearted, intolerant, jealous, spiteful rogue). Schnitzler, who knew as well as Herzl how little the latter's plays had fulfilled his youthful promise, consoled him by telling him how he had admired him as a student. Herzl's reply to the compliment shows him tired in body and spirit. "If you always saw me twenty paces ahead, at least you ought to know that this advantage of distance has been paid for with exhaustion; today, as I have told you, I sit upon a rock by the roadside and watch the others overtake and pass me by." Despair and self-contempt, the claim that he had interred himself in journalism as chastisement for the flippancy and vulgarity of his earlier writings run through an exchange of letters that overlap an essay on French anti-Semitism for the *Neue Freie Presse,* his exaltation of dueling to Regina Friedlander and his refusal to take part in a counteroffensive to the anti-Semitic libels then so common. He reaches the pessimistic conclusion, in January 1893, that in all probability France would soon experience a new revolution. "If I don't beat a hasty retreat to Brussels, in all probability they'll shoot me as a bourgeois, a German spy, a Jew or a capitalist." In this mood he had come to the belief that the best solution for the people as a whole was *un bon tyran,* a good dictator, while for the Jews the best solution was conversion to socialism if they lived in Germany, and to Catholicism in Austria.

For all his admiration for Bismarck and the Prussian state, Herzl knew Austria far better than Germany. It was the Austrian aspect of his solution that he elaborated to Moritz Benedikt of the *Neue Freie Presse* during his summer holiday in Austria. Herzl envisaged a bargain between himself, as leader of the Jews, and the Pope, as leader of the Catholics. "Help us against the anti-Semites," he saw himself saying, "and I will start a great movement for the free and honourable conversion of Jews to Christianity."[20] Herzl went on to explain what "free and honourable" meant to him: his mass conversion was to resemble neither the forced conversions of fifteenth-century Spain nor the conversions from conviction that had enriched the Church from the first century onward. "Free and honourable by virtue of the fact that the leaders of this movement—myself in particular—would remain Jews and as such would propagate conversion to the faith of the majority." The dramatist in Herzl prepared a grandiose stage. To the pealing of bells one Sunday at noon, great processions would converge on St. Stephen's cathedral. The older Jews, naturally with Herzl at their head, would remain outside the Christian shrine, content with having conducted the younger generation to the waiting fonts. "I could see myself dealing with the Archbishop of Vienna; in imagination I stood before the Pope—both of them were very sorry that I wished to do no more than remain part of the last generation of Jews—and sent this slogan of mingling of the races flying across the world."

Moritz Benedikt, a worldly Viennese who believed in social assimilation, rejected Herzl's idea of religious assimilation by the reference, not to the truth of Judaism, but to its long history. "For a hundred generations your line has preserved itself within the fold of Judaism. Now you are proposing to set yourself up as the terminal point in the process. This you cannot do and have no right to do. Besides, the Pope would never receive you." Herzl's idea, like most ideas, was not original. It echoed the philosophy of David Friedlander (1750–1834), a leader of the German Reform movement, a friend of Moses Mendelssohn and the first Jew elected to the Berlin City Council. Friedlander had been prepared to surrender the Talmud and ritual observances in favor of the assimilation of Berlin Jews to Protestant Christianity, provided too close acceptance of Christian dogma were not required. Favoring German rather than Hebrew for the purposes of prayer, Friedlander rejected belief in the Messiah. His whole family followed his counsel and received baptism, some during his lifetime, others after his death.

Herzl's more radical version of Friedlander's idea might have fared better in France. Only some five hundred Jews out of the entire Jewish population of France were, according to one observer of the 1890s,[21] truly orthodox. These were mostly from Eastern Europe; they lived in a shabby quarter and worshiped in *oratoires* (the French equivalent of *shuls*) very different from the lavish synagogues frequented by the rich. The overwhelming majority of French Jews, without having taken the "free and honourable" step recommended by Herzl for the Austrians, had already allowed the society in which they lived to modify their traditional practice. Michael R. Marrus, whom we have already quoted in another context, has listed the ways in which Catholic practices had affected those of the Jews. At the start of life infants were taken to the synagogue to be blessed while the collection plate had begun to be passed round at marriages. Boys were initiated into Judaism at the age of thirteen, girls a year earlier, in clothes exactly imitating those worn by Catholic children for First Communion. As life drew to its close, a rabbi was summoned to the deathbed while the corpse in its coffin was covered with wreaths and flowers. The organ was used in synagogues while, by a decision of 1865, French rabbis adopted the same dress as priests, with the exception that their collarband was white. A few years later a Grand Rabbi was to propose a "Sabbath" service for Sunday mornings.[22]

The idea of total assimilation was, in fact, advocated in France the same year that Herzl advocated it to Moritz Benedikt in Austria.

Bernard Lazare (who argued in print what Herzl had mooted in conversation) was five years younger than his Austrian confrere. His home town was Nîmes in the south of France. Though Nîmes was the center of an ancient Sephardic community, it is probable that Lazare's ancestors came from Alsace. In any case, Nîmes was his equivalent of Herzl's Budapest. Having completed his secondary studies, he moved north to Paris, where his closest friends were the Catholic poet Charles Péguy and the philosopher of anarchism, Georges Sorel. In one important way Lazare differed from Herzl: he belonged permanently to what may be imprecisely termed the Left. Yet he had his equivalent of Herzl's dalliance with Albia. Toward the end of the 1880s Jews escaping from Czarist pogroms arrived in France in increasing numbers. Lazare at this time was connected with an avantgarde magazine. He used it to publish two articles that "in none too gentle terms, denounced the victims of Czarist persecution."[23] Lazare supported what seemed a harsh point of view by elaborating a curious distinction between *juif* and *Israélite*.

> A *juif* was a Jew as portrayed in the traditional anti-Semitic caricature, a person who "is dominated by the unique preoccupation with

making a quick fortune," an individual "who make(s) money the
goal of all life, and the centre of the world." The *Israélite,* on the
other hand, was assimilated into French society, was much more refined, "limited in [his] desires," was either poor or of moderate circumstance, and had been settled for a long time in the place in
which he lived. French Jews were generally *Israélites;* German and
eastern European Jews were *juifs.* Lazare felt that anti-Semitic
charges were substantially correct when applied to these *juifs. Israélites,* he urged, should : reject association with these "money-
changers from Frankfort, Polish bartenders, Galician pawnbrokers,
with whom they have nothing in common." Building upon his anger, he called upon the *Israélites* to "kick out these lepers who cor-
rupt them; to vomit up the rottenness that wants to creep in"; they
themselves should assimilate to France.[24]

Some writers have speculated that Lazare may have discussed these
ideas with the Paris correspondent of the *Neue Freie Presse.* Herzl's
later references to Lazare (with whom he was to make a brief alliance) seem to indicate that he only came to know him in 1896.* In
1893 neither man made a point of cultivating his co-religionists;
neither man set foot in synagogue or *oratoire.* A further important
consideration makes it improbable that Lazare had discussed the
article he published on December 27, 1893, with Herzl. The *Israélites'*
only solution, he then proclaimed, was to lose themselves in the mass
of the nation. Only in this way could they escape from identification
with "the invading tribe" to which they had once belonged. At the time
this article appeared Herzl was in even worse health than when he
wrote to Arthur Schnitzler the previous year. In October the Russian Imperial Fleet had paid an official visit to Toulon. Herzl recorded
that he traveled south to report the occasion. His generally depressed
spirits may have made him particularly susceptible to the malaria then
endemic in this neglected part of France. A chance mosquito bite
was compounded, he believed, by the crass stupidity of the physicians
who treated him. "One of them injected quinine under my skin. From
this I got an abscess on the thigh which had to be operated on repeatedly. I walked with a cane like a cripple." When his cousin Jenö
Heltai (originally Eugène Herzl) wrote from Hungary asking for advice about visiting Paris, Herzl replied, in early December, that he
was still very weak and could reply but briefly.[25] It is to be doubted
whether at this time he would have had the psychic impetus to discuss with Lazare how French or Austrian Jews could escape from
identification with "the invading tribe" to which they had once belonged.

---

* "July 17, 1896: Talked with Bernard Lazare. Excellent type of a fine, clever
French Jew." *Complete Diaries,* p. 424.

CHAPTER 15

H erzl in Paris was considered a Viennese; his connection with Budapest was known only to those who, like him, had taken their origins in the eastern region of the Dual Monarchy. One of these was Samuel Friedrich Beer (1846–1912), a traditional sculptor with the tastes of an inventor. "Beerite," one of his inventions was a synthetic and quick-drying building material intended to replace plaster between bricks. His surviving sculptures include a bust of Washington Irving in New York's Washington Irving High School. In October 1894, toward the end of Herzl's third year of work in Paris, Beer was working on a bust of his fellow Hungarian. One sitting marked an important moment in Herzl's career.

The intimate talk with a practicing artist, the fact of his being this artist's subject reminded Herzl of his own estrangement from art, and then posed the question: as *what* was he being sculpted? Even for an ordinary man the sculptor's probing chisel compels an unnerving awareness of the self he daily takes for granted. A narcissist is moved more deeply: he is gratified by the artist's attention and saddened that he will never be as young again. Herzl had indeed learned to wear galoshes; he had not broken through to European fame. His reports were published, and therefore read, in Vienna, but in a newspaper owned and edited by Jews and considered primarily as a Jewish paper.[1] Herzl's name no more features in the memoirs of his gentile contemporaries than it does in most histories of the Austrian theater.[2] Perhaps to escape the force of such feelings both men (for Beer was no Rodin) began to discuss the Jewish problem in the two great cities of their empire of origin, Budapest and Vienna. Herzl later described more than once how the sitting with Beer gave him the idea for a play.[3] He said in one version:

> I worked myself up as I exposed to him the Jewish question in Austria. It vibrated inside me still as I left. On my way home the whole play came to me. The next day I said to him: "Beer, if I was not at the moment a day-labourer, but could take off to Ravello above Amalfi, I could write a play." Beer pulled an incredulous face. On the third day I stayed away from the sitting and remained away till the play was finished. When I returned I was fantastically tempted to tell him and read it through to him. However, I resisted and ascribed my absence to newspaper business.

The new turn in Herzl's life which led from Beer's studio is, like his marriage, fogged. The mystification in this case is not in regard to date, place or fact. It clouds the motivation for Herzl's return to creative writing, and the significance of the result.

Herzl began work on a new play, first entitled *The Ghetto*, then *The New Ghetto*, on October 21, 1894. The play was finished by November 8. His speed is the more astonishing when set against his commitments (which he fulfilled) as a correspondent. He was also in touch with Burckhard in Vienna about the new plays being performed in Paris and their suitability for Austrian production.

As soon as he had finished the play he wrote to Arthur Schnitzler giving the facts already quoted and making a proposal: "I do not want to be known as the author, at least temporarily, and certainly not for some months or years. I therefore require the help of a watertight, fire-proof friend who will give me his formal word of honour that he will keep silence and by no gesture betray what he knows, until I, equally formally, release him from his pledge. Are you willing to do this?" The name Herzl proposed to use was "Albert Schnabel." Even his family would not be let into the secret, which must remain dark to all eyes but four. Letters relating to the project must be sent care of the Paris *poste restante* and every such letter must start with the formula: "Today I have written to Albert Schnabel." Next Herzl demands Schnitzler's frankest judgment on the play—if he finds it bad, it won't worry Herzl. The pseudonym will be, for Schnitzler the critic, *ein Kugelpanzer*, a bulletproof waistcoat. Herzl adds that he plans to write four or five plays in this manner during the coming four to five years—meanwhile he'll let himself be despised as a journalist.

Schnitzler at this time was thirty-two. He had just finished his drama *Liebelei*, and was himself in search of a producer.

The four-act play Schnitzler took time off to read, to criticize and to promote contains fourteen named characters as well as two maids, a cook and a butler. It is set in the Vienna of the previous year. All but two characters (and the servants) are Jews, though one, Dr. Bichler, has been baptized for social reasons. Themes from Herzl's actual and imagined life are woven into a story with social implications.

The play begins with the marriage of Jacob Samuel (plainly Herzl's alter ego) to Hermine Hellman, second daughter of a rich Jewish couple. It ends with Jacob's death in a duel, shot by a retired captain of cavalry, Count von Schramm. Between these poles—the wedding reception in "a drawing room, elegantly furnished in the style of the late seventies, with much gilt"[4] and the book-lined study to which Jacob is brought home to die—Herzl's plot and dialogue convey a particular vision of Jewish society in Vienna, and its consequent problems.

The marriage (except that there is a synagogue ceremony, offstage) recalls his own. Jacob's bride—"pretty as a picture she looked, our Miss Hermine, in her white silk"—is a memory of Julie, just as Hermine's brother-in-law, Fritz Rheinberg, is a synthesis of the Naschauer brothers, Jacob and Wilhelm. The emotional shallowness of Hermine/Julie is baldly established. The play's comic character, Emanuel Wasserstein—arriving in a threadbare suit before the other guests, he prices the furniture like an auctioneer—reveals to Dr. Bichler that Hermine had previously been betrothed to him: the fact that she has chosen the admirable Jacob for her husband is accidental.

DR BICHLER   I can't believe it!

WASSERSTEIN   As I live and breathe! Or rather, as I lived and breathed a year ago, when this suit was still brand-new. In a way, she's the cause of my downfall.

DR BICHLER   What? Miss Hermine?

WASSERSTEIN   Of course! It takes a lot of money to marry one of the Hellman girls.

DR BICHLER   Herr Hellman isn't that rich.

WASSERSTEIN   Well, I wouldn't exactly rate him A1. Let's say, 100,000 guilders, most of it tied up in his business. If he should die—which I hope won't ever happen . . .

(*Dr. Bichler laughs.*)

WASSERSTEIN   In a nutshell, not much money, but a high scale of living. The girls were brought up to marry millionaires. When I fell in love with Miss Hermine, I said to myself, Wasserstein, I said, you'll have to become a millionaire! I took Rheinberg as my model—he's the other son-in-law, married Miss Charlotte three years ago. I went out with blood in my eye to win Miss Hermine. I went sweet on Portuguese debentures.

Dr. Bichler, the assimilated Jew, has done individually what Herzl had fantasized to Moritz Benedikt about on a collective scale the year before. In his conversation with Wasserstein (who explains how money can be lost on the stock exchange) Bichler mentions that he had not attended the synagogue service.

WASSERSTEIN	Oh, I forgot. You're a convert, aren't you?
DR BICHLER	The rabbi isn't very well disposed toward me, I know that much. With good reason, from his point of view. And I didn't wish to give offense to the devout Jews by my presence . . .
	(*Sound of a carriage approaching.*)
WASSERSTEIN	Tell me, why did you have yourself baptized, anyway?
DR BICHLER	It's really none of your business, my good fellow. But I won't evade the question. Mine was the solution of the problem on an individual basis.
WASSERSTEIN	Indivi. . . I don't quite follow you.
DR BICHLER	(*Sighs.*) Let's say it was an attempt at a solution . . . For between you and me, it solves nothing.

The religious Jew, Rabbi Friedheimer,* is introduced by Herr Hellman to Jacob—though like Julie's father he prefers to call him Jacques, *à la française.* The Rabbi's first words are addressed, however, to Jacob's brother-in-law.

> Herr Rheinberg, I hear the market is down.
> (Jacob's gentile friend, Franz Wurzlechner, asks in amazement):
> Does the Rabbi play the market too?
> (Jacob echoes his friend):
> I can hardly believe my ears, Rabbi! Are
> you interested in the Stock Market?
> (The Rabbi retorts with calm assurance):
> Not on my own account, my young friend; on
> account of our poor.
> (The Rabbi sits down and becomes the focus of attention. He continues, *somewhat unctuously,* in Herzl's stage direction):
> Yes indeed, when the market is good I have money for my
> poor. The Stock Exchange can be generous.

But if Hermine is shallow and the Rabbi disingenuous, the gentile Wurzlechner is cut from yet thinner card. He pays a surprise call on Jacob one morning (Jacob has been up all night working on the case of some socialist clients), offers him an interest-free loan (for Jacob,

---

* By some curious oversight, the Rabbi is omitted from the list of Dramatis Personae in Heinz Norden's translation of the play published by the Theodor Herzl Foundation, New York.

like Herzl, has learned how expensive a rich bride can be), then curtly announces his intention of annulling their lifelong friendship.

WURZLECHNER I don't think we'll be seeing each other any more.
JACOB (*Upset.*) Franz!
WURZLECHNER I'm sorry. (*Firmly.*) But I can't help it.
JACOB What on earth has happened?
WURZLECHNER It's you—you've changed. Your environment is different
—the company you keep. I don't belong there—with
these Rheinbergs, Wassersteins, the whole lot of them.
Can't you see? I can't take them—they rub me the
wrong way. And since your marriage I'm likely to run
into them at any time in your home—there's no escaping
them. It's not your fault—they're your people—though
I must say, sometimes I do get a little angry at you.
Somehow it doesn't seem quite fair. Anyway, let's call it
quits! Let's not just drift apart bit by bit, with pretended misunderstandings. Let's make it a clean break.
My feelings about you haven't changed. I'll be at your
service whenever you need me, as I know you'll be at
mine. But no more social meetings!

Wurzlechner expands his motives a moment later. He's going into politics. If he has "too many Jewish friends, brokers, speculators," he'll be branded a tool of the Jews. "It's true," Jacob admits. "You're right."

The play's two major themes are The Ghetto and Escape.

The market-playing Rabbi defends the ghetto on one level. "True, the ghetto was crowded and dirty, but the virtues of family life flourished there. The father was a patriarch. The mother (*he lays his hand lightly on that of Frau Samuel*) lived only for her children, and they honoured their parents. Don't belittle the Jewish quarter, my dear friend. Poor it is, but it's our home."

JACOB I don't belittle it. I only say we must get out of it.
RABBI And I tell you we cannot do it! When there was still a real
ghetto, we were not allowed to leave it without permission, on
pain of severe punishment. Now the walls and barriers have become invisible, as you say. Yet we are still rigidly confined to a
moral ghetto. Woe unto him who would desert it!

Yet as Jacob escorts the Rabbi to the door, he accepts this "Woe!"
"Outward barriers had to be cleared away from without, but the inner
barriers we must clear away ourselves. We ourselves, on our own!"

Herzl's conception of this inner ghetto and the escape from it was
hinted in the scene where Jacob, aggressive to the Rabbi, showed him-

self curiously passive to his gentile former friend. He offers Wurzlechner his hand.

> JACOB   I thank you for being so frank. I'm sure you must have
>   thought it over very carefully before you made up
>   your mind to hurt me like this. I thank you also for
>   your friendship all these years. I've learned a good deal
>   from you.
> WURZLECHNER   (*Controlling himself.*) You're joking . . . You learned
>   from me?
> JACOB   It's true—though at first without quite knowing it. I
>   learned big things and little—inflections, gestures, how
>   to bow without being obsequious, how to stand up
>   without seeming defiant—all sorts of things.

This is an important exchange. For it shows that to Herzl the escape
from the ghetto—the major theme of the play—involves the escape, not
so much from gentile oppression as from the bad qualities of the Jews
themselves. These are exemplified (and with what in a gentile writer
would seem a striking lack of balance) in the behavior of Rheinberg,
Jacob's brother-in-law. He uses every trick of the stock exchange
manipulator to ruin the odious von Schramm. The crisis of the play
comes when he succeeds. Von Schramm has lost everything and Jacob
implores his brother-in-law to be generous. The Rabbi lends his moral
support to Jacob.

> RHEINBERG   I can't agree with you. I have no obligations whatever
>   toward him. My brother-in-law only thinks I have. He's on
>   Schramm's side, I can't imagine why.
> RABBI   Because he believes, quite properly, that your enemies will
>   once again exploit a case like that against us Jews. I share
>   his opinion. That's why I'm here to ask you to help
>   Schramm.

Three attitudes to the ruin of von Schramm are shown in this
scene. Jacob wants to help him out of knightly noblesse; the Rabbi
wants to help him for prudential reasons; while Rheinberg (himself in
financial difficulties) argues that in the stock exchange, as elsewhere,
caveat emptor is the only maxim. At the climax of the scene von
Schramm invades the Rheinbergs' ornate drawing room. Jacob expresses his sympathy to von Schramm for his losses, while pointing out
that technically the count had not been cheated, but had panicked in
a stock exchange where only strong nerves triumph. He then changes
tack. He assails von Schramm for the criminal neglect that has led to

a mine disaster. The starveling miners have paid the price of the count's debauches. Tempers rise.

SCHRAMM   Your fine brother-in-law told me you were a fool. He said he
          was at odds with you . . . But now I understand it all. You
          were hand in glove with him.
JACOB   That's a lie!
SCHRAMM   You're just another dirty Jew!
JACOB   You'll take that back! . . .
SCHRAMM   And if I don't—you'll crawl as you did once before?
                    (*Butler enters.*)
          I know your kind. You'll crawl for your brother and for
          yourself. You dirty Jews are all the same!

On hearing the words "as you did once before," Jacob has flinched. For it is true that when challenged on a previous occasion, he had refused a duel, not out of cowardice, but out of concern for his father, then gravely ill. He now hurls himself at von Schramm and strikes him across the face. A duel, with Wurzlechner as his second, is now the result. Jacob is mortally wounded. Two points are made as he dies onstage. First: "O Jews, my brethren, they won't let you live again until you learn how to die." And then the final punch line: "I want-to-get-out. (*Louder.*) . . . out-of-the-ghetto."

Herzl linked the genesis of his play not only with the talk in Beer's studio, but with an incident that had occurred the previous summer. He had taken his family to Austria and had escaped for a holiday at Baden, with Ludwig Speidel, literary editor of the *Neue Freie Presse*. Herzl was already tiring of Paris. He was, though neither man then knew it, to take over Speidel's job two years later. One afternoon, as the two men tramped across the meadows at Hinterbrühl, they discussed what had become a burning problem.

"I understand what anti-Semitism is about," Herzl had said. "We Jews have maintained ourselves, even if through no fault of our own, as a foreign body among the various nations. In the ghetto we have taken on a number of anti-social qualities. Our character has been corrupted by oppression, and it must be restored through some other kind of pressure. Actually, anti-Semitism is a consequence of the emancipation of the Jews."[5] He developed a remarkably detached view of anti-Semitism and its likely results.

Anti-Semitism, which is a strong and unconscious force among the masses, will not harm the Jews. I consider it to be a movement useful to the Jewish character. It represents the education of a group by the masses, and will perhaps lead to it being absorbed. Education is accomplished only through hard knocks. A Darwinian mimicry will set in. The Jews will adapt themselves. They are like seals, which an act of nature cast into the water. These animals assume the habits and appearance of fish, which they certainly are not. Once they return to dry land again and are allowed to remain there for a few generations, they will turn their fins into feet again.[6]

These hopeful statements had been followed by a personal shock, less lethal than Jacob Samuel's, but to one of Herzl's personal sensitivity, profound. As his fiacre passed behind the Cholera Chapel on his way back to Baden, "two young fellows, one of them in cadet uniform, were passing by. I believe I was sitting huddled in thought. At that point I distinctly heard a cry from behind the carriage: 'Dirty Jew [*Saujude*]!'"[7] Herzl's first instincts had been those of Jacob Samuel—at least to scuffle with the urchins. But, hopeless, he had slumped back in his seat. The insult had not been directed at him personally: "for I was unknown to them, but at my Jewish nose and Jewish beard, which they had glimpsed in the semi-darkness behind the carriage lanterns."

Such bold ideas and poignant experience had fused in the play with which Schnitzler had to deal, first as critic, and then as middleman for Albert Schnabel.

Schnitzler had a warm heart and knew how easily a writer may be discouraged. He knew his first task would be the harder. His letter of November 17, 1894,[8] began by complimenting Herzl on his discovery of a new milieu for the stage, of new forms so far unattempted by other writers. He honestly admired the portrait of Wasserstein, the threadbare, unsuccessful Jew. In one scene, where Wasserstein explains himself to Hermine, his sentences ring with a pathos that still moves. "Just look at me. I have to buy everything for money. I have to pay for friendship, love. I even have to pay to have people treat me decently, as though I was always in a restaurant. Even when I'm flush, it's 'Herr von Wasserstein' to my face, and a smirk behind my back. (*Gently.*) I'm sorry for myself."[9] But even with Wasserstein, Schnitzler has to complain, Herzl underestimates his powers of characterization and makes his character too explicit about himself.

> This leads me to object to the very last sentence in the play which the dying Jacob Samuel is made to utter. It would be better to let him die wordless—this death says more, and says it better, than the dying man can. The dying man says: "Jews, brothers, they won't let you live again until you've learnt how to die."† But his death says: "This poor devil, noble as he is, must let himself be shot down because of a ridiculous brawl—just because he's born a Jew!"

---

† It is, perhaps, a tribute to Schnitzler's criticism that the words "until you've learnt how to die" are omitted, replaced by an ellipsis, in the English translation of the play.

There was a time when Jews were burnt at the stake by the thousand. They had learnt how to die. But for all that they were not allowed to live. Thus your drama, after a good start, gets on the wrong track. A good character to introduce might be a Jewish fraternity student who had issued thirty challenges, since he is a Jew. You could oppose to him another student, a member of a Catholic guild, who for reasons of conscience does not fight—and is therefore respected!

Schnitzler found particular fault with Hermine. The reader fails to imagine how such a superior person as Jacob Samuel could wish to marry her. He next finds fault with the gentile, Franz Wurzlechner; despite Herzl's efforts to be objective, to make him attractive, the result was a commonplace failure.

At least give him some stronger motivation for breaking with Jacob. Or if not, then hint at this infamous side of his character on his first appearance in Act One. Or let Jacob himself say that it will harm his new career to have traffic with Jews. Or better still, let Jacob plainly denounce his twists and turns. And as second for Jacob in the duel, I should prefer our newly invented student of the thirty duels—you could make him the nephew of the charming Wasserstein. Also "the Jew with the wounded sense of honour" does not satisfy me—give him somewhat more inner freedom. As he stands, he is unsympathetic because the conception does not hold up. Don't you agree? And here I see further still. There is a lack of strong Jews throughout the play. [*Die Figur des Kraftjuden fehlt mir geradezu in Ihren Stück.*] It is not even true, as you suggest, that all ghetto Jews were either despicable or despised. *There were others*—and it was precisely these whom the anti-Semites hated most. Your play is daring—I should like it to be defiant. Above all, don't make your heroes so resigned to die.

The play should certainly work on the stage, Schnitzler had concluded, if a theater could be found to put it on. But first, he looked forward to a second reading. In the interim Herzl might like to make some changes in the text in the light of his reactions.

Schnitzler had taken literally Herzl's request for frankness. That he was wrong to have done so was shown by Herzl's answer.

Having reread the piece, I can the better answer your objections. I don't find the characters "insufficiently sympathetic." But if I did, would that mean that I should falsify my misanthropy? Should I portray wonderfully noble and pure-hearted people even if I don't believe in their existence? No, my friend, that won't do. I refuse to emasculate myself for the sake of a possible success. I may be prejudiced, but I find the piece well done. I will by no means make a defense of the Jews or a rescue-attempt on their behalf. Let critics defend or attack. So long as I am produced, I have reached my goal. What happens next does not concern me. I care nothing for money, though I have little enough, nor for fame, though I have none at all. I do not wish to be a sympathetic poet. I want to speak out, bluntly, from the heart. And if this piece reaches the world, then I shall be eased, deeply, at heart.

Herzl concludes by saying that Schnitzler is right, he has other works in mind, which he has put temporarily aside. "If one day I acquire freedom from day-labour, the higher themes will come. I have a whole Spring within me—one day perhaps it will burst into flower."

Herzl's reply is revealing on three counts. The most obvious—it shows how unreal his request for frankness had been. Second, it shows how he misunderstands the onus of Schnitzler's criticism. Schnitzler, like Hartmann before him, had not found the characters he criticized unsympathetic, so much as unbelievable, their motivation insufficiently clear. As a work of polemic, Schnitzler had found the play damaging to the Jews, rather than a defense for them.

Proof that Schnitzler was not alone in this adverse reaction is found in an exchange of letters the following year. In May 1895 (after the failure of Schnitzler's efforts to place the play) Herzl wrote to Heinrich Teweles (1856–1927), then dramatic director of the German Landestheater in Prague. Once again Herzl was to use the stratagem of "Albert Schnabel," coupled with complex instructions about posting letters. Writing from Paris: "I shall have this letter sent to you from Vienna, because I want to have it registered, and here I would have to put down my name on the envelope. This would immediately be discovered in Prague."[10] Herzl lists the people who have already turned down his play: Brahm at the German Theater in Berlin; Blumenthal at the Lessing Theater; Mueller-Guttenbrunn at the Raymond Theater in Vienna. Leon Kellner gives us the original text of Herzl's German. Mueller-Guttenbrunn, "in order to doublecheck his opinion, gave it to a Christian and a Jew to read. The Christian said: this is dynamite. The Jew said: this is an affront to Jewry."[11]‡

There is more to this than a question of detail. The Jewish friend of Mueller-Guttenbrunn, like Schnitzler, had found the play potentially damaging to the Jewish minority. And in Prague itself the play was not accepted "owing to the opposition of the president of the Jewish community, who feared it might have some unfortunate consequences."[13]

‡ Professor Bein, in his published English version of the letter, compresses Herzl's words: "In order to doublecheck his opinion, he gave it to a Christian and a Jew to read. The Christian said: this was an affront to Jewry."[12]

The motives for obscuring this point are clear. To Herzl's hagiographers *The New Ghetto* "was a tremendous step forward in his development; it was the beginning of a new Jewish political method. Henceforth the Jewish question was to be lifted out of the trivial atmosphere of minor groups and obscure tea-party meetings, and put by the Jews on the stage of public action. It was like a fresh wind blowing suddenly through the choking atmosphere of a lightless room. It was a new attitude: decent pride."[14] In the same spirit André Chouraqui explains the use of the pseudonym. "Herzl wished to reach the public and force the discussion into the open. He was so unconcerned with his reputation that he envisaged publishing the play under the pseudonym Arthur Schnabel."[15]

This presentation finds little support in psychological truth. *The New Ghetto*, so far from marking the beginning of Herzl's new career, marks a last serious attempt to succeed in the old. The play was finally accepted for production at Vienna's Carltheater in December 1897. The police censor found it inopportune, since its attack on Jewish speculators might arouse sectarian applause; but permission was given provided that some twenty-four passages were deleted and that the Rabbi were not shown in ecclesiastical dress. It was finally performed in January 1898, to an enthusiastic audience of the author's friends.

The three years in Paris had consolidated Herzl in a position of enviable prestige. But the session with the sculptor focused his always alert attention on the question of what kind of prestige it was that he enjoyed. A fashionable life, based on a rented mansion and a carriage, was bought at a terrible cost. He had to slave behind the scenes preparing his long, immaculate cables to Vienna, dealing with the chaotic trivia of an evanescent decade in French politics. He was writing his name in a medium as insubstantial as water, the swiftly moldering pages of a daily paper.* His dreams of being an artist had faded. He had not even written a memorable *feuilleton* since the series that had won him his position in the summer of 1891. Not one of his plays had won him substantial fame or even money. In such a mood Herzl decided to make a new start as artist. If he could produce a challenging new play each year for four or five years, he could then leave Paris and in a new wind win fame as a European writer. He dreamed of escaping to a Sicilian fishing village, a good English hotel.

---

* Herzl preserved those of his articles that concerned French parliamentary life in a work published at the end of 1895, *Das Palais Bourbon,* named after the French debating chamber.

I would indulge in beautiful solitary thoughts and have not the least wish to win people's approval by writing down to them. I would watch the fishermen, as they flick their nets, a sight which has always intrigued me. In the evening I should sit down to a good dinner, at the same time smiling benevolently as the young English Misses of the day contrive love's follies with other young people. But I cannot. I sit in Paris, go to the Palais Bourbon or boring theatres, get cross with my colleagues and probably am worth no more than they.[16]

The use of the pseudonym is the key. It was the idea of a gambler. Against the sense that fate has been unkind, that previous works have not had the success they deserved, the pseudonym gives a second chance. The writer has the chance to fight under new colors, the face under the visor invisible, unknown.

The use of the pseudonym emphasizes what Herzl said with candor, that *The New Ghetto* was not a work of Jewish political action. "I will by no means make a defense of the Jews or a rescue-effort on their behalf." Nor could it be seen as such, as the two anonymous critics had made clear. To gentile audiences, the play would be dynamite, exhibiting a near-caricature of the minority about whom they were so ill-informed. To Jews it was indeed an affront, with its implication that they needed to remake themselves in a gentile fashion. The only audience for whom in 1894 the play might have worked was perhaps an audience Herzl did not rule out: men like his friend Alphonse Daudet who might be impressed by the pathos, perhaps grandeur of Jacob Samuel, a lonely phoenix on a pyre of IOUs and bills, thrown into a contrast as it was by its setting in a Jewish community not too different from the mental picture of it they already had.

Only inside the context of Herzl's work as a dramatist does the play represent a new direction. Hartmann had assailed *The Fugitive* as remote from life, its characters mustered from a theatrical museum. In *The New Ghetto,* seven years later, Herzl was attempting to be a realist. The milieu of the play is the Jewish society to which Herzl belonged, not the aristocratic society which he admired. His wife, his wife's relations and business associates are portrayed with little pity and much exaggeration. Only in Jacob Samuel, whom Schnitzler found insufficiently motivated, too like a figure in a dream, do Herzl's fantasies throb toward admiration. His obsession with dueling was of long standing. He had fought his one duel with honor, when a member of Albia; he had argued that a few good duels would do more for the Jewish cause than logical argument; his dream had solidified into details: he would challenge such Austrian anti-Semites as Georg von Schönerer or Prince Alois Lichtenstein. If he died, as Jacob Samuel dies, he would leave a letter that would tell the world how he had fallen victim to the most unjust movement of the age. If he won, he would deliver a heroic speech, first praising his dead opponent as a man of honor, then exalting the Jewish question in an oration worthy of Ferdinand Lassalle. "I would have compelled the respect of the judges, and the case against me would have been dismissed. Thereupon the Jews would have made me one of their representatives and I would have declined because I would refuse to achieve such a position by the killing of a man."[17]

This daydream of a *beau rôle* behind a pseudonym has a later echo in the composition of T. E. Lawrence's *Seven Pillars of Wisdom*. At literary parties "Aircraftman Shaw" would whisper to one guest after another, in strictest confidence, the secret of who he really was. Yet Lawrence won added fame from his book while Herzl's play had convinced neither Jews nor gentiles. If his play had succeeded, the pseudonym—a bulletproof waistcoat for himself as much as for anyone—would have been discarded. Even as things were it was not maintained long. In his original letter to Schnitzler he had spoken of resisting his temptation to tell first Beer, then Max Nordau, about *The New Ghetto*. By the spring he was confiding his secret to Teweles in Prague.

But his play's failure to win a European reputation for its author or Jewish approval for its theme was read with a gambler's relentless eye. He had staked an emotional maximum on a *colonne* and the croupier had coldly announced a zero. Herzl's dramatic impulse had failed on its obvious stage. The impulse would no more die than the urge for fame that was its companion. Surviving, it would find a different stage. He had already hinted what this stage would be, not only in his daydream of a successful duel, but in his correspondence with Schnitzler the previous year. Comparing himself with David Copperfield in the press gallery of the House of Commons, he had spoken of the chastisement that went with the acceptance of journalism. Then in a sudden tangent he had, after predicting the possibility of a new revolution, after recommending a good dictator, thrown out the hint of a new direction: "Sometimes I actually think of myself as a statesman."[18] By making plain his failure as an artist, *The New Ghetto* was important. It showed the need for some such radical departure.

PART FOUR

The Parnell of the Jews

1895

"I have decided to place myself at the head of an effort for the Jews . . ."[1]

CHAPTER 16

One known year—1895—was to change the life of Theodor Herzl as dramatically as the unknown day in which Saul of Tarsus, traveling to Damascus, became a Christian. Herzl's conversion to Zionism (a term coined by Nathan Birnbaum some years earlier) marked as radical a change as Saul's acceptance of the risen Jesus. Both men adopted, and then adapted, already existing movements. The result for both was an exhausting series of missionary journeys. Further comparisons are less precise. Saul the Jew became Paul the Christian thanks to an aural revelation that closely followed his participation in the stoning of Stephen. Herzl, the freethinker, claimed no similar intervention from outside himself; a contemporary of Sigmund Freud, he ascribed his change to an eruption from his unconscious.[2] Once converted, Paul taught that all men, slave or free, circumcised or uncircumcised, should be one in Christ; Herzl taught that the Jews should secede from gentile society. Each man had an ambiguous but different relationship to the Jewish religion. Paul in one sense rejected the Jewish Law, though in another his preaching brought aspects of it to a vast section of mankind. Herzl, while in one sense returning to Jewry, at the same time rejected the particularity of the Jewish tradition and urged the Jews to construct a nation-state like any other.

Herzl's conversion took place in an age that recorded each passing week in press and archive. Herzl described the context of his conversion and the course of action to which it led in a Diary he began "around Pentecost, 1895,"* and kept up until a last entry on May 16, 1904. In its complete and best edition† it runs to half a million words, or 1,631 pages.

This Diary, in part because he wrote it in a simple, unlabored style, but largely because of the intrinsic interest of what it tells, is his literary masterpiece. Its candor and detail make it perhaps the most revealing prose work of a period not poor in such achievements. Though primarily devoted to the Jewish question, and Herzl's solution, it incidentally throws vivid, sometimes lurid, torchlight on the end of one century and the beginning of another.

The Diary was begun after the fact of a conversion in process had become apparent to Herzl. The full implications of the conversion were yet to be worked out. He was in such haste to work them out that he did not sketch in four important factors in the period that went before. Two of these factors have entered myth. Two have not been mentioned at all. All four need consideration.

The factors that have entered myth are *The New Ghetto* and the Dreyfus case.

The New Ghetto, as we have suggested, was not the invasion of a new field so much as a last attempt in an old. The use of a pseudonym was a gauntlet to fate. If the play succeeded, then the playwright would return veiled to a literary career. The subplot in the play—the struggle of the coal miners against the tyranny of capital—suggests the kind of theme that as a new playwright Herzl might have tried.

But the old year died and the new year was born without the sudden surge to success that would have shown the gamble had succeeded. On January 19 Schnitzler wrote that his *Liebelei* had been accepted for production at the Burgtheater, but alas, there was no news of the acceptance of *The New Ghetto* in Berlin. Herzl was too disappointed fully to appreciate the pains to which Arthur Schnitzler had gone on behalf of "Albert Schnabel." Replying on Schnitzler on February 1,[3] Herzl spoke of his play as *"mein liebes Kindchen"* and of the sour taste left by its rejection. "It's not much help to tell oneself that one director is a blackguard, another a fool." His impulse was to throw the rubbish in the can; but he had begun well and would remain steadfast. His next letter to Schnitzler, written on February 14, constitutes one of the oddest valentines recorded. Marking a peak of desperation, it also showed a solipsistic remoteness

---

* The two Jewish holy days of Pentecost (Shevuoth) fell on Wednesday, May 29, and Thursday, May 30, in 1895. Herzl is referring to the Christian Pentecost, which his translator and editor (*vide* infra) render as "Whitsunday."

† *The Complete Diaries of Theodor Herzl,* ed. Raphael Patai, tr. Harry Zohn, New York, 1960.

from the feelings of others, being written to one whose friendship had been proved by his exertions. After a banal beginning, reproaching Schnitzler for not sending him literary news, he goes on:

> I have a great need of a good friendship. I am on the point of publishing an advertisement: "Man in prime of life seeks a friend to whom he can confide without fear all his frailties and absurdities." Or as they put it in the French papers: *On demande un ami désintéressé.* I don't know: am I too distrustful, or too diffident, or are my eyes too clearsighted? I find none such here among my acquaintances. One is too stupid, the next too treacherous, the third irritates me at my most sensitive point, when he takes advantage of a burgeoning familiarity . . . Tell me, do you, too, feel like this with a new friend?

The failure of Herzl's last attempt at being a serious playwright disappointed him as a writer, not as an evangelist. He can hardly have hoped that his play would console suffering Jews (and in particular those of Russia and Romania) even if it had been immediately and widely produced; for after Schnitzler's reaction, and that of the anonymous Jewish critic who found the play an affront to Jewry, he must have recognized that Jews, not gentiles, opposed its production. The notion that "it was in the nature of things that the German theaters should reject his play"‡ was as much a legend as that the writing of *The New Ghetto* meant at the time a first step in a campaign. But legend conceals certain truths. The writing of the play had focused Herzl's attention on a problem he had largely suppressed from conscious consideration; the play's inability to fire enthusiasm left his ambition wounded but not killed.

A more persistent legend has linked Herzl's conversion to the Dreyfus case. In this case the legend has its roots in the Herzl of a few years later, a man then battling as a politician and modifying his past in the interests of a cause. "The Dreyfus process,"* de Haas quotes Herzl as writing, "which I witnessed in Paris in 1894, made me a Zionist."[4] This was published in 1927; but when Herzl was still alive de Haas was more cautious. "Herzl has not confessed," he wrote in his entry on Herzl for the Jewish Encyclopaedia of 1904, "to what particular incident the publication of his 'Jewish State' in the winter of 1895 was due. He was in Paris at the time, and was no doubt moved

‡ André Chouraqui, *A Man Alone*, p. 81.
* "Process" is obviously an un-English attempt at *procès*, or "trial"; Herzl thus limits his conversion to the trial, which lasted, at the longest, from the arrest of Dreyfus on October 15 through the trial proper from December 19–22 to his degradation on Saturday, January 5, 1895.

by the Dreyfus affair."† It is possible that de Haas may have asked Herzl, a close acquaintance, what had been the agent of his conversion and that Herzl, on his guard, had been purposely vague. Once both Herzl and de Haas were dead, the connection between the Dreyfus case and Herzl's conversion became part of the legend.

Herzl's writings at the time do not confirm this causal connection. A glance at undisputed facts and dates shows indeed how unlikely such a connection would have been.

The Dreyfus case was not only the most impassioned controversy of the nineteenth century; it was also one of the longest, lasting indeed into the century that followed. Its beginning can be dated precisely. On September 26, 1894, Madame Bastian, an elderly cleaner employed at the German Embassy in Paris, delivered the contents of Colonel Schwartzkoppen's wastepaper basket to Major Henry, second-in-command of France's counterespionage bureau. Twenty-four years after the loss of Alsace-Lorraine, twenty years before the war that would win the region back, the Germans were extremely unpopular in Paris. Rummaging through the trove, Major Henry discovered, not the love letters of the military attaché, but a memorandum (known in accounts of the case as *le bordereau*) listing five documents that an anonymous vendor was willing to sell to the Germans. Only an officer who had recently served in the artillery, the men chosen to investigate decided, could know the details the traitor was offering to sell. There were four to five possible suspects. The handwriting of one—an Alsatian captain, Alfred Dreyfus—resembled that on the *bordereau*. On October 15 Dreyfus was arrested and the first stage of the case was completed when, just before Christmas, a court-martial sentenced him to degradation and imprisonment for life.

It is now possible, as it was not possible then, to extricate the bones of the case with untrembling fingers. Dreyfus was not arrested because of his connections with Germany, his grandfather's Judaism or his own adultery, though all these facts would be used against him by the unscrupulous; he was arrested because of the incorrect identification of his handwriting with that of the hidden traitor. The Army, which had acted in good faith at the start and which appointed Major Georges Picquart in July 1895 to reexamine the case, cravenly proceeded to defend its original error when in March 1896 Madame Bastian delivered new wastepaper, this time incriminating a Major Esterhazy, a Christian aristocrat with a grudge against France as large as his debts. The honest Picquart was transferred to Tunisia and from September 1896 onward Major Henry began forging evi-

† *Der Judenstaat* was in fact published in early 1896.

dence against him as well as against Dreyfus. As passions in press and café rose, the Army sank deeper and deeper into culpable deceit and injustice.‡ French society, which had at first been uninvolved, became violently divided on the subject, and thanks to the clamor of the Dreyfusards, led by Mathieu Dreyfus, the victim's admirable brother, and Emile Zola, who published his *J'Accuse!* on January 13, 1898, a series of new trials finally cleared the unfortunate prisoner of Devil's Island. Even then, the Army refused to make a radical admission of its šins. A second court-martial produced the absurd judgment that Dreyfus was "guilty of high treason with extenuating circumstances" and sentenced him to ten years imprisonment. Dreyfus then accepted a free pardon (although this implied his guilt) on the advice of his brother, who feared he could not stand another term of prison.

That Herzl "was no doubt moved by the Dreyfus affair" is indeed confirmed by a nearly contemporary account.* The spectacle of Dreyfus' degradation (which Herzl described in a cable to the *Neue Freie Presse*) was one to move pity in the hardest heart.

Yet at this early stage in the affair, the Jewish community in Paris was moved by another emotion—that of embarrassed indignation against a Jew who had apparently let his community down. Logically, the guilt or innocence of Dreyfus said nothing about the loyalty of other Jews. But French Jews knew from experience how the illogic of the rabble could be turned to violence. Some Jews were even more indignant than Christians. Two leading journalists, Isidore Singer and Joseph Aron, were in the midst of a courageous campaign against anti-Semitism at the time the news of the treachery was published. "Although there was no death-penalty for treason or espionage at the time, both felt that, if convicted, the traitor deserved to be executed; Aron believed that he should be shot, and Singer that he should be subjected to 'the pitiless penal code of Moses'—death by stoning, with the Grand Rabbi of France casting the first stone."[5]

At this early stage, the only people to be sure of the captain's innocence were those who knew him best, the immediate members of his family. "Madame Hadamard, Dreyfus's mother-in-law and the wife

‡ Before the non-French reader too roundly condemns the officers who took part in the suppression of truth, he should examine his own history. It is probable that he will turn up examples of similar corporate dishonesty. Seymour M. Hersh, writing in *The New Yorker* (January 29, 1972) about the slow uncovering of the Mylai massacre, reports: "The Army realized that it was dealing not only with the matter of serious war crimes but also with that of widespread deceit on the part of American officers, who, for various reasons, presumably including the desire to protect their own careers, had covered up virtually all the details of the massacre."

* Herzl's entry in his Diary for November 17, 1895.

of a wealthy Jewish diamond merchant, expressed this feeling in a number of newspaper interviews. How, she asked, could such a rich and devoted family man have committed such a crime?"[6] The rhetorical question flouted logic. Dreyfus was not a faithful husband; the annals of treachery show that no category of human being is ever ipso facto beyond suspicion. But Madame Hadamard, like his brother Mathieu, knew Alfred Dreyfus, and was morally certain of his innocence. Mathieu's campaign to prove this was less rhetorical. He knew that discretion was essential; simply to impugn a court-martial's verdict would not save his brother; evidence was required, and not emotion. For this reason Mathieu forced Lazare to hold back, till late 1896, what proved to be the first pamphlet defending Dreyfus. In describing the feverish impatience in which he passed a silent year and a half Lazare wrote: *"Je n'ai eu aucun confident de mes actions ni de mes désirs."*[7] We can hardly assume, therefore, that Herzl had heard from Lazare evidence exonerating Dreyfus. Even Lazare's evidence at this stage was largely intuitive, while Herzl was too busy with his duties as correspondent, his attempts to place *The New Ghetto* and then his Diary to play any role in the affair.

An aspect complicating the case was the personality of Dreyfus. Despite his mother-in-law's loyalty, his brother's affection, he was not an attractive martyr. Practicing Jews could hardly admire a man who had broken all ties with his ancestral faith. Although the '90s were not easily shocked, hypocrisy then as ever could condemn his liaisons with other women. In manner and appearance he was unappealing. His greatest champion, Major Picquart, had been adversely impressed by Dreyfus at his trial and later defended him out of principle only. In Proust's great novel, in which the affair plays an important role, Madame de Guermantes is made to remark: "What a pity we can't choose someone else for our innocent!" In real life the witticism was made by Madame Straus, born Geneviève Halévy.[8] The martyr's later acceptance of less than total vindication outraged many of his more idealistic supporters.

To have been a convinced Dreyfusard during the period of Herzl's conversion—winter and spring 1894–95—was as difficult for an honest observer as *not* to have been a Dreyfusard after Madame Bastian's new discoveries were known to implicate a different traitor. The statement that "the Dreyfus case made Zionists of Herzl and Lazare"† might be plausible if the conversion of these two men had taken place in 1896 or later. For Herzl to have become a Zionist at the time of Dreyfus' trial on the assumption that Dreyfus had been arrested as a

† Walter Laqueur, *Encounter*, August 1971.

Jew, and as a Jew could not expect justice, would have been as irrational as Drumont's certainty that as a Jew he could only be a traitor.[9] Herzl had less evidence for a Zionist interpretation of the case than Bernard Lazare. After writing two articles denouncing anti-Semitism,[10] Lazare had taken the trouble to meet the Dreyfus family in February 1895. This experience sufficed to convince him that there had in fact been a miscarriage of justice and as a result "the celebrated defender of anarchists and revolutionaries agreed to do everything he could for the wealthy Jewish family."[11]

In retrospect, the Dreyfus case has little logical connection with the views to which Herzl became committed in the period immediately after the trial. Another Jewish writer was to argue half a century later:

> There was no crisis that was "Jewish" in character. The fundamental issue in France was democracy itself: and it survived the crisis. Emancipation had not failed—it had worked. The fate of the Jew, Alfred Dreyfus, was. symbolic of the fate of French democracy and had roused the whole nation. Where, in all the world, a century before, would more than half a nation have come to the defense of a Jew? Had Herzl possessed a knowledge of history he would have seen in the Dreyfus case a brilliant, heartening proof of the success of emancipation. A world that had treated all Jews as Pariahs for 1500 years, had, within the space of a century, come to see half of a nation concerned to redress an injustice to one Jew.[12]

Herzl later gave his reasons for arguing a priori that a Jewish officer was incapable of committing an act of national treachery. "A Jew who, as an officer on the general staff, has before him an honourable career, cannot commit such a crime . . . The Jews, who have so long been condemned to a state of civic dishonour, have, as a result, developed an almost pathological hunger for honour, and a Jewish officer is in this respect specifically Jewish."[13] Members of any minority confronted by such a scandal find it easy to react in this instinctive manner. But the argument is irrational. Members of all minorities have committed crimes; no group has been proved exempt. The guilt or innocence of Dreyfus was to be determined, not by arguments as to whether Jews could not—or must—be traitors, but by the cold evidence that this particular officer had not committed the crime of which he was accused. Drumont and the converted Herzl were thus uncannily linked, and Herzl was to admit his debt to Drumont the summer of his conversion. "I owe to Drumont a great deal of the present freedom of my concepts, because he is an artist."[14] By "artist," Herzl probably meant a champion of instinctive judgments against rational, of the heart against the head.

To place Herzl's conversion in correct rapport with the failure of *The New Ghetto* and the distress of the Dreyfus trial has required some space. Far less is needed to describe the two other major factors affecting him as he approached his Damascus moment. But this does not make them unimportant.

Money, or its lack, had played its role in his life as in that of most writers. From the moment in August 1885 when he resigned his career as a government lawyer until the season, nine years later, when he wrote *The New Ghetto,* Herzl had been dependent on his parents or his pen for his livelihood. While Jacob Naschauer was alive, he could maintain a parental interest in Julie's dowry.‡ Herzl had found much of his Parisian existence irksome; his mother and father had visited France but disliked it and returned to Austria. He had consoled himself with the vision of a change, of becoming, perhaps, a politician. His salary was enough for him to maintain a rented house and carriage; his father's earnings as a stock agent were sufficient for minor loans and small-scale assistance. But he lacked the freedom and the funds for a political career.

Then on January 3, 1894, Herzl's own newspaper told its readers that after a long and painful illness the fifty-seven-year-old Jacob Naschauer had died in Budapest and would be laid to eternal rest in Vienna's central cemetery the following day. This change in the family situation, linked with his own boredom with Paris and his parents' disapproval of the frivolous city, may have helped Herzl to decide to move back to Vienna and to play a political role. *May . . . perhaps . . .* The reader must be protected from suppositions masquerading as facts. There is no ascertainable evidence that Julie's sudden access to new money influenced Herzl, though there is evidence from Herzl's wills that from now on he dipped into his wife's fortune on an increasing scale. (He attributed the need to do this to her extravagance.)[15] But the funds were considerable enough for Dr. Bein to quote them in guilders and marks in the German, 1934, edition of his biography.* We may state them in guilders and dollars. Jacob Naschauer's estate amounted to half a million guilders, or nearly a quarter of a million dollars.

The final circumstance was most important. Early in 1895 Herzl sent his family back to Vienna while he himself occupied a room at the Hotel Castille in the Rue Cambon. His return to a bachelor existence re-created the solitary situation that on previous occasions had

‡ The dowry was almost certainly involved in the family dissension at the time when Herzl's lawyer tried to secure Rabbi Güdemann's intervention.

* All reference to Jacob Naschauer's death and fortune has disappeared from the English version.

fired him to write. His job as Paris correspondent for the *Neue Freie Presse* had been won by the four *feuilletons* he had written when wandering alone in the mountains between France and Spain. Liberation from Julie suddenly gave him a new ability to dream and to create.

CHAPTER 17

Herzl's conversion cannot be linked with one particular event or moment; it was a process that began around the autumn of 1894 and was completed by the morning in May 1895 when he was ready to take his first action in the service of his new idea.

Great converts are usually men or women whose characters contain elements markedly at war; or two selves, one of which is latent or oppressed till it is released in its Damascus moment. Herzl is a striking instance. His appearance and his cast of mind were as fissured as his private life.

To those who met him in the 1890s Herzl's face balanced strength and delicacy. His resigned acceptance of comparative failure, his inner solitude were offset by an ambition as identifiable as his beard (often described as Assyrian), determined nose and bush-cut, strong black hair. Stefan Zweig wrote:

> It was a faultlessly handsome face. The soft, well-kept black beard gave it a clear almost rectangular outline, into which the clean-cut nose, set exactly in the middle, fitted well, as did also the high, slightly rounded forehead. But this beauty—perhaps almost too regular, too much like a work of art—was deepened by the gentle almond-shaped eyes with their heavy black, melancholy lashes— ancient Oriental eyes in this somewhat French face in the style of Alphonse Daudet, in this face which would have seemed slightly artificial or effeminate, or suggestive of the beau, had not the thousand-year-old melancholy of the soul shone through it.[1]

The melancholy throve in Julie's hothouse. A woman writer, now hardly remembered though in her day, 1926, awarded the Nobel

Prize for Literature, is to be heard with respect when she diagnoses what she took to be "the full tragedy of his life." Grazia Deledda did so on the basis of two meetings with Herzl which she remembered and assessed after a lapse of nearly thirty years. Both the meetings took place after his conversion and after he and Julie were settled in a suburban house in Vienna. In one, he had shown an earnest, even a prophetic self; in the second he had been with "his beautiful blond wife who—it became clear to me in a moment—found only torment in that which was life and fate to him. For that one hour, in her presence, he was . . . the witty feuilletonist—that and nothing more."[2] Grazia Deledda could not know that this woman whom he outwardly strove to please represented the walking graveyard of his adolescent dreams; still less could she know the secret sorrows of Julie, a rich girl for whom life had held nearly every promise but whose inner disappointment was as keen as her husband's. Only the compact between them, tensile as steel, forced each to act a public role.

What kept Herzl acting the drawing-room wit for Julie and her guests, what kept the melancholy from engulfing him as it had engulfed Kana was the urge Kana had recognized, "to get there," no matter the cost. It was made more urgent by Herzl's knowledge that he was unlikely to live as long as he had lived already. The impaired health that had prevented him joining the Austrian Army had been served ill by the strains of his Paris work and the stress of an unhappy marriage. If the Army physicians had discerned a heart tremor, this heart had been put in further jeopardy by the treatment he seems to have received for malaria. His visits to Baden and its sulphur springs had not effected more than transitory relief. With his flesh threatened, he had no consoling belief in a life hereafter.[3] If he was to get there, he must get there now. Posthumous reverence, for himself and his children, was a pallid consolation. He had suppressed all interest in religion since he left Budapest, if not earlier.

Yet an action connected with religion marked the approaching turn from playwright to politician. Shortly after writing *The New Ghetto*, he did something he had not done since boyhood. As with so many of his actions, it can be given a halo that fogs its significance. "For the first time since his departure from Pest," André Chouraqui writes, "he felt the need for prayer. At the synagogue in the Rue de la Victoire, overcome by emotion at the rhythm of the ancient music, a new course seemed to be demanded from him."[4] After such hagiography (other examples could be quoted)[5] it comes as a surprise to read Herzl's account of the occasion to the end.

"For the first time I went to the synagogue in the Rue de la

Victoire and once again found the services festive and moving. Many things reminded me of my youth and the Tabak Street temple at Pesth. I took a look at the Paris Jews and saw a family likeness in their faces: bold, misshapen noses; furtive and cunning eyes."[6] The account suggests a politician assessing his constituency or a doctor his patients, not a man in search of balm.

A little later—"some time before Easter"[7]—he called on Alphonse Daudet for a contribution to his newspaper. (Herzl had translated one of Daudet's plays into German.) In conversation, the two men got on to the topic of the Jews and Daudet confessed what was well known, that he was an anti-Semite. This confession appealed to the side in Herzl that had responded to some of Dühring's charges with assent. At his best in heated discussion, Herzl told his friend that he planned writing a book about the Jews.

"A novel?"

"I should prefer to write a man's book."

"But a novel can reach further. Think of *Uncle Tom's Cabin.*"

The mention of Harriet Beecher Stowe's attack on slavery inspired Herzl to further oratory. Even as a youth he had been persuasive; in maturity he could be overpowering, though people won today were sometimes lost tomorrow.

"*Comme c'est beau! comme c'est beau!*" was Daudet's reaction.

So encouraged by a man with a European reputation, Herzl, back in his hotel, returned to the theme for a novel he had begun the summer after Kana's death but which his promotion to Paris had left unfinished. Possibly he had been influenced by Schnitzler's complaint that *The New Ghetto* lacked "Jews of strength"; or possibly his new cast of mind was already dominant. Heinrich Kana—or Samuel Kohn—would no longer be the hero. The moods that had preceded his suicide would no longer be explored with loving interest. Instead, Kana would be the weaker friend of a positive hero. The new hero, Herzl himself, would learn of Kana's suicide just as he was leading a mass departure for the Promised Land. Instead of wasting tears, he would rage at the loss of talents that should have belonged . . . to the Jews.[8]

Herzl's final comment comes from among the truest pages he wrote, and the simplest: "How I proceeded from the idea of writing a novel to a practical program is already a mystery to me, although it happened within the last few weeks. It is in the realm of the Unconscious."[9]

His unconscious exploded so fast that at the time Herzl could only preserve random jottings, longer notes or copies of letters. Internal evidence shows that the earlier material was not included in his Diaries until the following April when he was permanently back in Vienna, once again living with Julie and the three children.[10] "This is where I interrupted the connected presentation at that time," he interjects on April 16, 1896; "for there followed several weeks of unexampled productivity during which I no longer had the peace to make a clean copy of my ideas. I wrote walking, standing, lying down, in the street, at table, at night when I started up from sleep."[11]

Herzl took his first political step when, suddenly, he wrote a letter to Baron Maurice de Hirsch, the leading Jewish philanthropist of his day. Born in Munich, de Hirsch had moved to Brussels as a young man, where he married Clara Bischoffsheim in the most spectacular Jewish wedding ever to have taken place in Belgium.[12] Enriched by building railways (particularly in the Ottoman empire), ennobled by the King of the Belgians, de Hirsch had become the intimate friend of the future Edward VII and the owner of a town house that had previously belonged to the Empress Eugénie. After the death of his only son, Lucien, at the early age of thirty-one, the Baron with his wife devoted his fortune to relieving Jewish distress. A convinced assimilationist (though he would serve kosher food for Jewish relatives and rabbis), the Baron believed in rescuing Jews from the ghetto and enabling them to live normal lives as agricultural laborers and tradesmen in such countries as the United States and Argentina. Six years earlier he had offered the enormous sum (by the standards of those days) of two million sterling pounds to found craft and agricultural schools for the depressed Jews of the Russian Pale. When this offer was turned down by the Czarist authorities, he diverted the money to establishing a Jewish Colonization Association whose purpose was similar to that for which Oswald Boxer had died in Brazil.

When Herzl had finished his letter, he left it on his hotel room desk for two weeks. When it still seemed valid after this lapse of time, he mailed it.[13] Herzl does not date the draft of the letter preserved in his *Diaries*, but it seems possible that it was composed on May 2, his thirty-fifth birthday. The letter, signed "Dr. Herzl, Correspondent of the *Neue Freie Presse*," requested the honor of being allowed to call on the Baron to discuss The Jewish Question. Herzl suggested Sunday as a convenient day (his need to cover parliamentary debates still keeping him busy) and emphasized that he did not want "to talk about a disguised or undisguised financial matter. It seems that the claims on you are so manifold that one cannot guard against the suspicion of unsavoury designs soon enough. I simply wish to have a discussion with you about Jewish political matters, a discussion that may have an effect on times that neither you nor I will live to see."[14]

Herzl was prudent to stress that he was not engaged in "a journalist's feat of extortion." De Hirsch was naturally skeptical of being approached by strangers. On May 20 he replied from his London residence, Bath House, at 82, Piccadilly. Would Dr. Herzl put what he had in mind in writing, and mark the envelope "Personal"? The multilingual Baron apologized for replying "in the handwriting of my secretary, and in French, but as the result of an old hunting injury to my right hand I am unable to hold a pen for any length of time." Herzl knew better than to commit his ideas to writing at this stage. Instead, his answer showed a shrewd understanding of human motives. "What you have undertaken till now," he told the man reputed to be the richest in Europe, "has been as magnanimous as it has been misapplied, as costly as it has been pointless. You have hitherto been only a philanthropist, a Peabody°; I want to show you the way to become something more."[15] The Baron was used to flatterers, not plain speakers; he was not used to being offered scope for the enhancement of himself. The Baron was intrigued. In a second letter from Bath House he announced that he would be paying a two-day visit to Paris and informed "Monsieur Herzl, 37 rue Cambon, Paris" that he would be at his disposal at 10:30 A.M. the following Sunday at two, Rue de l'Elysée.

Herzl admits that his letter had been carefully calculated. ". . . I saw that I had judged the man correctly and had hit him *at the place of least resistance* [Herzl used a Latin phrase]. Apparently my statement that he could become more than a Peabody had had an effect on him."

Herzl prepared himself for his encounter with careful attention to his thoughts and clothes. He had spent the previous day (the Sabbath to observant Jews) getting his notes in order; he divided them under three groups, *Introduction, Uplifting of the Jewish Race* and *Emigration*. But he had also taken time to break in a pair of gloves, so that they might still look new, but not fresh from the shop.[16] But despite his own maxim—"one must not show rich people too much deference" —Herzl was awed by the wondrous forms—old masters, tapestries, Boule—in which the Baron's wealth had found expression. A display case was thronged with Tanagra figurines. Few objects bring the past so vividly alive as these terra-cotta statuettes of the men and women of the Hellenistic Levant.[17] Unnamed artists used muted colors, tiny details to portray as they were the women, children, money-changers, actors of Alexandria, a society not far in spirit from the Paris of 1895. Herzl had time to examine them, for the Baron, in a tycoon's ruse,

° George Peabody (1795–1869) was the precursor of Andrew Carnegie in the line of American philanthropists. His name is associated with ugly brick tenements which he financed for the poor of London and other cities.

stepped into the billiard room quickly, gave his visitor an absent-minded handshake, before disappearing again to confer with other guests. Herzl armed himself against being too impressed. "The Baron, I thought to myself, must have hired someone to be in charge of good taste." The Baron, too, had armed himself for his meeting with the unknown intellectual. One of his philanthropic adjutants, known to Herzl from Vienna, would pass out through the same room where Herzl sat waiting: to remind the derider of Peabody of the range of de Hirsch's good works.

Once Herzl was alone with de Hirsch, he requested at least an hour in which to expound his ideas. Although the Baron smilingly agreed, Herzl never got through the twenty-two pages of notes he had prepared. Thus the later stages of his program may have already co-existed with the first. But the first stage is all that is recorded at the time.

Basically, Herzl attacked the idea of philanthropic resettlement with which the Baron was associated because it turned those whom it benefited into *shnorrers* (a Yiddish term for beggars) and did not attack the root problem of the Jews: their degeneration as a race. "Whether the Jews stay put or whether they emigrate, the race must first be improved right on the spot. It must be made strong as for war, eager to work, and virtuous. Afterwards, let them emigrate—if necessary." De Hirsch cannot be blamed if he felt that his visitor's future aim implied a present belief that the Jews were cowardly, reluctant to work and vicious. The ethos of *The New Ghetto* is still palpable. Jacob Samuel had been helped by his gentile friend to take a few paces from the ghetto, to look a man in the eyes, not to cringe. Herzl now wanted the Baron's support in doing for the Jewish masses what Wurzlechner had done for an imagined individual, or what membership in Albia had perhaps done for Herzl: to help them change gestures and inflections, cease to be subservient, stand up, to become, as a group, what Jacob Samuel had become as an individual. Herzl developed his ideas. They included the establishment of "huge prizes in the chief anti-Semitic countries for *actions d'éclat* [striking deeds], for deeds of great moral beauty, for courage, self-sacrifice, ethical conduct, great achievements in art and science, for physicians during epidemics, for military men, for discoverers of remedies and inventors of other products contributing to the public welfare, no matter what—in short, for anything great."

In this grandiose program Herzl saw a double value: it would improve the Jewish race and at the same time would foster favorable publicity. The Baron took the opposite view. He had long argued that a minority should, in effect, keep a low profile. He had once told his wife that the idea to encourage was that the only difference between

Jew and Christian was one of religious beliefs; the sooner they sat at the same workbench or tilled the same soil together, the better.[18] "All our misfortune," he now told Herzl, "comes from the fact that the Jews want to climb too high. We have too many intellectuals. My intention is to keep the Jews from pushing ahead. They should not make such great strides. All Jew-hatred comes from this."

Between the successful Baron (born in 1831) and the frustrated playwright (born in 1860) affinity of mind was hardly conceivable. Brought up before the concept of race invaded the brain of Everyman, happily married to a woman who shared his ideals, de Hirsch saw the Jews of Eastern Europe as pitiable fellow beings for whom as a Jew (however unobservant) he had the added responsibility conferred by a common religion. By June 2, 1895, Herzl's conversion had already solidified into its first conviction: the Jews could not assimilate to gentile standards in gentile society because that society would always find Jews alien. If the Jews were to become estimable by gentile standards, they could only do so as a self-governing nation-state. The spiritual liberation *The New Ghetto* had demanded was no longer enough. The Jewish millions could never become Jacob Samuels within a few steps of their ancient ghettos. They lacked the sensitivity, the education and the aristocratic courage. Herzl's remedy for this state of affairs was an intellectual construct and as such owed much to his university professors. It involved no necessary link with a particular group or a particular territory. It was an abstract solution for a concrete problem. On various later occasions he would accept now one, now another view of who the people requiring regeneration were and where they should go. Whitsunday 1895 shows him precise only on the need to secede. "To the Kaiser I shall say: let our people go! We are strangers here; we are not permitted to assimilate with the people, nor are we able to do so." He quotes himself as using the terms "national," "people" and "race" (but not terms connected with a religious community) to describe the "us" involved. He is silent on the place to which "we" are to go.

Herzl's use of the term "race" must be set, not only in the context of verbal heat, but in its time. This term, with its connotations of physical, biological difference, was popular with those who had lost their belief in traditional religions (which had solved the problem of identity on a creedal basis) and who had been shaken by Darwin's discoveries, or their popularization. It was used by anti-Semite and Jewish nationalist alike: by Disraeli as well as by Gobineau, by Moses Hess and Bernard Lazare as well as by Wagner and Houston Stewart Chamberlain. No man stood closer to Herzl in his year of conversion than Max Nordau, then a widely respected pundit. In 1892 he had written a

work entitled *Degeneration* which argued that since the artists he disliked—Baudelaire, Wilde, Nietzsche, Wagner—were physically degen-
erate, their works had no value and would not survive. Nordau (one
of the two Hungarian friends in whom Herzl had wanted to confide
the authorship of *The New Ghetto*) had first emphasized his break
with the ghetto tradition by changing his name (as son of Rabbi Süd-
feld) from the equivalent of "south field" to "northern meadow." A life
as physician, journalist and popularizer of science had carried the
break further. In another much read book, *The Conventional Lies of
Our Civilization,* he had attacked the Bible as younger than the Vedas,
inferior as literature to Homer and the European classics, childish as
philosophy and revolting as morality.[19] To one so radically divorced
from his religious background, terms taken from pathology fitted a
post-Darwinian world in which species warred for survival and in
which Cesare Lombroso (to whom *Degeneration* was dedicated)
taught that genetic defect, not misdirection of the will, accounted for
crime. Nordau used "degeneration" in its fullest pathological sense of
"a morbid change in the structure of parts, consisting in a disintegra-
tion of tissue, or in substitution of a lower for a higher form of structure."[20] His book went into numerous editions in the major languages
of Europe, including English. Like many scientific best sellers, it dated
quickly. "What startles us today," George L. Mosse wrote in 1968, introducing the first new edition for more than seventy years, "is not only
Nordau's psychology but also his use of moral judgments. Morality is
not connected with metaphysical truth or an inner quest for sincerity,
but rather what is 'useful' in terms of the progress of the species."[21] In
The Right to Love, a novel that appeared in the same year, Nordau
denied the right of individuals to have children if this endangered the
species. Once Herzl converted Nordau to his views, it is significant that
Nordau's only reservations concerned the question whether the Jews
were still "anthropologically fit for nationhood."[22] Herzl convinced
him on this point and two years later Nordau, on a solemn occasion,
used a chilling metaphor to express the particularity of the Jews. "Mi-
crobiology tells us that there exist tiny organisms which are perfectly
harmless, so long as they live in the open air, but become the cause of
frightful disease when deprived of oxygen. Governments and nations
may well beware lest the Jews in like case become a source of danger."[23]

Herzl's use of racial terminology was thus unsurprising for one of
his time and culture. The traditional Jewish teaching that Jews were
a holy people set apart for the service of Torah—and a people whom
outsiders could join only through conversion and wholehearted ac-

ceptance of the rules of Torah—was unacceptable to men who did not believe in the Jewish religion and who had broken with it in covert or overt fashion. Those who had been baptized without conviction, those who had married gentiles and no longer circumcised their sons or kept the food laws found in race a convenient solution for a problem of identity. Herzl used the term loosely, without deep commitment. When, later, he met a Jew with unattractive, almost African features, he rejected race for "nation," a term hardly more precise.

CHAPTER 18

———————

———————————

Baron Maurice de Hirsch had dominated the first stage of Herzl's program: he was "the big Jew of money"[1] who could fund the emigration while Herzl himself was "the Jew of the spirit" who could inspire it. But de Hirsch had found the notion of making Jews "strong as for war" so distasteful, or chimerical, that he had allowed his visitor to expound only six of his twenty-six pages of notes.[2] Back in his lonely but creative room Herzl put additional arguments into a letter of around two thousand words dated Whitmonday. He boldly confronted a problem that might be worrying de Hirsch—his own comparative youth. "In France, at my thirty-five years of age, men are Ministers of State and Napoleon was Emperor."[3] Having suggested his peers, he stressed that he had already counted the cost of transporting and feeding the migrating multitudes. But more important than matériel was the idea that would fire its users. Only an imponderable, such as a flag, could stir men to die.

"What! You do not consider the imponderable? And what is religion? Consider, if you will, what the Jews have endured for the sake of this vision over a period of two thousand years. Yes, visions alone grip the souls of men. And anyone who has no use for them may be an excellent, worthy, sober-minded person, even a philanthropist on a large scale; but he will not be a leader of men, and no trace of him will remain."[4] As a user of imponderables he cited the Bismarck who had created the German empire. The "philanthropist on a large scale" was de Hirsch, the absent interlocutor whom he alternately cajoled and menaced. For two days after he had posted the letter, he had an access of panic. De Hirsch might publish his letters to prove him mad. "But if he does, I shall smash him, incite popular fanaticism against him, and demolish him in print (as I shall inform him in due course)."[5]

Emigration, the first stage of his program, led of its own momentum to three further questions of equal weight. What kind of state should the Jews construct? where would they choose to site it? and how would they obtain it? He essayed all these problems in cerebration that kept him fevered from June 5 until at least June 16, the day in 1895 when he concluded "that for me life has ended and world history has begun."[6] In eleven days of bachelor existence, eating in bistros, he covered the equivalent of more than 130 printed pages; entries range from one sentence to a fifty-four-page "Address to the Rothschilds" composed on June 13. It is as though we witness the gestation of a romantic poem, the sources of whose inspiration are as interesting as the use made of them. All the factors that had influenced Herzl's intellectual and emotional formation—his family, his schooling, his study of law, his lessons in fencing, his plays, the newspapers he read as well as wrote for, the stock market from which his father earned his living—have created the deposit in the well from which rises his dream flower, a state for the Jews.

The first day records two ordinary events in the life of a correspondent. In office hours he visited the secretary of a senator in connection with a Hungarian named Nemes,[7] recruited irregularly into the Foreign Legion. (The visit sparked a daydream of how much better his own soldiers would behave.) That evening, by gaslight, at the Second Empire Opéra, he passed through Jean Louis Garnier's imposing foyer to watch a performance of *Tannhäuser*. In Vienna Herzl had not been a Wagnerite. Nor was *Tannhäuser*, musically, the composer's major work. Yet its spectacular processions and stirring fanfares fitted Herzl's present mood.[*] "We too will have such splendid auditoriums—the gentlemen in full dress, the ladies dressed as lavishly as possible. Yes, I want to make use of the Jewish love of luxury, in addition to all other resources." The sight of the Parisian audience sitting for hours "tightly packed, motionless, in physical discomfort" turned his thoughts back to the phenomenon of the crowd. The watchers were focused on imponderables: sounds, music, spectacle. "I shall also cultivate majestic processional marches for great festive occasions."[8] Nor was this the only time he mentioned Wagner during these fevered days. The biblical Exodus under Moses, he wrote,

[*] Carl E. Schorske's suggestion that Herzl may have felt "in Tannhäuser's morally liberating return to the grotto a parallel to his own return to the ghetto"[10] seems farfetched as well as inaccurate, since Tannhäuser does not return to the grotto once he leaves it (though in Act III he tries to).

bore the same relation to his scheme "as a Shrovetide play by Hans Sachs to a Wagner opera."[9]

Older and more substantial are the influences of his childhood and home. His dream of being an engineer has left its mark. Determined that his enterprise will be a Suez, not a Panama,[11] he envisages completely new cities, with their pipes and drains laid first. His cities will mix the grandiose with the *gemütlich*. "Build something of the order of the Palais Royal or the Square of St. Mark."[12] He foresees his own statue and hopes it will be more artistic than the one of Gambetta in the Tuileries.[13] Yet each city will be girt by forests, so that the effect is as much Garden City as Venetian. The statues in public gardens will be fashioned from Beerite; the same quick-drying material will cement glass bricks. Jeanette Herzl, with her passion for neatness and etiquette, would have approved the style. "All officials in uniform, trim, with military bearing, but not ludicrously so."[14] Her Germanic culture pervades his Utopia. "German theatre, international theatre, operas, operettas, circuses, café-concerts, Café *Champs Elysées*."[15] A tribute to her is the choice of language. "German is, *par la force des choses*, likely to become the official language. *Judendeutsch!* As the yellow badge is to become our blue ribbon."[16] Herzl was thinking of something like Swiss-German more than Yiddish. For Jeanette's influence is again palpable in the qualification that the language would be purged of "the Jewish jargons, Judeo-German, which has sense and justification only as the stealthy tongue of prisoners."[17] She would no less have approved the outlawing of the Jewish sense of humor. "One of the major battles I shall have to fight will be against the self-mockery of the Jews. This readiness to scoff represents, at bottom, the feeble attempt of prisoners to look like free men."[18] Yet Herzl makes a concession to the simply human. He had noticed that an Austrian friend on a visit to Paris was homesick for the coffee and whipped cream of the Habsburg capital. "Consequently I shall faithfully transplant Viennese cafes to the other side. With such little expedients I shall achieve the desired illusion of the old environment."[19]

The influence of Jacob Herzl is much less. Even so, his father will be the first senator in a Senate formed from the prominent Jews in the migration.[20] His father's familiarity with the world of bonds and stocks has rubbed off on the son who conjures with millions. "What are ten billion marks to the Jews? They are certainly richer than the French were in 1871, and how many Jews were among them!"[21]

His fraternity days are not forgotten. For "over there," as in student Vienna, dueling will play its role. But his creative frenzy melts and remolds the juvenile ordeal. Nineteenth-century Europe yields in one page to pagan Sparta, prototype for many daydreams of an ideal society. Dueling is to be virtually without restriction, "in order to have real officers and to impart a tone of French refinement to good society. Duelling with sabres is permitted and will not be punished, no matter what the outcome, provided that the seconds have done their share toward an honorable settlement. Every sabre duel will be investigated by the duelling tribunal only afterwards."[22] This body acquires a strange new function as his mind plays with the question of pistol dueling, "or the American type, if it really exists." Apart from deciding whether to allow or forbid a particular duel, the tribunal may have a secondary role unknown in modern Europe. Herzl imagines the court cleared even of the seconds while in strictest secrecy the judges order the would-be duelists to abstain from fratricidal slaughter and to kill instead a national enemy. "In this way the risk of death of the duel will be retained, and we shall derive wonderful benefit from it." Herzl may have remembered how the dread Krypteia, the secret police of Sparta, had ordered young bloods to pick off subject natives who might be dangerous. Secrecy pervades the imagined state. Herzl (his own security guarded by secret police) will "frequently make surprise spot inspections. (Highly important, so as to prevent *gaspillage* [waste] and officials lying down on the job.) Also get reports on malpractices from a secret Administrative Police."[23] But the crime most harshly punished will be "political agitation which can lead to the downfall of the State."[24] Herzl's suggested penalty is banishment, or in cases where an exiled agitator might do harm, death.

The reversals of previous attitudes that are common to all conversions underlie some of Herzl's legislation. Four such reversals may be noted. Like all writers, Herzl had had his bouts with censors. Freedom of the press will be limited, he now announces[25]; for those who go too far the pillory will be restored and fines imposed. "As a young man," Herzl admits, "I myself was a gambler—like Lessing, Laube, and many others who later became respectable men after all—but only because my craving for action had no other outlet."[26] Gambling would be forbidden in the new society, except in "refined card-clubs," restricted to members over forty years of age. Suicide (which had once appealed to him as a literary theme) now provoked him to a quest for drastic punishments. Unsuccessful suicide was easy to punish: those who tried it would be confined for life in insane asylums. It was harder to deal with those who succeeded. Dishonorable burial by night, after medical experiments on their corpses, was not enough. Their wills must be declared invalid and the publication of their literary works forbidden.[27] Only two years before, Herzl had recommended assimilation through the acceptance of either socialism or baptism. Now he bestows the contemptuous adjective of "cowardly" on assimilated, baptized Jews.[28]

Herzl shared the dislike for democracy of such Utopia builders as Plato and Sir Thomas More.† His aristocratic republic would find its nearest model in independent Venice,[29] and like Venice would be ruled by a Doge. The Doge and his senators would run the state according to the principles laid down in Herzl's Diary, and these would be kept secret. "When this book is published, the prescriptions for the organization of the government will be omitted. The people must be guided to the good according to principles unknown to them."[30] If Herzl were no longer living at the time, the editors were commanded to extract the administrative maxims and keep them in the Secret State Archives, where they would only be accessible to the government. The first Doge would be a Rothschild, provided, of course, the Rothschilds were won over.[31] Then, on his way to the Paris Grand Prix, on Sunday, June 9, Herzl had the thought that a later Doge might be his own son, Hans. In the temple thronged with the country's leaders he saw himself addressing the young man as "Your Highness! My beloved Son!" Tears stood in his eyes, Herzl assures us, as he surveyed in detailed imagination the future scene. Herzl cuirassiers led an impressive procession of artillery and foot soldiers from the Doge's palace. His wife and daughter play no role in his daydream.[32] But it indicates the role Herzl foresaw, at least intermittently, for himself. He would be Chancellor. A more accurate term for his function would have been the Latin *gestor*, but this was

† Herzl's nearly four years in Paris had left him with the highest respect for French culture but very little respect for the parliamentary system. The chapters of *Das Palais Bourbon* form a brilliant and public statement of his political attitudes at the time he was writing his Diary. "The people is and remains unable to conduct its business which is by magnitude and extent beyond its grasp." Yet the parliamentarian who conducts its business for it wears a mask. "It grows out of his natural face. At first he is sincere." The people themselves oversimplify issues: "if a great nation had the misfortune to possess the referendum, then in spite of all apostles of peace, it would be continually faced with war, on a Yes or No." The lingering disease of the French Republic seemed to him its failure to make a distinction between the principle of government and the form of the state. There were two principles of government: aristocratic and democratic. Whichever you chose, your state form must be the opposite. If the principle was aristocratic, the state must be democratic—in other words, a republic. If the principle was democratic, the state must be aristocratic—a monarchy. "The principle of government and the form of the State must moderate one another." These reflections were inspired by the parliamentary debates of July 1895.

rejected lest its English translation, "manager," might sound too commercial in Great Britain.[33]

The approval of the British Empire would be vital for the state. Some Anglo-Saxon customs would be copied. "I shall steer the *jeunesse dorée* toward English sports and in this way prepare them for the army."[34] Cricket as well as tennis would be played.

One influence striking by its absence is that of Judaism. Jewish clergy and places of worship, such as the temple, appear only as do Christian symbols and personnel in Wagnerian opera. "The High Priests will wear impressive robes" (these are not described in detail); "our cuirassiers, yellow trousers and white tunics; the officers, silver breast-plates."[35] For Judaism is simply part of the required imponderable and, like the Protestantism Wagner linked to German nationalism, it must somehow be made impressive, even at the cost of distorting its nature. Herzl thinks to import the Wonder Rabbi of Sadgora (a Hasid from Bukovina known for his piety and miracles) and install him "as something like the bishop of a province. In fact, win over the entire clergy."[36] Herzl was no more an orthodox Jew after his conversion (or for that matter a Jew of any recognized denomination) than Wagner was ever an orthodox Christian. Later the same summer he was to define his conception of God as being Spinozistic and having some resemblance to the natural philosophy of the monists. "I can conceive of an omnipresent will, for I see it at work in the physical world. I see it as I can see the functioning of a muscle. The world is the body and God is the functioning of it."[37] Everything which existed, including anti-Semitism, contained the divine Will to Good. A faith so vaguely defined is remote from the transcendent monotheism rooted in the revelation of Sinai—which Spinoza had been excommunicated for denying.

The second major question—which territory Herzl would manage, through which landscape his soldiers would gallop—preoccupied him comparatively little in the early summer of 1895. The abstract notion of a state preceded by some distance the concrete question of where to build it. The two regions he considered were very different. One was Palestine, the land in part of which Jews had maintained independent states from around 1000 to 586 B.C. Although he had yet to read J. L. Pinsker's *Auto-Emancipation*, a work suggesting much of his own program, he knew of the Lovers of Zion, an organization of Eastern European Jews headed by Pinsker until his death in 1891. Deeper within the creative well were memories of Rabbi Alkalai, his grandfather's hero and the preacher of a peaceful settlement of Jews in Palestine. "In Palestine's favor," Herzl now wrote, "is the mighty legend." But at the same time he listed three weighty objections. It was too close to the Russia and Europe that had corrupted the Jews. It was too small to allow for expansion. Jews were no longer accustomed to its climate.[38] Two references within two days—on June 11 and 12—show that at the moment of greatest pressure his imagination was turned toward Latin America, a continent decently remote from "militarized and seedy Europe."[39] If the Jews crossed the Atlantic, their state would not come to the attention of Europe for a considerable time.

"In South America we could at first live according to the laws, extradition treaties, etc., of the receiving state (vis-à-vis Europe)."

"Our defensive troops will always comprise ten percent of the male emigrants. In this way we shall get an army together unobserved, but will for a long time proceed cautiously, exploiting the enmities of the Republics and preserving their friendship through presents, bribes, loans, etc." In this first entry Herzl foresees the infiltration, then the conquest, of some unnamed territory south of Mexico. By the following day his emphasis had altered. "Those South American republics must be obtainable for money. We can give them annual subsidies. But only for about twenty years, i.e., until we are strong enough to protect ourselves; otherwise this would become a tribute which would be incompatible with our future dignity and the stoppage of which could lead to war." Even in this hesitant picture of transatlantic settlement, Herzl linked the state's dignity with a military preponderance akin to that of Germany in Europe. "The duration of these subsidies should be determined by the length of time indicated by our military head as sufficient for us to become *a match for all these republics together*." This need (the present author's emphasis) would have led the state into collision with the Monroe Doctrine, one probable reason why migration to South America was not explored further. But another entry makes clear how seriously Herzl for a while considered it. "If we move into a region where there are wild animals to which the Jews are not accustomed—big snakes, etc.,— I shall use the natives, prior to giving them employment in the transit countries, for the extermination of these animals. High premiums for snake skins, etc., as well as their spawn."[40] This entry clearly refers to somewhere more jungly than the Holy Land. Palestine, while harboring snakes, some venomous, boasted no wilder animals than the fox, jackal or hyena. By this date the wolf was rare.

When Herzl came to consider the third, and last, question—how to secure his territory—his mentors were British. Although his Diary was written in German, he used an English phrase, Society of Jews, or simply Society, for the body that would evolve into the state, and, another English phrase, Chartered Company, for the organism through which the Society would colonize. The last decade of the nineteenth century marked the high-water mark of European colonialism, and to every newspaper reader Great Britain was the colonial power par excellence. Just as all navies copied the British sailor suit, so Germany, Belgium and Italy proved their new status as nations by acquiring colonies in the British manner.‡ In May 1895 the new name Rhodesia had been officially bestowed on the latest British acquisitions: the rich region of southern Africa comprising Mashonaland and Matabeleland.

Two men—Jacob de Haas who knew him intimately, the German Kaiser who met him on three occasions—later linked Herzl's vision of how to obtain the territorial basis for a state with British actions in Africa. "The Jameson raid in the Transvaal," wrote the first, "had made a household word of chartered company, Herzl's favorite description of the medium of organized development."[41] Herzl informed the Kaiser that his plan was "to create a 'Jewish Chartered Company' for Palestine patterned after the 'British Chartered Company' for South Africa."[42]

The affinities—and differences—between the British empire-builder Cecil Rhodes and Herzl are of interest. Born six years before Herzl in a conventional Anglican parsonage, Rhodes had, at the age of seventeen, changed the direction of his life by taking a ship to Natal. While Herzl left Budapest at much the same age and became a writer, Rhodes became one of the century's great acquirers of wealth. He soon discarded Christianity for a roughhewn deism that saw human history as the struggle to produce a nobler type of humanity. Rhodes was the prophet of a complacent, victorious people. "Only one race, so it seemed to him, approached God's ideal type, his own Anglo-Saxon race; God's purpose then was to make the Anglo-Saxon race predominant, and the best way to help on God's work and fulfil His purpose in the world was to contribute to the predominance of the Anglo-Saxon race . . ."[43] Rhodes sought to expand an already swollen empire, not found one colony for one landless people. "In all that he did Rhodes was animated by a single and unchanging ambition—to found 'Homes, more Homes,' for the British race." Rhodes had more than a touch of megalomania. Asked by Dr.

‡ Between 1884 and 1885 Germany acquired South-West Africa, Togoland, Kamerun, New Guinea and Tanganyika. Leopold II of Belgium gained a million square miles of Congo in 1885. The same year Italy seized Eritrea, to be followed later by the acquisition of Somaliland. Between 1894–95 Japan was proving, by her first modern war against China, her right to rank as a modern state and therefore have colonies.

Jameson (author of the raid that precipitated the Boer War) how long he expected to be remembered, he paused for a moment, then answered without bravado, "I give myself four thousand years." Just as Herzl stood apart from the people he elected to lead (but with whom he was never entirely at ease), so Rhodes, a confirmed misogynist, was emotionally distant from the robber barons and pioneers he inspired. Some of his followers composed hagiography similar to that produced by the biographers of Herzl. "Today, sitting around the fires in the native kraals," one wrote as late as 1943, "the old men tell the younger (who in turn will pass it on to their sons) the true story—more wonderful than legend—of 'Lamula M'Kunzi' (Separator of the Fighting Bulls); the great white man who was their friend who brought about the lasting peace between the white men and the black—'Our Father and our Mother who never failed us.'"

The great achievement of Rhodes was to separate the Mashonas and the Matabeles from control over their land. How this was done Herzl had studied. The land to the north of Bechuanaland was ruled by Lobengula, king of the warlike Matabeles. In 1871 he had given the explorer Thomas Baines, along with another Englishman, Sir John Swinburne, a concession to explore his country's mineral wealth. Baines and Swinburne never took up their concession. The virgin territory, occupied only by Africans, was coveted by Boers from South Africa and Portuguese from Mozambique. To forestall them the British resident in Bulawayo had induced his friend, the king, to sign, in 1888, an agreement that he would look to no power but Britain, represented by her High Commissioner in Capetown, for support and assistance. Immediately thereafter Rhodes sent Alfred Beit and C. D. Rudd to persuade Lobengula to grant them a monopoly of the exploitation of the metals and minerals to be found in his kingdom. The Europeans offered in return 1,000 Martini-Henry rifles, 100,000 rounds of ammunition and a monthly subvention of £100. Having secured the new concession, Rhodes bought out the previous shareholders for £10,046. He then united all his interests in one giant South Africa Company with a share capital of one million sterling.

In deciding to exploit and colonize Lobengula's country through a chartered company Rhodes was using a formula based on recent British practice in North Borneo and the Niger valley. He had as enemies British liberals who feared that his schemes might lead, as they did, to the virtual dispossession of the natives. Rhodes skillfully used the press (in the person of W. T. Stead in particular) and a political group (the Irish Party in the British Parliament, for whose goal of Home Rule he expressed sympathy) to legalize his venture. In October 1889 Queen Victoria granted a Royal Charter of Incorporation to the British South Africa Company. The charter's geographical terms were deliberately vague, no northern limit being set to the company's sphere of operation. It was furnished with a sword and a veil of morality. An authorized armed police became the nucleus of a private army. A pledge to respect native civil law (subject to any British legislation that might be introduced) and to maintain freedom of trade and religion was linked with the expectation that in due course the blacks would be rescued from slavery and alcohol. The company's Board linked nobility (in the persons of the dukes of Fife and Abercorn) with astuteness (in the persons of Rhodes and Beit).

The charter went far beyond Lobengula's concession. It conferred on a commercial company rights hardly to be distinguished from sovereignty. It placed that company in a colonial situation in which it would almost certainly have to use the "police force" it had been allowed; it ensured that sovereignty would then devolve on the "race" supplying the soldiers.

The formula had worked. Having obtained his legal rights, Rhodes quickly arranged for British soldiers to be sent north from the Cape. After dealing with feeble incursions by Boers and Portuguese, they confronted the main and predictable threat—the natives. These were dismayed at the prospect of having their land divided up into farms for foreign settlers. With fruitless courage the Matabeles made a desperate attempt to evict the invaders. They were inevitably crushed, "machine guns," one account telling us, "being used with terrible effect upon the enemy."[44] The country was then thrown open to white settlers. The best land was later set aside for their permanent exploitation.

Herzl's stencil for obtaining a territory and then clearing it for settlement was cut after the Rhodesian model. Rhodes had backed his vision with a financial company drawing on the new wealth of Kimberley diamonds and Johannesburg gold. Herzl saw as his first priority the recruitment of de Hirsch, and then the Rothschilds. Rhodes had to convince his Imperial sponsor that his new colony would be to its advantage, and hence his efforts in the British press and Parliament. Herzl (once he found a sponsor) would have to convince it that a Zionist state would buttress its interests. Rhodes had at first pretended to befriend a local potentate, and then had crushed him. Herzl strove to use the more potent Sultan (once the choice had settled on Palestine) in the same manner as Rhodes used Lobengula.

One problem—that of the native population—presented itself in a more urgent form to Herzl than to Rhodes. Because the British already had many "Homes," settlement in Rhodesia would be limited and over a protracted period. Herzl envisaged millions of Jews arriving "on the other side" all at once. He had already complained that Palestine was not very large; he knew that it was already inhabited by a substantial population. Herzl confronted this problem with a resolution his followers have tried to conceal, preferring to portray their leader as naïve rather than informed or ruthless. A later Zionist slogan—"A land without a people for a people without a land!" —fits a mythology that banishes "Arab," or "Palestinian," from the indexes of most biographers. Like any other journalist Herzl depended on works of reference. His Paris office almost certainly contained Meyers Konversations-Lexikon or Baedeker's Palästina und Syrien. The most recent edition of each* gave the same figure, 650,000, as the population of Palestine, the great majority of which was Syrian, or Arab, while Greeks, Turks, Jews and Europeans were present in smaller numbers.

Herzl devoted twenty pages of his Diary, dated June 12, to reflections on the problem. He approached it with the assumption that the natives could be basically divided into the many poor and the landowning few. In regard to the former—tenant farmers or laborers—he foresaw the need for drastic expropriation without compensation. While insisting that "both the process of expropriation and the removal of the poor must be carried out discreetly and circumspectly,"[45] he is vague as to whether economic or physical force is to be used; he simply states that "we shall try to spirit the penniless population across the border by procuring employment for it in the transit countries, while denying it any employment in our own country."† He does not specify "the transit countries" in which the uprooted natives are to be given jobs. There are no transit countries, only an ocean, between Western Europe (where Herzl envisages the Jewish migration as starting) and the coast of Latin America. It is hard to see how the natives, having cleared the snakes from the land, could

---

* Meyers Konversations-Lexikon, 4th edition, vol. 12, 1888, p. 621; Baedeker's Palästina und Syrien, Leipzig, 1880, p. lxxxii.

† The original German is yet starker: *Die arme Bevölkerung trachten wir unbemerkt über die Grenze zu schaffen, indem wir ihr in den Durchzugsländern Arbeit verschaffen, aber in unserem eigenen Lande jederlei Arbeit verweigern.*

Die besitzende Bevölkerung wird zu uns übergehen. Das Expropriationswerk muss ebenso wie die Fortschaffung der Armen mit Zartheit und Behutsamkeit erfolgen. Theodor Herzl, *Tagebücher*, vol. 1, Berlin, 1922, p. 98.

then be smuggled into Holland. It is no easier in regard to Palestine, since Herzl's daydream plainly envisages the settlers arriving off Jaffa by ship, and not overland through Turkey and Syria. (They will dress for dinner on board ship, a later entry states.[46]) All that is clear is that most of the natives will have to leave.

For the property owners the expropriation will be voluntary. They will be encouraged to think that they are cheating the Jews, selling them things for more than they are worth.[47] But just as they will not be able to buy back what they have once sold, so the price they get will be kept down by a ruse. An army of local subagents "who must not know that their employer is himself a secret agent who takes instruction from the centralized 'Commission for Property Purchases'" will arrange a multitude of separate deals. "These secret purchases must be carried out *simultaneously* [Herzl's emphasis] as upon the pressing of an electric button. Our secret agents, who will appear over there as purchasers on their own account, will receive the signal: *Marchez!*"[48] The sales must be accomplished inside a week—otherwise prices would soar. Estate owners, too attached to their land or too old, will be offered "a complete transplantation—to any place they wish, like our own people. This offer will be made only when all others have been rejected. If this offer is not accepted either, no harm will be done. Such close attachment to the soil is found only with small properties. Big ones are to be had for a price."[49]

Herzl was no sentimentalist and admitted no supernatural restraints. He probably knew of his friend Nordau's remedy (formulated before Herzl converted him to Zionism) for "the problem of workers displaced by modern technology." It was a remedy typical of its age. "Displaced workers must settle on the soil, and if Europe lacked the space they must emigrate overseas. The emigrants would then take the place of the 'lower races' who were not surviving in the struggle of evolution."[50] Herzl seems to have foreseen that in going further than any colonialist had so far gone in Africa, he would, temporarily, alienate civilized opinion. "At first, incidentally," he writes on the pages describing "involuntary expropriation," "people will avoid us. We are in bad odor. By the time the reshaping of world opinion in our favor has been completed, we shall be firmly established in our country, no longer fearing the influx of foreigners, and receiving our visitors with aristocratic benevolence and proud amiability."[51]

This was not a prospect to charm a peon in Argentina or a fellah in Palestine. But Herzl did not intend his Diary for immediate publication.

CHAPTER 19

Herzl's period of mental ferment had coincided with the start of the French summer. His family had gone ahead to Vienna; friends had left on their vacations; only the parliamentarians, whose antics he had to describe for the *Neue Freie Presse,* maintained the activity of winter. The solitude possible in crowds fostered thought. His voluminous correspondence dwindled. He wrote two letters to Teweles in Prague about his play, then, as his frenzy calmed, another to Schnitzler on June 23. *The New Ghetto,* he wrote, was still being considered in Prague; but *etwas anderes, Neues, viel Grosseres* (something different, new, much greater)[1] now besieged him. But except for mentioning his coming return to Austria at the end of July, he said no more. His life had altered. When he was not writing in his room, or stalking the public gardens within reach of the Rue Cambon, he ate and drank in unfashionable places, such as a little *brasserie* near the Châtelet. He wanted to avoid human contacts. Acquaintances might tread on his toes, unaware of the brighter world from which he came.

Yet even a visionary confides in others, if only to assure himself that he sees more than hallucinations. Having failed with Baron de Hirsch, Herzl communicated something of his ideas to two other fellow Jews, one by post, the second in person.

Dr. Moritz Güdemann, now sole Chief Rabbi of Vienna, was also a respected writer on Jewish educational themes. In accord with his stated intention of winning the clergy, and because Güdemann could prove a useful emissary, Herzl wrote him three letters, on the June 11, 16, and 17.[2] In the first he boldly announced that he had decided to take the lead in an action on behalf of the Jews. If Güdemann would like to help, let him prepare a report on the present situation, moral and political, of the Jews in all Europe east of the Rhine, with particular emphasis on the effects of anti-Semitism. Herzl warned Güdemann that he also needed the help of a secular Jew and had in mind Salo Cohn, a friend of the rabbi's and a wealthy patron of Jewish writers. If Güdemann agreed, he should bring his completed report to Caux, near Lake Geneva, in seven days' time.

Herzl had chosen Caux with deliberation. The exalted scenery would lift his two associates "out of their everyday, narrow, restricted concepts." A literary parallel excited Herzl. Here Rousseau had discovered the social contract.

Güdemann replied by telegram. He could not manage the trip; nor could Salo, then absent at the North Cape.[3] The letter that followed two days later showed that the rabbi, who knew Herzl only as the writer who had married Julie Naschauer, had been astonished by his sudden interest in the Jewish cause. In his reply, Herzl admitted that he was not a practicing Jew; nevertheless, the problem of anti-Semitism had smoldered in his mind at least since the day he had read Dühring. He wanted Güdemann to play the role of envoy to the Rothschilds, not because he was dependent on them any more than on any other rich Jews, but because his plan, which he could not possibly summarize in a letter, required them to be informed, as Güdemann would in due course understand. The rabbi's duty would be to read Herzl's *Address to the Family Council* to Albert Rothschild, head of the Austrian branch of the dynasty, at his country estate of Gaming-Waldhofen outside Vienna. Herzl concluded the letter by greeting the rabbi "in trusting admiration as my first associate." The moment he had posted this letter doubts assailed him. He must write again. As he pictured the rabbi walking in the Austrian meadows, at their freshest in early summer, he recognized that one sentence in his letter of the previous evening—"I have the solution of the Jewish Question"—might seem presumptuous to the sixty-year-old and experienced rabbi. To prove that he was not insane Herzl inserted a few multiplication sums. No sooner had this letter sped on its punctual way (nineteenth-century posts were often quicker without planes than twentieth-century posts with them) than he pursued it with a telegram asking the rabbi not to open this postscript of a letter. As explanation he told a white lie: ONE OF FRIENDS INVOLVED WHOSE CONSENT HAD LIKEWISE BEEN PRESUPPOSED RAISES ABSOLUTE OBJECTIONS. MUST COMPLY. The real reason was rather different. It involved his second confidant.

Throughout his period of frenzy the only human being with whom he had been in personal contact was Friedrich Schiff, Paris correspondent of the Wolff Telegraphic Agency and a man whose loyalty made Herzl include him in his daydream as a future secretary. He also represented to Herzl the poor Jew as against de Hirsch, the rich one. Schiff had discerned with increasing alarm the signs of what he took to be megalomania in his friend, whose solitary life in the Rue Cambon, secretive meals and deliberate avoidance of old haunts could signify the early stages of a nervous breakdown. At first Schiff teased him. Herzl looked, he said, as if he had invented a dirigible airship, a project much under discussion at the time. Then (the day of his third letter to Güdemann) Schiff brought him to cold earth by remarking that Herzl's idea was not new: it had been tried in the previous century by Sabbatai Zevi. Schiff (and the Herzl who reports him) had his facts right but his dates wrong. Sabbatai Zevi had led his lemming-like followers toward Palestine in the seventeenth, not the eighteenth century. But Schiff and Herzl both remembered the false Messiah as an ominous warning. Jewish tradition had always linked the return to the Holy Land with the Messianic Age. To attempt a return by force was condemned by the Talmud.[4] Remembering his recent meditations Herzl suddenly saw that, like Zevi in the Jewish tradition (or according to some interpretations like Judas Iscariot in the Christian), he had been trying to accelerate the divine intention. Herzl now lapsed, not into the mystic's dark night of the soul, but the waking man's relief from nightmare. Schiff had saved him from making himself "either ridiculous or tragic."[5] He was prepared to be tragic—but not ridiculous. He took up his pen to rush off a new letter to Baron de Hirsch.[6] His first line stated bluntly: "I have given the matter up." Vividly, and for once with humor, he described how he had expounded his whole scheme to a sensible friend who was not a financier. (This to reassure de Hirsch that he was not frequenting rich men only.) His friend had been convinced to the point of tears: only the tears were those of pity, the conviction that Herzl was insane. Herzl himself still thought his idea sound. But the Jews were not ready for the Promised Land. "Still, I know where that land lies; within ourselves! In our capital, in our labor, and in the peculiar combination of the two which I have devised. But we shall have to sink still lower, we shall have to be even more insulted, spat upon, mocked, whipped, plundered, and slain before we are ripe for this idea."[7] Herzl would still value his idea, despite the smiles of outsiders, but would do nothing further to put it into practice. "Maybe this goes to show that I too am only a demoralized Jew. A Gentile would go through thick and thin for an idea of such power." But the dread of being laughed at, of looking like a Don Quixote sufficed to give him pause.

For that one evening.

The following morning, June 19, 1895, Schiff again called, this time about some bills that needed checking. Herzl found that he could do simple arithmetic more swiftly and accurately than the shaken Schiff. He was suddenly reconvinced. That same day he took the first symbolic step in nine years of missionary endeavor. Schiff had unknowingly shown him its direction, both by his disbelief and by his casual reference to Rabbi Güdemann as "insufficient."[8] Herzl decided to approach neither a millionaire nor a rabbi, but a childhood hero. Prince Otto von Bismarck, the former Chancellor and creator of the Second Reich, was now living in retirement, his angry brow wreathed with laurels. He was eighty years of age. If the gentile whom Herzl praised as "the greatest living empire builder"[9] sponsored his dream, the millionaires and rabbis would surely follow.

PART FIVE

The
Missionary Playwright
1895–99

Come to think of it, in all this I am still the dramatist. I picked poor people in rags off the streets, put gorgeous costumes on them, and have them perform for the world a wonderful pageant of my composition.[1]

CHAPTER 20

When Bismarck failed to answer Herzl's letter of June 19, 1895, disappointment no more stopped his spate than a weed-bound boulder obstructs a millrace. Nightweeds, daydreams. As the mania of summer cooled, as conversion solidified into a program, he acknowledged that Bismarck was a glorious and embittered has-been; the young Kaiser who had discarded him held the future. The approach to Bismarck led to nothing.* But the old man, to be dead within three years, was the first of a sequence of gentile figures he was to approach, Herzl's equivalents of the scattered eastern cities Paul had visited between his conversion and his martyrdom. It established a strategy that distinguished him from previous Zionists and irked some of his successors.†

To the biographer of Herzl there is a temptation, from 1895 onward, to merge him in the history of a political movement. This would drain his personality of its distinctive hues; he would wear a uniform, with other like-minded figures.

It would be equally absurd to contemplate Herzl in romantic isolation. His conversion would have had little significance if he had not strolled, with somnambulistic insight, onto a crowded stage. The conversion itself might not have lasted.

For conversions usually hide a thread of Ariadne, the possibility of retreat. Herzl's was no exception. Between June 17 and 19, 1895, he had all but abandoned any intention of political action. After Friedrich Schiff questioned his sanity, he had written to Baron de

----

* Bismarck later adverted to Herzl's vision as "melancholy fantasy."[2]
† For Chaim Weizmann's objections see his autobiography, *Trial and Error*, p. 45 and *passim*.

Hirsch that the Jews were not ready for Zionism and he had given the matter up.[3]

Herzl finally adhered to his interpretation of the Zionist idea because, despite all temptations to withdraw, it appeased emotional and intellectual needs in his psyche. The force of these needs, more than love for the Jews as such, held him to it. In finding personal fulfillment in a nationalist cause Herzl was in the tradition of other nineteenth-century nationalists, not least the leaders of the Italian Risorgimento. His discovery of the new part he intended to play implied a rejection of previous, unsatisfactory roles. His previous life had been marked by a series of misdirections. He had decided to be an engineer because he admired de Lesseps; he had joined a right-wing dueling club because he admired the manners of well-born youth; he had read law but practiced it only for a year; he had worked and won fame as essayist and playwright. Yet his false starts had all reflected something of the authentic Herzl and all would contribute something to the new leader. The movement he led, with its concentration on secession from Europe and state building, solved several vital problems. It raised others that would haunt his deathbed.

Herzl's last nine years were spent in motion, so that he seems an accelerated, railway-age version of the mythological wanderer. His restless missionary actions reimposed, or repermitted, a way of life that had previously liberated his creative spirit. In the movement of trains or the ships of the Lloyd-Triestino line he found the brief power to create again. Ideas surged as he traveled. On the train from Paris to Frankfurt he was to conceive the plot of a novel; a voyage to Egypt was to inspire a memorable essay. His new role made it, of course, unthinkable that he should cease to be the apparent husband of Julie; together they had to maintain the public fiction of concord. But at the same time his new role gave him excuses to leave home far more often than when the family had lived together in Paris. The kingly ability to move when he wished took some of the strain off sharing a house with Julie; she for her part had numerous friends and relations in Vienna with whom she could express her irritation at Theodor's absurd preoccupations. First in an apartment at 16 Pelikangasse in the ninth district, then from 1898 in a large suburban house surrounded by a wooded garden, it was easier to create the illusion of normal domestic life. Frustrated in her marriage, Julie expressed her emotions through her children, whose education at the hands of governess and tutors she supervised. The new situation satisfied her mother-in-law. Herzl's position as Jewish leader was more immediate in Vienna than his distant eminence in Paris. "She visualised him as 'king of the Jews' and saw herself as 'Queen Mother.'" So the Israeli psychiatrist Arthur Stern, in a fascinating study of Herzl's immediate family, and of how his attitude to his children was affected by his new position. Jeanette was her son's ally in insisting that the children be educated "like princes" and meet as few outsiders as possible. Herzl had a horror of infection and used this as pretext to isolate Pauline, Hans and Trude from other children. An observer heard one child ask another in the nursery: "Shall we have to go to school when Papa is king?" A visit to the Herzl home was considered a visit "at court," in Zionist circles.[4] This custom increased the children's dislike for their grandmother and their attachment to Julie.

Herzl's continence in marriage released almost superhuman reserves of energy. His output of words, in his Diary, in ephemeral journalism, in letters (over five thousand are preserved in Jerusalem), was exhausting but prodigious. Without the disgrace and financial loss of a divorce he had regained the liberty he had savored at Trouville, or in the Pyrenees before the fatal cable took him to Paris and the wearing of galoshes.

Yet it was no longer the gnawing, solitary creativity of the Spanish essays. It was the loneliness of the floodlit leader. Public applause could intoxicate a man who had preferred the theater to the press for its public quality. His Diary preserves compliments and plaudits as carefully as an actor's scrapbook. Two instances—since one easily surfeits on such fare—may suffice. A year after his conversion—in June 1896—he was to visit Bulgaria twice, first on his way to Constantinople and then on his return. On the first occasion: "I was hailed in extravagant terms as Leader, as the Heart of Israel."[5] On the second, making a politic visit to the Sofia synagogue: "I stood on the altar platform.‡ When I was not quite sure how to face the congregation without turning my back to the Holy of Holies, someone cried"—Herzl does not specify the language—"'It's all right for you to turn your back to the Ark, you are holier than the Torah.' Several wanted to kiss my hand."[6]

His new role gave the frustrated playwright an outlet for his talents. "Herzl, who failed in the theater, turned politics into theater. He became the director, stage manager, and reserved for himself the leading role. The play was the poignant salvation of a people, the plot was one man's vision and sacrifice, which would overcome all odds, the supporting cast was the rulers of the world's nations, and the backdrop was the grim tale of anti-Semitism and racial persecution in European history."[7]

‡ There is no altar in the synagogue; Herzl is using a term derived from churches.

If priority is given to emotional factors—appropriately highlighted in the above quotation from a psychoanalyst—it is because they come first, both in the development of the human being and in the development of Herzl's vision, where wild jottings precede the ordered *Address to the Rothschilds,* which itself precedes the writing of a more ordered statement. But Zionism appealed to Herzl's mind as well as to his emotions; it solved intellectual problems for him too. These concerned Judaism, both in its application to himself and as a sociological enigma of the modern world.

Herzl would never have embraced the Jewish religion from conviction. Involuntarily he had been born into the oldest minority in Europe and throughout his career this ancestral connection had warred with the voluntary choices of his mind. While his grandfather had blown the shofar horn and led the Kol Nidre prayers, his father's practices had grown more tepid as the family moved ever further from its frontier roots. Between his Budapest boyhood and 1894 he had not attended synagogue. Yet every time he bathed he was reminded that he was a Jew in the flesh; his grandfather had managed to attend his bar mitzvah, even if Herzl's Hebrew had been minimal and his "Confirmation's" main function had been the afternoon party at his parents' home. A new weakening of the tradition was evident in the generation of his children. Herzl and Julie, who disagreed on much, had agreed that Hans should not be circumcised. Herzl ate the non-kosher food Julie ordered for her kitchen and made no insistence that she should observe the ritual laws when Jewish guests were invited to meals. Thus Herzl was faced with the dilemma of being, in his own eyes, a freethinking European, but in the eyes of Europe, a Jew. He did not accept the traditional teaching that the Jews were a nation of priests set apart for the service of Torah; ancient Israel influenced his vision of a state for the Jews less than Hellas, Austria or England. His vision showed, not hostility to Judaism, but indifference or ignorance. "All will bare their heads," he writes, when picturing the arrival of the Jews in their new country. "Let us salute our flag!"[8] Thus casually he shows his remoteness from Jewish practice wherein the head is covered, not bared, on solemn occasions.* The thesis that the Jews formed, not a religious group, but a nation—the dominant social concept of the age—solved the problem of his relationship to the Jewish tradition as it had solved the problem of Moses Hess, who had discarded God and married a German whore. The Law of Moses could be dismissed much as an

---

* The strictly orthodox cover their heads at all times; other Jews cover their heads when entering a synagogue.

Englishman could dismiss trial by ordeal. Blowing the shofar horn could form, like Maypole dancing, a part of folklore. Circumcision could be maintained as a measure of hygiene, or discarded, as Englishmen had discarded the use of a bluish body dye known as woad.

But Herzl had a mind as tidy as his father's desk. The survival of the Jews into the nineteenth century had nagged Herzl's mind, as a problem, since his days as a law student. He saw its complexity. *The New Ghetto,* his novel and his Diary all show that he shared the stereotyped picture of Jews common in the society he frequented.† But unlike the racialists he was an optimist. He believed in the possibility of change. "For the learned, humiliated, sensitive Jew of the ghetto, he would substitute the rigorous, heroic, healthy farmer in his own land."[9] His vision of the world remained bifocal, one lens turned on the ghetto he wished to see abandoned, the other on the Europe whose values he wanted, even for the Jews. He constantly stressed the double use of Zionism. "Prayers will be offered up in the temples for the success of the project. And in the churches as well!"[10]

The Diary subtitled "of the Jewish Cause" and which lets us follow the development of Herzl's conversion until its final consolidation in action has, in the year 1895, three significant lacunae. The first covers the month between August 21 and September 20. It follows an important event, his reading of the *Address to the Rothschilds* to Rabbi Moritz Güdemann (whom we already know) and Dr. Heinrich Meyer-Cohn, banker, philanthropist and Lover of Zion.

Herzl had arrived by appointment in Munich on Saturday, August 17, 1895, where he ran into Güdemann in the hotel lobby. They joined Meyer-Cohn. Herzl immediately sensed that he was the wrong man: "a little Berlin Jew by his appearance" with trivial concerns.[11] Herzl then went to the synagogue, timing his arrival for the conclusion of the services. Herzl let the rabbi do the talking as he showed him round the beautiful temple. The three men then moved to luncheon in a private room at Jochsberger's kosher restaurant. Herzl warmed up, pleased to discover that Meyer-Cohn approved of the idea of Zion, relieved when the rabbi did not expostulate as Herzl expounded his Spinozistic conception of God and his belief that the purpose of humanity was to become as gods, knowing good and evil. After the meal Herzl began a reading of the *Address,* which lasted, with an unfortunate interruption at four, when Meyer-Cohn had a business appointment, until evening, when the session resumed in

† Dr. Charlotte Lea Klein has shown that similar stereotypes were found in English literature between the 1870s and 1933. (*Patterns of Prejudice,* vol. 5, no. 2, London, Institute of Jewish Affairs, 1971.)

Herzl's bedroom, he sitting on the bed, the others on the only two chairs. While Meyer-Cohn carped like a member of parliament at many details, the rabbi, who was known as an anti-Zionist, seemed carried away by Herzl's ideas. As they left for supper Güdemann exclaimed: "You remind me of Moses!"

Herzl tells us he laughingly rejected the thought. "Now as before I consider the whole thing to be a simple idea, a skillful and rational combination, which, to be sure, operates with large masses."

But Güdemann, even in his moment of fervor, recognized that Herzl convinced him as an artist, not as a theologian. He felt as dazed, he said, as someone who, expecting to hear important news, found, instead, two huge beautiful steeds.

At supper, again at Jochsberger's, all three agreed that the *Address* must not reach the audience it was intended for, "the Rothschilds, who are mean, despicable egotists." Instead, it should be given to the people, in the form of a novel. All three parted in exalted spirits.[12]

The vacant month contained "a great number of little things" which Herzl in part recorded in a long entry dated September 20. Güdemann waxed now hot, now cold, while his own newspaper was uniformly icy. On the positive side, he learned that Chief Rabbi Zadoc Kahn of Paris was an ardent Zionist, as was in England "Colonel Goldsmith"—Colonel Albert Edward Williamson Goldsmid—to the extent that he had wanted to charter vessels for the conquest of Palestine.[13] A landslide victory for the local anti-Semites took place in the Vienna City Council elections. "Toward evening I went to the Landstrasse district. In front of the polling place a silent, tense crowd. Suddenly Dr. Lueger came out to the square. Enthusiastic cheers; women waved back white kerchiefs from the windows. The police held the crowd back. A man next to me said with tender warmth but in a quiet tone of voice. 'That is our *Fuehrer!*'" More than declamations[14] and abuse these words convinced Herzl that anti-Semitism was deeply rooted in the hearts of the people.

The second gap in the Diary occurs between September 21 and October 15. Two opposed events made this a period of temptation. The *Neue Freie Presse*, on which he depended for his bread, refused point-blank to allow itself to be made a Zionist organ; except for one brief item, the newspaper was to publish nothing about Herzl as Zionist until his death. At the same time the Austrian government made him a flattering and surprising offer. In September 1895 Count Felix Badeni, a Pole and successful former governor of Galicia (a province with a Polish majority), had become Prime Minister. His mission was a renewed attempt to solve the main problem of the Habsburg empire: the harmonization of its nationalities. Trouble now centered on the Czechs. Badeni's efforts to appease them were assailed by the German nationalists, who decried any move toward the use of minority languages as a betrayal of a German empire. Between the empty dates in Herzl's Diary, Dr. Kozmian, the Prime Minister's friend and right-hand man, offered Herzl the editorship of the *Presse*, a daily paper older than the *Neue Freie Presse*, but long in the doldrums. Herzl records in great detail his gratifying reception by the Prime Minister of the empire and his own blunt speech. (The two men spoke in French.) Herzl stressed that he supported Badeni's policies from conviction, not as a lackey. "To my expressed desire that I be allowed to call on him at any time, *comme un ambassadeur*, he said, 'Non seulement je le permets, mais j'y tiens.'‡ We also talked about the conditions under which I would sever my connections with the *Neue Freie Presse*. I made it clear from the start that I always wanted to remember my old friends and would not carry on any injurious polemics against them—unless I was attacked first."[15]

Herzl refused the offer, but not because he sensed that Badeni, in his fight against German nationalism, might come to terms with Lueger. Indeed, when Badeni expressed his disdain for Lueger, Herzl boldly answered: "I believe Lueger's election as mayor must be validated. If you fail to do it the first time, you can never confirm him again, and if you fail to confirm him the third time, the Dragoons will ride."[16]

Herzl's refusal was tentative enough for the offer to be repeated a year later. By September 1896 Badeni was to have hardened his position into downright enmity to the liberal policies of the *Neue Freie Presse;* he now wanted a newspaper that would explicitly attack them. "The paper," Herzl summed up, "is to be liberal-conservative-anti-Semitic—in short an impossibility,—but swipe-ographically [he used the pun *diebographisch* instead of *typographisch*] produced exactly like the *N.Fr.Pr.*"[17]

The discussion with Kozmian and Badeni—or in view of Herzl's salaried position on the *Neue Freie Presse* the intrigue—is an unclarified mystery. What were Badeni's motives in approaching Herzl? What were Herzl's motives in at least considering the approach?

Badeni saw in Herzl not so much the journalist as the Jew. Former foreign correspondents were not rare in Vienna; as short-lived *feuilleton* editor of the *Allgemeine Wiener Zeitung* Herzl had not been outstandingly successful. Yet as a Jew who proclaimed that the Jews were a danger to European society and should be encouraged to

‡ Not only do I permit it—I insist on it."

migrate (which was probably all that Badeni then understood of Herzl's views) Herzl could be useful to a regime of compromise. Most Viennese Jews were staunch liberals; some were socialists. Badeni's efforts depended on balancing as many allies as possible against the Germans. To have Lueger and Herzl on his side might help outwit them.

Herzl's motives were more complex. Alex Bein's view that Herzl was attracted to Badeni "by his personal qualities as well as by his political outlook" may be right.[18] But at the time Herzl was attracted by anyone in power, since he needed any kind of status to convince his doubting Jews. His Diary entry of November 6, 1895, after he turned down Badeni's first proposal, shows this: "A deeply discouraging day. Community Councillor Stern and others came to the office. They are all people who expect salvation to come from the government and who go on bended knee to the ministers. Therefore, they would have believed in me if I had become Badeni's journalistic right-hand man. And so now I have no authority with them." Yet close collusion with Badeni probably would have finished Herzl as a Zionist. He was encouraged the same evening when Professor Isidor Singer, a leading economist of the Vienna school, assured him he had done rightly to refuse. "If I had accepted a semi-official position I would have disgraced myself and the cause."[19]

The objections were prudential only. Morally and intellectually Herzl might have found it possible to edit a *Presse* in the government's interest. He could have supported Badeni against the German nationalists and liberals if this Austrian government encouraged Jewish nationalism as it was in effect encouraging the nationalism of Czechs and Poles. By conversing in French he and Badeni had hinted their ambiguous stance, as Jew and Pole, to the Habsburg regime. Even the anti-Semitism of Badeni's allies could be reconciled with Zionism on a pragmatic basis: Lueger wanted to get rid of the Jews while Herzl wanted to remove the Jews from Europe.

The third gap in Herzl's Diary lasts, except for some twenty lines divided between four brief entries, from November 29, 1895, until January 18, 1896. These weeks were devoted to the formalization, in a pamphlet, of the ideas that had swirled in his mind during the early summer and which had found their first draft in the *Address to the Rothschilds*. This pamphlet was to be his major political statement. It is therefore important to describe two events that immediately preceded it. One affected the intellectual climate inside which he wrote, the other provided the encouragement his inspiration desperately required.

CHAPTER 21

In its evening edition of October 24, 1895, Herzl's newspaper published the full text of a rectoral address by his former professor at Vienna University, Anton Menger. Its title—"On the Social Tasks of the Science of Law"—will have ensured that Herzl read it carefully.

As with many university events, the ceremony had had a stormy start. The captains of Austria and Norica, two Catholic student associations, made a protest demonstration, since Menger was known to be anti-religious in general and anti-Catholic in particular. Wearing full dress and carrying swords—though they did not belong to one of the dueling fraternities—they were evicted after an uproar.

The retiring rector, Dr. Laurenz Müllner, then made the opening speech. His message—that a university could no longer divorce itself from contemporary problems, that thought must be fertilized by life— did not sound platitudinous in a university of 1895. Menger thereupon delivered his closely argued address, packed with information as well as opinions. Since he and his brother were anathema in Germany, he began with the pointed remark that the *Outline of a Civil Law Book for the German Empire* published in 1888 had run true to form in showing no concern whatsoever for the protection of the weak.* This fault was shared by other legal systems, whose general tendency was to protect privilege and property.

The new rector then defined three tasks confronting a science of law: the determination of law as it stands—which is dogmatic; the ex-

---

* The *Outline* referred to had inspired Menger to write his own *Civil Law and the Destitute Classes*, 1888.

trication of its sources—which is historical; and the adaptation of law to changing circumstances—which produces a *social* science of law.

The first approach dominated those countries (like England) with a common law; the result was often an intolerable type of law allied to a magnificent science of law. The Germans, he implied, were dominated by the second, historical approach. This, too, was inadequate. "Law is not, like the historical course of political and cultural conditions, a concluded whole, belonging to the past; on the contrary, law pushes into the present, its chief function being in the realm of practical activity, through ordering human existence in a rational manner."

The dominance of the historical approach led to traditionalism and abject respect for authority just at the moment when such things as universal suffrage, universal military service, the industrial revolution and compulsory education were effecting a radical transformation of society. These vital developments found hardly a mention in legal systems. As a monument to futility Menger again cited the German *Outline:* it had taken fourteen years to elaborate but had accomplished nothing.

Menger then went on to argue that the jurist must take cognizance of other countries and their laws and of the changes taking place in his own society. The most important of such changes concerned the altered conditions of power in bourgeois society. "Every order of law is a great system of power-relationships." Classes establish their own interests as laws, which claim to be objective. If this process were carried too far, law would lose its basis and become rationalized self-interest. The jurist's duty was to balance law and power, to prevent disaster. Menger cited as example the rising working classes: they were no longer slaves and the law must be changed to take account of this new condition.

Menger was no Marxist. Despite the great importance of economic development, he argued that it was an error to regard economic circumstances as the sole creators of state, law and religion. Politics were as important as economics: a battle, just as much as some new mode of production, could decide an economic system. As an instance of what a jurist could achieve, Menger cited the way his critique of the *Outline* had provoked the Germans into improving the second edition. Austria had an advantage over its great German neighbor in possessing a more flexible, less hidebound legal system. In conclusion, he summoned his students to create, as twentieth-century pioneers, a society and state that would be good to live in for all classes of people.

Menger's plea, for modernity achieved by the state through due process of law, had important implications for Herzl at this juncture in his career. With the lecture in mind, with a letter of introduction to

Chief Rabbi Kahn from Rabbi Güdemann in his briefcase, he set off for Paris, the steppingstone to London, the city which as early as June he had envisaged as the Zionist headquarters.[1] Once again motion helped him to clarify his thoughts. On the train he removed the mixture of threats and promises, directed to the Rothschilds as a family, which had been the scaffolding of his *Address*. He retained the impersonal arguments that would have appealed to Menger. On November 16 he read this pruned version to Zadoc Kahn, whom he does not seem to have met during his days as a Paris correspondent. Office made Kahn, like many ecclesiastics, a trimmer; his reaction to Herzl's ideas balanced a professed belief in Zionism with protestations of being a patriotic Frenchman. "Zadoc Kahn is of the breed of *little* Jews," was Herzl's irritable conclusion.[2]

Though France at this time played no important role in Herzl's plans, Paris gave him his first important convert. Max Nordau had been one of the two men, besides Arthur Schnitzler, to whom Herzl had felt tempted to talk about *The New Ghetto;* but during the summer of 1895 he had been absent from Paris. Now he proved the second person to understand Herzl's vision. But unlike Moritz Benedikt of the *Neue Freie Presse*, who had been the first, he also accepted it. He at once became Herzl's closest adviser. As he knew England well, he was in a position to brief Herzl before his visit.[3]

Still the most powerful country in the world, Britain had been a seedbed for Zionism long before it completed Jewish emancipation in 1890. Byron's *Hebrew Melodies*, George Eliot's *Daniel Deronda* were the literary froth on an underswell of gentile Zionism whose motives ranged from the lunatic to the Machiavellian. Clergymen and peers dreamed that the return of the Jews to Palestine would be followed by their conversion to Protestantism and the Second Coming of Christ. Cold-eyed statesmen saw the advantages to Britain of a Jewish state intruded into the Islamic Middle East and thus forever dependent on outside help. As early as 1838, when Britain had been at loggerheads with Muhammad Ali Pasha, the ruler of Egypt, Lord Palmerston had appointed the first British vice-consul in Jerusalem with a watching brief over the ten thousand or so Jews then inhabiting Palestine. Two years later Palmerston wrote to the British Ambassador in Constantinople: "It would be of manifest importance for the Sultan to encourage the Jews to return to, and settle in Palestine; because the wealth which they would bring with them would increase the resources of the Sultan's dominions; and the Jewish people, if returning under the sanction and protection and at the invitation of the Sultan, would be a check upon any future evil designs of Mohammed Ali or his successor . . ."[4]

Among British Jews support for a connection with Palestine was various and diffused, ranging from a paternalistic support for Jewish colonization shown by Sir Moses Montefiore to the fervor of the Maccabean Club. As their club's name suggested, the Maccabeans looked back with fiery nostalgia to the last semi-independent Jewish state in Palestine. One of its members was a thirty-one-year-old author, Israel Zangwill, famous for a recently published novel, *Children of the Ghetto.*

To meet his English confrere Herzl took a cab from Victoria Station. It made its way through repetitive, featureless streets in a northwesterly direction. Zangwill's father had been the poor peddler described in an earlier chapter; his son had, comparatively, prospered. Kilburn, a respectable suburb for those who serviced the Victorian dream, was an advance on the Whitechapel slum that had inspired Zangwill's writing. But compared with any of the streets in which Herzl had lived it was a sordid backwater. "Arrived a bit out of sorts. The house is rather shabby. In his book-lined study Zangwill sits before an enormous writing table with his back to the fireplace. Also close to the fire, his brother, reading. Both give one the impression of shivering southerners who have been cast up on the shores of Ultima Thule."[5]

The two Jewish nationalists found it hard to communicate. Herzl knew Hungarian, German and French, but rarely spoke Hungarian. He never spoke Yiddish. In his own phrase, he did not know enough Hebrew to ask for a train ticket.[6] Zangwill was ignorant of Hungarian and German but in addition to English knew Yiddish and Russian. Zangwill's French (the language they fell back on) was, Herzl wrote, inadequate. "I don't even know whether he understands me. Still, we agree on major points. He, too, is in favor of our territorial independence." They disagreed, however, on what constituted a Jew. Zangwill believed that the Jews were a race: a point of view Herzl had to reject "if I so much as look at him and myself."† He described his host as "of the long-nosed Negroid type, with very woolly deep-black hair, parted in the middle." Their discussion helped Herzl to sharpen his view of what Jewish nationalism meant. "All I am saying is: We are an historical unit, a nation with anthropological diversities. This also suffices for the Jewish State. No nation has uniformity of race." Herzl's view was more original than it seems. Until then it was commonly believed that a nation, as distinct from a race, must possess a common territory and a common language. This encounter in sooty Kilburn symbolized the lack of both.

---

† Yet Herzl was to go on using the term. For example, to a Jew who had embraced Islam: "I really do look upon you as a man of action, as a man of my race which I believe capable of any amount of energy."[7]

At the time of Herzl's visit Zangwill was a bachelor; he was later to marry a gentile, Edith Ayrton, novelist daughter of a distinguished fellow of the Royal Society. Zangwill was still unmarried when he first dined "at court" with the Herzls in the Vienna suburb of Währing. Although this visit took place later, it can be anticipated. It illuminates the contrasted characters of Theodor and Julie Herzl. Herzl had either failed to convey his impression of Zangwill's appearance, or Julie had paid no attention. "Mrs. Herzl," we are told by Leon Kellner, the second guest, "was visibly disappointed. She had probably expected a tall, well-built man, carefully groomed, dressed in the latest English mode, and displaying perfect society manners. Instead there sat down at her festive table which had been prepared with such loving care an average-sized gentleman of grotesquely Jewish appearance and awkward behaviour, with ill-fitting and neglected clothes."[8] The Herzls, and even more the Naschauers, had moved much further from Jewish tradition than the Zangwills. Even so, unless Herzl had taken literally Zangwill's theory that race was the link between Jews, there was a defiance of this tradition remarkable in the household of a Jewish leader. For "in honour of her guest Mrs. Herzl had prepared crabs for the first course. Zangwill did not know how to tackle the monster before him. He started back stiffly at the sight. He seized the crab with an effort at bravado and put it to his mouth. An outcry from Mrs. Herzl, a polite smile from the host—and we tried to show the impossible Englishman how to handle the beast on his plate. It was of no avail." To a traditional Jew crab was as forbidden a food as pork. But Julie could not support her guest's lack of *savoir-faire* and she left the room in silent protest as dessert was served. After the meal, when the three men were left alone, Zangwill stretched himself out full length on a chaise longue. Herzl raised an eyebrow but his dislike for informal conduct did not cloud his awareness of Zangwill's virtues. When next day Julie reverted to his peculiarities, Herzl came to Zangwill's defense: "Here we have a man who expends so much concern and thought on the care of his spirit that there remains nothing for externals."‡

‡ Although Leon Kellner wrote this memoir only a few weeks before he died, aged sixty-nine, in 1928, there seems to be no reason to doubt its essential accuracy. But the dating and some of the details are suspect. Kellner tells us that he first met Herzl in the fall of 1895, when the latter sent him a copy of *Der Judenstaat* and its English translation; he dates the dinner party as around "Derby Day in the spring of the following year." As Herzl's pamphlet (see Chapter 22) was not published until February 1896, and the English edition later, the meeting must have taken place in autumn 1896 and the meal in the spring of 1897. Was it dinner, however, or luncheon? Kellner records that Herzl "was not altogether sorry when I carried the English guest off to the races." Kellner also leaves us puzzled as to what method of cooking a crab would prompt even a neophyte to lift it to his mouth entire.[8]

Julie would have been happier to act as hostess to Herzl's next important London contact. But Sir Samuel Montagu, financier and Liberal member of Parliament, would have greeted dressed crab with outrage, not Zangwill's fumbling efforts to conform. When Herzl lunched at Sir Samuel's elegant town mansion three liveried footmen served kosher food. Herzl found the other members of the Montagu family "unfriendly, or merely wellbred," a sharp intuition, since the second son, Edwin Samuel Montagu, then a lad of sixteen, was destined to be one of the most eloquent opponents of the Zionist idea.* But when after lunch he found himself alone with Sir Samuel, the "good-natured patriarch" confessed that he himself felt more an Israelite than an Englishman. "He said he would settle in Palestine with his whole family. He has in mind a Greater Palestine rather than the old one."[10]

Next day, November 25, 1895, Herzl traveled all the way to Wales to meet the Colonel Goldsmid of whom he had heard in Vienna. Connected with one of the leading families of Anglo-Jewry, Goldsmid had been brought up a Christian, his parents having both been baptized. When as a young man in India he discovered this, he had indignantly reverted to the faith of his forebears while continuing to serve as a soldier of the Crown. He had eloped with his present wife (also a baptized Jew) and after a civil marriage in Scotland and her formal return to Judaism, they had been married in a synagogue. "I am an orthodox Jew," Goldsmid told Herzl. "This has not done me any harm in England."[11] At this time he was colonel-in-chief of the Welsh regimental district. He had previously worked for de Hirsch in Latin America and that experience had convinced him that Palestine was the only place to be considered: "like Montagu, he too thinks of a Greater Palestine."

Herzl was charmed by his evening at The Elms, Goldsmid's Cardiff home. The Viennese pianist Rosenthal, in Wales on a visit, was invited to play while Goldsmid's daughters, Rachel and Carmel, "listened in graceful poses. Truly, another world. In my mind's eye I could already see the aristocratic Jewesses of the coming era. Exquisite creatures with an oriental touch, gentle and dreamy. And as a piece of bric-à-brac there lay on the drawing room table a Torah scroll in a silver case."[12]

Herzl's chief difficulty in converting English Jews was his lack of

---

* "Zionism," he was to write in 1917, shortly before taking up the post of Secretary of State for India, "has always seemed to me to be a mischievous political creed, untenable by any patriotic citizen of the United Kingdom. If a Jewish Englishman sets his eyes on the Mount of Olives and longs for the day when he will shake British soil from his shoes and goes back to agricultural pursuits in Palestine, he has always seemed to me to have acknowledged aims inconsistent with British citizenship and to have admitted that he is unfit for a share in public life in Great Britain, or to be treated as an Englishman."[9]

English. He gave a speech to the Maccabeans in London, two thirds of which was in German (translated by the Zionist rabbi Simeon Singer) and the rest in French. Even so, his speech was applauded and he was unanimously elected an honorary Maccabee. "Then follow the objections, which I refuted. The most important of these: English patriotism." But despite his difficulties in communicating (and he resolved to take lessons to improve his English) and his failure to set up a Zionist Centre, success in England made him eager to get home and finish his pamphlet.

But the sooty metropolis immortalized by Gustave Doré lowered his health even while it raised his spirits. In transit through Paris he was found by Nordau (a physician as well as author) to be afflicted by a bout of bronchial catarrh.[13]

CHAPTER 22

Herzl used the weeks following his visit to England in November 1895 to complete his pamphlet. Mystery, or mystification, again clouds an event in Herzl's life. A plaque inscribed in French and Hebrew marks the Hôtel de Castille in the Rue Cambon, Paris. The French inscription reads as follows:

Ici en 1895, Théodore HERZL
Fondateur du Mouvement Sioniste
écrivit "L'Etat JUIF" livre prophétique
qui annonça la résurrection de l'Etat d'ISRAEL.[1]

Whether Herzl may be accounted the founder of the Zionist movement is arguable*; it is certain that he did not write *L'État Juif* in the Paris hotel.

For once Herzl himself is responsible for an error of fact. On a visit to Paris in 1899 he made the following entry in his Diary: "Out of piety I still stay at the old place where I wrote the *Jewish State* four years ago now."[3] His remembrance of the past had begun to be affected by his present vision; his state of health—he was suffering from palpitations and an irregular pulse—was poor. Two days later, after a visit to the Automobile Exposition, he had corrected his statement. "I suddenly found myself in the square bordered with mythological statues where, at exactly this season four years ago, I conceived the *Jewish State* while walking."[4] In both entries Herzl used the English phrase.

Herzl had indeed conceived the *idea* of a state for Jews while staying

---

* The term Zionism, used first by Nathan Birnbaum some years before,[2] stood for an idea—the return to Palestine—which the Hibbat Zion (Love of Zion) movement had advocated since its foundation in Russia in 1882.

in the Rue Cambon in June 1895. But the pamphlet to which the plaque refers was written in Vienna half a year later.

The pamphlet is first mentioned by name in his Diary on January 19, 1896. "Signed a contract with the publisher Breitenstein. He was enthusiastic when I read him a few passages from the text which I finished at last after long toil. I have changed the title—to *Der Judenstaat*."[5]

This new title means neither *L'État Juif* (the version on the plaque) nor *The Jewish State*, the translation given by the Diary's American editor in square brackets. It means: "The State of the Jews." The German for "The Jewish State" would have been *Der Jüdische Staat*.

His German title—*Der Judenstaat*—represents Herzl's original idea precisely: a state where Jews would form a self-governing majority, able to live as they wished, secure from pogroms. Yet the mistranslations were used on the English and French translations of his pamphlet which Herzl subsidized; by 1899 he himself was using *Jewish State* in his Diary. One reason for the change may be euphony. Like most writers of his day, Herzl valued a neat-sounding expression. But a more important reason was political. Herzl had soon discovered that, while the abstract notion of a state for the Jews appealed to gentiles or Jews without religious commitment, religious Zionists could only approve a state ruled by Torah. Sir Samuel Montagu, for example, disapproved when Herzl wrote him a letter on the Sabbath. Nearer home there was a sharper lesson. On Christmas Eve, 1895, taking time off from correcting his pamphlet, Herzl had been lighting the candles on his children's Christmas tree, watched by five-year-old Pauline, four-year-old Hans and two-year-old Trude, for the first time old enough to understand the exciting mystery. At that moment Rabbi Moritz Güdemann happened to call. He was visibly outraged by Herzl's adoption of a rite so intimately linked with celebrations of the birth of Christ. Herzl, for his part, was hurt: he would not let himself be pressured into breaking an annual rite. "Though I don't mind if they call it the Hanukah tree—or the winter solstice."[6]† Güdemann had felt doubts about Herzl as a Jew ever since the well-known journalist had written to him from Paris. The Christmas lights threw these doubts into relief.

In writing *Der Judenstaat* Herzl had been influenced, not by Judaism, but by his June visions as modified by the influence of Menger; only later were political considerations to impose an outward reconciliation with religious practice. In publishing the pamphlet, Herzl felt that he had burned his boats. On February 14, 1896, the eve of publi-

† An ancient Jewish ordinance forbade the aping of the gentiles. For *chukoth ha-goy*, see Leviticus XVIII: 3 and XX: 23. The Christmas tree was in fact more a pagan than a Christian symbol.

cation, he wrote: "This package of pamphlets constitutes the decision in tangible form. My life may now take a new turn."[7] When men burn their boats, they do so with tended flames. His pamphlet carefully censored much of what had gone into his Diary and his *Address*.

The Preface to *Der Judenstaat* leads with a bald pronouncement: "The idea which I have developed in this pamphlet is an old one: It is the establishment of a State for the Jews."‡

Two forces made a state for the Jews an urgent need and no Utopia: Jewish suffering and anti-Semitic fervor.° On August 21 in a letter to Güdemann Herzl had used a striking metaphor. "Another known quantity is the steam power which is generated by boiling water in a tea-kettle and then lifts the kettle lid. Such a tea-kettle phenomenom are the Zion experiments and a hundred other organized efforts to 'combat anti-Semitism.' But I say that this force is strong enough to run a great machine and transport human beings."[9] The figure is now used again word for word.

The Preface—which elaborates these points—is followed by an Introduction. Herzl suddenly changes course and, perhaps remembering Nordau's doubts as to whether Jews were anthropologically capable of state formation, disposes of the argument that Jews are dependent on host nations, their entrepreneurial function being that of parasites.

Here Herzl's modernism, his familiarity with the economic arguments of the Vienna school show at their happiest. The entrepreneurial function, he argues, is the major factor behind the progress associated with the nineteenth century, the transformation of peasant economies into complex, wealthy societies. Machines are the new slaves which make possible vastly increased productivity. "I approach this movement [anti-Semitism] as a Jew, yet without fear or hatred. I believe that I can see in it the elements of cruel sport, of common commercial rivalry, of inherited prejudice, or religious intolerance—but also of a supposed need for self-defense."[10] Anti-Semitism, a deep-rooted force, has made the Jews into one people, who cannot assimilate. To

‡ In German: *"Der Gedanke, den ich in dieser Schrift ausführe, ist ein uralter. Es ist die Herstellung des Judenstaates."* This important sentence, as first translated in the *Nouvelle Revue Internationale* (31,12,1896), correctly gives the meaning of *Herstellung* in French as *établissement*. In modern Zionist texts—for example, *The Zionist Idea*, ed. Arthur Herzberg, New York, 1959—the meaning is subtly altered to become: "The idea which I have developed in this pamphlet is an ancient one: It is the restoration of the Jewish State." The German for "restoration" would be *Wiederherstellung;* if Herzl had used it, it would have implied that he wanted the revival of the ancient state of Israel, which was far from his conception in *Der Judenstaat.*[8]

° Herzl naturally knew of Theodor Hertzka's *Freiland*, a Utopia set in Africa. An economist and a Jew, Hertzka had edited the *Wiener Allgemeine Zeitung* at the time when it had published Herzl's first *feuilleton*.

hope for their dissolution through interbreeding would require too long a delay: the process has only really started in the upper classes.

Herzl next concedes that by proclaiming "We are one people" he may be comforting the anti-Semites and discomforting those Jews, particularly in France, who have chosen to assimilate. Herzl answers that the exodus of dedicated Jews will ease things for those who want to stay where they are. Much Jewish philanthropy, he argues, is a tacit attempt to prevent Jewish immigrants from the east spoiling the position of the longer-settled.[11] Previous schemes for settlement—he was thinking of the efforts of de Hirsch in South America and of the Rothschilds in Palestine—have not solved the problem: they have merely transplanted anti-Semitism to new regions. Here he inserts the typical bold statement: "What is impractical or impossible on a small scale need not be so on a larger one. A small enterprise may result in loss under the same conditions that would make a large one pay. A rivulet is not navigable even by boats; the river into which it flows carries stately iron vessels."[12]

Before such stately vessels sail, Herzl tackles some misconceptions. He does not envisage a return to the desert, but, on the contrary, the transference of modern civilization *in toto*. While this will give unparalleled encouragement to Jews, it will also encourage an internal immigration of Christians into jobs the Jews have overcrowded. Three organs will be responsible for ensuring that the exodus is no piecemeal, haphazard venture, but an operation organized in the most modern style: the Society of Jews, local groups, and the Jewish Company.[13]

The next chapter of *Der Judenstaat* does not show Herzl at his best. The transition is abrupt and it is back to an emphatic but unemotional restatement of the Jewish predicament. Wherever Jews live in any number, the deterioration of their position is certain. This raises the urgent question: should we not leave? and if so, whither? It is hopeless to wait for an amelioration of the situation of Jews. The modern world forces Jews into the stock exchange as the medieval world had forced them into moneylending.

Only a grandiose plan can rescue them. It is useless to hope to turn them into peasants. When this had been tried in Hesse, the presence of Jewish farmers had simply aroused the hatred of their neighbors. It was as pointless as asking them to go to war armed with crossbows and not Krupp cannons.

Instead of reexamining the emotional roots of anti-Semitism, he prefers to analyze the political and economic factors that make it inevitable. Emancipation is the chief cause of modern anti-Semitism. Inside the ghetto the Jews had become a bourgeois people; on being allowed to come out, they formed a formidable rival to the native middle class. Yet because of the liberal laws passed by most European countries, the natives could not protect themselves by rescinding Jewish rights. The remote cause of anti-Semitism was thus the loss of the Jewish power of assimilation during the Middle Ages: "Its immediate cause is our excessive production of mediocre intellects, who cannot find an outlet downward or upward—that is to say, no wholesome outlet in either direction. When we sink we become a revolutionary proletariat, the subordinate officers of the revolutionary party; when we rise, there rises also our terrible power of the purse."[14]

The result is hatred between oppressors and oppressed. Again assimilation has the nagging power of an ancient scar. Herzl rejects it for two reasons. One carries less conviction than the other: it seems to be defensive. "I do not for a moment wish to imply that I desire such an end [as assimilation]. Our national character is too glorious in history and, in spite of every degradation, too noble to make its annihilation desirable. Though perhaps we *could* succeed in vanishing without a trace into the surrounding peoples if they would let us be for just two generations."[15] But the cogent objection is that the gentiles refuse this and as a result, he repeats, "We are one people."

All this is by way of introduction to the Plan.

"Let sovereignty be granted us over a portion of the globe adequate to meet our rightful national requirements; we will attend to the rest."[16] Neither here nor elsewhere in the pamphlet does Herzl discuss the natives; the frankness shown in the Diary is here lacking. The problem is posed simply as an abstraction. "To create a new State is neither ridiculous nor impossible. Haven't we witnessed the process in our own day, among nations which were not largely middle class as we are, but poorer, less educated, and consequently weaker than ourselves?"[17] The assumptions in this passage are important. Herzl had in mind such new states as Germany and Italy. In them Germans and Italians formed the overwhelming majority living on a long-possessed national territory. Herzl leaps the problem that Jews formed no such majority in any territory. The assumption that the Jews were mostly middle class shows his ignorance—at least up to this moment—of the situation of most European Jews.

"We will attend to the rest": through the medium of the Society of Jews, which would establish a scientific plan and political policies, and the Jewish Company, which would put them into execution. The Jewish Company would have two grand functions: liquidating the fortunes of Jews in the countries they were leaving and organizing commerce in the new country. Again the stress is on modernity. Rejecting earlier Zionists as exponents of folkweave, he explains his turn of thought with a revealing comparison: "Supposing, for example, we were obliged to clear a country of wild beasts, we should not set about it in the fashion of the fifth-century European. We should not take spear and lance and go out individually in pursuit of bears; we would organize a grand and glorious hunting party, drive the animals together, and throw a melinite bomb into their midst."[18]

The image of wild beasts evokes a jungle. But Herzl is as uncommitted as six months before to a particular land. "Two regions come to mind: Palestine and Argentina. Significant experiments in colonization have been made in both countries, though on the mistaken principle of gradual infiltration of Jews. Infiltration is bound to end badly. For there comes the inevitable moment when the government in question, under pressure of the native populace—which feels itself threatened —puts a stop to further influx of Jews." Which of the two possible territories was to be preferred? "The Society will take whatever it is given and whatever Jewish public opinion favors . . . Argentina is one of the most fertile countries in the world, extends over a vast area, is sparsely populated, and has a temperate climate."[19]†

"Palestine," on the other hand, "is our unforgettable historic homeland. The very name would be a marvelously effective rallying cry. If His Majesty the Sultan were to give us Palestine, we could in return undertake the complete management of the finances of Turkey. We should there form part of a wall of defense for Europe in Asia, an outpost of civilization against barbarism. The holy places of Christendom could be placed under some form of international extraterritoriality."

The pamphlet ends with a final assertion that the Plan is feasible. Two ironically contrasted factors will help achieve it: the knowledge of the rich that money can do anything in an industrial society balanced against the enthusiasm of the poor, who are ignorant of the powers of science. Herzl permits himself a prophecy:

"Once we begin to execute the Plan, anti-Semitism will cease at once and everywhere."[20]

For the publication of *Der Judenstaat* Herzl required a Jewish publisher. The first he approached—Sigmund Cronbach of Berlin—turned it down because he disliked its thesis. (Herzl noted, in retaliation, that Cronbach published a hairdresser's journal.) The second, Max Breitenstein of Vienna, contracted on January 19, 1896, to publish an edition of three thousand copies. The final proofs were ready by the end of the month. During the two weeks before publication Herzl read Pin-

† According to the thirteenth edition of the Encyclopaedia Britannica, Argentina's total population in 1895 was 3,954,911; its area was 1,083,596 square miles.

sker's *Auto-Emancipation,* the work that anticipated many of his own ideas. "A pity that I did not read this work before my own pamphlet was printed. On the other hand, it is a good thing that I didn't know it—or perhaps I would have abandoned my own undertaking."[21] On St. Valentine's Day a huge bundle containing the author's five hundred copies was delivered at 16 Pelikangasse; the following morning *Der Judenstaat* was displayed in Breitenstein's window at 5 Währingerstrasse. Herzl was now impatient for public response. Rumors circulated as to who was to review it and in what spirit. But no reviews had appeared by February 23 when a group of journalists whom he met at the Volkstheater told him that his pamphlet was the talk of Vienna. One of the group was Hermann Bahr, who had long ago made the speech that prompted Herzl to resign from Albia. Now a bearded writer of some success, Bahr told Herzl that he for one was going to attack him—people could not do without the Jews. Herzl smiled at his joke but thought only of reviews.

The first press notice that he saw was an editorial published on February 26 in the *Westungarischer Grenzbote.* The writer was Ivan von Simonyi (1834–1904), a Hungarian member of parliament who had founded the German-language paper to fight both Germans and Jews. He spoke in chivalrous terms of Dr. Herzl and showed by further laudatory editorials that this was no passing whim. On March 30 the Hungarian anti-Semite called on Herzl in person: "a mercurial, loquacious man with an astonishing amount of sympathy for the Jews. His conversation is a mixture of the sensible and the nonsensical; he believes in the ritual murder lie, but along with it has the brightest, most modern ideas. Loves me!"[22]

This eager and continued support from Simonyi—an anti-Semite who still believed that Jews used Christian blood at Passover—confirmed Herzl in his certainty that his ideas would appeal both to Jews and their enemies. It also consoled him at a time when other reactions to his pamphlet were discouraging. While one Jewish writer accused him of writing "the founding prospectus of a Jewish Switzerland," another characterized Zionism as "madness born of despair."[23] Nathan Birnbaum, who had invented the term, attributed Herzl's espousal of Zionism to desire for personal gain. ("Envious, vain, dogmatic," Herzl countered.[24]) Worst of all was the news, passed to him by his publisher just before Simonyi's visit, that Rabbi Güdemann had refused to lecture on *Der Judenstaat.* "My standpoint, he says, is political, whereas his is religious. From his point of view he must disapprove of my attempts to anticipate Providence."[25] Jewish hostility to his pamphlet was no idle matter. He had planned to be a Jewish leader, not a prophet or martyr. Yet he could not lead the Jews if the Jews refused him.

Immediately after Simonyi's encouraging support Herzl acquired, in place of the scrupulous Güdemann, two important new disciples: one only too anxious to see Providence accelerated, the other an intriguer to whom scruples were as remote as his homeland. Both were gentiles.

CHAPTER 23

A century's official frown is often balanced by a mad, secret smile. The age of Reason installed hermits in gothic grottos; the cellars of the Age of Steam abounded in books on magic and pyramidal prophecy. Herzl, the rationalist, had had no contact with this aspect of his age until, one March morning in 1896, it called on him in the person of a bearded clergyman. His first reaction was one of skepticism.

The Reverend William Hechler, born in India to a German father and British mother, had at one time tutored the son of Grand Duke Friedrich of Baden, the Kaiser's uncle. He was currently serving as chaplain to the British Embassy in Vienna. His lifelong ambition was to become Protestant Bishop of Jerusalem. No sooner had he read *Der Judenstaat* than he burst in on his ambassador to proclaim: "The fore-ordained movement is here!"[1] For some years Hechler had been devoting his leisure hours (and he rose daily at five) to the study of biblical prophecy and its relation to the present age. His key text was a verse in the book of Revelation: "The holy city shall they (the pagans) tread under foot forty and two months."[2] Hechler, like most of his kind, decided to read a month as "thirty years." But if one dated the prophecy from the fall of Jerusalem to the Romans in A.D. 70, Jerusalem should have been liberated in 1330. Since this reckoning did not work, Hechler took the initial point as A.D. 637, the year when Omar, father-in-law of Muhammad and his second Caliph, had won Jerusalem from its Byzantine bishop. This did work, even if the Arabs, with their stern monotheism, hardly deserved the description "pagan." This meant that the Jews would be returning to Palestine—and accepting Christ as their Messiah—in 1897–98.[3] Hechler's attitude to the Jews of his day was as ambivalent as Herzl's, though from another standpoint. "The Jews," he wrote, "are beginning to look forward to and believe in the glorious future of their nation, when, instead of being a curse, they are once more to become a blessing to all." The Zionists were "unconsciously fulfilling the Scriptures concerning the events, which the prophets tell us are to lead to the Lord's Second Coming, and they are doing this just as unconsciously as their forefathers fulfilled God's prophecies, when Christ came the first time and lived in Jerusalem."[4]

It surprised Herzl, whose mind had been shaped by agnostics like Menger, to learn that his movement was "biblical." He sensed something of the charlatan in the Reverend Hechler. He checked with his English teacher, for he was carrying out his resolve to improve his English. His teacher at once remarked that Hechler was a *Heuchler,* a German word for hypocrite or dissembler. Yet Herzl was at a juncture when any believer shored his own belief. A few days later he returned Hechler's call. The clergyman lived in one of the lofty palazzi which, with the Museum of Fine Art, formed the leafy quadrangle known as the Schillerplatz. As he slowly mounted four flights of stairs, he heard an organ. The staircase opened on a sunlit room lined from floor to ceiling with Bibles. Hardly had Herzl glanced at these treasures than his host extended a military staff map of Palestine on the carpet. He then pointed with prophetic finger at Bethel, the site, according to his calculations, of the new Temple.

The raptures of prophecy were interrupted by two English ladies, who had come to inspect the chaplain's collection. Once the two men were again alone, the sexagenarian Hechler sang his guest a Zionist song of his own composition. He accompanied himself on the organ.

Herzl was prepared to take Hechler at his face value if he could be useful. The hymn over, he confided what he wanted: contacts, on an ambassadorial level, with some statesman or ruler whose support for Herzl, or association with him, would convince the Jews. The ideal dignitary would be the Kaiser.

The clergyman immediately raised the question of money. Would Herzl pay his expenses for a Berlin visit? If so, he could raise the question with the court chaplain and two of the royal princes. Ill though he could afford the required hundred guilders, nag though Julie would if she found out, Herzl agreed. But as a quizzical Viennese, he saw that Hechler might strike the princes as an eccentric whose latest fad was the Jews. He instructed Hechler, therefore, to stress that he did not come at Herzl's behest. Thus, if all the old man wanted was a free trip to Berlin, Herzl would pay it, with open eyes. Yet Hechler's belief in his prophetic timetable was oddly moving. The clergyman patted the coat pocket in which he would carry his big map when the two of them would be riding round the Holy Land together. This simple gesture clinched Herzl's conviction that he was sincere.

Hechler had lifted Herzl to a peak of excitement; next day a visit from his parents' physician, Dr. Beck, cast him down again. Beck diagnosed a heart ailment caused by overexcitement. At the same time he spoke skeptically of Herzl's involvement in the Jewish question—none of his friends could understand his motives. One of Julie's brothers-in-law had given the same irritating report: the Jews in his circle could not understand why a man of Herzl's means and standing should involve himself in this affair.

Herzl had to be patient for a month before Hechler moved; and not to Berlin, as this proved needless. On April 14 the Kaiser visited Vienna. Hechler, having got in touch with friends in the Imperial retinue, suggested that he and Herzl should go on ahead to Karlsruhe, the residence of the Grand Duke of Baden and the Kaiser's next address. The Grand Duke was close to Wilhelm II, having played the leading role in the coronation of his grandfather, Wilhelm I. Herzl refused this tempting suggestion. He must go only on invitation. Hechler then asked for a photograph of Herzl—he wanted to prove to his courtly friends that the Zionist leader was physically different from their picture of a Jew. As luck would have it, April 14 was also Jacob Herzl's birthday; for his father's present Herzl had had his photograph taken; he had spare copies.

That evening he secured a box at the opera diagonally opposite the Kaiser. He studied him closely throughout the performance. He noted a general stiffness, an occasional affability and laughter, but above all, the way his left hand rested forever on the hilt of his sword. Herzl was later to construct a theory of the Kaiser's personality on the basis of his withered left arm. The deformity was the Imperial equivalent of the Jewish burden. The Kaiser, supreme war lord of industrial Europe, had a defect that would have disqualified him (as Herzl had been disqualified) from service as a simple soldier. His shiny uniforms, his gleaming helmets were glittering distractions from his defect.[5]

Hechler set out the next morning on the longish trip to Karlsruhe. A week of anguish for Herzl followed. Telegrams telling him to delay, telegrams telling him to hope. He began to think that the clergyman was deluded and that he would have to write off his expenses as cheerfully as possible. April 21, 1896, was a day of crisis. No word from Hechler but in the press the report that the Kaiser had left Karlsruhe for Coburg. Feeling that gentile promises might be deceptive, Herzl returned to his first target, de Hirsch. The previous day he had begun a long letter to Nordau in Paris asking him to board the millionaire for a few millions to be used as baksheesh in Turkey. Palestine was an Ottoman possession and Constantinople, not Europe, might provide the key. An hour after he posted the letter a news item plunged him into despair. On the Hungarian estate to which he had invited the great ones of Europe, including the Prince of Wales, Baron Maurice de Hirsch had died. Herzl was full of regrets. He had not even sent him *Der Judenstaat;* he had hesitated about writing to Nordau. "The moment I decide to do, he dies. His participation could have helped our cause to success tremendously fast. In any case, his death is a loss to the Jewish cause. Among the rich Jews he was the only one who wanted to do something big for the poor. Perhaps I did not know how to handle him properly."[6]

Then, as if to swing him back to gentile targets, a telegram arrived from Hechler. Herzl was to hasten to Karlsruhe. This meant that he would be received by the Grand Duke. "A curious day. Hirsch dies, and I make contact with princes."[7]

Herzl in Karslruhe prepared for his audience with characteristic care. There were photographs of the Duke on display in the shopwindows of the small, neat capital. He studied them. The Duke seemed a well-meaning, commonplace person of seventy. (He was destined to outlast Herzl by three years.) Herzl listened attentively as Hechler told him how he had primed his former employer for this important meeting. Hechler had worked on his emotions to secure his interest. He knew that as former tutor he was associated in the Grand Duke's mind with his dead son Ludwig. At this moment a red sandstone mausoleum was being completed near the place where his dead pupil had been wont to play. As tears coursed down the bereft father's cheeks, Hechler consoled him with a Psalm. He carefully chose one in which Zion featured. He also appealed to vanity. The Grand Duke had already played an important role in the creation of the German empire. What if he were to play his part in the founding of a second state? "For the Jews will become a great nation." The Grand Duke had three reservations: Herzl's status as mere scribbler; concern lest support for Zionism might seem prompted by a desire to get rid of his Jews; the dread that their massive exodus might mean a drain of capital.

Herzl rejected Hechler's suggestion that he should wear tails: the meeting was intended to be incognito. "So I wore my trusty Prince Albert. Externals increase in importance the higher one climbs, for everything becomes symbolic."[8] This maxim dictated the hiring of a cab for the few steps to the castle door. Herzl strove valiantly not to be impressed by the soldiers on guard, the princely portals. But the spectacle of regimental banners dating from the 1870 war against France filled him with awe. Aware of this, Hechler maintained a merry prattle with the refrain that dukes were only human. But at the same time he cautioned Herzl to unglove his right hand, in case a ducal hand were offered. This precaution, in the event, at first proved needless. After polite bows, the three men sat up in armchairs not calculated to give ease during two and a half hours of conversation.

Herzl, not the Duke, who was modest, exaggerated the importance of the dukedom. It was true that Grand Duke Friedrich had paraded the troops before Kaiser Wilhelm I in 1871; but his importance under the Imperial system was symbolic at best. When Herzl, seeking his support for political Zionism, said he was the Kaiser's adviser, the Grand Duke retorted: "I advise him, but he does what he pleases." The importance of the meeting was also symbolic. The Grand Duke could not guarantee an introduction to his nephew, still less the Czar. But Herzl had entered the outerworks of German power. He could outline his idea and refute the immediate objections. Zionism, he argued, would have a double benefit: it would drain off the surplus Jewish proletariat and would keep international capital under control. He spoke, too, in larger terms. A Jewish state in Palestine would serve the interests of Europe. "We would restore to health the plague-spot of the Orient. We would build railroads into Asia—the highway of the civilized peoples. And this highway would then not be in the hands of any one Great Power."[9]

The meeting ended with, at last, a handshake. Its only firm result was an agreement that Herzl should write to the Grand Duke from time to time. Nevertheless Herzl's spirits soared. He had been received by a ruler, and although Baden was a subordinate entity, hints and whispers could make the occasion impressive to skeptical Jews.

Though he owed this success to Hechler, Herzl still did not entirely trust him. The long train journey back to Vienna by way of Munich gave him time to reflect. "There is much pedantry, exaggerated humility, pious eye-rolling about him—but he also gives me excellent advice full of unmistakable good will. He is at once clever and mystical, cunning and naïve." One piece of advice concerned a key question if the state were to be in the Levant—its boundaries. On the train from Munich Hechler, who had made a side trip to Basel, again brought out his maps. "The northern frontier ought to be the mountains facing Cappadocia; the southern, the Suez Canal. The slogan to be circulated: The Palestine of David and Solomon."[10]*

Herzl did not exempt Hechler from racial prejudice.

* The mountains facing Cappadocia must be the Taurus range, which patrol the southern frontier of what is now Turkey. Herzl probably had the vaguest notion of the limits of the Davidic kingdom. No Jewish state had ever exercised effective control over the coastal plain, inhabited by Phoenicians and Philistines, let alone Sinai, Lebanon and northern Syria.

His criticisms are excellent, although it is then that his anti-Semitism occasionally comes through. Self confidence on the part of a Jew seems insolence to him. When it was getting dark, he even treated me to a downright anti-Semitic story. He had once put up a Jew at his home, and by way of thanks the Jew had robbed him. A Talmudic scholar, to whom he told his troubles, answered him with a comparison of flowers and nations, saying that the rose was the English, the lily the French, etc., the fat thistle on the dung-heap the Jewish flower.[11]

European potentates were only one objective in Herzl's strategy. The other was the Ottoman Sultan, the only man who could, if he would, sell Palestine to the Zionist movement. In approaching the Sultan and his government at Constantinople Herzl was aided by another gentile adjutant, an eccentric in a more urbane fashion and a man whom he was to sum up as "the most interesting figure I have had to deal with since I have carried on the Jewish cause."[12]

Philip Michael de Nevlinsky's origins as a Polish aristocrat inclined him to anti-Semitism; but his own experiences of oppression had enlarged his sympathies. He had grown up in a part of Poland occupied by Russia and had lost his lands and social position when, as a young man, he took part in an unsuccessful revolt against Czarist rule. Thereafter lifelong exile turned the sprig of an aristocracy into a rootless, charming, extravagant, multiple agent. "Since I cannot shape the policy of my nation, I don't care a fig for anything. I go on artist's tours in politics, like a piano virtuoso—that is all."[13] His first bought loyalty had been to Austria-Hungary, but having lost the possibility of fidelity to Poland, Nevlinsky saw nothing wrong in taking money from Poland's oppressors. He was like many Poles a fluent linguist, and ideas and loyalties were as fluid in his mind as tongues. In one year, when the Habsburg police took the trouble to check his earnings, they discovered that Russia, as well as Serbia, Romania, Turkey, Italy and France, had contributed to his income. An amusing, cynical talker, Nevlinsky had one solid asset: his excellent knowledge of the Grande Porte, as the government in Constantinople was known in Europe. He had acquired this between 1874, when the Austrian Foreign Minister Andrassy appointed him to the Habsburg Embassy in Constantinople, and 1878, when he was recalled because of scandalous debts.

The Ottoman empire was ruled at this time from Yildiz, a park containing a number of comparatively flimsy and unostentatious buildings; from here the last great Sultan, Abdul Hamid II, played his long defensive game against a grasping Europe. Being slight and hook-nosed, pusillanimous and so afraid of assassination that he could not bear corridors, Abdul Hamid was outwardly one of the least impressive rulers in history. Indeed, his greatness seems small when set against such early sovereigns of his dynasty as Muhammad II, who took Constantinople, or Suliman the Magnificent, whose guns were dragged to the suburbs of Vienna. But astuteness in politics does not consist in copying periods of strength in periods of weakness; it consists of knowing one's weakness (if one is weak) and using what assets remain to protect or prolong existence. Like other sultans, Abdul Hamid had been brought up in the harem but had acquired there, not a debilitating appetite for concubines, but the concubine's skill at intrigue. He played off the powers as a woman might play off lovers. He knew that his neglected provinces, his strategic deserts were coveted in the west. Some states preferred to keep him weak but intact, for fear that bits should go to others. Others were eager for an instant division of spoils in the Balkans, Africa and Asia. The one power that had not tried for a slice of Ottoman territory was Germany and the result was a particular friendship between the Sultan and the Kaiser.

All this was known in Europe thanks to ambassadors and journalists. But Nevlinsky could offer more than political analysis. He had mastered the jungle, trackless to the uninitiate, which surrounded the austere little Sultan's kiosk. Tradition made Ottoman officials as venal as experience had made Nevlinsky. After leaving Turkey he had kept up his friendships at the Porte and in Vienna consolidated a reputation as an expert by starting a news agency. This produced a daily sheet entitled *Correspondance de l'Est* (devoted to information from the Levant and Eastern Europe) and a daily supplement, *Österreichische Korrespondenz*, which reported on the internal affairs of the Habsburg empire. These publications were façades for influence-peddling and intrigue.†

Herzl had defined his policy toward the Ottomans on May 3, 1896, to Dionys Rosenfeld, editor and publisher of a German-language newspaper produced in Constantinople. "We shall bestow enormous benefits upon Turkey," Herzl told him, "and confer big gifts upon the intermediaries, if we obtain Palestine. This means nothing less than its cession as an independent country. In return we shall thoroughly straighten out Turkey's finances."[15] Rosenfeld, eager for the gifts, claimed to be on good terms with Izzet Bey, the Sultan's Arab favorite. He stressed that the moment was propitious for disbursement, since Turkey was in worse financial straits than usual. But Herzl hesitated. He needed someone of both skill and weight to be his envoy. A

† At the time of Nevlinsky's death, three years later, the subscription to the *Correspondance de l'Est* was found to consist of twelve copies daily.[14]

resident journalist, dependent on Ottoman good graces, would hardly
be the man to impress and convince. Besides, despite two conversions,
first to Greek Orthodoxy, then to Roman Catholicism, Rosenfeld was
by origin a Jew. Seigneurial tact would be needed, seigneurial accepta-
bility, since the envoy would have to address his blandishments, promises, threats to those near the throne, as otherwise much mischief
could be done. Turkish nerves were raw when money was mentioned.
For in the nineteenth century a weak country that got into debt could
easily lose its independence. The classic example had been Egypt, still
in theory a province of the Sultan's empire. In 1875 the Egyptian
Khedive had been turned off his throne by Anglo-French pressure because of his inability to pay off his Western moneylenders. This had
been merely the first stage in the reduction of Egypt to that of a veiled
protectorate, with a full-scale British occupation, in 1882. The dread
of a similar action against himself kept the Sultan awake in his melancholy park where giant night birds swooped over fragile minarets and
the Koran was recited during the hours of darkness. At the same
time, in offering to buy Palestine for some undisclosed financial support, Herzl's envoy had the considerable problem that, in the summer
of 1896, his patron held no recognized position whatsoever in Jewry;
the funds at his disposal were his salary from the *Neue Freie Presse*
(considerably reduced as this was from his Parisian stipend), his father's scrapings and Julie's dowry. An impresario was needed who
could conjure a pyramid from such trifles as the audience with the
Grand Duke of Baden.

Nevlinsky's name had been suggested to Herzl on February 21,
1896, by Dr. Saul Rafael Landau, a native of Galicia and as such
acquainted with many Poles. Something in Landau's word portrait told
Herzl that Nevlinsky was his man. In response to Herzl's telephone
call, Nevlinsky visited him on May 7. The Pole immediately claimed
to have read and admired *Der Judenstaat*.‡ Furthermore, he had discussed it with no less a person than Sultan Abdul Hamid on his latest
trip to Turkey. This seems the contact man's typical flattery. Even so,
his report that the Sultan would never part with Jerusalem, because it
contained the Mosque of Omar, showed a clear understanding of
the Sultan's political vision, which regarded Islam as the one bond
for a threatened empire. The Sultan—Nevlinsky continued with equal
shrewdness—had little understanding of money. Ottoman decline
vis-à-vis Europe was largely due to disdain for the commerce that
since the seventeenth century had made Western Europe powerful as

‡ This may have been more than a compliment. According to one source[16]
Nevlinsky's wife Maria, a former actress, was Jewish by origin; she may have
brought the book to his attention.

well as rich. One further remark—that the Sultan would prefer to abandon Anatolia sooner than the Holy Land—makes odd reading in the twentieth century, when a Turkish republic based on Anatolia is all that remains of the Ottoman empire. Yet Nevlinsky was in effect saying what Atatürk, the creator of the Turkish Republic, would repeat: the cosmopolitan Ottomans despised the Turks—or "villagers"—of Anatolia. The dynasty regarded its prime mission as religious. This required them to hold Constantinople (their greatest historical prize) and to safeguard the three holy places: Mecca, focus of Islamic prayer; Medina, tomb of the Prophet; and Jerusalem, point of departure for Muhammad's mystical night journey into heaven.

The urgent problems facing the Sultan in the 1890s were the Greeks (anxious to win Crete for their independent kingdom) and the Armenians. The Armenians posed the graver threat, since they inhabited, not peripheral islands, but the geographical center of the empire: for however little Abdul Hamid thought of Anatolia, the great plateau bounded by sea to the north and west and by deserts and mountains to the east and south was the imperial turntable; on it communications to the other sections largely depended. It was also a reservoir of soldiers. The Armenian question had now brought Nevlinsky to Vienna en route to Western Europe. As friend of the Sultan he was on a confidential mission to the exiled Armenian leaders. He was to propose a deal: if they held their hand and abstained from the guerrilla action they were known to be planning, the Sultan would initiate more liberal policies in their regard. He was also interested in inducing the European press to be less harsh to Turkey. As the Jews were influential in the press, they too formed part of his mission.

Herzl's extraordinary ability to convince other men was shown by his effect on the aging and cynical adventurer. Of course Herzl dropped his inevitable hint: "The Jewish cause will bring you greater returns than the Armenian."[17] Nevlinsky stressed in return that he indeed expected ample reward if anything came of his mission. Yet the Polish aristocrat (unlike the Ottoman Sultan) had a keen understanding of the value of money and a shrewd perception of how little Herzl had. Herzl's further offer to intervene with the Armenians was as chimerical. Yet Nevlinsky agreed, before setting off on May 10 for Brussels, to add the Zionist account to his ledgers.

Once again Herzl endured weeks of anxious waiting. He was aware as Nevlinsky that he was attempting a conjuring trick. "Great things need no solid foundation," he wrote two days after the Pole's departure. "An apple must be put on a table so that it will not fall. The earth floats in mid-air. Similarly, I may be able to found and stabilize the

Jewish State without any firm support. The secret lies in motion."[18]
He was determined that when Nevlinsky got back they would take the
train to Turkey.

Herzl maintained his stability in the interim through ceaseless action. He tried to persuade Nordau to work on the Armenians (Nordau
cabled back the one word "No!"[19]), to arrange an interview for Nevlinsky with Lord Salisbury, the British Prime Minister (this, too, naturally came to nothing). He planned a big speech to the London
Maccabeans that summer—but he would need to have more to show
than an audience with one Grand Duke. He pushed ahead with the
English, French and Russian translations of his pamphlet, all of which
he subsidized himself. The English version was the first to be printed;
its translator, Sylvie d'Avigdor, reported on May 21 that Sir Samuel
Montagu had presented a copy to Gladstone.[20] On June 2, 1896, Gladstone's guarded reply provided the one occasion in his lifetime on
which the *Neue Freie Presse* referred, noncommittally, to Herzl's connections with Zionism. It followed a *feuilleton* from Tolstoy's estate
near Moscow saying that the sage had also read the pamphlet but opposed its thesis. Though most Jewish students at Vienna University
favored assimilation, a Zionist faction proposed to recruit a battalion
of between one and two thousand volunteers and land them at Jaffa.
"I advised them against this fine Garibaldian idea, because these thousand men, unlike the men of Marsala, would not find a nationally prepared population awaiting them. The landing would be suppressed
within twenty-four hours, like a schoolboys' prank."[21]* From Constantinople Rosenfeld wrote naggingly that his contact wanted to know the
precise funds at Herzl's disposal, "because he would be risking his
head if the negotiations broke down."[23]

Herzl soothed his irritations with thoughts of what Nevlinsky was
achieving. But removed from Herzl's fascination, Nevlinsky had allowed his enthusiasm to cool. When he returned to Vienna he avoided
Herzl for three days and when Herzl at last got hold of him, he spoke
out frankly: Herzl's project was regarded as Utopian in journalistic
circles, and, not surprisingly, in financial and governmental circles too.
The director of the Landesbank had declared it a fantasy; his own editor Benedikt had called it madness.[24] In an obvious attempt to cancel the trip Nevlinsky stressed that the Ottomans were too preoccupied
with Crete to think of Zion.

* This quotation is interesting for showing that Herzl had no illusions about the
likely attitude of the Palestinians to a Zionist invasion. But even in the Italian
case, Cavour's representative in Naples admitted that, out of the seven million inhabitants of the newly annexed Kingdom of the Two Sicilies, there were not a
hundred believers in Italian unity.[22]

Yet a week later, on June 15, 1896, Herzl was writing his Diary on the train to Constantinople. He had boarded the Orient Express at Vienna in the evening. Nevlinsky had been convinced and was to join the train when it passed through Pesth at two in the morning. Nevertheless, Nevlinsky had kept his wits. Herzl was given a shopping list of vegetable baksheesh for friends in Turkey: asparagus, peaches, strawberries, grapes, all imported from France, all from Sacher's, Vienna's most expensive hotel. Herzl kepts his wits, too. The hotel could supply but a fraction of the gigantic order and he did not bother to charge his hamper elsewhere. Of his two new disciples the eccentric clergyman cost him far less money.

CHAPTER 24

The pages Herzl devoted to his first visit to Constantinople contain material he would have worked up into a *feuilleton,* had his mission not precluded so frivolous a product. He was visiting the Ottoman capital at a moment suited to its peculiar melancholy and decay. If Gorky was right and a full moon over a river is best evoked by the description of a piece of broken glass glittering in the mud, then the pages describing Herzl's attempt to secure a territorial basis for his *Judenstaat* evoke much more than their theme. Above all they evoke the mixture of sensitivity and push that co-existed in their author.

He was in Constantinople from June 17, 1896, until June 28. The train journey had had, as was usual with Herzl, its advantages. Nevlinsky was able to introduce him to three fellow travelers who gave him a first taste of the men with whom he would be dealing: Ziad Pasha was diminutive, elegant, Parisian in manner; Karatheodory, jovial, plump, white-bearded, showed a serious side in his reading of a history of Russia when he was not talking; Tewfik, a young pasha, quoted old editorials from the *Neue Freie Presse* as evidence of his modern turn of mind. Ziad repeated what Nevlinsky had told him:

"Under no circumstances will you get Palestine as an independent country; maybe as a vassal state."

"That would be hypocrisy from the start," Herzl had answered. "Every vassal thinks only of how to become independent."[1]

Herzl was entering a world where appearances counted for even more than in Western Europe. At Sofia his troops appeared, a motley collection of Zionists whose presentation of red roses and grandiloquent terms of address astonished ordinary travelers on the train. But

Nevlinsky was not outdone. His arrival was saluted by a Bulgarian church dignitary in impressive robes. When the train drew into Stamboul the pashas' turn came. Already formally arrayed, the sooner to make their way to Yildiz, they were hailed by a welcoming horde of relations and friends.

Herzl was welcomed by two Greek journalists and Baron Berthold Popper, an Austrian Jew whose father, ennobled in 1867, had been a business associate of Jacob Naschauer. Across the Bosporus busy with ships they could see Haidarpasha, the terminal of the railway thrusting south through Anatolia toward its ultimate destinations of Mecca and Baghdad. Popper was currently bargaining for the contract to build the section from Alexandretta (the modern Iskanderun) to Damascus.

The way from Stamboul to Pera-Beyoglu, the Europeanized section of the city to the east of the Golden Horn, led through seedy streets opening on glimpses of vast, domed mosques. "We drove through this astonishingly beautiful, dirty city," Herzl wrote.[2] "Dazzling sunshine, colorful poverty, dilapidated buildings. From a window of the Hotel Royal our view extends over the Golden Horn. The houses on the slopes are situated among greenery, and it looks like grass growing between stones—as if nature were slowly recapturing this crumbling city." Herzl and Nevlinsky occupied a suite at the Royal Hotel, their bedrooms sharing a parlor with a long green damask sofa. As soon as Nevlinsky had changed, he went to Yildiz, leaving Herzl to take a drive round Pera and then saunter in good humor down the bumpy streets to the old bridge. But Nevlinsky's humor was not good when he returned, later than expected. The Sultan was ill with a boil and Izzet Bey was hostile to the project now that too many people were counting on commissions. An after-dinner stroll took them to an open-air concert hall where an Italian company was performing light opera. In the audience Nevlinsky spotted the son of the Grand Vizir. Herzl exploited his luck with journalist's boldness. Within minutes the young man had joined them on a bench while Herzl explained his mission and asked the young man to arrange a meeting with his father. Like others who knew the Middle East, the Grand Vizir's son pointed out that a Jewish occupation of Palestine would outrage Islamic feelings. Nor did Herzl advance his case in defining his projected state as an "aristocratic republic." "Republic" was a seditious word in Turkey. Nevertheless the amiable young man promised to do his best.

The following day—June 18—Herzl had interviews with men who exemplified the influences at work on the Sultan. Since Nevlinsky thought that Russian influence was currently strong at Yildiz, Herzl made his first call at the Russian consulate in Pera on Yakovlev, the dragoman: "gaunt, tall, dark-haired, with a narrow face, a scraggly beard, and small, slit-like eyes." Herzl opened by announcing his intention to visit the Czar through the intervention of a member of his family. (He meant the Prince of Wales, whom he had never met.) Yakovlev countered by conveying his unfavorable impression of the Jews he had met when Consul in Jerusalem. They had, he said, tried to wriggle out of the taxes they owed the Consulate, claiming to be Turks when it was inconvenient to be Russians, and vice versa. Herzl remarked in answer that considering the persecutions to which his people had been subjected, it was no wonder if they displayed moral defects. His next call took him to the sprawling palaces that commanded the last prong of Europe. Herzl found Topkapı, the onetime headquarters for a militant empire, "a decaying, old, dirty, imposing building, humming with the most remarkable activity." The Secretary-General to the Grand Vizir, a youngish, handsome army doctor, led them to his master, a stooped, once tall old man with a wrinkled, withered face and white beard. Two pairs of prayer beads lay on the desk before him. After diplomatic banalities, which his Secretary translated carefully, the Grand Vizir got down to business. What terms was Herzl proposing? Although on the train Herzl had agreed with Nevlinsky that twenty million might be reasonable—two million for Palestine itself, eighteen to rescue Turkey from its creditors—he refused to commit himself. The interview ended and the Secretary, as a kindness, showed Herzl a particularly good view of the narrows between Europe and Asia, at the same time squeezing his hand.

The next call was at the Foreign Office. Mehmet Nuri Bey—whom Herzl mistook for an Armenian—was the son of a French convert to Islam by a Circassian mother. Educated in France and with the reddish hair of a European, he affected to disdain his colleagues, proclaiming himself the one-eyed man in the kingdom of the blind. Though only two years Herzl's senior, he had been Chief Secretary for Foreign Affairs since 1893. Quickly comprehending Herzl's idea, he introduced him to the First Dragoman, Daoud Effendi, an Ottoman Jew. Daoud protested that the Jews were well off in the Turkish empire and were loyal to the Sultan. It was largely true. Ever since the Spanish persecutions the Ottoman empire had welcomed Jews, who were particularly numerous in Salonika and Smyrna. Daoud was a tall, fat man with a short, gray beard. The soldiers on guard presented arms with a great clatter as he passed. Daoud sensed that his own position, as well as that of his co-religionists in other regions of the empire, might be endangered if it were thought that a Jewish movement was going to follow the Greeks, Bulgars and Armenians in demanding a portion of the Sultan's realm. Daoud showed his apprehension by imploring Herzl to have someone else introduce him to the Foreign Minister.

A final interview ended Herzl's first morning in this complex city. Nishan Effendi was an Armenian in charge of the Press Bureau. He and his underlings scoured the European press for references to Turkey. They were not pleased with some recent articles in the *Neue Freie Presse.*

Nevlinksy returned that evening to their parlor with news from Yildiz so bad that he ordered but a half bottle of champagne, in sign of mourning.

"Nothing doing," he told Herzl. "The Grand Seigneur won't hear of it." The bottle open, he went on to report what the Sultan had said: "If Herr Herzl is as much your friend as you are mine, then advise him not to take another step in this matter. I cannot sell even a foot of land, for it does not belong to me, but to my people. My people have won this empire by fighting for it with their blood and have fertilized it with their blood. We will again cover it with blood before we allow it to be wrested away from us. The men of two of my regiments from Syria and Palestine let themselves be killed one by one at Plevna.° Not one of them yielded; they all gave their lives on that battlefield. The Turkish Empire belongs not to me, but to the Turkish people.† I cannot give away any part of it. Let the Jews save their billions. When my Empire is partitioned, they may get Palestine for nothing. But only our corpse will be divided. I will not agree to vivisection."[3]

Herzl's reaction to the disappointment showed an artist's recognition of a grand gesture and a diplomat's second sense, since his words would surely get back to Yildiz. He was touched, he told Nevlinsky, by the truly lofty words of the Sultan, though they temporarily dashed his hopes. There was a tragic beauty in a fatalism that accepted death and dismemberment, yet fought, even passively, to the last breath.

Next day, Friday, was marked by the selamlik, an important weekly occasion when just before noon Abdul Hamid would be driven from his palace enclosure to pray in the white mosque by the bright

---

° A town in the modern Bulgaria where an Ottoman army was besieged by Russians and Romanians in 1877.

† In German, "*Das türkische Reich gehört nicht mir, sondern dem türkischen Volk.*" Herzl is quoting in German what Nevlinsky told him either in German or French. Nevlinsky did not speak Ottoman Turkish. While it was customary for Europeans to speak of the Turkish empire, Sultan Abdul Hamid saw himself as Sultan-Caliph of an Islamic, not a Turkish, empire. He probably spoke of the Ottoman empire and the Ottoman people.

blue Bosporus. Troops—"sturdy, sinewy, sun-tanned fellows, full of energy . . . hardship-defying"—marched up; cavalry regiments trotted down the hill; Zouaves in red and green turbans practiced the goose step taught by their German military advisers; buglers held horns to their lips ready to blow. The Ottoman elite—pashas on horseback or in carriages, small boys dressed as officers, the Sultan's sons and other princelings drawn up on horseback with two gray-bearded tutors, the Chief Eunuch, three royal coaches containing veiled ladies—all waited for the man who claimed, as Caliph, to be the Prophet's successor as head of the Islamic community on earth.

The Sultan arrived in a half-open landau which he shared with Osman Pasha, the sixty-five-year-old soldier whom he had honored with the title Gazi, or Conqueror, after the heroic defense of Plevna, in which so many Arabs had died. As the hoofs of horses clopped between a close-packed hedge of officers and guards, Herzl studied the Sultan with the same care he had devoted to the Kaiser. He was slight and sickly, his most outstanding features a large hooked nose and a medium-sized brown beard that appeared to be dyed. Those who are being stared at often know. Abdul Hamid stared sharply back at the two Europeans standing on a nearby terrace; after the prayers were over—they lasted about twenty minutes—the sultan stared again.

The fairy-tale splendor of the selamlik, with its aura of power, doomed whatever followed to seem an anticlimax. The dancing dervishes Herzl was taken to see were not to his taste. The music struck him as homespun, the dance itself like "a sort of *chaîne anglaise* in a quadrille," suddenly turning to dizzy whirling. The appearance of the dervishes, their gestures—in white garments, their cloaks abandoned—their left palm toward the ground, the right turned up, reminded him of Loie Fuller, an American dancer whose sinuous movements had caused a sensation at the Folies Bergères Herzl's first year in Paris.

That Friday afternoon Herzl met a Romanian denizen of the Yildiz jungle: Také Margueritte, a bibulous favorite of the Grand Vizir. He was also a gossip and a mischief-maker. After retailing stories about Baron Popper's exploits, he told Herzl that Nevlinsky had asked him, in Herzl's name, to drop the matter of Palestine.

Herzl discussed tactics with Nevlinsky in their shared parlor. At the start of the new Turkish week—Saturday, June 20—Herzl suggested an interim loan to the Sultan of two million; even though the money might be lost in a bottomless drain, it could induce a compliant mood. It was vital for Herzl that he should not return to Europe empty-handed. Nevlinsky reported a countersuggestion that came from Izzet: the Jews should acquire some other territory and then trade it to the Sultan for Palestine, along with a loan. Herzl's comment: "I immediately thought of Cyprus. Izzet's idea is good, and it shows that he is thinking with us and for us. He declines a personal share in it. But he has his family in Arabia, numbering—1500, for whom something would have to be done." Nuri Bey, whom Herzl met again that afternoon, made yet a third proposal. Instead of trying to get Turkey off the financial hook, the Jews should join those dangling it: i.e., they should infiltrate the Commission of Bondholders. Herzl was easily swayed by considerations of personal affinity and there were resemblances between himself, a Hungarian Jew with Germanic leanings, and Nuri, a half European with considerable contempt for the society he ostensibly served. Herzl was to write that Nuri had the most intelligent mind in the Foreign Office. Here Nevlinsky showed the sharper acumen. He damned Nuri's proposal out of hand. If the Jews infiltrated the Bondholders, they would become as detested as the members of the commission.

Although Nevlinsky was never to win Herzl the Sultan's acquiescence, he was brilliantly successful at procuring him the right introductions. The following day, Sunday, the two men were received at Yildiz by Izzet Bey, at this time the favorite with most influence on the Sultan. Yildiz Park, with some of its tawdry buildings under repair, typified the slipshod empire. "It looks rather shabby. The individual offices look like beach cabins. Even the room of Izzet Bey, the all-powerful, is small and paltry. Izzet's desk, a smaller one for his secretary, a few armchairs, and a curtained four-poster (in case he has to spend the night there on continuous duty); that is all." It was as typical of Eastern bureaucracy that Izzet received another caller, a Jewish jeweler with a silver pendulum clock ordered by the Sultan for the physician who had lanced his boil. After finishing with him, Izzet gave Herzl just fifteen minutes. The Syrian Arab struck him as intelligent but tired. Their meeting accomplished nothing, though its conclusion instructed Herzl in the baksheesh-giving then customary, each of the flunkys and doorkeepers holding out a shameless hand. Nevlinsky and Herzl drove east along the Bosporus to Bebek and a waterside café. Only when they were seated out of earshot of listeners did Nevlinsky reveal what he had accomplished the previous day with the Grand Vizir: he had kept silent earlier lest Herzl inadvertently let Izzet know.

The Sultan, Nevlinsky said, had recently been angered at the way the *Neue Freie Presse* had written about Turkey—and this after Abdul Hamid had granted Bacher (with Benedikt, the paper's editor and publisher) an audience. It was therefore impossible for Herzl to be received as a journalist. But he could be received as a friend—if in the meanwhile Herzl showed some earnest of that friendship. Herzl must influence the press in London, Paris, Berlin and Vienna to handle the Armenian question in a more understanding spirit; he must also persuade the Armenian leaders to submit to the Sultan, who in return would be generous with concessions. "To me all my peoples are like children I might have had by different wives"; the Sultan had used a comparison unthinkable in a Western society. "They are my children, all of them; and even though they have differences of opinion among themselves—with me they can have none." In apparently assuming that Herzl could work such miracles, the Sultan was, in fact, putting him to a test. If Herzl claimed to be able to solve the enigma of Ottoman finances, let him show his prowess in the smaller problem of the Armenians. Herzl said that he was prepared to try, but if the Sultan received him first, it would strengthen his position. No, Nevlinsky said, *afterwards:* and then he would also confer on him a high decoration.

Herzl's impatience to reach the Sultan made him fidget through a firemen's exhibition, and then the recital by a Polish violinist at the house of Madame Gropler, one of Constantinople's few hostesses; her husband was a Pole who had settled in Turkey after the same unsuccessful revolt that had ruined Nevlinsky. Herzl seems to have inspired her with affection and later the same year he sent her photographs of Pauline, now aged six, Hans, aged five, and Trude, three.

But an evening sail on the Bosporus calmed his nerves. "The veils of evening slowly draped themselves around the beautiful, white, proud castles where the harem wives dwell, the widows of former sultans and the widows (sic) of the present one. For he does not live with them." But that his mind was still not focused, these sentences show.

On Monday Herzl returned refreshed to the attack. At all costs Nevlinsky must secure him his interview: his position with the financiers and Maccabees of London depended on it. He used Také Margueritte to secure an appointment for Tuesday with the Grand Vizir and then at once wired Benedikt in Vienna that he would cable him the whole interview, provided the *Neue Freie Presse* stressed the amiability of his reception. Benedikt wired back that he would do all Herzl wished. The interview with the Vizir lasted one and a half hours. They were painful, since Herzl had to take notes on his knee against a barrage of sun. It was routine stuff. More interesting was a vignette of Ottoman manners. As Herzl and Také returned across the Golden Horn bridge, a beggar boy whined for baksheesh even after Herzl had tipped him. Herzl begged Také to rid them of him. This Také did by spitting full in the lad's face. Half an hour later, back at the hotel, they joined Nevlinsky in the parlor. Nevlinsky was busy writing. Brusquely he ordered Také: "Ring!" Obediently Také pulled the bell rope. His humility avenged the boy. When Herzl commented on the double incident to Nevlinsky, the latter philosophized: "*Ici on reçoit des crachats et on les rend.*"‡

Would Herzl get his Imperial interview? Wednesday was a day of encouraging suspense. The Sultan sent a message that he should not leave. Herzl at once filed a pro-Turkish article for his paper. In the afternoon he sailed to the Austrian Ambassador's residence for a conversation. The Ambassador compared politics to chess. This banality was followed by an evening excursion: dinner by the sea; a moonlit return across the water toward a skyline of minarets and domes, Také Magueritte drunk as a lord.

Nevlinsky's original warning that the time was inauspicious for Herzl's visit was borne out. On Sunday there had been rumors of bloodshed in Crete, of the massacre of an Ottoman battalion by Druse irregulars, of an Armenian incursion from Russia that left three hundred Muslims dead. On Thursday yet more killings were reported, this time from near Lake Van. And tomorrow would be another Friday, a second selamlik, further hours in which nothing could get done. Herzl did what he could. He sent his interview with the Grand Vizir by the hands of a passenger traveling to Vienna on the Orient Express.

Nevlinsky used a womanizer's idiom to maintain Herzl's spirits. The Turks, he was sure, were willing to give Palestine to the Jews; the Porte was simply acting like a whore affecting to be coy. After the second selamlik, Nevlinsky met the Sultan, while Herzl went for a drive. In the evening Nevlinsky reported. (Herzl was never sure how much he could rely on Nevlinsky's truthfulness, which added to the tension.) The Sultan had thanked Herzl for the article in the *Neue Freie Presse.* He welcomed Izzet's proposal—that the Zionists secure some other territory, then offer it in exchange. Herzl seems to have taken this report at its face value; to a student of the Sultan's psychology it might have seemed an exercise in his favorite strategy, procrastination. His promise, "In any case, I shall receive Herr Herzl—sooner or later," was another example. But Herzl was in a mood where gnats were dragonflies.

Nevlinsky recounted an interesting exchange.

‡ "Here one gets spat on and spits back."

The Sultan: "Must the Jews have Palestine? Couldn't they settle in some other province?"

Nevlinsky: "Palestine is their cradle; that is where they wish to return."

The Sultan: "But Palestine is the cradle of other religions as well."

Nevlinsky: "If they cannot get Palestine, they will simply go to Argentina."

A discussion had then followed in Turkish (which Nevlinsky did not understand) with Izzet. From the mention of "Salonika" it was possible the Sultan thought of offering northern Greece.[4]

But Saturday came, then Sunday, the day for Herzl's departure, with nothing more than hints and promises. The Sultan's chamberlain, Nevlinsky told him, was more influential than all the ambassadors: for he was a trusted dreamer; the Sultan acted on his dreams. The Prince of Bulgaria, did he but know it, owed his throne to one such dream.

From this wonderland Herzl decided to salvage what he could. He asked Nevlinsky straight out to get him a decoration. "I have never given a hoot for decorations, and I don't give a hoot now. But for my people in London I badly need a sign of favor from the Sultan." That evening, after being shown the Sultan's treasures at Topkapı and Dolmabahçe—he was rowed to them by eight sturdy boatmen in the Sultan's caïque—he returned to the hotel to find Nevlinsky sweating in his underwear, writing a letter.

"He sends you this," said the Pole, casually handing him a box. It contained the Commander's Cross of the Mejidiye Order.[*]

While Herzl the politician was frustrated—and the second-class bauble summarized a journey that cost three thousand francs and was fruitless except in rhetoric—Herzl the artist reappeared. Behind the would-be leader of the Jews lurked the successful essayist, the genuine artist. "I loved the view of the Golden Horn from our hotel windows. Whistler-like dusk and nights aglow with lights, wonderful rosy morning mists; the thick violet and grey-blue splendor of the evening vapors. The big ships disappearing in the fog and then emerging again. On moonlit nights, light powdery veils. Today it is sunny. The heights over there—Eyub, I believe—stretch between two sheets of blue. Above, the delicate sky; below, the oily waters on which the silver strokes of oars flash."

A week later he was back in London, making bricks for his political

---

[*] An order founded by Abdul Hamid's father, Sultan Abdul Mejid, in 1852. The impressive decoration had seven silver rays and crescents with stars surrounding a gold medallion, whose enamels and jewels depended on its class. There were six classes; Herzl's was the second.

structure from the wisps of straw he had gathered in this beautiful ruin whose only protection was that everyone wanted it. "None of the pirates will let any of the others enjoy this beauty—and so perhaps it will remain unplundered."[5]

CHAPTER 25

H is reception by the Grand Duke of Baden, his calls on Ottoman officials established the two poles of Herzl's gentile strategy. But his strategy only made sense if he were acknowledged by the Jews as their *gestor*. The Kaiser's elderly uncle was too lightweight a potentate, the Sultan too *rusé* and hesitant, for handshake or decoration to have results. But if such exalted circles took Herzl seriously, so might the Jews; and if the Jews—preferably the millionaires, failing them the learned, or as a last resort the masses—accepted him as their leader, then when he next knocked on kingly portals in Europe or Turkey, he could do so with effect. Herzl was thus in the position of a conjurer who had to maintain three plates in the air at once. If one fell to the ground, the two others would follow. Rejection by gentile statesmen, a final veto from the Sultan would obstruct his mission. But if the Jews withheld their support, the mission was finished before it began. His offer to rid Europe of its revolutionaries and financiers would then sound as preposterous as his offer to pay the Sultan's debts. Only if he had the backing of the Jews could Herzl speak with authority in Europe and Asia.

The Sultan had asked for a loan of two million as evidence of Herzl's authority. The City of London was at this time the world's richest source of capital. A week after leaving Turkey Herzl was entering the House of Commons as the guest of Sir Samuel Montagu. Grandiose externals worked their effect. "At the sight of these imposing parliamentary trappings—after all, externals have a dramatic effect—I experienced a touch of dizziness such as I had felt that time in the ante-chamber of the Grand Duke of Baden. At the same time I began to understand why the English Jews should cling to a country in which they can enter this house as masters."[1] Montagu confided some exciting news: the Hirsch Foundation had at its disposal ten million sterling. But this was the last good news from the rich. An atmosphere of hesitation fogged this London visit, of suspicion, of failure. Montagu's last word was that he would adhere to the movement only if three conditions were met: the Great Powers must consent; the Hirsch Foundation must turn over its millions; and Edmond de Rothschild, the leading member of the French branch of the dynasty, must join the committee. Montagu also expressed grave doubts about the mass meeting in the East End which Herzl had engaged to address on July 12, 1896. Herzl replied that he did not want a demagogic movement: "but if the worst came to the worst—if the aristocrats proved too aristocratic—I would set the masses in motion, too."[2]

The mass meeting of jubilant, hat-waving, hurrahing East Enders showed how his Turkish visit was seen in a drab background. Yiddish posters proclaimed, incorrectly, that Herzl had been received by the Sultan. One speaker compared him to both Moses and Columbus. Herzl had been intoxicated by his grip on his hearers. He felt wafted to extremes. He antagonized the English Lovers of Zion when, at a meeting at Bevis Marks synagogue, he laid his cards on the table: he was opposed to infiltration or undefended colonies. "I said I wanted only the kind of colonization that we could protect with our own Jewish army."[3] The meeting ended in uproar. The weather echoed his mood. "My dear child," he wrote to Julie in one of the rare letters to his wife that have survived, "Two quick words before I embark— in bad weather—for Boulogne. I hope the God of the seas will be merciful to me. Tomorrow I am in Paris, I do not want to stay there longer than absolutely necessary, because until now my vacation was nothing but very tiring, although very successful, work. I yearn for recuperation. Many hearty kisses to you and the beloved children. Your faithful Papa, Theodor."[4]

In Paris on July 18 Herzl called on Baron Edmond de Rothschild at his business headquarters in the Rue Laffitte. The baron was fifteen years older than Herzl. If only de Rothschild would grant what the late Baron de Hirsch had refused, Herzl could proceed in his negotiations with the Sultan as nuncio of the aristocrats, not tribune of the masses. But de Rothschild proved even colder than de Hirsch. A dispiriting interview began with the banker revealing that Colonel Goldsmid had concluded that Herzl's schemes were downright dangerous. The rest was so dismal that Herzl could hardly bring himself to record it. The head of the wealthiest Jewish family in Europe felt that his financial interests, far from being safeguarded by Zionism (the argument Herzl had advanced in his *Address*), were imperiled by it. As patron of several philanthropic but unprofitable colonies in Palestine, de Rothschild feared that Herzl's intrigues might put his colonists at risk.

Having failed to win a single millionaire, Herzl now set out to conquer the Jewish communities. His eventual success—a triumph of noise and drama as well as of organization—was to delete the traces of enemy positions. The struggle to convince the Jews proved tougher than charming gentile politicians or bribing Ottoman officials. The stakes were high and Herzl attacked with a gambler's frenzy. If he lost, he would be scorned as an idle dreamer and discredited even as a writer. If he won, his secret boast, "I shall associate with the mighty of this earth as their equal,"[5] would be sober fact. Since the winners in history have the power, at least temporarily, to write it, his enemies would be traduced or posthumously transformed into supporters. Dr. Moritz Güdemann's *Nationaljudentum*,* the pamphlet in which he wrote down his considered objections to Jewish nationalism, would be condemned as a work of "cowardly vagueness" composed at "the wishes of the upper class of Viennese Jewry."[6] At the time, it was Herzl who seemed vague, Herzl whose allies seemed to be dubious. Güdemann had welcomed Herzl's apparent return to Judaism and had been carried away by the boldness of his ideas. Yet he openly disapproved of the Herzl family's failure to practice even a minimal Judaism and knew that *Der Judenstaat* was in no sense a blueprint for a state based on Torah. On reflection, safe from Herzl's personal fascination, he compared him with apprehension to Sabbatai Zevi. The false Messiah, first mentioned by Schiff on June 17, 1895, was to occur repeatedly in the minds of the doubtful. For example, on March 29, 1896, the day before the visit of his anti-Semitic admirer von Simonyi, Herzl had attended the Seder of the Jewish student association, Unitas. Otto Friedmann, a distinguished member of Herzl's former faculty, then expounded the significance of the festival to the Jewish students. "I sat next to him. Later he spoke briefly with me in private, reminded me of Sabbatai Zevi, 'who enchanted all people,' and winked in a way that seemed to say that I ought to become such a Sabbatai. Or did he mean," Herzl paused as he assessed the remembered wink, "that I already *was* one?"[7]

The damning comparison with Sabbatai Zevi was to be made far more explicitly by one of the most brilliant and stirring Jewish preachers of his age. Born in Russia in 1859, Chaim Zundel Maccoby had

* In it Güdemann asked: who was more assimilated, the nationalist Jew who ignored the Sabbath, or the practicing Jew who felt himself a German?

studied the Prophets as a child of six and in his early adolescence became an inspired exponent of Love of Zion; he traveled all over Russia preaching the peaceful settlement of the land. His Zionism was religious and non-political; his soul would have revolted from any attempt to evict the other people living in Palestine. His success as a preacher (or maggid) gave him the name by which he is now remembered, the Kamenitzer Maggid. In 1890, at the age of thirty-two, he came to London, where his preaching won him an enthusiastic following among other emigrants from Russia. His characteristic gentleness is shown by an interview given by his daughter in her extreme old age.[8]

> "What did your father teach you children regarding meat eating?"
> "Oh," she replied, "that it was cruel, cruel."
> "What did he do about the shank bone for Seder?"
> "He substituted another egg for it."

The Kamenitzer Maggid greeted Herzl with prophetic denunciation. A disbeliever† could not be a true Jewish leader. On the contrary, he could only be a Sabbatai Zevi done up in the trappings of the nineteenth century. "Maccoby attacked him with sharp and scathing words, declaring him to be a false Messiah to be shunned." But Herzl's followers in the East End, some of them recruited from the Maggid's former disciples, began to break up the rabbi's meetings. Their pressure induced the Federation of Synagogues to forbid him from mentioning Zionism in his sermons; he was finally ordered to withdraw from all communal work in London. He died in 1916 "a disappointed, embittered and heartbroken man."[10] Yet his greatest injuries were to be posthumous and Orwellian. By 1928 the Maggid had been virtually included in Herzl's retinue: "The immigration of a number of Jewish nationalists, which, already in 1887, led to the foundation of the Kadimah in the East End of London, and the impassioned pulpit addresses of the Reverend Chaim Z. Maccoby, the famous Kamenitzer Maggid, produced, at the beginning of the '90s, a popular agitation in favour of Jewish nationalism."[11] Four decades later a Hall of Education was to be established in the Maggid's memory at Bar Ilan University in Israel. A fund-raising pamphlet, with a résumé of his life, a list of patrons and two pages of tributes, so far from mentioning his conflict with Herzl and his rejection of political

---

† The Maggid believed that Herzl had confessed his atheism to Asher Myers, then editor of the *Jewish Chronicle*. Herzl's religious position, which he himself defined as a species of monism, was nearer to agnosticism, though with overtones of an evolutionary theism.[9]

Zionism, says: "his outpourings of mind and heart paved the way to the ultimate success of Zionism."[12] It is as if Cardinal Newman were to be memorialized without word of his conflict with Cardinal Manning.

It would have been easier for Herzl the freethinker if he could have dismissed opposition to his ideas as the result of religious crankery or shallow self-interest. This he could not do. Some of his briskest opponents were cultured, experienced men whom he had to respect. They saw serious dangers in his plans and the manner in which he tried to advance them. Three such critics may stand for all: a courageous journalist, an astute Minister of Finance and a pioneering social scientist. We know that Herzl respected the integrity of all three.

Dr. Joseph S. Bloch (1850–1923), the first of the three to meet Herzl, was a member of the Austrian parliament, a learned rabbi, and as editor of the *Österreichische Wochenschrift,* the most consistent opponent of anti-Semitism in the German-speaking world. His weekly, which specialized in refuting racialist libels, was read in most Jewish households. Bloch combined learning in the traditional Jewish modes with a profound secular education. Bloch's first reaction to Herzl, when he met him at a meeting of the Austro-Israelite Union in a Vienna restaurant, resembled Güdemann's: he was surprised at finding him at all interested in Jewish affairs. "Herzl was known," Bloch later wrote,[13] "as a consummate man of the world and a favourite master of the conversational art, whose *feuilletons,* with their air of ironic superiority, very rarely touched upon the fate of the Jews and then only to shower icicles of delicate ridicule upon it." Bloch believed, with Güdemann, that the Jews were a religious community held together by the faith of Moses; for him, the fact that Jews felt nothing in common with a Jew who accepted some other religion proved this hypothesis to be true.

Five days later Bloch accepted an invitation to the house of an architect friend to hear Herzl read what was to become *Der Judenstaat.* Bloch was relieved that in the version he then heard neither Zion nor Palestine was mentioned. "Palestine is the old homeland of the Jews," he explained. "It is the symbol of prophetic expectations and longings. However, its position at the frontier of Asia, Africa and Europe had always made it a bone of contention between the big neighbouring countries, and we Jews should not lay our heads on this sickbed once again."[14]

A few days later Herzl called on Bloch in some embarrassment. Several of his friends had convinced him that only the magnetic word "Palestine" would inspire Jews to migrate. Bloch implored Herzl to read the history of the Holy Land from earliest times. He would then find that it had only been independent under David and Solomon and that thereafter a long succession of peoples had made it their battlefield. Bloch joined the ranks of those who had mentioned Sabbatai Zevi. To correct Herzl's idea of Judaism he lent him a book by Adolf Jellinek, joint Chief Rabbi with Güdemann until his death in 1893. This taught Jews that their homes could be more fitting temples of the living God than the long-destroyed Temple. "The altar in Jerusalem was destroyed, the Jew could bring no offerings, and the Talmud taught that the most splendid altar is your heart. Be generous to the poor, for to aid a single father and sustain his children is worth more in the eyes of God than if you slaughtered a hundred bulls in His honour; do philanthropic deeds; study the Torah and stamp its spirit of justice and love upon your actions, and then you will never have need of a blood sacrifice."[15]

Though Herzl plainly had no intention of reviving a sacrificial cult in a rebuilt Temple, Bloch feared that his program would lead to violence and suffering. He quoted a saying by Austria's greatest dramatic poet, Franz Grillparzer: "From humanity by way of nationality to bestiality."[16] The anti-Semitic jest that Palestine would make a good mousetrap for the Jews might also prove true.

Soon after the publication of *Der Judenstaat*, early in 1896, Bloch introduced Herzl to his second critic, Leon Ritter von Bilinski (1846–1923). Bilinski and his wife, though Catholics, were both of Jewish origin and maintained a warm sympathy for Jews. Brought up in Galicia, Bilinski had a brilliant career at Lvov University, whose rector he became at the early age of thirty-two. In 1883 he had been elected to the Austrian parliament and at the time he met Herzl he was Minister of Finance. (He was to fill the same function in the independent Poland set up after the First World War.) Bilinski had heard wild tales of Herzl and agreed to meet him only on condition that both men swore to keep their meetings confidential. Bilinski's posthumous Memoirs omit any reference to Herzl nor does Bilinski's name appear in Herzl's Diary.‡ But twelve hundred typewritten pages describing his contacts with Herzl were given by Bilinski to Bloch, who bequeathed them to a namesake, Chaim Bloch, who has released enough to show the statesman's attitude. The quantity of the notes proves how seriously each man took the other.[17]

‡ Herzl was probably more than willing to exclude Bilinski and his criticisms from his Diáry, which was kept with a political purpose. While mentioning his meetings with Joseph S. Bloch, he does not record the arguments against Zionism that he heard from him.

As a politician, Bilinski was in daily touch with the makers of Habsburg policy. Already in 1896 Austrian anti-Semites were finding ammunition in Herzl's arguments, as would the followers of Drumont once *Der Judenstaat* had appeared in its French translation. Von Schönerer, for example, told Bilinski that he thought Herzl entirely right and that the only solution for the Jewish problem was for the Jews to be given a territory and made to go to it. The argument that Drumont and his followers took up in *La Libre Parole* was that the Jews consisted of a separate people that could not assimilate. Herzl's often repeated thesis when dealing with gentile statesmen—that Zionism would siphon off elements dangerous to their host countries—could have lethal results. Anti-Semites approved of Herzl for authenticating their own accusations against the Jews. "If the malicious propaganda that the Jews are a danger to the world and that they are revolutionaries continues," Bilinski noted, "the Zionists will, instead of establishing a Jewish State, cause the destruction of European Jewry."* Bilinski shared the view of Bloch—and that of Emperor Franz-Josef†—that nationalism was in itself destructive. Von Schönerer wanted a war, because German nationalism would rise from the wreckage of the Habsburg empire; Herzl foresaw a Jewish nation-state arising as a result of a war that would similarly destroy the Sultan's empire. "Herzl doesn't want to admit that he is a fanatic nationalist," Bilinski wrote. "But, truthfully, is not nationalism identical with fanaticism? The notion that any Jew who is not an adherent of the Zionists and is not a nationalist is not a Jew—is not original.

---

* Herzl has been accused of writing for *La Libre Parole*. Neither inquiry from one such accuser nor careful investigation of the back numbers of the journal from 1895 to 1904 has substantiated this accusation. Drumont was served by a team of writers who signed their articles; it was equally alien to Herzl's proud temperament to use a pseudonym, particularly on such an issue as the Jewish question and in such a journal. What is certain is that Herzl badgered his friend Daudet to get Drumont to review *L'État Juif*[18] and that Drumont did so. Herzl's translated pamphlet was published in the *Nouvelle Revue Internationale*, half in the issue of December 31, 1896, half in the issue of January 15, 1897. Drumont's long and signed article, "*Solution de la Question Juive*," was published in *La Libre Parole* on January 16, 1897. Two days later Herzl noted in his Diary that three Paris friends had sent him the issue, "in which Drumont gets off a highly flattering editorial about me and promises more." Drumont praised Herzl for agreeing to so many of the charges made against the Jews by their opponents. He praises the Zionists of Herzl's persuasion *for not seeing in us fanatics, maniacs, savage and heartless beings, but citizens who exercise the right of self-defence.*[19] (author's italics)

† On Herzl's argument that civic equality was "a misfortune because it led to assimilation and intermarriage," Franz-Josef commented to Bilinski: "What would have become of this Herzl if there were no equality of rights? Herzl's collaboration with the German nationalists, the mortal enemies of the Monarchy, gives me constant concern."[20]

The German nationalists proclaim the same things. Herzl uses all kinds of journalistic fireworks to create dissension between the Powers. But when war breaks out the Jews will be the first victims."[21]

Bilinksi was one of two thinkers to predict at this early stage that Herzl's program would arouse hostility to the Jews in the Middle East, a region where European-style prejudice was still unknown.‡ "The anti-Semites who are today recommending the Zionist plan will later incite the mobs in Palestine and Syria too and then the concentration of Jews in Palestine will be of no avail to the Zionists."[22]

Bilinski's prediction of a clash with the Arabs can be approximately dated to a period at least two years after his first meeting with Herzl. The second prediction can be dated precisely. On December 9, 1899, Ludwig Gumplowicz published an essay on *The Sociological Interpretation of History*. Although this essay had nothing to do with Zionism, Gumplowicz was a Jew and in a letter of December 11 Herzl asked the leading sociologist to express his attitude to "this mad movement" [Zionism]. He also posted some of his writings to Gumplowicz. The latter was old enough to be Herzl's father. He took advantage of his seniority to write a withering retort. The Zionists, he replied, were historically wrong. The Jews had about as much connection with Palestine as nineteenth-century "Aryans" had with India: "In *Palestine* were their ancestors as little as the ancestors of the Palestinians in Egypt." He referred to some literary documents bequeathed by his son Max which even cast doubt on the "Semitic" origins of Polish and Russian Jews. "This is your *historical* foundation. And now your *political naïveté*. You want to create a state without bloodshed? Where have you ever seen such a thing? Without force and without cunning? So very openly and honestly,—on shares?"[23] Gumplowicz (who died before the publication of even an edited version of the Diary) based his judgment of Herzl on his numerous declarations and speeches. For by the time Gumplowicz wrote Herzl had achieved a pulpit and a forum.

The pulpit was a weekly newspaper in German entitled *Die Welt*. The Jewish star, or Magen David, fitted snugly between the article and the noun.[24] It was published in Vienna at 9, Türkenstrasse.

Launching the newspaper consumed more money and psychic energy than Herzl could afford. But by the night of June 6, 1897,

‡ This is not to say that Jews had never suffered in Islamic countries. They had, along with Christians and Muslim heretics. But Islamic law, based on the Koran, recognized Jews with Christians as "people of the Book," monotheists who deserved toleration. What prejudice existed was based on unrationalized prejudice or commercial rivalry. Prejudice based on racial doctrines, the type of the new anti-Semitism, was not known.

the paper was out. Herzl described himself as "utterly exhausted," a phrase that henceforth appears with metronomic regularity in his Diary. There had been the Zangwill visit, the need to plan a Whitsun *feuilleton* and the insidious fear that Benedikt might use *Die Welt* as an excuse to dismiss him. His mother as well as Julie showed intermittent fears that he might lose his one solid source of income.

The prime aim of the newspaper was to diffuse the Zionist viewpoint inside the Jewish communities. But at the same time, Herzl wrote to Sidney Whitman, an English traveler who enjoyed the Sultan's friendship, and to Ahmed Midhat, the Sultan's favorite journalist, that *Die Welt* existed to serve the Ottoman cause. In this connection Whitman had raised two questions. Would the Jewish settlers owe allegiance to the Sultan? How, without dispossessing the natives, would the Jews obtain the land they needed? Herzl's reply, in the light of earlier entries in his Diary, was hardly frank. "The immigrant Jews in Palestine would become subjects of HM the Sultan," he wrote, "on condition of an absolutely guaranteed *self-protection.** The necessary land purchases would be made entirely without constraint. It cannot be a question of 'dispossessing' anyone at all. Ownership is a private right and cannot be violated. The Sultan's private domains could be paid for in cash according to their value, if he desires to sell."[25]

Herzl's preoccupation with *Die Welt* is shown by a curious slip in a reference to his son's birthday. Ending the fourth volume of his Diary he noted: "June 10, 7th birthday of my Hans." It was in fact the sixth.[26]†

More important than the pulpit was the forum: the first Zionist Congress. The idea of such a rally of Zionist sympathizers had been stimulated by his exasperation with Baron de Rothschild. "You were the keystone of the entire combination," Herzl quotes himself as telling the baron. "If you refuse, everything I have fashioned so far will fall to pieces. I shall then be obliged to do it in a different way. I shall start a mass agitation, and that way it will be even harder to keep the masses under control."[27] Two days later he had instructed the faithful de Haas in London "to organize the masses."[28]

Another stimulant was "a good letter" he received when resting at Aussee on August 1, 1896.[29] Chief Rabbi Zadoc Kahn proposed the convening of "a secret conference" representing the largest Jewish communities. Kahn knew of the rift with de Rothschild and wished

---

* English in original.

† Herzl refers infrequently to his children in his Diary. It is curious that out of the five references to their birthdays or age, he gets the age wrong on three occasions. (*Complete Diaries,* pp. 560, 1136 and 1158.)

to reconcile these two prominent Jews. The conference should be secret so as not to arouse Rothschild fears; it could provide alternative backing for Herzl. Though his immediate reaction was one of assent, Herzl did not want a secret conclave. If the Jewish masses were to be organized, they must be seen to be organized; if there was a conference, it must be as spectacular as possible.

More than a year passed before the Congress took place. The first intention was to hold it in Munich, but the Jewish community in that city protested officially and after briefly considering Zurich, Herzl decided on Basel, a smaller Swiss town. The Congress was to last from August 29 to 31, 1897. Premises were finally secured in the shape of the town casino, a hall normally used for concerts or gambling. Its delegates numbered two hundred, including the Reverend Hechler and two other Christian Zionists. Far from being a secret gathering, the Congress was conducted with the maximum publicity. Reporters from at least a dozen major newspapers, including the London *Times,* the New York *Herald,* the *Frankfurter Zeitung* and *L'Écho de Paris,* attended, as well as representatives of the Swiss and Hebrew press.

The delegates (women as well as men) varied greatly in age and profession. By and large they came from neither of the extremes. Rothschilds and other millionaires were neither present, nor, on Herzl's persuasion, mentioned in the speeches. The poor were spoken about but largely absent. It was a middle-class coming-together of unelected delegates prompted to speak for what they considered to be their nation. They were very much of the same class that had espoused German and Italian nationalism. Left to themselves they would have seemed a somewhat dowdy crowd. But they were not left to themselves. Months before, Herzl had decided that all delegates to the opening, morning session should wear evening dress.

> This worked out splendidly. Formal dress makes most people stiff. This stiffness immediately gave rise to a sedate tone—one they might not have had in light-colored summer suits or travel clothes —and I did not fail to heighten this tone to the point of solemnity. Nordau had turned up on the first day in a frock coat and flatly refused to go home and change to a full-dress suit. I drew him aside and begged him to do it as a favor to me . . . He allowed himself to be persuaded, and in return I hugged him gratefully. A quarter of an hour later he returned in formal dress.

From this elegant scene Herzl sent off commemorative postcards to each of his children, his parents and even Julie, though the Naschauers as a whole disapproved of Zionism. He wrote them at the presidential table which he had approached with icy calm until he found among the telegrams and other mail the very first letter from Hans, then just over six. Sending the postcards was, he wrote, his first lighthearted action since he had started the movement.[30]

Three days of verbal excitement produced two resolutions that are still of interest: one, of thanks and devotion, was cabled to the Sultan; the other was a concise definition of the Zionist program:

> The aim of Zionism is to create for the Jewish people a home in Palestine secured by public law.
> The Congress contemplates the following means to the attainment of this end:
> 1. The promotion, on suitable lines, of the colonization of Palestine by Jewish agricultural and industrial workers.
> 2. The organization and binding together of the whole of Jewry by means of appropriate institutions, local and international, in accordance with the laws of each country.
> 3. The strengthening and fostering of Jewish national sentiment and consciousness.
> 4. Preparatory steps towards obtaining government consent, where necessary, to the attainment of the aim of Zionism.[31]

In one important detail the Basel program was less candid than Herzl's *Judenstaat;* in another it was firmer. The mention of a home, not a state, was a tactical maneuver by Max Nordau. "I did my best," he wrote much later, "to persuade the claimants of the Jewish state in Palestine that we might find a circumlocution that would express all we meant, but would say it in a way so as to avoid provoking the Turkish rulers of the coveted land. I suggested 'Heimstätte' as a synonym for 'State' . . . This is the history of the much commented expression. It was equivocal, but we all understood what it meant. To us it signified 'Judenstaat' then and it signifies the same now."[32] The program bluntly decided on which territory was wanted. Argentina was not to be mentioned again; when another territory in another continent was proposed, the resulting storm was to hasten Herzl's death.

Herzl left the first Congress in a state of exhilaration. "Were I to sum up the Basel Congress in a word—which I shall guard against pronouncing publicly—it would be this: At Basel I founded the Jewish State. If I said this out loud today, I would be answered by universal laughter. Perhaps in five years, and certainly in fifty, everyone will know it."[33] The fact that the Congress—the realization of the Society of Jews—had taken place, that it would be reconvened, that it could claim (to those who accepted the claim) to represent the Jewish nation gave Herzl a new position in the world, for he had been elected its President. His presidential deportment, the result of his frequent attendance at French parliamentary debates, was designed to impress observers like Nevlinsky or Hechler who could report to their patrons. Nevlinsky had caused him concern. As a Polish aristocrat, what would he say about the Jews, and what would the Jews say about him? Herzl resolved to keep him apart . . . "Yet if only because of Nevlinsky, I must give the Congress a certain *style*."[34]‡ Exhilaration gave increased energy. On his way back to Vienna he was in such haste to get the Congress reports into an expanded issue of *Die Welt* that he alighted from the train at the Austrian border to cable instructions to the twenty-two-year-old student who was editing the paper in his absence.[35] The Congress had filled the wells of Herzl's self-esteem. Though the general language was German, one speaker had hailed him in Hebrew as King. But his nerves suffered. Entries in his Diary stab his emotions like butterflies on pins . . . Mrs. Sonnenschein of the *American Jewess* after one wrangle: "They will crucify you yet—and I will be your Magdalene" . . . "Four or five people were always talking to me at the same time. An enormous mental strain. I felt as though I had to play thirty-two games of chess simultaneously": or conduct an egg dance. He listed some of the eggs. His own newspaper: he must not give it a pretext to dismiss him. The Orthodox Jews: for their sake attending synagogue in a top hat, he had found the few Hebrew words of blessing more of an ordeal than his inaugural speech. The claims of Austrian patriotism. The Ottoman Sultan: the plan to detach a province of his empire might contrast oddly with the cable of loyalty. The Czar: the Russian ill-treatment of Jews was an argument for Zionism, but at some stage the Czar might be useful. The Christian churches: they might be concerned for the holy places. He then paused—only to find further eggs. Edmond de Rothschild; the Lovers of Zion, whose English members had stayed away; and not least, the personal jealousies and conflicts of the Zionists. For in truth he commanded "only boys, beggars and prigs. Some of them exploit me. Others are already jealous or disloyal. The third kind drop off as soon as some little career opens up for them."[36]

Herzl had always been suspicious. As his exhilaration subsided, he was suddenly convinced that Nevlinsky was a traitor. For when the two of them discussed the next steps to take in Turkey, Nevlinsky casually revealed that he had been in contact with Baron Edmond de Rothschild. The Pole reported the millionaire's hostility to Zionism

‡ *Tournure* in the original.

and his belief that the publication of *Der Judenstaat* had already done damage to the colonies supported by de Rothschild in Palestine.

Herzl controlled his anger only from fear of what harm "this scoundrel" could work him in Turkey if he wished.[37]

CHAPTER 26

"These days," Herzl wrote, halfway between the first Congress and the second, "I always live in a railroad atmosphere. The train speeds, or the station is deserted."[1] Politically, the year showed little advance; the visit to Turkey still seemed fruitless. He was thrown back to the world of imagination, and his family. Three ideas that came to nothing are described in his Diary: a verse drama in Renaissance costume, a novel about a newspaperman who swings from German nationalism to Zion, a play about Moses. In January 1898, he published a brief "Autobiography" (*Jewish Chronicle*, January 14, 1898) in which he claimed to have been caned at school for not attending to his scripture lessons.* *The New Ghetto*, thanks to its author's new celebrity, was first performed in Vienna in January and in Berlin in February; while *The Fugitive* had its last performance at the Burgtheater. In March there was tantalizing news: the Kaiser was going to Palestine in October, to dedicate a church and show his friendship for the Sultan. Hechler, who had a church conference to attend in Berlin, would urge the Kaiser to meet Herzl.

From the strain of hope he turned, when in Vienna, to his family. Their new house at 29 Haizingergasse in Währing was healthy and secluded; it had the protection of trees, which he had thought so vital for the new towns "over there." On June 10 Hans was seven and his father gave him a Zionist flag. "Shield of David with six stars in the six triangles. The seventh on top. In the middle field, the Lion of Judah . . ."

* Joseph Patai suggests that this and much of the "Autobiography" exemplifies Herzl's humor and is not to be taken literally. "The fact is that the teachers in his school did not administer physical punishment."[2]

But despite Herzl's precautions, Pauline was again ill that summer. Visitors "at Court" saw her lying in bed, a hot-water bottle to her heart. As is inevitable in a loveless marriage, each parent blamed the other for neglect and both spoiled the child further. Pauline developed a craving for attention she was never to outgrow. Her illness, probably rheumatic fever, permanently impaired her health. But by early August, as he took his annual vacation, Herzl could tell his editor that Pauline was almost better. This may have been to excuse his departure for Basel, where the second Congress opened on August 29. It was as exhausting as the first, but less exciting. His thoughts wafted balloon-like from the presidential table. He was back in some meadow of his youth, whether near Salzburg or Vöslau, he could not be sure. "A green meadow at eventide, a tall tree by my path, a little house —I no longer know whether a farm house or a parsonage—an infinite, fragrant peace."[3] The delegates were discussing the foundation of a bank.

Then, on September 10, 1898, something happened. As the Empress Elizabeth of Austria walked from her Geneva hotel to board a ferry, an Italian anarchist plunged a stiletto in her back. In his Sunday sermon the Reverend William Hechler told his Embassy congregation: "In the whole history of the world no such week has passed before."[4] Since apocalypse had entered everyday, the clergyman dashed off a letter to his ducal patron in Baden. It was largely devoted to Herzl's role in the prophecies of Revelation. But not entirely. Hechler had good news of his own. The Kaiser, in Vienna for the Empress' funeral, had inspected a small Palestine museum that the Ambassador had allowed Hechler to set up at the Embassy. In view of his forthcoming visit to the Holy Land, the Kaiser had been interested in Hechler's temples and charts. There was a further triumph. Hechler was about to make his own first pilgrimage to Palestine. (This was thanks to Dr. Herzl's friends, who were paying him a thousand guilders.[5]) The clergyman had a practical end in mind: to organize a search for the Ark of the Covenant, surely hidden intact on Mount Nebo to the east of the Jordan. The German Ambassador in Constantinople should induce the Sultan to cede Transjordania to the Kaiser, and then, "when the Ark of the Covenant is found, His Majesty will possess it with the two tables of stone with the 10 Commandments written by God on mount Sinai, and probably the original MS. of the 5 books of Moses, written by Moses, which were hid in the Ark and which will prove how foolishly so called 'Higher Criticism' tries to make out that Moses could not have written this and that, etc. etc."[6]

So much for the blissful Hechler.

For Herzl, too, the assassination had been followed by some successes. In a number of strenuous interviews he had expatiated on the advantages of Zionism for Germany's internal health as well as on the desirability of a German protectorate over Palestine. His hearers had been three of the most influential men in the German empire.

Herzl was fortunate in the man who was German Ambassador in Vienna from 1894 to 1902. Count Philipp zu Eulenburg was a literary dilettante, in Herzl's phrase, only too willing to meet a distinguished man of letters. He represented, as the Kaiser's most intimate friend, one side of that mercurial ruler's temperament. For the Kaiser was not only the war lord whom Herzl had diagnosed as compensating for his withered arm in militaristic poses; he had a genuine love of art and music, inherited perhaps from his grandfather, Queen Victoria's consort. But the arts had changed since the heyday of Tennyson. The Parnassus of the '90s was a symbolist rockscape of perverse scents and slippery places. Eulenburg (after being made a prince in 1900) was to have a fall as dramatic as Wilde's and of the same nature. But this was to be when Herzl was no longer living. The Eulenburg of September 16, 1898, gave Herzl no sense of foreboding, only a sense of closeness to power.

In response to a letter from Herzl, the Ambassador had wired him at Unterach on the Attersee saying that he would be available at the German Embassy at nine in the morning on the day before the funeral. Herzl returned to Vienna in haste. The interview began, a little late, with Eulenburg all smiles as Hechler, in shirt sleeves, put the last touches to his museum. The count impressed Herzl as "a tall, elegant man, on life's downward slope. Somewhere around 55, but he still seems to have a future. Imperial Chancellor, perhaps?"[7] Eulenburg, who was in fact fifty-one, had the famed Prussian reserve, "locked tight like an iron safe": but the hard, blue eyes could suddenly glow soft and hint the unsafe side. He spoke amiably to his handsome Jewish visitor, but could not promise to present him to the Kaiser on this occasion. The Emperor would be too busy conferring with Bernhard von Bülow, his Foreign Secretary.

Perhaps because both men had artistic interests, perhaps because Herzl already felt affinity with the Prussian he was to know best, he was with Eulenburg held back by none of his customary shyness. He spoke with emphasis. Two Zionist congresses proved that Jewish nationalism existed as a force. He had first thought that England would be its most natural sponsor. "But it would be even more welcome to me if it were Germany. The Jews of today are predomi-

nantly German in culture.† But I am not saying this because I am at
the German Embassy, but because it is true. Proof: the official language of the two Basel Congresses."[8]

The mention of England was clever. England stirred a complex of
reactions in the Kaiser and his circle, admiration and jealousy warring
for first place. The Indian empire which the odious Prince of Wales
would inherit from the Kaiser's beloved grandmother (who was to die
in his arms, not Edward VII's) had been amassed from a huddle of
Mogul possessions that had some resemblance to the Sultan's ram-
shackle domains; the notion of penetrating the Middle East as the
friend of the Sultan, then   transforming the Ottoman ruins into a
German equivalent of British India was one of the Kaiser's daydreams.
Eulenburg at once proposed that Herzl should meet von Bülow the
following morning.

That von Bülow received Herzl so quickly—in his private apartments, with trunks open but unpacked—seemed to confirm that the
Germans were indeed interested in the idea of a new protectorate.
As Foreign Secretary, von Bülow had followed a policy of colonial
expansion. But unlike Eulenburg von Bülow aroused—despite the alleged possession of artistic leanings—all Herzl's shyness. "In Bülow's
presence I unfortunately became a vain writer and strove harder to
make polished *mots* than to talk seriously to the point."[9]

The point Herzl did stress was calculated to appeal to a Prussian
whose conservative feelings had been outraged by the murder of an
Empress: Zionism was an antidote to socialism, which was in any
case alien to the Jewish temperament. Von Bülow looked impressed
when he was informed that Zionism had already won many Jewish students from this destructive creed. But he kept the conversation on a
casual level: in a moment he must be off to meet his master at the station. But first he felt impelled to deny the rumors that the Kaiser was
an anti-Semite: he was merely opposed to "the destructive Jews." Von
Bülow was not encouraging, however, when Herzl proposed that the
All-Highest might receive him on the train. But Herzl refused to despair. During the Embassy dinner that followed the funeral, he had
Hechler sit in the doorkeeper's quarters, having first sent his card
upstairs to Eulenburg. Herzl, with a new pair of black gloves and a
crape band round his top hat, waited hopefully in the offices of *Die
Welt*. Neither messenger nor telephone called him to the station. He
had to return to Währing and Julie's comments.

---

† Herzl was either arguing to make a point or, despite his contacts with Poles
and Russians at the Congress, was still unaware that their culture was far from being German.

Before his next important interview Herzl made a rapid descent on England to make speeches and raise funds. He traveled by way of Holland and in Amsterdam received Eulenburg's reply to the memorandum with which Herzl had followed up his Vienna meetings. Eulenburg reaffirmed that the Kaiser was interested in Herzl's movement and was willing to receive a Zionist deputation in Palestine.[10] Greatly heartened, Herzl addressed a mass meeting of ten thousand in London's East End. "Very picturesque among my *supporters* [English in original] was the Catholic Father Ignatius. In his black pleated monastic habit, with his medieval evangelist's pulpit gestures, his beautiful, clear profile, his spirited speech, he was a joy to listen to and to look at." The priest's assertion that Zionism was the Judaism of God might not silence a doubtful rabbi but it aroused enthusiasm in the East End crowds.‡

Herzl's next destination was Berlin, where Eulenburg had told him he would be spending some days at Liebenberg, his country house. To Herzl's disappointment, there was no message waiting at his hotel. Could Prussian air turn the would-be poet back into the Junker? Herzl was almost late for the train, having lingered over the problem of what to wear. He had finally decided on his gray frock coat and trousers, although a light-colored suit would normally have been suitable for a country visit. Yet to come informally attired might have given the impression that he thought himself a guest. Eulenburg seemed to approve the garb he chose and, after introducing him to his family, led him on a proprietorial stroll in a park gaudy with autumn leaves. The Kaiser's friend spoke so encouragingly that Herzl was left dazed with hope. As he thanked him, Eulenburg made a puzzling rejoinder: "Perhaps the moment will come when I shall claim favors from you." "Henceforth," Herzl replied, "you will find in me a devoted and grateful man." Back in his hotel room he searched, vainly, for clues to Eulenburg's meaning. But whatever these mysterious favors were, Herzl would grant them. "Everyone

‡ The Zionists were understandably confused as to who it was who had endorsed their cause. While Herzl describes the Reverend Leycester Lyne as a Catholic, de Haas, who was also present, calls him "that rare picturesque Father Ignatius, a monk of the Protestant order of St. Benedictine (sic)."[11] Father Ignatius—the Reverend Joseph Leycester Lyne—was one of the most eccentric figures of the nineteenth-century Anglican Church. He claimed, like Herzl, to have been mercilessly flogged at school (St. Paul's) for having even then shown too pronounced an interest in Jewish matters. (Contemporaries deny the authenticity of the flogging.) Determined to revive monasticism in the Church of England, he lived a life of pious absurdity worthy of Ronald Firbank's *Valmouth*. On one occasion he and a Sister Gertrude took an "Infant Oblate"—a child dressed as a monk—to Rome, where the Italians misunderstood his motives.

who comes into contact with me shall get the opposite of the proverbial opinion of the Jews."[12]

Possibly Eulenburg foresaw even then that his private life might require defending by a skillful pen. But apart from this puzzle, the interview exhilarated Herzl. Some Jews might shake their heads over a protectorate; but since even Herzl did not want a monarchy, no one else could. "To live under the protection of this strong, great, moral, splendidly governed, tightly organized Germany can only have the most salutary effects on the Jewish national character."[13]

Herzl now waited for the Kaiser's summons. So as to lose less time when the command came, he put on his number-one patent-leather boots. But in vain. He had, instead, to make do, the following day, with the Kaiser's uncle, his Foreign Secretary and his Imperial Chancellor. All three meetings took place at Potsdam; he traveled on the same train as von Bülow.

The warmth of his reception by the Grand Duke of Baden prompted Herzl to a rare exclamation of personal attachment. "I don't even remember all the kind words with which he greeted me. I only know that I love and venerate this wise, good, and great man. Never in my life have I met a man so truly aristocratic . . ."[14] Baden chatted freely about the great period of German unification: Herzl pinched himself to make sure he wasn't dreaming. "Here was one of the greatest men of the greatest period of Germany speaking in this way with me, a plain journalist." The royal sage surveyed the European scene. In Russia any action, however ruthless, could be expected. In England, the Church was favorable to Zionism, if the government had not yet acted. In France there would shortly be a dictatorship. For Germany, the great hope was a vast program of naval expansion. "With admiration I listened to these exalted, mature thoughts, surrendering to their calmness without even being acquainted with their details. I suggested to him that he disseminate these views among the people in some easily grasped and entertaining form, and placed my pen at his disposal for this. That would be the most effective propaganda against the Socialists."

After Eulenburg and Baden, his meeting with von Bülow came as a disappointment. This was due, he felt, to the presence of Prince Chlodwig von Hohenlohe, the Imperial Chancellor. He sensed an immediate antipathy as Hohenlohe, now in his eightieth year, addressed him questions. Would the rich Jews—the Jews comfortably installed in Berlin, for example—leave their stock exchange to follow him? How much territory was Herzl requesting? As far north as Beirut—or farther?[15]

Herzl parried these questions. The poor would follow him. The Zionists would ask for what they needed—the more Jews came, the more land they would require. It would, of course, be purchased from its present owners in accordance with civil law.

And who were these?

"Arabs, Greeks," Herzl answered, "the whole *mixed multitude* [English in original] of the Orient."

And what was the Turkish reaction to his idea of founding a state there?

Herzl quoted the Grand Duke of Baden as saying that the German Ambassador in Constantinople, Herr Marschall, was encouraging.

Von Bülow, who was to succeed Hohenlohe as Chancellor two years later, here interrupted: no such reports from Marschall had come before his eyes.

Herzl construed Hohenlohe as an anti-Semite and the coldness of both men as due to a wish to frustrate a brilliant master. Herzl was unfair to Hohenlohe. The Chancellor had upheld liberal principles throughout a long political career; although a Catholic, he had supported Bismarck's *Kulturkampf* and had openly opposed the doctrine of papal infallibility. He was also a convinced believer in the innocence of Dreyfus and the guilt of Esterhazy.[16] His questions had been severely to the point. Herzl had casually mentioned the availability of a sum of ten million pounds. Would the rich Jews in fact put up this sum? Since Turkey was Germany's friend, it was vital to know the Turkish attitude to the Zionist plan. Did Herzl know exactly whose land he wanted to obtain and had he fixed boundaries in mind? All these questions needed clear answers. Herzl's answers were vague or negative. The only racialism in the exchange was in Herzl's reference to the mixed multitude of the Orient. The imprecision of what territory he required, the odd inclusion of "Greeks" in the Levant may have helped convince both statesmen that Eulenburg had involved their master in a romantic scheme whose serious espousal would damage German interests in the east.*

Herzl refused to be discouraged. He won from von Bülow a promise that he should be allowed to deliver an address in Jerusalem; he should submit it for advance approval in Constantinople; the Kaiser would receive him there or in Palestine.

Even if Zionism turned out to be "the jilted darling of the Kaiser," its progress could only be helped by the adventure. As companions in adventure Herzl took with him four German-speaking Jews, all

---

* There were more Germans than Greeks living in Palestine at this period, a considerable number of Protestant colonies having been established there.

bearded, all roughly of his own age, but with usefully contrasted skills. Max Isidor Bodenheimer, thirty-three, was a lawyer; a charter would require skill if it were to be precise and ambiguous at the same time. David Wolffsohn, forty-two, a successful merchant, was Herzl's chief counselor on financial matters; money was the instrument for bringing pressure on the Sultan and for assisting colonization. Josef Seidener, Herzl's exact contemporary, had had experience of land purchase in Palestine some years earlier. Dr. Moses Schnirer, thirty-seven, was a physician as well as Vice-President of the Zionist Inner Actions Committee; he could look after the health of his companions while advising on problems of hygiene for the future state.

Max Bodenheimer has left an account of the farewell tea party at Herzl's Währing home.[17] Wolffsohn and Schnirer went on ahead to the station. Herzl's father, gray-haired, gray-bearded, kindly, seemed rather dubious of the project. His mother sat proudly confident of her son's judgment. The children romped. Julie, blond, pretty, still vivacious, allowed Seidener to use his engineering talents to measure her foot for a pair of Turkish slippers—as though to signal her indifference to the delegation's purpose. Herzl's own comment on the farewell also survives. "Taking leave from my loved ones was quite hard this time. I could very well stay in my beautiful house, with my lovely children, whose rosiest childhood is passing without my enjoying it; who are growing up without my observing the delightful details of their development." Projecting his own suspiciousness on others, he took seriously a warning that the Turks might kill him. If this happened, only his parents would be inconsolable. His children were young enough—Pauline eight, Hans seven and Trude five—to recover. He never thought of Julie on such occasions.

On the Orient Express the adventurers seemed at last to be moving toward an attainable objective. Herzl discussed with Bodenheimer Hohenlohe's question of how much land they would require. Bodenheimer suggested boldly:

"Area: from the Brook of Egypt to the Euphrates.† Stipulate a transitional period with our own institutions. A Jewish governor for this period. Afterwards, a relationship like that between Egypt and

---

† Herzl's German text reads "*Gebiet: Vom Bach Ägyptens bis an den Euphrat.*" In his edition of the Pentateuch and Haftorahs, Dr. J. H. Hertz glosses "the brook of Egypt" (1 Kings VIII: 65) as "the southern limit, now called Wadi el-Arish." The same verse gives the northern limit of Solomon's brief-lived kingdom as Hamath, again glossed by Dr. Hertz as "on the Orontes, the modern Hama." Hebrew has separate words, *nachal* and *nahar,* for "brook" and "river" respectively; while Luther's Bible distinguishes *Bach* from *Fluss,* the Authorized Version uses "river" for both.

the Sultan.‡ As soon as the Jewish inhabitants of a district amount to ⅔ of the population, Jewish administration goes in force politically, while local government (communal autonomy) always depends on the number of voters in the community."[18] Herzl confided to his Diary that he found Bodenheimer's ideas excellent "in part." He does not indicate what points of disagreement divided the two men as their train swung through the Balkans toward the Turkish frontier.

On this his second visit Herzl was uninspired by Constantinople: "all the scenes already familiar and therefore lacking the interest of those first days two years ago." His thoughts were focused on the Kaiser. There were disquieting moments, as when Bodenheimer, calling at the German Embassy, was coldly informed that Ambassador Marschall (who may have learned from von Bülow how he had been misquoted) knew no Dr. Herzl. Only by using all his push, by imploring letters first to von Bülow, then to the Kaiser himself,[19] did he achieve the dreamed-of audience, just before the last possible ship sailed for Alexandria, the necessary transit point for reaching Jaffa. His impressions, when at last he met the great man, could only be expressed poetically. Herzl felt as though he had strayed into the enchanted forest where the unicorn is said to dwell. All at once he was confronted by a magnificent woodland creature, with on its forehead but a single horn. Its appearance surprised him less than the fact that it existed. "And my astonishment grew when the one-horned creature began to speak in a very friendly human voice and said, 'I am the fabled unicorn.'"[20]

The interview took place on the afternoon of October 18, 1898, at the guest palace specially built for the Kaiser in the grounds of Yildiz. Herzl had paid his usual attention to his dress: frock coat with gloves of a particularly delicate gray. Wolffsohn drove with him, taking with him a clothesbrush; on the box sat "a sly-looking Jew who appears to have police connections." After long, fidgeting waits, after icy doubts as to whether the Kaiser would appear and whether he would be received, Herzl was finally summoned to an upstairs room. The Emperor, dressed in a dark hussar uniform, came almost as far as the door in welcome and offered Herzl his hand.

It is easy to smile at the court circular prose with which Herzl conveys his impressions at this peak moment of his existence. "His

‡ Egypt (although in fact occupied by a British army) technically enjoyed autonomy under a hereditary Khedive who acknowledged the Ottoman Sultan as his overlord. Herzl and Bodenheimer seem to have contemplated an autonomous Jewish Palestine with the German Kaiser as nominal overlord. As Egyptians held Ottoman citizenship, the implication is that the inhabitants of *Der Judenstaat* would have been German citizens.

great sea-blue eyes . . ." "fine, frank, genial and yet bold . . ." "his fine, serious face . . ." Yet this was the apogee of European royalty, when Europe ruled most of the world and kings ruled Europe. With the glamour of pop stars and the power of presidents, they could compel servility from the cynical and agreement from the stubborn. Herzl found himself echoing the Kaiser's hostility to republican France.

"I often wonder," the Kaiser said, "what is to become of that country. It is valuable, after all. The French spirit constitutes the spice, the pepper, for the other cultures—the Attic salt. Of course, too much pepper is no good. But what is going to happen to France?"

"Your Majesty, I think that it will crumble from within," was Herzl's answer. "It is fine indeed in literature and arts, and it is the refinement of decadence."

Kaiser, Herzl and von Bülow all agreed: Paris was the place for a good time, for cafés and night clubs.

But Herzl was doing business. He did not allow the Kaiser to get away with the remark that there were Jewish elements in Germany he would prefer transported to Palestine, the usurers, for example, at work among the peasants in Hesse . . . Herzl launched into a counterattack on anti-Semitism. Von Bülow countered by arguing that the Jews had forgotten their debt to the house of Hohenzollern and were active in all the opposition parties. This gave Herzl the chance to restate his thesis: Zionism would siphon off the Jews from the parties of revolution.

If the content of the interview was less impressive than the fact that it took place, it ended with the Kaiser, too, coming down to business:

"Just tell me in a word what I am to ask the Sultan."

Herzl chose the Rhodesian phrase: "A *Chartered Company*—under German protection." He used the English words, to make his point clearer.

The Kaiser's right hand, strong enough for two, shook Herzl's; then the Emperor marched first out of the door.

From Constantinople the five Zionists sailed through the Greek seas—where they docked long enough at Peiraeus to pose for a photograph beside the caryatid porch on the Acropolis, inspiration for much Viennese building—to Alexandria, where they boarded a smaller vessel, the *Russia*, for the last lap of the journey. They had now entered the world of myth. Herzl's arrival at Jaffa on October 26, 1898, shows how swiftly the events in his life could be remolded. David Wolffsohn has been quoted for the following account.

When our ship left Port Said, bound for Jaffa, it was evening. All
of us knew that we should land in Palestine the following morning.
And all of us, myself included, retired to our cabins for the night.
Only Herzl did not think of resting, but remained on deck.

I was sound asleep—for it was already long past midnight—when
I heard some one calling: "David! Are you sleeping, my friend?"
I felt a hand pass gently over my face as the voice continued:
"Don't you want to see our mother Zion, David? Get up—the light
of morning is already shining on the towers of Jaffa! We can
already see their gleaming!"

Rising from my bed, I was amazed to see Herzl attired as for an
audience with an emperor. His face glowing, his eyes shining, he
exclaimed: "Come, David, get dressed! Let us go see our beloved
motherland!"

I dressed and we went up on deck, whence we could see the
pointed minarets of Jaffa beckoning to us. We fell into each
other's arms, and tears rose to our eyes as we whispered softly: "Our
country! Our mother Zion!"

Wolffsohn supposedly gave this account "one evening soon after his
return."[21] Herzl's account, written down the day following his arrival
in Palestine, has the candor and exactitude that compel belief. The
only sight that impressed him on the voyage, he writes, was the Suez
Canal: it eclipsed anything he saw in Greece. He suffered from the
heat throughout the trip. The five bearded men shared one cabin,
which became unbearably stuffy. The first night out, Herzl crept
away from his companions at three in the morning; he spent the
whole of the last night asleep on deck. Then "when it grew light, we
began to peer towards the Jewish* coast. Toward seven o'clock the
first bit of land, two dots of mountains on the right, was sighted by
Wolffsohn." Herzl evokes the contrasting emotions felt by the different passengers as they approached Jaffa: the Arabs who had been
with them all the way from Constantinople, the old German pastor
from South Africa, the Russian muzhik whose pilgrimage took him in
the foul-smelling hold, the Romanian Jewess with a sick daughter in
Jerusalem. Herzl's own emotion seems to have been anxiety that
the Turkish authorities might prevent him landing. As a precaution
he had already written out a cable of complaint to be sent to the
Kaiser. But it proved needless. The five men were met without fuss
by a Cook's launch which landed them on a pier. (All five wore the
white cork helmets then considered imperative for survival in the

* A curious expression, since even in ancient times the coastline had been dominated by gentiles, Phoenicians in the north and Philistines in the south.

colonies.) German police were already present for the Kaiser's arrival. Herzl and his companions drove to a noisy hotel in the Arab town.[22]

Palestine—a very small segment of which Herzl saw on his nine-day visit—has suffered more from the mythologists than Herzl himself. When the forerunners of political Zionism were trying to encourage Jews to migrate there, its fertility was stressed. Sir Moses Montefiore, who visited the Safad region on May 24, 1839, saw "groves of olive-trees, I should think more than five hundred years old, vineyards, much pasture, plenty of wells; also fig-trees, walnuts, almonds, mulberries, etc., and rich fields of wheat, barley, and lentils."[23] A generation later, Laurence Oliphant, a Christian advocate of Jewish settlement, rode his horse through another region, the plain of Esdraelon. Though owned by a Lebanese banker named Sursock, the plain supported, in 1883, some five thousand Arab farmers scattered in thirty villages.

> Readers will be surprised to learn that almost every acre of the plain of Esdraelon is at this moment in the highest state of cultivation; that it is perfectly safe to ride across it unarmed in any direction, as I can testify . . . It looks today like a huge green lake of waving wheat, with its village-crowned mounds rising from it like islands; and it presents one of the most striking pictures of luxuriant fertility which it is possible to conceive . . . Some idea of the amount of grain which is annually grown in their portion of the plain of Esdraelon alone may be gathered from the fact that Mr. Sursock himself told me that the cost of transporting his last year's crop to Haifa and Acre amounted to $50,000.[24]

Later Zionists were to write in other terms. André Chouraqui, for example: "After nineteen centuries, the country was in a deplorable state of neglect; jackals and swamps were its real masters; it was as bare, bleak and barren as the most lamentable visions of the prophets."[25] Two factors—besides the wish to make propaganda—could account for bleak visions of the Holy Land by later Zionists. Some settled there after the First World War, when the region had been reduced to starvation, its population diminished by a third, as Turkish retribution for Arab support of the Allies. Others, coming like Herzl on brief visits, arrived in late summer or early autumn, delectable seasons in Europe or America, but parched in the Middle East, where harvest takes place as early as May and where the grass is bleached pale until the first rains of winter.†

† That this was also true of the Greek islands, even in classical times, is shown by the famous line of Sappho:
   I am paler than grass, I seem to be not far short of death . . .
                                                      Fragment 31.[26]

Herzl found the country at its most bleached and desolate. He was attracted by neither the Arabs, the Zionist settlers nor the Jews in Jerusalem. He was to leave with only one attractive memory—a group of Jewish lads on horseback imitating an Arab fantasia—and one trophy. This was a photograph of some use in Zionist propaganda. Even this had to be faked.

Herzl had spent his first day and second morning visiting several of the Jewish settlements that already existed and which had been founded by Lovers of Zion or philanthropists. The oldest of these was the 600-acre Mikveh Israel, an agricultural school with around one hundred pupils. The most prestigious was Rishon le-Zion, which the Rothschilds had rescued from bankruptcy in 1884 and which by the time of Herzl's visit covered more than 2,000 acres. Around six hundred Jewish settlers tended some million and a half vines. Herzl had returned to his Jaffa hotel on the evening of October 27, exhausted by the heat. Hechler turned up and through him Herzl sent a message to August zu Eulenburg, Philipp zu Eulenburg's cousin and the Kaiser's Court Marshal, to say that he would station himself on the highway outside Mikveh Israel school the following morning, on the Kaiser's itinerary. Already feeling ill, Herzl managed to get out to the school (a few miles outside Jaffa) the following morning and took up his position in a dark suit and cork hat beside agricultural machinery. A *mixed multitude* (Herzl repeated the English phrase) of Arab beggars, women, children and horsemen lined the dusty road. At nine o'clock a rising commotion announced the imminent approach of the royal party. Grim-looking Turkish cavalry came first, casting martial glances at the crowd. Herzl had trained the children's choir, he tells us, to sing the Imperial anthem, "Hail to Thee in Victor's Crown!" Reining up, the Kaiser leaned from his horse to exchange a few gentlemanly banalities about the heat, the country's prospects and the need for irrigation. On the sideline stood Wolffsohn with his Kodak, eager to preserve for eternity a scene that could be made to say more than the Kaiser said: not least to the Jews, whose non-Zionist representatives, the Rothschild administrators, were looking, according to Herzl, timid and out of sorts.

But when the Jaffa photographer developed the negatives—which Wolffsohn valued at more than ten thousand marks—one, Herzl wrote, "showed only a shadow of the Kaiser and my left foot," while the other was completely spoiled.

A photographic transplant was later performed. The result: a much reproduced photograph showing the Kaiser bending from his horse to greet Dr. Herzl, erect in light tweeds, his Assyrian beard in profile, his cork helmet in his left hand. Immediately behind the Kaiser (his spiked helmet trailing a veil) is a tricorn bunch of pennants, with a star visible. The symbolism is clear: backed by flags that evoke Sultan, Kaiser and Zionism, the German Emperor greets his local protector, or *gestor*, Theodor Herzl.

How was the picture contrived?

The reader must keep in mind four photographs, which may be termed A, B, C and D. A is the picture that showed only a shadow of the Kaiser and Herzl's left foot. B is the picture that was totally spoiled. C is a picture showing the stooped Kaiser on a white horse stationed just in front of another veiled, helmeted figure (probably August zu Eulenburg) on a dark horse with a white blaze, behind them the tricorn pennants; the white horse's head is cut off and a smallish cork helmet obtrudes from the right. D is what Dr. Bein publishes as the "rectified" photograph. This—the picture that was used to illustrate the biography of de Haas, among other works—shows the Kaiser, on the *dark* horse with blaze, bending to Herzl in a *lightly* colored tweed suit and holding a different white helmet (it has a dark band) from that photographed in picture C. Those who achieved the photographic transplant must have performed the following operations:

1. They removed zu Eulenburg (or whoever the second figure was) from his black horse with white blaze.

2. They transferred the stooped Kaiser from his white horse on to the now vacant black horse.

3. They inserted a snapshot of Herzl in light clothing in front of the black horse and to the rear of the Kaiser's horse.

4. They imposed a larger, different cork helmet.

This leaves only one mystery unsolved. Is photograph C (reproduced in Dr. Bein's book opposite photograph D) the same as photograph A? It seems unlikely. C shows the Kaiser fairly clearly, even less of a "shadow" than he is in D.

Herzl (the historical figure in the dark suit who had felt ill all morning) was slightly feverish by the time he and his friends caught the Jerusalem train. It left the station late and they thus went up to the Holy City on the Sabbath by public transport. Herzl records:

> Sitting in the cramped, crowded, scorching compartment was torture. While crossing the dismal, desolate countryside I developed a fever and grew more and more feverish and weak as we rode further into the Sabbath. For, because of the delayed train, and to Wolffsohn's extreme chagrin, we found ourselves travelling into the Sabbath. The moon was full when we arrived in Jerusalem. I

would have gladly driven the half hour's distance‡ from the station
to the hotel; but the gentlemen made long faces, so I had to resign
myself to walking to the city, weak with fever though I was. I
tottered all over the place on my cane.

For Jerusalem as it was Herzl took away bitter feelings. Everything
conspired against him: not only the Germans, whose attitude seemed
to have changed, and the local Jewish leaders, who avoided him, but
the international situation. A local conflict between England and
France in the Sudan—the Fashoda Incident—threatened a European
war and for some hours it seemed as though the Kaiser might cut
short his visit and not receive the Zionist delegates at all. Herzl was
later to regret that he had not insisted on introducing his companions
to the Kaiser in public, on his triumphal entry into Jerusalem. When
the interview was finally arranged, there were absurd, small problems. Bodenheimer, who had no good silk hat, could find only a
grotesque substitute and a suit with cuffs so wide that his shirt sleeves
continually slid into sight. Schnirer suggested they all take a bromide
to calm their nerves. Herzl insisted instead that they all eat lightly, to
keep on their toes. They drove to their interview in a carriage, but the
event was an anticlimax. The German party were staying in an en-
campment, there being no suitable accommodation in Jerusalem itself.
The Kaiser and von Bülow were sitting in the Imperial tent. Wilhelm II wore his same veiled helmet with gray colonial uniform and
brown gloves, and, which struck Herzl as odd, held a riding crop in
his right hand. The interview was strictly formal. Herzl was permitted
to introduce his four companions by name; but at no point were Wolffsohn and Bodenheimer included in the conversation, which in any
case was brief. Herzl was allowed to read his address (previously
amended in accord with the instructions of German officials) but the
Kaiser's reply to it was noncommittal. He spoke of the need for water
and trees; he remarked that all settlements, those of the Jews as well
as of the German "Templars," could serve as models to the natives
for what might be done to improve the land. Then the Kaiser asked
if Herzl knew von Bülow. The question must have hurt Herzl, who
had met the Foreign Secretary three times before. Von Bülow quoted
a tag from Pindar: ἄριστον μὲν ὕδωρ. "Best is water." Herzl was not to
forget it.* But there was little else to remember. The Kaiser had
read the temperatures at Ramleh: 88° F. in the shade, 106° F. de-

‡ The mythmakers have been undeterred by the publication of Herzl's own account in his Diary. Itzhak Raphael, as late as 1954, says that Herzl "refused to
desecrate the Sabbath by riding into town from the station."[27]
* The phrase was to reappear as epigraph to his *feuilleton,* "*Eine Reise nach
Ägypten,*" published in 1903.

grees in the sun. But the atmosphere in the tent had been arctic and the attitude of the Kaiser's aide de camp showed the departing delegates how Zionist stock had slumped since the meeting in Constantinople.

Herzl's one wish was now to escape from Palestine. The anxiety that troubled his remaining hours was not without cause. Dr. Aharon Mazie, a Rothschild physician, was spreading the rumor that Herzl had come to convert the Jews to Protestantism. If the Turks had their wits about them, they might get rid of Herzl while they had their chance.

Forced to spend a further night in Jaffa, he had himself rowed from one vessel to another in the harbor. Besides the Kaiser's men-of-war and a Turkish steamer bound for Constantinople, there was a boat going to Beirut, several freighters, one of them Russian with four days' loading still ahead, and the yacht of James Gordon Bennett, owner of the New York *Herald*. Herzl asked all the civilian vessels, except the Turkish, if they could get him out. He finally settled for the *Dundee*, a small British freighter of 350 tons shipping oranges to Alexandria the following day. The Arab plantations of Jaffa gave their name to a world-famous variety of citrus.

His companions, dragged from their beds to catch the freighter, sulked: all except the faithful Wolffsohn. The passage to Alexandria was rough. The five men slept on deck, heaving under the stars. His companions seem not to have shared his mood when in Alexandria he enthused over the manner in which Khedive Ismail had created whole new quarters on barren sand. From the cable office he wired his father: had the audience been reported? The reply came: AUDIENCE KNOWN. Herzl transferred to the *Regina Margherita*, an Italian ship, with soaring spirits.

These were dashed in Naples. First there was the news that Nevlinsky was ill and could not go to Constantinople. (This was malingering, Herzl felt sure.) Then came their first reading of the communiqué, published on November 2 in Jerusalem, describing the Kaiser's visit to Palestine. Munich's *Allgemeine Zeitung*, after relating the visit to the Mosque of Omar under the guidance of the Governor-General of Syria, reported that the Kaiser had called on the Roman Catholic and Greek Catholic patriarchs. "They received him at the entrance to their residences surrounded by their clergy. Later the Kaiser received the French consul and a Jewish deputation which gave him an album with views of the Jewish colonies in Palestine. In reply to an address by the leader of the Deputation, the Kaiser replied that all those endeavours could count on his benevolent interest that aimed at an improvement of agriculture in Palestine in the interests of the prosperity of the Turkish empire and that fully respected the sovereignty of the Sultan."[28]

What had happened, between the state room in Yildiz and the tent near Jerusalem, to chill the Kaiser? The Grand Duke of Baden told Herzl, in a letter of December 5, 1898, that his Imperial nephew had disliked "the way your co-religionists live and carry on in the city of Jerusalem. They made an unfavourable impression on the Kaiser, particularly because many small tradesmen engage in speculations of all kinds and of an unsavoury nature there. The prominence of these businessmen, he feels, makes a repulsive impression and harms the cause which you promote."[29]

But there were stronger reasons. The German government probably had two main aims in planning the Kaiser's visit to Palestine. By his spectacular dedication of the Protestant Church of the Saviour and his no less spectacular gift of the piece of land associated with the Blessed Virgin's Assumption† to the German Catholic Society of the Holy Land, the Kaiser was attempting to unite his empire's two great Christian sects. On the level of foreign policy, the visit was part of the German drive to the east. As the London *Times* commented at the time,[30] "The Ottoman Empire receives its rifles from Mauser, its cannon from Krupp." Support for Zionism would not please German Christians and, it was soon evident, would anger the Sultan. Eulenburg was later to tell Herzl that the Sultan's opposition was the decisive factor. "The Sultan rejected the Kaiser's suggestion regarding the Zionists so brusquely that it was not possible to pursue the matter further. We were anxious to remain on good terms with him. As a guest the Kaiser could not of course press the subject."[31] An immediate consequence of Herzl's visit was, in fact, a new hardening of Ottoman opposition to Jewish settlement.‡

An official German *aide-mémoire* shows that still other factors damned the notion of a German protectorate. Neither France nor England would have welcomed an expansion of German influence so close to the Maronites of Lebanon (in France's case) or to the Suez Canal (in the case of Britain). Nor was Herzl a German subject. His protestations that a Jewish Palestine would be eternally loyal to Germany were taken no more seriously in Berlin than his professions of loyalty to the Sultan were taken in Constantinople.[32]

Most of these objections would have been foreseen by any normally

---

† Or in the Orthodox tradition, the Dormition.

‡ *The Jewish World* reported on November 11, 1898, that at a meeting of the Anglo-Jewish Association, "Mr. Nissim Behar of Jerusalem reported . . . that difficulties were being placed by the government authorities on the landing of foreign Jews. Mr. S. M. Adler said it was the fault of political Zionism."

informed official. But Herzl the visionary and Wilhelm the poseur had allowed themselves to be tempted across the frontier between actuality and dream. Their chief aide had been Philipp zu Eulenburg, himself an amateur poet. Von Bülow had never taken the scheme very seriously. His Memoirs state that the Kaiser's brief interest in Zionism was prompted by the wish to rid Germany of elements he did not particularly like. The Memoirs also show that if the Zionists could add to photographs, the Germans could subtract from history. Von Bülow states flatly that "the Kaiser refused to receive the Zionist representatives in Zion."[33] *

The Sultan had said the first and last word: while his empire remained in being, Palestine was not for sale. The Sultan never swerved from his belief that the Holy Land formed part of his sacred trust, both as Caliph of Islam and as Sultan of the Arabs, who formed nine tenths of the country's population.

It says much for Herzl's extraordinary pertinacity that despite so clear a refusal he continued pushing. He returned to Vienna to find Nevlinsky as ill as the cause. Yet Herzl insisted to himself that No was still Perhaps and that Nevlinsky was the man to turn Perhaps into Yes.

---

* It is curious that the two other Germans closest to the project of a German protectorate also deny that the Zionist deputation was officially received in Palestine. The Kaiser admits to having met Herzl in Constantinople: "a clever, very intelligent man with impressive eyes, Dr. Herzl decidedly was an enthusiastic idealist with an aristocratic mentality." But he states baldly that "I greeted him on *one* subsequent occasion: when I passed a Jewish farming settlement in Palestine." (This author's emphasis.) Philipp zu Eulenburg later wrote that the reason he regretted not having accompanied his cousin, August zu Eulenburg, to Palestine was that Herzl was granted an audience with the Kaiser neither in Jerusalem nor Constantinople: "for *I* would have pushed that audience through for him."[34]

PART SIX

The
Desperate Intriguer
1899–1904

The wind blows through the stubble. I feel the autumn of my life approaching. I am in danger of leaving no work to the world and no property to my children.[1]

CHAPTER 27

O n April Fools' Day, 1899, Philip Michael de Nevlinsky died in a
room overlooking the Bosporus. He had been accompanied to
Constantinople's Hotel Bristol by his wife, family and a Jewish physician for an invalid's last throw. His sudden death had repercussions on
Herzl that showed themselves in turn in changes of health and character. Politically he had lost his guide to Yildiz, in one of whose
mazelike turnings he had thought to find the key to Palestine. He had
also lost a replacement for Kana and Boxer, a friend whose optimism
buoyed his spirits, whose panache aroused his admiration and whose
egoism did not impair his own. Of course he had called him a
scoundrel, but Herzl knew his own nature well enough to distrust his
suspicions. His Diary, the prime witness to the change in Herzl, re-
verts to Nevlinsky's death with a grief made sharper by a sense of
guilt. He had allowed him, with a diagnosed heart disease, to become
the first martyr of political Zionism. Yet his memory was not to remain unsullied.

From May 18 to July 29, 1899, a Peace Conference, the first of a
long series of vain attempts to limit armaments, was in session at
The Hague. It was sponsored by the young Czar Nicholas II, which
ensured the presence of the representatives of some twenty-six states
and many idealists. Prominent among these was Baroness Bertha von
Suttner, formerly secretary to Alfred Nobel and known to Herzl as a
contributor to his newspaper. Her friendship, Herzl thought, might
gain him access to the Czar. He went to Holland for a few days in
mid-June. The baroness showed her liking for him by including him
among the guests at a dinner in celebration of her twenty-third wed-

ding anniversary. Among the other guests were Captain Scheine of the Russian Navy, Léon Bourgeois, French representative at the conference, and the French Ambassador to The Hague.[2]

One of the lesser delegates was the same Nuri Bey whose intelligence Herzl had admired on his first visit to Constantinople. Nuri was still Chief Secretary for Foreign Affairs. To escape the humanitarian merry-go-round, Herzl invited Nuri to dine with him tête-à-tête in the salon next to his hotel room. The Ottoman (for the half-French Nuri was in no sense a Turk) riddled the image of Nevlinsky as a pure-souled martyr. After speaking guardedly of "the deceased," he soon warmed to denigration. Nevlinsky, he confided, had cheated Herzl from the start, had never brought Herzl's proposals to the attention of the Turkish authorities, but instead had offered to spy on the Zionists in their behalf. Mahmud Nedim, the Ottoman Ambassador in Vienna, had colluded with the Pole in return for being allowed to sleep with his wife. Nuri's cruel summation: *une sale canaille.*

In this company, after these revelations, Herzl was encouraged to tell a politician's lie. He needed, he said, a chartered company.

Could he, Nuri asked, get the Kaiser's backing?

"I said vigorously: *'Oui!'* "

"He replied: *'Alors la chose est faite.'* "[3]

Herzl had not enjoyed robust health since he had left Budapest. At the time of his student dissipations he had contracted a venereal disease for which, in those days, the best hope was that it might become mildly chronic. He had twice been rejected for Army service. While a Paris correspondent he had bouts of aging illness that may have been connected with his earlier sickness. But now the references in the Diary to ill health become insistent. Two forms of suffering are mentioned: palpitations of the heart and cerebral anemia, or blackouts. Before going to The Hague he had taken an eight-day rest cure at Bad Nauheim. But only three days after dining with Nuri he was in Paris and feeling ill. "My heart is badly strained. I suffer from palpitations and an irregular pulse."[4] A later entry describes his cerebral anemia. He was talking with colleagues in the office of *Die Welt*, whose financial losses, all paid by himself, must have contributed to the strain. "My consciousness suddenly blacked out and my perception grew blurred, although I was able to observe myself closely during the spell and even cracked jokes with Schalit and Reich, the secretaries."[5] A carriage took him to Währing, where the doctor prescribed a period of rest. He did not take it. These attacks could come on anywhere and at any time. One June evening, on a visit to Paris, he was driving in the Bois de Boulogne when he fainted in the carriage. He lay sprawled on two park benches in the bushes till the spell passed, then drove home "with greatly diminished consciousness."[6] (The background this time was Nordau's nagging.) On another occasion he had an attack while catching up with a pile of literary contributions. "I didn't mention it to anyone. My parents could find out and get excited about it. It wouldn't make my wife any more loving either."[7] Julie was persuaded that his absurd obsessions were making him sick and exhausting her dowry. She was never afraid to put her persuasions into words.

These spasmodic attacks reached a climax in the summer of 1900. The fourth Zionist Congress, unlike its Basel predecessors, was to take place in London. Although it was the first week in August, a severe chill forced Herzl to his bed on the day of his arrival. He was staying at the Langham Hotel in Bayswater. To Herzl (who was ignorant of medicine) the symptoms indicated malaria, or perhaps pneumonia; his secretary, who was not a physician, considered it as his first true heart attack.[8] His temperature of over 104° F. fired delirious visions in which his two English nurses assumed weird shapes. Although he managed to take part in the social functions of the Congress, including a Rothschild garden party, he was only recovering from the wear and tear of his London illness by the end of August; as late as September 28 he was still listless and devoid of energy.[9]

Physical illness took intermittent toll of his mental alertness; his temper splintered. Comparatively minor matters excited him out of all proportion. Just before the Peace Conference, he mislaid the letter Eulenburg had sent to him in Amsterdam the previous year. Since it affirmed the Kaiser's interest in Zionism it was important and he wanted it photographed. At the same time he had to write an editorial about the return of Dreyfus from Devil's Island. This kept him up late. When a friend, Alexander Marmorek, arrived next morning with a camera, Herzl could not find the letter. A desperate search all over the house was fruitless. A drive into Vienna, to the Türkenstrasse offices of *Die Welt*, to his parents' flat: nothing! Then his father suggested he should look in the garden at their country house just outside the city. There the letter lay, on a bench, among a cluster of firs. "As chance would have it, in twenty-four hours the gardener had not been there to clean up, nor had our children, who tear up all letters. Nor had there been any rain, which would have soaked the letter and completely destroyed it."[10]

Although one of his English nurses, a Catholic, had thought his
appearance reminiscent of Christ's,* his untouched photographs were
to reveal an increasing puffiness of face; his Diary hints similar inroads
on his once fastidious spirit, a bloating of its capillaries by megalomania.† As early as the aftermath of his first Turkish journey, he had
been conscious at a workingman's meeting in London of his legend
being born. "The people are sentimental; the masses do not see clearly.
I believe that even now they no longer have a clear image of me. A
light fog is beginning to rise around me, and it may perhaps become
the cloud in which I shall walk."[13] Shortly after Nevlinsky's death
he granted an interview to the wife of a. Latin American diplomat.
She described him as "the Apostle of Zionism" and attributed to him
remarks that unmistakably echo, to a Christian, one greater than any
Apostle. Palestine he described as "that land which seems dead today but which is only sleeping, ready, like Jairus' daughter, to rise
from the grave." He declared his intention "to drive the hucksters
and the filth that dishonor Jerusalem out of that holy city." To a Hebrew writer‡ he confided a childhood dream—unmentioned hereto-
fore—in which the Messiah carried him up to Moses, who said that
he was the child for which he had prayed.[14] At the same time he
became increasingly harsh to the Jews. A general statement made
just before his fortieth birthday—"I have thought of a good epitaph
for myself: 'He had too good an opinion of the Jews.' "[15]—is balanced
by innumerable angry snapshots: "The Jerusalem Jew Navon Bey
called on me with projects—a badly Parisianized Oriental Jew, type
of red Oriental Jew, face of a bird of prey, furtive crook."[16] After
Hechler and "good bishop Bramley Moore" went to an Irvingite
church, where the bishop put on his episcopal vestments to ask God's
advice on their duty with respect to Zionism, he wrote: "These simple
Christian hearts are much better than our Jewish clerics who think
of their wedding fees from the rich Jews."[17]*

These hostile judgments may have reflected a secret admiration
for those he criticized. They certainly reflect, in the apostle of Jewish
nationalism, a recurrent psychic unease.

* To Dr. Leibster at the Langham Hotel.[11]

† Apropos of two Austrian diplomats who, unlike the Germans, neglected to return Herzl's cards: "They treat me as though I were air, these idiots of whose
existence not a soul will any longer have an idea when my name will shine through
the ages like a star."[12]

‡ Reuben Brainin; see Bein, op. cit., English edition, pp. 11–14.

* Edward Irving (1792–1834), a minister of the Church of Scotland, established the principles on which, shortly after his death, a "Catholic Apostolic
Church" was founded. William Bramley-Moore had published in 1897 his *Mar-
turia: or the Testimony of the Ancient Records and Monuments in the British
Museum to the Historical Accuracy of the Holy Scripture*: a title after the Reverend Hechler's heart.

The causes of the psychic unease that ran in tandem with physical illness are not hard to discern. He was besieged by money worries, always the most corrosive. These affected him, not only as the leader of an ambitious movement, but as the father of three young children.

As early as May 25, 1898, when *Die Welt* had run for just less than a year, he spoke with "my dear L. Kellner" about the future. If Herzl predeceased him, Kellner should become editor-in-chief of *Die Welt* and publish the Diary in installments. "The paper itself is, of course, the property of my children, because during the period I have been working on behalf of the Jews, I have neglected to earn for them."[18] If Hans survived him and grew to manhood, he should take over the paper and from its profits pay his sisters an allowance. But hard fact, in the year following his failure in Palestine and Nevlinsky's death, deflated euphoric hopes. He was still defraying the expenses of *Die Welt;* out of fifty thousand guilders already spent on Zionism, no less than twenty-five thousand had gone on a paper that would continue to run at a loss throughout his lifetime.† The demands of his family and his political movement forced him to cling to his position on the *Neue Freie Presse,* though the men in charge there, Bacher and Benedikt, remained implacably opposed to his ideas. After the third Congress in August 1899, which first bored, then irritated him, and finally only proved that the movement still existed, he returned to Vienna. The contrast between acclaim and lordship at Basel and his subordinate status in Vienna irked. "I must return again to my vile servitude at the *Neue Freie Presse* where I am not allowed to have an opinion of my own. It is a question of a measly few thousand guilders which I, being the head of a family, must not give up."[19] The demands of political action, expressed through middlemen, journalists or informers, were insatiable. The coarsening of spirit that is worked by ambition tangled in monetary cares found in Julie a target. He was spending her money as well as his own on the movement and *Die Welt.* To admit this would be to put himself on the defensive. He took the offensive in a manner that left her no power to reply. In 1899, while he was preparing his speech for the third Congress, his imagination linked Pauline's illness of the previous summer with his grudges against Julie. He began roughing out a play, *The Sinful Mother,* which, renamed *Gretel,* was under rehearsal for the Raimund Theater in Vienna by March 1900. A laudatory review of its first performance appeared in the *Neue Freie Presse* of April 5, under the initials F. Sch. These belonged to Friedrich Schutz, who worked under Herzl in the paper's literary section. (It was the paper's policy to report Herzl the writer while remaining silent about Herzl the politician.) The

† *Die Welt* finally suspended publication in July 1914.

play's chief character is Marianne Winter, a hysterical, sensual young woman who, "through all manner of compromise and speculative calculation," has become the wife of Dr. George Winter, a reserved Vienna lawyer. She has an adulterous liaison with a frivolous young sophisticate, Edgar Böheim. Her sins are promptly punished in the serious illness of her daughter, Gretel. In an ecstasy of guilt Marianne confesses her adultery to her husband. The child, roused by her parents' altercations, starts from her pillows, only to sink back and mutter her bedtime prayer:

> I am tired, I go to rest;
> Close my eyes:
> Father, may thy eyes
> Watch o'er my bed.

As Gretel recovers, the gulf between frivolous wife and serious husband widens. One afternoon as Gretel is taken out on her first walk—laden with dolls she hops impatiently from foot to foot—Marianne has the certainty that her child will be taken from her. When Gretel returns from the park, she finds her mother slain by her own hand.

Some in the Vienna audience will have seen in Marianne and Edgar Böheim portraits of Julie and the anti-Zionist Naschauers. This was in April. The following month—on May 23, 1900—he carried his offensive further, but this time in private. He wrote a will that his conception of knightly behavior would not have allowed him to draft even five years earlier. Everything, including kind words, was left to his parents, the property being in trust for his children. A clause stipulated that "the relatives of my parents, my wife Julie Naschauer or her relatives, must not receive anything." Seven weeks later he added a yet harsher codicil: "Of the dowry of my wife, Julie Naschauer, only about 20,000 guilders are still left. The enormous expenditures which were forced upon me by her, consumed during the past eleven years, approximately 55,000 guilders, in addition to my hard earned money. Now my income begins to improve, perhaps I will succeed in replenishing the dowry so that she will receive the original amount at the time of my death. I desire that she deposit the above amount with the court and that she receive only the usufruct thereof until the end of her life."‡

Household expenses, Julie's dresses, losses to Naschauer in-laws at cards,[21] small sums for Hechler, the need to bargain over large sums for men like Nuri, these were trifles compared with the millions he

‡ The testament of Herzl has been translated into English and edited by N. M. Gelber, who adds that "unquestionably he had contributed both his own and his wife's fortune to the cause to which he devoted his life as well."[20]

must command if he were to put right the finances of the Ottoman empire and colonize part of it. (Herzl estimated the Ottoman *dette* as nominally eighty-five million sterling, or twenty-two million at its current quotation.[22]) Herzl shared the colonial assumptions of Cecil Rhodes but lacked his financial genius and never won an equivalent of the Rand mines to back his ventures. All he had was a hypothesis: that Jewish financial power, whose conspicuous existence had damaged the Jews hitherto, could be used to help them.[23]

But neither de Hirsch, whom he had approached first, nor the Rothschilds, whom he had exhorted in his *Address*, had disbursed a penny. The first Zionist Congress of 1897 had embodied Herzl's vision of a Society of Jews; Max Bodenheimer had then proposed a National Fund which would embody Herzl's vision of a Jewish Company, the equivalent of the British South Africa Company that had enabled Cecil Rhodes to colonize the domains of King Lobengula. Herzl had then predicted that 1898 would see the establishment of what was provisionally named the Jewish Colonial Bank. This bank would be based on London and have a share capital of two million sterling, divided into one-pound shares. The bank was again predicted for the following year at the second Congress; the coming journey to Palestine made it yet more urgent. The bank was indeed registered in London on March 20, 1899, and a week later the subscription list was opened. But only 200,000 shares were subscribed for, 50,000 less than the required minimum. Although by the time of the third Congress the bank edged up to the requisite total, it was still sadly short of what Herzl had envisaged. As might be expected of a bank founded for a political purpose by a President who was an inspired but interfering amateur, it produced headaches more than profits. Accusations of maladministration were investigated and found to be baseless. Yet the bank caused constant ill feeling, not least when Herzl created special Founders Shares which gave control of the bank and were restricted to people whose Zionism he could trust. In all financial matters David Wolffsohn was his faithful assistant; but even Wolffsohn's patience had almost reached the breaking point by early 1900.

This summary of Herzl's money worries consumes a few lines of print. Yet the anxiety they caused clouded week after slow week of Herzl's life. Their repercussions glint angrily through the records of those days. The Diary reflects this new, worried diarist and loses its clear, exciting line. It becomes the documentation of parochial wrangles, tedious as old bridge scores. Herzl is conjuring, not now with three, but with a dozen plates: a nagging bank manager clutches his coattails from behind.

Only new contacts with men of power could strike fire from his pen. Then the old skill at rapid portraiture flashes from the dull pages of transcribed letters, the references to ill health, the doubts about close associates and the silence on his private life. Places had temporarily lost their power to inspire. On his last three visits to Turkey he described his intrigues, not their background. "Beauty no longer moves me," he wrote.[24]

His continued Turkish intrigues, expensive, drawn out and finally futile, were made possible by his discovery of a wondrous replacement for Nevlinsky. Arminius Vámbéry was an adventurer and explorer to rank with his contemporary, Sir Richard Burton. Born to Orthodox Jewish parents in Hungary, Vámbéry had first embraced Islam to enter the Ottoman service and then Protestant Christianity to become professor of oriental languages at Budapest. When Herzl met him for the first time on June 17, 1900, Vámbéry's extraordinary life grew no more ordinary in his old man's telling. "This limping, 70-year-old Hungarian Jew who doesn't know whether he is more Turk than Englishman, writes books in German, speaks twelve languages with equal mastery, and has professed five religions, in two of which he has served as priest," fascinated Herzl, who added: "with an intimate knowledge of so many religions he naturally had to become an atheist."[25] In strictest confidence Vámbéry confided that he was a secret agent of both Turkey and Great Britain. He had further assets. He was rich. He was a personal friend of Sultan Abdul Hamid, with whom he would eat, in the Turkish manner, squatting on the floor. (Herzl had no such powers of adaptation. He found the custom of using the same utensils for a succession of little dishes abhorrent. The son of Jeanette Herzl insisted on a fresh plate, knife and fork for each of fifteen courses. He believed this impressed the Turkish servants even more than his baksheesh.) The Sultan had asked Vámbéry, like Nevlinsky before him, to improve the Turkish name in the European press. This gave Herzl his cue. Vámbéry should advise the Sultan to invite Herzl to Constantinople (his mere presence there would raise Abdul Hamid's credit) and entrust him with the task.

Certainly cleverer than Nevlinsky, Vámbéry was probably also more courageous. He wrote vividly of travels that had taken him in great discomfort throughout central Asia. But his character showed that a man who frivols with religion does not keep his soul intact. Under the influence of this nineteenth-century Mr. Norris, a coarser, less honest Herzl temporarily replaces the idealist who had sought to behave and write with noble candor. Herzl becomes the admiring, colluding nephew. *Vámbéry bácsi* (Uncle Vámbéry, as Herzl asks to be allowed to call him in Nordau's manner) becomes the rogue who first amuses and then instructs. Herzl and his associates begin to use code: the Sultan, for example, is *Cohn* and Yildiz *the factory*. The code is a necessary cloak. The Diary (written in Herzl's beautiful hand) carries items that even the charitable must recognize as two-faced. For example, in one letter Vámbéry refers to his friend the Sultan (of whom after his deposition he was to write an illuminating memoir*) as the *mamzer ben-nide* (foully conceived bastard)[26]; yet in a letter of obsequious loyalty to the Sultan Herzl refers to "my excellent friend, Professor Vámbéry, who is such a profoundly devoted servant of Your Imperial Majesty."[27] General statements similarly clash. "At present I can see only one more plan: See to it that Turkey's difficulties increase; wage a personal campaign against the Sultan; possibly seek contact with the exiled princes and the Young Turks†; and, at the same time, by intensifying Jewish Socialist activities stir up the desire among the European governments to exert pressure on Turkey to take in the Jews."[28] This Machiavellian plan contradicts both Herzl's sermons to the German conservatives on Zionism as an antidote to socialism and a characteristic profession of loyalty to the Commander of the Faithful: "The greatness and power of the Ottoman empire are the only hope of the Jewish nation, and it is as a faithful Jew that I wish to earn, not for myself but for my brethren, the good will of the great Caliph."[29]

Herzl's last three visits to the caliphal capital—in May 1901, in February, then July 1902—showed the disadvantages of being his mother's son, of looking on the east as barbaric and of failing to recognize Ottoman tactics as part of a serious strategy of defense. Without this aloof contempt—which he shared with most Europeans of the day—he might have underestimated his opponents less and saved time, perhaps his health. When as we shall see he came to regard another Eastern people with sympathy, it was already too late: by then the Zionist engine was out of his control and he, though wiser and pain-taught, was too weak to profit. His description of eating with the leading members of the Ottoman regime—a signal honor—attests this aloofness: "Another loathsome meal with those innumerable barbaric dishes which, according to the Oriental custom, have to be forced down with exclamations of delight. Veritable snake food."[30] The Kaiser, or Cecil Rhodes, might have felt the same. Herzl also underrated the system that kept the Sultan's empire, if not intact, then

* "Personal Recollections of Abdul Hamid II and His Court," *The Nineteenth Century*, June 1909.

† The Young Turks were to overthrow Abdul Hamid in 1909 and institute a nationalistic, racist dictatorship that antagonized the non-Turkish elements in the Ottoman empire.

in being. Incapable of resisting Europe in arms (until a peasant army led by a military genius fought for its own soil at Gallipoli), the Turks used the arts of diplomacy to fend off foreigners eager for slices of their land. One of these arts was procrastination. "Two moods," Herzl says of his long waits in Constantinople for a favorable answer, "may be recorded as ever-recurring ones. The anxiety at Yildiz, which increases in the hours of waiting. Then, the feeling while speaking with them that they aren't really serious at all. They are like sea foam. Only their expressions are serious, not their intentions."[31] In fact, Ottoman intentions, as distinct from Ottoman appearances, were both serious and normal. They wanted their state to survive. At the same time they were admittedly short of money. This Austrian journalist with the waxy skin and the long, square beard was offering to correct finances as tangled as jungles, or in a figure Herzl used more than once, to act the part of Androcles to the Turkish lion. The Turkish officials, far less naïve than they seemed, were curious to see what he could offer. Were Jewish millions at the disposal of their guest? If so, they could be useful. Though Palestine itself was not for sale, concessions and deals in other regions could be considered. Mesopotamia, for example, was suggested as a possible region for Jewish settlement in February 1902. Just as Herzl used his Turkish decoration (which he despised) to impress Western Jews, the Turks could use him (whose financial power they doubted) to coax more money from other financiers, such as the French. Again, as a journalist Herzl could influence the press of Austria and other countries to be more understanding about Turkish problems. For Herzl had given color to a myth—that Jews controlled the Western press—which was long to survive in the Middle East.

Far from being shifty, the Ottoman attitude was consistent from start to finish. The Sultan's first statement to Nevlinsky is echoed by the message he sent Herzl on his fifth and last visit: "The Israelites can be received and settled in the Ottoman Empire under the condition that they be installed, not together, that is, dispersed, in the places adjudged suitable by the government, and that their numbers be fixed in advance by the government. They will be invested with Ottoman citizenship and charged with all the civic duties, including military service, as well as being subject to all the laws of the land like Ottomans."[32] The Sultan was thus welcoming the Jewish victims of Romanian and Russian anti-Semitism in a period when even Bernard Lazare had urged Frenchmen to close their doors against Eastern Jews and when England was pondering measures to restrict immigration. In demanding that the Jews should accept military service and obedience to the laws of the empire, the Turks were demanding what the United States also demanded of immigrants. They were also things that Herzl had agreed to on more than one occasion. The rub came over the place: Herzl's insistence that they be allowed to settle in Palestine seemed evidence to the Turks of what Europeans such as the Grand Duke of Baden implied with a heavy wink—that once the Jews were in Palestine in a large number they would imitate former Ottoman vassals, such as the Bulgarians, and declare their independence. Herzl's remark, "Only when one has an army of a million men can one begin to do things in a country without diplomacy,"[33] may have seemed original to its maker. To the Turks, whose army had once been the strongest in Europe, it was a truism. Once the Zionists had such an army, they could do what they liked.

Herzl's eagerness to obtain a charter and the Ottoman determination not to give it made Herzl's one meeting with the Sultan a mixture of banality and misunderstanding. He had gone to Constantinople assured by Vámbéry (to whom he promised 300,000 guilders) that the charter would come this year. His youngest daughter Trude had been tearful because he might be away (he was) for May 20, her birthday. But at last, on May 18, 1901, he had reached the inner sanctum of Yildiz. He sat in an armchair across from the divan on which sat "the Master," a sword dangling between his legs: "small, shabby, with his badly dyed beard which is probably freshly painted once a week for the selamlik. The hooked nose of a Punchinello, the long yellow teeth with a big gap on the upper right. The fez pulled low over his probably bald head; the prominent ears 'serving as a trousers-protector,' as I used to say about such fez-wearers to my friends' amusement— that is, to keep the fez from slipping down onto the trousers. The feeble hands in white, oversize gloves, and the ill-fitting coarse, loud-coloured cuffs. The bleating voice, the constraint in every word, the timidity in every glance."[34] The interview lasted two hours. Herzl offered to settle the debt, provided His Majesty made a gesture of support to the Jews. The Sultan's secretary blurted in with a proposal: the court jeweler, a Jew, might repeat some kindly, pro-Jewish phrase of the Sultan's to the press. Herzl brushed this aside: he wanted, he said, to enlist world Jewry in the cause of Turkish development. The Sultan replied that the empire was indeed rich—only that morning a cable from Baghdad had reported the discovery of oil fields richer than those in the Caucasus. But after meandering talk of money, solutions, mutual esteem, the conversation got nowhere. The only achievement to offset Trude's disappointment was represented by the blue envelope handed to him the following day by the same secretary who had mentioned the court jeweler. It contained a present from the Sultan, a stickpin set with a golden-yellow diamond.[35]

Herzl had given baksheesh to the Sultan's servants. The Sultan now gave baksheesh to Herzl. He was never to give more.

CHAPTER 28

As one of his enduring characteristics Herzl had the ability to stroll from reality into fiction, to find fertility in writing when reality was arid. For nearly three years one last great dream—expressed in his one serious novel*—served as a crystalline mirror through which he could step when the everyday seemed dull or hopeless.

The theme was first set down when Herzl was on the train from Paris to Frankfurt on July 2, 1899. He was returning from a London visit devoted to niggling questions of the bank. His original title for a looking-glass novel about a future state for the Jews was *The New Zion*. The idea had shimmered beside him through the tedious third Zionist Congress in August 1899. On August 30—once again in movement, this time on an omnibus jolting from central Vienna to his suburban home in Währing—he hit on a better title. *Altneuland* (*Old-New Land*) would have echoes of the famous synagogue, Altneuschul, in Prague.

The dream novel made no progress for another eighteen months—since in the interim the dream element had invaded everyday, with his discovery of Vámbéry and his interview with the ruler of Wonderland, another name for Yildiz. He referred to the novel once more, on November 8, 1899, when his losses on *Die Welt*, his lack of support from Kaiser or people turned him desperately back to writing as a means of livelihood. "In order to get some grist for my mill, I now have even revised my old farce *Muttersöhnchen* and included a part

---

* At the age of nineteen he wrote what he later called "a bad, youthful novelette," *Hagenau*, which remained unpublished until March 1900, when Bacher, short of material, persuaded Herzl to publish it in the *Neue Freie Presse*. It appeared as *Die Heimkehr* (*The Homecoming*), the work of "H. Jungmann."[1]

for the comedian Girardi. There is no literary work that would be more loathsome to me. And there will probably be reproaches levelled at me when it becomes known that I as 'prophet' am performing such *basse besogne.*† But what am I to do? Zionism is costing me money and must not yield me anything. On the other hand, I have done myself very great harm as a 'German writer,' and they don't quite dare perform me." In this mood he again thought of *Altneuland,*[2] as he did on June 3, 1900, when swinging between Vámbéry's hopes that the Sultan would grant a charter and his own more realistic despair. "Or shall we hear a categorical No from Yildiz? If this came, I would resume work on my novel *Altneuland.* For then our plan will be only for the future and a novel."[3]

A year's activity in the real world intervened. It included some domestic relief. "The fantasies moved past while I walked up and down in my children's room. The children were being bathed and put to bed, as they are every evening. They made their daily jokes, draped bedclothes around themselves after they had been undressed, lustily sang their way into the bathroom, danced into their beds, and said their evening prayers; today I made them say a Hebrew prayer in addition to the German one."[4]‡ And then, in March 1901, he was again enmeshed in disappointments. Lord Rothschild refused to meet him in London; a legacy of 200,000 guilders from a drunk Russian Zionist, Georg Taubin, was contested and Vienna irked him so much that he thought of moving to London (Julie agreed but his parents did not). In this baffled mood he returned with relief to his Utopia. "I am now industriously working on *Altneuland.* My hopes for practical success have now disintegrated. My life is no novel now. So the novel is my life."[5] Once again a pause. He was interrupted by two new disappointments: one, his fourth visit to Turkey, the other his first contact with the gentile millionaire whose role in history might foreshadow his own. After his meeting with the Sultan in May 1901 Herzl had gone to London to exploit its resonance with British Jews. While there, Joseph Cowen, an English Jewish businessman who had attended the first Zionist Congress, contacted William Thomas Stead, the journalist ally of Cecil Rhodes, on Herzl's behalf. For Herzl had hit on a new way of getting Palestine. The South Africans—and as early as 1896 he had thought of enlisting "the South African goldmine billionaire Barnato"[6]—could secretly buy up the bonds of the Turkish

† Lowly tasks, or hackwork.
‡ The incident has all the ring of truth; but the inclusion of the Hebrew prayer reminds us that the Diary was intended for eventual publication. Herzl's knowledge of Hebrew was so rudimentary that when he wanted to recite a sentence it had to be written out for him in Latin characters.

dette. Herzl would then have a double message: to the Sultan, liberation from debt—if he surrendered Palestine; to the Jews, Palestine, if they paid the South Africans for what they had spent, plus of course their profit. Stead replied to Cowen:

"I told him [Rhodes] that Herzl would come and see him any day that was convenient; that he wanted to discuss with the one founder of States that modern times had produced. Rhodes said: 'If he wants any tip from me, I have only one word to say, and that is: let him put money in his purse.'"[7] Rhodes, who was pro-German on racial grounds, told Stead that he believed "Asiatic Turkey ought to be turned over to Germany, since England could not rule the whole world." Rhodes, like Herzl, had been charmed by the Kaiser. But on March 27, 1902, Herzl wrote bleakly: "Cecil Rhodes is dead. For a time I had him in mind as a fund raiser. I didn't manage to get together with him. My helpers in England proved a failure in this instance."[8] He now resumed his novel in earnest and by April 30, 1902, the manuscript was finished. It was published in the first week of October the same year.

Altneuland has the distinction of being the only Utopia fashioned by a man whose ideas have also led directly to the creation of a state. As a novel, it has affinities to science fiction, which Leslie A. Fiedler has described as "that largely Jewish product"[9]; as such it is the final manifestation of Herzl's admiration for de Lesseps. In structure it is a story woven round an unusual friendship between two men. Dr. Friedrich Loewenberg—Jewish, Viennese, handsome, unhappy, twenty-three and a doctor of laws—reads an advertisement similar to the one Herzl had once thought of inserting in the French press: "Wanted: An educated, desperate young man willing to make a last experiment with his life. Apply N. O. Body, this office."* After a vulgar evening party at which Ernestine Loeffler, the rich girl he loves, rejects him for a broker with a squint and damp palms, Friedrich answers the advertisement and is led to Mr. Kingscourt, a former Prussian officer who has become a millionaire in America at the cost of being cuckolded by his nephew. As a result he has become a hater of the human race in general and of women in particular. "It is human to be base, and every opportunity is a pander. Avoid human beings if you would not have them wreck you." Having purchased an archipelago in the South Seas and a yacht, he now seeks a permanent male companion. "I must remind you that you are undertaking a life-long obligation. At least, it must hold for the rest of my life. If you come

* The novel has been translated and published in New York as *Old-New Land* by Lotta Levensohn, preface by Emmanuel Neumann.

with me now, there will be no going back. There will be no women."
Friedrich accepts.

Before the two men depart, Friedrich helps the family of a starving
Jewish urchin, David Littwak, to migrate to Palestine.

On their journey south the two adventurers visit, at Kingscourt's
suggestion, the Palestine of 1903. The Holy Land is painted in dreary
colors. "The alleys [in Jaffa] were dirty, neglected, full of vile odors.
Everywhere misery in bright Oriental rags. Poor Turks, dirty Arabs,
timid Jews lounged about—indolent, beggarly, hopeless." In Jerusalem
they are both revolted by the appearance of the beggars praying at
the Wailing Wall. The two men sail away through the Suez Canal to
an island paradise where they spend twenty open-air years as Robinson
Kingscourt and Jewish Man Friday.

In 1923 the two friends come back. Neither has tired of the other,
but the elderly Kingscourt's curiosity, not Friedrich's, has returned
them to the threshold of the world. The first surprise is the Gulf of
Suez, no longer bustling with international shipping. "At Port Said
they disembarked. There was a lively freight traffic in the harbour,
but the shabby bazaars no longer swarmed with the vivid, multicolored, polyglot pageant that had once been typical of the town. This
had been the crossways for all who travelled from East to West, and
from West to East. The most fashionable globetrotters had been
accustomed to pass through Port Said; but now, except for the natives,
only a few half-drunken sailors lounged before the dirty cafés."
Palestine's new position at the center of a nexus of railways has
emptied Port Said of tourists. The two hasten to Haifa, now the best
port in the eastern Mediterranean. Here coincidence arranges that
David Littwak, the once starving beggar boy, is about to step into an
electric launch. A politician, destined to be elected President before
the tale is told, David guides the two strangers around the New
Society.

The characters in the novel are nearly all transcriptions of people
who had played parts in the story of Herzl's life. His judgment on
them, and the patterns which he arranges for them, are thus of great
interest to his biography, wherein so much of his intimate life has been
shrouded with man-made clouds.

Friedrich, summed up in the title of the first section as "an educated,
desperate young man," is obviously Herzl himself: but the Herzl of
pre-Zionist days. Kingscourt, whom Friedrich describes as "the best
and only friend I have in the world," bears a physical resemblance to
Philipp zu Eulenburg. Kingscourt embodies Herzl's admiration for

Prussian values†; his reliance on a male friend indicates that Herzl had registered, perhaps unconsciously, what was to be Eulenburg's historically most important characteristic.‡ David Littwak is David Wolffsohn, Lithuanian by birth and future successor to Herzl as President of the Zionist World Organization, and guardian to one of his daughters. Kana and Boxer are mentioned by name in the opening pages; other associates appear as minor characters. Even Richard Wagner, cause of Herzl's first brush with racialism, reappears in code (to those who knew the name of the musician's real father) as Rabbi Dr. Geyer, a demagogue who is defeated at the polls.

The roles allotted to Herzl's intimates are most significant. Pauline (to whose memory *Altneuland* was dedicated) is reborn as Miriam, the serious-minded schoolteacher whom Friedrich finally marries at the request of Miriam's dying mother. The woman whom Herzl had married in real life, Julie Naschauer, is portrayed as Ernestine Loeffler; her family of rich, assimilated Jews are depicted more cruelly than the Jews of *The New Ghetto*. At the opera—where he attends a music drama based on the story of Sabbatai Zevi—Friedrich sees Ernestine and her daughter. "At first he was under an odd illusion. Ernestine Loeffler had not changed in the least in twenty years . . . There were the same delicate young features, the same tender young form. But he realized his error after a moment. This young girl was not Ernestine, but Ernestine's daughter. Mrs. Weinberger was the fat, faded, gaudily dressed woman in the next seat. She was looking up to him, smiling an invitation, and nodded vigorously in response to his bow." A long illusion, preserved in happy reveries on Kingscourt's island, crumbles. "In his dreams he had always seen her in her youthful form. His sudden glimpse of the natural process of aging was a shock. He felt a sense of shame, but also of relief. That he should have been heartsick over this woman! Was it possible?"

The one character unrelated to experience is the solitary Palestinian. During his visit to Palestine Herzl had met no Arabs; except for reflecting that they might clear swamps for the settlers,[10] he seems to have given them little thought. One letter from Herzl to an Arab has been published, though it is not one of the letters Herzl copied into his Diary.* It dates from March 19, 1899, in the immediate

---

† "By the way, if there is one thing I should like to be, it is a member of the old Prussian nobility." *Complete Diaries*, July 5, 1895.

‡ The scandal surrounding Eulenburg and the so-called "Camarilla" at the Kaiser's court marked the first important rift between the Kaiser and his people.

* Translation of French original published in *From Haven to Conquest: Readings in Zionism and the Palestine Problem Until 1948*, ed. Walid Khalidi, Beirut, The Institute for Palestine Studies, 1971, p. 91.

aftermath of his Palestinian journey and a few days before the death
of Nevlinsky. Its Arab recipient was Youssuf Zia al-Khalidi, member
for Jerusalem in the Ottoman parliament of 1877 and in 1899 Mayor
of Jerusalem. The Mayor, as spokesman of the Arab majority in
Palestine, had been perturbed by the intentions of the five Zionist
delegates who had been seen in Jaffa and Jerusalem during the
Kaiser's visit. The mayor had written to Zadoc Kahn, the Chief Rabbi
of France, expressing the friendliest feelings toward the Jews but
anxiety over Zionist intentions for his country. Kahn passed his letter
to Herzl, who personally replied to his objections. The Jews, he
wrote, were neither backed by a bellicose power nor were themselves
warlike. The holy places were the property of all mankind, and as
such were sacred. "You see another difficulty, Excellency, in the
existence of the non-Jewish population in Palestine. But who would
think of sending them away? It is their well-being, their individual
wealth which we will increase by bringing in our own." Herzl answered
the Mayor's plea that the Jews should choose somewhere else to
settle, by the veiled threat that they might indeed do so—to Turkey's
detriment. As a loyal Ottoman, Khalidi should support, not oppose,
the Zionist plan.

Altneuland's "Reschid Bey"† is a wealthy Arab who, like the Jews
in the New Society, speaks German and delights in the Garden City
amenities provided by the settlers. One of David Littwak's best friends,
he lives in a comfortable house, married to a cultivated though secluded wife. Reschid Bey ridicules Kingscourt's suggestions that the
Muslims might have regarded the Jews as intruders. "You speak
strangely, Christian. Would you call a man a robber who takes nothing
from you, but brings you something instead? The Jews have enriched
us."

Whether the poorer Palestinians have been spirited across the border is left vague, as are the borders. Tyre, Sidon, Damascus and
Tadmor (the rebuilt Palmyra) are certainly on the Jewish railway; the
land east of the Jordan is part of the state. There is a similar vagueness
about Palestine itself. The names are biblical but the electric trains
move through a scenery that could well be a hotter Scandinavia.
There is no army—because universal peace has banished war. Religious intolerance is a thing of the past.

The overpowering sweetness and light, the avoidance of the knotty
problems he had not avoided in his Diary give weight to Emanuel
Neumann's judgment, in his preface to the U.S. edition, that Herzl's
purpose in writing *Altneuland* was to make propaganda, though Mr.

† So written in Herzl's German; it should be pronounced "Rasheed."

Neumann limits this to inspiring the Jewish people with faith and confidence in the Zionist idea. As a work of propaganda, or public relations, it was equally directed to gentiles. Herzl presented copies of the book to, among others, the Sultan, the Austrian Prime Minister and the King of Italy.[11] It even contained compliments. "You will be interested to know," David Littwak tells his guests, "that railway fares are very low here. We have adopted the system of fares in vogue in Baden during the reign of the kindly, wise Grand Duke of Baden." The Grand Duke was a first-day recipient of an inscribed copy.‡

But, even more, *Altneuland* is an expression of Herzl the dreamer. As he says in the Epilogue: "Dreams are not so different from Deeds as some may think. All the Deeds of men are only Dreams at first. And in the end, their Deeds dissolve into Dreams."

In *Altneuland* the dream has taken over at the expense of the conscious intent. The narrative exhibits Herzl's deepest emotions, his bitterest as well as his most hopeful feelings. It also exhibits the liberal idealist behind the politician who wrote the Diary. In his dream he is more truthful about his aims, if less candid about their implications. Two strands in his imagination visibly unite: his youthful delight in science; his maturer espousal of free thought. In the month before he wrote his first notes, Herzl had hit on the idea of "mutualism" (he used the English word), shortly after contemplating "the American 'Cleveland Car,' the best automobile available," at the Paris Automobile Exposition of 1899. "Mutualism strikes me as the middle road between capitalism and collectivism. Producers' and consumers' cooperatives are only beginnings, suggestions of the mutual principle."[12] A month after his first notes he wrote one of his most characteristic sentences: "The chief tenet of my life: Whoever wishes to change men must change the conditions under which they live."[13] Under the same date—August 6, Vienna—he added no less sincerely: "My testament for the Jewish people: Make your State in such a way that the stranger will feel comfortable among you."

Kingscourt, enslaved by David's infant son, Fritzchen, feels so comfortable in the New Society that he, the Protestant Junker, asks to join it. It seemed less comfortable to many Zionist Jews. Some ardent nationalists (such as Asher Ginsberg, who wrote in Hebrew under the name Ahad Ha-Am) met it with hostile uproar. To such critics, the kind of state envisaged by Herzl represented not the survival of the Jews, but their cultural obliteration. Altneuland is

‡ Ernst von Koerber, Prime Minister of Austria 1900–4, received his copy two months later, on December 9, 1902. Herzl wrote: "Please accept my new book *Altneuland* (a political novel, an ideal solution of the Jewish Question) as a token of my sincere respect." Cf. Diary for this date.

indeed what Herzl had told the Prussians it would be, an outpost of German culture in the Middle East. Hebrew words punctuate the German only as *parbleu!* or *mon Dieu!* punctuate historical novels about France; Hebrew festivals are part of the folklore. But the language, culture and ethos are German, the manifestations of what Kingscourt perceptively calls a Mosaic mosaic, the tesserae all being imported from Europe. As Herzl's translator, Lotta Levensohn, points out, Herzl so insists that there is nothing new in Altneuland, only the transplanatation of things already existing when he wrote, "that it was clear he attributed no creative powers whatsoever to the Jews. Adapt and develop existing facilities, ideas and institutions they could and did in the *Old-New Land,* and with superb results. But in all those years no new ideas or schools are born in any field of thought or activity. Culturally and in every other way, the country is a collection of copied models."[14] In his haste Herzl seems to accept by default the teaching of those European racialists who confined creativity to the Aryan peoples. This may be because he was more intent on a positive affirmation: civilization was something any people could, by their efforts, rise to share in. The Jews had been prevented from doing so by centuries of anti-Semitism. "And all that time Judaism had sunk lower and lower. It was an 'elend' in the full sense of the old German word that had meant 'out-land,' the limbo of the banished."[15] In a state of their own the things that had differentiated them from other peoples would wither away; they would be a nation like other nations. The humanist maxim *Nil humani a me alienum puto***** is inscribed over the Peace Palace which dominates a Jerusalem wherein all private dwellings have been banished from the Old City. "Religion had been excluded from public affairs once and for all. The New Society did not care whether a man sought the eternal verities in a temple, a church or a mosque, in an art museum or at a philharmonic concert."[16] The Jews had failed to assimilate as individuals; in Altneuland they had assimilated as a people. The fact that there is nothing distinctively Jewish about Altneuland, that any group could construct such a society from the materials available in 1899, the year of the Peace Conference, is one message of the book. For to Herzl what seemed distinctively Jewish was simply the result of gentile persecution.

Although the book ends with two deaths—that of Miriam's mother

---

* Sic in the U.S. edition. The full quotation is usually written *Homo sum; humani nil a me alienum puto.* (I am a man, and reckon nothing human alien to me.) Its author is the Latin playwright Terence, 195–59 B.C.

and the New Society's first President—*Altneuland* is a work of optimism, unlike many other projections of the future. Its sunshine comes from the world into which Herzl habitually escaped from personal wrangles and worries over cash.

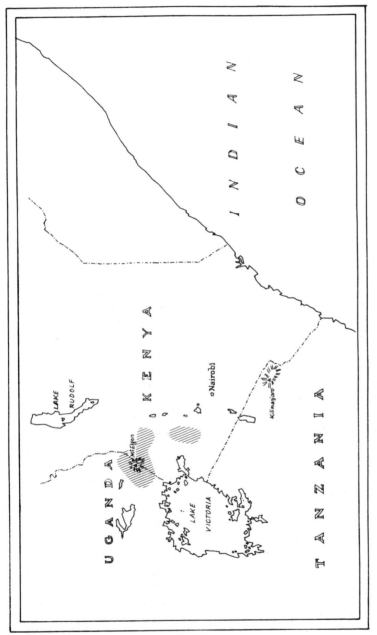

Modern East Africa. Shaded areas show the depopulated (fertile, upland) areas proposed for Jewish settlement in 'Uganda' – mostly in modern Kenya.

CHAPTER 29

Bitter reality dragged Herzl from his daydream. For some time Julie had been ill with an internal complaint. Passing through Paris in early June 1902, he wrote that he himself was now "an aging and famous man." The days of his youth, despite their melancholy, had been preferable. Then he had been a writer. Now he had become world-famous as a Jewish propagandist; yet this role could not satisfy his deepest longings. "As a writer, particularly as a playwright, I am held to be nothing, less than nothing. People call me only a good journalist. And yet I feel, I know, that I am or was a writer of great ability, one who simply didn't give his full measure because he became disgusted and discouraged."[1] In London he was invited to give evidence before a Royal Commission appointed to report on the problem of a vast new influx of Russian Jews. He intended to outrage Rothschild, the first practicing Jew to be made a British peer, in particular and the assimilated English Jews in general. He would define the dilemma facing the British: either they must break with their tradition of granting asylum to refugees, or leave their own working class "unprotected." One way out was for the British to grant not Palestine, but Cyprus to the Jews.

The thought of acquiring Cyprus was not new. On his first visit to Turkey Herzl had toyed with the idea of obtaining the island so as to use it as a bargaining counter for persuading the Sultan to surrender Palestine. He had later been in correspondence with Davis Trietsch, who, as an advocate of Jewish settlement in Cyprus, had been the first Jewish nationalist to approach British officialdom (in his case, the High Commissioner in Nicosia) with a view to the colonization of territory controlled by Britain. Trietsch had embarrassed Herzl at the fifth Zionist Congress by trying to have the Basel program of 1897 amended to read: "Zionism strives to create for the majority of Jews a Home in Palestine *and in its neighbouring lands* secured in every respect."[2]

Then, on the evening of June 9, he returned from the theater to his London hotel to find a telegram from Vienna summoning him home. Jacob Herzl was seriously ill. Although he tried to persuade himself that it might be an attack of pneumonia, he secretly knew that it was death. Next day was Hans's eleventh birthday.

Just before he caught the train to Dover, a second telegram confirmed that his father had died, painlessly, of a stroke. Among Herzl's flooding regrets, an island: his father had died without reading the last pages of *Altneuland*. Back in Vienna he took a strange decision: his father would be given only temporary burial in the Döblinger Friedhof. This cemetery was the most beautiful in the city: "beyond its walls one sees the vast sweep of green hills and valleys whose graceful undulations rise and fall past Grinzing and Sievering to the Kahlenberg."[3] His mother seems to have shared Herzl's determination that within the foreseeable future Jacob Herzl would be reburied in some such state as *Altneuland* had pictured.

But the location of this state had suddenly become in doubt. From 1902 until 1904 Herzl considered acquiring Cyprus, the Sinai Peninsula, "Uganda,"* Mesopotamia, Mozambique, the Congo and Libya. Cyprus, Sinai and Uganda were taken seriously enough as Jewish destinations for discussion of their acquisition to be conducted at the highest levels. About Herzl's burning desire to acquire one or other of these territories by a British charter, there is no debate. The debate concerns his motives. Did he wish to acquire one or other of these places as solutions for *Judennot* (Jewish need)? as steppingstones to Palestine? or substitutes for it? His actions above provide the key.

Early in July 1902, the bereaved Herzl was back in London. Now that he was to give evidence before the Royal Commission, he was received by Lord Rothschild. Rothschild foresaw that the two "jackasses," on the commission—Arnold White and Evans Gordon—planned to call Herzl to support their hostile viewpoint. "Dr. Herzl is certainly the exemplary Jew," he envisaged them saying, "and he declares that a Jew can never be an Englishman."[4] Yet it was the cautious Lord Rothschild who first let fall the incautious word "Uganda." After luncheon and coffee Herzl had asked Rothschild if he would now

---

* "Uganda" was, as we shall see, an imprecise description for territory in British East Africa, or the modern Kenya.

like to hear his "scheme" (he used the English word). Rothschild agreeing, Herzl pulled his chair closer to the elderly financier's better ear.

"I want to ask the British government for a colonization charter."

"Don't say charter. The word has a bad sound at the moment."

"We can call it whatever you like. I want to found a Jewish colony in a British possession."

"Take Uganda!"

"No. I can only use this . . ." And because there were other people in the room, Herzl wrote on a slip of paper: "Sinai Peninsula, Egyptian Palestine, Cyprus." Herzl reports that when he asked the financier if he agreed, Rothschild pondered the paper with a smirk, then answered:

"Very much so."

Herzl pushed a further note toward him: "Prevent the Sultan from getting money."

Rothschild commented that though he had indeed stopped Romania getting money (because of its anti-Jewish policy), this chore was beyond him. If the Powers wanted railroads built through Anatolia, he could not stop them.

Herzl now mentioned a further territory. "The Sultan offered me Mesopotamia."

Rothschild was astounded.

"And you refused?"

"Yes."[5]

Shortly afterward Herzl left on what was to prove his fifth and last visit to Constantinople. Even if Mesopotamia (the future Iraq) might be unsuitable for colonization, the exploitation of its minerals might be worth consideration. But no deal was arranged with the Sultan. Herzl now placed all his hopes on his London contact, Leopold Jacob Greenberg,† being able to arrange a meeting with the one man who could help him settle Jews in a British possession. This man, Joseph Chamberlain, Secretary for the Colonies since 1895, received him on October 20, 1902. To keep the appointment Herzl had fled his newspaper like a schoolboy from school, and like a schoolboy he feared punishment or expulsion.

At being granted an hour in which to explain himself to "the famous master of England," Herzl. was so impressed that his rough-and-ready English trembled while the Colonial Secretary's impassive

---

† Greenberg, a journalist and small publisher, had known Chamberlain in Birmingham, when both men had been ardent radicals. In 1906 Greenberg was to buy the *Jewish Chronicle* with assistance from the Jewish Colonial Trust and become the first Zionist editor. He died in 1931.

mask gave no encouragement. But warming to his theme, Herzl wrung a laugh by comparing his fruitless negotiations with the Sultan to carpet-haggling. He used the relief to state what he wanted: "Cyprus, El Arish and the Sinai Peninsula."

Chamberlain took the territories in the order Herzl had raised them. Cyprus, which came under his jurisdiction, had a population of Greek Christians and Turkish Muslims. He could hardly crowd them out for the sake of immigrant Jews; on the international level Greece and Russia would cause an uproar, and on the island there would be a trades-union resistance such as already opposed immigration into England. As Colonial Secretary in the Conservative government headed by Arthur James Balfour, Chamberlain could do nothing against the will of the indigenous population. (Provided, he implied, this population were white; for if Herzl could show him "a spot in the English possession where there were no white people as yet," they could talk about that.‡[6]) Since everything was in the open in England, a political tempest would batter any discussion of Herzl's proposal.

"I replied," Herzl had his answer ready, "that *not everything in politics is really disclosed to the public—only results, or whatever may happen to be needed in a discussion.*" Herzl then summarized the way in which his plan could be put into action. Once a Jewish Eastern Company for settling Sinai and El Arish had been established, "the Cypriots will begin to want that golden rain on their island, too. The Moslems will move away, the Greeks will gladly sell their lands at a good price and migrate to Athens or Crete."[7]

But Chamberlain considered that he had disposed of Cyprus. He moved on to Herzl's alternative, El Arish. He first consulted a map to

‡ Julian Amery, the biographer of Joseph Chamberlain (*Life of Joseph Chamberlain*, London, 1951), confirms the accuracy of Herzl's account but also illuminates the motives of his hero. "Chamberlain . . . was the first among British statesmen to see in Zionism both an end to the ancient Jewish problem and a means of advancing the interests of the British Empire" (p. 256). The Rand gold mines in South Africa were largely controlled by Jews; on the prosperity of the Rand Chamberlain largely counted for the reconstruction of South Africa. Like his Prime Minister, Balfour, Chamberlain was also worried by the Jewish poblem in Britain itself. "As a result of Russian persecution towards 1900 . . . nearly 100,000 Jews had settled in Britain" (p. 259). A concentration of Jews and Jewish money in Sinai or elsewhere, indebted to Britain, would serve British foreign policy ("a Jewish colony in Sinai might prove a useful instrument for extending British influence into Palestine proper, when the time came for the inevitable dismemberment of the Ottoman Empire" [p. 261]) and siphon off immigrants whose cheaper labor was deplored by the British trade unions. Amery agrees with Denis Judd (*Balfour and the British Empire*, London, 1968, p. 99) that Chamberlain was personally anti-Semitic, although he was a close friend of Alfred Rothschild and maintained extensive Jewish connections.

discover where this was, reminding Herzl of a store owner who had forgotten the precise location of something he wanted to sell. Finding it in Sinai, well within the frontiers of Egypt, he pointed out that it did not come under his jurisdiction. Any advance in that direction would therefore depend on Lord Cromer, Britain's minister plenipotentiary in Cairo.

His interview with Chamberlain reveals much of the Herzl of this terminal period. His desperation to secure a territory had clouded his lawyer's brain. In the letter that had led up to the interview, he had written to Greenberg: "I should like to interest Mr. Chamberlain in a settlement of the Jews on a major scale in the British possessions."[8] Yet neither Cyprus nor Sinai was juridically a British possession at this time. In 1878, in return for a promise of British support against the Russians, the Sultan had allowed Britain, as a base for this purpose, to administer Cyprus, which remained in theory part of his empire. El Arish and the Sinai Peninsula were part of Egypt, whose Khedive, Abbas II, ruled a vassal state also under the suzerainty of the Sultan. Britain had occupied Egypt in 1882 as an ally of the then Khedive; the official title of her representative, Lord Cromer, was "British agent and consul general." In his demand for Cyprus, Herzl forgot his own arguments about a people's need for a home; he assumed that the Cypriots would abandon their villages for money. Almost certainly the villagers would have proved as stubborn in parting from their land as the fellahin in Palestine. Years ago he had written in his Book of Folly: "The only interesting play is the one backstage."[9] His remark to Chamberlain—italicized by the present writer—shows his acceptance of political deception. Many nationalists have justified deceit in the interests of the nation. This defense would assume that Herzl intended to mislead the British public and the Greeks and Turks of Cyprus. The same pretext could, of course, be used to deceive the Jews: in their own interests, as Herzl saw them.

Herzl in any case read Chamberlain's reaction to his request for Cyprus as a definitive No. Next day, despite an appeal from Rothschild (who had begun to admire him) for Cyprus rather than El Arish, Herzl did not mention the island when he was received in audience by the Foreign Secretary, Lord Lansdowne. At first he found Lansdowne merely a pleasant, modest English gentleman, and not particularly bright. But this kind of Brahmin had evolved through centuries its own bland mode of cooling an enthusiast. Herzl stumbled through his arguments, relieved to depart with a request from the Foreign Secretary to submit a memorandum and a promise to give

Greenberg (at this moment his most prized collaborator[10]) an introduction to Lord Cromer.

The months between November 1902 and March 1903 fell into two divisions. In the first period, Herzl's flagging spirits were revived when Greenberg was given a friendly reception by the authorities in Egypt. In the second period, when Greenberg had gone back to Egypt with explicit instructions to work for a charter, Herzl was torn by anxiety and suspicion. He was learning the painful lesson that a political movement is like a bicycle: if you stop moving, you fall off. Without success, his movement would stop moving. But only self-deception kept him hopeful about the chances of securing, under British pressure, an Egyptian charter to develop Sinai. The man who had watched the debates at the Palais Bourbon with shrewd discernment now seemed to have lost a clear distinction between fantasy and fact. When he came to describe his Egyptian negotations,* his report reflected this. "After long negotiations our agent received from the Egyptian Government a statement in which they declared themselves in agreement with the principle of the proposed charter." This was untrue. On February 22, 1903, the Egyptian Foreign Minister, Butros Ghali, explicitly rejected any notion of a charter.

"In accordance with the Imperial Firmans, the Khediviate can under no pretext or motive give up, in whole or in part, any of the rights inherent in the Sovereign Power.

"Consequently, the entire idea of a concession of a charter must be formally discarded."[11]

The Egyptian government was prepared, like the Sultan, to welcome Jewish refugees and give them tax concessions as well as land, provided they became "local subjects": which was plainly stated to mean that Jews who were not already Ottoman subjects (as Egyptians were) must produce a certificate from their countries of origin attesting that there was no objection to their becoming Ottomans and that these countries would claim no right to them as subjects or protected persons.

The Egyptian government's refusal to consider a charter of the kind Herzl wanted led to a coldness between himself and Greenberg. Greenberg, not entirely sure what Herzl wanted, had tried to get as much from Egypt as he could. He made the mistake of cabling Herzl a congratulatory message based on the offer of lands. Herzl was torn by painful emotions, one of them suspicion. He felt that while he was confined to his journalistic work in Vienna, Greenberg was making a bid for Zionist leadership. When he pressed Green-

* At the sixth Zionist Congress, in 1903.

berg to define the Egyptian offer, he received a coded reply: DOCU-
MENT AGREES TO CONCEDE TERRITORY IN LEITH (Sinai Peninsula) TO
CHECK (Jewish Eastern Company) UPON REPORT OF RABBIS (members
of the commission) AND TO CREATE OF TERRITORY A MUNICIPALITY.
LATTER WAS ALTERNATIVE TO JAM (charter).[12] Herzl suspected that the
disobedient Greenberg was trying to get the concession made out to
himself. When Herzl heard that the Sultan's Commissioner in Egypt
was proving obstructive, he cabled clear instructions:

PEREXILE (you may promise) COHNSMAN (Turkish Commissioner)
BOTH (two) GUY (thousand) MONTHS (pounds) AFTER (after) RU-
MOREN (charter signed by) CHISEL (Egyptian government). Green-
berg had not done this.[13]

That, instead of revolting, Herzl's associates cooperated in what
must have seemed a harebrained scheme testified to his ascendancy
as leader. It also testified to his followers' dependence, as subordinate
leaders, on some shared success. But Herzl's references to the sums of
money they demanded, and in many cases received, imply that enthusiasm for El Arish was scant. Greenberg took sums from the
Colonial Trust far in excess of his needs; Colonel Goldsmid, given a
hundred pounds for his expenses in January, was by March demanding a hundred and fifty more to send to his wife, as well as a letter of
credit for expenses. Herzl was particularly irked when Leon Kellner—
"I have an old liking for him"—refused to write a monograph on what
the ancients had to say about Pelusium and Lake Sirbonia (the part of
Sinai just east of the Canal) unless he were paid five hundred
guilders.[14] Fortunately for his associates, Herzl lavished money like
a gambler piling chips against a luckless run.

A commission of experts left Trieste on February 2, 1903 for
Egypt, to investigate the feasibility of constructing a *Judenstaat* in
Sinai. Perhaps they would have more luck with geography than
Greenberg with diplomacy. For when Greenberg returned to Europe
later in February, he still had no charter. He avoided Vienna and
Herzl and went instead to Paris to confer with Nordau. He sent the
letter from Foreign Minister Butros Ghali, with his own report, by
post to Herzl.

Herzl dismissed the report with cold irritation; it seemed "the
masterpiece of a not completely loyal agent." For in contradiction to
his own words at the next Congress, his Diary shows[15] his plain recognition that "the granting of a Charter is flatly refused." But Herzl
controlled his feelings. An alienated Greenberg might get too close to
Rothschild. His reply was polite. Nevertheless sarcasm rasped the
final paragraph.

"Mrs. Greenberg must be pleasantly surprised to see you again after such a short absence. Please give her my regards. She probably thought as I did that you would be gone longer and would only return with the Charter or with the Commission."[16]

On March 18, he wrote to Lord Rothschild asking him to convene in Paris a meeting of the men who handled the Hirsch Trust. Herzl reported that three members of the commission had already returned, while five were still surveying the southern mountainous region of Sinai. "But even the results which are already at hand in the reports and memoranda show that the territory we have in mind is suitable for a great settlement. In addition, we have received a written preliminary assurance from the Egyptian government, granting the desired settlement to the Zionist Movement in principle."[17] Neither of these assurances was true. They revealed the same desperation as his readiness to risk his health in a new journey. It would start the same day. "I am leaving for Cairo to put things in order with Lord Cromer and the Egyptian government." His address would be Shepheard's Hotel.

CHAPTER 30

Herzl, like his experts, took ship from Trieste, then the major port of the Habsburg empire. "Blue days, extremely sunny and wind-wafted. The continent has sunk beyond the horizon. For a while one can look back and see it grow pale like the days of one's youth, its lines as perfumed. In front lies the glorious sea, the Adriatic . . ." The *Semiramis* put in briefly at Brindisi with its cracked Roman column and living misery.

The column and the peculiar misery are linked by the fact that the place has always been a port. Rome's fortunate general landed here and the column will commemorate him forever. And this peculiar misery? The beggars, men and women alike, have eaten away faces, collapsed noses. They lack an arm, a leg. What cursed ground is this? It is a port. Here excited sailors would come ashore from the seas of all the world and these old beggarwomen were once Italian girls. From the gangway to the Post Office, where one posts one's last greetings to Europe, the cripples line the way. The one constable is rough. He screams himself hoarse, brandishes his cane and laboriously upholds an unthreatened order. He does this to impress the travellers from the big steamer. Many heroic actions have no deeper prompting . . . It was cruel what he did to a blind man who, led by a boy, held out his hand. He shoved the old man with the child behind railings, and closed the door. No need to lock it since the blind man could put up no resistance. At first the prisoner wailed to the boy that he was losing the ship, would take no pennies; his lamentations grew louder so that an observer could have taken him for the blinded, exiled king of tragedy. Only when the ship weighed anchor did the angry

despot open the railing door and let the old man totter forth.
Wailing, pulling at the boy's hand, he walked the length of the
harbour lamenting his bad luck to all he passed. A ship that would
have earned him a few pence was for him a shipwreck. His pain
could not have been greater if he had been a shipowner whose
vessel had gone to the sea-bottom. But in such cases the poor are
better off than the rich, for their losses are more easily made up.
The weeping, blind, old man was our last sight of Europe.[1]

Thus once more Herzl turned from the drab world of squabbles,
telegrams, disappointments, moral corrosion, to the bright world of
prose. The five-thousand-word *feuilleton* he wrote for the *Neue Freie
Presse* had as its epigraph von Bülow's Greek quotation from Pindar:
"Best is water." It began, "Between two dreams lies Egypt. The first
was going there, the second is getting back." It grew as they cruised
through the middle sea, the academic among them fishing for Homeric tags till, south of Cape Matapan, the sea rose and the numbers
at the captain's table shrank. Then in Alexandria, where they arrived
early on March 23, 1903, he evoked the world which he had first
rejected for Paris and which now drew and repelled him at the same
moment, "The sun rises and illumines red, saffron, blue; misery
bristles in narrow lanes; mysterious women in black glide past, veils
secured at the bridge of the nose with a brass coil, leaving free the
eyes. At the station, uproar. In all these catastrophes, it is a question
of one, at most of two piastres. The same expense of lungpower and
rudeness that a porter uses here, to extract an extra piastre, could, in
a civilized country, easily make him a member of parliament. The
value of rudeness rises precisely with the culture of a people."

Just as *Altneuland* had watered his disappointments, so his vision
of the Nile waters his arid mission. The tourist's impressions—the
eternal river, the loaded camels disregarding the Age of Steam—these
are the routine impressions of Egypt. Yet his prose is also steeped in
the melancholy of a poet who sees in each sad image the mirror of
human fate. In Egypt Herzl seems to be saying goodbye to the physical world. "The fellah family crouches by the well, watching the
buffalo go round and round and round. Morning, noon, evening, the
sun will glare from the enchanted sky. The buffalo continues to circle.
If the owner is compassionate, he blindfolds its eyes. The animal sees
nothing of heaven, but also nothing of its constant track." Then the
delta of canals and villages suddenly attains a climax in stately houses,
gardens, turrets, mosques: the capital of Egypt.

A sick man's passivity breathes from the lines as Herzl watches
the "masked ball" of Cairo from the hotel veranda facing Ezbekiah

Gardens and the Opera. "You sit on the terrace with a flywhisk and let things come to you, pass you. Colours and cries. A hundred different propositions from guides and traders. The childishness, the squalor of the East. But in its midst a few stern, watchful, first-class policemen. A platoon of Highlanders march past in tartan trousers, jaunty young men—the Occupation. Other English gentlemen, officers, wear the tarboush, which is higher than the Turkish fez. It is wonderful how they know how to keep order, without brutality, without tropical frenzy." The essay now becomes a tribute to the British, the first foreigners not to oppress the wretched Egyptians. The world of politics has reappeared. The *Neue Freie Presse* will be read at the Vienna Embassy (Hechler will see to that) and the translation of Dr. Herzl's compliments will be sent to Cairo. But to his Diary, which will not soon be published, Herzl confides impressions that go deeper than the standard admiration for the forces of occupation. By the time he writes them down, March 26, he has been received by Evelyn Baring, the first Earl of Cromer. One of Britain's greatest proconsuls, Cromer had earned, as a young man, the nickname "Overbearing"; Herzl found him "the most disagreeable Englishman I have ever faced."[2] Cromer, for his part, had dismissed his Jewish visitor as "a wild enthusiast"[3]; Herzl's visit is unrecorded in Lord Zetland's biography of Cromer, although this was published as late as 1932. Depressed, Herzl had attended a lecture by Sir William Willcocks, the world's foremost authority on irrigation, and found it "dreadfully boring."

> What interested me most was the striking number of intelligent-looking young Egyptians who packed the hall. They are the coming masters. It is a wonder that the English don't see this. They think they are going to deal with *fellahin* forever. Today their 18,000 troops suffice for the big country. But how much longer? It is the same English boldness and cold-bloodedness which makes them give the notes of the Bank of England only weak metal backing. This boldness makes them magnificent *merchant adventurers* [English in original]; but it also always makes them lose their colonies later.[4]

The English might lose their empire—he would like to come back in fifty years to find out—but Herzl was increasingly aware as he waited that he would leave Egypt without the colony he sought. Herzl's presence in Egypt went unnoticed. The social columns of the *Egyptian Gazette* spoke of such fellow visitors as the Grand Duke of Hesse-Darmstadt and the Queen of Portugal. At the opera Ermete Novelli was announced in a guest appearance as Edmund Kean on

March 31 and as Oedipus (both plays in French) on April 1. The famous Egyptologist Maspero lectured on "The Old Empire Tombs at Sakkara" under the auspices of the Ladies' Club. At night there was a small dance at Shepheard's. The music drifted up to the room where Herzl lay in anguish. The weather was still cool at night, sinking to 45° F.; but by day it was beginning to reach 70° F. According to ancient Coptic tradition, serpents opened their eyes on March 25; the next day frogs and reptiles spawned and the plague of flies began. Distinguished guests booked passage for home and started to pack.

The commission's report proved unhelpfully forthright. "The country," the dusty explorers reported, "is quite unsuitable for settlers from European countries."[5] Under pressure from its Zionist members, the report conceded that part of what was now desert could, if water were provided, support a sizable population. Herzl's idea was to use the Nile, by pumping it under the Suez Canal. This suggestion displeased in different ways the British, the Egyptian government and, if they were allowed to hear of it, the mass of Egyptians. The British, who regarded the Suez Canal as their jugular, refused to consider even its momentary closure. The Egyptian government, aware of its nationalist hotheads, knew how these would react to talk of establishing a foreign colony on Egyptian soil. There had been a precedent. When de Lesseps had secured his concession to build the Canal, he had also obtained a concession to develop the lands beside the Sweet Water Canal which brought drinking water from the Nile to such cities as Ismailia and Port Said. Fearful that the French might establish a foothold in Egypt, and aware of what they had already done to Algeria, the Khedive Ismail had revoked this concession at considerable expense to Egypt. Water was the most valuable commodity in the country. Without the Nile, Egypt would have formed a swathe of the desert which stretched west from the Red Sea to the great Sahara. In Egyptian villages peasants fought neighbors they suspected of using too much of the precious liquid. If there was any extra water to be used, it should be expended, not on watering a foreign colony in Sinai, but in enlarging the area of land the fellahin could cultivate.

When the Austrian Lloyd's steamer *Bohemia* sailed from Alexandria on April 4, the passenger list was published in the *Egyptian Gazette*. It was headed by "*Le Comte et la Comtesse Bissingen, Le Comte Ledochowsky, Le Baron et la Baronne Herring et famille*"; it passed by way of other forgotten notables to include, two thirds of the way down, Dr. Herzl. The list closed with "*3 femmes de chambre, 1 valet.*" It was an age that knew how to assess importance.[6]

CHAPTER 31

Yet Herzl had sailed not entirely hopeless. He forced himself to think that the known objections to Sinai might yet be overruled. Disillusion came swiftly. On May 11, 1903, the Egyptian government formally rejected the whole project. On May 14, Cromer, the real power in Egypt, wrote to Lord Lansdowne that while he had done his best to obtain a fair hearing for Dr. Herzl and his colleagues, "I am, however, now decidedly of the opinion that the matter should be dropped."[1] He gave reasons for his opinion. If either of two possible schemes were to go through—the irrigation of some 60,000 acres to the east of the Canal through siphoned Nile water, or the irrigation by rain water of land near El Arish—the British government would have to exert "far stronger pressure than the circumstances of the case would in any degree justify." The Egyptian government, on whom such pressure would have to be applied, was not, Cromer explained, inspired by anti-Jewish prejudice in rejecting the scheme. Their opposition was prompted by two main thoughts: expert opinion, both British and Egyptian, had concluded that the scheme was impracticable, and no one wanted to be associated with an expensive fiasco; politically, in the complex tangle of sovereignties and legal rights that constituted Egypt, it would be calamitous "if a large cosmopolitan society were allowed to settle in the Sinai Peninsula, for objects which are avowedly political and which are, to say the least, difficult to reconcile with the interests of the Sultan, who is Suzerain of Egypt."

Herzl recognized that he had visited Egypt in vain. "I thought the Sinai plan was such a sure thing," he wrote on May 16, "that I no longer wanted to buy a family vault in the Döbling cemetery, where my father is provisionally laid to rest. Now I consider the affair so wrecked that I have already been to the district court and am acquiring vault No. 28."²

The disinterring of a beloved human being is a harrowing experience. Herzl's secretary, A. H. Reich, a Viennese, was entrusted with the task of moving Jacob Herzl to a new grave. He implored Herzl, whose health had been causing him concern, not to attend. But at the last moment, when the coffin lay in its new place, Herzl suddenly appeared at the graveside. As he stared into the pit he swayed, overcome by emotion. He turned to Reich. "Soon—very soon—I, too, shall lie down there."³

The rejection of Sinai propelled Herzl in two strange new directions. One was toward East Africa, in the last attempt to build a state in his lifetime; the other was toward Russia, and his last important political relationship. Since he remained a star performer in the egg dance he had described at the first Zionist Congress, he continued to toy with other ventures. On one of Cromer's visits to London, El Arish was again requested and again refused. The Sultan was once more asked for Palestine, though this time the area was confined to "the vilayet of Acre." (The Sultan's Arab favorite, Izzet Bey, was offered a new bribe, this time of twelve thousand pounds, if he contrived a charter.) On May 25, 1903, Herzl waited on the Portuguese Ambassador in Vienna and asked for permission to colonize Mozambique. (The answer was evasive.) On July 12 the same year he asked a rich Belgian banker to ask King Leopold for similar permission in the Congo. (The banker refused.) The strangest suggestion—which Herzl pondered for more than six weeks before rejecting it—came from a Swede who had turned Turk, "Ali Nuri Bey." Two hired cruisers, screened by merchant vessels, should enter the Dardanelles at night, shell Yildiz in the morning and install a new Sultan pledged to give the Jews a chartered right to colonize Palestine.⁴＊

East Africa and Russia, the regions of Herzl's last serious involvement, generated passion and opposition. In conjunction they inspired the first serious challenge to his position as leader. Death not only aborted the challenge but made it possible to conceal the aims of each venture with reticence or obfuscation. To uncover Herzl's true intentions it is no longer possible to rely on what he wrote in his Diary.

＊ An interesting anticipation of Winston Churchill's ill-fated Dardanelles project in World War I.

He had become less candid and in his last weeks wrote nothing. Facts must be used as paleontologists use fragments of bone.

The investigation can begin with one such fact. In April 23, 1903, Herzl again called on Joseph Chamberlain, who now received him as a friend.[5] The aging Colonial Secretary had just returned from a trip to South Africa (to do with the ending of the Boer War) which had also taken him to Egypt and East Africa. In Cairo, when Chamberlain raised the Sinai project, Cromer made clear his opposition. Then, farther south, just before Christmas, he had inspected a major achievement of the British empire: the nearly completed railway linking the east coast and the great Lake Victoria in the heart of Africa. It was 584 miles long, and had cost five million pounds to build. It had not only quadrupled down-traffic freight in the preceding year but had opened up a great new region for European settlement. Chamberlain had noted land empty of inhabitants along the railway line, between Nairobi and the Mau escarpment. He wrote in his diary for December 21, 1902: "If Dr. Herzl were at all inclined to transfer his efforts to East Africa, there would be no difficulty in finding suitable land for Jewish settlers." Now that he again met Dr. Herzl face to face, he brushed aside further discussion of El Arish. "I have seen a land for you on my travels," he said kindly, "and that's Uganda. It's hot on the coast, but farther inland the climate becomes excellent, even for Europeans. You can grow sugar and cotton there. And I thought to myself, that would be a land for Dr. Herzl. But of course he wants to go only to Palestine or its vicinity."

The correspondence between Herzl (who used Greenberg as his representative) and the British authorities showed that this was no longer the case.† On May 25, 1903, Greenberg was assuring Chamberlain of Herzl's intention of giving his suggestion "his immediate earnest consideration," but asking for a precise definition of the territory involved. "Mr. Chamberlain wishes me to say," came the reply from the Colonial Office, "that he did not refer to any particular place, but that in his view the most favourable territory is between Nairobi and the top of the Mau escarpment, but that if Dr. Herzl is disposed to consider the matter, it would be necessary that his Agents should visit the Protectorate and make their own report on the most suitable spots."

† The original copies of Herzl's *Jewish Colonisation Scheme* (annotated in red ink by Lord Lansdowne), of Greenberg's letters, of the replies by officials of the Colonial and Foreign Offices, of memoranda from British officials and other interested parties in East Africa are preserved in London, at the Public Record Office and the Foreign Office.

The lack of precision over what is plainly part of Kenya might at first sight confirm Herzl's poor opinion of Chamberlain's geography. But in the case of "Uganda" the Colonial Secretary had an excuse. As recently as April 1902, there had been a reshuffling of territories inside the empire, the eastern province of the Uganda Protectorate having been reallocated to British East Africa. The eastern province[6] comprised much of what is now the western highlands of Kenya, a healthy upland plateau stretching from the southern shore of Lake Rudolf due south along the edge of the Laikipia and Kikuyu escarpments to the border with what was then German East Africa and is now Tanzania. Since the plateau was some 8,000 feet above sea level, its average temperature ranged from 66° to 73° F. It was free of fever and thanks to internecine wars, largely free of natives. The area Chamberlain thought to offer (see relevant map in the illustrations) was about the size of Yorkshire, England's largest county, or some 6,000 square miles. Although Herzl had been requested by Chamberlain, through the Colonial Office, to submit, "if he wishes," a memorandum, the tentative nature of the proposal was constantly emphasized, and its dependence on the final decision of the Foreign Office. Greenberg submitted Herzl's memorandum for "New Palestine" on July 13, 1903. Lord Lansdowne's marginal comments survive in red ink. "This seems right," he comments, when Herzl proposes that the Zionists should bear the expense of any expedition of investigation. But "I fear it is throughout an *imperium in imperio* [an empire within an empire]," is his final assessment. The British were not prepared to gratify a "hankering after the semblance of sovereignty"; the powers enjoyed by a British County Council were the stated maximum.[7]

Since Easter, 1903, the Bessarabian town of Kishinev had been frequently mentioned in the press. The Czarist police possibly encouraged, certainly did nothing to prevent, pogroms that left forty-seven Jews dead and another ninety-two severely injured. Kishinev first appears in Herzl's Diary on May 19. He mentions the town in a dignified but friendly letter to the man in control of the Russian police, Minister of the Interior Vyacheslav Plehve.

Now hardly remembered, the name of Plehve had in those days a resonance of evil later echoed by that of Adolf Eichmann. The fact that Plehve operated within an ostensibly Christian society and was getting old at the time of his greatest power may to some extent have reduced his impetus for cruelty. Like Eichmann, he was a functionary rather than a fanatic. His career had been favored by the assassination of the liberal Czar Alexander II. Despite his efforts to liberalize the conditions of Russian Jews, Alexander had been met by sedition in which Jews played a considerable though largely non-violent role.‡ Plehve, a police officer, won recognition for his zeal in hunting down the assassins. In 1884 he became deputy Minister of the Interior, in 1894 head of the Imperial Chancellery and in 1899 State Secretary for the Grand Duchy of Finland. Himself the son of Russified German parents, Plehve became the leading exponent of the new policy of Alexander III, which aimed to make Russian nationalism the cement of empire. As such he persecuted not only Jews but Finns, Poles, Armenians and Russian nobles with liberal tendencies. When the last Czar, Nicholas II, succeeded Alexander III in 1894, he sometimes sided with Plehve, and sometimes with his more liberal Minister of Finance, de Witte. Since the weak young Czar patronized the leaders of the Black Hundreds, whose sport was pogroms, and since the Jews were naturally disposed to revolt against the injustice of their state, Plehve saw in anti-Semitism a policy that would win him his master's favor. De Witte, his enemy, confirms what Plehve was to tell Herzl: "personally he had nothing against the Jews . . . He possessed enough intelligence to understand that he was following an essentially wrong policy. But it pleased Grand Duke Sergey Alexandrovich (the brother of Alexander III) and apparently his Majesty; consequently Plehve exerted himself to the utmost."[8] The Kishinev pogrom was thus no aimless violence. Plehve intended it as a warning to the Jewish community, with whose rabbis and exiled leaders he was already in contact: if they would put a stop to Jewish participation in the revolutionary movement, Plehve would remove their disabilities and halt the pogroms. Plehve was well-informed about the Zionist movement (which in Russia antedated Herzl) thanks to a network of informers. While he condemned its emphasis on a distinctive Jewish "nationality," he approved its intention of removing the Jews from Russia.

Herzl had approached Plehve's master, the Czar, as early as 1899. On November 22 that year he had drafted a letter explaining Zionism which the Czar's kinsman, the Grand Duke of Baden, had forwarded to St. Petersburg. In developing his ideas Herzl used an expression—"the Zionist plan for the final solution of the Jewish question"[9]—which was to have sinister connotations on later lips. On Christmas Day the Czar had replied in polite French to the Grand Duke: he had read M. Herzl's memorandum with lively interest, but although the theory

‡ Most Jews adhered to the Social Democratic or Marxist parties, which opposed assassination. One exception was Hirsch Lehert. He shot the Governor of Wahl for having whipped May Day demonstrators.

of Zionism could help promote the inner tranquillity of Europe, he saw few practical prospects for it, even in the distant future.[10]

The Czar's rebuff put Russia out of Herzl's mind, though he remained aware of the potential resources of the Pale of Settlement. The Kishinev pogrom, on top of his failure in Turkey and Egypt, made him think of Russia again. Encouraged by word from an intermediary[11] that Plehve looked forward to making the acquaintance of so interesting a personality as Dr. Herzl and would wholeheartedly support "emigration without the right of re-entry," Herzl took the St. Petersburg train. From August 7 to 17, 1903, he was in Russia. Apart from some perfunctionary comments on droshky drivers and over-gilded churches, his Diary recounts business only. For the first time the question naggingly intrudes as to whether his account is candid. In Vilna, on August 16, he received a letter from Sir Clement Hill of the Foreign Office in London. It officially suggested that the Jews should examine Uganda with a view to a possible British offer of land there. If Herzl had privately decided to work for East Africa, he faced serious problems as he compiled a Diary that had been planned all along as a Zionist text for publication in *Die Welt*. The Basel program of 1897 demanded the colonization of Palestine and nowhere else. When Trietsch had tried to extend the formula to include Cyprus, there had been trouble. Herzl had long known—and now saw for himself—how the Zionism to be found in Russia and Poland differed from his own. With great reluctance he had rejected Europe, because Europe, it seemed, rejected the Jews; he had wanted to obtain a territory in which Jews could show that they too could run a state on liberal European lines. The Eastern Zionists did not reject Europe, because they had never known it; they exalted all that was Jewish, preferred Hebrew to Yiddish and regarded Palestine as their national territory by right. Aware of such strong feelings, Herzl had reiterated that he, too, wanted Palestine. If he accepted Africa, it must appear that he only did so as a second-best. To move the ardor of the Russian Jews to a New Palestine in Africa would require subterfuge as well as effort.

The relationship between Herzl and Plehve seems to have started cool but soon grown warmer.[12] Plehve—"a bit obese, . . . a sallow, serious face, grey hair, a white moustache, and remarkably youthful, energetic brown eyes . . ."—showed an initial distrust. When Herzl requested a piece of paper on which to note down questions, so as not to interrupt the Minister's flow of words, Plehve tore a leaf from a small pad but "ungenerously detached its printed heading before giving it to me, as though he were afraid I might misuse it." But the frankness with which Herzl stated his terms commanded the Minister's respect. Herzl undertook to silence Jewish revolutionaries (the main objective of Plehve's policy) and to organize an exodus of such scope as Plehve had not dared envisage. In return for these concessions Herzl set out three demands:

1. Russia should induce the Sultan to issue a charter allowing the Jews to colonize Palestine, but with the exception of the holy places.

2. Russia should help finance the emigration through taxes levied on rich Jews.

3. The "loyal organization" of Russian Zionist societies should be permitted.

With some quibbling, Plehve agreed and he stated the agreement as he saw it in a letter Herzl was to use. He meanwhile asked for a memorandum from Herzl. This provided an opportunity to set the record straight for future readers of the Diary. The memorandum Herzl presented to Plehve showed him active for Palestine. It could be produced as evidence of his loyalty to the Basel program.

Although his Russian journey achieved little, it is important for what it reveals of Herzl's true intentions. By this time he knew Constantinople well enough to know that most Turkish policies were inspired by dread of Russia. The Czars had expanded their relatively small eighteenth-century kingdom until it had become a vast empire stretching to the frontiers of China and Japan. The expansion had been largely at the expense of Turkish-speaking peoples. Russia had encouraged the Greeks, Bulgars and Serbs to revolt against Turkey. For these reasons Turkey had first had an alliance with Britain and now had an alliance with the Kaiser. Strong Russian backing for the Jewish colonization of Palestine would have had one predictable effect: to close the Holy Land to Jewish immigration as long as the Ottoman empire remained in being.

If Herzl went to St. Petersburg in a serious effort to secure Palestine, his journey made no sense. If he was determined to secure East Africa, it did. That he was so determined is proved by perceptive witnesses and his own actions on his return.*

The sixth Zionist Congress was due to open in Basel in the last week of August. He hastened from Russia, spending only one night with his family, on holiday at Altaussee. His strategy at the Congress is a further

* One contemporary witness was Chaim Weizmann, destined to be the first President of a Jewish state in Palestine, who examined the documents and letters to do with the Uganda scheme in London during the summer of 1904. Greenberg, Weizmann wrote on August 24, 1904, "only acted as an obedient soldier *par ordre* of Herzl, who *wanted* Africa at any price."[13]

guide to his intentions. Herzl's account in his Diary is brief. It begins as follows:

> August 31, Constance, on Lake Constance.
> The difficult great Sixth Congress is over.
> When, completely worn out, I had returned from the Congress building, after the final session, with my friends Zangwill, Nordau, and Cowen, and we sat in Cowen's room around a bottle of mineral water, I said to them:
> "I will now tell you the speech I am going to make at the Seventh Congress—that is, if I live to see it.
> "By then I shall either have obtained Palestine or realized the complete futility of any further efforts.†
> "In the latter case, my speech will be as follows:
> " 'It was not possible. The ultimate goal has not been reached, and will not be reached within a foreseeable time. But a temporary result is at hand: this land in which we can settle our suffering masses on a national basis and with the right of self-government. I do not believe that for the sake of a beautiful dream or of a legitimistic banner we have a right to withhold this relief from the unfortunate.' "

He would emphasize that he, too, had become a *Lover of Zion* (he used the English, not the Hebrew, phrase), that the decision for East Africa had produced a split in the movement centered on his person and that he would therefore resign.

In prefacing his account of the sixth Congress with an imagined speech for the seventh, Herzl shows what he was working for in the last August of his life. On Friday, August 21, Herzl reported to the Great Actions Committee of the Zionist movement on his two related accomplishments: the journey to meet Plehve and his reception of the British offer. Little evidence survives to illuminate this meeting. Nevertheless, two things are clear. Herzl showed himself embittered by a lack of appreciation for what he had done while encouraged that even the East European Zionists seemed ready to accept Uganda. The meeting was adjourned for the start of the Sabbath and next morning Herzl attended the synagogue services as had become his Congress habit. Immediately they were over he summoned a small caucus of leaders to Joseph Cowen's room to show them the British document. Assured of its impact, he left them alone to prove that he was not trying to persuade them. That evening the Greater Actions Committee again dis-

---

† Since the seventh Congress was scheduled for the following year, and since there was no likelihood of an Ottoman collapse in the interim, it is clear which Herzl thought the likelier of these alternatives.

cussed the Plehve letter. Opponents of Herzl's policy were later to argue that neither of these meetings empowered him to put the British "offer" before the Congress; Herzl on the other hand affirmed that he had been so empowered. It is likely that he deliberately left the issue vague, knowing that when he addressed the Congress in the morning, the effect on dispirited leaders of what he had to say would be electric. He was right. Herzl for the last time showed his dramatic gifts. He announced to the assembled delegates that, a short time ago, the "British government had placed a portion of British East Africa at the disposal of the Congress for the purpose of carrying out a scheme of Jewish colonization. This territory while administered by Jews would be under British suzerainty."[14] Vast enthusiasm greeted this first public recognition of the Jewish entity by a great power. Herzl's next step was to have a resolution voted upon, not accepting the British "offer," but appointing a committee of investigation similar to the one that had already reported on Sinai. The voting was conducted with elaborate fairness, the motion being translated into all the languages spoken by the delegates, including Hebrew. The resolution was approved by 295 votes to 177; but about a hundred delegates abstained.

Herzl's expectations, or hopes, can be inferred. The commission could only report favorably on the fertility and climate of the Nairobi region. Plehve could be expected to promote a wave of emigration. Russian intervention at the Porte (or even rumors of such intervention) could be expected to bolt the doors on Palestine. Herzl could then found his secular, African New Palestine while the Lovers of Zion chased their chimerical dreams further north without harming his.

But the Congress was no ordinary democratic parliament in which a majority of 295 to 177 was sufficient to silence the rest. The impassioned Nay-Sayers, as the Zion-Zionists called themselves, were more likely to secede and plot than accept their defeat. The whole movement was weak enough already in the eyes of the world. A major schism would mean final disaster. As the leader of a faction inside a faction Herzl could negotiate with no one. He therefore went to great lengths to conciliate his Nay-Saying opponents. Zionist funds, it was conceded, would not be used to finance the committee's travels. And then, before his closing speech, a friend wrote out for him, in Latin characters, the Hebrew sentence: "If I forget thee, O Jerusalem, may my right hand wither!" He delivered this with conviction and was heard with applause.

The question posed by Herzl's words and actions is simple: was he still a Zionist in terms of the Basel program? The answer is complex. As

Herzl's health failed, as he no longer spoke clearly for himself, his cast of mind was ambiguous enough for a later rectification as radical as the rectification of Wolffsohn's snapshot. His disinclination to speak frankly was certainly prudent. Hostility among his opponents hardened to the point where they planned to unseat him the following year. Some were prepared to express their disapproval in more violent ways. Herzl's chief ally was believed to be Max Nordau. In December, Nordau attended a Hannukah ball with his wife at the Salle Charras in Paris. It was a Zionist occasion. Suddenly, toward midnight, a twenty-four-year-old Russian Jewish student of chemistry advanced on Nordau and shrieking "Death to the East African!" fired two shots. He missed Nordau but shot a bystander in the leg.

An enraged Nordau willingly received Raphael Marchand, correspondent of the *Libre Parole,* at his Pigalle home. It says much for the weakened position of Herzl at this juncture that Marchand, in his report of the interview on December 21, 1903, referred to Nordau as *"le chef du sionisme."* Nordau, undiplomatic in his indignation, firmly blamed the Russians (as did Herzl) for the attempt on his life and defined his view of Zionism bluntly: "the reconstitution of Jewish nationality on an independent territory . . . It is not a question of religion, but exclusively of race, and there is no one with whom I am in greater agreement on this point than M. Drumont." Nordau justified the rejection of Palestine not only by the Sultan's refusal to part with the Holy Land but also by the perils of becoming isolated, like the Armenians, in a Turkish sea. In praising Uganda as a "wonderful country whose climate and countryside recall southern England," Nordau was almost certainly echoing Herzl, who had visited Alfred Austin, the British poet laureate, at his home in Kent in 1900. He had then been delighted by a gentle spring landscape balanced by blazing logs in the evening fireplace.

Herzl's true attitude becomes easier to understand if two myths are first dispelled: the first, that Herzl felt a passionate attachment to Palestine, and the second, that in accepting East Africa he was prompted by compassion for Jewish suffering. His Diary shows how little he saw of Palestine during his one brief visit and how little that pleased him; *Altneuland* embodies a dream whose location and scenery are unimportant. As to Jewish suffering he had always opposed the traditional remedy of charity. This does not mean that he was not a compassionate man. It means rather that Zionism was for him a national movement. Only in thé long run could it bring physical ease to suffering Jews. In rejecting charity he was on common ground with his opponents inside the movement. "The problem of meeting the pressure of Jewish need was not the business of Zionism, whose task it was to concentrate on the achievement of its ultimate objective even if it could not, in the interim, be of any assistance to the suffering Jewish masses."[15] So Dr. Alex Bein, summarizing the standpoint of Herzl's opponents at the sixth Congress. In fact, neither of the two places Herzl so desperately sought—El Arish or East Africa—could have brought anything but toil and pain to the first generation of emigrants from Russia. Herzl had been distressed by the heat of Jaffa in October; summer in scorching Sinai would have tortured the sick, the young and the old; it would take much time and effort to build a comfortable society in Uganda.

Why, then, did Herzl strive for Africa?

He certainly yearned to accomplish something grandiose in his lifetime. But by 1903 ambition had found routine channels. He insisted on being obeyed as a leader, but was too sick, too doomed, to indulge further dreams of a royal court, even though in Vilna, on his way out of Russia, he heard a young man shout for the day when "King Herzl" would reign. Julie was a sick woman, her health apparently no better than his own. That he might be responsible for her sickness was a thought to push from him, but no less surely, a reproach to return at night. His neglected children were another reproach. Pauline, never entirely recovered from her illness, one shoulder higher than the other, was spoiled and moody; photographs showed how much she differed, and would differ, from his idealized sister whose name she bore. Separated from other children, aware of the rift between their parents, resentful of their grandmother, the personalities of Hans and Trude were already affected by their past, their future was already clouded. Hans was an attractive, reticent boy of twelve. But it was hard to imagine him as Crown Prince under the African sun.

To Zionists reluctant to abandon Zion, Herzl advanced the argument Nordau put forward in a speech of support at the sixth Congress: East Africa would be a *Nachtasyl*, an overnight shelter, as well as a training ground for the eventual assault on Zion. These were debating points. Herzl knew well that if East Africa were won, if the Russian Jews were forced to migrate and if the doors to Palestine were closed, then East Africa would absorb the available resources of the Jews. Under his leadership they could construct a state resembling Altneuland. Uganda, so far from being a steppingstone to Palestine, would be a decisive stride in the opposite direction.

Three considerations could account for why Herzl wanted to take this African step away from Palestine. Only one has been considered in previous accounts. This was his clear recognition by 1903 that the Sultan had always meant what he said about refusing any form of Jewish autonomy in Palestine. Yet if Herzl had wanted Zion and nowhere else, he could have associated himself with the Russian Zionists who wished to build up a solid body of settlers on the ground imbued with Hebrew culture. These would form the nucleus for a state when, in the Sultan's phrase, his empire became a corpse. Loyalty to his formula—first a charter, then colonization—was one factor turning Herzl away from Palestine.

But the two unconsidered considerations were perhaps stronger.

In more buoyant days Herzl had coined the epigram: "The enemy is the iron circlet of the nation."[16] Then the natives had been shadowy abstractions; he was not sure if they wore Arab or Amazonian dress. But his leadership of a movement with Middle Eastern ambitions had made him think about the potential enemy. As early as 1897 he was being visited in Vienna by Mustafa Kamil, the youthful Egyptian nationalist. "This young Oriental makes an excellent impression," he wrote at the time: "he is cultivated, elegant, intelligent, eloquent."[17] Then he had only considered how he might use Kamil, whose chief purpose was to get the British out of Egypt. The British might support a Jewish Palestine with rail connections to the Persian Gulf. But his visit to Egypt had impressed him strongly. The country had inspired his pen while the assertive intelligence of the young Egyptians at the public lecture showed that Mustafa Kamil was not alone. In recognizing the force of Egyptian nationalism he showed more perception than Lord Cromer, who seems to have imagined that the Egyptians would indefinitely support an occupation. The following year, toward the very end of his Diary, he suddenly notes: "There is an Arab movement which intends to make a descendant of Muhammad Caliph. The Caliphate was stolen by Sultan Selim.‡ Now it might be restored, as a sort of papacy with Mecca as Rome."[18] Herzl had, it seems, recognized a nationalism similar to his own, and established in place. In his reflective moments he probably foresaw the circlet of enmity that could surround the Jewish colonization of Palestine: not from the Turkish masters but from the Arabs, who owned nearly all of the country, and their brothers (at least as close to them as Austrian Jews to Russian) in Egypt and other lands. He probably calculated that a depopulated part of Africa would prove a less menacing place for Jewish settlement. Farther south his hero Cecil Rhodes had shown what white men could achieve.

A third consideration was compelling on a different level. Chaim

‡ Selim I conquered Egypt from its Mameluke Sultans in 1517 and took prisoner the last Abbassid Caliph, whose prestige was by this time entirely symbolic.

Weizmann, who first saw Herzl at the second Congress, was distressed by what he termed his clerical leanings.* To us who have followed Herzl through his freethinking, dueling youth and his detached and cynical Parisian experience, this seems at first sight surprising. His only contacts with a religious tradition had been in his boyhood, when his family lived next door to the synagogue and when his grandfather from Semlin had spoken of his hero, Rabbi Alkalai. His schooling had been German and secular in spirit; by his late teens he had dismissed Moses as a fraud. His marriage to Julie Naschauer not only completed his separation from Jewish practice but gave him three children who, according to traditional law, were doubtfully Jewish. Yet his involvement with Zionism had inevitably put him in contact with religious Jews and made him think about the religion he had hitherto ignored. At the second Congress he made a much quoted remark: "Zionism is a homecoming to Jewishness even before a return to Jews' land."† At the time this affirmation was tactical and ambiguous, like his annual visits to the synagogue. Certainly it was not followed by any return in the Herzl ménage to the dietary laws. But it signified that he and the East Europeans were moving in opposite directions. Weizmann and the Russian Zionists were moving away from a religious background; Talmudic studies and their rabbinical teachers represented a familiar past which they wished to transcend in a nationalistic future. Herzl was a dying man whose secular background, formed by the skeptical tradition of the eighteenth century and the scientific tradition of the nineteenth, influenced by the waves of German and Hungarian nationalism, was receding from him; he found himself immersed in a present where everything was related, in one way or another, to the Jewish tradition. As an artist, Herzl was sensitive to the arguments of Talmudic scholars, even when they opposed him. Joseph Samuel Bloch, the courageous editor, was perhaps the first to tell him of the Talmudic teaching that forbade the Jews from taking Palestine by force or establishing a state there. The same tradition had been asserted in a major sermon by Chief Rabbi Adler in London. Adler had explicitly condemned political Zionism and Herzl's role in it. "It is distinctly an-

---

* "He had excessive respect for the Jewish clergy, born not of intimacy but of distance. He saw something rather occult and mysterious in the Rabbis . . . His leaning toward clericalism distressed us, so did the touch of Byzantinism in his manner. Almost from the outset a kind of court sprang up about him, of worshippers who pretended to guard him from too close contact with the mob." (*Trial and Error*, New York, 1949, p. 45)

† *Der Zionismus ist die Heimkehr zum Judentum noch vor der Rückkehr ins Judenland.*" In the German the word *Judentum* is difficult to translate. Formed like *Deutschtum*, it means the sum total of being Jewish rather than Judaism, as which it is sometimes translated.

nounced that our redemption is to be effected by Divine interposition at such time as seemeth good in God's sight, when it pleases Him to send the Messiah, and when the nations of the world shall with one accord unite and help Israel to return to the land of their fathers."‡

The Talmud had full force only for a believing Jew, and this Herzl never became. But the sight of his father's coffin, his awareness that he too would soon be dead came in the context of his discovery of what Judaism said about Palestine and the Return. His own secular thought ran the risk of becoming entangled in an ancient and powerful tradition. His intellectual position was close to that of Israel Zangwill. Placed by his marriage to a gentile in an ambiguous relationship to Judaism, Zangwill became increasingly opposed to building a state in Palestine "on the grounds that it would require the re-establishment of the ancient Jewish form of worship, with all its rites, such as sacrifices, etc; we could not, therefore, lead a modern life there."[19] Since the Talmud stated that only the Messiah should lead the Jews back from exile, Herzl was placed in an agonizing position. As a bad Jew, he could not be the Messiah. If he was not the Messiah, he could only be a figure of doom, as Bilinski had warned, bringing horror first upon his family and finally upon the people he was setting out to save. And even if the Talmud were only mythology, those who believed in its truth could damagingly affect the fabric of his liberal, secular state. East Africa thus represented a way of escape. In that virgin landscape, unburdened by any association with a theocratic past, "the Jews that want it," in the words he had used seven years earlier when writing *Der Judenstaat*, "will have their State, and they will deserve it."* In such a state, his children and those of Zangwill and Nordau could with honor create a society whose blueprint lay in the writings of Herzl.

‡ Preached at the North London Synagogue on Sabbath, November 12, 5659-1898, the sermon was published the same year under the title *Religious Versus Political Zionism*.

* *"Die Juden die wollen werden ihren Staat haben und sie werden ihn verdienen"*: these words form the last sentence of the introduction to *Der Judenstaat*.

CHAPTER 32

That Herzl's interest in Uganda represented a resolve to swerve from Palestine becomes plainer when we probe the seriousness of the British offer and the obstacles, other than Zionist objections, to its success. For the purposes of the sixth Zionist Congress, Herzl and his allies exaggerated the concreteness of the offer, and its scope. The London *Times* published a telegraphed correction to its report of Herzl's opening speech: the territory in British East Africa offered by the British government to the Zionists was not to be "under the suzerainty of England," but it was to be invested with local Jewish autonomy under British control.[1]* Nordau told the Congress that if necessary the Jews could now establish themselves in British East Africa "generously placed by Great Britain at the disposal of Jewish autonomous colonization." Zangwill similarly spoke of a British "offer" when reporting to an enthusiastic meeting of the English Zionist Federation in early September.[3]

The British government went no further in 1903 than their suggestion that the Zionists might explore British East Africa with a view to some possible form of settlement; nothing approaching national independence was considered from the British side. At the time of the sixth Congress the British Foreign Office quickly disposed of exaggerated reports. They did so by releasing to *The Times* a letter to Greenberg from Sir Clement Hill (the official whose letter had reached Herzl in Russia) stressing that Britain was only prepared to *consider* a Jewish

* In another context Herzl exaggerated the extent of the territory "offered." Writing to Izzet Bey on December 12, 1903, he implied that Britain had offered an area of between 180,000 and 270,000 square miles.[2]

settlement and that in any event it would reserve to itself most rights, including "the power to reoccupy the land if settlement should not prove a success."⁴ On September 7, 1903, the same newspaper reported Lord Delamere's complaint that "giving this fine land to the Jews would be handing it over to aliens." Delamere was himself buying land in East Africa at the time.

Just as Cromer had turned down Sinai, after an apparent effort to be fair, so in East Africa, Sir Charles Eliot, Britain's High Commissioner in Mombasa expressed increasing disapproval of the scheme, while apparently giving it fair consideration. A letter to Sir Charles Eliot from Lord Lansdowne shows that as early as October 1903 the High Commissioner was showing reluctance "to give up to a colony of Jewish settlers some of the most valuable portions of the Protectorate"⁵; the letter also shows that in London the whole scheme was still tentative. Eliot's long reply to Lansdowne's letter, written on November 4, began by suggesting that in any case a smaller area farther north than Chamberlain's first proposal, and not including Nairobi, would be more suitable. This was the Gwas Ngishu Plateau, "a grassy plain, well-watered and possessing a temperate climate. In August I myself found it disagreeably cold, but this objection would doubtless not be felt by Jews from Central Europe. The plain is surrounded by forests which yield good timber, and is practically uninhabited, owing (as I have explained in the despatch above cited) to tribal wars, but not to any defect. The position is sufficiently isolated to protect the Jews from any hostile demonstration of other races, and to admit the free exercise of such autonomy as is given them; it is also sufficiently distant from the coast to ensure a very considerable addition to the traffic of the Uganda Railway."⁶ But unlike Chamberlain's territory, the Gwas Ngishu Plateau was not along the railway, but some distance from it. Eliot had clear opinions as to the extent of Jewish autonomy. "I hardly think it would be advisable to have anything more than Jewish municipalities, nor is it likely that Eastern Jews would want more. For most Orientals 'the national life' means the religious life, in the large sense of the whole domain covered by religious observances." Eliot added that his own experience of Jews in Russia, Turkey and Morocco did not inspire him with enthusiasm for the scheme. He was skeptical about claims that Jews made good agriculturists and feared that if they started by working the fields, they would soon revert to the role of middlemen or would finance British settlers, whom Eliot made it plain he would prefer to Jews. He expressed the fear that a Jewish presence in the territory might frighten off such British settlers.

Eliot produced further negative opinions. He forwarded a letter from the Bishop of Mombasa: "to suffer the whole tract of country mentioned above to pass into the possession of say only low-class Jews will tend to cause stagnation in that development of truly Christian religious life in the African tribes which we all are eager to witness. It will be no concern of them to lift their heathen neighbours into the element of Christian civilization."[7] As the British became aware that not many Zionists wanted to colonize East Africa, at least not immediately, British reluctance to tie up large areas of valuable land became more marked. At the same time, despite Greenberg's protests, the British refused to consider granting more than the "power to regulate Jewish observances and as much local autonomy as a County has under a County Council in England."

Eliot delivered what he hoped would be a *coup de grâce* on March 24, 1904. The situation, he wrote, had changed. Before, there were not enough settlers for the land; now there was not enough land for the settlers. "This being so I can no longer recommend to your Lordship the establishment of a Jewish colony in this Protectorate even on the Gwas Ngishu Plateau. I have no antipathy to Jews and no objection to an isolated Jewish community, but long experience of Eastern Europe has convinced me that it is not politic to allow distinct Jewish settlements among Christians. Such an arrangement seems to inevitably result in racial conflicts."[8] The British held the project open only out of an unwillingness to go back on their word.†

Against these frustrating clouds, Herzl once more took refuge in a train. He reached Venice in the middle of January 1904. "I couldn't be bothered," the Diary entry vividly suggests his mood, "to put on my dinner jacket for the 1½ Englishmen in the Grand Hotel, so I went to Bauer's Austrian Beer House." There he was approached by the last of the many eccentrics he had attracted all his life. Four years younger than Herzl but like him Hungarian-born, Berthold Dominique Lippay was court painter to the recently elected Venetian Pope, Pius X. (Pius had reason to favor Habsburg subjects, the Austrian veto having prevented the election of Cardinal Mariano Rampolla.) Over their beer the two men made quick plans for Herzl's last missionary journey. The nineteenth of January found Herzl and the painter traveling south together on the train. In Rome Lippay promised to introduce Herzl to the Pope while in Vienna Herzl promised to do the same for Lippay with David Gutmann, a Jewish millionaire with a virtual monopoly over coal.

Travel no longer soothed his nerves; he described his sleep in Rome's

---

† As late as July 26, 1904, Lord Lansdowne wrote in red ink on a minute detailing Zionist objections to East Africa: "We shall be fortunate if the project falls through." By this time Herzl was dead.

Hotel Quirinal as becoming "worse and worse."[9] But a change of scene, new contacts with the great could still stimulate his mind. In Rome he was to meet the King of a nation-state and the head of a supranational Church.

Before meeting King Victor Emmanuel III, Herzl took a leisurely drive round the center of the city. His engineer's imagination was stirred to new life. If he obtained Jerusalem, he would construct a Diaspora Street, lined with architectural samples from all the countries in which the Jews had lived. But the climb to the royal antechamber at the Quirinal Palace caught the dreamer's breath. Yet Herzl's eyes had not lost their sharpness (in the King's shortness he found an equivalent of the Kaiser's arm) nor his tongue its fluency, as the two men chatted like students. The King showed the realism of his family. The Jews, he pronounced, would inevitably get Palestine—they must wait, though, till they had half a million Jews there. To Herzl's objection that they weren't allowed in: "Bah! Everything can be done with baksheesh."

"But I don't want that. Our project means investments and improvements, and I don't want them undertaken as long as the country isn't ours."

The King laughed and quoted an Italian saying to the effect that this would be making improvements *in casa di altri.*‡

Once again Sabbatai Zevi intruded. One of the King's ancestors had conspired with the false Messiah. Which prompted a royal question: were there still Jews who awaited the Messiah?

"Naturally, Your Majesty, in the religious circles. In our own, the academically trained and enlightened circles, no such thought exists, of course."

Lest the King mistake him for a rabbi, Herzl stressed that the Zionist movement was purely nationalist. He made a joke. When in Palestine he had avoided riding a white horse or donkey, so that no one would embarrass him by mistaking *him* for the Messiah.

The King said he was pleased at the apparent Zionist abandonment of East Africa. His professed reasons—that he loved the power of an idea and could even sympathize with the young extremist who had tried to kill Nordau—may not have been his real ones. Italian imperial ambitions were directed to East Africa, where Eritrea and Somalia had been acquired already and where Uganda's neighbor, Ethiopia, remained a target.*

‡ "In the house of someone else."
* To be temporarily achieved in the 1930s, under the same King, who added Emperor to his titles until the defeat of Fascist Italy by the Allies.

Despite the King's attitude, Herzl made a renewed bid for an alternative to Palestine. He suggested channeling surplus Jews into Tripolitania (then an Ottoman possession) "under the liberal laws and institutions of Italy."

The King repeated his earlier phrase: "But that again is the house of someone else."

"But the partition of Turkey is bound to come, Your Majesty."

The spirit of these exchanges was little different from the spirit of previous talks with Emperor, Grand Duke or Colonial Secretary. But on January 25† he was received by the ruler of a kingdom defined by its founder as not of this world. Born a peasant, Giuseppe Sarto was to reign over the Catholic Church until 1914; fifty years after his death he would be proclaimed a saint, the first Pope to be canonized since Pius V in the sixteenth century. Herzl's susceptibility to his opponents —shown in his admiration for the firmness of Abdul Hamid's first words on Palestine—was shown in his conversation with a man who opposed him, politely, but with all the majesty of the Church. Herzl had come resolved not to kiss the Pope's ring. But having decided not to do this (which Lippay said was a most necessary gesture), his refusal nagged him throughout the interview. His fears that he might have offended the Pope were probably groundless; but Pius, who noticed that Herzl wore his Ottoman decoration, addressed him throughout as Commendatore, or Commander, not Signore or Dottore. Herzl though used to worldlings could recognize the genuine when he saw it. The Pope's bucolic touches, his huge pinches of snuff, his sneezes into a giant red handkerchief compelled his respect. "He is a good, coarse-grained village priest," he wrote afterward, "to whom Christianity has remained a living thing, even in the Vatican."

But the Pope's attitude to Zionism was firm.

"We cannot give approval to this movement. We cannot prevent the Jews from going to Jerusalem—but we could never sanction it. The earth of Jerusalem, if it was not always holy, has been made holy by the life of Jesus Christ. I as head of the Church cannot possibly say otherwise. The Jews have not recognized our Lord; we therefore cannot recognize the Jewish people."

Herzl recited, he tells us, "my little piece about extraterritorialization, *res sacrae extra commercium*. It didn't make much of an impression. *Gerusalemme*, he said, must not get into the hands of the Jews."

The Pope gave his reasons:

> "There are two possibilities. Either the Jews will cling to their
> faith and continue to await the Messiah who, for us, has already

† The Feast, as the Pope pointed out, of the Conversion of St. Paul.

appeared. In that case they will be denying the divinity of Jesus and we cannot help them. Or else they will go there without any religion, and then we can be even less favourable to them.

"The Jewish religion was the foundation of our own; but it was superseded by the teachings of Christ, and we cannot concede it any further validity. The Jews, who ought to have been the first to acknowledge Jesus Christ, have not done so to this day."

It was on the tip of Herzl's tongue to say, "That's what happens in every family. No one believes in his own relations." But instead he said: "Terror and persecution may not have been the right means for enlightening the Jews."

The Pope's rejoinder struck Herzl as magnificent in its simplicity.

"Our Lord came without power. He was poor. He came in peace. He persecuted no one. Only later did he grow in stature. It took three centuries for the Church to evolve. The Jews therefore had time to acknowledge his divinity without any pressure. But they haven't done so to this day."

"But, Holy Father, the Jews are in terrible straits. I don't know if Your Holiness is acquainted with the full extent of this sad situation. We need a land for these persecuted people."

"Does it have to be *Gerusalemme?*"

"We are not asking for Jerusalem, but for Palestine—only the secular land."

"We cannot be in favour of it."

There was one papal question Herzl only remembered to insert two pages later in his Diary. "He spoke of the Temple at Jerusalem. It had been destroyed forever. Did I suppose that one ought to reconstruct it and perform the sacrificial services there in the ancient way?" Herzl does not record his answer.

His last night in Rome Herzl had a strange dream. He and the Kaiser were alone in a small boat at sea.

CHAPTER 33

I n May 1904 Herzl's doctors ordered him to take the waters at Franzensbad, an Austrian spa. His last official act was a meeting in Vienna with the Foreign Minister. His last entry in his Diary was made on the sixteenth, when he transcribed a letter to Jacob Schiff, an American millionaire. Three days earlier, at the head of a letter to Plehve in French, he had written the two English words *broken down*. These two May entries were inspired by a recent visit from Dr. Nissan Katzenelson, the Zionist physician who had accompanied him to Russia. Katzenelson reported that Schiff, a non-Zionist humanitarian,* was prepared to negotiate a loan for Russia (then involved in its expensive but unsuccessful war with Japan) provided something were done for the Jews. "But it is understood," Herzl added, "that this good deed would also have to bring him [Schiff] more than the standard rate of interest."[1] The entries were signposts pointing nowhere. By the end of July neither Herzl nor Plehve would still be living.

The period from May 16, when Herzl ended his Diary, to July 3, when he ended his life, resemble one of those blanks in ancient maps which cartographers filled with giants or mermaids. While Herzl's body was in the hands of his doctors, the leaders of his movement controlled the rest. The puppetmaster was in the hands of his puppets.

The doctors (at least four are known to have been involved[2]) must have known that they could not save his life; their difficulties were compounded by their vagueness as to his complaint. Such aids to the diagnosis of heart conditions as blood tests, electrocardiographs and

---

* As late as 1917 Schiff was against reestablishing a Jewish nation.

catheter studies were not available in 1904. The consensus at the time was that Herzl was suffering from progressive disease of the heart muscle, or myocarditis chronica.[3] As early as 1936 Dr. Wolf Guttmann of Prague rejected this diagnosis, which a more recent physician describes as "a very vague term, which could mean anything, or as one suspects nothing, showing the confident ignorance of the physicians."[4] Guttmann suggested that Herzl's final illness was "the first decompensating phenomena of a heart disease acquired in earlier years."[5] Apparently ignorant of Herzl's earlier medical history, Guttmann ruled out the presence of "a specific infectious or toxic noxa, for which we find no support in the whole life of Herzl." If the cause for his rejection for Army service had been cardiac murmur, the most likely modern diagnosis would be subacute bacterial endocarditis. This disease was then invariably fatal, took months to kill and had subtle effects on the system: low-grade fever, anemia, listlessness and gradually increasing weakness. The scarred heart valve (and no evidence survives to show whether it was the mitral or aortic) would have become infected. The most common agent was Streptococcus viridans. Some such simple cause as a tooth infection, leading in turn to manipulation by the dentist, could have released a shower of bacteria into the bloodstream. An abscess in the soft tissues of the skin could have had the same effect.[6] Or it could have been the delayed result of his Vienna youth. A recent study has shown that before the discovery of antibiotics the gonococcus was the precipitating cause of up to 26 per cent of cases of bacterial endocarditis.[7]

Whatever the physical cause, emotional stress had played an aggravating role. The public strain of the sixth, "Uganda," Congress had been severe. As the Russian Nay-Sayers "swept like a torrent swollen by the melting snows of spring out of the Congress," one eyewitness noticed the effect on Herzl: "In one tense minute he grew old. I saw his face pale, his muscles twitch. In one poignant moment he saw the futility of Zion's dream: he saw confusion instead of fusion, disunion instead of union . . . Perhaps he felt that, strong man as he was, he had somehow failed."[8]

But his domestic situation provided a cause of stabbing tension.

According to the ordinary calendar, his son Hans had been thirteen on May 10, 1904. The Jewish calendar was slightly different. By its reckoning, Hans completed his thirteenth year on May 18; his bar mitzvah celebration should have taken place either the following day, a Thursday, or more probably, on Saturday.[9] But since he had never been circumcised, he could not be regarded as a son of the Covenant and would not be called up to read his portion of the Hebrew scripture. The anguish as Herzl recognized that his son, the Crown Prince of a Jewish movement, was not eligible for this important ceremony can easily be conjectured. The ambiguous status of his children now worried him more than his relationship with Julie.

On May 9, the day before his son's thirteenth birthday, Dr. Katzenelson had been with him at Franzensbad. The two men were taking a gentle walk in the town when Herzl suffered a bad heart attack. It was early in the season and the Kaiserstrasse was empty. Katzenelson looked in vain for someone who could fetch a doctor, but managed to help his leader to a bench, where he shortly recovered. Katzenelson later described the incident in *Die Welt*,[10] the Zionist weekly. He had tried to comfort Herzl by pretending that the attack had been brought on by the slight gradient in the street and their too quick pace. Herzl refused such comfort. The third bell had rung for him and he could face death calmly. His comfort was that he had spent his last years to some effect. Both men conversed in German and Herzl's next words were as follows: *"Ich war doch kein allzu schlechter Diener der Bewegung, meinen Sie nicht?"* ("I wasn't altogether too bad a servant *of the movement,* don't you think?") The words are important because they provide one instance of how Herzl's ikon was to be rectified. Dr. Bein's German *Biographie* of 1934 carries the words as quoted.[11] But in the English version his translator has changed them to read: "I was not altogether a poor servant *of my people,* don't you think?" Herzl's precise candor had been softened to sentimental rhetoric.

Once Herzl fell ill, a process of pious embalmment had begun, its purpose his survival (and utilization) as an ikon after death. Nothing has survived from the sickroom that could disturb the picture. "Authentic particulars" of the last phase were given in *Die Welt* and published in English by the *Jewish Chronicle*. After Franzensbad—where he got no better—he moved to Edlach, near Reichman, where he had married Julie.

> Here at first his condition betokened some improvement, but a fortnight ago serious symptoms of irregular action of the heart appeared with all their terrible pains and sufferings. He suffered greatly from shortness of breath. However, the careful treatment of the physicians in attendance, and the marvellous devotion of his wife, who for weeks had had the patient in her sole charge, succeeded partially in overcoming the disease and aroused hopes among his friends that the danger might be averted. He even took walks in the garden. This is said to have brought about the

disaster. Probably through a chill last Saturday (July 2nd) inflammation of the lungs set in. The poor weakened sick heart—the doctors immediately recognised—could not resist this new complication. The night from Saturday to Sunday was very bad. The patient was aware of his grave condition and, although he had hitherto managed to conceal from his mother his serious state of health, insisted on her, together with his two younger children, being hastily summoned from Aussee. On Sunday morning sudden signs of collapse ensued. Camphor injections were constantly made, and his words were: "Shall I still see my mother?" In the afternoon such a remarkable improvement took place that the opinion gained ground that he would yet survive this severe attack. When his mother arrived he was able to embrace her and the children. He was quiet and in almost a good humour. At a quarter to five he expressed the wish to take a little sleep. Dr. Siegmund Werner, his faithful attendant for some days, who was alone in the room with him, had left the bedside for a moment when he heard a deep sigh. When he hastily turned round Dr. Herzl had breathed his last.[12]

The *Jewish Chronicle* received a telegram from its special correspondent dated July 6. It gave a version of Herzl's last words that commends itself both for its psychological truth and early date: "How I wish to rest."

Additions to these accounts lack conviction. Hechler had been allowed to visit Herzl and in his dotage remembered, for a hagiographical publication, his hero saying: "Give them all my greetings, and tell them that I have given my heart's blood for my people."[13] When these words were published, Hechler was known only in Zionist circles; his ambition of being made Protestant Bishop of Jerusalem was unfulfilled. The reliability of his memory is not confirmed by his dating his visit to Herzl in July 1903 and placing it in "Herzl's home at Edlach."

Herzl's disappearance had crucial implications for the leaders of his movement as well as for his family.

His funeral was designed to exalt the dead leader as a living talisman against his own last chapter. A special correspondent of the *Jewish Chronicle* wrote:

> In a beautiful spot overlooking the hills surrounding Vienna, Theodor Herzl has just been laid to his eternal rest. I have never witnessed such an enormous concourse of people assembled round a grave since the interment of Beaconsfield at Hughenden. The library at Herzl's residence had been converted into a mortuary, and there the body had remained since the removal of the remains from Edlach. It had been encased in a lead coffin, which, in its turn, was placed into a plain japanned tin shell. Mounted on

trestles, it was covered with a creped Zionist flag, and although in an adjoining room were magnificent floral tributes, on the coffin itself was only a simple bouquet, evidently placed there by one of his nearest and dearest. Surrounded by huge brass candelabra with lighted candles, ward was kept by a constant bodyguard. The funeral service began at ten o'clock, when the near relations and political friends of the deceased leader gathered in the improvised mortuary. The two cantors, with their choir, beautifully sang *Tefillah Lemoshé*, after which the coffin was conveyed to the hearse. In accordance with Dr. Herzl's explicit instructions, his funeral was conducted, so far as simplicity was concerned, as that of a poor man. There were only two mourning coaches, these conveying the widow and the bereaved mother, with the son and some other female relatives. The rest of the vast gathering fell into marching line and walked from the house to the cemetery behind the hearse. It was a wonderful gathering, composed of men and women from many lands. Cheek by jowl with the correctly attired Western Jew one noticed the caftaned heavy-bearded Jew from Galicia, and side by side with the dark-eyed Roumanian was the fair-skinned North German. But on every face was the mark of a huge and lasting sorrow, the look that comes with an irreparable personal loss.[14]

After the body was laid in the vault with Jacob Herzl, the same witness tells us, Hans Herzl recited the Kaddish while David Wolffsohn, in place of an address, called on the mourners to join him in the oath with which Herzl had concluded the controversial sixth Congress: "If I forget thee, O Jerusalem, may my right hand wither!"

Wolffsohn was later to launch an appeal for financial help to Herzl's family: at least 100,000 guilders of Herzl money had been spent on the movement. In return *Die Welt* published a statement from the widow which then appeared as "Letter from Madame Herzl" in the *Jewish Chronicle* of July 29, 1904. After thanking innumerable well-wishers for their sympathy, Julie wrote:

If I did not publicly take part in the life's work of my beloved husband, it was because I feared still further to encourage him in his restless and worrying labours, and because I foresaw an end which, unhappily, has come all too soon. His work was however and will ever remain sacred to me. I will serve the Zionist movement with all my strength, and will do all that is possible to initiate my children in the life's work of their father, and to make them worthy champions in the movement for the deliverance of our people, for which he strove. I hope thereby to act in the spirit of my beloved dead, and also to give expression to my love for his life's work.

This statement, and probably the tribute to Julie's devoted nursing of her husband,† formed part of a campaign by Herzl's associates to conceal truths that embarrassed them acutely.

Chaim Weizmann, a young Nay-Saying chemist with a great future in the Zionist movement, heard the news of Herzl's death in Geneva. He was shaken by it. Even so, he decided not to attend the funeral but to set off instead for England, by way of Paris. His protest made, he visited Vienna in August and went to the Döblinger cemetery. He described his "very nasty feeling that we are standing amidst the ruins of the case, and that the deceased himself contributed quite a bit to it. Herzl, *for his own sake,* died in time."[15] He recounts the extreme hostility to Julie among the leading Zionists. His correspondence at the time suggests the reasons. In the week following Herzl's death, he had met Nordau in Paris. Nordau categorically rejected the suggestion that he should succeed Herzl. He gave three reasons. First, he did not consider his private life sufficiently "national." Second, he would encounter strong resistance in the Zionist milieu, which would not forgive him what had been forgiven Herzl. Third, he did not believe in the cause: he was unwilling to play with a façade that had no solid building behind it; Herzl had been able to do this, thanks to his belief in his own personality.[16] Nordau made it plain to Weizmann that what he was not forgiven was his marriage to Anna Kaufmann, the widow of his friend Richard Kaufmann, and a gentile. It is curious in this connection that Nordau said *"Mir kam der Zionismus zwei Jahre zu spät"* ("Zionism reached me two years too late"). Herzl, according to his Diary, won Nordau's allegiance as early as November 1895. Yet Nordau only married Anna in 1898. The implication seems to be that in the early years of Herzl's Zionism, the secular philosophy of *Der Judenstaat* and *Altneuland* was still paramount; the *Judentum* to which Herzl spoke of returning involved no necessary connection with the rules of Torah.

Nordau's plight indicated an area for rectification in the preparation of the Herzl ikon. The Zionists had overlooked Herzl's marriage; but now that he was dead his reputation had to be shielded from its effects.

Despite her statement in *Die Welt,* neither Julie nor any of her children played any further role in the Zionist movement. Julie in any case had little time. Although as a bride she had been strikingly robust, by her mid-thirties, during her last two years as Herzl's wife,

---

† The *Die Welt* reference to "the marvellous devotion of his wife, who for weeks had the patient in her sole charge" is plainly hyperbole. Herzl moved from one medical establishment to another, had the care of at least four physicians, while Julie's health was itself the cause of grave and justified concern.

her state of health caused more anxiety than his. Her three years of widowhood were spent in nursing homes at Homburg, Wiesbaden and Königstein; death came to her at Bad Aussee in 1907. If like Crown Princess Stephanie she suffered for her husband's youthful dissipations, then she endured a disease described as wickedly damaging in women.[17] "In compliance with her clearly expressed desire that her traces should be wiped out completely, she was cremated in Gotha. She had willed the urn containing the ashes to her son Hans, but it was lost in an unexplained way."[18] Julie's drastic decision—since cremation was no more practiced by Jews than by Catholics—may have been taken from a willingness to spare her husband's followers embarrassment. If she were not considered Jewish by *halacha*, her burial would have posed problems akin to those of her wedding.

The strong-willed Jeanette Herzl outlived her daughter-in-law and died in Vienna in 1911. It seems that her grandchildren disliked her as heartily as they loved their mother.[19]

Once his mother was dead, Hans underwent circumcision. This was probably more at the suggestion of his guardian, Joseph Cowen, than of his grandmother. Hans, who inherited his father's good looks and intellectual powers, was sent to England for his education. From Clifton College he won a scholarship to Cambridge, where he had a nervous breakdown. Noted for his correct, kindly and sympathetic manner, he never married. Under the prodding of psychiatrists, he is said to have had normal, if extramarital relations with women in Paris, though he preferred continence. Although the Zionists provided munificently for the Herzl children, their fortune was invested in Austrian bonds. As Hans was in England, and naturalized by 1914, his bonds were confiscated in the war and he never obtained any redress. He lived in considerable poverty, earning what he could from translations but having to watch every penny. He was more interested in religion than politics and passed through several variants of the Christian faith before being baptized as a Catholic by Friar Arthur Day, S.J., on October 19, 1924. But he soon lapsed. His attitude to his father was also complex. He displayed a portrait of him in his rooms at Cambridge and carried a memorial sonnet by Israel Zangwill in his wallet; but he could not bear to hear Herzl's name mentioned. His great attachment was to his sister Pauline, and this contrived his death.

Pauline had probably never fully recovered from the physical effects of rheumatic fever; the consequent spoiling by her parents also left its mark. Adolescence, coinciding with her father's death, triggered an explosion of animal vitality that doomed her to a life as short as her mother's, and as sad. After an unsuccessful stint as a children's nurse, she became by turns an unfaithful and childless wife, a frequenter of Jazz Age night clubs and the patient of countless psychiatrists. When she fell seriously ill in 1930 from morphine addiction, Hans hurried from England to her Bordeaux bedside. Thinking her on the mend, he returned to England, only to be summoned back. On his way through Paris he surprised Anna Nordau and her daughter Maxa at home.[19] He seemed to them distraught but parted from them the same evening without saying what seemed on the tip of his tongue. In Bordeaux, where Pauline was dead, he had wild delusions of being able to revive her corpse and then dreams of being buried with her in one grave. "My life was bad," he wrote, "and bad is the end. After the death of my dearest sister, a man who condemns himself for what he has done should not leave the execution of the verdict to others."[20] Like his father's best friend, he commited suicide, shooting himself in his hotel bedroom.

On March 5, 1903, Herzl had added a codicil to his will. (This was before he changed course for Uganda). "I wish to be interred in a metal coffin in the vault next to my father, and to remain there until the Jewish people will transfer my remains to Palestine. Likewise the coffins of my father, of my sister Pauline, buried in Pest and of members of my immediate family (mother and children) should be brought to Palestine. My wife only if she so desires in her last will." This wish was granted in the case of Herzl himself in 1949. But Hans and Pauline remain buried in Bordeaux, under a Hebrew tombstone.

Unlike the introspective Hans and the uncontrolled Pauline, Herzl's third child was clinically insane. Trude's guardian, David Wolffsohn, withdrew her from her Viennese secondary school when she was seventeen. Thereafter her life alternated between mania and depression. Alone of Herzl's children she contracted a lasting relationship. Her husband was Richard Neumann, a rich industrialist twenty-six years older than herself and already father of three children by a divorced wife. Trude underwent treatment, Neumann recorded, in fourteen different psychiatric institutions. Frenzy, gloom, noise, coquetry, aggression, suspicion, co-existed with flashes of erudition, surges of love, the last of which found expression in enough letters to her husband to be bound in two volumes. She also wrote to such important figures as President Roosevelt and the Kaiser. She approached the King of England with the bizarre suggestion: "I should like to reign: would it be quite impossible to get me the British throne?" After Edward VIII abdicated, she urged his restoration.

In 1942 Trude was removed by the German authorities from the Steinhof Asylum and sent to Theresienstadt, where she was joined by her husband, then an inmate of an old people's home. With her, Dr. Bein believes, Trude carried a bulky key to the understanding of her father's life. "Most of the letters between Herzl and Julie were in the possession of Margaret-Trude . . . who evidently took them along when she was deported by the Nazis to Theresienstadt."[21] This explanation is as mysterious as anything in the story. Theodor Herzl was a major figure in Nazi demonology. The letters had plainly been withheld from biographers for reasons that would have interested the manic rulers of the Third Reich. That his surviving daughter could have retained them in an asylum under German occupation seems improbable, that she could have lugged them to a concentration camp and there destroyed them, all but impossible. The correspondence was more likely suppressed much earlier; at the latest after the death of Hans.

"In Theresienstadt," Arthur Stern tells us,[22] "Trude attracted immediate attention by her well-kept clothes and luggage, her charm and elegance. 'I am Herzl's daughter, I wish to establish special, personal contact with the highest Jewish authorities in Theresienstadt.' The head of the hospital looked after her and soon arranged for her transfer to the psychiatric ward of the camp. It would appear that she was nursed and cared for as well as conditions allowed, given extra allocations of food to supplement the usual starvation rations." Either these proved insufficient (and Dr. Stern surmises that she was starved) or she was overcome by grief at her husband's death. She died in March 1943, leaving one son, Stefan Theodor Neumann, the last of Herzl's descendants. This young man is said to have looked like his grandfather. During the Second World War he served as a captain in the British Army and immediately after the war visited Palestine on his way to and from India. In 1946 Neumann was posted as commercial attaché at the British Embassy in Washington. He ended Herzl's line by jumping from a bridge in the American capital on November 26, 1946.‡

‡ His motives may be explained in the folder of papers he handed to Mr. Eliyahu Eilat, then representative of the Jewish Agency in Washington. These have not been published. It is possible that the belated discovery of some family secret may have overturned the balance of his mind.

EPILOGUE

H erzl survived as an inspiring symbol to thousands outside his immediate circle. The first artist to be fascinated by him was Ephraim Lilien (1874–1925). Lilien used Herzl's features for those of Moses in illustrations to the Bible and in a stained glass window.[1] In most ways Herzl was very unlike the biblical Moses, who is described as the most humble of men. But one circumstance that he shared with Moses contributed to his appeal. Just as Moses had approached the ancient Hebrews from the heart of the Egyptian culture that oppressed them, so Herzl had left the cafés of Paris, the theaters of Vienna, to lead the Jews of modern Europe to a Promised Land. Yet it was not only Zionists whom Herzl impressed. "Till Dr. Herzl came to me," Plehve had time to say, before being assassinated outside a St. Petersburg station, "I did not know there were Jews who did not crawl."[2] This testimonial is less striking than Clemenceau's: "He was a man of genius, not to be confounded with a man of talent. There are plenty of men of talent in the world. Men of genius are rare."[3] The old statesman claimed that in his nights of retirement he was visited not only by Goethe, Galileo, Washington and Socrates, but by Theodor Herzl. Sigmund Freud, who took much magic out of dreams, saw Herzl in his sleep: "a majestic figure, with a pale, dark-toned face framed by a beautiful, raven-black beard, with infinitely sad eyes."[4]

But as a prophet of Jewish power Herzl inspired nightmare no less than dreams. The year of the first Zionist Congress, his greatest triumph, witnessed the birth of another durable myth with a Hungarian connection: Bram Stoker's *Dracula* was published in June 1897, two months before Herzl posted the commemorative postcards to his children. And if to his followers Herzl combined the passion of a Mazzini with the presence of a Moses, to later anti-Semites he loomed as a conspirator with the uncanny powers of the undead. It is not surprising that a man who had decided to lead the Jews should attract the lightning of their enemies. But some of his actions and words encouraged the force he had hoped to exorcise. Early anti-Semitism (if it may be called that) was based either on religious bigotry or the dislike of the strange. The examples of the first have been frequent in this book: its force could be expected to diminish with the spread of education. The classical example of the second can be found in the works of the most notorious anti-Semite of the twentieth century, who came to Vienna shortly after Herzl's funeral. "Once, when passing through the Inner City, I suddenly encountered a phenomenon in a long caftan and wearing black sidelocks. My first thought was: Is this a Jew? They certainly did not have this appearance in Linz. I watched the man stealthily and cautiously; but the longer I gazed at that strange countenance and examined it feature by feature, the more the question shaped itself in my brain: Is this a German?"[5]

Religious bigotry and xenophobia have both led to persecutions; both could be expected to diminish with civilization. But history shows that when the heterodox or the strange is also considered dangerous persecution can turn to genocide. The Protestants hounded Elizabethan Catholics when it was thought that they were in league with Spain; the once tolerant Turks massacred the Armenians when they feared that the Armenians were plotting to destroy the Turkish empire at its heart. Witch-hunting is only possible when men believe in devils. Herzl's statement that *"Nous sommes un peuple, un peuple un"* was what had most impressed de Boisandré, the man who wrote his obituary for *La Libre Parole*.[6] Herzl's characteristic mixture of promises and threats, his insinuation that this one omnipresent people could pay the Sultan's debts or destroy his empire, that they could foment revolution or subsidize the status quo may have inspired the still untraced author of *The Protocols of the Elders of Zion*. Certainly the 1917 edition of that conspiratorial fantasy claims a connection. "These Protocols," wrote the monk Sergei Nilus in his preface to what a British author has called a Warrant for Genocide,[7] "are nothing else than a strategic plan for the conquest of the world, putting it under the yoke of Israel, the struggle against God, a plan worked out by the leaders of the Jewish people during the many centuries of dispersion, and finally presented to the Council of Elders, by 'the

Prince of the Exile,' Theodor Herzl, at the time of the first Zionist Congress, summoned by him at Basel in August 1897." Hitler died in his bunker still believing in the authenticity of this fantastic myth.

But those who follow Herzl stage by stage, who note his candor, his feeling for the striking phrase, his love of publicity, would find it as hard to believe that Herzl wrote the turgid Protocols as that the Zionist delegates would have heard them out or that the journalists (and Philip Nevlinsky) would not have remarked them.

If then this search for the historical Herzl has removed from Herzl's dark hair the hagiographer's halo and the demonologist's horns; if Herzl has been discovered as a man who cast a handsome, if sometimes vain reflection in the mirror; and if in the background to his life the variety of the Jews and their attitudes to Judaism has been evident, not the monolithic power feared by their enemies, then the book will have served part of its purpose. More will have been served if Herzl appears, not only as one of the most characteristic figures of nineteenth-century Europe, but as a man of rich complexity who spoke truly for himself when, in his early twenties, he wrote to his closest friend:

"The basic feeling of life is grief and joy comes only when, for a brief while, grief abates."[8]

NOTES

Chapter 1: pages 3-10

1. Theodor Herzl, "An Autobiography," *Jewish Chronicle*, January 14, 1898.
2. The Dohány-utca synagogue is described and illustrated in *A 90 Éves Dohany-utcai Templom*, Budapest, 1949.
3. The first rabbi is Professor Sándor (in his English writings Alexander) Scheiber of the Orthodox Rabbinical Seminary, Budapest; he made the comment in conversation with the author. The second quotation is from an article by Dr. André Ungar (rabbi of Temple Emanuel, Westwood, N.J.) in *Conservative Judaism*, winter 1971: "Hungary: A Sentimental Journey."
4. The quotations about the Pesth and Hungary of 1858 are to be found *passim* in the 1858 edition of Murray's *A Handbook for Travellers in Southern Germany*.
5. For William Tierney Clark (1783–1852) see the Dictionary of National Biography.
6. The statistics and references to the hygienic conditions of nineteenth-century Budapest and Berlin can be found in the thirteenth edition of the Encyclopaedia Britannica.
7. Grant, A. J., and Temperley, Harold, *Europe in the Nineteenth and Twentieth Centuries* (1789–1939), London, Longmans, 1927, p. 283.

Chapter 2: pages 11-21

1. Circumcision not a sacrament: see Jewish Encyclopaedia, New York and London, Funk and Wagnalls Co., 1903, vol. IV, article by Aaron Friedenwald, M.D., late of Baltimore. Rabbi Meir is quoted as saying that a non-Jewish physician could if necessary perform the operation; as could women, slaves and even children.
2. Samuel Raphael Hirsch, *Judaism Eternal*, London, Soncino Press, 1956, vol. 2, pp. 230–31.
3. Genesis XVII: 10–14, in *The Pentateuch and Haftorahs*, Hebrew Text, English Translation and Commentary, ed. by Dr. J. H. Hertz, C.H., Late Chief Rabbi of the British Empire, London, Soncino Press, 5720-1960.
4. Exodus IV: 24–26, ibid., p. 221.
5. Joshua V: 2–9, ibid.
6. See Howard Carter's *The Tomb of Tut Ankh Amen*, 3 vols., London, Cassel & Co., 1923–33, for a photograph of this iron dagger.

7. Jewish Encyclopaedia, article already cited.

8. Book of Jubilees, XV: 26–27.

9. I here follow Dr. Alex Bein, *Theodore Herzl, A Biography*, London, Horovitz Publishing Co., East and West Library, 1957, p. 8, though Raphael Patai, editor of *The Complete Diaries of Theodor Herzl*, tr. Harry Zohn 5 vols., New York, Herzl Press and Thomas Yoseloff, p. 1860, transliterates the Hebrew as Binyamin Z'ev.

10. Hirsch, op. cit., vol. 1, p. 233.

11. Ibid., p. 149.

12. Deuteronomy XXVIII: 10–14, in *The Pentateuch and Haftorahs*, op. cit., p. 866.

13. These curses (and others) occur in Deuteronomy XXVIII between vv. 15 and 50.

14. *Pirke Aboth, The Ethics of the Talmud: Sayings of the Fathers*, ed. with introduction, translation and commentary by R. Travers Herford, New York, Schocken Books, 1962, p. 30.

15. Dr. I. Grunfeld in a preface to his translation of Samson Raphael Hirsch's *Horeb, A Philosophy of Jewish Laws and Observance*, London, Soncino Press, 1962.

16. Bein, op. cit., p. 5.

Chapter 3: pages 23-33

1. Bein, op. cit., p. 7.

2. Max Bodenheimer in *Im Anfang der Zionistischen Bewegung*, ed. H. H. Bodenheimer, Frankfurt a.M., 1965, p. 110.

3. Bein, op. cit., p. 10.

4. For Yehudah Alkalai, see article in Jewish Encyclopaedia.

5. Jewish Encyclopaedia, article on Purim of Buda.

6. Jacob de Haas, *Theodor Herzl, A Biographical Study*, 2 vols., New York, The Leonard Co., 1927, vol. 1, p. 30. The same story, told to de Haas by Herzl in 1896, also appears in Adolf Friedemann's *Das Leben Theodor Herzls*, Berlin, 1914.

7. de Haas, op. cit., p. 31.

8. This extract from Disraeli's Life of Lord George Bentinck is quoted in the Jewish Encyclopaedia article on the Earl of Beaconsfield, 1903.

9. Bein, op. cit., p. 8. The photograph is no. 7 in his book.

10. de Haas, op. cit., p. 31, gives the story that "Lobel Herzl was a mystic and practised 'white magic' or Caballa," but adds that he was inclined to think such stories had been fabricated by local gossips after Lobel's great-grandson became famous. The New Standard Jewish Encyclopaedia spells it "Kabbalah."

11. Bein, op. cit., p. 9.

12. Photograph no. 5, Bein, op. cit.

13. Joseph Patai, "Herzl's School Years," *Herzl Year Book*, vol. 3, Herzl

Centennial Issue, New York, Herzl Press, 1960, gives a detailed account of Herzl's education in Hungary.

14. John Pudney, *Suez: de Lessep's Canal*, London, Dent, 1968, p. 20.

15. Joseph Patai, *vide supra.*

Chapter 4: pages 35-44

1. *Complete Diaries*, p. 117.

2. Ibid., p. 28.

3. Ibid., p. 127.

4. Ibid., p. 122, conclusion to a letter to Bismarck of June 19, 1895.

5. Joseph Patai, *Herzl Year Book*, vol. 3; in the Hungarian edition of his life of Herzl Patai reproduces Herzl's mark card.

6. Joseph Patai, *Herzl Year Book*, vol. 3: I have transposed the order of two sentences.

7. Jacob Wassermann, *Mein Weg als Deutscher und Jude* (German edition, 1921); English translation, S. N. Brainin, New York, Coward-McCann, 1933, pp. 12–14.

8. Ibid., p. 14.

9. Article on "Reform Judaism," New Standard Jewish Encyclopaedia, ed. Cecil Roth and Geoffrey Wigoder, London, W. H. Allen, 1970, p. 1609.

10. Bein, op. cit., p. 14.

11. Ibid., p. 12.

12. Acts of the Apostles II: 1–4. Jerusalem Bible.

13. Exodus XIX: 5, 6, in *The Pentateuch and Haftorahs*, op. cit., p. 291.

14. Passage in Israel Zangwill's *Children of the Ghetto* quoted as description of Moses Zangwill, Israel's father, in Joseph Leftwich's *Israel Zangwill*, London, James Clarke, 1957, p. 72.

15. A phrase of Wassermann's, op. cit., p. 6.

16. Professor John George Robeson (author of *History of German Literature*) in essay on Heine, Encyclopaedia Britannica, 13th ed., vol. 13, p. 215.

Chapter 5: pages 45-51

1. The Gymnasium was still standing, as was the church, in October 1971.

2. "An Autobiography," *Jewish Chronicle*, January 14, 1898. "At the Gymnasium, which was called the Evangelisches Gymnasium, the Jewish boys formed the majority . . ."

3. For Herzl's knowledge of Hungarian, see Alexander Scheiber, *Herzl Year Book*, vol. 3.

4. Oscar Briliant, referring to R. W. Seton-Watson, *Racial Problems in Hungary*, London, 1908, in article on Hungary in Encyclopaedia Britannica, 13th ed.

5. Quoted in *The Economist*, London, August 21, 1971.

6. Graham Greene, *A Sort of Life*, London, 1971, p. 117.

7. Joseph Patai, *Star over Jordan, The Life of Theodor Herzl*, tr. from Hungarian by Francis Magyar, New York, Philosophical Library, 1946 [original Hungarian, 1932], p. 26 and *passim*.

8. de Haas, op. cit., for example: p. 57. "As always he had been nervous in the presence of strangers, a weakness he diligently tried to conquer."

9. Bein, op. cit., p. 21.

10. Herzl's "An Autobiography," *vide supra*. Herzl uses the word *Schriftsteller*.

11. Bein, op. cit., p. 22.

12. Bein, op. cit., p. 22. "He guarded every keepsake of hers like a sacred relic." Joseph Patai recounts the annual visit to Budapest.

13. Phrases of Herzl's, quoted by Alex Bein, p. 21.

Chapter 6: pages 55-59

1. Herzl to Heinrich Kane, 30 August 1883, Herzl-Kana Correspondence, Central Zionist Archives, Jerusalem.

2. Simone de Beauvoir, *The Second Sex*, p. 299.

3. Raoul Auernheimer, *Das Wirtshaus zur verlorenen Zeit*, Vienna, 1948; translated and abridged extract, "Beard of the Prophet," in *Herzl Year Book*, vol. 6, New York, Herzl Press, 1965.

4. Norman Cohn, *Warrant for Genocide*, London, Eyre & Spottiswoode, 1967, p. 171, gives Marr as "the probable inventor of the word 'anti-semitism'"; Cohn translates the title as *The Victory of Jewry over Germandom, considered from a non-denominational point of view*. I have translated Marr's *Judenthum* as "Jewishness" in order to keep Marr's double suffixes and also because *Judenthum* becomes important later in Herzl's life.

Chapter 7: pages 61-67

1. "Autobiography," op. cit.

2. Bein, op. cit., p. 25.

3. Arthur Schnitzler's correspondence with Herzl; *Midstream* VI, November 1960.

4. Hans Kohn, "Zion and the Jewish National Idea," *The Menorah Journal*, 1958.

5. Incidents and quotations from *The Life and Opinions of Moses Hess*, by Isaiah Berlin; Lucien Wolf Memorial Lecture, December 1957, Jewish Historical Society of England.

6. Bein, op. cit., p. 182.

7. From the Preface to *A Musician's Problem*, being part of *The Case of Wagner*, written by Friedrich Nietzsche in Turin, May 1888.

8. Aphorism 40 in Selected Aphorisms from Nietzsche's *Retrospect of His Years of Friendship with Wagner*, Summer 1878, vol. 8, Oscar Levy ed., tr. Anthony M. Ludovici, Edinburgh, 1911.

9. Ibid., Aphorism 41.

10. Preface to *A Musician's Problem, vide supra.*

11. Ernest Newman, *The Life of Richard Wagner,* London, Cassell, 1945, vol. 3, p. 275.

12. Nietzsche wrote in January 1874; *The Use and Abuse of History* comes in *Thoughts Out of Season,* tr. Adrian Collins, ed. Oscar Levy.

13. Epilogue to *A Musician's Problem, vide supra.*

14. *A Musician's Problem,* p. 5.

15. Ibid., Preface.

16. *Retrospect of His Years of Friendship with Wagner,* op. cit., Aphorism 76.

17. See Carl E. Schorske, "Politics in a New Key: an Austrian Triptych," *Journal of Modern History,* December 1967.

18. Adolf Hitler, *Mein Kampf,* tr. James Murphy, London, 1939, p. 94.

19. Bein, op. cit., p. 26.

Chapter 8: pages 69-77

1. Leon Kellner, *Theodor Herzls Lehrjahre* (1860–1895), Vienna, 1920.

2. R. S. Morton, *Venereal Diseases; Studies in Social Pathology,* London, Penguin, 1966, p. 30.

3. Fritz Judtmann, *Mayerling: The Facts Behind the Legend,* London, George G. Harrap, 1971; original ed., *Mayerling ohne Mythos,* Vienna, 1968.

4. To the present author, whose Oxford B.Litt. thesis he was supervising; with reference to Algernon Charles Swinburne, whose pathological masochism was denied by Harold Nicolson in his *Swinburne* as late as 1926, then conclusively proved by the publication of G. Lafourcade's *La Jeunesse de Swinburne* two years later.

5. The *Jugendtagebuch* was published in *Theodor Herzl Jahrbuch,* ed. Tulo Nussenblatt, Vienna, 1937; the letters to Kana repose in the Central Zionist Archives (CZA), Jerusalem.

6. de Haas, op. cit., pp. 37–38.

7. Bein, op. cit., p. 62.

8. Judtmann, op. cit., p. 20.

9. Dr. T. Nussenblatt, "Theodor Herzl Before the Commission on Fitness for Military Service," *Judische Welt,* July 31, 1936.

10. Information received from Dr. T. H. M. Stewart, Ottawa General Hospital.

11. CZA, letter addressed "Herrn H. Kana, Doktor," from Pesth, March 5, 1882.

12. CZA, letter from Baden, August 30, 1883.

13. CZA, letter dated November 22, 1883.

14. *Jugendtagebuch,* p. 47.

15. For Boswell's malady, see *Boswell's London Journal 1762–1763,* ed. Frederick A. Pottle, London, 1950.

Chapter 9: pages 79-89

1. Cf. Carl Schorske, op. cit., *passim.*
2. Eric Nemes, Hungarian-born Paris art expert, in letter to the author.
3. Fritz Hartung, *Deutsche Verfassungsgeschichte,* Stuttgart, 1950, p. 255.
4. Jüdisches Lexikon, vol. 1. Congress of Berlin.
5. Anatole Le Roy-Beaulieu, *Israël chez les Nations,* Paris, 1893, pp. 55–56.
6. "Autobiography," 1898.
7. Bein, op. cit., p. 30.
8. Ibid., p. 89.
9. *Theodor Herzl Jahrbuch,* ed. Nussenblatt, p. 22 onward.
10. Kellner, op. cit., pp. 127–34.
11. Ibid., p. 18.

Chapter 10: pages 91-96

1. Gustav Kobbé, *Complete Opera Book,* ed. and revised by Earl of Harewood, London, 1954.
2. My debt to Robert Gutman's *Richard Wagner: The Man, His Mind and His Music,* London, 1968, is evident throughout this discussion of *Parsifal* and its significance.
3. George Heer, *Quellen und Darstellungen zur Geschichte der Burschenschaft und der deutschen Einheitsbewegung,* vol. 16, Heidelberg, 1939.
4. See Herzl's letter of resignation, whose text is printed in full on pp. 27, 28 of Kellner, op. cit.
5. Bein, op. cit., *passim.*
6. Letter to Dankwart, April 4, 1883, printed on p. 29, Kellner, op. cit.
7. CZA, letter dated August 30, 1883.
8. CZA, letter 16, The Month of Affliction.
9. Peter Loewenberg, op. cit., p. 156.
10. *Theodor Herzl Jahrbuch,* for these two quotations under cited dates; ed. Nussenblatt.
11. Herzl's own term in "Autobiography," op. cit.

Chapter 11: pages 99-107

1. "*Ich glaube, von Anfang an ist jeder gut, oder wie ich es nenne, echt . . . Dann tritt etwas ein, vielleicht nur der Verlauf der Zeit, und sie werden unecht.*" From "*Der Gedankenleser*" (The Thought Reader), last essay in *Neues von der Venus,* Leipzig, 1887.
2. For Herzl's university influences, see in particular Joseph Adler, *The*

Herzl Paradox: Political, Social and Economic Theories of a Realist, New York, Hadrian Press, 1962.

3. "Autobiography," op. cit., 14.1, 1898.

4. Herzl's letter to Kana, May 28, 1885, quoted by Kellner.

5. "Autobiography," op. cit., "In Salzburg I spent some of the happiest hours of my life. I would have liked to have stayed in the beautiful town, but, as a Jew, I could never have advanced to the position of a Judge."

6. Bein, op. cit., English version, p. 48.

7. "*Gestern war Grande Soirée bei Treitel. An die 30–40 kleine, hässliche Juden und Jüdinnen. Kein tröstender Anblick.*" Kellner, op. cit., p. 127.

8. Kellner, op. cit., p. 48. This letter is placed immediately after one dated August 3, 1883; internal evidence, such as a reference to Berlin, indicates that it was written after November 1885.

9. Josef Fraenkel, *Theodor Herzl: Des Schöpfers Erstes Wollen*, Wien, Fiba Verlag, 1934, *Vorwort*, translation by D.S.

10. "Autobiography," op. cit.

11. Fränkel, op. cit.

12. Olga Schnitzler, *Spiegelbild der Freundschaft*, Salzburg, Residenz Verlag, 1962, p. 81.

13. Bein, op. cit., English version, p. 66.

14. Kellner's eighth chapter, "On The Wrong Road," gives this estimate along with other criticism of Herzl the playwright.

Chapter 12: pages 109-122

1. Kellner, op. cit., p. 92.

2. I owe these important details to Mrs. Therese Nickl's researches in the pages of the Vienna directory, *Der Wohnunganzeiger von Adolph Lehmann*, as well as in Vienna's Zentralfriedhof where the Naschauers are buried.

3. Bein, op. cit., German version, p. 106. "*Ungleich seinem Vater, der sich mehr für jüdische Literatur und Philosophie als für den Erwerb interessierte, war er der richtige Vertreter jener ersten Generation emanzipierter Juden, denen die Emanzipation vor allem den raschen wirtschaftlichen Aufstieg ermöglichte.*"

4. Bein, op. cit., English version, p. 62.

5. André Chouraqui, *A Man Alone*, tr. from *Théodore Herzl: Inventeur de l'état d'Israël* by Yael Guiladi; Keter Publishing House Ltd., Jerusalem, 1970, p. 39.

6. Nussenblatt, op. cit., pp. 49ff.

7. Kellner, op. cit., p. 60.

8. Bein, op. cit., German edition, p. 88.

9. Kellner, op. cit., p. 61.

10. Joseph Fränkel, op. cit., introduction to *Sein Hoheit*, translation by D.S.

11. "*Schonungslos sind wir nur gegen die Nahestehenden.*" *Herzl-Worte*, zusammengestellt von Felix A. Theilhaber, Berlin, 1921, p. 87.

12. Kellner, op. cit., gives the dates of composition as January 25–Feb-

ruary 1; he also gives the complete text of Ernst Hartmann's letter of advice, dated February 7, 1887. *Inter alia: "Studieren Sie mehr nach dem Leben als in der Welt, die Ihr Kopf malt . . . Bilden Sie nach lebenden Modellen anstatt nach den Gipsmodellen eines Theatermuseums."*

13. Kellner, op. cit., p. 71.

14. F. Freund, "Das Alltägliche," *Neues von der Venus*, Leipzig, 1887, p. 181.

15. Ibid., "Mentor und Telemach," p. 227.

16. Bein, op. cit., German edition, p. 118.

17. Martha Hofmann, *Theodor Herzl, Werden und Weg*, Frankfurt-am-Main, 1966, p. 29.

Chapter 13: pages 123-131

1. See "The Testaments of Herzl," N. M. Gelber, *Herzl Year Book*, vol. 3, p. 259.

2. In *The New Ghetto*, written 1894, Act II, scene 9.

3. *"Über Verlobungen lacht man in Theater immer herzlich, weil die Schadenfreude uns allen geboren ist." Herzl-Worte*, p. 86.

4. Youth Diary, May 2, 1882, *Theodor Herzl Jahrbuch*, ed. Nussenblatt.

5. In "The Chief Rabbi and the Visionary," in *The Jews of Austria, Essays on Their Life, History and Destruction*, London, 1967, edited by himself, Josef Fränkel explains how the *Memoirs of Rabbi Moritz Güdemann* (1835–1918), written for his family, never published and possibly since destroyed, came into his hands for a few days before the Second World War.

6. See photostat of wedding certificate.

7. Herr Michael Waissnix still retains the slate tablets on which the names of the temporary tenants were chalked.

8. See *Liebe, die Starb vor der Zeit*, Vienna, 1970, both for the Schnitzler-Olga Waissnix correspondence (ed. Heinrich Schnitzler and Therese Nickle) and in particular for Olga's letter of June 12, 1890, describing Hélène Naschauer's marriage the following summer.

9. Chouraqui, op. cit., p. 9, states that Hans's birth "was welcomed in lyric accents by Theodor," and claims that *"Der Sohn"* was written on this occasion. It was in fact published the previous year.

10. S. R. Hirsch, *Judaism Eternal*, p. 231.

11. See Bein, op. cit., German edition, p. 108; also English edition, pp. 63–64.

12. Josef Fränkel reproduced the cover of the musical score in his *Theodor Herzl, A Biography*, London, "Ararat" Publishing Society, 1946.

13. I owe this information to a letter from Madame Maxa Nordau of September 21, 1972.

14. "Die Kinder sind unsere gröster Lehrmeister." *Herzl-Worte*, p. 87.

15. See Kellner's chapter on Kana for text of this and following letter.

16. The portrait was reproduced on front cover of *Hadassah Magazine*, January 1972.

17. *"Spielwut und Sparwut sind nur verschiedene Grade desselben Passion." Herzl-Worte,* p. 91.

18. According to Fränkel, "The Chief Rabbi and the Visionary," *vide supra.*

19. Kellner, op. cit., p. 152.

20. *Complete Diaries,* p. 12.

Chapter 14: pages 133-144

1. *Anfang einer spanischen Reise* (1: *"Luz, das Dorf";* 2: *"Zur Brücke von Spanien";* 3: *"Die Geckenküste";* 4: *"König Kind"*) was reprinted in Theodor Herzl, *Feuilletons,* Wien, Verlag Banjamin Harz, 1911, pp. 111–51.

2. *"In Tarbes, dem Hauptorte der Pyrenäen, fügte ich meinem letzten Willen ein Kodizill hinzu. Ich verbot in dem kategorischen Tone, welcher zur Feinheit solcher Schriftstücke gehört, dass meine Reste hier bestattet würden, falls mich die Langweile hinwegraffen sollte. Denn ich möchte beinahe noch lieber in Tarvis leben, als in Tarbes begraben sein. Zu meinem Erstaunen erwachte ich aber am andern Morgen und konnte die Reise nach Pierrefitte fortsetzen."*

3. Kellner, op. cit., p. 152.

4. Maurice Magnus, *Memoirs of the Foreign Legion,* London, Martin Secker, 1924.

5. *Complete Diaries,* p. 42.

6. *Herzl-Worte,* p. 93. (from *Palais-Bourbon*)

7. February 11, 1891. *"Mann muss es nur in der richtigen Entfernung betrachten."*

8. Norman Cohn, op. cit., p. 46, discusses the true significance of these two letters.

9. Lieselotte Schmidt, "Édouard Drumont—Emile Zola: Publizistik und Publizisten in der Dreyfus-Affäre," inaugural dissertation for Ph.D. in Philosophical Faculty of the Free University of Berlin, 20.12.1962.

10. Israel Cohen, *Theodor Herzl, Founder of Political Zionism,* New York, Thomas Yoseloff, 1959, p. 64.

11. Malcolm Hay, *The Pressure of Christendom on the People of Israel for 1900 Years,* Boston, 1960, p. 188.

12. Jean Bouvier, *Les Rothschild,* Paris, 1960, p. 48.

13. Michael R. Marrus, *The Politics of Assimilation,* Oxford, 1971, p. 317, for quotation from Les Archives Israélites, 3.10.1889.

14. Marrus, op. cit., pp. 90, 91.

15. Alan Neame, *The Happening at Lourdes,* London, Hodder & Stoughton Ltd., 1968.

16. For attitude to Lourdes, see Bein, op. cit., English edition, p. 70.

17. Bein, op. cit., English edition, pp. 79–80, gives a compressed version of the critique; longer version of it in German edition, pp. 132ff.

18. Israel Cohen, op. cit., p. 64.

19. For letters between Herzl and Schnitzler, see Olga Schnitzler, *Spiegelbild der Freundschaft*, Salzburg, 1962, ch. on Herzl.

20. *Complete Diaries*, p. 7.

21. See Marrus, op. cit., p. 59, who quotes an editorialist in *Univers Israelite*, 16.12.1898.

22. Marrus, op. cit., pp. 58ff.

23. Ibid., p. 169.

24. Ibid., pp. 169–70.

25. *Three Unknown Herzl Letters*, op. cit.

Chapter 15: pages 145-157

1. Moritz Benedikt, first editor with Eduard Bacher, then publisher of *Neue Freie Presse*, to Herzl: "Until now we have been considered as a Jewish paper but have never admitted it." *Complete Diaries*, p. 246.

2. For example, Joseph Gregor, *Geschichte des Österreichischen Theater*, Wien, 1948.

3. *Complete Diaries*, p. 11; my text Olga Schnitzler, op. cit., pp. 86ff. Also for other quotations from letters to and from Schnitzler.

4. All quotations from Heinz Norden's translation, *The New Ghetto*, New York, 1955; I change gulden to guilders.

5. *Complete Diaries*, p. 9.

6. Ibid., p. 10.

7. Ibid., p. 11.

8. Olga Schnitzler, op. cit., pp. 90ff.

9. P. 72, Norden translation.

10. Alex Bein's tr. and ed. *Herzl Year Book*, vol. 1, 1958, p. 304.

11. Leon Kellner: "*Er hatte es, um seine Meinung überprufen zu lassen, einem Christen und einem Juden zu lesen gegeben. Der Christ sagte: das ist eine Dynamitbombe. Der Jude sagte: das ist eine Beschimpfung des Judentums.*"

12. Bein, op. cit., p. 305.

13. Israel Cohen, op. cit., p. 62.

14. Bein, op. cit., English edition, p. 107.

15. Chouraqui, op. cit., p. 77.

16. Olga Schnitzler, op. cit., p. 92.

17. Bein, op. cit., English edition, p. 88.

18. Ibid., p. 78. *Staatsjuristen*-might also be translated as "politician."

Chapter 16: pages 161-169

1. Herzl to Chief Rabbi Moritz Güdemann, June 11, 1895; de Haas, op. cit., p. 58.

2. *Complete Diaries*, p. 13.

3. Olga Schnitzler, op. cit., ch. on Herzl.

4. de Haas, op. cit., p. 50. De Haas gives the source as "an essay quoted in Kellner's collection, but wrongfully described as having appeared in the *North American Review* in 1899."

5. Marrus, op. cit., p. 213.

6. Ibid., p. 215.

7. Robert Gauthier, *"Dreyfusards!" Souvenirs de Mathieu Dreyfus et Autres Inédits,* Paris, 1956, p. 86.

8. George D. Painter, *Marcel Proust, A Biography,* London, Chatto & Windus, 1959, vol. 2, p. 329.

9. See *"L'Âme de Dreyfus,"* by Édouard Drumont, *La Libre Parole,* December 26, 1894; reprinted in H. R. Kedward, *The Dreyfus Affair, Catalyst for Tensions in French Society,* London, Longmans, 1965, p. 59.

10. *"La Justice,"* November 17, 1894, and *"L'Écho de Paris,"* December 31, 1894.

11. Marrus, op. cit., p. 181.

12. Elmer Berger, *The Jewish Dilemma,* New York, Devin-Adair, 1946; chapter "For Free Jews in a Free World," pp. 169–208.

13. Bein, op. cit., English edition, pp. 114–15.

14. *Complete Diaries,* p. 99.

15. N. M. Gelber, "The Testaments of Herzl," in *Herzl Year Book,* vol. 3, pp. 257–68.

Chapter 17: pages 171-179

1. From "King of the Jews" in *Theodor Herzl: A Memorial,* ed. Meyer W. Weisgal, New York, 1929.

2. Maria E. Delle Grazie, "Father and King, A Remembrance of Herzl's Views on Jewish Destiny," also in *A Memorial,* p. 40.

3. "We are bad soldiers, because we are devoid of honor, because there is nothing for us beyond death." *Complete Diaries,* p. 71.

4. Chouraqui, op. cit., p. 80.

5. Bein, for example, p. 118 (English edition).

6. *Complete Diaries,* p. 11.

7. Ibid., p. 12.

8. Ibid., p. 13.

9. Ibid., p. 13.

10. Ibid., p. 24.

11. Herzl says (ibid., p. 24) that the notes were dated and that he would ask his father to enter them in the Diary.

12. For Baron de Hirsch, see Samuel J. Lee, *Moses of the New World, The Work of Baron de Hirsch,* New York, Thomas Yoseloff, 1970. For marriage, p. 102.

13. For the letter and its circumstances, see *Complete Diaries,* pp. 13–17.

14. Ibid., p. 14.

15. Ibid., p. 16.

16. For Herzl's preparations, and for the account of his visit to de Hirsch, see ibid., pp. 17–24.

17. Describing the Tanagra statuettes in the Greco-Roman Museum in Alexandria, E. M. Forster says they "were at first connected with funeral rites and later placed in the tomb from the sentiment that prompts us to drop flowers, especially when the dead person is young. They have mostly been found in the tombs of children and women. They are the loveliest things in the Museum." *Alexandria*, New York, Doubleday, 1961, p. 129.

18. Samuel J. Lee, op. cit., p. 16. The following direct quotation: *Complete Diaries*, p. 22.

19. Max Nordau, *The Conventional Lies of Our Civilization*, Chicago, 1895, p. 61.

20. Oxford English Dictionary.

21. *Degeneration*, tr. from 2nd ed. of the German work; reprinted New York, Howard Fertig, 1968; Introduction by George L. Mosse, p. xxiii.

22. *Complete Diaries*, p. 276.

23. In the closing paragraphs of Nordau's address to the 1897 Zionist Congress: quoted by David Baron in *The Ancient Scriptures and the Modern Jew*, London, 1900.

24. "Israel Zangwill is of the long-nosed Negroid type, with very woolly deep-black hair . . . his point of view is a racial one—which I cannot accept if I so much look at him and at myself." *Complete Diaries*, p. 276.

Chapter 18: pages 181-192

1. *Complete Diaries*, p. 26.
2. Ibid., p. 25.
3. Ibid., p. 27.
4. Ibid., p. 28.
5. Ibid., p. 37.
6. Ibid., p. 105.
7. Ibid., p. 33. Patai has Nemec; probably Herzl used the French *c* to terminate the Hungarian name Nemes.
8. Ibid., p. 33.
9. Ibid., p. 38.
10. Op. cit., p. 375.
11. *Complete Diaries*, p. 63.
12. Ibid., p. 38.
13. Ibid., p. 40.
14. Ibid., p. 33.
15. Ibid., p. 40.
16. Ibid., p. 56.
17. Ibid., p. 40.
18. Ibid., p. 106.
19. Ibid., p. 60.
20. Ibid., p. 42.

21. Ibid., p. 29.
22. Ibid., p. 58.
23. Ibid., p. 52.
24. Ibid., p. 62.
25. Ibid., p. 65; also see ibid, p. 170: "We shall impose extensive but firm limits on public opinion, especially in the beginning."
26. Ibid., p. 68.
27. Ibid., pp. 57 and 127.
28. Ibid., p. 36.
29. Ibid., p. 39.
30. Ibid., p. 55.
31. Ibid., p. 39.
32. Ibid., p. 57.
33. Ibid., p. 47.
34. Ibid., p. 57.
35. Ibid., p. 40.
36. Ibid., p. 34.
37. Ibid., p. 231.
38. Ibid., p. 56.
39. Ibid., pp. 69–70 and 92.
40. Ibid., p. 98.
41. de Haas, op. cit., p. 99.
42. *Vide* unpublished Memoir in the State Archives Berlin-Dahlem, quoted in *Herzl Year Book*, vol. 6, p. 61.
43. Arthur F. Basil Williams, *Cecil Rhodes*, New York, Greenwood Press, 1968, p. 50.
44. Besides Williams, op. cit., see, for this last quotation, article by Alfred Peter Hillier and Frank R. Cana on Rhodesia in the thirteenth edition of the Encyclopaedia Britannica; also J. G. McDonald, *Rhodes, A Heritage*, London, Chatto & Windus, 1943; also Lewis H. Gann, *A History of Southern Rhodesia: Early Days to 1934*, London, Chatto & Windus, 1965.
45. *Complete Diaries*, p. 88.
46. Ibid., p. 212.
47. Ibid., p. 88.
48. Ibid., p. 90.
49. Ibid., p. 90.
50. *Degeneration*, op. cit., p. xix.
51. *Complete Diaries*, pp. 88–89.

Chapter 19: pages 193-196

1. Kellner, op. cit., p. 157.
2. See *Complete Diaries*, under relevant dates, for texts of Herzl's letters to Güdemann.
3. Ibid., p. 102.
4. See footnote to page 29.

5. *Complete Diaries*, p. 115.
6. Ibid., p. 115, dated June 18.
7. Ibid., p. 116.
8. Ibid., p. 126.
9. Ibid., p. 120.

Chapter 20: pages 199-206

1. *Complete Diaries*, June 10, 1895, p. 67.

2. Ibid., p. 438.

3. Ibid., p. 115.

4. Arthur Stern, "The Genetic Tragedy of the Family of Theodor Herzl," *The Israel Annals of Psychiatry and Related Disciplines*, vol. 3, no. 1, April 1965.

5. *Complete Diaries*, p. 368.

6. Ibid., p. 402.

7. Peter Loewenberg, op. cit., p. 167.

8. *Complete Diaries*, p. 91.

9. Loewenberg, op. cit., p. 171.

10. In "The Jewish State," as edited by Arthur Hertzberg in *The Zionist Idea; A Historical Analysis and Reader*, New York, Harper Torchbooks, 1959, p. 225.

11. *Complete Diaries*, p. 230.

12. Ibid., p. 233.

13. Ibid., pp. 242–43.

14. Ibid., p. 244.

15. Ibid., p. 256.

16. Ibid., p. 261.

17. Ibid., p. 469.

18. Bein, op. cit., English edition, p. 153.

19. *Complete Diaries*, p. 266.

Chapter 21: pages 207-213

1. "Our headquarters will be in London because in matters of civil law we must be under the protection of a great nation which is not anti-Semitic at the present." *Complete Diaries*, p. 144.

2. Ibid., p. 272.

3. Ibid.

4. George Kirk, *A Short History of the Middle East*, London, 1945, p. 147. See also Adel Ismail, *Histoire du Liban*, Paris, 1955.

5. *Complete Diaries*, p. 276.

6. Ibid., p. 171.

7. To Arminius Vámbéry, June 21, 1900; *Complete Diaries*, p. 967.

8. *Theodor Herzl: A Memorial*, pp. 73–74.

9. Document dated August 23, 1917, CAB24/24, marked Secret, *Circulated by the Secretary of State for India*.

10. *Complete Diaries*, p. 280.

11. Ibid., p. 282.

12. Ibid., p. 283.

13. Ibid., p. 284.

Chapter 22: pages 215-222

1. See *Guide Juif de France*, Paris, 1971, p. 50, for a photograph of the plaque.

2. Cf. Walter Laqueur, *A History of Zionism*, London, 1972, p. xiii.

3. *Complete Diaries*, p. 848.

4. Ibid., p. 851.

5. Ibid., p. 286.

6. Ibid., p. 285.

7. Ibid., p. 299.

8. Harrap's Standard German-English Dictionary, 1967, agrees with Muret-Sanders, 1897, published about the time Herzl was writing, in giving the primary meaning of *Herstellung* as establishment, creation; Muret-Sanders gives a secondary meaning with *Wieder* in brackets, as restoration, while Harrap gives this meaning as archaic. Grimm cites examples from Goethe and Schiller for the use of *Herstellung* as an abbreviation for *Wiederherstellung*. If the pamphlet harked back to the state of David, it might be possible to argue for "restoration" as the correct translation. Such harking back is absent.

9. *Complete Diaries*, p. 237, for first use of figure.

10. Arthur Hertzberg's edition of *Der Judenstaat*, in *The Zionist Idea*, p. 209.

11. Ibid., p. 212.

12. Ibid., p. 213.

13. Ibid., p. 214.

14. The translation given by de Haas, op. cit., p. 79.

15. Herzberg, op. cit., pp. 219–20.

16. Ibid., p. 220.

17. Ibid., p. 220.

18. Ibid., p. 221.

19. Ibid., pp. 222–23.

20. Ibid., p. 225.

21. *Complete Diaries*, p. 229.

22. Ibid., p. 317.

23. The first, Anton Bettelheim (1851–1930), in *Münchner Allgemeine Zeitung:* "We reject Herzl's *Judenstaat* with greater distaste than the meanest anti-Semitic pamphlet." The second, Dr. Julius V. Gans-Ludassy (1858–1922), in *Wiener Allgemeine Zeitung*, which he edited 1894–1902, when he took over editorship of the *Neue Freie Presse*.

24. *Complete Diaries*, p. 308.

25. Ibid., entry for March 26, 1896, p. 316.

Chapter 23: pages 223-233

1. *Complete Diaries,* p. 310.
2. Revelation XII:2. The Jerusalem Bible translates as "pagans," earlier versions as "gentiles."
3. Hechler works out his prophecies in a letter to the Grand Duke of Baden, March 26, 1896, reproduced in facsimile in *Herzl, Hechler, the Grand Duke of Baden and the German Emperor: 1896-1904,* documents found by Hermann and Bess Ellern and reproduced in facsimile, Tel Aviv, Ellerns' Bank Ltd., 1961.
4. Ellern, op. cit., item 15, p. 7.
5. *Complete Diaries,* pp. 462–64.
6. Ibid., p. 323.
7. Ibid., p. 323.
8. Ibid., p. 331. For the interview with the Grand Duke of Baden: pp. 328–41.
9. Herzl probably refers to Britain and its desire to monopolize control of the Suez Canal area.
10. *Complete Diaries,* p. 342.
11. Ibid., p. 342.
12. Ibid., p. 390. For Nevlinsky, see N. M. Gelber, *"Philipp Michael de Newlinski: Herzls Diplomatic Agent,"* in *Herzl Year Book,* vol. 2, 1959.
13. *Complete Diaries,* p. 390. I have changed "I don't care a *rap,*" to *"fig."*
14. Israel Cohen, *Theodor Herzl,* p. 208.
15. *Complete Diaries,* p. 344.
16. Dr. Louis Poborski to N. M. Gelber, op. cit., p. 118.
17. *Complete Diaries,* p. 346.
18. Ibid., p. 348.
19. Ibid., p. 349.
20. Ibid., p. 354.
21. Ibid., p. 356.
22. Denis Mack Smith, *Victor Emmanuel, Cavour, and the Risorgimento,* London, 1971, p. 34. The original source occurs in *La Liberazione del Mezzogiorno e la Formazione del Regno d'Italia,* Carteggi di Camillo Cavour: 5 vols., Bologna, 1949–54.
23. *Complete Diaries,* p. 359.
24. Ibid., p. 362.

Chapter 24: pages 235-244

1. *Complete Diaries,* p. 367. All the material in this chapter is based on pp. 366–403 of the *Complete Diaries.* References are only provided for certain, more important quotations.
2. Ibid., p. 370.
3. Ibid., p. 378.

4. Ibid., p. 395.
5. Ibid., p. 399.

hapter 25: pages 245-257

1. *Complete Diaries*, p. 411.
2. Ibid., p. 416.
3. Ibid., p. 420.
4. *Some Early Herzl Letters*, ed. Alex Bein, *Herzl Year Book*, vol. 1, p. 310.
5. *Complete Diaries*, p. 42.
6. Dr. Shalom Spiegel, *Theodor Herzl: A Memorial*, p. 92.
7. *Complete Diaries*, p. 317.
8. *Jewish Vegetarian*, London, autumn issue, 1967.
9. See Julius Jung, *The Light* (Journal of the Federation of Orthodox Synagogues), London, September 1967.
10. See article by Minnie Timkin, *Jewish Review*, March 3, 1971.
11. Paul Goodman, *The Rise of English Zionism*, *Theodor Herzl: A Memorial*, p. 77.
12. Pamphlet (undated) entitled *Kamenitzer Maggid Hall of Education / at Bar Ilan University / Israel: Rabbi Chaim Zundel Maccoby 1858–1916*. Professor Sir Isaiah Berlin, C.B.E., M.A., F.B.A., who salutes "the memory of this brave man whose political courage was very great," gives no indication of the precise direction in which the Maggid's courage had been deployed.
13. Chaim Bloch, "Theodor Herzl and Joseph S. Bloch," *Herzl Year Book*, vol. 1, p. 156.
14. Ibid., p. 157.
15. Adolf Jellinek, *The Talmud, Two Speeches*, Vienna, 1868.
16. Bloch, op. cit., p. 159.
17. N. M. Gelber, "Herzl's Polish Contacts," *Herzl Year Book*, vol. 1, pp. 211–19.
18. See facsimile of Daudet letter in André Chouraqui, *Théodore Herzl: Inventeur de l'état d'Israël*, Paris, Éditions du Seuil, 1960.
19. *"Ils ne voient pas en nous des énergumènes, des maniaques, des êtres barbares et sans coeur, mais des citoyens qui usent du droit de légitime défense."*
20. Bloch, op. cit., p. 155.
21. Gelber, "Herzl's Polish Contacts," p. 214.
22. Ibid., p. 215.
23. Werner J. Cahnman, "Scholar and Visionary, The Correspondence between Herzl and Ludwig Gumplowicz," *Herzl Year Book*, vol. 1, p. 177.
24. Herzl's *Complete Diaries*, p. 556, shows the typography.
25. Ibid., p. 551.
26. Ibid., p. 560.
27. Ibid., p. 428.

28. Ibid., p. 430.

29. Ibid., p. 447.

30. Ibid., p. 581.

31. Walter Laqueur, *The Israel/Arab Reader; A Documentary History of the Middle East Conflict,* London, Weidenfeld and Nicolson, 1969, p. 11.

32. Christopher Sykes, *Cross Roads to Israel,* London, Collins, 1965, p. 32.

33. *Complete Diaries,* p. 581.

34. Ibid., p. 578.

35. Erwin Rosenberger, "The First Congress," *Herzl Year Book,* vol. 1, p. 288.

36. *Complete Diaries,* pp. 585, 586, 578, 577.

37. Ibid., p. 587.

Chapter 26: pages 259-276

1. *Complete Diaries,* p. 609.

2. Joseph Patai, "Herzl's School Years," *Herzl Year Book,* vol. 3, p. 55.

3. *Complete Diaries,* p. 651.

4. Cf. Hechler's letter to Grand Duke of Baden, September 26, 1898, reproduced in Ellern, op. cit., item 15, p. 2.

5. *Complete Diaries,* p. 665.

6. Letter cited in note 4, ibid., p. 4.

7. *Complete Diaries,* p. 662.

8. Ibid., p. 664.

9. Ibid., pp. 665–68, for Bülow interview.

10. Text of letter from Rominten, dated September 27, 1898, preserved in Eulenburg's handwriting in Central Zionist Archives and translated in *Herzl Year Book,* vol. 6, pp. 63–64.

11. de Haas, op. cit., p. 237.

12. *Complete Diaries,* p. 694.

13. Ibid., p. 693.

14. Ibid., pp. 697–700, for interview with Grand Duke of Baden.

15. Ibid., pp. 701–4, for interview with von Bülow and Hohenlohe.

16. *Denkwürdigkeiten des Fürsten Chlodwig zu Hohenlohe-Schillingsfürst,* Stuttgart, vol. II, 1907, p. 533.

17. Henriette Hannah Bodenheimer, *Im Anfang der Zionistischen Bewegung,* Frankfurt a.M., 1965, p. 110.

18. *Complete Diaries,* p. 711.

19. Ibid., pp. 716, 717, for text of letter to Kaiser.

20. Ibid., p. 722.

21. To Z. H. Masliansky, described as "Dean of Zionist propagandists in this country [the United States]," *Theodor Herzl: A Memorial,* p. 76.

22. All Herzl quotations about his visit to Palestine come between pp. 737–65, *Complete Diaries.*

23. Quoted in Nevill Barbour's *Nisi Dominus, A Survey of the Palestine Controversy,* London, Harrap, 1946, p. 32.

24. L. Oliphant, *Haifa, or Life in Modern Palestine*, London, 1887, pp. 59, 60.

25. Chouraqui, *A Man Alone*, p. 136.

26. Denys Page, *Sappho and Alcaeus*, Oxford, 1955, p. 20.

27. *The Mizrachi Woman*, vol. 27, no. 4 (December 1954), p. 6.

28. *Allgemeine Zeitung*, München, November 3, 1898.

29. Quoted by Bein, *Herzl Year Book*, vol. 6, p. 76.

30. *The Times*, London, October 28, 1898.

31. *Complete Diaries*, p. 1,021.

32. Ellern, op. cit., item 47. Ellern attributes the *aide-mémoire* to the German Foreign Office, in reply to a letter from the Grand Duke of Baden.

33. Von Bülow, *Denkwürdigkeiten*, Berlin, 1930, vol. 1, p. 254.

34. See essay by Bein, "Herzl's Meeting with the Kaiser," *Herzl Year Book*, vol. 6, for manuscript sources for the quotations from the Kaiser and Eulenburg.

Chapter 27: pages 279-290

1. *Complete Diaries*, p. 1,062.

2. See Bertha von Suttner, *Memoiren*, Stuttgart, 1908.

3. *Complete Diaries*, p. 848.

4. Ibid., p. 849.

5. Ibid., p. 968.

6. Ibid., p. 1,155.

7. Ibid., p. 1,206.

8. A. H. Reich, *In Memoriam*, published in *A Memorial*.

9. *Complete Diaries*, p. 979.

10. Ibid., p. 841.

11. S. S. Sarna, *Early British Zionism;* unpublished typescript of twelve pages, the property of Mr. N. M. Brilliant.

12. *Complete Diaries*, p. 1,461.

13. Ibid., p. 421.

14. Ibid., p. 874. Herzl reprints the interview.

15. Ibid., p. 942.

16. Ibid., p. 1,158.

17. Ibid., p. 1,161.

18. Ibid., p. 637.

19. Ibid., p. 863.

20. *Herzl Year Book*, vol. 3, pp. 257–68.

21. *Complete Diaries*, p. 1,051.

22. Ibid., p. 1,196.

23. Ibid., p. 451.

24. Ibid., p. 1,105. Two days later he qualifies this statement: "Excursions to the Bosphorous whose beauty finally did stir even my hardened heart."

25. Ibid., p. 961.

26. Ibid., p. 967.

27. Ibid., p. 1,164.

28. Ibid., p. 960.

29. Ibid., p. 1,181.

30. Ibid., p. 1,339.

31. Ibid., p. 1,334.

32. Ibid., p. 1,341.

33. de Haas, op. cit., p. 80.

34. This description is his final recollection as he sails away on the *Principessa Maria. Complete Diaries*, p. 1,128. There is another description of the Sultan two days earlier, p. 1,112.

35. Ibid., p. 1,122.

Chapter 28: pages 291-299

1. *Complete Diaries*, p. 920.

2. Ibid., p. 886.

3. Ibid., p. 959.

4. Ibid., p. 1,040.

5. Ibid., p. 1,071.

6. Ibid., pp. 370, 409 and 514.

7. Ibid., p. 1,169.

8. Ibid., p. 1,265.

9. Leslie A. Fiedler, *Waiting for the End, the American Literary Scene from Hemingway to Baldwin*, Harmondsworth, England, Pelican Books, 1967, p. 76.

10. *Complete Diaries*, p. 741.

11. Ibid., p. 1,356. On January 23, 1904, Victor Emmanuel III of Italy asked to see a copy of the book, "if possible not in German." On February 23, 1904, Herzl sent him a translation which had appeared in an American magazine.

12. Ibid., p. 852.

13. Ibid., p. 856.

14. *Old-New Land*, New York, 1960, p. xix.

15. Ibid., p. 252.

16. Ibid., p. 259.

Chapter 29: pages 301-308

1. *Complete Diaries*, p. 1,283.

2. See Oskar K. Rabinowicz, "Davis Trietsch's Colonization Scheme in Cyprus," *Herzl Year Book*, vol. 4, pp. 119–206.

3. G. Sil-Vara, *Theodor Herzl: A Memorial*, p. 21.

4. *Complete Diaries*, p. 1,292.

5. Ibid., p. 1,294.

6. Ibid., p. 1,361.

7. Ibid., p. 1,361.

8. Ibid., p. 1,355.

9. *"Interessant ist nur das, was hinter den Kulissen gespielt wird,"* *Herzl-Worte*, p. 89.

10. *Complete Diaries*, p. 1,372.

11. The text of this letter, as of other documents to do with Herzl's Egyptian negotiations, *Herzl Year Book*, vol. 1, p. 114 *et passim*.

12. *Complete Diaries*, p. 1,425.

13. Ibid., p. 1,417.

14. Ibid., p. 1,430.

15. Ibid., p. 1,428.

16. Ibid., p. 1,430.

17. Ibid., p. 1,437.

Chapter 30: pages 309-312

1. The *feuilleton* that appeared in the *Neue Freie Presse* on April 12, 1903, was published in book form in vol. 2 of Herzl's *Feuilletons*, Berlin, 1903.

2. *Complete Diaries*, p. 1,446.

3. Letter from British Agency, March 28, 1903; cf. Raphael Patai, "Herzl's Sinai Project," *Herzl Year Book*, vol. 1, p. 116.

4. *Complete Diaries*, p. 1,449.

5. See *Report of the Sinai Technical Commission*, Appendix to Raphael Patai, op. cit.

6. All quotations about theaters, visitors, in the *Egyptian Gazette*, portions of which were printed in French.

Chapter 31: pages 313-326

1. *Herzl Year Book*, vol. 1, p. 120.

2. *Complete Diaries*, p. 1,491.

3. A. H. Reich, *In Memoriam*, in *Theodor Herzl: A Memorial*.

4. *Complete Diaries*, p. 1,498, for interview with Count Paraty; p. 1,511 for letter to Franz Philippson; pp. 1,614–17, 1,619–20 for Ali Nuri Bey and his scheme. Herzl proposed a twelve thousand pounds bribe to Izzet Bey on December 12, 1902, p. 1,574.

5. For Chamberlain interview, *Complete Diaries*, pp. 1,473–75.

6. *Atlas of Uganda*, Department of Lands and Surveys, Uganda, 1962.

7. F. O. Document 785. Cecil James Barrington Hurst, assistant to the legal adviser to the Foreign Office, has annotated Herzl's *Jewish Colonisation Scheme* with critical notes typed in black. Using red ink, Lord Lansdowne has ticked portions of the Memorandum which he approves (such as Herzl's suggestions about taxation), has underlined some of Hurst's strictures and added, beside his comment on the *imperium in imperio*, "But there might be natives within the assigned area and it would be necessary to provide for their protection."

8. *Memoirs of Count Witte,* London, 1921, p. 380.

9. *Complete Diaries,* p. 888.

10. Czar's letter reproduced in facsimile, Ellern, op. cit., p. 79.

11. The intermediary was Paulina Korvin-Piatrovska, Polish author, Zionist sympathizer and friend of Plehve. *Complete Diaries,* p. 1,514.

12. Plehve interview, *Complete Diaries,* pp. 1,522–32.

13. Weizmann, The Letters and Papers of, vol. 3, Series A, Sept. 1903–Dec. 1904, ed. Meyer W. Weisgal, Oxford, 1972, p. 332.

14. *The Times,* August 24, 1903.

15. Bein, op. cit., English edition, p. 457.

16. *"Der Feind aber ist der eiserne Reifen der Nation,"* Herzl-Worte, p. 11.

17. *Complete Diaries,* p. 527.

18. Ibid., pp. 1,616–17.

19. Weizmann Papers, op. cit., p. 77: in a passage where Weizmann comments that Zangwill, like Nordau, "is completely hypnotized by Herzl."

Chapter 32: pages 327-332

1. *The Times,* August 26, 1903.

2. *Complete Diaries,* p. 1,575.

3. For Nordau, *The Times,* August 25, 1903; for Zangwill, at meeting of the English Zionist Federation, September 5, 1903, *The Times,* September 7, 1903.

4. This letter, dated August 14, 1903, was sent to Greenberg on receipt from Chamberlain of the letter from Greenberg of July 13, 1903, containing Herzl's scheme for an African Jewish settlement. *The Times* published Sir Clement Hill's letter on August 26, 1903.

5. Lansdowne's letter of October 15, 1903, refers to a dispatch of the fourteenth numbered 459 "which will indicate how far H.M. Government would be prepared to go in furthering the scheme."

6. Sir Charles Eliot's letter of November 4, 1903, was written from Commissioner's Office, Mombasa.

7. Eliot included the bishop's letter in a dispatch of March 24, 1904.

8. The above dispatch confirmed in more detail a telegraphic dispatch of February 11, 1904. This also referred to a large grant of land to the East Africa Syndicate.

9. *Complete Diaries,* p. 1,592; he made the entry at 5 A.M. For the rest of Herzl's stay in Rome, for his interviews with King Victor Emmanuel III and the Pope, see ibid., pp. 1,591–1,607.

Chapter 33: pages 333-341

1. *Complete Diaries,* p. 1,628.

2. Besides Dr. Siegmund Werner, we hear of Dr. A. Konried and Professors Singer and Ortner: Nussenblatt, op. cit., p. 284.

3. Ibid.: *"Dr. A. Konried bezeichnet als die Todesurache Chronische Herzmuskelentzündung: Myocarditis chronica. Die Professoren Singer und Ortner die Herzl behandelten namen eine fortschreitende Herzmuskelerkrankung an."*

4. Dr. T. H. M. Stewart in association with Dr. Jules Eli Harris, Ottawa General Hospital.

5. Dr. Wolf Guttmann, Nussenblatt, op. cit., pp. 284ff.

6. Not to be ignored, and not ignored by Guttmann, the chronic suppuration in the wake of his treatment for malaria contracted at Toulon.

7. Stephen J. Kraus, *Complications of Gonococcal Infection,* The Medical Clinics of North America: Symposium on Venereal Diseases, 56, no. 5, 1972, pp. 115–25.

8. S. Alfred Adler, *Jewish Chronicle,* July 8, 1904.

9. According to information given to the author by Mark Braham.

10. May 20, 1910.

11. Bein, op. cit., German edition, p. 682; English edition, p. 500.

12. *Jewish Chronicle* version of *Die Welt* story, July 15, 1904.

13. From *The First Disciple,* in *Theodor Herzl: A Memorial,* 1929.

14. *Jewish Chronicle,* July 15, 1904.

15. *Weizmann Papers,* op. cit., p. 328.

16. Ibid., Letter to Zvi Aberson of July 9, 1904.

17. R. S. Morton, op. cit., p. 60.

18. Arthur Stern, op. cit., p. 111.

19. Madame Maxa Nordau in a letter to Dr. M. Clarke dated September 21, 1972.

20. Stern, op. cit., p. 104.

21. *Herzl Year Book,* vol. 1, p. 310, footnote.

22. Stern, op. cit., p. 108; as for other details of Trude's plight.

Epilogue : pages 343-345

1. Alfred Werner, "The Tragedy of Ephraim Moses Lilien," *Herzl Year Book,* vol 2.

2. Israel Zangwill, *Jewish Chronicle,* July 15, 1904.

3. *Clemenceau Remembers Herzl,* as told to Pierre Van Paassen, *Theodor Herzl: A Memorial,* p. 27.

4. Leo Goldhammer, *"Herzl and Freud";* in *Herzl Year Book,* vol. 1, p. 195.

5. Adolf Hitler, *Mein Kampf,* tr. James Murphy, London, 1939, pp. 58–59.

6. *La Libre Parole,* A. de Boisandré, July 11, 1904.

7. See Norman Cohn, op. cit., p. 69.

8. Letter to Heinrich Kana, September 4, 1882, Central Zionist Archives, Jerusalem. *"Schmerz ist das Grundgefühl des Lebens und die Freude ist nur dann, wenn zufällig der Schmerz eine Weile nicht ist."*

APPENDIX I: HERZL'S PLAYS

1884 *Tabarin:* Drama in One Act; 1885, New York.

1885 *Muttersöhnchen* (Mother's Little Boy): Comedy in Four Acts.

1885 *Seine Hoheit* (His Highness): Comedy in Three Acts; 1888, Prague, Berlin, Vienna, Breslau.

1887 *Der Flüchtling* (The Fugitive): Comedy in One Act; 1889, Vienna.

1888 *Wilddiebe* (Poachers): Comedy in Four Acts, in collaboration with Hugo Wittmann (1839–1923); 1888, Vienna.

1889 *Was wird man sagen?* (What Will People Say?): Comedy in Four Acts; 1890, Prague, Berlin.

1889 *Prinzen aus Genieland* (Princes from Genie-Land): Comedy in Four Acts; 1891, Vienna.

1890 *Die Dame in Schwarz* (The Lady in Black): Comedy in Four Acts, in collaboration with Hugo Wittmann; 1891, Vienna.

1890 *Des Teufels Weib* (The Devil's Wife): Text for Operetta; 1890, Vienna.

1894 *Die Glosse* (The Marginal Note): Verse Comedy in One Act.

1894 *Das Neue Ghetto* (The New Ghetto): Drama in Four Acts: 1898, Vienna; then Berlin and Hamburg.

1899 *Unser Kätchen* (Our Katie): Comedy in Four Acts; 1899, Vienna and Prague.

1899 *Gretel* (original title, *Die Sündige Mutter,* or The Guilty Mother): Drama in Four Acts; 1900, Vienna.

1900 *Solon in Lydien* (Solon in Lydia): Conundrum Play; 1903, Prague.

1900 *I Love You* (English title in German original): Comedy in One Act; 1900, Vienna.

APPENDIX II: HERZL'S MARRIAGE

On the most important event in Herzl's personal life the documentation is all but non-existent: any discussion of it must be based more on a priori reasoning than reported facts. For more than half a century the one, over-used source was Leon Kellner's laconic sentence published in 1920: "The nuptials [in German *Hochzeit*] took place on July 25, 1889, at Reichenau, in the Rax and Schneeberg district."[1] The succeeding biographers have simply reworked this statement, though Mr. Josef Fraenkel wisely gave no month[2] while Dr. Bein, in his German *Biographie*, gave the correct date, June 25, only to have the incorrect date restored by his English translator.[3] Josef Patai (who also got the right date) made a one-word addition to Kellner's account by describing the nuptials as *ünnepélyes*, which his English version translates as "festive." M. André Chouraqui, at the end of a line of hagiographers, has the following description: "The engagement was quickly celebrated and the marriage fixed for July 25, 1889. At Reichenau near Vienna, with great ceremony, Theodor Herzl and Julie Nashauer [sic] were united in matrimony."[4]

The false date posed problems which writers on Herzl were to confront in different ways. Pauline was born on March 29, 1890. While M. Chouraqui, the committed Zionist, writes that Julie "gave birth prematurely,"[5] the uncommitted Peter Loewenberg writes: "There is no record of this child having been premature. If she was a full-term baby, we may say from all the evidence that she was a child of love."[6] The establishment of the correct date—June 25—removes this problem.

But other problems remain. These almost certainly stem from the conflict of two legal systems, Austro-Hungarian state law and *halacha*, the Jewish traditional law.

According to Thomas Dolliner's authoritative *Handbuch des österreichischen Eherechts*, Vienna, 1849, vol. 1, marriage in the Dual Monarchy was a civil contract and belonged to the state (p. 59). The only impediments to marriage were those laid down by the state: madness, mistaken identity, lack of means, adultery, pregnancy (of the bride by a third party), omission of publication of banns, solemn religious vows, existing marriage tie, consanguinity, being a minor, forced consent or difference of religion (p. 63). Marriage between an unbaptized Jew and a Christian was invalid in Austria-Hungary; even a marriage between, for example, a Hungarian Jew and a Protestant Prussian woman solemnized in Berlin (which recognized interfaith unions) was not recognized as valid in the Dual Monarchy.[7] Other religious impediments had no validity. A Jewish marriage (ibid., vol. V, author Ignaz Grassl) was also a state marriage; like Catholics and Protestants, Jews were subject to the state law of marriage. Emperor Josef II (1785–86) had suppressed the rabbinical courts (which till then had decided on Jewish marriage) and had subjected Jewish marriage to the civil law (ibid., p. 10). The one concession to Jewish tradition covered consanguinity, on which the Jewish laws were freer: but even here a certificate of the relationship had to be submitted to ensure that state laws were not being violated. A Jewish marriage was required to be performed by a rabbi or a religious teacher of the *Hauptgemeinde* (chief Jewish community) of one of the couple, in the presence of two witnesses (p. 49, para. 127). Rabbis or religious teachers were required by state law to keep a marriage register according to the law of the land or be subject to fines or corporal punishment, with subsequent permanent dismissal from their functions (ibid., para. 131). In 1868 the basic law relating to marriage was modified in the Austrian empire. (See *Verfassungs und Staatsgrundgesetze; Allegemeines Bürgerliches Gesetzbuch*, ed. Leo Geller, Vienna, 1898.) Under the new law a couple whose pastor (the German *Seelsorger* covers priest, minister and rabbi) refused for any reason to celebrate the marriage were given the right to be married before a secular authority, the *Bezirksbehörde*. This civil authority would send an extract of the marriage certificate to the religious authority who had refused to conduct the marriage. "The pastor who had refused to celebrate the marriage must on reception of the marriage certificate from the secular authority enter up, in the register delivered to him by the state for marriages, in continuous order with the preceding entry, the particulars of the marriage and of the witnesses thereto" (ibid., p. 187).

To sum up: in the eyes of the Austrian state both Theodor and Julie were Jews (since they had not been baptized and were children of parents known to be members of the Jewish community) and eligible as such for a marriage which should be by a rabbi or religious teacher but could be by a civil authority and which had to be registered in the marriage registry of the Leopoldstadt Jewish community. For them to have married in any other way would have been impossible, unless they had both accepted baptism. The modern form of secular marriage in a registry office only became possible in Austria after the 1938 Anschluss with Nazi Germany, when more onerous burdens were to be placed upon Jews. The fact that Herzl's marriage was registered, "in continuous order with the preceding entry," in the Leopoldstadt Jewish community register establishes that neither Theodor nor Julie had been baptized. It does not, unfortunately, tell what kind of religious ceremony, if any, accompanied the festive *Hochzeit* at Reichenau.

So much for the position of Dr. Theodor Herzl and Fräulein Julie Naschauer in the eyes of the state of which both were subjects. The rabbis who maintained *halacha* had different criteria. To them, the question of "Who is a Jew?" was decided on the basis of the mother's status. On the one hand, a change of religion did not remove Jewishness. "The apostate, even the apostate who does great harm to Jewry, is classified as a Jew who has sinned. A *cherem* (ostracism) may deprive him of all privileges, may consign him to an ass's funeral; but as long as he lives, he remains under obligation, and his children are Jews."[8] On the other hand, no *pro forma* conversion (similar to the social baptisms often performed in those days) could confer Jewishness. If Julie's mother, or maternal grandmother, was not Jewish according to *halacha*, Julie herself was not a Jew and her children would not be Jewish either. A non-Jewish woman could only become Jewish (at least in the religious climate of nineteenth-century Vienna) by a thoroughgoing conversion accompanied by domestic adherence to Jewish law over a period of time.

That this conflict between two legal systems explains the marriage in Reichenau is confirmed by Jacob Naschauer's decision to marry another of his daughters, Helene, in the same place and the same month of the following year.[9]

APPENDIX II: NOTES

1. Op. cit., p. 93: *"Die Hochzeit fand am 25. Juli, 1889 zu Reichenau im Rax-und-Schneeberg-Gebiet statt."*

2. *Theodor Herzl, A Biography,* op. cit., p. 41.

3. Op. cit., p. 63. "On July 25, 1889, the marriage was celebrated in the watering-place of Reichenau."

4. Op. cit., p. 40.

5. Ibid., p. 41.

6. Op. cit., p. 158.

7. *Österreichische Gesetze,* Erste Abteilung Österreichische Justizgesetze, Wien, 1882, Band I, Verfassungs und Staatsgrundgesetze, Allgemeines Bürgerliches Gesetzbuch, Part I, ch. II, Von dem Eherechte, p. 54, note 4.

8. Gerald Abrahams, *Jewish Chronicle,* January 22, 1971.

9. Schnitzler-Nickl, op. cit. Letter from Olga Waissnix in Reichenau to Arthur Schnitzler, June 12, 1890: *"Dienstag grosse Hochzeit Helene Naschauer. Miese Braut, mieser Bräutigam, alles greulich."*

APPENDIX III: HERZL'S YOUTH DIARY

The text of this important document only came to light after Hans Herzl's suicide. It fell to Mrs. Sala Leftwich, wife of the English Jewish author Josef Leftwich, to go through Hans's personal effects at Hampden House, a seedy lodging house for impecunious gentlemen near London's Euston Station. The notebook containing the Youth Diary was the only valuable find. Hans had been lent it by Reichenfeld, one of Herzl's three executors, some time before in the hope that the record of his father's early struggles might encourage his son. That Hans appreciated its value is shown in the last will and testament he drew up shortly before his death; the entry also testifies to his extremely scrupulous nature:

> I have a little notebook with MS notes by my father, which I think is worth a trifle. Someone may even be willing to offer a fairly large sum for it. Probably not less than £10 and not more than £50. Whichever it is I should like it to go to my cousin Frida Czopp. She is good-hearted and has never had a real chance. But first £40 to "Bill" Exner. I owe £40 to my old sergeant Bill Exner and £10 to Mr. Edward Good, antique jeweller, who advanced me that sum in return for a translation I made of a little book of his.

Mr. Josef Leftwich offered the notebook to a leading Zionist organization, who were not interested. Zalman Reisen then acquired it for the Jewish Scientific Institute in Vilna. Tulo Nussenblatt's version gives two thirds of the original; a Hebrew translation by Jacob Steinberg was published in Tel Aviv in 1934; the original manuscript is now in the Yiddish Scientific Institute, Fifth Avenue, New York City.

BIBLIOGRAPHY

NOTE   Instead of listing newspapers and periodicals separately, I have enclosed them in parentheses. I have listed Herzl's own works in this bibliography, and not in a separate section.

Adler, Rev. Dr. [Hermann]. *Religious Versus Political Zionism.* London: Alfred J. Isaacs & Son, 1898.
Adler, Joseph. *The Herzl Paradox: Political, Social and Economic Theories of a Realist.* New York: Hadrian Press, 1962.
Amery, Julian. *Life of Joseph Chamberlain.* London: 1951.
(*Archives Israélites*, Paris.)

Barbour, Nevill. *Nisi Dominus, A Survey of the Palestine Controversy.* London: Harrap, 1946.
Baretz, Leon. *Réalités et Rêveries du Ghetto.* Geneva: La Revue Juive de Genève, 1934.
Bein, Alex. 1. *Theodor Herzl Biographie.* Vienna: Fiba-Verlag, 1934.
   2. *Theodore Herzl, A Biography* (tr. Maurice Samuel). London: Horovitz Publishing Co. Ltd., East and West Library, 1957.
Bentwich, Norman, and John M. Shaftesley. "Forerunners of Zionism in the Victorian Era," in *Remember the Days, Essays in Honour of Cecil Roth.* Jewish Historical Society of England: 1966.
Berger, Elmer. *The Jewish Dilemma: The Case Against Jewish Nationalism.* New York: Devin-Adair Company, 1946.
Berlin, Isaiah. *The Life and Opinions of Moses Hess.* Jewish Historical Society of England: 1957.
Bithell, Jethro. *Modern German Literature 1880–1950.* London: Methuen, 1959.
Bodenheimer, Henriette Hannah. *Im Anfang der Zionistischen Bewegung.* Frankfurt a.M.: Europäische Verlagsanstalt, 1965.
Bouvier, Jean. *Les Rothschild.* Paris: Club Français du Livre, 1960.
Braham, Mark. *Jews Don't Hate—How a Jewish Newspaper Died.* Sydney: Nelson, 1970.
Brodetsky, Selig. *Memoirs. From Ghetto to Israel.* London: Weidenfeld & Nicolson, 1960.
Bülow, Bernhard von. *Denkwürdigkeiten.* Berlin: Ullstein, 1930.

Calder-Marshall, Arthur. *The Enthusiast, An Enquiry into the Life, Beliefs and Character of the Rev. Joseph Leycester Lyne, alias Fr. Ignatius.* London: Faber, 1962.

Chapman, Guy. *The Dreyfus Case, A Reassessment.* London: Rupert Hart-Davis, 1955.

Chouraqui, André. 1. *Théodore Herzl: Inventeur de l'état d'Israël.* Paris: Éditions du Seuil, 1960.

   2. *A Man Alone;* tr. Yael Guiladi. Jerusalem: Keter Publishing House, Ltd., 1960.

Cohen, Israel. *Theodor Herzl, Founder of Political Zionism.* New York: Thomas Yoseloff, 1959.

Cohn, Norman. *Warrant for Genocide, the Myth of the Jewish World-Conspiracy and the Protocols of the Elders of Zion.* London: Eyre & Spottiswoode, 1967.

Czerwinski, A. *Brevier der Tanzkunst.* Leipzig: 1887.

Dubnow, Simon. *Weltgeschichte des Jüdischen Volkes,* vol. x. Berlin: Jüdischer Verlag, 1929.

Elbogen, Ismar. *A Century of Jewish Life.* Philadelphia: The Jewish Publication Society of America, 1945.

Eliot, Sir Charles. *British East Africa.* London: Edward Arnold, 1904.

Ellern, Hermann and Bess. *Herzl, Hechler, The Grand Duke of Baden and the German Emperor: 1896–1904.* Documents found by, and reproduced in facsimile. Tel Aviv: Ellern's Bank Ltd., 1961.

Encyclopaedia Britannica, 13th edition.

Epstein, Isidore. *Judaism.* London: Penguin, 1959.

Fraenkel, Josef. 1. *Theodor Herzl: Des Schöpfers Erstes Wollen.* Vienna: Fiba-Verlag, 1934.

   2. *Theodor Herzl, A Biography.* London: "Ararat" Publishing Society Limited, 1946.

   3. *The Jews of Austria, Essays on Their Life, History and Destruction.* Ed. by Josef Fraenkel. London: Vallentine, Mitchell, 1967.

Gann, Lewis H. *A History of Southern Rhodesia: Early Days to 1934.* London: Chatto & Windus, 1965.

Gauthier, Robert. *'Dreyfusards!' Souvenirs de Mathieu Dreyfus et Autres Inédits.* Paris: Julliard, 1956.

Georg, Manfred. *Theodor Herzl, sein Leben und sein Vermächtnis.* Berlin: R. A. Höger, 1932.

Grant, A. F., and Harold Temperley. *Europe in the Nineteenth and Twentieth Centuries (1789–1939).* London: Longmans, 1947.

Gray, John. *Archeology and the Old Testament World.* New York: Thomas Nelson, 1962.

Gregor, Joseph. *Geschichte des Österreichischen Theater: von seinen Ursprüngen bis zum Ende der Ersten Republik.* Vienna: Donau-Verlag, 1948.

Gross, Felix. *Rhodes of Africa.* London: Cassell, 1956.

Grunwald, Kurt. *Türkenhirsch: A Study of Baron Maurice de Hirsch, Entrepreneur and Philanthropist.* Jerusalem: 1966.

Gutman, Robert. *Richard Wagner: The Man, His Mind and His Music.* London: Secker and Warburg, 1968.

Haas, Jacob de. *Theodor Herzl, A Biographical Study,* 2 vols. New York: The Leonard Company, 1927.

Hartung, Fritz. *Deutsche Verfassungsgeschichte.* Stuttgart: K. F. Koehler, 1950.

Hay, Malcolm. *The Pressure of Christendom on the People of Israel for 1900 Years.* Boston: Beacon Press, 1960.

Hechler, Rev. William H. 1. *The Jerusalem Bishopric.* London: 1883.
    2. *The Restoration of the Jews to Palestine.* London: 1884.

Heer, Georg. *Quellen und Darstellungen zur Geschichte der Burschenschaft,* vol. 16. Heidelberg: Carl Winters Verlag, 1939.

Hegedüs, Géza. *Heltai Jenö.* Budapest: Szépirodalmi Könyvkiadó, 1971.

Herford, R. Travers. *Pirke Aboth, The Ethics of the Talmud: Sayings of the Fathers; Text, Complete Translation and Commentaries.* New York: Schocken Books, 1962.

Hertz, Dr. J. H. *The Pentateuch and Haftorahs; Hebrew Text, English Translation and Commentary.* London: Soncino Press, 5720-1960.

Hertzberg, Arthur. *The Zionist Idea; A Historical Analysis and Reader.* New York: Harper & Row, 1959.

Herzl, Theodor
    A. For general list of dramatic works, see Appendix.
    The New Ghetto, 1895, tr. Heinz Norden. New York: The Theodor Herzl Foundation, 1955.
    B. 1. *Neues von der Venus.* Leipzig: F. Freund, 1887.
    2. *Das Buch der Narrheit.* Leipzig: F. Freund, 1888.
    3. *Das Palais Bourbon, Bilder aus dem französischen Parlamentsleben.* Leipzig: Duncker und Humbolt, 1895.
    4. *Der Judenstaat, Versuch einer modernen Lösung der Judenfrage.* Vienna: M. Breitenstein, 1896.
    5. *Philosophische Erzählungen.* Berlin: Gebrüder Paetel, 1900.
    6. *Altneuland.* Leipzig: H. Seemann, Nachfolger, 1902. (An English translation by de Haas appeared in *The Maccabaean,* New York, 1902–3; but quotations in this book are from *Old-New Land,* tr. by Lotta Levensohn, preface Emanuel Neumann, New York: Bloch Publishing Company and Herzl Press, 1960.)
    7. *Feuilletons,* 2 vols. Berlin: Wiener Verlag, 1903.
    8. *Zionistische Schriften,* 2 vols. Berlin: 1905.

9. *Theodor Herzls Tagebücher*, 3 vols. Berlin: Jüdischer Verlag, 1922–23.

10. *Herzl-Worte:* a collection of aphorisms, etc., by Felix A. Theilhaber. Berlin: Welt-Verlag, 1921.

Herzl Year Book, ed. Raphael Patai, vol. 1, 1958; vol. 2, 1959; vol. 3, Herzl Centennial Volume, 1960; vol. 4, 1962; vol. 5, Studies in the History of Zionism in America: 1894–1919, 1963; vol. 6, 1965. New York: Herzl Press.

Hess, Moses. *Rom und Jerusalem.* Leipzig: 1862.

Hillier, Bill. *Israel and Palestine.* London: Consultative Committee of Peace Organisations, 1968.

Hirsch, Samson Raphael. 1. *Judaism Eternal,* 2 vols. London: Soncino Press, 1956.

2. *Horeb, A Philosophy of Jewish Laws and Observances,* tr. Dr. I. Grunfeld. London: Soncino Press, 1962.

Hofmann, Martha. *Theodor Herzl, Werden und Weg.* Frankfurt a.M: 1966.

Hohenlohe-Schillingsfürst, *Denkwürdigkeiten des Fürsten Chlodwig zu.* Stuttgart: 1907.

Hubman, Franz. *The Habsburg Empire.* London: Routledge & Kegan Paul, 1972.

Ismail, Adel. *Histoire du Liban.* Paris: Gustave-Paul Maisonneuve, 1955.

Jacobs, Rabbi Dr. Louis. 1. *Jewish Values.* London: Vallentine, Mitchell, 1960.

2. *Principles of the Jewish Faith.* London: Vallentine, Mitchell, 1964.

Jerusalem Bible. London: Darton, Longman & Todd, 1966.

(*The Jewish Chronicle,* London, weekly.)

Jewish Encyclopaedia, New York: Funk & Wagnalls Company, 1903.

The New Standard Jewish Encyclopaedia, ed. Cecil Roth and Geoffrey Wigoder. London: W. H. Allen, 1970.

(*The Jewish World,* London, weekly.)

Judd, Denis. *Balfour and the British Empire.* London: Macmillan, 1968.

Jüdisches Lexikon. Berlin: Jüdischer Verlag, 1927–30.

Judtmann, Fritz. *Mayerling: The Facts Behind the Legend,* tr. Ewald Osers. London: Harrap, 1971.

Katona, József. *A 90 Éves Dohány-Utcai Templom; Az Országos Magyar Zsido Múseum Kiadása.* Budapest: 1949.

Kedward, H. R. *The Dreyfus Affair, Catalyst for Tensions in French Society.* London: Longmans, 1965.

Kellner, Leon. *Theodor Herzls Lehrjahre (1860–1895); nach den handschriftlichen Quellen.* Vienna: R. Löwit, 1920.

Khalidi, Walid, ed. *From Haven to Conquest: Readings in Zionism and the Palestine Problem Until 1948.* Beirut: Institute of Palestine Studies, 1971.

Kirk, George E. *A Short History of the Middle East.* London: Methuen, 1948.

Klein, Charlotte Lea. *Jews in English Literature. Patterns of Prejudice,* vol. 5, no. 2. Institute of Jewish Affairs, London: 1971.

Kohn, Hans. "Zion and the Jewish National Idea." *The Menorah Journal:* 1958.

Laqueur, Walter. 1. *The Israel/Arab Reader; a Documentary History of the Middle East Conflict.* London: Weidenfeld & Nicolson, 1969.

2. *A History of Zionism.* London: 1972.

Lee, Samuel J. *Moses of the New World, The Work of Baron de Hirsch.* New York: Thomas Yoseloff, 1970.

Leftwich, Joseph. *Israel Zangwill.* London: James Clarke, 1957.

Le Roy-Beaulieu, Anatole. *Israël chez les Nations.* Paris: 1893.

(*Libre Parole,* Paris.)

Lipson, E. *Europe in the Nineteenth Century 1815–1914.* London: Adam & Charles Black, 1916, 1960.

Loewenberg, Peter. *Theodor Herzl: A Psychoanalytic Study in Charismatic Political Leadership,* from *The Psychoanalytical Interpretation of History,* ed. Benjamin B. Wolman. Basic Books: 1971.

Marmorstein, Emile. *Heaven at Bay, the Jewish Kulturkampf in the Holy Land.* Oxford: 1969.

Marrus, Michael R. *The Politics of Assimilation; a Study of the French Jewish Community at the Time of the Dreyfus Affair.* Oxford: 1971.

Menger, Anton. *Civil Law and the Destitute Classes.* Vienna: Tubingen, 1888.

Morton, R. S. *Venereal Diseases: Studies in Social Pathology.* London: Penguin, 1966.

Murray's *Handbook for Travellers in Southern Germany.* London: John Murray, 1858 and 1863.

(*National Review,* London.)

Neame, Alan. *The Happening at Lourdes.* New York: Simon & Schuster, 1969.

(*Neue Freie Presse,* Vienna.)

Neumann, I. *Lehrbuch der venerischen Krankheiten und der Syphilis.* Vienna: 1888.

Newman, Ernest. *The Life of Richard Wagner.* London: Cassell, 1945.

Nietzsche, Friedrich. 1. *The Case of Wagner; Nietzsche contra Wagner, etc.,* tr. Anthony M. Ludovici. London: J. N. Foulis, 1911.

2. *Thoughts Out of Season,* tr. Anthony M. Ludovici, Part 1, *Richard Wagner in Bayreuth.* London: 1914.

Nordau, Max. 1. *Degeneration,* tr. from 2nd German edition, introduction by George L. Mosse. New York: Howard Fertig, 1968.

2. *The Conventional Lies of Our Civilization.* Chicago: 1895.

(*Nouvelle Revue Internationale.*)

Nussenblatt, Tulo, ed. *Theodor Herzl Jahrbuch.* Vienna: Dr. Heinrich Glanz Verlag, 1937.

Oliphant, L. *Haifa, or Life in Modern Palestine.* London: 1887.

Painter, George. *Marcel Proust, A Biography,* 2 vols. London: Chatto & Windus, 1959 and 1965.
Parkes, James. 1. *The Foundations of Judaism and Christianity.* London: Vallentine, Mitchell, 1960.
 2. *Anti-Semitism.* London: Vallentine, Mitchell, 1963.
Patai, Josef. *Star over Jordan, the Life of Theodore Herzl,* tr. Francis Magyar. New York: Philosophical Library, 1946.
Pinsker, Leo. *Auto-Emancipation.* Berlin: 1882.
Pudney, John. *Suez: de Lessep's Canal.* London: Dent, 1968.

Sachar, Abram Leon. *A History of the Jews.* New York: Knopf, 1970.
Scheiber, Alexander. *Hebräische Kodexüberreste in Ungarländischen Einbandstafeln.* Budapest: 1969.
Schmidt, Lieselotte. *Édouard Drumont—Emile Zola: Publizistik und Publizisten in der Dreyfus-Affäre,* doctoral dissertation, Philosophical Faculty of Free University of Berlin, 1962.
Schnitzler, Arthur. Correspondence with Olga Waissnix, ed. Therese Nickl and Heinrich Schnitzler, *Liebe, die starb vor der Zeit.* Vienna: Molden, 1970.
Schorske, Carl E. "Politics in a New Key: an Austrian Triptych." *Journal of Modern History.* Chicago: December 1967.
Smith, D. Mack. *Victor Emmanuel, Cavour, and the Risorgimento.* London: Oxford University Press, 1971.
Sokoloff, Alice Hunt. *Cosima Wagner, A Biography.* London: Macdonald, 1970.
Sokolow, Nahum. *History of Zionism (1600–1918),* 2 vols. London: Longmans, 1919.
Stein, Lorenz von. *Geschichte der Sozialen Bewegung in Frankreich von 1789 bis auf unsere Tage.* Leipzig: 1850.
Stern, Arthur. "The Genetic Tragedy of the Family of Theodor Herzl." *Israel Annals of Psychiatry and Related Disciplines.* April 1965.
Suttner, Bertha von. *Memorien.* Stuttgart: 1908.

Tibawi, A. L. *A Modern History of Syria, Including Lebanon and Palestine.* London: Macmillan, 1969.
(*The Times,* London.)

Wasserman, Jacob. *My Life as German and Jew,* tr. S. N. Brainin. New York: Coward-McCann, 1933.
Weisgal, Meyer W., ed. *Theodor Herzl: A Memorial.* New York: 1929.

Weizmann, Chaim. 1. *Trial and Error* (autobiography). London: 1949; New York: Schocken Books, 1966.

    2. The Letters and Papers of, vol. 3. Series A. Sept. 1903–Dec. 1904. ed. Meyer W. Weisgal. Oxford: 1972.

(*Die Welt*, Vienna, Cologne, Berlin, 1897–1914.)

Williams, [Arthur F.] Basil. *Cecil Rhodes*. New York: Greenwood Press, 1968.

Witte, Count Sergei Yulievich. *Memoirs of Count Witte*, tr. and ed. by Abraham Yarmolinsky. London: Heinemann, 1921.

Yale, William. *The Near East*. London: Mayflower Publishing Co., 1958.

Zangwill, Israel. 1. *Children of the Ghetto*. London: Heinemann, 1892.

    2. *Speeches, Articles, and Letters*, ed. Maurice Simon. London: Soncino Press, 1937.

Zweig, Stefan. *The World of Yesterday* (*Welt von Gestern*). London: Cassell, 1943.

INDEX

Abbas II, 305
Abdul Hamid II, Sultan, 55, 220, 263ff.,
   245, 253, 267, 287ff., 292, 293, 303ff.,
   344; copy of *Altneuland* to, 297; first
   Zionist Congress cables, 255; and
   Kaiser's visit, 259, 262, 268, 275, 276;
   Vámbéry and, 286ff.
Abdul Mejid, Sultan, 243n
Abrahams, Gerald, 110n
Adler, Chief Rabbi, 325–26
Adler, S. M., 275n
Africa. *See* East Africa; South Africa;
   specific places
Ahad Ha-am (Asher Ginsberg), 297
Ahmed Midhat, 253
Akademische Lesehalle, 61–63, 66, 79
Albert, Prince, 49
Albia, 83–85, 92, 93–95
Alexander II, Czar, 47, 317
Alexander III, Czar, 317
Alexandria, 32, 274, 310
Ali Nuri Bey, 314
Alkalai, Yehudah, 27, 28–29, 186
Altneuland (Herzl), 291–99, 322
Amalfi, 118–19
Amery, Julian, 304n
Anatolia, 231
Andrassy, Julius, Count, 228
Anti-Semitism, 80–83ff., 91–94, 136–
   42, 204ff., 217–19, 220, 251, 344 (*see
   also* specific groups, persons, places);
   and Dreyfus case, 165–67; Marr
   creates term, 59
Arabs, 223, 295–96, 324. *See also* spe-
   cific countries
Argentina, 220
Ark of the Covenant, 260
Armenians, 28, 231, 232, 241
Arndt, Karl Ludwig, 71n
Aron, Joseph, 165
Auernheimer, Raoul, 57
Austin, Alfred, 322
Austria(ns), 9, 25, 28, 36, 46, 55–67,
   73, 141ff., 249ff. *See also* specific
   cities, rulers
Auto-Emancipation (Pinsker), 186, 221
Avigdor, Sylvie d', 232

Bacher (editor), 136, 240–41, 283, 291n
Baden, Frederick, Grand Duke of, 225,
   226–27, 264, 265, 275, 289, 297, 317
Baden (spa), 73–74, 95, 135, 151, 152
Badeni, Count Felix, 204–5, 206
Bahr, Hermann, 93, 221
Baines, Thomas, 189
Balfour, Arthur James, 304
Bar Kokhba, Simon, 17
Basel, Zionist Congresses in: first
   (1897), 253–56, 285, 318; second,
   260, 325; third, 283, 291; fifth, 302;
   sixth, 319–20ff., 327, 334, 337
Bastian, Mme., 164, 166
Beauvoir, Simone de, 56–57
Beck, Dr., 225
Beer, Samuel Friedrich, 145
Bein, Alex, 26, 50, 71, 102, 107, 111n,
   154n, 168, 206, 272, 323, 335, 341,
   373
Beit, Alfred, 189
Bela IV, 5
Belgium, 18, 188
Benedikt, Moritz, 136, 142, 232, 240–
   41, 283
Bennett, James Gordon, 274
Berlin, 6, 7, 43, 81, 103–4, 120, 121,
   263–65 (*see also* specific residents);
   Congress of, 55, 80–81; Napoleon's
   Decrees, 36
Berliner Tageblatt, 117
Bernhardt, Sarah, 65
Bernstein, Aaron, 39
Bible, and circumcision, 12–14
Bibliography, 379–82
Bilinski, Leon Ritter von, 250–52
Birnbaum, Nathan, 161, 215n, 221
Bismarck, Otto von, 36, 55, 80–81, 196,
   199
Bizet, Georges, 65
Bloch, Chaim, 250
Bloch, Joseph S., 249–50
Bloch, Maurice, 138
Blumenthal, Oscar, 120, 154
Blunt, Wilfrid, 134
Bodenheimer, Max Isidor, 266–67, 273,
   285

THE INDISPENSABLE ROUSSEAU
Compiled and presented by John Hope Mason

The ideas of Jean-Jacques Rousseau (1712-78) have had a seminal influence on the modern world. His most important political work, *The Social Contract*, became a handbook of the French Revolution; his book on education, *Emile*, radically changed people's attitudes to children; his novel *The New Heloise* and his autobiographical *Confessions* were key documents in the birth of the Romantic movement.

This book provides a comprehensive introduction to Rousseau's ideas, containing extracts from all his major works and lesser-known texts. It includes an introductory outline of his thoughts and relates each work to its context in his life.

'We all know that Rousseau was not a "one book man"; but it has been very difficult for the general reader and ordinary student to get beyond *The Social Contract*, so much did Rousseau write in so many forms. So one is deeply in debt to Mr Hope Mason for providing a marvellously well chosen and well introduced anthology of Rousseau's writings. The ordinary English reader can at last get him in perspective.' Bernard Crick

'This is a deeply interesting, invaluable book...a brief biography...a list of key-words...well-translated selections...a well-judged, never intrusive commentary.... It would only be a very flowery chap indeed who could recommend this book too highly,' David Williams, *Punch*

'A marvellous primer which skilfully combines biography, comment and explanation with a comprehensive selection of Rousseau's writings. He has also contributed a modest and lucid and illuminating introduction.' Polly Devlin, *Vogue*

£5.95

Sybille Bedford
ALDOUS HUXLEY   A Biography

Volume One   The Apparent Stability   £2.95

'Here a gifted novelist with a keen intellect recounts the early life of an
author notable for the liveliest of minds, encyclopaedic knowledge and
an intense feeling for all the arts. Miss Bedford, intimate from her
girlhood with Huxley and his first wife, portrays their delightful,
contrasting characters most vividly; and she weaves the letters and
reminiscences of their friends into her narrative with consummate
skill. The book displays the art of biography at its finest.'   Raymond
Mortimer, *Sunday Times*, 'Choice of the Year'

'A feast of entertaining anecdotes ... observations, conversations,
quotations, and pleasant gossip.'   Harold Acton, *Books and Bookmen*

'This beautiful book is worthy of its subject.'   C. P. Snow, *Financial
Times*

Volume Two   The Turning Points   £2.95

'Miss Bedford has done a fine piece of work worthy of a fine subject.
Aldous Huxley is likely to be remembered for a long time to come, and
those interested in his writings will here find abundant material for
further thought (for, heaven knows, he was a stimulator of thought
himself).'   Christopher Sykes, *The Listener*

'Her treatment of his character is as masterly as anyone alive could
have managed. She had many advantages, she lived in his ambiance for
years, stayed for long periods with him and his first wife Maria, was
able to study some of Maria's private writings. Miss Bedford, though a
young woman at the time, didn't lose her balance. She has a
percipience about them both, which is tolerant, experienced, and the
reverse of sentimental. This picture of Aldous is as accurate as we are
ever likely to get.'   C. P. Snow, *Financial Times*

Molly Lefebure
SAMUEL TAYLOR COLERIDGE
A Bondage of Opium

'The first absorbing, original, convincing book about Coleridge to
have been written for many years.' Geoffrey Grigson, *Country Life*

'This study ... is important, because the author is not only expert in the
literature of the period, but also has a professional knowledge of drug
addiction.' Anthony Storr, *Sunday Times*

This full and balanced study of Samuel Taylor Coleridge solves one of
the greatest problems which has faced scholars of his work: why a man
of such obvious genius, intellectually endowed beyond all his
contemporaries, seemed so unscrupulous and dishonest in his
plagiarizing of other people's work. Molly Lefebure puts forward a
wholly convincing answer, examining an area of Coleridge's life which
has long been underestimated or misunderstood: his drug addiction.

'The story of Coleridge's decline is admittedly one of the most
poignant pages in literary history, and Miss Lefebure tells this story
with sympathy and intelligence.' John Cornwell, *The Times
Educational Supplement*

'For several days I was as hooked as any junkie on this stunning
biography.' Jilly Cooper, *Sunday Times*

£3.95

Sissela Bok
LYING
Moral Choice in Public and Private Life

Lying is a penetrating and useful examination of one of the most important yet ignored aspects of public and private life.

'Sissela Bok has written a well-argued, honest, and balanced book about the moral complexities of lying. If everyone had the respect for reason and moral principle that is so forcefully expressed in these pages, they would certainly be less wicked, and might even, as she suggests, be less unhappy.' Professor Bernard Williams

'Everyone will say Sissela Bok's book is wonderfully timed. All should know that it is also wonderfully incisive and informative' John Kenneth Galbraith

Sissela Bok is a philosopher who teaches ethics and decision-making in medicine at the Harvard Medical School. She is the author of numerous articles on medical ethics, has worked in hospitals on human experimentation committees and was a member of the Ethics Advisory Board to the Secretary of Health, Education and Welfare under the Carter administration.

£3.95

Other anthologies edited by Terry Carr:

THE BEST SCIENCE FICTION OF THE YEAR (THREE VOLUMES)
AN EXALTATION OF STARS
INTO THE UNKNOWN
NEW WORLDS OF FANTASY
NEW WORLDS OF FANTASY 2
NEW WORLDS OF FANTASY 3
ON OUR WAY TO THE FUTURE
THE OTHERS
SCIENCE FICTION FOR PEOPLE WHO HATE
   SCIENCE FICTION
THIS SIDE OF INFINITY
UNIVERSE 1
UNIVERSE 2
UNIVERSE 3
UNIVERSE 4

With Donald A. Wollheim:
WORLD'S BEST SCIENCE FICTION: 1965–1971
   (SEVEN VOLUMES)

Universe 5

RANDOM HOUSE ⌂ NEW YORK

Universe 5

EDITED BY

Terry Carr

Library of Congress Cataloging in Publication Data
Carr, Terry, comp.
UNIVERSE 5.
CONTENTS: Busby, F. M. If this is Winnetka, you must be Judy.—Le Guin,
U. K.   Schrödinger's cat.—Effinger, G. A. How it felt. [etc.]
1. Science fiction, American.   I. Title.
PZ1.C2339Uk [PS648.S3] 813′.0876 74-9090
ISBN 0-394-48562-9

CONTENTS

Universe 5

IF THIS IS WINNETKA,
YOU MUST BE JUDY

by F. M. Busby

F. M. Busby sold his first sf story in 1957, but it wasn't till he retired from his job as a communications engineer a couple of years ago that he began to write regularly. He attended the Clarion-West sf writers' workshop in Seattle and has become a frequent contributor to science-fiction magazines and original anthologies, besides selling his first novel, Cage a Man, to New American Library and the Science Fiction Book Club.

The following novelette shows why he's been so successful: Busby has a firm grasp on the interplay between Idea and Character in science fiction. In fact, except for a few differences made possible by the increased freedom of the field since it left its pulp days behind, this story might have appeared in one of the

classic issues of Astounding Science Fiction *during the "Golden
Age": in tone and idea-exploration it would not seem out of place
beside the early trend-setting stories of Heinlein, Sturgeon and
Asimov.*

THE ceiling was the wrong color—gray-green, not beige.
Alert, well-rested but still unmoving after sleep, Larry Garth
thought: It could be the Boston apartment, or possibly the one in
Winnetka—or, of course, someplace new. Throwing off the covers
and rolling over, he put his feet over the side of the bed and sat
up. His back did not protest; cancel Boston.

The walls were gray-green also, the furniture stained walnut.
Yes, Winnetka. As a final check before going into the bathroom,
he raised the window shade and looked out. It had been a long
time, but he recognized the details. Winnetka for sure, and he was
thirty-five or thirty-six; there were only about two years of
Winnetka. One question of importance remained: Judy, or
Darlene?

The bathroom mirror agreed with him; he was at the time of
the small mustache; he'd seen the thing in pictures. He didn't like
it much, but spared it when he shaved; it was bad policy, at
beginnings, to introduce unnecessary change.

He went back to the bedroom and got his cigarettes and lighter
from the bedside stand, hearing pans rattle in the kitchen. Judy, or
Darlene? Either way, he'd better get out there soon. As soon as he
checked his wallet—first things first.

He lit a cigarette and leafed through the cards and minutiae
that constituted his identity in the outside world. Well . . .
knowing himself, his driver's permit would be up-to-date and all
credit cards unexpired. The year was 1970. Another look outside:
autumn. So he was thirty-five, and the pans clattered at the hands
of Judy.

Just as well, he thought. He hadn't had the breakup with Darlene, but he knew it was, had to be, hectic and bitter. He'd have to have it sometime, but "sufficient unto the day . . ." Now, his wedding with Judy was only days or weeks distant—but he didn't know which way. The trees across the street were no help; he couldn't remember when the leaves turned color here, or began to fall. Well, he'd listen; she'd let him know . . .

In a plastic cover he found an unfamiliar card, with a key taped to one side. He drew it out; the other side was more than half-filled with his own small neat printing, mostly numbers. The first line read: "1935–54, small misc. See chart. 8/75–3/76. 2/62–9/63. 10/56–12/56." There was much more: wonder rose in him. And then excitement, for suddenly the numbers made sense. Months and years—he was looking at a listing of the times of his life, in the order he had lived them. "9/70–11/70" caught his eye—that was *now*, so he wasn't married to Judy yet, but would be before this time ended. And the crudely dated record listed six more life-segments between this one he was beginning and the one that had ended yesterday! He scanned it, scowling with concentration. Automatically he took a ball-point from the stand and completed the final entry, so that it read: "12/68–9/70."

He'd never kept records before, except in his head. But it was a good idea; now that his later self had thought of it, he'd continue it. No, he'd *begin* it. He laughed, and then he didn't laugh. He'd begin it because he'd found it; when and how was the actual beginning? He grappled with the idea of circular causation, then shrugged and accepted what he couldn't fully understand—like it or not, it was there. He looked again at the card, at the signposts on his zigzag trail.

A short time, this one, ending a few days after the wedding. Then about seven months of being twenty and back in college; probably it would be when he found the sense to quit that farcical situation, in which he knew more of many things than his instructors did, but very little of what his exams would cover. He looked forward to seeing his parents again, not only alive but in good health. They'd nag him for quitting school, but he could jolly them out of that.

And next—no, he'd look at it again later; Judy would be getting impatient. A quick look at the other side. Below the key was printed *First Mutual Savings* and the bank's address. The key was numbered: 1028. So there was more information in a safety-deposit box. He'd look at it, first chance he got.

He put on a robe and slippers; the last time with Judy, in 1972–73, her freedom from the nudity taboo was still new and strange to her. Shuffling along the hall toward breakfast, he wondered how the record he'd just seen was lost, wiped out, between now and that time. Did he later, in some time between, change his mind—decide the knowledge was more harm than help? He came to the kitchen and to Judy, with whom he'd lived twice as husband, but never met.

"Morning, honey." He moved to kiss her. The kiss was brief; she stepped back.

"Your eggs are getting cold. I put them on when I heard the water stop running. There's a cover on them, but still . . . what took you so long, Larry?"

"It took awhile to think myself awake, I guess." Looking at her, he ate with little heed to temperature or flavor. She hadn't changed much, going the other way. Red-gold hair was pinned up loosely into a swaying, curly mass instead of hanging straight, and of course she was bundled in a bulky robe rather than moving lithely unencumbered. But she had the same face, the same ways, so different from his first time with her. That was in the late, quarreling stages, five years away, when she drank heavily and was fat, and divorce was not far off. He did not know what went so wrong in so short a time between. Now at the start, or close to it, he wished he could somehow rescue the fat drunk.

"More coffee, Larry? And you haven't even looked at the paper."

"Yes. Thanks. I will, now." Damn! He had to get on track better, and fast. "Well . . . what's new today?"

He didn't care, really. He couldn't; he knew, in large, how the crises and calamities of 1970 looked in diminishing perspective. The paper's only use was to orient him—to tell him where in the middle of the movie he was, what he should and should not know. And today, as on the first day of any time, he looked first for the exact date. September 16, 1970. His wedding was six weeks and three days ahead of him, on Halloween. And this day was Wednesday; the bank would be open.

As if on cue, she asked, "Anything special you need to do today?"

"Not much. I want to drop in at the bank, though. Something I want to check on." That was safe; she'd know about the bank. He kept only essential secrets. "Anything you'd like me to pick up at the groshry?" He remembered to use their joke-pronunciation.

"I'll look. I have a couple of things on the list, but they're not urgent."

"Okay. Come here a minute first, though." Short and still slim, she fit well on his lap, as she had two years later. The kisses became longer.

Then she pulled back. "Larry. Are you sure?"

"Sure of what?" He tried to bring her to him but she resisted, so he relaxed his grip. "Something on your mind, Judy?"

"Yes. Are you sure you want to get married again, so soon after . . . ?"

"Darlene?"

"I know you had a hideous time, Larry, and—well, don't get on that horse again just to prove you're not afraid to."

He laughed and tightened his hold; this time she came close to him. "Proving things isn't my bag, Judy. To myself, or to anybody."

"Then why do you want to marry me, when you have me already? You don't have to—all you have to do is not change, stay the same for me. So why, Larry?"

"Just old-fashioned, I guess." It was hard to kiss and laugh at the same time, carrying her to the bedroom. But he managed, and so did she, her part.

She got up first; the "groshry" list was ready when he was dressed to leave. Their goodbye kiss was soft.

Downstairs, he recognized the car with pleasure—a year-old Volvo he knew from two and five years later; it was even more agile and responsive now.

The drive to the bank gave him time to think.

In his early time-years the skips were small, a day or two, and his young consciousness took them for bad dreams—to wake with unfamiliar sensations, body changed and everything out of size. Much later, waking in a hospital, he learned they were real.

"Do you use drugs, Mr. Garth?"

"No, I don't." A little grass now and then wasn't "drugs." "I'd like to know why I'm here."

"So would we. You were found lying helpless, unable to talk or coordinate your movements. Like a baby, Mr. Garth. Do you have any explanation, any pertinent medical history?"

So this is where I was, he thought. "No. I've been under a lot of pressure." That was probably safe to say, though he didn't know his body-age or circumstances. But in some thirty consciousness-years he'd learned to keep cover while he got his bearings in a new time. And eventually, as he hoped and expected, they told him most of what he needed to know about himself, and let him go. As sometimes happened, his research into the parameters of now was largely wasted; the time lasted only a dozen or so days. But the waste was not total, for when the following time came to him, he would still remember.

Once as a four-year-old he woke to middle age and panicked, screaming for his mother. He remembered being taken to the hospital that time, and did not look forward with pleasure to waking in it. But what had been would be. And he was certain there was at least one more infancy skip to be lived down someday.

At first he did not talk of these things in "home" time because he had no speech. Then he remained silent because he thought it was the same for everyone. And finally he kept his counsel because he realized no one could help or understand, or even believe.

Once in his seventh consciousness-year he woke with a throbbing joy at his groin; the woman beside him overrode his bewilderment and fulfilled his unrealized need. It was a time of a single day, and he hadn't seen her again. He didn't know the time-year or where he was, but he knew enough to say very little. He kept the situation as simple as possible by saying he was tired and didn't feel well, remembering just in time that grownups say they're not going to *work* today—he almost said *school*. He got away with it, and his confidence improved.

There were other dislocations from his early time-years, but none major until he went to sleep aged nineteen and woke to spend seven months as a forty-year-old man, twice-divorced. He wondered what was wrong, that twice he had failed in marriage. His unattached state simplified his adjustment, but after a time he became convinced that he'd lost twenty years and was cheated. But the next skip was to an earlier time, and then he began to know the way of his life.

The changes came always during sleep, except for the one that came at death. He didn't know how old he died; his brain's constricted arteries would not maintain an attention-span of any useful length. Inside him, his brief thoughts were lucid, but still the effect was of senility. How old, though? Well, he'd once had a year that included his seventieth birthday and golf, an operation for cataracts, a lawsuit successfully defended and a reasonably satisfying state of potency. So when he came to the last, he knew he was *damned* old.

Having died, he still feared death. It would be merely a

different way of ending. For he had no clear idea how much of his life had been lived, back and forth in bits and pieces. One day he would use up the last unlived segment, and then . . . he supposed he simply wouldn't wake up. At his best estimate, he had lived something less than half his allotted time-years. He couldn't be sure, for much of his earlier conscious time was unmeasured.

Dying itself was not terrible; even his senile brain knew he had not yet filled all the blank spaces of his life. The pain was bad, as his heart fought and for a time would neither function nor gracefully succumb, but he had felt worse pain. His mind lost focus, and came clear only for a few seconds at the end. He died curious, wondering what might come next.

It was the other book end; the circle closed. He was trapped, constricted, pushed. Pressured and convulsed, slowly and painfully. Finally cold air reached his head and bright light stabbed at his eyes; at the consciousness-age of perhaps thirty, he was born. Except for the forgotten instinctive rapture of feeding, he found the newborn state unpleasant.

Filling early skips involuntarily, he dipped twice again into infancy. The first time bored him almost to apathy; he could neither see clearly nor move well. The second time, better-learned, he concentrated on his wide-open senses, trying to understand the infant condition. He found the experience instructive, but still was glad when next he woke adult.

Relationships with others were ever difficult; always he came in at the middle of the second feature, unsure of what had gone before and of correct responses to people he was supposed to know. He learned to simulate a passive streak that was not his by nature so that his friends would accept the quiet necessary to each new learning period. He cheated no one by this small deceit; it was as much for their benefit as his. And while he stayed in one time, at rest between zigzag flights, his friends and lovers—and their feelings—were real to him, of genuine concern. When he met them again, before or afterward, it pained him that they could not also know and rejoice in the reunion.

Early in his experience he sometimes fumbled such reunions. Now he knew how to place the time and adjust his mental files to produce only acceptable knowledge for the year.

There was no way he could pursue a conventional career with organizational status and seniority, and at the end of it a pension. Hell, he couldn't even finish college. Luckily, at his first major change, when he skipped from nineteen to forty, he found himself a published author of fiction. He read several of his works and enjoyed them. In later times, half-remembering, he wrote them, and then others that he had not read. His writings never hinted at the way of his own life, but a reviewer said of them: "Garth presents a unique viewpoint, as though he saw life from a different angle."

It was a strange life, he thought. How did they manage it? Living and seeing solely from one view that plodded along a line and saw only one consecutive past.

So that they could never, ever understand him. Or he, them.

He had attuned so easily to the car and the locality, hands and feet automatically adjusting to four-on-the-floor and quick brakes and steering, that, daydreaming, he nearly drove past the turnoff to First Mutual Savings. But from the right-hand lane, braking and signaling quickly, he made his turn without difficulty. He found a slot at the end of a parking row, well away from the adjacent car in case its driver was a door-crasher.

He didn't know the bank, so he walked in slowly and loitered, looking around with care. The safety-deposit counter was to his left; he approached it. On it, a marker read "Leta Travers"; behind the desk was a gray-haired woman, spectacularly coiffed, who wore marriage rings. He couldn't remember how people in this suburb in this time addressed each other in business dealings. Well, it couldn't be too important . . .

"Good morning, Mrs. Travers."

She came to the counter. "Mr. Garth. Going to change your will again?"

What the hell! No; she was smiling; it must be a "family joke." Damn, though; how had he later come to set up such a stupid thing? He knew better than that, *now*.

Well, go along with it. "Yep. Going to leave all my millions to the home for retired tomcats." But he'd have to kill this for later, or else change banks. Or some next-time, off-guard, it could be bad. Maybe that's why he dropped the records . . . wait and see.

Leta Travers led him to the aseptic dungeon, where their two keys together opened Box 1028. Saying the usual polite things, she left him to its contents.

The envelope was on top. He didn't like the label: *This Is Your Life* with his signature below. That was show-off stuff. Or dumbhead drunk. He'd brought a pen; with it, he scribbled the designation into garble. He thought, then wrote: *Superannuated; For Reference Only.* He repeated the phrase subvocally, to fix it in his mind.

He unfolded the envelope's contents and was impressed. There were two major parts, plus some side-trivia he could study later. The last looked interesting, but it had waited and could wait awhile longer.

First was an expanded version of the card in his wallet: a chronology of his consciousness, more exactly dated than he could verify from memory. Somehow, later, he'd checked these things more closely. He couldn't imagine how to do it. Or maybe, along with the dumbhead labeling, he had taken to putting exact dates to inexact recalls. He didn't like to think of his mind going so flyblown, and determined to watch against such tendencies.

He skimmed without going deeply into memory. The list seemed accurate; he'd have to look more closely later. The second paper described his life from a different aspect: by time-years it showed the parts he'd had and what he'd known and guessed of what had gone between. At the back was a summary in chart form.

Both parts went well past his own experience, as the card had done. He looked at the first and read, after the college section: "February 6, 1987, through March 4, 1992. Three years wonderful with Elaine and the others, then two so terrible as she died and afterward. She died November 10, 1990, and we are alone."

He could not read any more; he couldn't make sense of it. Elaine—how could she die so soon? He was *counting* on her, someday, for a lot of good years: now and then, as it would happen. Suddenly he could see a reason for destroying records— he'd rather not know of the end of Elaine. But obviously he hadn't thought that way afterward, or the papers wouldn't be here before him. Something else must happen, later, to change his mind.

He knew Elaine from two times: first when their matured marriage was joined fully to that of Frank and Rhonda. Only two months then. And later, starting when they were six months married, he had the next year and a few months more. And she was the person he most wanted, most loved . . . and most missed.

He couldn't take any more of it, not yet. He needed to study and memorize the record, but not here, not now. Well, Judy wasn't nosy; he could take it home. He put the envelope in a pocket. Everything else went back in the lock-box; he pushed it in to click its assurance of security. All right; time to go.

At the counter he thanked Mrs. Travers. "And I've decided to leave my will alone from now on," he said. "The retired tomcats will just have to do the best they can."

She laughed, as he'd hoped she would. "Well, whatever you say, Mr. Garth."

"True," he said, "it's my nickel, isn't it? Well, then . . . see you again, Mrs. Travers, and thank you."

He walked toward the door.

The black-haired girl walked by as he came out to the sidewalk, and before he could think, he called to her. "Elaine!"

She turned; frantically he tried to think of a non-incriminating excuse. But her eyes went wide, and her arms; she ran to him and he could not resist her embrace. "Larry! Oh, Larry!"

"Uh—I guess I made a mistake," he said. His mind churned uselessly. "Perfectly natural. I guess I do look like a lot of other people."

She shook her head, scattering the tears that leaked onto her lashes. "No mistake, Larry." Her hands gripped his upper arms; he could feel the nails digging in. "Oh, think of it! You too, Larry! You too!"

His mind literally reeled; he felt dizzy. He breathed deeply, and again, and a third time. "Yes," he said. "Look. Elaine—let's go someplace quiet and have coffee or a drink or something. We've got to talk."

"Oh, yes! We have to talk—more than any other two people in the world."

They found a small bar, quiet and dimly lit, and sat at a corner table. Three men occupied adjacent stools at the bar; across the room a couple talked quietly. The bartender, scowling in concentration, mixed something in a tall glass.

Larry looked at Elaine, ten years younger than he had ever seen her. She aged well, he thought; the little lines at the corners of her eyes hadn't advanced much by the time they were married. The gray eyes themselves did not change, and the line of her chin was durable. The black hair was longer than he'd seen it; the few threads of gray were yet to appear. He could close his eyes and see the slim body under her bright dress; he felt desire, but remotely. More important now were things of the mind—of both their minds.

The bartender was coming to their table. "Vermouth on the rocks?" Larry said. "You always like that."

"I do?" She laughed. "That's right; I do, later. Well, perhaps this is where I begin to acquire the taste. All right."

He ordered the same. Both were silent while the drinks were brought. He started to raise his glass in a toast, but she didn't wait.

"How much have you had, Larry? Of us?"

"I haven't met you. Except now, of course. I had the last half of our first year and most of our second." He showed her the envelope. "I have the dates here. And earlier I had a few weeks in the middle, in '85, when we were with Frank and Rhonda. I was pretty young; it really confused me at first."

She nodded. "I should have known then. I've had that part too, and suddenly you seemed withdrawn, you wouldn't talk. Then, gradually, you came out of it."

"How much have you had, Elaine? I mean—how much do we have left, together? Not too long from now I get the last—" Good Lord! What was he *saying?* "Elaine—have you had, uh, your death yet?"

She nodded. "Yes. It wasn't as bad as it probably seemed. I looked awful and smelled awful, toward the end, I know. And made noises, from the pain. But that was just my body. Inside, except for seeing how all of you hurt for me, I was pretty much at peace; the pain was out there someplace where I hardly felt it.

"Poor Larry! I gave you a bad time, didn't I?"

"I haven't had that time yet. I'll be having it pretty soon, though."

"You'll *what?* How can you know that?" Her face seemed to crumple. "Oh! We're not the same, after all?"

He took her hand. "Yes, we are. It's—I keep records, or I will. And I found them, written in the time just before now." He showed her the lists from the envelope. "Here—you can see what I've had, up to here, and what I'll be having up through the time that ended a couple of days ago."

She recovered quickly and studied his life-records with obvious fascination. "But this is marvelous! I never thought of doing it; I don't know why. It's obvious, when you think about it. Stupid me!"

"Stupid me too, Elaine," he said. He sipped his drink. The ice had melted; the taste was watery. "I didn't think of it either, until I saw it on paper."

"But that means you did it because you'd done it." She grasped the circularity of the process instantly—which was more than he had done.

"Larry, do you mind if I mark on this—the chart here—a little bit? In pencil? I want to see how much we have left together." Quickly she drew neat lines. "Both *knowing*; won't that be— what's a bigger word than 'wonderful'?"

"Whatever it is, it fits." Impatience gripped him. "Well, how does it look?"

"Better than I expected, but not as good as I'd like. Damn! I've met you and you haven't met me. Then here, late in 1980, we overlap; we've both had a couple of months there. And you've had most of 1981 and a little of '85, and I've had nearly all of '85 and all of the last three years. Oh, dammit! See here? Out of our ten years, one or the other of us has already had nearly six. Not knowing. Not *knowing*, Larry!" She wiped her eyes and gulped from her glass.

"Yes, Elaine; I feel the same way. But what's lived is lived; we can't change it."

"Can't we?" She raised her face to him, shaking back the hair that had fallen forward. "What if—what if the next time you've had and I haven't, I just *tell* you? Or the other way around? Why not, Larry? Why the hell not?"

He shook his head, not negating her but stalling. The idea had come to him too, and the implications rocked him. Not her, though—God, how he loved that bold mind! But he needed time to think.

"I'm not sure, Elaine. What would happen? We were there, you see, and we *didn't* tell, either of us, our selves who remembered sitting here right now. Why didn't we?" He was still holding her hand; he squeezed it once and let go. "Was it because of something we decided in the next few minutes? Or hours, or days?

We've got to think, Elaine. We've got to think in ways no one's ever had to think before."

She smiled. "You're sure of that? There are two of us. Maybe there are others."

"Maybe. I've watched, and never—what are the odds against recognition? If I hadn't been off-guard, you know, I'd never have given myself away."

"But I'm so glad you did. Aren't you?"

"Of course, Elaine. Christ, yes! I mean, even if it's only the four years . . ."

"But maybe we could have *more*. The overlap—you see?—the parts we've both had, where neither of us knows about the other—there's not much of it."

"No, there isn't." He signaled the bartender, holding up a glass and extending two fingers of the hand that raised it. "Elaine, we don't have to decide this right away. Put it on the back burner and let it simmer. Let's talk about us. For instance, how old are you?"

She laughed. "I thought your memory was better than that. I'm two years and five days younger than you are."

It was his turn to chuckle. "I don't mean body-years. How old in consciousness-years?"

"Oh. I call them life-years. About twenty-four, I think, give or take a couple. And you?"

"Close to forty; I can't be exact about it either."

The bartender brought filled glasses, collected his money and went back to the bar, all silently.

"Getting old and cautious, are you, Larry? No, I don't mean that. We learn to be cautious; we have to. It's just that *this*—not to be alone with the way I live—I'll take *any* risk. Any risk at all, Larry." She sipped vermouth; the ice clinked as her hand shook slightly. "But yes, let's talk about us.

"You asked about my death," she said. "Have you had yours? Or what's the oldest you've been?"

"I had it, and I don't know; I was senile. You're all right on the inside, but you can't keep track for very long. But I was damned old; I know that. Because I was seventy for a while once, and still in pretty good shape."

"And I died at fifty-three. God *damn* it, Larry!"

"Elaine!" What could he say? "Sometimes quality counts more than quantity."

She made a disgusted grimace and a half-snort. "Some quality! Do you remember any of my life history? Well, I'm with my first husband, Joe Marshall, and he's just making a start on drinking himself to death. It takes him fifteen years, as I recall. Oh, I can't complain about my childhood, or college, or even the first five years of the marriage, what I've had of it. But I've also had four of the next eight, before the divorce. In three times, separated and out of sequence. No, Larry. When it comes to quality, it's all in the times with you. With you and our other two."

"Those were good times for me too," he said. "But you know something? I tried to feel alike to everybody, the way we were supposed to. And I was with all three of you *before* the time you and I were alone earlier, but I felt more yours than Rhonda's, anyway." He paused and drank. "I wonder if somehow the body gives feedback, under our conscious memory."

Her mind looked at him from somewhere far behind her eyes. "I don't know. Sometimes there are hunches . . . feelings . . ." She shook her head and smiled. "Larry, how is it with you now?"

"Mixed up, for one thing. I've probably told you, maybe in some time you've had and I haven't, about my first two marriages—what I knew of them. Well, you can see here on this diagram—I woke up today between wives."

"Today? You're just beginning a time today?"

"Yes. Judy's living with me; we get married in about six weeks."

"Judy? She's the lush, isn't she?"

"Not now, and not two years from now. Maybe I'd had only the bad end of it when I told you about her—yes, that's right. Someday I'll find out what happened, I expect. I just hope it isn't my fault. But it probably is . . ."

"You can't afford to think that. You didn't ask to be born zigzag, any more than I did. If we can take it, why can't they?"

"Can we take it, Elaine?"

"We're doing it, aren't we?" She looked at her watch. "Oh, I have to go! Joe—my husband—I'm an hour late! He'll be drunk again if I don't hurry."

"Yes. All right. When can we see each other?"

"I don't know yet, but we will. We have things to settle, you and I. You're in the phone book?" He nodded. "I'll call."

She stood, and he with her. She started to move away, but he took her arm. "Just a minute, Elaine. It's been a long time." They kissed long, before they moved apart and walked out.

"I go this way," she said. "It's only a few blocks. Don't come with me."

He stood looking after her, at the grace of her walk. After a few steps, she turned. "I'll call you tonight," she said. "We can meet tomorrow, if I'm still here. Still now, I mean."

"Well, you have to be, is all." They smiled and waved; then he turned and walked to the parking lot.

When he unlocked his apartment door, he almost knocked Judy off the ladder; she nearly dropped the picture she was hanging. "Oh, it's you!" she said. "Here, catch this." Off-balance, she leaned to hand him the picture. Her hair was hanging loose, brushed smooth, and her robe was open. She descended, and closed the robe before she turned to face him.

"Have you had lunch, Larry? I waited awhile, but then I got hungry and had mine. I'll do yours if you want, though why I should when you're so late . . ."

He started to say he wasn't hungry, then realized he was; he'd missed lunch. "Go ahead with what you're doing, Judy; I'll make a sandwich. My own fault; I got hung up." From the refrigerator he took bread, meat to slice, pickles and a jar of mustard. "When we're both done, let's have a beer and chat some."

She went back to her task, picture in one hand, hammer in the other and tacks silencing her mouth. Climbing a ladder, he thought, does a lot for a good round butt.

He knew what he wanted to talk about. A trip out of town, a fictitious assignment. A pre-honeymoon, by about ten years, with Elaine.

Keeping cover was one thing; he'd always had to do that. Lying was something else, he found, as he and Judy talked, sipping beer from bottles as though it were champagne from frosted goblets. The beer went well, after his sandwich.

"I'm not sure yet," he said, "but I may need to cut out for the last of this week and the weekend." He knew his slang had to be a little out of date, one way or the other, but always there was some leeway in speech patterns. "Let you know for sure, soon as I can."

"Sure, Larry. I wish I could go with you, but you know I'm tied this weekend."

"Sure." He hadn't known it, but it helped. "Next time, maybe."

She was vital and desirable, Judy. Mobile mouth, bright hair, lithe body carrying no more than five excess pounds, all nicely hidden. No genius, but a good mind and compatible nature. And in bed, like a mink with its tail on fire. So why could he not cleave to her? Because she was of the other species, the one that lived along a single line and knew nothing else.

And was that the reason she would become a fat, surly drunk? He wished he knew, and that it didn't have to happen.

Dinner wasn't much to brag about. "Leftovers Supreme," said Judy; her grin was wry. They were drinking coffee when the phone rang.

It was Elaine; he put her on "Hold." "Business stuff," he said to Judy. "I'll take it in the other room so you can read your book." Again, it hurt to lie; Judy didn't deserve lies.

On the bedroom extension: "Elaine?" The connection was noisy.

"Yes, Larry. I've been thinking."

"So have I. We need more time."

She laughed through the circuit noises. "Yes. We always do."

"I mean, time to ourselves. To think, and talk together." He paused, surprised to find himself embarrassed. "And to have each other, if you'd like that. I would."

She was silent for a moment. "What's the matter? Are you hard up? Has your lush gone dead?"

Anger! "You have no right to say that. You don't know her. And why—?"

Her voice came softly, almost drowned in the crackling sounds. "All right, Larry, so I'm jealous. Sorry about that. Shouldn't have said it. I'm a little drunk, boozing along with Kemo Sahib before he passed out a while ago. Leaving myself untouched, as usual. It does make me bitchy, when he spends all evening working up to nowhere. I wish I knew what he does with it."

"I wish I knew a lot of things," he said. "But never mind that. What do you say—Elaine, let's just take off for a few days; the hell with everything. Okay?"

She waited longer than he liked. Then, "I can get away with it if you can." Another pause. "And we can talk? Everything?"

"That's what I was hoping."

"All right, Larry. I'll be in that same bar tomorrow, about noon. Or a little later; I'm not much for being on time. But there. With my suitcase."

"Yes. Yes, Elaine. And goodnight."

"Cautious Larry. It's all right; I can wait for you to say the rest." The phone went dead, dial tone blurting at his ear. He listened as though there were meaning in the noise, then hung up and went back to Judy.

She was reading, TV on but the sound off; he'd never understood that habit, either time he'd known her. It's not so alone, was all she ever said.

"Like a beer or anything?" he said. "I think I'll have one or two, look at the paper a little. And then crap out early."

"With or without?"

"Huh?"

"Me."

"Oh. With."

"Good. Yes, I'd like a beer with you, Larry."

That part was good. Instead of reading, they talked. After a while, he told her about his "assignment"—not what or where, but when. "I'll be leaving tomorrow morning, not too early, and be back Monday. Maybe Sunday night."

"Yes. Well, with luck I'll be too busy to miss you properly."

He began to laugh, but stopped. For he didn't expect to be missing Judy.

He finished his beer and went to the refrigerator. "Another, honey?"

"No, but you go ahead and have one while I shower." He did, then showered also.

Later, plunging together and close to all of it, he found his mind was with Elaine. Fantasy in sex was nothing new, but this reality deserved better. He almost failed to climax then; when he did, it was minor, a mere release. But he had good luck with Judy-the-unpredictable; she made it big and asked no questions. He was glad of that much.

Elaine, suitcase and all, arrived as the bartender set drinks on the table. "Am I late, Larry?" He shook his head; they kissed briefly.

"Where do you want to go?" he asked. "Anyplace special?"

"Yes, I think so, if you like the idea. If you don't think it's too far." She sipped the chilled vermouth. "There are some lakeside cabins a little north of Fond Du Lac. I was there once, with the great white bottle-hunter."

"Oh? Memories?"

She made a face. "He hated it; I loved it."

"Do you remember the name of the place? Maybe we should call first."

She shook her head. "It's past the season. School's started; all the little sunburns are back in their classrooms."

"Okay. I'll take the chance if you will."

They left their drinks unfinished.

The cabin was at the north end of the row, adjoining a grove of maples. The inside was unfinished, the studding exposed, but the bed was comfortable and the plumbing worked. They sunned beside the lake, swam a little, and dined on Colonel Sanders' fried chicken. Correct dinner attire was a towel to sit on.

"Tomorrow we'll go out and eat fancy," he said, "but tonight we're at home."

"Yes, Larry. Just don't lick your fingers, or I'll swat you."

Indian summer cooled in twilight; they had waited for the heat to slacken. Now, he thought, comes our time together. It did, and not much later, again.

Then they sat side by side on the bed. He brought a wooden chair to hold cigarettes, ashtray and two bottles of cold beer. For a time they talked little, busy smoking, sipping beer, touching each other and smiling. It's just the way it was, he thought.

He touched the breast, small and delicately curved, that was nearest him.

"I was never much in that department, was I?" she said.

"Beauty comes in all sizes, Elaine."

"Yes, but you know, I felt so one-down, with Frank and Rhonda. She was so damned superbly—uh, endowed, it just killed me." She was smiling, but she stopped. "It did, you know. Literally."

He was running his hand through her hair, bringing it over to brush slowly across his cheek and then letting it fall, over and over. "I don't understand."

"Larry, I knew I had a lump. For more than a year, before you found out and made me see a doctor—what was his name? Greenlee."

"But why—?"

"I didn't have much, and I was afraid of losing what I had. So I tried to think it wasn't serious. And the worst—I don't know if I should even tell you . . ."

"Come on, Elaine. You and I can't afford secrets."

She butted her cigarette with firm straight thursts. "All right. Greenlee told me, after the examination, that if I'd gone to him earlier I could have gotten by with a simple mastectomy at *worst*, and not too much of a scar. But I couldn't take the idea, Larry. So I put it off, and ended up with that ghastly double radical, all the muscles, all that goddamned radiation and—*you* know—and even that was too late." Her eyes were crying but she made no sound.

"Jesus, Elaine!" He had to hold her, because there was nothing else he could do. And besides, he had to hold her.

Finally he spoke. "You just made up my mind for me; you know that?"

"About what?"

"What you said. Next time we're together we tell each other, even though we didn't. If we can; I'm not sure. But if we can—look; the record says I'm with you again, right after this time and then a few months back in college. And first thing, I'm going to try to tell you. About how we're the same, and then about the cancer too."

"But I've lived that, Larry. And died of it."

He was up and pacing. He laughed shortly, without humor, and went to the refrigerator. He set two fresh beers on the chair and sat again.

"I've never tried to change anything before, Elaine. I guess I thought it couldn't be done. Or I was too busy keeping cover to think of making waves. I don't mean I followed any script; I didn't have one. But I went along with how things were, and it all seemed to fit. Not now, though." He gripped her shoulder and turned her to face him. "I don't want you to die as you did."

He was really too tired for sex, he thought. But he found he wasn't.

They planned to stay until Monday, but Sunday came gray, cold with wind and rain. So for breakfast, about ten o'clock, Larry scrambled all the remaining eggs, enough for four people. They had more toast than they could manage, and gave the rest to a hungry brood of half-grown mallards.

In the cabin, luggage packed. "I hate to leave, Larry."

"I know. Me too." He grinned. "We could stop at a motel for seconds if you like."

She shook her head. "No. It wouldn't be the way it is here." So they didn't. Except for a mid-afternoon snack break, he drove nonstop, and pulled up to let her off at her apartment house.

"It can't be as good, Elaine, but we've got to see each other anyway. I'm only here through November ninth."

"I don't know how long I am, of course. But, yes—I have to see you."

After the kiss she walked inside without looking back. He drove home, trying to put his mind in gear for Judy.

But Judy wasn't there, and neither were her possessions.

The letter was on the kitchen table:

> I'm sorry Larry but I'm bugging out. I don't know what's wrong but I know something is, you aren't the same. It's not just you going off this weekend, I need people to be the same. I love you, you know that Larry, but you changed on me. The day you went to the bank you came up different. I need you to be the same to me, I need that. So I'm bugging out now. Don't worry, I'll call off all the wedding present stuff, you won't be bothered with it. I do love you when you were the same and I'll miss you a lot.
>
> Judy

Well. She didn't say where she was going; it could be anywhere. The hell with unpacking; get a beer, sit down and think it out.

Two cigarettes later, the memory came—the time she told him about this.

"Remember when I ran out on you, Larry? I was really spooked; I don't know why, now. And I never knew how you found me. You didn't even know I *had* a cousin Rena Purvis." He laughed and memorized the name, as he did all things concerning his future in someone else's past.

Rena Purvis' number was in the book. He dialed the first three digits, then thought a moment and hung up. He dialed Elaine instead.

A man's voice answered. "H'lo? Who'that?" Kemo Sahib had a good start.

How to play it? "Mr. Marshall? Mr. Garth here. I have the report Mrs. Marshall requested early last week."

"S'okay. I'take it, fella."

"I'm sorry—Mrs. Marshall's instructions . . . would you put her on the line, please?"

"I said I'take it. Or leave it. Take it or leave it. Get it?"

"Perhaps Mrs. Marshall could call me back? Mr. Garth?"

The slurred voice harshened. "Saaay—you' the bastard she was off with, right?"

The hell with it. "The very bastard, Joe; the very same. Your own stupid fault, Joe—waste not, want not. Now, are you going to put Elaine on the phone, or am I going to come over there and show you just how much of a bastard I can be if I put my mind to it?"

It took Marshall three slams to get his phone safely on the hook; the crashes hurt Larry's ears. That was dumb of me, he thought—or was it? Should he get over there in a hurry? No. Whatever else Elaine felt about her husband, she wasn't afraid of him . . . and the slob had sounded completely ineffectual. So, give it a few minutes . . .

It took twenty; then his phone rang. "Hello. Elaine?"

"Yes, Larry. Joe . . ."

"Any trouble? I can be there fast."

"Noise trouble, is all. As usual. He's settled down; he's telling his troubles to his glass teddy-bear. What in the world did you say to him?"

"Sorry. I tried to play it nice but he wouldn't. So I laid the truth on him. Maybe I shouldn't have?"

"No, that's all right. I'd already told him, and that he and I are through. We were talking about changing things, Larry? I'm doing it. I don't know if it will work; I lived through four years with him after this, so probably I get stupid and relent. But for now, I've had it." She paused. "But you're the one who called. What is it?"

He told her, reading Judy's letter aloud. ". . . and then I didn't call her. And maybe I shouldn't go bring her back, even though I did. Because I think I made her a lush, not being the same, not being able to be the same. What do you think?"

"I think you're not through talking yet, and I'm not done listening."

It wasn't easy, but he had to laugh. "Yes, Elaine. Will you come live here?"

"Where else?"

"Tomorrow?"

"I haven't unpacked my suitcase."

"Shall I come get you?"

"No. I'll take a cab."

"All right. You have the address?"

"Yes. And number 204, right?"

"I'll leave the door unlocked. Hell, I'll leave it open!"

Time, stolen from a programmed future, was sweet. Despite everything, he felt occasional guilt about Judy. But she didn't call, and neither did he. Joe Marshall called several times, more or less coherently. Larry always answered, gently, "Forget it, Joe." Elaine simply hung up at first recognition.

All too soon, like Judgment Day, came November ninth. They made a ceremony of it, with dinner in the apartment from none other than Colonel Sanders. Larry did not lick his fingers. Later, in bed, they did everything slowly, to make it last until . . . whenever.

He woke. Elaine's face was close above his; her smile was wistful. "Hello, Larry. Do you *know*?"

To see, he had to push her soft hair aside; the ceiling was gray-green. "I *know*. But what's the date?"

"November tenth, 1970." Her voice was level, cautious.

He whooped. He kissed her with fierce joy, with elation; he kissed her out of breath. "Elaine! We changed it! I didn't skip!" Tears flowed down her cheeks, around her laughing mouth.

For the second part of their celebration he scrambled eggs in wine; it was messy, he thought, but festive.

"How much can we count on, Larry?"

"I don't know; we can't know." He held up the envelope with its carefully detailed records. "But this is useless now."

"Yes. Don't throw it away yet. I want to see where you've been, and talk about it together."

"All right. We can sort it out later."

It was a new life; he set out to live as though it would be endless. They couldn't marry, but Elaine filed for divorce. Joe Marshall filed a countersuit. It didn't matter; no law could force her to live away from Larry Garth.

New Year's Eve they drove to Chicago for dinner and night's lodging at the Blackhawk. The occasion was a thorough success.

The ceiling was silver, with fleeting iridescent sparkles. He came awake slowly, feeling minor aches one by one. Whatever this was, it was no part of college. For one thing, he hadn't often slept double there, and now a warm body pressed against him.

He turned to see. Only a brief spill of hair, salt-and-pepper, closely cut, showed between covers and pillows. He drew the cover away.

She *would* age well, he thought. Then Elaine opened her gray eyes.

He had to say it fast. "I'm new here, Elaine. Straight from 1970. Nothing in between."

"Nothing? Oh, Larry, there's so *much*. And I've had only a little of it myself. Back and forth—and it's all so different."

"From . . . before, you mean?" His fingers ruffled her hair, then smoothed it.

"Yes." Her eyes widened. "Why, you don't *know* yet, do you? Of course not; you can't."

"Know what, Elaine?"

"How much have you had after 1970? How many years?"

"How much have I used up? I don't know—twelve years? Fifteen, maybe. Why?"

"Because it's *not* used up; it's all new!" Her hand gripped his wrist tightly, to the edge of pain. "Larry, I came here from '75—from a time I'd had *before*, married to Joe. But this time I was with you. This time we're together all the way."

He couldn't speak and his laugh was shaky, but his mind flashed. I'll have to die again, he thought—or will I? And then: We've gained ten years together; could we make it twenty? I've never had the actual wedding to Darlene! What if . . .

But he said only, "There's a lot to tell, isn't there?" And so much he wanted to ask, when there was time for that.

"Yes." She turned her face upward, wriggled her head and neck hard into the pillow, then smiled. "I saw Judy once, in '74. She married a lawyer and had twins. And she wasn't a lush."

"I'm glad."

"I know. You were when I told you then too."

He laughed. "What lives we lead, Elaine. What lives . . ."

Then he remembered. "But *you*. Are you—?" The bulky comforter hid her contours. Two breasts, one, or none? He told himself it didn't matter. She was alive, wasn't she?

"Oh, I'm fine, really," she said. "It worked. Of course the scar was horrid at first. To me—*you* never seemed to mind. But it's faded now; you can hardly see it."

"How long—?"

"It's been five years." She must have seen the question in his face; she shook her head. "No; I don't know how long I live—or you. This is the oldest I've been. And I haven't known a *you* who's been older."

"Elaine? How old are we now?"

She smiled, and then her mouth went soft and full. She pushed the cover back and turned to face him squarely. He looked and saw that she had lost nothing of herself, save for the tribute to the years. Part of him that had been prepared to comfort and reassure her took a deep breath and relaxed.

"How old?" she said. "Old enough to know better, I suppose, but I hope we don't.

"Does it matter? We'll have time enough to be young."

One of them reached out, and the other responded.

SCHRÖDINGER'S CAT

by Ursula K. Le Guin

People who try to impose categories on fiction only create logical traps for themselves—this box for "hard science" stories, that box for "new wave" stories . . . And then someone like Ursula Le Guin (The Left Hand of Darkness, The Lathe of Heaven) comes along and trips the lid of the box, and the categorizers are caught inside it, or outside it.

Here's a delightful story that uses a famous physics anomaly as the motif for a narrative of the Earth falling into uncertainty. Is it "hard science"? Is it "new wave"? Try not to answer.

.   .   .

AS things appear to be coming to some sort of climax, I have withdrawn to this place. It is cooler here, and nothing moves fast.

On the way here I met a married couple who were coming apart. She had pretty well gone to pieces, but he seemed, at first glance, quite hearty. While he was telling me that he had no hormones of any kind, she pulled herself together, and by supporting her head in the crook of her right knee and hopping on the toes of the right foot, approached us shouting, "Well, what's *wrong* with a person trying to express themselves?" The left leg, the arms and the trunk, which had remained lying in the heap, twitched and jerked in sympathy.

"Great legs," the husband pointed out, looking at the slim ankle. "My wife has great legs."

A cat has arrived, interrupting my narrative. It is a striped yellow tom with white chest and paws. He has long whiskers and yellow eyes. I never noticed before that cats had whiskers above their eyes; is that normal? There is no way to tell. As he has gone to sleep on my knee, I shall proceed.

Where?

Nowhere, evidently. Yet the impulse to narrate remains. Many things are not worth doing, but almost anything is worth telling. In any case, I have a severe congenital case of Ethica laboris puritanica, or Adam's Disease. It is incurable except by total decephalization. I even like to dream when asleep, and to try and recall my dreams: it assures me that I haven't wasted seven or eight hours just lying there. Now here I am, lying, here. Hard at it.

Well, the couple I was telling you about finally broke up. The pieces of him trotted around bouncing and cheeping, like little chicks, but she was finally reduced to nothing but a mass of nerves: rather like fine chicken-wire, in fact, but hopelessly tangled.

So I came on, placing one foot carefully in front of the other, and grieving. This grief is with me still. I fear it is part of me, like foot or loin or eye, or may even be myself: for I seem to have no other self, nothing further, nothing that lies outside the borders of grief.

Yet I don't know what I grieve for: my wife? my husband? my children, or myself? I can't remember. Most dreams are forgotten, try as one will to remember. Yet later music strikes the note and the harmonic rings along the mandolin-strings of the mind, and we find tears in our eyes. Some note keeps playing that makes me want to cry; but what for? I am not certain.

The yellow cat, who may have belonged to the couple that broke up, is dreaming. His paws twitch now and then, and once he makes a small, suppressed remark with his mouth shut. I wonder what a cat dreams of, and to whom he was speaking just then. Cats seldom waste words. They are quiet beasts. They keep their counsel, they reflect. They reflect all day, and at night their eyes reflect. Overbred Siamese cats may be as noisy as little dogs, and then people say, "They're talking," but the noise is further from speech than is the deep silence of the hound or the tabby. All this cat can say is meow, but maybe in his silences he will suggest to me what it is that I have lost, what I am grieving for. I have a feeling that he knows. That's why he came here. Cats look out for Number One.

It was getting awfully hot. I mean, you could touch less and less. The stove-burners, for instance; now, I know that stove-burners always used to get hot, that was their final cause, they existed in order to get hot. But they began to get hot without having been turned on. Electric units or gas rings, there they'd be when you came into the kitchen for breakfast, all four of them glaring away, the air above them shaking like clear jelly with the heat waves. It did no good to turn them off, because they weren't on in the first place. Besides, the knobs and dials were also hot, uncomfortable to the touch.

Some people tried hard to cool them off. The favorite technique was to turn them on. It worked sometimes, but you could not count on it. Others investigated the phenomenon, tried to get at the root of it, the cause. They were probably the most frightened ones, but man is most human at his most frightened. In the face of the hot stove-burners they acted with exemplary coolness. They studied, they observed. They were like the fellow in Michelangelo's "Last Judgment" who has clapped his hands over his face in horror as the devils drag him down to Hell—but only over one eye. The other eye is busy looking. It's all he can do, but he does it. He observes. Indeed, one wonders if Hell would exist if he did not look at it. However, neither he nor the people I am talking about had enough time left to do much about it. And then finally of course there were the people who did not try to do or think anything about it at all.

When hot water came out of the cold-water taps one morning, however, even people who had blamed it all on the Democrats began to feel a more profound unease. Before long, forks and pencils and wrenches were too hot to handle without gloves; and cars were really terrible. It was like opening the door of an oven going full blast, to open the door of your car. And by then, other people almost scorched your fingers off. A kiss was like a branding iron. Your child's hair flowed along your hand like fire.

Here, as I said, it is cooler; and, as a matter of fact, this animal is cool. A real cool cat. No wonder it's pleasant to pet his fur. Also he moves slowly, at least for the most part, which is all the slowness one can reasonably expect of a cat. He hasn't that frenetic quality most creatures acquired—all they did was ZAP and gone. They lacked presence. I suppose birds always tended to be that way, but even the hummingbird used to halt for a second in the very center of his metabolic frenzy, and hang, still as a hub, present, above the fuchsias—then gone again, but you knew something was there besides the blurring brightness. But it got so that even robins and pigeons, the heavy impudent birds, were a blur; and as for swallows, they cracked the sound barrier. You knew of swallows only by the small, curved sonic booms that looped about the eaves of old houses in the evening.

Worms shot like subway trains through the dirt of gardens, among the writhing roots of roses.

You could scarcely lay a hand on children, by then: too fast to catch, too hot to hold. They grew up before your eyes.

But then, maybe that's always been true.

I was interrupted by the cat, who woke and said meow once, then jumped down from my lap and leaned against my legs diligently. This is a cat who knows how to get fed. He also knows how to jump. There was a lazy fluidity to his leap, as if gravity affected him less than it does other creatures. As a matter of fact there were some localized cases, just before I left, of the failure of gravity; but this quality in the cat's leap was something quite else. I am not yet in such a state of confusion that I can be alarmed by grace. Indeed, I found it reassuring. While I was opening a can of sardines, a person arrived.

Hearing the knock, I thought it might be the mailman. I miss mail very much, so I hurried to the door and said, "Is it the mail?" A voice replied, "Yah!" I opened the door. He came in, almost pushing me aside in his haste. He dumped down an enormous knapsack he had been carrying, straightened up, massaged his shoulders, and said, "Wow!"

"How did you get here?"

He stared at me and repeated, "How?"

At this, my thoughts concerning human and animal speech recurred to me, and I decided that this was probably not a man, but a small dog. (Large dogs seldom go yah, wow, how, unless it is appropriate to do so.)

"Come on, fella," I coaxed him. "Come, come on, that's a boy, good doggie!" I opened a can of pork and beans for him at once, for he looked half-starved. He ate voraciously, gulping and lapping. When it was gone he said "Wow!" several times. I was just about to scratch him behind the ears when he stiffened, his hackles bristling, and growled deep in his throat. He had noticed the cat.

The cat had noticed him some time before, without interest, and was now sitting on a copy of *The Well-Tempered Clavichord* washing sardine oil off its whiskers.

"Wow!" the dog, whom I had thought of calling Rover, barked. "Wow! Do you know what that is? *That's Schrödinger's cat!*"

"No, it's not; not any more; it's my cat," I said, unreasonably offended.

"Oh, well, Schrödinger's dead, of course, but it's his cat. I've seen hundreds of pictures of it. Erwin Schrödinger, the great physicist, you know. Oh, wow! To think of finding it here!"

The cat looked coldly at him for a moment, and began to wash its left shoulder with negligent energy. An almost religious expression had come into Rover's face. "It was meant," he said in a low, impressive tone. "Yah. It was *meant*. It can't be a mere coincidence. It's too improbable. Me, with the box; you, with the cat; to meet—here—now." He looked up at me, his eyes shining with happy fervor. "Isn't it wonderful?" he said. "I'll get the box set up right away." And he started to tear open his huge knapsack.

While the cat washed its front paws, Rover unpacked. While the cat washed its tail and belly, regions hard to reach gracefully, Rover put together what he had unpacked, a complex task. When he and the cat finished their operations simultaneously and looked at me, I was impressed. They had come out even, to the very second. Indeed it seemed that something more than chance was involved. I hoped it was not myself.

"What's that?" I asked, pointing to a protuberance on the outside of the box. I did not ask what the box was, as it was quite clearly a box.

"The gun," Rover said with excited pride.

"The gun?"

"To shoot the cat."

"To shoot the cat?"

"Or to *not shoot* the cat. Depending on the photon."

"The photon?"

"Yah! It's Schrödinger's great *Gedankenexperiment*. You see, there's a little emitter here. At Zero Time, five seconds after the lid of the box is closed, it will emit one photon. The photon will strike a half-silvered mirror. The quantum mechanical probability of the photon passing through the mirror is exactly one-half, isn't it? So! If the photon passes through, the trigger will be activated and the gun will fire. If the photon is deflected, the trigger will not be activated and the gun will not fire. Now, you put the cat in. The cat is in the box. You close the lid. You go away! You stay away! What happens?" Rover's eyes were bright.

"The cat gets hungry?"

"The cat gets shot—or not shot," he said, seizing my arm, though not, fortunately, in his teeth. "But the gun is silent, perfectly silent. The box is soundproof. There is no way to know whether or not the cat has been shot until you lift the lid of the box. There is NO way! Do you see how central this is to the whole of quantum theory? Before Zero Time the whole system, on the quantum level or on our level, is nice and simple. But after Zero Time the whole system can be represented only by a linear combination of two waves. We cannot predict the behavior of the photon, and thus, once it has behaved, we cannot predict the state of the system it has determined. We cannot predict it! God plays dice with the world! So it is beautifully demonstrated that if you desire certainty, any certainty, you must create it yourself!"

"How?"

"By lifting the lid of the box, of course," Rover said, looking at me with sudden disappointment, perhaps a touch of suspicion, like a Baptist who finds he has been talking church matters not to another Baptist as he thought, but to a Methodist, or even, God forbid, an Episcopalian. "To find out whether the cat is dead or not."

"Do you mean," I said carefully, "that until you lift the lid of the box, the cat has neither been shot nor not been shot?"

"Yah!" Rover said, radiant with relief, welcoming me back to the fold. "Or maybe, you know, both."

"But why does opening the box and looking reduce the system back to one probability, either live cat or dead cat? Why don't we get included in the system when we lift the lid of the box?"

There was a pause. "How?" Rover barked distrustfully.

"Well, we would involve ourselves in the system, you see, the superposition of two waves. There's no reason why it should only exist *inside* an open box, is there? So when we came to look, there we would be, you and I, both looking at a live cat, and both looking at a dead cat. You see?"

A dark cloud lowered on Rover's eyes and brow. He barked twice in a subdued, harsh voice, and walked away. With his back turned to me he said in a firm, sad tone, "You must not complicate the issue. It is complicated enough."

"Are you sure?"

He nodded. Turning, he spoke pleadingly. "Listen. It's all we have—the box. Truly it is. The box. And the cat. And they're here. The box, the cat, at last. Put the cat in the box. Will you? Will you let me put the cat in the box?"

"No," I said, shocked.

"Please. Please. Just for a minute. Just for half a minute! Please let me put the cat in the box!"

"Why?"

"I can't stand this terrible uncertainty," he said, and burst into tears.

I stood some while indecisive. Though I felt sorry for the poor son of a bitch, I was about to tell him, gently, No, when a curious thing happened. The cat walked over to the box, sniffed around it, lifted his tail and sprayed a corner to mark his territory, and then lightly, with that marvelous fluid ease, leapt into it. His yellow tail just flicked the edge of the lid as he jumped, and it closed, falling into place with a soft, decisive click.

"The cat is in the box," I said.

"The cat is in the box," Rover repeated in a whisper, falling to his knees. "Oh, wow. Oh, wow. Oh, wow."

There was silence then: deep silence. We both gazed, I afoot, Rover kneeling, at the box. No sound. Nothing happened. Nothing would happen. Nothing would ever happen, until we lifted the lid of the box.

"Like Pandora," I said in a weak whisper. I could not quite recall Pandora's legend. She had let all the plagues and evils out of the box, of course, but there had been something else, too. After all the devils were let loose, something quite different, quite unexpected, had been left. What had it been? Hope? A dead cat? I could not remember.

Impatience welled up in me. I turned on Rover, glaring. He returned the look with expressive brown eyes. You can't tell me dogs haven't got souls.

"Just exactly what are you trying to prove?" I demanded.

"That the cat will be dead, or not dead," he murmured submissively. "Certainty. All I want is certainty. To know for *sure* that God *does* play dice with the world."

I looked at him for a while with fascinated incredulity. "Whether he does, or doesn't," I said, "do you think he's going to leave you a note about it in the box?" I went to the box, and with a rather dramatic gesture, flung the lid back. Rover staggered up from his knees, gasping, to look. The cat was, of course, not there.

Rover neither barked, nor fainted, nor cursed, nor wept. He really took it very well.

"Where is the cat?" he asked at last.

"Where is the box?"

"Here."

"Where's here?"

"Here is now."

"We used to think so," I said, "but really we should use larger boxes."

He gazed about him in mute bewilderment, and did not flinch

even when the roof of the house was lifted off just like the lid of a box, letting in the unconscionable, inordinate light of the stars. He had just time to breathe, "Oh, wow!"

I have identified the note that keeps sounding. I checked it on the mandolin before the glue melted. It is the note A, the one that drove Robert Schumann mad. It is a beautiful, clear tone, much clearer now that the stars are visible. I shall miss the cat. I wonder if he found what it was we lost?

HOW IT FELT

by Geo. Alec Effinger

Geo. Alec Effinger has been writing a series of stories about the far future of humanity that contrast the miracles of our technology in that distant time with the matter-of-fact quality of the life then. See, for two examples, "The Ghost Writer" in Universe 3, and the following dry narrative of the last person on Earth who could feel emotion.

A STUDIED carelessness. It was a phrase that held a peculiar fascination for her; its paradox of attitudes struck her as sophisticated in a way that she herself was not. Adopting a studied carelessness of manner could make her appear more sophisticated to her friends.

It was late at night when Vivi came to this conclusion. She was standing beneath an immense tree in the congregation area of her home. The tree was one of her favorites; its bark was tough, black, scored with a vertical network of furrows. Its limbs were dressed with dangling shawls of Spanish moss, which Vivi had created in imitation of Alhu's trees. Vivi's friends, for the most part, had never seen Alhu's, and they frequently remarked on Vivi's imagination. She always smiled but said nothing when they complimented her.

The stars frightened her, and as she stood beneath her tree she kept her eyes down, refusing to look through the tangle of leaves into the threatening face of the night. She tried instead to imagine how her friends would react when she assumed a new personality. Moa would be the first to notice. Moa was always the first; Moa would raise her eyebrows and whisper something in Vivi's ear: how bored Moa was growing, how tired Moa was of wandering through a lifetime without events, how much Moa welcomed Vivi's eccentricities. Moa would kiss Vivi as a reward. They would spend the day in repetitious sexual gratifications.

But then it would become dark. Vivi would be terrified by starlight, seized by a hatred of the moon. As always, Moa would not understand, and she would return to her own home. Vivi would be alone, as she was every night.

Vivi sighed. Even her fantasies were empty.

The branches above her head rustled. Vivi laughed bitterly. *It won't work,* she thought. *You can't trick me that way.* Vivi didn't look up into the muttering boughs where stars waited like determined voyeurs among the leaves. She felt the rough side of the tree a final time, rubbing her fingers painfully over the stone-hard ridges. Still staring into the grass at her feet, she moved slowly away.

A thin wall ran across the congregation area, roughly parallel to the narrow brook. The wall was seven feet tall and four times that in length. It contained various devices which dispensed food and drink, as well as whatever other luxuries her companions required. Another wall, beyond the grove of the congregation area, held the transportation unit. Still other service units, scattered about the several square miles of her open-air house, provided everything Vivi or her friends could ever desire.

The carefully trimmed lawn changed to clumps of grass, then to isolated brownish stalks of weed growing in a narrow track of sand and pebbles. Vivi sat down at the edge of the brook. She dipped her hand in the water; it was a pleasantly warm temperature, the same temperature as the air in her home. The temperature of both was constant. Trees grew along the opposite side of the brook, and their leafy branches prevented the stars' reflections from frightening Vivi. She was bored. She was young, but she was bored. Nevertheless, she couldn't yet retire to her sleeping area. It was still too early in the night to lie on her back and stare at the evil constellations, letting the infinite horror of space invade her mind. If she did that too soon, then nothing would be left to pass the remainder of the night. She couldn't face that possibility.

"Vivi!"

She turned around; the thin wall blocked her view of her visitor, but she recognized the voice. It was Moa. "I'm here by the brook," said Vivi.

Moa walked around the wall and joined Vivi at the edge of the water. "I thought you'd be here," said Moa. "I want to show you something."

Vivi felt a sudden excitement. "Have you found something new?" she asked.

"I'm not certain," said Moa. "You'll have to help me."

"Of course," murmured Vivi, a little disappointed.

"I've brought Tagea. I hope you don't mind. He's waiting in your passagerie. He gave me the idea."

"No," said Vivi. "I don't mind."

"Good," said Moa, standing and pulling Vivi up beside her. "Let's use your transportation unit. It'll be quicker." The two women splashed across the brook and through the small stand of trees. They came out on a wide meadow which was part of Vivi's sleeping area. It was here that, during the daylight hours, she and Moa shared the often tedious pleasures of their bodies. Vivi did not have to keep her gaze fixed on the ground; alone no longer, she found no terror in the stars. She wondered what new thing Moa had discovered.

She comes to me more often than to any of the others, thought Vivi. *It is because I have emotion. It is because I can entertain varying states of mind. Moa cannot. None of the others can. Only I. And the price of this lonely talent is panic.* Vivi walked beside Moa, trying to hold her pace down to Moa's languid speed. On the far side of the meadow was a ravine. They climbed down into it; Vivi enjoyed the humidity, the feel of the mud beneath her bare feet, even the biting of her insects. She glanced at Moa. Her companion's expression was no different than it ever was. Moa was without emotion.

They scrambled up the other side of the ravine. Vivi saw the man Tagea waiting by the wall. He said nothing when the two women appeared. Moa led the way, and Vivi followed. They stepped through the portal of the transportation unit; the unit, tied into the TECT system buried deep beneath the surface of the earth, transported them to Moa's chosen destination. Vivi blinked rapidly as she walked across the threshold. Wherever they were, it was now bright daylight.

"This is a new world," said Moa.

"I found it a few years ago," said Tagea. "It amused me, but now I've given it to Moa."

Vivi yawned; it was the first outward sign of her new campaign of studied carelessness. She would be unimpressed, not at all curious. She said nothing. She could see that Moa was disappointed.

"That sun in the sky is the center star of the Wheel of the Sleeper," said Moa. "I recall your hatred of stars. I remember that this star seems specially malignant to you. We have come here for several reasons, one of which is to prove to you that you have nothing to fear."

"Ah, Moa," said Vivi quietly, "you won't understand. It is not a product of objective thought, this terror I feel. It is something else, something which you cannot share. It is my burden alone."

"It is your *illness* alone," said Tagea. He stared at Vivi, shielding his eyes with both hands against the glare of the odd sun. Vivi did not answer, though her anger almost caused her to scream. But that would not have been in keeping with her new self.

"Are you unwell?" asked Moa. "You do not appear to be as unsteady in your responses. You are repressing the irrational personality that is your chief asset."

Vivi shrugged. Moa took her hand and led her across a field of waving blue grasses. Tagea followed them; Vivi could hear him muttering to himself. It was a habit of his whenever it was obvious that he was being excluded from the immediate sexual situation. The three people walked for several miles. Vivi was becoming increasingly fatigued; at first, the magenta tint of the sky intrigued her, but that lasted only a hundred paces. The irritating tickle of the grass occupied her for another hundred. Then there was nothing. The horizon was empty. There was only Moa, still holding her hand, and Tagea's smug monologue behind them.

Why are we here? thought Vivi. Surely in her search for diversion, Moa had found something of interest. It must lie beyond the endless blue sea of grass. Vivi couldn't allow herself to ask the question aloud, however. She was establishing her character. Moa, who had no emotions, needed time to notice and analyze the difference.

It was a difficult thing being the only person left with true feelings. Vivi often cursed her emotions; they interfered with her relations with Moa and the others. Vivi was more of a creature, a temporary entertainment, than an equal to them. She wished that she could throw her feelings away, strip them off as all the other people had done generations before. But then again, she was glad of her affliction. Her emotions helped her pass the awful hours. She never had to search the world—and other worlds—for amusement.

"You are oddly silent," said Moa.

"It is a mood," said Tagea. "Several of her moods include silence. I would have thought you'd have cataloged them all by now. Perhaps this is 'spite' again. Or 'petulance.' We've had them all before. I have long since grown weary of them. They are so limited."

"Is he right, Vivi?" asked Moa. "Is it another emotion?"

"Oh, I don't know," said Vivi. "I'm just being quiet. Is there something I should be saying?"

"No, of course not," said Moa. "But you're usually more responsive." Vivi only shrugged once more.

They emerged finally from the broad prairie, coming out on the bank of a small, muddy river. On the opposite bank was a collection of artificial buildings. Vivi forgot her new personality for a moment and gasped in surprise.

"Those are homes," said Moa. She sounded pleased that Vivi had at last reacted. "They're like our homes, in a way, except that these low-level creatures trap themselves within physical limits. They must be surrounded by the products of their labor. It is a peculiar and annoying form of pride."

"I ought to defend them," said Tagea. "After all, I discovered them. They think I'm some kind of universal authority. It was amusing for a short time, but it didn't last."

Moa frowned. "You can't protect them now," she said. "You gave them to me."

"Yes," said Tagea. "I had no intention of interceding. I was only considering alternatives."

"Are you going to kill them?" asked Vivi. She said it with her air of studied carelessness so that it didn't seem to matter to her whether Moa answered or not.

Moa walked down to the river's edge. She scooped up a handful of stones. "TECT will help me, even here," she said. "Watch." Moa extended her arms. The water began to churn violently. Rocks from the bed of the river and from the solid ground tore themselves loose and piled up to make a bridge. "I won't kill those creatures directly," said Moa. "Maybe indirectly. We'll see."

Vivi crossed the rock span behind Moa and Tagea. She wondered at how simple it had been to graft a new point of view onto her personality. It was no effort at all to maintain her unconcerned attitude; it was now the most natural thing to wander about with her companions, unimpressed, unaffected, somewhat weary. Moa was already puzzled by Vivi's behavior, but Tagea, the possessor of decidedly inferior mental powers, hadn't yet noticed. Vivi felt less than she had anticipated; she had hoped for a different wealth of worldliness, but had acquired little that was remarkable. She understood that this was how Moa had lived her entire life, without measurable degrees of emotion. It was an attractive quality in Moa. Vivi hoped it would be the same in herself.

"Look," said Tagea. He pointed toward the nearest of the buildings. A small gathering of creatures had formed.

"What do you think of them?" said Moa.

"Nothing, as yet," said Vivi lazily. "I noticed that they have covered their bodies with furry containers, even though the sun is uncomfortably warm."

"Do you wish to converse with them?" asked Tagea.

"Don't you want to love them, or be afraid?" asked Moa.

Vivi stretched and yawned. "Are we in a hurry to return?" she said. Moa shook her head. Vivi waited. Moa raised her eyebrows and shook her head once more.

The creatures shouted at them as the three walked through their town. Moa and Tagea took no notice. Vivi was startled by the creatures' appearance at first, but after a short time she found their ugliness monotonous. Moa led the way beyond the stinking settlement; Vivi noticed that her feelings were fewer and weaker than ever before. She was pleased. She walked across a broad, stony plain and climbed several low hills on the far side. At the top of the tallest of these hills, Moa turned and pointed back in the direction they had traveled. "There," she said. "That's the community of the native creatures. You can see the smoke."

"It is much more pleasant here," said Vivi.

"The path is unbearably steep," said Tagea. "The rocks in the soil are uncomfortable to walk upon. We will only have to repeat the journey to get home."

"Where we are, TECT is," said Vivi. "TECT will take us home from here."

"I had planned to walk all the way back to the point where we arrived on this world," said Moa. "It will be an adventure."

"Yes," said Vivi. "An adventure."

"Boring," said Tagea.

"Be seated," said Moa. Vivi and Tagea glanced at each other, then made themselves as comfortable as possible in the dry dust of the hilltop. Moa licked her lips and walked a few steps away from them. She faced away from the creatures' village toward a vast, gray body of water in the distance. "That is an inland sea," she said. "It is larger than any sea on our world except the sunset ocean." Moa raised her hands toward the water. Perspiration appeared on her brow and on her upper lip. She held her position for many minutes. Vivi said nothing. Tagea was not even watching. Moa's body glistened with sweat. Her concentration was complete; her connection with TECT deepened until Moa quivered with a dangerous power.

"I've seen this before," said Tagea. "I think I've seen *everything* before."

"So have I," whispered Vivi. "But there's no one that can match the taste and delicacy of Moa's technique. I had hoped that we'd see something new, though."

"There's still time," said Tagea. "We'll be here for quite a while, if I know her."

The outline of the giant sea was blurred by distance. Still, Vivi could see that it was changing shape. Moa pointed one hand at the water, but swung the other slowly toward the neighboring hills.

Carefully coordinating her devastating strokes, Moa splintered the ground at the edge of the ocean, and crushed the small mountains that stood between her and the water.

The hills turned from a rich blue to an ashen gray. Moa pulled moisture from them, desiccated them, crumbled the ancient bones of rock into a fragile powder. The hills collapsed in great clouds which obscured Vivi's vision for a long while. Moa waited until the storm she had created subsided; the day ended with Moa standing, posing. Tagea slept. Vivi practiced her lack of passion. At dusk the air cleared. The dust settled into low mounds on the plain, white and sterile. Moa let loose the waters of the sea through channels and fissures she built among the dead hills. The water rolled quickly, noisily at first until Moa gestured. The ocean became sluggish and thick. The water contracted.

The night passed quietly. Vivi watched the ocean shrink in its new course until the entire inland sea had shriveled to the size of a small pond. By then it was nearly dawn.

"Have I missed anything interesting?" asked Tagea.

"A pyrotechnic display," said Vivi. "Much more energetic than her usual, I suppose. Watch."

The pond that was all that remained of the ocean sat between two mounds of white powder. The water was a dark green. Moa pressed her fingers together, and the water bubbled. It shrank even further, rolling into a sphere of black substance. The sphere wasted away into a mere ball the size of a fruit, the color of the powdery hills. Moa extended her hands, and the ball began to spin. The ball bounced across the distance separating the hills from their creator. It became lighter, finally rolling as softly as a hairball to its finish at Moa's feet. She nodded and bent to pick up the round clump of stuff. She held it for a moment and dropped it back again. She forgot it. Moa said nothing.

Tagea yawned, and Vivi merely stared. Moa was not yet finished; she had only begun to block out her work. Vivi could not visualize the totality of Moa's project and thus could not understand the reasons behind each of her specific, sure touches.

Still, Vivi did not wonder. She would not give Moa that ever again.

After a time Moa stopped. Her arms fell to her sides at last, her bunched back muscles relaxed. To Vivi, Moa seemed to shrink, to withdraw within herself. She became human again. Moa turned to her friends and sighed. "I will study your reactions now," she said.

"A trifle overdone, don't you think?" asked Tagea.

"You always say that," said Moa. "I don't care to hear your opinion. I want to relish our Vivi's. This has all been for her benefit."

"I have seen it before," said Vivi. "Not all together, of course. But you're only stringing one trick after another. I want something different."

Moa stared. "Where is your dismay now?" she asked. "Where is your awe? I need it, Vivi. I'm hungry."

"I'm tired," said Vivi.

"Give me your fear," said Moa. Vivi said nothing. Moa turned toward the village of the creatures. She merely pointed. There was a distant, hollow noise, and the settlement disappeared in a muffled explosion.

"You killed them all," said Vivi.

Moa nodded. She made the ground open up beneath the wreckage of the town. Just as suddenly, as the debris tumbled into the crack, she made the earth close up. There was no sign that any living thing had ever passed by that place.

"We must delight our friends with this," said Vivi. "This is no doubt an entertaining moment. But it has gone on too long. You've always lacked discipline, Moa."

"Yes," said Tagea. "Let's go back now."

Moa's eyebrows twitched. "I've never known anger," she said. "I've never known hatred or admiration. But frustration is common enough among us. It is an itch. It must be scratched, one way or another." She put out her hand again. Tagea jumped to his feet as though he were a marionette. His face contorted in pain. His arms and legs wobbled in the cool evening breeze; they looked as if there were no longer any bones inside to give them a normal human shape. Still Tagea jerked about. Finally, Moa let him fall to the ground. He collapsed into a heap like a doll filled with sawdust. His corpse turned bright, glossy pink. Vivi moved quietly to his side and touched him. His skin was hard and cold, like polished stone. As Vivi watched, Moa turned Tagea's body into a small, perfect cube of pink crystal.

"Tagea?" asked Vivi.

"He's right there," said Moa. "How do you react?"

Vivi looked up with an expression of studied carelessness. "He was more tiresome than he knew," she said.

Moa raised her hand again. Vivi raised her own. The two women stared at each other. At last, Moa dropped her arm. "I'm dead," she said. "You were my only pleasure."

"It's a pity you can't enjoy all this for its own sake," said Vivi, indicating the ruined world.

"I used to," said Moa. "Many years ago."

"I'm going home." Vivi contacted TECT and gave the mental order to be transported back to her house. When she arrived, it was once again night. She was very tired; she went to her sleeping area. Vivi was strangely glad that she was alone.

The meadow was cool, her sleeping temperature. The air was filled with pleasant flower scents. Vivi's birds twittered in the distant trees. She lay in the tall grass, preparing herself for her day's greatest, final pleasure. She opened her eyes to the stars, waiting for the wave of utter horror to sweep through her.

It never happened.

THE NIGHT IS COLD,
THE STARS ARE FAR AWAY

by Mildred Downey Broxon

Mildred Downey Broxon was raised in Rio de Janeiro and
now lives on a houseboat in Seattle with her husband and a boa
constrictor named Sigmund. A former psychiatric nurse, she
attended the Clarion-West sf writers' workshop in 1972 and sold
her first story to Clarion III.

"The Night Is Cold, The Stars Are Far Away" is the second story
she's sold; of it she says, "I wrote this while studying the
overturning of the geocentric theory in astronomy class, and
wondering what would happen to a race living in a one-planet
system with little or no axial tilt, therefore no seasons, etc., and no
reason to think that everything did not, in fact, revolve around
them."

INAR stepped out of the gray dead-earth tower and rubbed his eyes; age and the nightwatch combined to make him tired. His fur was graying and brittle, his eight-fingered hands were stiff, and his eyes were clouding. The breeze was chill; he shivered in his cloak and wrapped his long thick tail around his neck. The glow of approaching dawn was dimming the stars; it was time to go home, time to crawl into his darkened cubicle and sleep the daylight hours away while the rest of the world went on about its business.

His neighbors regarded him as an eccentric, the mad old one who had wasted his life watching the stars. He was harmless, all agreed, and the Mother cherishes fools. But his own children had forsaken the work and him. Inar wondered if his mother had felt so alone. But no; she, of course, had relied on him to carry on.

"Long ago," she had said, standing small and bent beside the tower, "our entire family watched the sky and hoped. Now there are only my brother, myself, and your father."

"What happened to all the others?" he said. The sun was warm; he wanted to play, not spend his nights in the dusty old tower. But his duty was plain.

"They grew old and died. Some say the Mother of All receives us no matter what we believe." She crouched by the tower wall and wrapped her arms against the wind. "Your brother has left us. He has gone into the service of the Mother. And since your uncle had no sons or daughters, only blindthings, there is no one left but you, Inar, to carry on. Find a good wife, one who will help you. Raise children, not blindthings. Remember to watch the sky."

Out of love and respect he had promised that night, and for the rest of the nights of his life he had watched, he and his wife. His wife had worked with him, talked to him, supported him until the Mother of All took her in the last childbirth, took her and the child conceived too late and born too soon—and that was many sixty-fours of days ago.

Now he was alone, for his promise could not bind his sons and daughters, who laughed and called him mad. They never came to the tower.

"Why? You have watched since you were a child, and your mother and father watched before you, and their parents before them. The sun circles us and the stars are jewels on the nightcloak of the Mother."

A cold sharp wind sang through him and he huddled inside his thin cloak. Was his family, indeed, cursed with blindthings and madness, cursed by the misdeeds of Ancestor Caltai who had, in the dim back-reaches of time, committed them all to the skywatch?

He rose and went into the tower to gather his notes and cover the mirror against the dust and heat of day. Pulling open the ancient metal door, he stood looking into darkness. The curved mirror shone dimly on the floor, gathering skylight, now intensifying the faint glow before dawn. Above hung another mirror, angled to focus on his working platform halfway up the wall. He climbed the ladder, put away his notes, and climbed painfully back down. He shook out the soft silvery cloth and draped it over the mirror.

Outside again, he stood on the hillside looking down at the city of Asdul and wondered why he did not merely curl up in some part of the tower and sleep till dusk. He supposed if he did his neighbors would come looking for him, concerned, asking stupid questions, raising dust to foul the mirror; they worried for his health and wanted him to be cared for. He did not want care; he did not want to be humored like a blindthing.

It was light enough now that he could see a figure, risen early or still up late, coming up the path to the tower. It would be rude to lock the door and leave, though he did not welcome visitors. He stood and waited.

As the figure drew closer, walking briskly, he thought for a moment he saw his eldest son, and he felt a sudden joy. But he was wrong, of course: his eldest son had grown portly and smug and never left the city. It could not be him; Inar had seen little of him lately.

"Grandfather?" The visitor had reached the tower and stood, cape thrown carelessly back, tail curved about his body.

Inar blinked, "Oh. Ah—"

"Shavna," the youth said.

"Oh, yes. Shavna." Inar looked at him more closely. "I have not seen you for some time—you have grown. My eyes are no longer young—"

The youth shifted from one foot to another. Inar realized he was rambling on like an old fool. "What brings you here, Shavna?"

"I rose early to speak with you; I know you are a daysleeper." He looked at the tower. "I have questions to ask you, questions my parents would not answer."

"Such as?"

Shavna avoided his eyes and crouched low to the ground, running a hand through the live-earth there. "People say that the family carries a curse, and that is why my brother was a blindthing. People say you are mad, and that you do not believe in the Mother of All." He looked at Inar then, his eyes large. "People say my great-great-grandfather Caltai was mad as well."

"People have been quite talkative," Inar said. "But surely you have heard these whispers all your life. They are no secret to me. Why do you come here now?"

Shavna's fingers found a small plant growing in the live-earth. He touched it gently and withdrew his hand. "Because now I wish to marry, and I wonder if it is true, as they say, that madness is passed on. And there are the blindthings—"

Inar sighed. "It is true our family has produced many more blindthings than other families have. I do not know whether it has anything to do with Ancestor Caltai. And I cannot answer you about the madness; for if I am mad, my speech is only raving."

"You do not sound like the madmen I have aided in the market," Shavna said. "Would you tell me the story of Ancestor Caltai, then, and explain what you do here?"

Inar watched the rising sun touch the mountains beyond Asdul. "Your parents could have told you the story as well. They know it."

"They said to ask you." Shavna arranged himself on the ground and wrapped his tail around his feet.

Inar settled his stiff limbs into a semblance of comfort and drew his cloak against the dawn breeze. "Very well. Long ago, when your great-great-grandfather Caltai was still young—before he married—he lived in M'larfra."

"That's far to the south," Shavna said. He sat straighter. "I have studied the maps in school. I thought only barbarians lived there."

"All strangers are barbarians to some," Inar said. "The M'larfrans are nomads, wanderers, driven by the wind and the sand and the sun. They had a custom regarding their young: when a man or woman was ready to wed, he or she went out to the desert alone to consider how to have a good marriage and how to raise children. The young person had to list all the mistakes his parents had made, resolve not to make the same mistakes himself, and then—most important—forgive his parents. If he did not forgive them, he knew his own children would never forgive him for the mistakes he would make in turn.

"Each one sought solitude as best he could; Ancestor Caltai was strong and healthy, and he walked far into the desert until he came to one lone seng tree. There he crouched in its small shade and thought.

"The sun was hot, as it always is in M'larfra. He sat for hours, thinking, then looked up surprised, for the Mother of All seemed to have sent him a vision, and he did not consider himself worthy of visions.

"He saw a bright gleam in the air and felt the ground shake. Sand flew in a fountain and settled again; he went to see what had happened. He thought it was close-by.

"He walked farther than he had expected, and found plants shattered and small sunskimmers dead. At last he came to the crest of a sand-hill and looked down into the next hollow where a metal form lay partly buried in the sand. He was not afraid; the Mother lives in the sky, and he thought she had sent him a gift. He went closer and saw a hole in the side of the metal object, and on the sand, a white figure sprawled. When he came yet closer, he could see that the being—for such it was—was much larger than he. It lay on the sand; he came up to it and greeted it with word and gesture of reverence. For it had, indeed, come from the sky.

"When he touched the figure, Ancestor Caltai was surprised to hear it speaking—"

The youth was astonished. "It came from the sky, and it spoke M'larfra-speech?"

"No. As the story goes, it spoke no clear words at all—it spoke to his knowing. It did not seem to know where it was; it sounded sick and hurt, and spoke as those who rave in fever."

"How could that be? How could it speak without language?"

"It had some device for speaking to strangers. Pictures and ideas formed in Caltai's mind. Or so the story goes."

"Oh," said the youth. "What did it say—think?"

"It wept inside," Inar said, "for it was dying, and alone. It had made an error, and had crashed its ship—"

"Its ship? In the desert? You said it came from the sky!"

"It thought of a ship, a sky-ship, that had crashed. It thought of stars, and it looked once at our sun and moaned. For its sun was golden, not silver, and it was far from home. And as it thought of its sun, it thought of our world, like a ball of earth and water, spinning around the sun, a ball of flame."

"It was, perhaps, ill to madness," Shavna said.

Inar continued. "The pictures were quite clear. It thought of its own world, green like old copper and blue like young lichen. It revolved around a burning golden sun, and around the sun were its sister worlds, hot and cold and far away. Then it thought again of our world, where it now lay injured, and it thought 'one-planet system' and 'no astronomy'—by which it meant study of the stars. It thought also of ideas Caltai could not understand; the pictures that formed made no sense."

"It must have been raving in madness," Shavna said.

"If so, then from where did it come? Would the Mother drop a child and let it die? Have you ever heard madness like this madness? Madmen rave of things they know, not of things they know not."

"True."

"The creature looked away from the sky and saw Caltai, and it was afraid. Caltai was sorry for it, hurt and lost as it was, and made the sign for 'no harm'; the creature seemed to understand. But then grief replaced its fear, and it thought about 'interference,' and it cursed itself for a fool.

"Caltai made the sign for 'whence came you?' but the creature either did not understand or would not answer. It looked up again at the sky and thought of 'sun' and 'home.' Then it turned to Ancestor Caltai and waved its arms, pounded the sand, and pointed over the hill, thinking *'Run! Poison! Danger! Death!'*

"He did not want to leave the injured thing, until it thought about a poison-explosion and great destruction. Then he was afraid. As he left, the creature was growing weaker, and thinking of flying home, but it was near death and much confused, and mostly it felt pain and loneliness. Caltai left, and a short time after he was over the crest of the sand-hill, there was a bright orange flash, thunder threw him to the sand, and when he could stand again he saw a strange-shaped cloud.

"Later, when his fear left, he crept back over the sand-hill; there was no creature, no large silvery shape, nothing but a bowl of hot green glass. So he went home."

"How did his people receive his story?" Shavna asked.

"Badly. They said the sun had addled his brains, that he had been on the desert too long, or that he had not been on the desert long enough. They wanted to take care of him. Only one person believed him: the girl he was to marry. She too had been on the desert, and she too had seen the light fall from the sky, and the flash later. But she had not seen the creature, and of course it was gone. When they returned, the sands had covered even the bowl of glass.

"They talked about what this might mean, but they came to no conclusion, so they decided to come to Asdul, where the wise men live. They took space on a fishing boat, worked a hard, cold, salty passage, and landed here. They spoke to many, and no one could understand their story; finally it was suggested they attend People's Day at the University and ask the wise men themselves.

"They waited in the crowded hall with the other questioners, and when their turn came, some laughed, even though this is forbidden. But one wise man listened with interest, and asked to see them privately.

"They sat in his cool courtyard and drank sweet water while he explained what they must do; for, after all, if the creature came from heaven, it came from the Mother, and if it came from another world, it brought ideas not yet conceived.

"The wise man explained that his studies left him no time, but that they could watch the sky for him; they could watch to see if another creature arrived, and while they watched they could also study the stars.

"For, as he explained, if the creature's tale was true, that the world moved around the sun, and the stars were other suns farther away, then as the world moved, one should see a change in pattern among the stars."

"Why?" asked Shavna.

"Walk around the tower. The green light on the Mother's temple will shift closer to the white light on the University, and then shift back again."

Shavna was silent a moment. "I have seen it," he said.

"The wise man taught them how to observe the stars; he gave

them a scrying mirror, and told them how to watch by night, and how to make metal plates to record what they had seen. He told them that if they found anything they should tell him, and he gave them money with which to live; but he died old with no reward, and so did your Ancestor Caltai.

"The story would have ended there, but Caltai and his wife had taught their children—all but the blindthings, of which they had many—and their children taught theirs. Out of reverence for their parents they watched, though they lost hope after a time and the family was cursed with blindthings, as if the stock had become tainted. Finally the duty to parents strove against duty to the Mother of All. My brother was the first to defect; he entered the priesthood. Of my children, none followed me. My wife died long ago. Now I watch alone."

"Do you think your work has reason?" Shavna said.

"Yes, I do. Most of the time. Why should a goddess watch over us? Why, if she watches, does she not prevent evil? Why did she not keep my wife from dying in the healers' temple? Why were my nephews all blindthings?"

The youth stood. "I wonder too. Show me what you do, and how. Show me how you make the records on the metal plates, and how you watch the sky. Tell me the names you have given the stars, and where they live."

The old one looked at him. "You really want to learn?" His voice was shaking.

"I want to understand if this is madness or a new knowledge."

Inar showed him the scrying mirror, the same as the diviners used, but ground perfect and smooth. He told how the wise man had helped his great-great-grandparents construct it. He showed him the tower, and how it pointed at the sky and kept the lights of the city from the mirror. He climbed stiffly up to his desk to show him the metal plates and the blackening chemicals; he told him how the bright stars made black streaks on the plates.

Then, with a feeling of shame, he showed him the first few plates taken by Ancestor Caltai, the plates he had taken last night, and the careful measurements that showed them to be the same, always and eternally the same.

"That means the world does not move," Shavna said. "It means you are wrong, and the stars are not suns but jewels. Why do you keep watching?"

Inar looked down at the black-streaked plates in his hands. "I promised," he said. "I was very young, and I promised. There is no one to release me from my vow. Either Ancestor Caltai was wrong or—I do not know."

When he looked up, Shavna was gone.

He locked the tower door with a new combination and hobbled down the hill toward home. The stars were all gone, and the city was stirring, ready to rise and face the sun.

Inar awoke toward afternoon and opened the door of his lightproof, soundproof cubicle. He bowed toward the skulls of his mother and father and donned eye-protectors before facing the harsh light of day. Long dark-adaptation had made his eyes sensitive, and the day was not his time to work.

He slid open his doorway and looked down the hall. One of his female neighbors was returning from food-buying.

"Inar," she said, "how are you? What great things did you discover last night?" She ruffled her fur and laughed. "How are your sons and daughters?"

"They are well."

They were not "well" according to Inar's values, but he knew she enjoyed teasing him. She was doubtless glad his children, at least, were "normal."

He walked down the long gleaming hallway to the outer door. He had not eaten; there was no food in the house. He sometimes wondered what he would do if he were no longer accorded Privilege. The storekeepers did not grudge his status, but he always chose the cheapest items, the bruised fruit, the wilted vegetables. He was grateful for the Privilege the Mother gave madmen, fools, and blindthings, but he was also ashamed, and today the shame killed his hunger. He went, instead, to the tower.

The sun was white on the yellow vegetation, the sky was deep-blue, and the air was hot. Inar did not enjoy the bright daytime; he went instead into the cool dark tower where the walls provided shade.

He relaxed in the dim dust-smelling silence. This was his home, not the tiny rooms in the housing project, not the city streets where he was a figure of pity, but here.

He climbed slowly to his desk and ran his fingers over the records of the night before: "The Eyes of the Lover rose above the rim of the tower at 425 nocks, hour 3.2 after sunset. By hour 7.1 the Eyes were 79 nocks dawnward from overhead."

He could have taken the notes out and sight-read them, he could have seen the star tracks on the metal plates, but he preferred to stay in the tower where it was cool and dim and quiet, where he was at home.

He should, he knew, compare his observations again with those made by his grandparents and his parents to see if there might somehow be a change, but he was discouraged and afraid. All his ancestors had failed to see any change in position among the points of light. It was obvious to any intelligent being that if the earth moved, the stars would shift position, for, as he had told Shavna, if one walked around the tower, the lights of the city seemed to shift. But how much more comforting to believe that the lights in the sky were jewels on the nightcloak of the Mother of All, who turned slowly through the night to keep her child, the earth, from harm.

All sky-things rotated about the earth. It was obvious. The sun, the silver fastening on the cloak of the Mother, rose and set always in the same place.

If, instead of the Mother's cloak, there was unimaginable vastness speckled with tiny lonely suns, then nothing circled the earth, the Universe was cold and empty, the Mother did not live, and they were all alone.

Inar smiled bitterly. No wonder Shavna had left. Sometimes he too wondered if Ancestor Caltai had sat too long in the sun and had come home raving. His own position of Privilege showed what people thought. And sometimes when he was discouraged, even he looked up at the night sky, and instead of shrieking empty space, saw the jewel-studded cloak of a protecting Mother.

He edged down the ladder toward the shelf where he kept the collected records of generations. He took measuring instruments, selected a streaked plate from the records of his grandfather, and crouched on the ground. He wanted to be certain; he measured and re-measured, and finally closed his eyes in defeat.

The same, always the same, made with the same instruments, readings taken night after night, lifetime after lifetime, and yet there was no shift among the stars. They rose earlier each night, but in the same fixed patterns. The earth did not move.

He slumped discouraged on the live-earth floor, holding the metal plates in his stiff and tired hands. Why go on? Why not go back to Asdul, sleep at night and wake during the day as other people did? Why not enjoy the brief time he had left? Why give up the world for an ancient dream, an old delusion?

As he sat, the sky grew redder and the shadows lengthened. His mind was numb.

Had he slept, or had he merely stared entranced as shadows fell across the metal plates? When the knock came, he was startled, and the plates clattered to the floor.

He rose on aching limbs and shuffled toward the door. It was Shavna who stood there, with one other, a young female. Shavna's cape swirled carelessly about him; he stood close to the young woman.

"I have thought all day, Grandfather," he said. "I do not believe Ancestor Caltai was mad, nor do I think you are mad.

There is a mystery here, and you are trying to solve it as best you know. That does not make you mad."

The last glow faded from the sky; one by one the brightest stars came out. The twin stars, the Eyes of the Lover, were the brightest of all.

The young woman spoke. "Shavna told me of your watching, and how you and your ancestors have watched for generations to see any change among the stars, the change that would mean the world moves."

"Yes," said Inar. He was tired, and he had lost hope. The young woman reminded him of his long-dead wife.

"I have noticed," she said, "that if you walk around Asdul the city lights shift position, but if you look at the mountains beyond the city, the mountains themselves do not appear to change, though that does not mean you are standing still. If you travel for many days, you can see a change even in the mountains.

"What if the stars are very far away, farther than we can imagine? We might not be able to see a shift even if there is one. There might be other ways to tell if the world moves, ways we ourselves can measure. I would learn what you know."

Inar looked up at the Mother's cloak. It was no longer warm, no longer enveloping. There was no cloak, nothing but endless distances and tiny scattered suns. There was no one there to shield the world from harm. What difference does it make if the world moves? he wondered. But it was too late for such thoughts.

The Eyes of the Lover stared blindly down; they did not see him. He shivered and took Shavna and the woman inside out of the empty night.

MYSTERIOUS DOINGS IN THE METROPOLITAN MUSEUM

by Fritz Leiber

When critics discuss the evolution of science fiction, they speak of the writers who brought real literary values into what began, in this country, as an almost exclusively pulp-oriented genre; the names Theodore Sturgeon, Ray Bradbury and Kurt Vonnegut are usually invoked. Yet the writer who has won more awards in this field than any other, at last count, is Fritz Leiber. Maybe it's because he's been more versatile than the others, his output ranging from adventurous sword-and-sorcery tales (the Fafhred-Grey Mouser series) to grim warnings of possible futures ("Coming Attraction") to pungent satires on our world (A Spectre Is Haunting Texas).

Or maybe it's simply because Leiber is a man of strong personal vision who has the literary tools with which to express himself forcefully year after year. His present story for Universe *is a short one, a preposterous jape about a convention of bugs, but it shows Leiber at his irrepressible best—there's not a single human character in the story, yet it manages to say more about humanity's foibles than most sf novels filled with struggling, soul-searching men and women acting out troubled destinies against starry backdrops. (Besides—and not at all incidentally— it's a wickedly funny piece.)*

THE top half of the blade of grass growing in a railed plot beside the Metropolitan Museum of Art in Manhattan said, "Beetles! You'd think they were the Kings of the World, the way they carry on!"

The bottom half of the blade of grass replied, "Maybe they are. The distinguished writer of supernatural horror stories H. P. Lovecraft said in *The Shadow Out of Time* there would be a 'hardy Coleopterous species immediately following mankind,' to quote his exact words. Other experts say all insects, or spiders, or rats will inherit the Earth, but old H. P. L. said hardy coleopts."

"Pedant!" the top half mocked. " 'Coleopterous species'! Why not just say 'beetles' or just 'bugs'? Means the same thing."

"You favor long words as much as I do," the bottom half replied imperturbably, "but you also like to start arguments and employ a salty, clipped manner of speech which is really not your own— more like that of a death-watch beetle."

"I call a spade a spade," the top half retorted. "And speaking of what spades delve into (a curt kenning signifying the loamy integument of Mother Earth), I hope we're not mashed into it by gunboats the next second or so. Or by beetle-crushers, to coin a felicitous expression."

Bottom explained condescendingly, "The president and general secretary of the Coleopt Convention have a trusty corps of early-warning beetles stationed about to detect the approach of gunboats. A Coleopterous Dewline."

Top snorted, "Trusty! I bet they're all goofing off and having lunch at Schrafft's."

"I have a feeling it's going to be a great con," bottom said.

"I have a feeling it's going to be a lousy, fouled-up con," top said. "Everybody will get connec. The Lousicon—how's that for a name?"

"Lousy. Lice have their own cons. They belong to the orders *Psocoptera, Anoplura,* and *Mallophaga,* not to the godlike, shining order *Coleoptera.*"

"Scholiast! Paranoid!"

The top and bottom halves of the blade of grass broke off their polemics, panting.

The beetles of all Terra, but especially the United States, were indeed having their every-two-years world convention, their Biannual Bug Thing, in the large, railed-off grass plot in Central Park, close by the Metropolitan Museum of Art, improbable as that may seem and just as the grassblade with the split personality had said.

Now, you may think it quite impossible for a vast bunch of beetles, ranging in size from nearly microscopic ones to unicorn beetles two and one-half inches long, to hold a grand convention in a dense urban area without men becoming aware of it. If so, you have seriously underestimated the strength and sagacity of the coleopterous tribe and overestimated the sensitivity and eye for detail of Homo sapiens—Sap for short.

These beetles had taken security measures to awe the CIA and NKVD, had those fumbling human organizations been aware of them. There was indeed a Beetle Dewline to warn against the approach of gunboats—which are, of course, the elephantine, leather-armored feet of those beetle-ignoring, city-befuddled giants, men. In case such veritable battleships loomed nigh, all accredited beetles had their directives to dive down to the grassroots and harbor there until the all-clear sounded on their ESP sets.

And should such a beetle-crusher chance to alight on a beetle or beetles, well, in case you didn't know it, beetles are dymaxion-built ovoids such as even Buckminster Fuller and Frank Lloyd Wright never dreamed of, crush-resistant to a fabulous degree and able to endure such saturation shoe-bombings without getting the least crack in their resplendent carapaces.

So cast aside doubts and fears. The beetles were having their world convention exactly as and where I've told you. There were bright-green ground beetles, metallic wood-boring beetles, yellow soldier beetles, gorgeous ladybird beetles and handsome and pleasing fungus beetles just as brilliantly red, charcoal-gray blister beetles, cryptic flower beetles of the scarab family with yellow hieroglyphs imprinted on their shining green backs, immigrant and affluent Japanese beetles, snout beetles, huge darksome stag and horn beetles, dogbane beetles like fire opals, and even that hyper-hieroglyphed rune-bearing yellow-on-blue beetle wonder of the family *Chrysomelidae* and subfamily *Chrysomelinae Calligrapha serpentina*. All of them milling about in happy camaraderie, passing drinks and bons mots, as beetles will. Scuttling, hopping, footing the light fantastic, and even in sheer exuberance lifting their armored carapaces to take short flights of joy on their retractable membranous silken wings like glowing lace on the lingerie of Viennese baronesses.

And not just U.S. beetles, but coleopts from all over the world—slant-eyed Asian beetles in golden robes, North African beetles in burnished burnooses, South African beetles wild as fire ants with great Afro hairdos, smug English beetles, suave Continental bugs, and brilliantly clad billionaire Brazilian beetles and fireflies constantly dancing the carioca and sniffing ether and generously spraying it at other beetles in intoxicant mists. Oh, a grandsome lot.

Not that there weren't flies in the benign ointment of all this delightful coleopterous sociability. Already the New York City cockroaches were out in force, picketing the convention because they hadn't been invited. Round and round the sacred grass plot they tramped, chanting labor-slogans in thick Semitic accents and hurling coarse working-class epithets.

"But of course we couldn't have invited them even if we'd wanted to," explained the Convention's general secretary, a dapper click beetle, in fact an eyed elater of infinite subtlety and resource in debate and tactics. As the book says, "If the eyed elater falls on its back, it lies quietly for perhaps a minute. Then, with a loud click, it flips into the air. If it is lucky, it lands on its feet and runs away; otherwise it tries again." And the general secretary had a million other dodges as good or better. He said now, "But we couldn't have invited them even if we'd wanted to, because cockroaches aren't true beetles at all, aren't *Coleoptera;* they belong to the order *Orthoptera,* the family *Blattidae—blat* to them! Moreover, many of them are mere German (German-Jewish, maybe?) Croton bugs, dwarfish in stature compared to American cockroaches, who all once belonged to the Confederate Army."

In seconds the plausible slander was known by insect grapevine to the cockroaches. Turning the accusation to their own Wobbly purposes, they began rudely to chant in unison as they marched, "Blat, blat, go the *Blattidae!*"

Also, several important delegations of beetles had not yet arrived, including those from Bangladesh, Switzerland, Iceland and Egypt.

But despite all these hold-ups and disturbances, the first session of the Great Coleopt Congress got off to a splendid start. The president, a portly Colorado potato beetle resembling Grover Cleveland, rapped for order. Whereupon row upon row of rainbow-hued beetles rose to their feet amidst the greenery and sonorously sang—drowning out even the gutteral *blats* of the crude cockroaches—the chief beetle anthem:

> "Beetles are not dirty bugs,
> Spiders, scorpions or slugs.

Heroes of the insect realms,
They sport winged burnished helms.
They are shining and divine.
They are kindly and just fine.
Beetles do not bite or sting.
They love almost everything."

They sang it to the melody of the Ode to Joy in the last movement of Beethoven's Ninth.

The session left many beetle wives, larval children, husbands and other nonvoting members at loose ends. But provision had been made for them. Guided by a well-informed though somewhat stuffy scribe beetle, they entered the Metropolitan Museum for a conducted tour designed for both entertainment and cultural enrichment.

While the scribe beetle pointed out notable items of interest and spoke his educational but somewhat long-winded pieces, they scuttled all over the place, feeling out the forms of great statues by crawling over them and reveling inside the many silvery suits of medieval armor.

Most gunboats didn't notice them at all. Those who did were not in the least disturbed. Practically all gunboats—though they dread spiders and centipedes and loath cockroaches—like true beetles, as witness the good reputation of the ladybug, renowned in song and story for her admirable mother love and fire-fighting ability. These gunboats assumed that the beetles were merely some new educational feature of the famed museum, or else an artistry of living arabesques.

When the touring beetles came to the Egyptian Rooms, they began to quiet down, entranced by art most congenial to coleopts by reason of its antiquity and dry yet vivid precision. They delighted in the tiny, toylike tomb ornaments and traced out the colorful murals and even tried to decipher the cartouches and other hieroglyphs by walking along their lines, corners and curves. The absence of the Egyptian delegation was much regretted. They would have been able to answer many questions, although the scribe beetle waxed eloquent and performed prodigies of impromptu scholarship.

But when they entered the room with the sign reading SCARABS, their awe and admiration knew no bounds. They scuttled softer than mice in feather slippers. They drew up silently in front of the glass cases and gazed with wonder and instinctive reverence at the rank on rank of jewel-like beetle forms within. Even the scribe beetle had nothing to say.

Meanwhile, back at the talkative grassblade, the top half, who was in fact a purple boy tiger beetle named Speedy, said, "Well, they're all off to a great start, I don't think. This promises to be the most fouled-up convention in history."

"Don't belittle," reproved the bottom half, who was in reality a girl American burying beetle named Big Yank. "The convention is doing fine—orderly sessions, educational junkets, what more could you ask?"

"Blat, blat, go the *Blattidae!*" Speedy commented sneeringly. "The con's going to hell in a beetle basket. Take that sneaky click beetle who's general secretary—he's up to no good, you can be sure. An insidious insect, if I ever knew one. An eyed elater—who'd he ever elate? And that potato bug who's president—a bleedin' plutocrat. As for that educational junket inside the museum, you just watch what happens!"

"You really do have an evil imagination," Big Yank responded serenely.

Despite their constant exchange of persiflage, the boy and girl beetles were inseparable pals who'd had many an exciting adventure together. Speedy was half an inch long, a darting purple beauty most agile and difficult for studious gunboats to catch. Big Yank was an inch long, gleaming black of carapace with cloudy red markings. Though quick to undermine and bury small dead animals to be home and food for her larvae, Big Yank was not in the least morbid in outlook.

Although their sex was different and their companionship intimate, Speedy and Big Yank had never considered having larvae together. Their friendship was of a more manly or girlish character and very firm-footed, all twelve of them.

"You really think something *outré* is going to happen inside the museum?" Big Yank mused.

"It's a dead certainty," Speedy assured her.

In the SCARAB room silent awe had given way to whispered speculation. Exactly what and/or who were those gemlike beetle forms arranged with little white cards inside the glass-walled cases? Even the scribe-beetle guide found himself wondering.

It was a highly imaginative twelve-spotted cucumber beetle of jade-green who came up with the intriguing notion that the scarabs were living beetles rendered absolutely immobile by hypnosis or drugs and imprisoned behind walls of thick glass by the inscrutable gunboats, who were forever doing horrendous things to beetles and other insects. Gunboats were the nefarious giants, bigger than Godzilla, of beetle legend. Anything otherwise nasty and inexplicable could be attributed to them.

The mood of speculation now changed to one of lively concern. How horrid to think of living, breathing beetles doped and brainwashed into the semblance of death and jailed in glass by gunboats for some vile purpose! Something must be done about it.

The junketing party changed its plans in a flash, and they all scuttled swifter than centipedes back to the convention, which was deep into such matters as Folk Remedies for DDT, Marine Platforms to Refuel Transoceanic Beetle Flights, and Should There Be a Cease Fire Between Beetles and *Blattidae?* (who still went "Blat, blat!").

The news brought by the junketters tabled all that and electrified the convention. The general secretary eyed elater was on his back three times running and then on his feet again—click,

click, click, click, click, *click!* The president Colorado potato beetle goggled his enormous eyes. It was decided by unanimous vote that the imprisoned beetles must be rescued at once. Within seconds Operation Succor was under way.

A task force of scout, spy, and tech beetles was swiftly told off and dispatched into the museum to evaluate and lay out the operation. They confirmed the observations and deductions of the junketters and decided that a rare sort of beetle which secretes fluoric acid would be vital to the caper.

A special subgroup of these investigators traced out by walking along them the characters of the word SCARAB. Their report was as follows:

"First you got a Snake character, see?" (That was the s.)

"Then you get a Hoop Snake with a Gap." (That was the c.)

"Then Two Snakes Who Meet in the Night and have Sexual Congress." (That was the a.)

"Next a Crooked Hoop Snake Raping an Upright or Square Snake." (The r.)

"Then a repeat of Two Snakes Who Meet in the Night, et cetera." (The second a.)

"Lastly Two Crazy Hoop Snakes Raping a Square Snake." (The b.)

"Why all this emphasis on snakes and sex we are not certain.

"We suggest the Egyptian delegation be consulted as soon as it arrives."

Operation Succor was carried out that night.

It was a complete success.

Secreted fluoric acid ate small round holes in the thick glass of all the cases. Through these, every last scarab in the Egyptian Rooms was toted by carrying beetles—mostly dung beetles—down into deep beetle bunkers far below Manhattan and armored against the inroads of cockroaches.

Endless attempts to bring the drugged and hypnotized beetles back to consciousness and movement were made. All failed.

Undaunted, the beetles decided simply to venerate the rescued scarabs. A whole new beetle cult sprang up around them.

The Egyptian delegation arrived, gorgeous as pharaohs, and knew at once what had happened. However, they decided to keep this knowledge secret for the greater good of all beetledom. They genuflected dutifully before the scarabs just as did the beetles not in the know.

The cockroaches had their own theories, but merely kept up their picketing and their chanting of "Blat, blat, go the *Blattidae*."

Because of their theories, however, one fanatical Egyptian beetle went bats and decided that the scarabs were indeed alive though drugged and that the whole thing was part of a World Cockroach Plot carried out by commando Israeli beetles and their fellow travelers. His wild mouthings were not believed.

Human beings were utterly puzzled by the whole business. The curator of the Met and the chief of the New York detectives investigating the burglary stared at the empty cases in stupid wonder.

"Godammit," the detective chief said. "When you look at all those little holes, you'd swear the whole job had been done by beetles."

The curator smiled sourly.

Speedy said, "Hey, this skyrockets us beetles to the position of leading international jewel thieves."

For once Big Yank had to agree. "It's just too bad the general public, human and coleopterous, will never know," she said wistfully. Then, brightening, "Hey, how about you and me having another adventure?"

"Suits," said Speedy.

M IS FOR THE MANY

by J. J. Russ

J. J. Russ is not Joanna Russ; his first name is Jon, he's married and has a young daughter, and he's a psychiatrist who practices in California. His poems and stories have appeared in Cimarron Review, The Smith, San Francisco Magazine *and* Fantastic.

Here he tells a deft, acerbic story of the relationship between love and need. (Well, one of the relationships, anyway.)

WHEN Nyta was angry she kicked the resilient gray bag in which Rey was suspended. If the impact interfered with her husband's trances, he never admitted it, but it gave Nyta satisfaction nonetheless. Her leg swung, clad in golden mesh disks, and with every swing she felt her toe sink into the fluid-filled sack. Every time, Rey's floating body must have jolted slightly inside. But the bag never burst and Rey never woke and nothing was any different.

Time was going by.

Lery turned, watched her for a moment instead of the kaleidoscopic patterns on the screen. "Mommy," he asked, "why you kick the bag?"

"Because I'm mad at Daddy, baby."

"Why you mad at Daddy?"

"Because . . . there's nobody else to be mad at." Nyta went on kicking until her leg was weak, but the exercise changed nothing. Lery would soon be five, the time for Bupop to take him the way they had taken Alba. In only two weeks she would be sealed in the partment with Rey and their bags and the screen. *Without a baby.* The thought made her shudder.

She coaxed Lery into her arms and cradled his head. His silken brown hair that grew in overlapping curls, his endless questions, his moist and curious eyes—soon they'd just be memories to wish inside her bag.

But two weeks is a long time.

Rocking, she crooned the song remembered from her child-hood, an ancient lullaby full of words she didn't understand. "Rock-a-bye baby on the treetop. When the wind blows, the cradle—"

"Mommy!" Lery shook himself out of her arms. "I wanna watch the screen." He ran away and reactivated the shifting three-di-mensional patterns that he now preferred to her songs.

As usual, Lery complained when she took over the screen for motherhood hour. Nyta held him firmly on her lap and smiled at the five other women who seemed to be sitting in her partment.

"My, Lery's getting so *big,*" Mercia said, cuddling her ten-month-old twins against her breasts. "Your work is almost over!"

"I know." Nyta held onto her smile.

Simi, the oldest of their group, stroked the furry animal on her lap. "You should be proud. From a little nothing, you've helped him grow to where he's ready to take his own place in the world." The other women applauded.

"It wasn't hard," Nyta said. "He's so cute." She hugged him tightly and ignored his squirming.

Simi adjusted the diaper around the hole cut for her animal's tail. "Soon you'll be needing a substitute, like me. I tried synthetic babies, but the tiny things don't grow. It's unnatural." The animal blinked. Its bright eyes were surrounded by rings of pink flesh and its nose was flat and broad. "Dandy here is so much nicer."

Ugly, Nyta thought. *Not like a baby, not like my Lery.*

By dinnertime Nyta decided, and told Rey while they were eating. He plucked another food container from the wall beside the screen and chewed serenely. He grinned ecstatically, just as he did after all his trances.

"They'll never let you. Forget kids and sack up. Use your bag, like me." Rey didn't seem to notice her new golden drape. As usual, he avoided looking at Nyta, making her feel fat and ugly, conscious of flesh sagging from curves he'd once admired.

"I don't want to! You know what happens when I trance." Remembering the nightmares, she pressed her arms over her heavy breasts. "I mean it. I want to keep Lery."

Rey shrugged. Although he was four years older than Nyta, his lean face was unlined, his cool gray eyes were clear and unworried. "*I* don't care. But you know the law."

Nyta interrupted quickly. "That's why we'll ask Bupop." She shook her long brown hair. "I *need* a baby . . . a child."

"Okay, okay." Rey put up his palms defensively. "But what's so special about *him?*" He shrugged his shoulder in the direction of Lery.

"I just need him." Nyta incinerated food containers in the low, shining sposal, wincing with each brief flash.

"Why you need me?" Lery asked.

Nyta smiled. She loved answering his questions. "Because . . . I do. Because you're nice. Because I love you."

Rey laughed dryly, without malice. "You'd better think up something better for Bupop. They're tough about things like this."

"But they'll have to understand." Compulsively, Nyta fingered the slack skin under her chin.

"You know what they'll tell you." He began to edge back to his bag.

"Rey!" She closed her eyes tightly and put thoughts out of her head by singing, "Rock-a-bye baby . . ."

"Bye-baby, bye-baby," her son echoed.

After Rey untranced the next morning, they summoned Bupop on the screen. There was a breathtaking shimmer of colors, accompanied by throbbing and passionate music. A resonant voice bellowed: *"Be fruitful and replicate!"* And then the colors condensed into a gray-haired man who seemed to be sitting in front of the screen. He nodded his head graciously in the direction of Nyta and Rey.

"Bureau of Population," he said. "May I help you?"

"I want to keep my baby!" Nyta blurted immediately to the controller, and then blushed and bit her tongue. She had to ask just right . . .

"I see." The gray head bobbed, apparently unoffended. "And you are . . ."

"Rey and Nyta Jonsn," Rey said, "partment F829-Q19484-J, *sir.*"

The man closed his eyes for a moment and a faint humming came from his skull. "You've given us one child so far?"

"Alba." Nyta's eyes watered.

"You know two's quota, of course?"

"Yes, sir, but so fast . . . my son's due to go in a few weeks—"

"Surely that's no surprise, my dear." There was compassion in the controller's face that made Nyta hopeful. "You know," he went on, "we nurture all children from their fifth birthdays, ensuring standard adjustment and sparing you all that bother"—he frowned only briefly—"of draining interdependencies."

"But Lery's *still* a baby. He needs me."

"Now, now." The compassionate man smiled warmly. "Surely you yourself remember when you were taken, the joy of freedom, the excitement of independence, the warmth of your first bag."

Nyta remembered mostly the nightmare trances that began in her bag, memories of her parents being sealed behind her, feelings of burial and suffocation. "Lery's special," she said. "And I'm a good mother for him. You'd see . . ."

"I'm certain you are. But you have use of offspring for five years only. After that"—his head shook slowly—"they are free."

"Then I want another!" Nyta's voice broke.

"Nyta!" Rey apologized to the controller. "She knows it's impossible, sir."

"Never mind." The controller's tone was mellow with patience. "That's what I'm for, isn't it?" Leaning forward, he stared into Nyta's eyes. Close up, she noticed that his eyes had no lids, and that they were spinning slowly around the pupils. "Now, my dear, you must realize we cannot allow exceptions. If we take three children from you, how can we deny others?"

Nyta wanted to kill him. "Not everybody wants—"

"Our partments are full. No one, you understand, may do more than replace himself. When there are excess or premature deaths we make exceptions . . ." Somehow, lidlessly, he closed his eyes again and again his skull hummed. Nyta hugged herself tightly and gnawed her lip. "In your case"—the controller waved a benevolent hand from side to side—"we cannot."

Nyta felt numb.

"Of course, you still have time." The controller smiled faintly and his voice brightened. "Pretransfer offspring are yours. None of our affair."

Rey nodded. "That's right."

"Quota, my dear. Quota cannot be exceeded."

Not Lery . . . Lery's special, she thought.

"That's what I told her, all right." Rey grinned.

Lery, impatient with the monotonous screening, asked, "What's kota?"

Nyta cupped her hands over his ears.

The gray-haired man gave a last paternal nod. "I suggest you consider substitutes. Also, use your bag. Happy dreams," he said, and vanished from the partment.

"You heard him," Rey said. "Sack up!"

"Men," Simi told her that afternoon, "they just don't understand. All they think about is their bags and orgasmic trances and new permutations on the matrix programmer."

"Sounds like my Jun, all right." Mercia giggled.

"They don't know what it's like to feel a baby grow in your own belly," Simi went on, "or to care about something little and helpless more than for yourself. Even an animal like my Dandy here." Simi stroked the long-tailed animal, whereupon it turned its lips out in a snarl and tried to bite her hand. "Men don't understand. They think only about themselves—big babies, all of them."

"*My* husband says he likes babies," a newlywed said, and then blushed. "We have a double bag. He says when the baby comes he'll help take care of it."

"*Help.*" Simi pronounced the word like an insult. "You'll see."

Nyta looked again at Simi's animal, which now had closed its eyes and wedged its ugly face in Simi's armpit. "Where do you get animals?" she asked. "Are they expensive?"

Nyta's first animal had long ears, was white and furry with pink eyes and big front teeth. She bought it from Simi's dealer, a curio vendor on an obscure channel. He guaranteed authenticity, but couldn't tell Nyta its name. She enjoyed petting it until Lery killed it while trying to unscrew its head.

Next she bought a playful green-eyed carnivore that delighted her with the vibrations of its throat against her skin. But when it punctured Rey's bag with its needle-sharp claws, causing his fluid to run low during an exceptionally inventive trance, he insisted that it be returned. Nyta cried for hours, thinking of how she could have cuddled it when Lery was gone.

The last animal, also the smallest, was gray and tapered at both ends. Its rear sloped to a long bare tail, and its head was pointed in a whiskered snout, always nibbling. It liked to snuggle in Nyta's warm lap until one evening, surprised at being squeezed, it snapped at her finger. A red drop quivered on the fingertip. Without thinking, Nyta grabbed the animal by its tail and dropped it into the sposal. As the wriggling body dropped, the sposal widened its metallic iris. Nyta changed her mind—too late—and the animal vanished with a white flash and faint sizzle.

Lery was watching. "Mommy, why you 'pose the an'mal?"

"Because I was angry. Because it hurt me." Nyta sucked the wounded finger, feeling cold and empty. It was only four days before Lery's birthday.

"What if I hurt you?"

"You wouldn't hurt me, would you, baby?"

"Yeah!" He ran laughing back to the screen.

Again, Nyta kicked the quivering bag that held Rey ecstatic, alone. She aimed at where the bag had healed over the animal's claw-holes. At the screen Lery giggled at incongruously tinted patterns. In front of her, Rey's sack swung and bobbled. Nyta's own container hung beside it on the matrix rack, dry and empty, waiting. She used it only for sleep, with minimum transition. Even then . . .

"Do you have to buy animals? They're so damn messy," Rey said. "And you don't even know how to take care of the things after you get them." Rey hadn't noticed Nyta's new translucent beige drape. "You can wish them in the bag anyway, for free."

"The *bag*. That's all you ever say!" She glared at the food trays flashing in the sposal.

Lery jumped up, his eyes gleaming. "After I leave, will I have a bag then? Will I?"

"Sure you will," Rey said. "No more bed, but a bag of your very own."

Nyta bit her lip. "Do you have to talk about leaving now? There's still a while yet."

Lery marched around in a circle. "I'm gonna have a bag! I'm gonna have a bag! Four days, four days, I'm gonna have a bag!"

Nyta stood up.

"You look awful." Rey tapped her hand lightly with his fingers still, always, slightly damp with remnant fluid. "Really, you ought to use your bag. For your own good." He smiled the way he used to . . . he was a baby himself, really, with his big head and small bottom. Nyta wanted to hug him, but knew that he'd pull away.

"Maybe you're right," she said. "I will, I promise. Tomorrow."

She hated climbing into the slack cavity, feeling the warm fluid rise around her, the faint sting of wire tentacles linking their poised charges to the nerves of her scalp. Floating in darkness, Nyta regretted her promise. The principle was simple— just wish for something, anything, and the bag would make it seem to happen. But her trances never went right.

She wanted to climb out, but there was no choice. In three days the bag would be all she'd have. She loved Lery so much, more than she'd loved anyone, even Alba. He was too excited lately, but still . . .

Bobbing in tepid fluid, snared in an electrified silver web, Nyta wished: *She was pregnant again. Her breasts swelled taut, her emptiness filled, her belly rose until it was hard to breathe. Months swept past as her womb crescendoed, and Nyta hummed and sang, brimful of life and melody. A fetus kicked under her ribs. And then it was time for pain, a surf of pain that tore her open and receded, leaving a baby, born in the caul, between her legs. And the caul was an elastic sack, opaque, gray, thick. Nyta slit it open with her fingernails. Inside was another bag, darker and tougher. This one she tore open with her teeth. Inside was another. And another. Nyta screamed.*

But there was no sound.

"Well, feeling better?" Rey was all loose joints and cool smile.

"It happened again." Nyta shook. "I told you. I need something *real*."

"Real? What's the difference?" Rey's smile became patronizing. "How do you know what's real? For all I can tell, I'm in my bag right now, except I don't think I'd wish to have you . . . like this."

"I need something I can hug, like Lery. Something that hugs me back."

"Then just wish for it, like me."

"But I can tell the difference."

"That's crazy." Rey walked to the matrix rack, punched for an indeterminate trance, and stepped inside his bag. "There *is* no difference," he said.

"You're lucky," Mercia told Nyta, "lucky to be getting free. The twins never give me a moment's rest." She rocked her babies, one nestled in the bend of each elbow, but did not manage to frown.

"You think so?" Nyta said.

"Of course, dear," Simi interrupted. "You've done your maternal duty, grown your Lery from nothing at all . . ." Nyta noticed that Simi had replaced her furry animal with a gleaming green cylindrical one without legs. There was a bandage on Simi's left forearm. "Not like some people who *call* themselves women, and never have any at all."

"Why not?" the newlywed said. "We've got so many people anyway. According to Bupop—"

"Bupop," Simi said in a haughty voice, "is not a mother. And neither are you yet, darling."

Nyta kept stealing looks at Mercia's twins. It wasn't fair. There were *two* babies with round faces, smiling and sucking little mouths. Soon she wouldn't have any. *Lery* . . .

Simi's green animal kept trying to glide up her shoulder, and she batted it down with a scolding finger. "Naughty," she said. "Listen to Mommy, now!"

There's still two days with him, Nyta thought. *Long, long days.*

Lery was at the screen almost all the time now, absorbing the pretransfer information in the shape of animated pastel spheres, obelisks and tetrahedrons. He watched with a new intensity, punctuated with gusts of laughter that seemed to Nyta to be sucked from her own lungs.

For no reason she fussed around the partment, pretending to clean its unsoilable interior. Rey had given up on her and was in his bag almost constantly. It sagged, pulsing slightly, and the circulation of the fluid hissed with a subdued whisper.

Nyta spent a long time wiping the sealed front door. Except for the delivery hatch, it hadn't been open since her daughter was dragged out—how long ago? Alba, her blond hair trailing, had cried, much to Rey's embarrassment. "She's like you," he had said, intending a rebuke.

Nyta had only nodded. "Yes, I know."

Nyta loved that crying, loved comforting her babies when they had cried. Lery hardly cried at all any more.

She felt confused. Rey thought she was crazy, trying to hold onto her baby. Simi said she should feel proud. Here she was, doing cleaning when nothing gathered dust. Stains erased themselves, dirt disintegrated, anything broken healed itself within a few days. The translucent windows on which colored patterns changed endlessly were spotless: *mauve, saffron, magenta, tur-*

quoise . . . Even without a baby she'd have the full screen and proscenium, the bags hanging from the matrix rack, food cooked to her whim in an instant, her friends on the screen every day, the sposal to annihilate whatever she didn't want . . .

"Lery!" She felt a rush of affection. "Please!"

He came reluctantly, dragging his feet and glaring at her. "Tomorrow I can do what I want."

Despite his words, Nyta wanted to bury him under her kisses. "But today we can talk. It's our last day," she said.

Lery sat beside her, really not much bigger than the wrinkled baby she had suckled almost five years ago. He fidgeted and craned his neck in the direction of the screen.

"Isn't there anything you want to say?" she asked.

"No."

"But, baby, today's our last day."

"*No.*" He refused to look at her. Even when he tried to be angry, he was beautiful. There was a cute tug at his lower lip, the wrinkling of his chin—that special look.

"Then suppose I ask you some questions?" Without an answer, she continued, "Do you remember the games we played with the food boxes? Do you remember when the stacks of them fell down, how much we laughed?" Nyta glowed with the memory. Lery had laughed like music then. He liked to hang gurgling from her neck and didn't watch the screen.

"Those were *baby* games," he said now.

"Then . . . do you remember when you played magic and promised to break open the door? You said you'd take me out and we'd run all day and never see a wall. Do you remember?"

"I was dumb then," he said, giggling. "That sounds dumb!"

"Remember the fuzzy animal we had a few weeks ago? The one with the long white ears? It wiggled its whiskers and you liked to tickle it."

"That an'mal was crummy. Its head broke and you couldn't even make it fix itself."

Nyta knew she should stop asking. Everything with Lery had

always been so special . . . he was just excited now. She was spoiling everything, spoiling even the past.

"Then tell me," her tightening voice kept on, "tell me what you're going to do *after* you leave."

Lery came alive. His small body weaved back and forth with anticipation. "I'm gonna get a bag. It'll be like the ones you and Daddy have. And I'll go in it and I'll have anything I want in it and I could go in or out anytime I want to."

"Oh." Nyta saw that he meant it. In a flash his face seemed to merge with two others, just for an instant. *No.* A hard chill spread through her stomach. "Will you think of me when you're in the bag?"

Her son laughed, a high unchildish cackle that cut her like teeth. "Course not! The bag's not for that!"

Nyta tried to stop, but she had to know. "Then . . . when will you think of me?"

"I won't." Lery looked puzzled. "Will they make me?" Again his face blurred into others, a quick, buck-toothed boy, a girl with long brown hair and narrow lips. *Not again . . .*

"No," Nyta sighed. "They won't make you." She thought of the controller, his gray head humming, eyes slowly spinning, saying *quota, my dear, quota.* She pinched Lery's arm, hard, digging in her long thumbnail, hoping that he would cry, become her baby again.

"Hey!" he shouted, and punched her in the breast.

"Lery, I'm your mother. You will remember me, baby, you will, honey, won't you?"

"You're only my mommy," he said, "till tomorrow."

Tomorrow. Lery somewhere in a bag just like his father, floating and dreaming under silver mesh, forgetting everything. Forgetting *her.* Then just the partment left, the screen with her stupid friends, the hiss of Rey's fluid, colors on the windows, treacherous animals. And her empty bag, waiting. She'd hoped to wish Lery back in the bag, to have him forever with his games, his tears and soft smile. Now there was no Lery.

"Mommy, why you lift me?"

For the first time she didn't answer him.

The sposal opened as it always did, just wide enough, allowing Lery's waving arms to clear by a fraction of an inch. The flash was so bright that for several minutes Nyta could see it etched in black wherever she looked. *Just like the other two.* The hole in her vision soon disappeared.

She forced herself to cry by singing the ancient, the incomprehensible lullaby. "Rock-a-bye baby . . ." She sang as she had sung to all her babies: first Alba, then Sundy, Krin, and, of course, Lery. Nyta enjoyed the crying and savored her feelings, a mixture of loss with a surge of depthless mothering warmth that would bring forth another baby. Inside, inside her.

Rey was not surprised. "You might have saved us that embarrassing Bupop nonsense, though." He agreed to replace Lery as soon as possible, and would arrange for his bag to collect semen from him and transfer it to Nyta in hers. Things would be better, he hoped, since a baby would keep her happy for another five years.

But Mercia was appalled. "*I'd* never abort *my* babies," she said. "Especially not *that* old. How could you, Nyta!"

"Don't be so quick to judge," Simi told her. "I've aborted one too, you know, darling. Only six months old, but still . . ." Simi's long green animal quivered its red tongue in the air.

"But three! What kind of woman would do that? Tell me, Nyta, what kind of woman are you?"

"A mother," Nyta said.

Already her thoughts were full of the new baby, its tiny sucking mouth, its miniature fingers and toes, its new skin under her hands. All hers, her baby. Before the end of the meeting she noticed Mercia tipping up the faces of her twins, looking first at one and then the other, as if she were thinking, *Which? Which one?*

THE NIGHT WIND

by Edgar Pangborn

AFTER some years away from the future world of his classic novel Davy, *Edgar Pangborn has recently returned to it in stories such as "Tiger Boy" (Universe 2) and "The World Is a Sphere" (Universe 3). It's a self-consistent background ranging over many centuries after the destruction of our present civilization and the slow growth of a new culture founded in superstitious fear of the holocaust that nearly annihilated humanity.*

In that fear-ridden world Pangborn finds men and women who try to be as human as they can, and he tells their stories . . . such as the following warm and moving tale of a particular kind of monster, not really a mutant, and his coming of age.

.   .   .

At Mam Miriam's house beyond
Trempa, Ottoba 20, 402

I WILL do it somewhere down this road, not yet but after dark; it will be when the night wind is blowing.

Always I have welcomed the sound of the night wind moving, as the leaves are passing on their secrets and sometimes falling, but falling lightly, easily, because their time to fall is come. Dressed in high colors, they fall to the day winds too this time of year, this autumn season. The smell of earth mold is spice on the tongue. I catch scent of apples ripening, windfalls rich-rotten pleasuring the yellow hornets. Rams and he-goats are mounting and crazy for it—O this time of year! They fall to the day winds echoing the sunlight, the good bright leaves, and that's no bad way to fall.

I know the dark of autumn too. The night wind hurts. Even now writing of it, only to think of it. Ottoba was in me when I said to my heart: I will do it somewhere down this road, I will end it, my life, for they believe it should never have begun. (I think there may be good spirits down that road. Perhaps the people I met were spirits, or they were human beings and spirits too, or we all are.) And I remembered how Father Horan also believes I ought never to have been born. I saw that in him; he believes it as the town folk do, and what we believe is most of what we are.

For three days I felt their sidelong stares, their anger that I would dare to pass near their houses. They called in their children to safety from me, who never hurt anyone. Passing one of those gray-eyed houses, I heard a woman say, "He ought to be stoned, that Benvenuto." I will not write her name.

Another said, "Only a mue would do what he did."

They call me that; they place me among the sad distorted things—armless or mindless or eyeless, somehow inhuman and corrupted—that so many mothers bear, or have borne, folk say, since the end of Old Time. How could a mue be called beautiful?

When I confessed to Father Horan, he shoved his hands behind his back, afraid he might touch me. "Poor Benvenuto!" But he said it acidly, staring down as if he had tasted poison in his food.

So I will end it (I told the hidden self that is me)—I will end it now in my fifteenth year before the Eternal Corruption that Father Horan spoke of can altogether destroy my soul; and so the hidden self that is me, if that is my soul, may win God's forgiveness for being born a monster.

But why did Father Horan love me once, taking something like a father's place, or seem to love me? Why did he teach me the reading of words and writing too, first showing me how the great words flow in the Book of Abraham, and on to the spelling book and so to all the mystery? Why did he let me see the other books, some of them, the books of Old Time forbidden to common people, even the poets? He would run his fingers through my hair, saying I must never cut it, or rest his arm on my shoulder; and I felt a need, I thought it was loneliness or love, in the curving of his fingers. Why did he say I might rise in the Holy Amran Church, becoming greater than himself, a bishop—Bishop Benvenuto!—an archbishop!

If I am a monster now, was I not a monster then?

I could ask him no such questions when he was angry. I ran out of the church though I heard him calling after me, commanding me to return in God's name. I will not return.

I ran through the graveyard, past the dead hollow oak where I saw and heard bees swarming in the hot autumn light, and I think he stood among the headstones lamenting for me, but I would not look back, no, I plowed through a thicket and ran down a long golden aisle of maple trees and into Wayland's field (where it happened)—Wayland's field all standing alive with the bound shocks of corn, and into the woods again on the far side, only to be away from him.

It was there in Wayland's field that I first thought, I will do this to myself, I will end it, maybe in that wood I know of; but I was afraid of my knife. How can I cut and tear the body someone called beautiful? And so I looked at the thought of hiding in a shock of corn, the same one where I found Eden idle that day, and staying in it till I starved. But they say starving is a terrible death, and I might not have the courage or the patience to wait for it. I thought too, They will look for me when they know I'm gone, because they want to punish me, stone me, even my mother will want to punish me, and they would think of the cornfield where it happened and come searching like the flail of God.

How bright they stand, the bound stalks in the sun, like little wigwams for the field spirits, like people too, like old women with rustling skirts of yellow-gray; their hair is blowing! Now I know I will remember this when I go on—for I am going on without death, never doubt it, I promise you I shall not die by my own hand.

I saw two hawks circling and circling in the upper wind above Wayland's field. I thought up to them: You are like me, but you have all the world's air to fly away in.

The hawks are bound to the earth as I am, they must hunt food in the grass and branches, men shoot arrows from the earth to tear their hearts. Still they enter regions unknown to us, and maybe they and the wild geese have found an easy way to heaven.

Into the woods again on the far side of Wayland's field I hurried, and down and up the ravine that borders it, shadowed ground with alder and gray birch and a cool place of ferns I know of where sunlight comes late in the morning and mild. The brook in the ravine bottom was running scant from the dry weather, leaves collecting on the bodies of smooth shining stones. I did not go downstream to the pool but climbed the other side of the ravine and took the path—hardly that, merely a known place where my feet have passed before—to the break in the trees that lets you out on this road, and I thought: Here I will do it, somewhere farther on in the shadows.

It is wider than a wood-road and better kept, for wagons use it now and then, and it is supposed to wind through back ways southeast as far as Nupal, ten miles they say or even more—I never believed much of what I hear about Nupal. The trading of our village has always been with Maplestock, and surely nobody goes to Nupal except those tinkers and gyppos and ramblers with their freaky wagons, squirrel-eyed children, scrawny dogs. A sad place it must be, Nupal, more than seven hundred crammed into the one village, as I hear it. I don't understand how human beings can live like that—the houses may not be standing as horridly close together as folk tell. Maybe I'll see the place in passing. I've noticed a dozen times, the same souls who sniggle about with ugly fact until it looks like fancy will turn right-about and ask you to believe that ugly fancy is fact.

I went down the road not running any more, nor thinking more about Father Horan. I thought of Eden.

Then I thought about my mother, who is going to marry Blind Hamlin the candlemaker, I'm told. She wouldn't tell me herself, the winds told me. (Toby Omstrong told me, because he doesn't like me.) Let's hope the jolly wedding isn't delayed by concern over my absence—I am not coming back, Mother. Think of me kindly while tumbling with your waxy man, or better, think of me not at all, the cord is cut, and anyhow didn't you pick me up somewhere as a changeling?

Hoy, there I was on your doorstep all red and nasty, wrapped up in a cabbage leaf! Likely story. But we can't have it thought that *you* gave birth to a monster, even one begotten by a little shoemaker whose image you did your best to destroy for me. (But I saved some pieces, I try to put them together now and then. I wish I could remember him; the memories of others are not much more help than wind under the door, for people don't understand what I want to know—small blame to them, they can't hear the questions I don't know how to ask—and I think your memories of him are mostly lies, Mother, though you may not know it.) "He was a poor sad soul, Benvenuto." Was he, Mother? "He broke my heart with his unfaithfulness, Benvenuto." But Blind Hamlin is going to stick it back together with mutton-fat, remember? "He drank, you know, Benvenuto, that was why he could never make a decent living." Why, I will drink to you, Mother, I will drink to the wedding in Mam Miriam's best apple brandy before I leave this poor empty house where I am writing.

Don't destroy Blind Hamlin, Mother. I don't like him, he's a crosspatch bag of guts, but don't destroy him, don't whittle him down as you must have scraped my father down with the rasp of words—but I forget, I am a changeling. Poor Blind Hamlin!—there may be witchcraft in it, Mother. It troubles me that a man who can't see makes candles for those who will not. Don't destroy him. Make another monster with him. I'd like a monster for a half-brother—but there, never mind, I'm not coming back to Trempa, make all the monsters you wish. The world's already full of them.

I am not writing this for my mother. She will not be the one to find it here. Whoever does—I pray you, read this page if you like and the one before it that begins "She wouldn't tell me herself"—read and then throw away, in God's name. For I would like the truth to be somewhere in the world, maybe in your head, whoever you are, but I don't wish to slap my mother in the face with it, nor Blind Hamlin either. Blind Hamlin was never unkind to me. I am all soreness, the tenderest touch smarts on a burned skin. I will mend. I don't hate my mother—do I hate anyone?—is it a sign of my monsterhood that I don't hate anyone?—or if I do, I will *mend,* I'll cease hating wherever I am going, and even forget. Especially forget. Read those pages and throw away and then, you too, forget. But save the rest, if you will. I don't want to die altogether in your mind, whoever you are.

Down that road I came. I think I left behind me most of what had appeared certain in the world; the new uncertainties are still to find. Where did I encounter you? Who are you?—oh, merely the one supposed to find this letter. So then you are not the new person I need to find—someone not Eden, nor Andrea whom I loved, but some other. But with Andrea I understood that heaven would open whenever he looked on me.

In that road through the woods beyond Wayland's field the trees stand close on either side, oak and pine and enormous tulip trees where the white parrots like to gather and squabble with the bluejays, and thickets that swell with a passion of growth wherever an opening like that road lets through the sun. Oaks had shifted into the bronze along with the clear gold of maple trees when I passed by, yet I saw few leaves fallen. You remember some of the wise prophets in Trempa have been saying it'll be a hard winter, with snow in January for sure. The Lord must save a special kind of forgiveness for the weather prophets—other kinds of liars have some chance of learning better. As I looked along the slender channel of the road, I saw the stirring of distant treetops under the wind, but here that wind was hushed, cut to a modest breeze or to no motion at all. And suddenly the stillness was charged with the fishy loathsome reek of black wolf.

It is a poison in the air and we live with it. I remember how it has always happened in the village: days, weeks, with no hint of the evil, and when we have forgotten and grown careless, then without warning the sour stench of them comes on the air, and we hear their rasping howl in the nights—nothing like the musical uproar of the common wolves who seldom do worse than pick up a sheep now and then—and people will die, ambushed, throat-torn, stripped of flesh and bones cracked for the marrow. Some tell of seeing the Devil walk with them. He teaches them tricks that only human beings ought to know. He leads them to the trail of late travelers, to lonely houses where a door may be unlatched, or someone seized on the way to shed or outhouse. And yet they do say that black wolf will not attack by day; if a man comes at him then, even if he is at his carrion, he may slink off; now I know this is true. At night black wolf is invincible, I suppose. The smell hung dense on that woodland road, coming from all around me, so that I could not run away from it.

I had my thin strength, and a knife; my knife is from the hands of Wise Wayland the Smith, and there is a spell on it. For look you, no harm comes to me if I am wearing it. I was not wearing it when Andrea's family moved away and took him with them—all the way to Penn, God help me. I was not wearing it when they came on me with Eden in Wayland's field and called me monster.

In fear I went ahead, not trying for quiet because no one ever surprises black wolf. I came on the beast on the far side of a boulder that jutted into the road, but before that I heard the sounds of tearing. It had ripped the liver from the body. Blood still oozed from all the wounds. Enough remained of the face so that I knew the man was old Kobler. His back-pack was not with him, nor any gear, so he had not been on his way to the village. Perhaps he had been taken with some sickness, and so the wolf dared to bring him down in broad day.

By this time Kobler will be expected in the village. They'll wonder why he doesn't come marching to the General Store with his stack of reed baskets and Mam Miriam's beautiful embroideries and such-like, and slap down his one silver coin, and fill his back-pack with the provisions for Mam Miriam and himself. True, he was never regular in the timing of his visits; another week or two might go by before anyone turns curious. People don't think much unless their convenience is joggled, and old Kobler was so silent a man, never granting anyone a word that could be held back—and Mam Miriam herself hardly more than a legend to the town folk—no, I suppose they won't stir themselves unduly. All the same I must leave, I must not be caught here by those who would stone me for their souls' benefit. Nothing keeps me in this house now except a wish to write these words for you, whoever you are. Then I will go when the night wind is blowing.

It was an old dog wolf, and foul, alone, his fangs yellowed. He held his ground hardly a moment when I walked down on him with the knife of Wayland flashing sunlight on his eyes. I did not understand immediately that Kobler was past help—then the wolf moved, I saw the liver, I knew the look on the old man's mask was no-way meant for me. Jon Kobler, a good fellow I think, Mam Miriam's servant, companion, and more. He shrank from the world as she did, nor do I see how you could hold it against either of them, for often the world stinks so that even a fool like me must hold his nose. It will not harm them now if I tell you they were lovers.

The wolf slunk off through the brush into a ravine. It must have been the power of Wayland's knife—or is it possible that black wolf is not so terrible as folk say? Well, mine is a knife that Wayland made long since, when he was young; he told me so.

He gave it to me on the morning of the best day of my life. Andrea had come to me the day before, had chosen me out of all the others in the training yard—although I seldom shone there, my arm is not heavy enough for the axe or the spear-throwing, and in archery I am only fair, undistinguished. He challenged me to wrestle, I put forth my best, almost I had his shoulders down and he laughing up at me, and then presto! somehow I am flung over on my back and my heart close to cracking with happiness because he has won. And he invited me to go on the morrow with him and some of his older friends for a stag hunt through Bindiaan Wood, and I had to say, "I have no knife, no gear."

"Oh," says Andrea, and April is no kinder, "we'll find extra gear for you at my father's house, and as for a knife of your own, maybe Wayland the Smith has one for you."

I knew that Wayland Smith did sometimes make such gifts to boys just turning men, but had never imagined he would trouble with one so slight-built as I am and supposed to be simple-minded from the hours with the books. "You do hide your light," says Andrea, whom I had already loved for a year, scarcely daring to speak to him. He laughed and pressed my shoulder. "Go to ancient Wayland, do him some little favor—there's no harm in him—and maybe he'll have a knife for you. I would give you mine, Benvenuto," he said, "only that's bad magic between friends, but come to me with a knife of your own and we'll make blood brotherhood."

So the next morning I went to Wayland the Smith with all my thoughts afire, and I found the old man about to draw a bucket of water from his well, but looking ill and drooping, and he said, "O Benvenuto, I have a crick in my arm—would you, in kindness?" So I drew the water for him, and we drank together. I saw the smithy was untidy with cobwebs, and swept it out for him, he watching me and rambling on with his tales and sayings and memories that some call wanton blasphemies—I paid little heed to them, thinking of Andrea, until he asked me, "Are you a good boy, Benvenuto?" His tone made me know he would like to hear me laugh, or anyway not mind it, indeed I could hardly help laughing at a thousand silly notions, and for the pleasure of it, and the joy of the day; and that was when he gave me this knife I always carry. I don't think I answered his question, or at least only to say, "I try to be," or some such nonsense. He gave me the knife, kissed me, told me not to be too unhappy in my life; but I don't know what one must do to follow that counsel, unless it is to live the way all others do, like baa-sheep who come and go at the will of the shepherd and his dog and must never stray from the tinkle of the wether's bell.

Oh, yes, that day I went on the hunt with Andrea, armed with the knife that was given me by Wayland Smith. We killed a stag together, he marked my forehead, with our own blood then we made brotherhood; but he is gone away.

There was nothing anyone could have done for old Kobler except pray for him. I did that—if there's anything to hear our prayers, if the prayers of a monster can be noticed. But who is God? Who is this cloud-thing that has nothing better to do than stare on human pain and now and then poke it with his finger? Is he not bored? Will he not presently wipe it all away, or go away and forget? Or has he already gone away, forgotten?

You will not have me burnt for these words because you will not find me. Besides, I must remember you are simply the unknown who will happen on this letter in Mam Miriam's house, and you may even be a friend. I must remember there are friends.

When I rose from kneeling beside the poor mess that was what remained of Kobler, I heard rustling in the brush. That wolf had no companions or they would have been with him tearing at the meat, but perhaps he was rallying from his fright, hungry for something young and fresh. I understood too that the sun was lowering, night scarcely more than an hour away. Night's arrival would be sudden in the manner of autumn, which has a cruelty in it, as if we did not know that winter is near but must be reminded with a slap and a scolding. Only then did I think of Mam Miriam, who would expect Kobler's return.

When was the last time any of you in Trempa saw Mam Miriam Coletta? I had not even known she was daughter to Roy Coletta, who was governor of Ulsta in his time. Or was this only something she dreamed for me, something to tell me when perhaps her wits were wandering? It doesn't matter: I will think her a princess if I choose.

She was twenty-five and yet unmarried, hostess of the governor's mansion at Sortees after her mother's death, and she fell in love with a common archer, one of the Governor's Guard, and ran away with him, escaping from her locked bedroom on a rope made from a torn blanket. O the dear romantic tale! I've heard none better from the gyppos—their stories are too much alike, but this was like some of the poems of Old Time, especially as she told it me, and never mind if her wits wandered; I have ceased speculating whether it was true.

You think the archer was this same man who became Poor Old Kobler, marching into town fortnightly with his back-pack and his baskets, and the embroideries by a crazy old bedridden dame who lived off in the Haunted Stone House and wouldn't give anyone the time of day?

He was not. That archer abandoned her in a brothel at Nuber. Kobler was an aging soldier, a deserter. He took her out of that place and brought her to Trempa. He knew of the old stone house in the woods so long abandoned—for he was a Trempa man in his beginnings, Jon Kobler, but you may not find any bones to bury—and he took her there. He repaired the solid old ruin; you would not believe what good work he did there, mostly with wood cut and shaped out of the forest with his own hands. He cared for her there, servant and lover; they seem not to have had much need of the world. They grew old there, like that.

Rather, he did, I suppose. When I saw her she did not seem very old. Why, I first heard talk and speculation about them (most of it malicious) when I was six years old; I think they must have been new-come then, and that's only nine years ago. Yesterday or perhaps the day before, nine years would have seemed like a long time to me. Now I wonder if a thousand years is a long time, and I can't answer my own question. I am not clever at guessing ages, but I would think Mam Miriam was hardly past forty; and certainly she spoke like a lady, and told me of the past glories as surely no one could have done who had not known them—the governor's mansion, the dances all night long and great people coming on horseback or in fine carriages from all over the county; she made me see the sweaty faces of the musicians in the balcony, and didn't she herself go up one night (the dance at her tenth birthday party) to share a box of candy with them? She spoke of the gardens, the lilac and wisteria and many-colored roses, the like you never saw in Trempa, and there were odd musky red grapes from some incredible land far south of Penn, and from there also, limes, and oranges, and spices she could not describe for me. Telling me all this simply and truly, she did seem like a young woman, even a girl—oh, see for yourself, how should I know? There she lies, poor sweet thing, in the bed Jon Kobler must have made. I have done what I could for her, and it is not much.

I am wandering. I must tell of all this as I should, and then go. Perhaps you will never come; it may be best if you do not.

I prayed for Kobler, and then I went on down the road—despising the wolf but not forgetting him, for I wish to live—as far as its joining with the small path that I knew would take me to Mam Miriam's. There I hesitated a long while, though I think I knew from the start that I would go to her. I don't know what it is in us that (sometimes) will make us do a thing against our wishes because we know it to be good. "Conscience" is too thin a word, and "God" too misty, too spoiled by the many who mouth it constantly without any care for what they say, or as if they alone were able to inform you of God's will—and please, how came they to be so favored? But something drives, I think from within, and I must even obey it without knowing a name for it.

You see, I had never followed that path. No one does. The road like the old stone house itself is haunted. Anyone who ventures there goes in peril of destruction or bewitchment. So far, I am not destroyed.

Once on the path—why, I began to run. Maybe I ran so as to yield no room in my thought to the fear that is always, like black wolf, waiting. I ran down the path through a wilderness of peace. There were the beeches, gray and kind—I like to imagine something of peace in their nearness. I know that violence might be done in the presence, in the very shadow of the beech trees, as in any other place where the human creature goes; a little corner of my mind is a garden where I lie in the sun not believing it. In their presence on that path I ran without shortness of breath, without remembering fear, and I came to the green clearing, and the house of red-gray stone. It was growing late, the sun too low to penetrate this hidden place. In shadow therefore I came to Mam Miriam's door and pounded on the oak panel. But gossip had always said that the old woman (if she existed at all outside of Jon Kobler's head, if he didn't create those dazzling embroideries himself out of his own craziness and witchcraft) was bedridden and helpless. So my knocking was foolish. I turned the latch and pushed the heavy sluggish thing inward, closing it behind me, staring about half-blind in the gray light.

The house is trifling-small, as you will see if you dare come here. Only that big lower room with the fireplace where Jon cooked, the bench where he worked at his baskets, clogs, wooden beads, and this other room up here with the smaller hearth. There's this one chair up here where I sit now (Kobler used to sit beside his love's bed, you know) and the little table I write on, which I am sure they used drawn up beside the bed for their meals together, for the night pitcher of water she no longer needs. You will be aware now that she did exist. There's the roll of linen cloth—Kobler must have gone all the way to Maplestock to buy that—and some half-finished table mats, pillow slips, dresser covers. There's her embroidery hoop, the needles, the rolls of bright yarns, and thread—I never knew there were so many sizes and colors. And there she too is lying. She was; she lived; I closed her eyes.

I looked about me in that failing evening, and she called from upstairs, "Jon, what's wrong? Why did you make such a noise at the door? You've been long, Jon. I'm thirsty."

The tone of her voice was delicate, a music. I cannot tell you how it frightened me, that the voice of a crazy old woman should sound so mild and sweet. Desperately I wanted to run away, much more than I had wanted it when I stood out there at the beginning of the path. But the thing that I will not call Conscience or God (somewhere in the Old-Time books I think it was called Virtue, but doubtless few read them)—the thing that would never let me strike a child, or stone a criminal or a mue on the green as we are expected to do in Trempa—this mad cruel-sweet thing that may be a part of love commanded me to answer her, and I called up the stairway, "Don't be afraid. It's not Jon, but I came to help you." I followed my words, climbing the stairs slowly so that she could forbid me if she chose. She said no more until I had come to her.

The house was turning chill. I had hardly noticed it downstairs; up here the air was already cold, and I saw—preferring not to stare at her directly till she spoke to me—that she was holding the bedcovers high to her throat, and shivering. "I must build you a fire," I said, and went to the hearth. Fresh wood and kindling were laid ready, a tinderbox stood on the mantel. She watched me struggle with the clumsy tool until I won my flame and set it to the twigs and scraps of waste cloth. That ancient chimney is clean—the fire caught well without smoking into the room. I warmed my hands.

"What has happened? Where is Jon?"

"He can't come. I'm sorry." I asked her if she was hungry, and she shook her head. "I'm Benvenuto of Trempa," I told her. "I'm running away. I must get you some fresh water." I hurried out with the pitcher, obliged to retreat for that moment for my own sake, because meeting her gaze, as I had briefly done, had been a glancing through midnight windows into a country where I could never go and yet might have loved to go.

Why, even with gray-eyed Andrea this had been true, and did he not once say to me, "O Benvenuto, how I would admire to walk in the country behind your eyes!"

I know: it is always true.

(But Andrea brought me amazing gifts from his secret country, and nothing in mine was withheld from him through any wish of mine. I suppose all the folk have a word for it: we knew each other's hearts.)

I filled the pitcher at the well-pump downstairs and carried it up to her with a fresh clean cup. She drank gratefully, watching me, I think with some kind of wonder, over the rim of the cup, and she said, "You are a good boy, Benvenuto. Sit down by me now, Benvenuto." She set the cup away on the table and patted the edge of the bed, and I sat there maybe no longer afraid of her, for her plump sad little face was kind. Her soft too-white hands, the fingers short and tapered, showed me none of that threat of grasping, clinging, snatching I have many times seen in the hands of my own breed. "So tell me, where is Jon?" When I could not get words out, I felt her trembling. "Something has happened."

"He is dead, Mam Miriam." She only stared. "I found him on the road, Mam Miriam, too late for me to do anything. It was a wolf." Her hands flew up over her face. "I'm sorry—I couldn't think of any easier way to tell it." She was not weeping as I have heard a woman needs to do after such a blow.

At last her hands came down. One dropped on mine kindly, like the hand of an old friend. "Thus God intended it, perhaps," she said. "I was already thinking, I may die tonight."

"No," I said. "No."

"Why should I not, my dear?"

"Can't you walk at all?"

She looked startled, even shocked, as if that question had been laid away at the back of her mind a long time since, not to be brought forth again. "One night after we came here, Jon and I, I went downstairs—Jon had gone to Trempa and was late return-ing—I had a candle, but a draft caught it at the head of the stairs—oh, it was a sad night, Benvenuto, and the night wind blowing. I stumbled, fell all the way. There was a miscarriage, but I could not move my legs. An hour later Jon got back and found me like that, all blood and misery. Since then I have not been able to walk. Nor to die, Benvenuto."

"Have you prayed?" I asked her. "Have you besought God to let you walk again? Father Horan would say that you should. Father Horan says God's grace is infinite, through the intercession of Abraham. But then—other times—he appears to deny it. Have you prayed, Mam Miriam?"

"Father Horan—that will be your village priest." She was considering what I said, not laughing at me. "I believe he came here once some years ago, and Jon told him to go away, and he did—but no charge of witchcraft was ever brought against us." She smiled at me, a smile of strangeness, but it warmed me. "Yes, I have prayed, Benvenuto . . . You said you were running away. Why that, my dear? And from what?"

"They would stone me. I've heard it muttered behind windows when I passed. The only reason they haven't yet is that Father Horan was my friend—I thought he was, I'm sure he wanted to be, once. But I have learned he is not, he also believes me sinful."

"Sinful?" She stroked the back of my hand, and her look was wondering. "Perhaps any sin you might have done has been atoned for by coming out of your way to help an old witch."

"You're not a witch!" I said. "Don't call yourself that!"

"Why, Benvenuto! Then you do believe in witches!"

"Oh, I don't know." For the first time in my life I was wondering whether I did, if she in all her trouble could be so amused at the thought of them. "I don't know," I said, "but you're not one. You're good, Mam Miriam. You're beautiful."

"Well, Benvenuto, when I am busy with my embroideries, I sometimes feel like a good person. And in Jon's embraces I've thought so, after the pleasure, in the time when there can be quiet and a bit of thinking. Other times I've just lain here wondering what goodness is, and whether anyone really knows. Bless you, am I beautiful? I'm too fat, from lying here doing nothing. The wrinkles spread over my puffy flesh just the same, like frost lines coming on a windowpane, only dark, dark." She closed her eyes and asked me, "What sin could you have done to make them after stoning you?"

"The one I most loved went away last spring—all the way to Penn, Gold help me, and I don't even know what town. I was lonely, and full of desire too, for we had been lovers, and I've learned I have a great need of that, a fire in me that flares up at a breath. In Wayland's field a few days ago, where the corn shocks are standing like golden women, I came on someone else, Eden—we had been loving friends, though not in that way. We were both lonely and hungry for loving, and so we comforted each other—and still, in spite of Father Horan, I can see no harm in it—but Eden's people found us. Eden is younger than me—was only driven home and whipped, and will suffer no worse, I hope. Me they call monster. I ran away from Eden's father and brother, but now all the village is muttering."

"But surely, surely, boy and girl playing the old sweet game in an autumn cornfield—"

"Eden is a boy, Mam Miriam. The one I love, who went away, is Andrea Benedict, the eldest son of a patrician."

She put her hand behind my neck. "Come here awhile," she said, and drew me down to her.

"Father Horan says such passion is the Eternal Corruption. He says the people of Old Time sinned in this way, so God struck them with fire and plague until their numbers were as nothing. Then he sent Abraham to redeem us, taking away the sin of the world, so—"

"Hush," she said, "hush. Nay—go on if you will, but I care nothing for your Father Horan."

"And so God placed upon us, he says, the command to be fruitful and multiply until our numbers are again the millions they were in Old Time, destroying only the mues. And those who sin as I did, he says, are no better than mues, are a *kind* of mue, and are to be stoned in a public place and their bodies burned. After telling me that, he spoke of God's infinite mercy, but I did not want to hear about it. I ran from him. But I know that in the earlier days of Old Time people like me were tied up in the marketplaces and burned alive, I know this from the books—it was Father Horan taught me the books, the reading—isn't that strange?"

"Yes," she said. She was stroking my hair, and I loved her. "Lying here useless, I've thought about a thousand things, Benvenuto. Most of them idle. But I do tell you that any manner of love is good if there's kindness in it. Does anyone know you came here, Benvenuto?" She made my name so loving a sound!

"No, Mam Miriam."

"Then you can safely stay the night. I'm frightened when the night wind blows around the eaves, if I'm alone. You can keep the fright away. It sounds like children crying, some terror pursues them or some grief is on them and there's nothing I can do."

"Why, to me the night wind sounds like children laughing, or the wood gods running and shouting across the top of the world."

"Are there wood gods?"

"I don't know. The forest's a living place. I never feel alone there, even if I lose my way awhile."

"Benvenuto, I think I'm hungry now. See what you can find downstairs—there's cheese, maybe sausage, some of the little red

Snow Apples, and Jon made bread—" Her face crumpled and she caught at my hand. "Was it very bad—about Jon?"

"I think he was dead before the wolf came," I told her. "Maybe his heart failed, or—a stroke? I've heard black wolf won't attack in broad day. He must have died first in some quick way, without pain."

"Oh, if we all could!" That cry was forced from her because her courage had gone, and I think it was only then that she really knew Jon Kobler was dead. "How could he go before me? I have been dying for ten years."

"I won't leave you, Mam Miriam."

"Why, you must. I won't allow you to stay. I saw a stoning once in Sortees when I was a girl—or maybe that was when my girlhood ended. You must be gone by first light. Now, find us some little supper, Benvenuto. Before you go downstairs—that ugly thing over there, the bedpan—if you would reach it to me. God, I hate it so!—the body of this death."

There's nothing offensive in such services, certainly not if you love the one who needs them: we're all bound to the flesh—even Father Horan said it. I wished to tell her so, and found no words; likely she read my thought.

Downstairs everything had been left in order. Jon Kobler must have been a careful, sober man. While I was busy building a fire to cook the sausage, arranging this and that on the tray Jon must have used, I felt him all around us in the work of his hands—the baskets, the beads, the furniture, the very shutters at the windows. Those were all part of a man.

In some way my own works shall live after me. This letter I am finishing is part of a man. Read it so.

When I took up the tray, Mam Miriam smiled at it, and at me. She would not talk during our meal about our troubles. She spoke of her young years at Sortees, and that is when I came to learn those things I wrote down for you about the governor's mansion, the strange people she used to see who came from far off, even two or three hundred miles away; about the archer, the elopement, all that. And I learned much else that I have not written down, about the world that I shall presently go and look upon in my own time.

We had two candles at our supper table. Afterward, and the night wind was rising, she asked me to blow out one and set the other behind a screen; so all night long we had the dark, but it was not so dark we could not see each other's faces. We talked on awhile; I told her more about Andrea. She slept some hours. The night wind calling and crying through the trees and over the rooftop did not waken her, but she woke when for a moment I took my hand away from hers. I returned it, and she slept again.

And once I think she felt some pain, or maybe it was grief that made her stir and moan. The wind had hushed, speaking only of trifling illusions; no other sound except some dog barking in Trempa village, and an owl. I said, "I'll stay with you, Mam Miriam."

"You cannot."

"Then I'll take you with me."

"How could that be?"

"I'll carry you. I'll steal a horse and carriage."

"Dear fool!"

"No, I mean it. There must be a way."

"Yes," she said, "and I'll dream of it awhile." And I think she did sleep again. I did, I know; then morning was touching the silence of our windows.

The daylight was on her face, and I blew out the candle, and I told her, "Mam Miriam, I'll make you walk. I believe you can, and you know it too." She stared up at me, not answering, not angry. "You are good. I think you've made me believe in God again, and so I've been praying that God should help you walk."

"Have I not prayed?"

"Come!" I said, and took her hands and lifted her in the bed. "Come now, and I'll make you walk."

"I will do what I can," she said. "Set my feet on the floor, Benvenuto, and I will try to lift myself."

This I did. She was breathing hard. She said I was not to lift her, she must do it herself. "There's money in the drawer of that table," she said, and I was puzzled that she should speak of it now when she ought to be summoning all her forces to rise and walk. "And a few jewels brought from Sortees, we never sold them. Put them in your pocket, Benvenuto. I want to see you do that, to be sure you have them." I did as she said—never mind what I found in the drawer, since you have only my word for it that I did not rob her.

When I turned back to her, she was truly struggling to rise. I could see her legs tensing with life, and I believed we had won, even that God had answered a prayer, a thing I had never known to happen. A blood vessel was throbbing fiercely at her temple, her face had gone red, her eyes were wild with anger at her weakness.

"Now let me help," I said, and put my hands under her armpits, and with that small aid she did rise, she did stand on her own legs and smile at me with the sweat on her face.

"I thank you, Benvenuto," she said, and her face was not red any more but white, her lips bluish. She was collapsing. I got her back on the bed Jon Kobler made, and that was the end of it.

I will go into the world and find my way, I will not die by my own hand, I will regret no act of love. If it may be, I will find Andrea, and if he wishes, we may travel into new places, the greater oceans, the wilderness where the sun goes down. Wherever I go I shall be free and shameless; take heed of me. I care nothing for your envy, your anger, your fear that simulates contempt. The God you invented has nothing to say to me; but I hear my friend say that any manner of love is good if there's kindness in it. Take heed of me. I am the night wind and the quiet morning light: take heed of me.

SURVIVAL PROBLEMS

by Kris Neville

Kris Neville is an underrated writer in this field, probably because he isn't particularly prolific; a chemist specializing in plastics research, he writes only as a sideline. But he sees the trends of our lives in constantly unexpected ways, and his sense of humor is as sly as that of any writer in science fiction—as he's shown in stories such as "Ballenger's People," "Medical Practices among the Immortals," and the following wry tale of people trying to cope with the future (but the present keeps getting in the way).

JOE WHITE, top plastic specialist with the Research Department of the American Mortuary Society, under contract with the National Institutes of Health, won the Survivor's Lottery.

Word traveled up the managerial ladder to Mr. Braswell himself. Mr. Braswell, head of the society, announced that he would attend the testimonial banquet in person: a rare event.

Mr. Braswell, now seventy-three, appeared no older than fifty. Since before White was born, Mr. Braswell had been taking Go-Slow injections. These, while slowing his metabolic rate and thereby extending his life span, unfortunately slowed down the mental processes correspondingly.

Attendance at the testimonial was intentionally restricted to White's immediate associates, Mr. Braswell, and Mr. Braswell's personal physician, Dr. Franklin. The press was excluded, and White's bodyguard remained outside.

The attendees could not, of course, fill the banquet room they rented, so they formed into a little huddle around the corner bar.

White drank three martinis, although he was not accustomed to drinking.

Gladys Rosenwald, one of his two assistants, kept pace with him. "I guess you won't even be here tomorrow to help us," she said. "What do you know about that? Well, I'll say this, if it hadn't been for you, I don't know where we'd be right now. We wouldn't be nearly as far along, I'll tell you that!"

Mr. Braswell and Dr. Franklin hung back on the periphery of the group. White kept eying them nervously. "I never thought Mr. Braswell himself would come down to see me off," White said to Alf Sherman, the project engineer.

"This is good publicity," said Sherman. "It's going to get our own project off with a real bang!" Sherman put down his drink. "Joe, we are going to miss you. But I look at it this way: we're losing a man, but you're gaining a world."

"I'll be out in a few years," White said. "As soon as the international situation with China quiets down."

"I wouldn't be too optimistic."

"I wouldn't be, either, Joe," said Pete Remington, his other assistant. "It looks pretty bleak right now, with all these

Communist-inspired food riots among the starving in India. I don't think it's over a year away—at the most!"

"Let's not talk about things like that tonight, eh?" Sherman suggested. "Let's forget all that for tomorrow. Do you know when you're leaving yet, Joe?"

Sherman passed around the tranquilizers, and they all selected the dosage appropriate to their degree of concern.

"Day after tomorrow," said White.

Sherman put his arm over White's shoulder. "I think that calls for another drink. Let's all have another drink."

The bartender obliged.

"Now, Joe," Sherman said, "while we're waiting for the dinner and all to start, I'd like to talk to you a minute, just you and I."

"Sure, Alf."

"Let's step over here." They withdrew along the bar.

"As you know, Joe," said Sherman, "we're encapsulating General Feather in the morning. I don't need to tell you how much this means! This is the thing we've been working for, for the last two years, and, Joe, we need you there with us. I know this is an awful lot to ask, but is there any way you can see your way clear to making it in to work tomorrow morning, just for the time until we get the general done? I'll consider it a personal favor to me, Joe. It wouldn't seem right if you weren't there. If anything went wrong, you'd always blame yourself, if you weren't there. Isn't that true? You know that's true. Always blame yourself for it, feel bad about it . . ."

"Gosh, Alf—"

"Not only for me, of course, but for the whole society. It's done a lot for you."

"Well . . ."

"Bottoms up, Joe."

"I've already had three."

"Come on, bottoms up! This is your farewell party!"

"Uh . . . okay, bottoms up! Bottoms—ugh, Jesus Christ! Wow!"

"Now, Joe, what do you say?"

"That was a strong one. Yes. Wow! Alf, I . . . Well, Alf, I won't . . . whew! . . . let you down . . ."

"Good man," said Sherman. "I knew you'd come through. This calls for a drink, and I'll be sure to have somebody over to your new place the first thing to pick you up, how's that?"

When dinner arrived, Sherman told Miss Rosenwald, "I'm getting swacked!"

"Me, too! I don't know when I've been so swacked. It takes your mind off things."

Mr. Braswell himself sat with White at the head of the table. Sherman introduced Mr. Braswell. Mr. Braswell stood up and surveyed the faces as if trying to remember where he was. He handed the watch to Sherman, who, in turn, handed it to White.

At length Mr. Braswell said, "Good afternoon, ladies and gentlemen."

They waited.

"I am very," he began and then hesitated. He thought for a while. "Allow me to introduce, uh, a man who . . . who . . . has . . . That reminds me of a story."

They waited.

"Never mind," Mr. Braswell said. "That reminds me of a story. No. I already told that, didn't I? This young man . . ."

Into the lengthening silence, Sherman supplied the name.

"Yes, slipped my . . ." The silence elongated.

"Mind," said Dr. Franklin.

"Yes, mind. I guess I've talked too long already. So now I turn it over to . . ."

White stood uncertainly. "I sure do thank you, Mr. Braswell."

Hands were applauding. He looked over the audience.

"I sure do thank you for coming down here tonight. Thanks, everybody. As you know, I took part in this national lottery. Out of all the people that took part on the male side, my name just came out. Out of all those people. That's democracy. I feel good about that. I guess there's no point in trying to kid anybody that I don't feel good about that. Now, let me have another little sip of this drink. Thanks. Ah. I want to thank Mr. Braswell. And I want to thank all of you for this watch. I sure do appreciate it. As I was saying, they're going to put me and this girl in suspended animation down in this big lead vault somewhere in the Midwest, which is a secret, of course, where it is, somewhere, about a mile underground, and then if there's this war they're all talking about, we'll be left to start the race over again, Americans starting the race over again, which is very important, really, if somebody doesn't do something about it, when the timer goes off about five thousand years from now when it's not so radioactive anymore. Well, you all know how that goes.

"I do want to thank you again for the watch. I'm not much good at thanking people, but I really mean it when I say thanks for the watch. You know what I mean? It's very good, and I'll have a lot of use for it where I'm going to keep time with. Well, you know, I never got much practice in thanking people growing up, and . . .

"I was just lucky to have my card come up: it could have been anybody in good health, in their twenties, I mean. But I feel I'm a symbol. It makes you think, I mean, it's a symbol of how America looks forward to the future, by spending ninety-seven billion dollars on that vault, more than it cost to go to Mars, because the trip's longer, actually, when you look at it . . . and it's not just the money, it's the concern for the human race, and democracy, and that a little guy like me could . . .

"What we have is everybody really facing up to the survival problem we're confronted with, which refutes those people who say the American people are morbidly preoccupied with death and won't do anything about all the real problems and all these troubles we have at home and also abroad, because we've got our eyes on really important things that mean something, you know what I mean, and also all those people who don't know what they're talking about and say we're . . . indifferent to the future, and have lost all sense of what it means to be alive, this will show them. It shows you how much this country cares.

"Well, you know, I kind of got drunk tonight, and I think we all kind of got drunk tonight, except Mr. Braswell, who didn't drink much, and I think what we ought to do, what I think we ought to do is all go home and get some sleep so we can be up fresh and alert when we encapsulate General Feather in the morning!"

Anyone who has thought about the problem of the proper encapsulation of a corpse comes to recognize that it is a substantial technological challenge.

Basically, two methods could be employed:

METHOD I

Method I involves placing the corpse in some convenient container and pouring a liquid plastic over it. The plastic may subsequently be converted to an impermeable, corrosion-resistant solid by heat or some form of chemical reaction. The plastic, in addition to possessing very low viscosity, must be formulated to provide extreme durability and must be stable to light and normal weathering conditions.

Ideally, the potting compound should be water-clear when hardened, in order that the finished product can be seen without distortion. Most plastics, unfortunately, particularly when cast in larger masses, tend to discolor somewhat during the hardening reaction, which involves the liberation of heat. Additionally, it is difficult (even with vacuum impregnation) to get a bubble-free casting of any size. And finally, minimum build-ups cannot be obtained. In thicker sections, shrinkage with all known plastics is prohibitive, even the best of them exerting pressures as high as 5,000 psi on the corpse itself, leading to undesirable aesthetic effects, as has been amply demonstrated by animal research with mini-pigs.

METHOD II

Method II, dip coating, overcomes most of the above problems but presents its own. Essentially, by the dip-coating method, the corpse, suitably suspended, is immersed in a vat of liquid, removed, and allowed to drain. With proper formulation, a smooth, continuous coating is deposited. This is then subsequently cured in an oven.

Normally the dip-coat method employs a long pot-life compound which is capable of fairly rapid cures at only moderately elevated temperatures. In no case, for rather obvious reasons, should the curing temperature be permitted or required to increase above that of boiling water.

Method II had been selected by White and his fellow researchers at the American Mortuary Society, under contract with the National Institutes of Health.

On the morning following White's farewell party, the staff met.

"Remember, everybody," Sherman said, "General Feather is going on public display, and public acceptance of encapsulation will depend on how well we do today. This is it! This is what we've been working for, for the past two years!"

In anticipation of demand, a production line had been established. It was capable of handling up to twenty corpses at one time. The corpses would be rolled out, properly suspended by piano wires from the overhead trolley system, positioned, and then simultaneously immersed in a tank some forty feet long, four feet wide, and nine feet deep. The tank was loaded to seven feet with the liquid plastic compound, the remaining two feet being an allowance for ullage. Glass windows in the tank permitted inspection during processing.

White performed last-minute checks. The temperature was within allowable limits of plus or minus two degrees Fahrenheit. He checked other aspects of the process. This done, he measured the thixotropic index of the plastic and corrected it by the addition of a diluent.

"Well," he said, "I guess it's all or nothing."

They brought General Feather in and dipped him.

White and the rest watched in silence as the bubbles rose and broke.

"Okay," said White at length. "Lift him out slow, now . . . There. There. Hold it, hold it! Okay. Let him drip for a little while, I think we've got it!"

"It's just beautiful!" said Miss Rosenwald.

"It's too early to tell," said White. "Let's wait to see how he cures out."

They swiveled the general to the cart, attached him to the fixture there, and wheeled him into the 150°F. warm room.

They drank coffee and talked for thirty minutes, then they brought General Feather out. White inspected the general critically. "There's a few bubbles to patch up, but I guess that's all. I'd say he's good for a thousand years or so . . . if he isn't caught in the blast area."

Sherman let out a sigh. "Joe, we sure appreciate this. I knew nothing could go wrong with you here."

"I didn't do anything Gladys or Pete couldn't have done just as well. Look. I hate to run like this, but they've got a big program laid out for me, instructions and things, and training, you know. . . ."

"And I better rush over to tell Mr. Braswell," Sherman said. "He told me to be sure to come over and tell him personally just as soon as it was over." Sherman extended a hand. "Goodbye, Joe. And thanks."

"Yeah," said Remington in the embarrassment of parting. "Goodbye, Joe, we'll see you on TV. Good luck."

White left with his bodyguard.

Sherman went to the roof and flew his helicopter to Mr. Braswell's estate. The butler met him and together they went to tell Mr. Braswell the good news.

.　　　.　　　.

Two weeks later an unfortunate accident during an inspection tour of a bacteriological warfare installation brought distinguished customers to the Research Center: the President of the United States, the Chief of Staff, the Secretary of Peace, the Speaker of the House, the Minority Leader of the Senate, a newspaper photographer, and two Eagle Scouts.

"Oh, God!" Sherman said. "Do you think we're big enough to handle this one? The process is still in the experimental stages. If only Joe were here!"

"Damn!" cried Miss Rosenwald. "Why did it have to happen right now? This is one I hate to tackle. There's too much at stake!" She puffed nervously at her cigarette, thoughts of bacteriological warfare calling up the threat of cancer.

Remington paced the floor. "Hey!" he said at length. "Do you suppose they'd let Joe come up for this one? Jesus! *This is it!*"

"I'm going to find out. That's exactly what I'm going to do! I'm going to take this straight to the top!"

Sherman did.

At the emergency meeting of the Cabinet, the first order of business was introduced by the new President:

"As you know, we've got a problem over at the American Mortuary Society. I think you'll all agree that it's a matter of national prestige that the job be done right. Well, their staff feels the encapsulation process is not yet quite fully developed, and they feel they would like to have this White fellow on hand to help out on this one, in view of its importance. We could put him back within twelve hours or so. That's what I think we ought to iron out first."

There followed a lengthy discussion. The new President clearly favored one course, whereas the new Secretary of Peace persuasively favored the opposite:

"There's more to it than appears on the surface, Mr. President. Under normal circumstances, I'd go along. But every moment

White was above ground there'd be the possibility he might be assassinated, for no matter how law-abiding most of us are, there are always a few nuts running around loose who just seem to enjoy shooting public figures for no reason at all. I can't tell you how much that would affect our moral posture and increase the undeserved reputation we have in certain uncommitted countries for being a violent nation. That was a matter of foremost concern to your predecessor and mine, sir. If anything like that happened, I hesitate to predict the repercussions in many foreign countries on the fence, and the black mark it would give us there. I say, now that we've gotten them both safely underground and hidden, let's leave well enough alone."

In the end, it was decided that they must go ahead without White.

Preparations were made.

All eight were to be processed at the same time: Together in Life, Together in Death. There was a ring of democracy to it. The President of a great nation would stand with two Eagle Scouts side by side in niches of honor throughout the future serving as an example for a hundred generations as yet unborn and reverberating consequences to eternity. They were known as the Eight National Martyrs for Peace, and a number of solemn ceremonies were planned throughout the free world.

As is inevitable with such matters of state, a tight schedule must be adhered to, to accommodate TV commitments, speaking engagements, etc. From first to last, there could be no hitch or delay.

Miss Rosenwald and Remington and Sherman nervously made the final preparations and took the final precautions.

"We've got to hurry," Sherman said. "The nation is waiting. They'll arrive in exactly six minutes. Everything okay?"

"Well," said Remington, "the thixotropic index is off."

"Hurry up!"

"I am hurrying!"

Miss Rosenwald added the diluent.

"It's not coming up right," Remington said in mild alarm and harsh exasperation. "Add some more!"

"I'm afraid to add any more! We might lose flow control in the oven, and we'd just streak them all up, and they'd look awful!"

"We've just got a few minutes!" said Sherman. "For God's sake, hurry!"

"I am hurrying!"

"What are we going to do now?"

"They're waiting on us!" cried Sherman. "All over the free world! There's at least a billion people out there waiting for us!"

"I know! I know! For God's sake, I know! What else can we do now?"

"How about raising the temperature a little?" Miss Rosenwald asked. "I've seen Joe do that with the swine. That will make it more fluid without bothering the flow control in the oven."

"Good; good."

"How's this, Pete?"

They waited for the tank to come up to the new temperature.

"Now?"

"Better."

"A little more."

"Just a *little!*"

"Here?"

"Hurry, please!"

"A little more?"

"How's this?"

They waited.

"Whew!" said Remington. "There. That's done it. Good. We're in specification. We're ready, Alf."

"And not a minute too soon," Sherman said. "Here they come!"

The corpses came in from the overhead entrance, two morticians still putting the last touches on them. Sherman signaled the operator. "Okay, bring them on down!"

Down they came.

"Hold it! They look okay, Pete?"

"They're in position just right."

"Lower away!" ordered Sherman. "Gently, now, gently, now. . . . Good!"

When the plastic closed over the last head, Sherman and Remington and Miss Rosenwald all said simultaneously, "Thank God!"

"It's coming okay," Miss Rosenwald said, allowing herself the first pill of the day.

They watched the bubbles.

"Whew!" Sherman said. "Five minutes."

"Better make it ten," Remington said. "It's still a little thick. We've got to get penetration." He stepped back from the monitor.

They waited. It seemed an eternity.

"Take 'em out!" Sherman said.

"A little bit more," Remington said. "This could be critical here. Let's not goof it by hurrying." He turned to Miss Rosenwald. "What's the temperature set at? The thixotropic index—"

"Oh, look," said Miss Rosenwald dreamily, with interest but without alarm.

"What?"

Taking another pill, Miss Rosenwald said, "It's taking off so pretty. It's at one hundred and eighty, one hundred and eighty-five—"

"A hundred and—oh, my God!" cried Sherman. "Pull 'em out! *Pull 'em out!*"

The control technicians responded promptly.

There was the twang of parting piano wires.

"Dear Jesus," said Sherman.

Remington sprang to the ladder and scrambled up. He reached down into the tank and felt the smooth, glass-hard surface of the compound. He stared down into the clear, solid block with horror. It was beginning to acquire a faint amber cast.

"Oh, dear me," said Sherman. "Is there . . . is there going to be much shrinkage?"

Remington turned away. "Quite a bit, I'm afraid," he said softly. "This is one of the biggest castings I've ever heard of."

Sherman stumbled from the room and made his way, almost unseeing, to the helicopter on the roof.

He flew over the grief-stricken city of Washington, D.C., a city suffering through the seventh national day of mourning so far this year. His heart went out to the American people.

Mr. Braswell's butler greeted Sherman.

"I've got to see Mr. Braswell!"

"I'm sorry, sir, Mr. Braswell cannot be disturbed."

"He's got to be! This can't wait! It's too important!"

The butler led Sherman to Mr. Braswell's room. The private nurse protested and then stepped aside to permit them to enter.

Mr. Braswell lay in the center of a king-sized bed. He looked very small and crumpled. He was breathing so slowly it could scarcely be noticed.

"He'll live a real long time now," the butler said. "He just had Dr. Franklin give him a huge increase in the Go-Slow injection. As I told you, he can't be disturbed."

"Don't he look sweet?" the nurse said. "How far removed he is now from all the cares of this troubled world!" She bent over Mr. Braswell and listened intently for a minute. "Gee," she said. "If he just stopped breathing entirely, I think Mr. Braswell could live forever!"

PASSION PLAY

by J. Michael Reaves

J. Michael Reaves is a native Californian now in his early twenties; in 1972 he traveled to Michigan State University to attend the Clarion-East sf writers' workshop, sold his first story to Clarion III and used the money to buy a typewriter. Judging from the following sharply etched tale of a girl taking advantage of a strange talent (his second sale), I expect his investment will prove to be a boon for lovers of science fiction.

THE hitch-hiker was barely visible far ahead, a stick figure where the road joined the flat gray horizon. The dust that clung like dry paint to the windshield and the heat waves from the black asphalt blurred Sherry's vision. But still she felt certain it was a "he."

The knowing made her smile—the lovely feeling of knowing she would be right.

She half listened to Ellis' voice droning just above the rattling clatter of the old truck's engine, telling her interesting things about animal life that she had no desire to hear. Ellis would stop for the hitch-hiker if she wanted him to. She smoothed her hair back, fingers sliding over the blond tangles slick with sweat, and wondered, Would it be worth stopping?

Yes.

"Stop for him," she said, leaning over close to his ear. It was the sort of command best delivered in a husky tone, breathed just above a whisper. But the '62 Chevy pickup forced conversation to be carried on in shouts. Sherry refused to bellow, and so she leaned close to Ellis' ear, rubbing the tips of her fingers over the back of his neck, feeling sweat and dust like a thin layer of mud. An eighth of an inch behind her smiling face, she shuddered in pure disgust. No ripple of it showed on the surface.

"Stop for him, Ellis."

His foot began pumping the worn-out brakes in time to the rubbing of his neck.

She was almost able to see the pink dot of his face as he walked slowly backward down the highway. To not even see his face, and to *know* that it would be worthwhile to stop, she thought. A lovely, lovely feeling.

Ellis didn't believe in feminine intuition, in Sight. He would grumble and curse, but he would stop. It was good to let him have some resentment left. It kept him thinking that the decisions were still his.

But instead of protesting, Ellis merely said, "Wonder where in hell he came from. Man'd die after a few hours in this heat without a car."

The truck lurched onto the shoulder in front of the hitch-hiker.

The way he walked, Sherry thought, watching him as he approached the truck. There was such an easiness to it. It made her think of—

"At least he's not a nigra," she said.

—John Frank, the black man they had hired to fix the roof last fall.

And then he was opening the door and sliding in, fast, because Ellis' heavy foot was on the gas pedal, sending the truck back onto the road again. The rattle of gravel and sand against the frame died away, and Sherry looked at the hitch-hiker.

She felt again the satisfaction of being right. She had known he would be different.

And so he was.

His face was tanned and unwrinkled—baby-smooth, and yet lean. She watched him settle back against the seat, relaxing against the plastic covering. His hair was black and short, almost furlike. There was no trace of a beard.

And he was not sweating.

She looked at his face, dry and still in the whistling hot wind. His eyes were closed, but she would see their color soon.

Different, she thought. How different . . . no, she told herself. Don't look too long, or you'll find out too soon. She wanted to be intrigued awhile longer. It had been so long since she had been interested in anybody.

She looked at his hands, pale and slim, with tapering fingers. Lucille Ballentine's hands had looked like that.

"What happened, mister?" Sherry snapped her head around in surprise, saw Ellis looking across her at him. Sitting next to Ellis, she could smell the animal odor of his shirt, could see the yellow circles under his arms. Ellis had been driving for almost eight hours. Sherry almost wrinkled her nose in distaste; almost, but not quite.

"My car broke down." His voice was quiet, and right in the middle; a neutral tone.

Sherry expected Ellis to say that they hadn't passed any abandoned cars. Instead he simply said, "That happens."

She sat between them, feeling the contrast, feeling repugnance push her away from Ellis, from his grimy clothes and damp skin, toward the hitch-hiker. "What's your name?" she asked.

"Kyle." He hadn't looked at her once—she still did not know what color his eyes were. If she moved another quarter inch, she would be touching him . . .

Not yet. She was still enjoying the mystery too much. To touch him would be to absorb more knowledge, just to brush against him would tell her what she didn't want to know so soon.

Ellis had resumed his lecture, which had started on desert life and progressed to animals in general, reciting scraps of knowledge remembered from old *Reader's Digest* articles. One large hand gripped the steering wheel while he talked; the other rested on the door. The sun had tanned that arm darker than its mate during the three days he had been driving.

"You take your reptiles, your snakes and lizards," he said. "Protective coloration—they look just like the dirt they crawl around in. There's some can even change their color to match their background. That's how they stay alive, y'know. Or some attach themselves up with the dominant life-form in the neighborhood, like those birds that live on rhinoceroses. It's called a defense mechanism."

"Ellis," Sherry said, looking at him wearily. "We're *not* interested." Ellis grunted, and changed the subject, flashing an irritated glance her way. The look surprised her—usually that tone of voice forbade any resentment on his part.

"Bad place to have a breakdown," Ellis continued. "Gets up to a hundred-twenty in the shade this time of year. That's killing weather."

And Kyle's skin was so smooth, and dry—and pale. Sherry looked from the brown of Ellis' arm to the pink of Kyle's face. Was there the slightest hint of darkening, down to the first button of his shirt?

It was time, she decided, to learn a little bit more. Sherry put her hand lightly on his, and felt—

Thunder! Gunshot!

—And the color of his eyes as he looked at her . . .

The truck was jolting toward the right, the blown-out tire dragging them toward the shoulder. Ellis wrestled it to a stop, twisted the key out of the ignition. He got out of the cab, walked around to the right front tire, and let go with a curse and a kick.

Kyle was still looking at her. "What's your name?"

She knew her confusion showed. "Sherry."

"Sherry." He smiled, opened the door, and went out to help change the tire.

Sherry watched the two of them working. A stripe of sunlight lay across her thighs, making her hose hot and itchy. She touched her tongue lightly with a fingernail and wondered if she should be afraid.

His eyes were brown. The dark chocolate brown of John Frank's, the walnut-brown of Lucy Ballentine's. Gooseflesh burned along her arms from that touch.

She watched them changing the tire, Ellis doing most of the talking. Three years with Ellis; the challenge, the satisfaction, and now the boredom of being in command. He would do anything she told him to, even quit his job and move from Arkansas to California, for the privilege of her body. She watched the easy way Kyle lifted the tire into place, back muscles stretching the faded blue shirt he wore. Then, quickly, one hand went to the rear-view mirror, twisted it so she could see her face. Her complexion was chapped, and her hair stringy from the hot dry air. She reached for her purse and was dabbing salve on her cheeks when Kyle and Ellis got back in the cab.

The road stretched long and straight, like pulled taffy, toward the swollen red sun. Night came almost without a dusk. They rode without saying much for another hour, until the lights of a small motel showed on the horizon.

"Stopping here," Ellis said. It looked clean, and more important for what she had in mind, there was only one other car parked in the gravel lot. Sherry smiled.

Ellis went in to sign for a room. When the glass door to the motel office swung shut behind him, Sherry said quickly, "Why don't you stay here for the night, and we'll take you on with us tomorrow?"

And waited, breathing lightly, for his answer.

"I could hitch the rest of the way tonight," he said. And by the tone of it, she knew that he was playing with her. She turned her head, and stared at him. His eyes were hidden in the darkness— the red *Vacancy* light flashed a band of crimson across his chest.

"I know you'll stay," she said.

"How do you know?"

"Same way I knew I wanted to pick you up. Same way I knew you were—different." She smiled at him. "I can usually tell about things like that. Mother used to say I had Sight." She put her hand on his arm again.

Kyle grinned, and she ran her tongue over her dry lips. "You're a sensitive girl, Sherry. Just how different am I?"

"I hope to find out." She reached into her purse, pulled out a ten and a five. "You take a room here. After Ellis goes to sleep . . ."

He looked at the money. "What makes you think I won't take it and leave?"

She glanced at the motel office door, then leaned over and kissed him. His lips were dark and full, soft and womanly . . .

"You'll stay," she told him. It was meant to be a sultry whisper, full of confidence. It came out a gasp, full of pleading.

Suddenly confused, she slid over to the door, opened it, and started toward the motel office. As she reached the door, Ellis came out.

"Number seventeen," he said and handed her the key. As she started across the parking lot, she saw Kyle stroll into the office. A few minutes later, he was unlocking the door to number fifteen.

Another hour or two, she thought, and no more mystery.

She was in bed by the time Ellis was out of the shower, her eyes closed so she wouldn't have to see him walk damp and naked across the floor. The thought of his paunchy belly on hers, weight crushing her into the mattress, puffing his way to climax and beginning to snore almost before he rolled off, disgusted her. But he made no attempts, merely laced his fingers behind his head and stared up at the ceiling. After a moment he mused, "That Kyle's a strange one, ain't he?"

He's tired from driving, she thought. Good. "Strange how?"

"Why, it's fairly obvious how, at least to me. I guess a woman wouldn't notice it, though." Ellis chuckled.

"Ellis, what are you talking about?"

"He's gay, is all."

"*What?*" An image of Kyle, smoothly strong and tall . . . the easy way he had lifted the tire, his relaxed form sitting beside her . . . "Gay? *Kyle?*"

"Plain as can be," Ellis said. He chuckled again. "I always wondered why anyone would care to play on that side of the fence. But seeing one as pretty as he is, I can almost understand—"

"Ellis!" she shouted. "You quit talking like that!"

For a moment he was silent. Then, "Why's it bothering you, Sherry?"

"What do you mean?" She didn't like the tone of his voice. "It's not bothering me. Now, go to sleep."

"Not right yet. I think I deserve an answer."

"Ellis, go to sleep!"

He said nothing else—the silence gathered and grew. Finally he reached over and turned the light out.

Gay. She thought of a night, not quite a year gone, when she had stayed at Lucy Ballentine's house while Ellis and Lucy's husband went moon-fishing. The two of them sleeping in the same bed, lying close together and touching . . .

She waited until Ellis began snoring. Then she dressed and went out the door. She walked along the sidewalk, swearing softly as one bare foot came down on a piece of gravel. At his door she stubbed her toe against the cement porch. The pain made her sit down for a moment, holding her foot, tears squeezing out of her eyes.

When she was able to stand, without thinking she knocked. Then she realized what she was doing, and before he could make it worse by saying "Come in," (or "Stay out"? she wondered), she opened the door and stepped inside.

Kyle was sitting up in the bed, the sheet pulled across him. "Hi," she said. Quietly, almost shyly. And began to undress.

She had put on her clothes for a reason, instead of just throwing a coat on. She watched Kyle as she undressed, trying to read his expression in the dim light. She had done this before, more than once—there had been a time when she had been paid to do it. Ordinarily she would move slow as chilled oil, tugging buttons loose on her blouse one by one; swaying slightly, sliding material over her shoulders and down her arms to let it drop on the floor. She would look through lashes at her audience, tongue against her lips, as she let her skirt fall. And following it, with just enough movement, would be her stockings, and the black napkin-lace of her panties.

It was one of the things that kept Ellis in line, kept him chained to her. The sight of her preparations; the prelude to bed. But this time it was different—this time she hurried, fumbling buttons, tossing her blouse away, yanking her skirt down her hips, stepping quickly out of underwear. No tantalizing, no baiting this time. It would take too long.

And then she stood beside the bed staring at him. Remembering the two times in her life when she had been satisfied by someone other than herself—once by John Frank, and once by Lucille Ballentine. The mingled feelings of desire and guilt . . .

He was staring into her eyes, his gaze brown and deep. Feeling her thoughts, her desires; *knowing*, she thought, somehow. "Kyle," she whispered. Then she turned the sheet back, let it flutter to the floor like a dying ghost.

And saw:

Skin clear and smooth, woman's skin on a man's body. The hairlessness of the chest, the darkening flesh.

"You're not—" she said.

"I'm different. You said you could tell." The voice was a man's voice, and a woman's voice, and neither.

"You're not *human*," Sherry whispered.

"It doesn't matter, does it?" And it didn't, it didn't; the rushing of her blood, the moistness . . . she still *wanted* him—

As she watched, his skin grew darker, blacker. Above the erect penis were the lips of a vaginal slit.

"No . . ." she whimpered just before he kissed her. His kiss was that of John Frank, firm against her mouth. And his hands were Lucy's hands, the softest she had ever known.

John Frank was in the county jail back home, for carnal knowledge of a white woman. And Lucy Ballentine had suffered a nervous breakdown in fear of lesbian tendencies.

"No," she said again as Kyle pulled her down to the bed. "*No!*" she screamed, and pushed both hands against the soft black shoulders. There was a moment of pain, and then she was grabbing her clothes and running out the door. Behind her, she could hear the sound of Kyle's laughter . . .

She was sobbing by the time she reached her room, screaming by the time Ellis had gotten out of bed, bewildered, demanding to know what was wrong. She told him what had happened, again and again, scratching at his chest to make sure he understood, until a sudden, intense pain against her cheek stopped the crying and the explaining. For an instant she did not know what had happened. Then she realized—he had slapped her.

He had slapped *her*.

"Ellis?" she murmured. A small sound, totally lost in her throat.

"You goddamn bitch," he said. "Sherry, you've done it now."

She sat quietly in a chair and watched him dress. He picked up the suitcases and carried them out to the truck—after a moment, realizing that she was alone, she followed him outside.

The truck's engine was running, and the headlights were on. Ellis slung the suitcases into the back.

Yes, she thought. Let's leave—leave now, before—

The door to number fifteen was open. Sherry watched the woman walking across the gravel of the parking lot toward the truck, toward Ellis, who was busy tying down the luggage.

"Ellis," Sherry said.

"Just shut up, okay?" He pulled a knot tight.

The woman stopped beside Ellis, leaned against the fender, smiled at him. "You going west?" she asked.

The skin was whiter than it had been yesterday. The hair was lighter, and the eyes—were blue. Only the smile and the voice were the same.

"Ellis!" Sherry screamed. But there would be no evidence under those clothes for any accusations she made against Kyle.

He ignored her. "I am," he replied.

"I could use a ride."

"I'm sure my wife won't mind," Ellis said. "She'd better not, at any rate. Right, Sherry?"

"You send her away," she said desperately. "Ellis, you send her away this minute. You even think such thoughts as that, and I'll—I'll leave you! I'll leave you this minute, I swear I will!"

He would do as she said, like always. But that woman, that *thing*, was smiling at him, and one hand was touching him, stroking his arm.

She remembered what that touch had been like.

Ellis looked at her. His eyes were hard.

"Leave, then," he said. He pulled her suitcase loose, dropped it on the gravel.

Sherry stood by the road watching the two red taillights disappear below the horizon. Just wait until he finds out, she thought. He'll be back. When he learned what sort of creature it was, he'd get rid of it, leave it, kill it, and come back for her. He couldn't throw her over like that, and not even . . .

Not even for another *woman* . . .

After a long time of waiting, the eastern sky began to gray. She tried to ask the one other guest at the motel for a ride, but couldn't seem to make him understand what had happened. Afterward, she picked up her suitcase and began to walk. For a while, she held her thumb out, hopefully. But the few cars that passed her did not stop.

THE RUBBER BEND

by Gene Wolfe

Gene Wolfe, who wrote that remarkable book The Fifth Head of Cerberus, *as well as outstanding shorter works such as "The Death of Dr. Island" (Universe 3), appears now with a story much less weighty than these earlier ones . . . but in its distinctively Wolfean way it's as far-out as anything he's written. You'll recognize it easily as a parody of the Sherlock Holmes stories, but don't be misled: far from a simple bit of fluff, it's a complex and ingenious story that deals with one of the most puzzling questions in relativity: If all four space-time dimensions are equivalent, how is it that we perceive one so differently from the rest?*

.   .   .

IT WAS a dark and stormy night—not actually night but late afternoon, and raining buckets. I share an apartment with March B. Street, the human consulting engineer-detective, and I recall that when I came home that afternoon, Street ventured some deduction to the effect that it must be raining, since the water was still streaming off me and onto the carpet, and I remarked that it was a nice day out for ducks, a little witticism I have often found to have a remarkably calming effect on my patients, though of course—I am a bio-mechanic, you see—its use is somewhat dependent on the weather; though I am over fifty, my seals are still tight and I think I may boast that you won't find another robot my age with fewer rain leaks anywhere.

Where was I? Oh, yes. It was on a dark and stormy afternoon in October that I was first introduced to the weird and sinister business which I, in these reports, have chosen to refer to as *The Affair of the Rubber Bend.*

Street waited until I had dried myself off and was about to sit down with the paper, and then said sharply, "Westing!"

I confess I was so startled that for an instant I froze in a sort of half-crouch with my hips perhaps four inches above the seat of the scuffed old Morris chair next to Street's antique telespectroscope; had I known at the time how significant that posture was to be, in the eldritch light of the disappearance of Prof. Louis Dodson and the haunting of—but perhaps I am in danger of anticipating my story.

"Westing," Street continued, "for goodness' sake sit down. Hanging in the air like that, you look like a set of tin monkey bars flunking Darwin."

"It's only natural," I said, taking my seat, "for you humans to envy the somewhat greater coordination and superior muscular effectiveness we possess, but it is hardly necessary—"

"Quite. I'm sorry I startled you. But I had been thinking, and I want to talk to you. You are, are you not, a member of the Peircian Society?"

"Certainly," I said. "You know perfectly well, Street, that on the first Monday of each odd-numbered month I absent myself from this apartment—good lord, have I missed a meeting?" I had risen again and was actually trying to recall what I had done with my umbrella when I caught the error. "No, you're wrong for once, Street. This is October. October isn't—November is, of course, but today's Tuesday. Our meeting's five days off yet."

"Six," Street said dryly, "but I didn't say you were late for the meeting; I simply asked if you were still a member. You are. Am I not correct in saying that the purpose of the society is to discuss—"

In my eagerness I interrupted him. "To prove that the works signed 'Damon Knight' were actually written by the philosopher Charles Sanders Peirce, of course. And they were, Street. They were. It's so obvious: Peirce, the otherwise unknown founder of Logical Positivism—"

"Pragmatism," Street said.

"They are almost the same thing. Peirce, as I was saying, lived in Milford, Pennsylvania—a minute hamlet since buried under the damned waters of the Delaware—"

"You don't bury things under water."

"—thus conveniently destroying certain evidence the historical establishment did not want found. Note these points, Street: a village the size of Milford could hardly expect one such man in five hundred years; it had—this is what we are supposed to believe—two in less than fifty. Knight—"

"Knight also lived in Milford?"

"Yes, of course. Knight appeared shortly after Peirce—supposedly—died. Peirce, at the time of his supposed death, was being sorely hounded by his creditors. Peirce grew a thick beard, obviously to keep from being recognized later as Knight. Knight also grew a beard to prevent his being recognized as Peirce. Can't you see, Street . . ." I paused.

"You pause," Street remarked. "Has something struck you?"

"Indeed it has. You, Street, have become engrossed in this most fascinating of historical, scientific, and literary puzzles. You will apply your immense abilities to it, and in a short time we will know the truth."

"No."

"No?"

"I only apply those abilities you have flatteringly called immense to puzzles which hold out some possibility of remuneration, Westing. I merely wished to know if you were still a member of the Peircian Society. You are, and I am content."

"But surely—"

"There is a favor I would like you to do for me—it may be rather an inconvenience for you."

"Anything, Street. You know that."

"Then I want you to live for a few days with a friend of mine—be his houseguest. It shouldn't interfere with your practice, and I'll set up a gadget to relay your calls."

"I could go to a hotel—"

"I'm not trying to get rid of you, Westing; it's your presence there I want—not your absence here."

"Street, does this have something to do with—"

"The Peircian Society? No, not at present; in fact, Westing, I wish you'd forget I ever mentioned that. Put it completely out of your mind. A friend of mine—his name is Noel Wide, by the way—wishes to have a good bio-mechanic near at hand in the evenings. Ordinarily he calls a neighbor of his, but the fellow is on vacation at the moment. He asked if I could suggest someone, and I told him I'd try to persuade you to fill in. If you are willing to go, I want you there tonight."

"Tonight?"

"At once. Collect your medical bag and emergency self-maintenance kit and be on your way."

"Street, you're not telling me everything."

"I am telling you everything it's politic to tell you at the moment, and it's important that you don't miss dinner at Wide's. If you are sincere in wanting to go, go now. Here—while you've been jabbering I've written out the address for you."

"Dinner? Street, you know it isn't necessary—we robots don't—"

Something in his look stopped me. I collected the accouterments he had suggested and took my departure; but as I left I noted that Street, now calm again, had picked up the book that lay beside his chair, and as I read the title an indescribable thrill shot through me. It was *A for Anything*.

The address to which Street had dispatched me proved to be an old brownstone in a neighborhood that held a thousand others. It had once had, I observed as I plodded toward it through the downpour, a sort of greenhouse or conservatory on its roof, but this was now broken and neglected, and its shattered panes and rusted ironwork, dripping rain, looked as dejected as I felt. At my knock the door, which was on a chain-guard, was opened by a robot younger (or as Street would say, "newer") than myself. I asked if he was Mr. Wide.

He grinned mechanically, and without offering to unchain the door, replied, "He lives here, but I'm Arch St. Louis—you want in?" I observed that he sported a good deal of chrome-and-copper trim, arranged in a manner that led me to think better of his bank account than of his taste. In answer to his question I said, "Please," and when he continued immobile I added, "As you see, I'm standing in the wet—I'm Dr. Westing."

"Why didn't you say so?"

In a moment he had opened the door and shown me in. "Here," he said, "I'll get you some red-rags to wipe yourself off with. Don't take the cold reception to heart, Doc; we have unpleasant company from time to time."

I stifled the impulse to remark that birds of a feather assemble in groups, and asked instead if it would be possible for me to see Mr. Wide, my host.

St. Louis glanced at his watch. "Five minutes, he's down in the plant rooms. He'll be up at six."

"The plant rooms?"

"In the basement. He grows mushrooms. Come on into the office."

I followed him down a short corridor and entered a large and beautifully appointed chamber fitted out as something between an office and a parlor. A small desk near the door I deduced to be his; at the other side of the room stood a much larger desk with a scattering of unopened correspondence on its top, and behind it an immense chair. I walked over to examine the chair, but my awed perusal of its capacious dimensions was interrupted by the labored sighing of an elevator; I turned in time to see a pair of cleverly disguised doors slide back, revealing the most bulky robot I have ever beheld. He was carrying a small basket of tastefully arranged fungi, and holding this with both hands so as (at least, so it seemed to me) to have an excuse to avoid shaking hands with me, he marched across the room to the larger desk, and seating himself in that gargantuan chair, placed the basket squarely before him.

"Mr. Wide," St. Louis said, "this is Doc Westing."

"A pleasure, Doctor," Wide said in a thick but impressive voice. "You have come, I hope, to stay until my own physician returns?"

"I'm afraid there has been a mistake," I told him. "I am a bio-mechanic, with no experience in robot repair. My patients—"

"Are human. Indubitably, Doctor. It is not for me, nor for Mr. St. Louis, that your services may be required. I frequently entertain human guests at my table."

"I see," I said. I was about to ask why his guests should require the services of a bio-mechanic when St. Louis caught my eye. His eloquent look told me more plainly than words could that I would be wise to hold my peace until he explained later.

"You are clearly fatigued, Doctor," Wide was saying. "Perhaps you will permit my associate to show you to your room, and afterward give you a tour of the house."

I admitted I could do with some freshening up.

"Then I will expect you for dinner."

As the sliding doors of the elevator closed behind us, St. Louis grinned and gestured toward the control panel. "See those, Doc? Push one. Your room's on three."

I pressed the button marked 3. The elevator remained immobile.

"They're phonies; leave it to Arch."

Addressing no visible person he said loudly, "Take 'er down, Fritz. Plant rooms." The elevator began a gentle descent.

"I'm afraid," I began, "that I don't—"

"Like I said, the buttons are phonies. Sometimes the cops want to bother Mr. Wide when he's down in the plant rooms or up in the sack thinking great thoughts. So I herd 'em in here, press the button, they see it don't work, and I take off that access plate there and start playing around with the wires. They're dummies too, and it works good on dummy cops. Like it?"

I said I supposed such a thing must often be useful, which seemed to please him; he treated me to his characteristic grin and confided, "We call it the St. Louis con, or sometimes the old elevator con. The real deal is the house has a built-in cyberpersonality, with speakers and scanners all over. Just ask for what you want."

"I thought," I ventured as the elevator came to a halt, "—I mean, weren't we going up to my room?"

"I'm showing you the mushrooms first," St. Louis explained, "then you'll have a clear shot upstairs until dinner, and I'll have a chance to do some chores. Come on, they're worth seeing."

We stepped out into semidarkness; the ceiling was low, the

room cool and damp and full of the smell of musty life. Dimly I could make out row upon row of greenhouse benches filled with earth; strange, uncouth shapes lifted blind heads from this soil, and some appeared to glow with an uncanny phosphorescence. "The mushrooms," St. Louis said proudly. "He's got over eighteen hundred diffcrent kinds, and believe me, he gets 'em from all over. The culture medium is shredded paper pulp mixed with sawdust and horse manure."

"*Amazing*," I said.

"That's why he wants you here," St. Louis continued. "Wide's not only the greatest detective in our Galaxy, he's also the greatest gourmet cook—on the theoretical end, I mean. Fritz does the actual dirty work."

"Did you say Mr. Wide was a detective?"

"I may have let it slip. He's pretty famous."

"What a striking coincidence! Would you believe it, St. Louis, my own best friend—"

"Small Universe, isn't it? Does Street cook too?"

"Oh," I said, "I didn't know you knew him; no, Street's hobby is collecting old machines, and scientific tinkering generally."

"Sometimes I wish Wide's was, but he cooks instead. You know why I think he does it?"

"Since no one but a human being can eat the food, I can't imagine."

"It's those add-on units—you noticed how big he was?"

"I certainly did! You don't mean to say—"

St. Louis nodded. "The heck I don't. Add-on core memory sections. His design is plug-to-plug compatible with them, and so far he's sporting fourteen; they cost ten grand apiece, but every time we rake in a big fee he goes out and buys his brains a subdivision."

"Why, that's incredible! St. Louis, he must be one of the most intelligent people in the world."

"Yeah, he's smart. He's so smart if he drops something on the floor I got to pick it up for him. But it's the image, you know. He's eighty inches around the waist, so he figures he's got to do the food business. You ever hear of *Truffles et Champignons à la Noel Wide*? He makes it with sour cream and sauerkraut, and the last time he served it we almost lost two clients and an assistant district attorney."

"And he's giving one of these dinners tonight? I'm surprised that anyone would come."

St. Louis shrugged. "He invites people who owe him a favor and don't know; and then there's a bunch who'll turn up darn near regularly—some of the stuff's pretty good, and it's a sort of suicide club."

"I see," I said, rapidly checking over the contents of my medical bag mentally. "Am I correct in assuming that since, as you say, there is a great deal of cooking done in this house, you are well supplied with baking soda and powdered mustard?"

"If it's got to do with food we've got tons of it."

"Then there's nothing to worry—"

I was interrupted by the sound of the elevator doors, and Wide's deep, glutinous voice: "Ah, Doctor, you have anticipated me—I wished to show you my treasures myself."

"Mr. St. Louis tells me," I said, "that you have mushrooms from all over the Universe, as well as the Manhattan area."

"I do indeed. Fungi from points exotic as Arcturus and as homely as Yuggoth. But I fear that—great as my satisfaction would be—it was not to expatiate upon the wonders of my collection that I came." He paused and looked out over the rows of earth-filled benches. "It is not the orchid, but the mushroom which symbolizes our society. I used to grow orchids—were you aware of that, Doctor?"

I shook my head.

"For many years. Then I acquired my eighth unit of additional core." Wide thoughtfully slapped his midsection—a sound deeply reverberant, but muted as the note of some great bronze gong in a forgotten catacomb of the temple of Thought. "I had no sooner gotten that unit up, than the insight came to me: *No one can eat orchids.* It was as simple as that: *No one can eat orchids.* It had been staring me in the face for years, but I had not seen it."

St. Louis snorted. "You said you came down here for something else, boss."

"I did. The client is here. Fritz admitted her; she is waiting in the front room with a hundred thousand credits in small bills in her lap."

"Want me to get rid of her?"

"There has been another apparition."

St. Louis whistled, almost silently.

"I intend to talk to her; it occurred to me that you might wish to be present, though Dr. Westing need not trouble himself in the matter."

A sudden thought had struck me: If, as it had appeared to me earlier that evening, Street had had some ulterior motive in sending me to this strange house, it was quite probable that it had to do with whatever case currently engaged Wide's attention. I fenced for time. "Mr. Wide, did I hear you say 'apparition'?"

Wide's massive head nodded slowly. "Thirteen days ago the young woman's 'father,' the eminent human scientist Louis C. Dodson, disappeared. Since that time an apparition in the form of Dodson has twice been observed in his old laboratory on the three thousand and thirteenth floor of the Groan Building. Miss Dodson has retained me to investigate Dodson's disappearance and lay the phantom. You appear disturbed."

"I am. Dodson was—well, if not a friend, at least a friendly acquaintance of mine."

"Ah." Wide looked at St. Louis significantly. "When was the last time you saw him, Doctor?"

"A little less than two months ago, at the regular meeting. We were fellow members of the Peircian Society."

"He appeared normal then?"

"Entirely. His stoop was, if anything, rather more pronounced than usual, indicating relaxation; and the unabated activity of the tics I had previously observed affecting his left eye and right cheek testified to the continuing functioning of the facial nerves."

I paused, then took the plunge. "Mr. Wide, would it be possible for me to sit in with you while you question his daughter? After all, death is primarily a medical matter, and I might be of some service."

"You mean, his 'daughter,' " Wide said absently. "You must, however, permit me to precede you—our elevator is insufficiently capacious for three."

"He's hoping she'll object to you—that'll give him an excuse to threaten to drop the case," St. Louis said as soon as we were alone. "And that elevator'll hold five, if one of 'em's not him."

I was thinking of the death of my old acquaintance, and did not reply.

Alice Dodson, who sat on the edge of a big red leather chair in front of Wide's desk, was as beautiful a girl as I had ever seen: tall, poised, with a well-developed figure and a cascade of hair the color of white wine. "I assume," Wide was saying to her as St. Louis and I emerged from the elevator, "that that diminutive glassine envelope you hold contains the hundred thousand in small bills my cook mentioned."

"Yes," the girl said, holding it up. "They have been microminiaturized and are about three millimeters by seven."

Wide nodded. "Arch, put it in the safe and write her out a receipt. Don't list it as an addition to the retainer, just: 'Received of Miss Alice Dodson the sum of one hundred thousand credits, her property.' Date it and sign my name."

"I've already given you a retainer," Miss Dodson said, unsuccessfully attempting to prevent St. Louis's taking the envelope, "and I just stopped by here on my way to the bank."

"Confound it, madame, I conceded that you had given us a retainer, and I have no time for drollery. Tell us about the most recent apparition."

"Since my 'father' disappeared I have entered his laboratory at least once every day—you know, to dust and sort of tidy up."

"Pfui!" Wide said.

"What?"

"Ignore it, madame. Continue."

"I went in this morning, and there he was. It looked just like him—just exactly like him. He had one end of his mustache in his mouth the way he did sometimes, and was chewing on it."

"Dr. Westing," Wide said, turning to me, "you knew Dodson; what mood does that suggest? Concupiscent? (We must remember that he was looking at Miss Dodson.) Fearful?"

I reflected for a moment. "Reflective, I should say."

Miss Dodson continued: "That's all there was. I saw him. He saw me—I feel certain he saw me—and he started to rise (he was always such a gentleman) and"—she made an eloquent gesture—"puff! He disappeared."

"Extraordinary."

"Mr. Wide, I've been paying you for a week now, and you haven't gone to look at the ghost yet. I want you to go in person. Now. Tonight."

"Madame, under no circumstances will I undertake to leave my house on business."

"If you don't I'm going to fire you and hire a lawyer to sue for every dime I've paid you."

"However, it is only once in a lifetime that a man is privileged to part the curtain that veils the supernatural." Wide rose from his huge chair. "Arch, get the car. Doctor, my dinner for tonight must be postponed in any event; would you care to accompany us?"

During the drive to Dodson's laboratory I ventured to ask Miss Dodson, with whom I damply shared the rumble seat of Wide's Heron coupe, her age. "Eight," she replied, lowering her eyes demurely.

"Really? I had observed that your attire is somewhat juvenile, but I would have taken you for a much older girl."

"Professor Dodson liked for me to be as young as possible, and I

always tried to make him happy—you know, for a robot you're
kind of a cuddle-bear."

It struck me then that if Miss Dodson were, in fact, to take
Wide off the case, I might recommend my friend Street to her;
but since for the time being Wide was still engaged, I contented
myself with putting an arm gently across her shoulders and
slipping one of my professional cards into her purse.

"As you see, Doctor," Wide explained when we had
reached the three thousand and twelfth floor, "Dodson both lived
and worked in this building. This floor held his living quarters, and
Miss Dodson's—they shared most facilities. The floor above is his
laboratory, and to preserve his privacy, is inaccessible by elevator.
As this is your home, Miss Dodson, perhaps you should lead the
way."

We followed the girl up a small private escalator, and found
ourselves in a single immense room occupying the entire three
thousand and thirteenth floor of the building. Through broad
windows we could see the upper surface of the storm raging
several miles below; but this was hardly more than a background,
however violent and somber, to the glittering array of instruments
and machines before us. Between our position by the escalator
and the large clock on the opposite wall three hundred feet away,
every inch of floor space was crammed with scientific apparatus.

"I left the lights *off*," Alice Dodson remarked in a shaken voice,
"I know I did. You don't suppose that *he*—"

"There!" St. Louis exclaimed, and following the direction
indicated by his outthrust finger, I saw a black-clad figure bent
over a sinister machine in the center of the laboratory. While St.
Louis muttered something about never going out on a murder case
without a gun again, I seized a heavy isobar from a rack near the
door.

"You won't need that, Westing," a familiar voice assured me.

"Street! What in the world are you doing here?"

"Earning my pay as a consulting detective, I hope. I am here at the instigation of Mr. Noel Wide."

Miss Dodson, still apparently somewhat shaken, looked at Wide. "Is this true?"

"Certainly. Madame, because you found me at my desk when you called, you supposed me inactive; in point of fact I was, among other activities, awaiting Street's report."

"You were working the crossword in the *Times!* Your house told me."

"Confound it! I said among other activities."

"Here, now," Street intervened. "Quarreling lays no spooks. From the fact that you are here, Wide, I assume there has been some recent development."

"There has been another apparition. Miss Dodson will tell you."

"Since my 'father' disappeared," Miss Dodson began, "I have entered his laboratory at least once every day—you know, to dust and sort of tidy up."

"Pfui!" Wide interjected.

Seeing that both Street and Wide were giving Miss Dodson their complete attention, I took the opportunity to speak to Wide's assistant. "St. Louis," I asked, "why does he make that peculiar noise?"

"Every once in a while he gets too disgusted for verbal, and wants to write out a comment on his printer—"

"Why? Interior printers are fine for notes, but I've never heard of using them to supplement conversation."

"Oh, yeah? Did you ever try to *say*: °#@&!°!!?"

"I see your point."

"Anyway, he doesn't like women mucking around a house, but his printer don't work; he got clarified butter in it one time when he was trying to make *Currie Con Carne mit Pilz à la Noel Wide*, so when he tries to feed out the paper he makes that noise."

"You say," Street was asking Miss Dodson, "that when you saw him he was *sitting*? Where?"

"Right there," she said, indicating a low casual chair not far from us.

"But, as I understand, in both the earlier apparitions he was *lying down*?"

The girl nodded voicelessly.

"May I ask precisely where?"

"The f-first time—pardon me—the first time over on a day bed he kept over there to rest on. The s-second—"

"Please try and control yourself. Dr. Westing can administer medication if you require it."

"The second time, he was on a chaise longue he had put in for me near his favorite workbench. So I could talk to him there."

"And his behavior on these two occasions?"

"Well, the first time I had been so worried, and I saw him lying there on the bed the way he used to, and without thinking I just called out, 'Snookums!'—that's what I always used to call him."

"And his behavior? Give me as much detail as possible."

"He seemed to hear me, and started to get up . . ."

"And disappeared?"

"Yes, it was terrible. The second time, when he was on the chaise, I was carrying some dirty beakers and Erlenmeyer flasks over to the sink to wash. When I saw him there I dropped them, and as soon as I did he disappeared."

Street nodded. "Very suggestive. I think at this point we had better examine the day bed, the chaise longue, and that chair. Tell me, Miss Dodson, of the five of us, which is closest in height to the professor?"

"Why . . ." She hesitated for a moment. "Why, Dr. Westing, I suppose."

"Excellent," said Street. We all trooped after him as he crossed the huge laboratory to the day bed Alice Dodson had indicated. "Westing," Street murmured, "if you will oblige me."

"But what is it you wish me to do?"

"I want you to lie down on that bed. On his back, Miss Dodson?"

"More on his side, I think."

"And try," St. Louis put in, "to look like a genius, Doc." Wide shushed him.

"Don't hesitate to arrange his limbs, Miss Dodson," Street told her; "this is important. There, is that satisfactory?"

The girl nodded.

Street whipped a tape rule from his pocket and made a series of quick measurements of my position, jotting down the results on a notepad. "And now, Miss Dodson, please give me the date and time when you saw the professor here—as exactly as possible."

"October twelfth. It was about ten-twenty."

"Excellent. And now the chaise."

At the chaise longue we repeated the same procedure, Miss Dodson giving the date and time as October 18th, at ten minutes to eleven.

When I had been measured in the chair as well, Street said, "And today is October twenty-fifth. At what time did you see the professor?"

"It was about one o'clock this afternoon."

While Street scribbled calculations on his pad, Wide cleared his throat. "I notice, Street, that the time of this most recent apparition would seem to violate what might earlier have appeared to be an invariable rule; that is, that Dodson's ghost appeared at or very nearly at ten-thirty in the morning."

Street nodded. "If my theory is correct, we shall see that those significant-looking times were mere coincidences, arising from the fact that it was at about that time each day that Miss Dodson entered this room. You did say, did you not, Miss Dodson, that you came *every day?*"

The girl shook her head. "I suppose I did, but actually the first apparition frightened me so much that I didn't come again until—"

"Until the eighteenth, when you saw him the second time. I suspected as much."

"Street," I exclaimed, "you understand this dreadful business. For heaven's sake tell us what has been happening."

"I shall expound my theory in a moment," Street replied, "but first I intend to attempt an experiment which, should it succeed, will confirm it and perhaps provide us with valuable information as well. Miss Dodson, your 'father'—like myself—dabbled in every sort of science, did he not?"

"Yes, at least . . . I think so."

"Then is there such a thing as a wind tunnel in this laboratory? Or any sort of large, powerful fan?"

"He—he was interested in the techniques air-conditioning engineers use to make their systems as noisy as possible, Mr. Street. I think he had a big fan for that."

After a ten-minute search we found it, a powerful industrial-grade centrifugal fan. "Exactly what we need," Street enthused. "St. Louis, you and Westing take the other side of this thing. We want to set it up on the lab bench nearest the escalator."

When we had positioned it there, Street turned to the girl and said, "Miss Dodson, at this point I require your fullest cooperation—the success of this experiment depends primarily upon yourself. I have placed the fan where you see it, and I intend to spike the base to the top of the bench and permanently wire the motor to make it as difficult as possible for anyone to disconnect. I want your solemn word that you will not disconnect it, or interfere with its operation in any way; and that you will exert your utmost effort to prevent any other person whatsoever from doing so before November seventh."

"You think," the girl said in so low a tone that I could scarcely make out the words, "that he is still alive, don't you?"

"I do."

"If this fan runs all that time, will it bring him back to us?"

"It may help."

"Then I promise."

"Even should the professor be restored to you, it must remain in operation—do you understand? It might be wise, for example, to persuade him to take a brief holiday, leaving the fan untouched."

"I will do my best," the girl said. "He likes the seaside."

Street nodded, and without another word walked to the wall, threw one of the main circuit breakers, and began soldering the fan-motor leads into a 220-volt utility circuit. Under Wide's direction St. Louis and I found hammers and a gross of heavy nails, with which we secured the base to the benchtop.

"Now," Street announced when all our tasks were complete, "once again I shall require cooperation—this time from every one of you. I shall stand here at the circuit breaker. The rest of you must scatter yourselves over this entire laboratory, each taking a section of it as his own responsibility. When I turn on the fan, things will begin to blow about. What we are looking for will, I think, be a slip of notebook paper, and when you observe it, it will be at a distance of about seventy-six centimeters from the floor. Seize it at once—if you wait for it to settle we are lost."

We did as he asked, and no sooner was the last of us in position than the huge fan sprang into life with hurricane force. A tremendous wind seemed to sweep the entire laboratory, and several pieces of light glassware went over with a crash.

Keeping my eyes fixed, as Street had suggested, at a height of seventy-six centimeters above the floor, I at once observed a sheet of paper fluttering in the machine-made wind. I have often observed that a scrap of paper, blown about, will seem to appear when its surface faces me and disappear when it is edge-on, and for an instant I assumed that the peculiar character of this one stemmed from a similar cause; then I realized that this was not the case—the sheet was, in fact, *actually disappearing and reappearing* as it danced in the gale. Street and I both dived for it at once. He was a shade the quicker; for a split second I saw the tips of his fingers vanish as though amputated by some demonic knife; then he was waving the paper overhead in triumph.

"Street!" I exclaimed, "you've got it! What is it?"

"There's no need to shout, Westing. If you'll step back here behind the inlet we can talk quite comfortably. I was relying upon a brilliant scientist's habitual need to reduce his thoughts to paper, and it has not failed me."

"What is it?" I asked. "Can I see it?"

"Certainly," Street said, handing me the paper. Miss Dodson, Wide, and St. Louis crowded around.

The note read:

$$160 \text{ cm} — 4:00$$
$$159.5 — 2:00$$
$$159.0 — 12:00$$

$$d = 14,400 \text{ sec/cm} \times h$$

"Brief," Street remarked, "but eminently satisfying. The great scientist's calculations agree astonishingly well with my own."

"But, Street," I protested, "it doesn't tell us anything. It's only a formula."

"Precisely the way I have always felt about those prescriptions of yours, Westing."

Wide said, "I think it's time you reported, Street."

"It will take only a few moments now for me to begin the rescue of Professor Dodson," Street told him. "And then we will have some minutes in which to talk. Have you ever practiced yoga, Mr. Wide? No? A pity."

Before our astonished eyes Street proceeded to stand on his head, assuming the posture I believe is known as "The Pole." We heard him say in a distinct voice, "When you grow tired of this, Professor, you have only to use the escalator. Use the escalator." Then with the agility of an acrobat he was upright again, slightly red of face.

"I believe, sir," Wide said, "that you owe us an explanation."

"And you shall have it. It occurred to me today, while I sat in the lodgings I share with Dr. Westing, that Professor Dodson's disappearance might be in some way connected with his membership in the Peircian Society. That he was a member was stated in the dossier you passed on to me, Wide, as you may recall."

Wide nodded.

"I began my investigation, as Dr. Westing can testify, by rereading the complete works of Peirce and Knight, keeping in mind that as a Peircian Dodson ardently believed that the persecuted philosopher had arranged his own supposed death and reappeared under the *nom de guerre* of Knight; certainly, as the Peircians point out, a suitable one—and particularly so when one keeps in mind that a knight's chief reliance was upon that *piercing* weapon the lance, and that Knight was what is called *a freelance*.

"I also, I may say, kept before me the probability that as both a Peircian and as a man of high intellectual attainments Dodson would be intimately familiar with what is known of the life and work of both men."

"Do you mean to say," I exclaimed, "that your reading led you to the solution of this remarkable case?"

"It pointed the way," Street acceded calmly. "Tell me, Westing, Wide, any of you, what was Charles Sanders Peirce's profession?"

"Why, Street, you mentioned it yourself a moment ago. He was a philosopher."

"I hope not. No, poor as that shamefully treated scholar was, I would not wish him in so unremunerated a trade as that. No, gentlemen—and Miss Dodson—when his contemporaries put the question to Peirce himself, or to his colleagues, the answer they received was that Peirce was a physicist. And in one of Knight's books, in an introduction to a piece by another writer, I found this remarkable statement: *It deals with one of the most puzzling questions in relativity, one to which Einstein never gave an unequivocal answer: If all four space-time dimensions are equivalent, how is it that we perceive one so differently from the rest?* That question is sufficiently intriguing by itself—conceive of the fascination it must have held for Dodson, believing, as he did, that it had originated in the mind of Peirce."

"I begin to see what you are hinting at, Street," Wide said slowly, "but not why it affected Dodson more because he thought Peirce the author."

"Because," Street answered, "Peirce—Peirce the physicist— was the father of pragmatism, the philosophy which specifically eschews whatever cannot be put into practice."

"I see," said Wide.

"Well, I don't," announced St. Louis loudly. He looked at Miss Dodson. "Do you, kid?"

"No," she said, "and I don't see how this is going to help Sn—the professor."

"Unless I am mistaken," Street told her, "and I hope I am not, he no longer requires our help—but we can wait a few moments longer to be sure. Your 'father,' Miss Dodson, decided to put Knight's remark to a practical test. When you entered the room this evening, I was in the act of examining the device he built to do it, and had just concluded that that was its nature. Whether he bravely but foolhardily volunteered himself as his own first subject, or whether—as I confess I think more likely—he accidentally exposed his own person to its action, we may never learn; but however it came about, we know what occurred."

"Are you trying to say," I asked, "that Dodson discovered some form of time travel?"

"We all travel in time, Westing," Street said gravely. "What Professor Dodson did—he had discovered, I may add parenthetically, that the basis for the discrimination to which Knight objected was physiological—was to bend his own perception of the four dimensions so that he apprehended verticality as we do duration, and duration as we do verticality."

"But that formula," I began, "and the note itself—"

"Once I understood Dodson's plight," Street explained, "the question was quantitative: How was vertical distance—as seen by ourselves—related to duration as perceived by Dodson? Fortunately Miss Dodson's testimony provided the clue. You will remember that on the twelfth she had seen Dodson lying on a day bed, this being at approximately ten-thirty in the morning. On the eighteenth, six days later but at about the same time, she saw him on her chaise longue. A moment ago I measured your position, with you posed as the missing man had appeared, but I still did not know what portion of the body governed the temporal displacement. The third apparition, however, resolved that uncertainty. It took place seven days and two hours and ten minutes after the second. Dodson's feet were actually lower this time than they had been in his first two appearances; his center of gravity was scarcely higher than it had been when he had half reclined on the chaise; but his head was considerably higher—enough to account nicely for the time lapse. Thus I located the 'temporal determinant'—as I have been calling it to myself—in the area of the frontal lobes of the brain. When you were lying on the day bed, Westing, this spot was fifty centimeters from the floor; when you were in the chaise, seventy-four centimeters; and when you sat in that low chair, ninety-two and one-half centimeters. From these figures an easy calculation showed that one centimeter equaled four hours of duration. Dodson himself arrived at the same figure, doubtless when he noted that the hands of that large clock on the wall appeared to jump when he moved his head. As a true scientist he expressed it in the pure cgs system: vertical displacement times fourteen thousand four hundred seconds per centimeter equals duration."

"And he wrote it on that slip of paper."

Street nodded. "At some time in our future, since if it had been in the past we could not have put the paper in motion, as we did, by setting up a fan in the present with assurances that it would remain in operation for some time. Doubtless he used one of the laboratory benches as an impromptu writing desk, and I have calculated that when he stood erect he was in November sixth."

"Where we will doubtless see him," Wide said.

"I think not."

"But, Street," I interrupted, "why should that note have undergone the same dislocation?"

"Why should other inanimate objects behave as they do? Unquestionably because they have been in contact with us, and there is, as far as we know, no natural opposing force which behaves as Dodson. There was, of course, some danger in grasping the note, but I counted on my own greater mass to wrench it from its unnatural space-time orientation. I had noted, you see, that Miss Dodson's descriptions of her 'father' did not state that he was nude, something she would undoubtedly have commented on had that been the case—ergo, he could be said to bend his clothing into his own reference frame."

"But why did he vanish," Miss Dodson demanded tearfully, "whenever he saw me?"

"He did not vanish," Street replied, "he simply stood up, and, standing, passed into November sixth, as I have already explained. The first time because he heard you call his name, the second because you startled him by dropping glassware, and the third time because, as a gentleman of the old school, he automatically rose when a woman entered the room. He doubtless realized later that he could reappear to you by taking his seat once more, but he was loath to frighten you, and hoped he could think his way out of his predicament; the hint he required for that I believe I have provided: you see, when I stood on my head just now I appeared to Dodson at about the time he suffered his unfortunate accident; the formula I have already quoted, plus the knowledge that Dodson had vanished thirteen days ago, allowed me to calculate that all I need do was to place my own 'temporal determinant'—the area of my frontal lobes—fourteen centimeters above the floor."

"But where is he now?"

Street shrugged. "I have no way of knowing, really. Obviously, he is not here. He might be at the opera or attending a seminar, but it seems most probable that he is in the apartment below us." He raised his voice. "Professor! Professor Dodson, are you down there?"

A moment later I saw a man of less than medium height, with

white hair and a straggling yellow mustache, appear at the foot of the escalator. It was Professor Dodson! "What is it?" he asked testily. "Alice, who the hell are these people?"

"Friends," she sobbed. "Won't you please come up? Mr. Street, is it all right if he comes up?"

"It would be better," Street said gently, "if you went down to him. He must pack for that trip to the seaside, you know." While Miss Dodson was running down the escalator, he called to the man below, "What project engages you at the moment, Professor?"

Dodson looked irritated, but replied, "A monograph on the nature of pragmatic time, young man. I had a mysterious—" His mouth was stopped with kisses.

Beside me St. Louis said softly, "Stay tuned for Ralph the Dancing Moose," but I was perhaps the only one who heard him.

Much later, when we were returning home on the monorail after Street had collected his fee from Wide, I said: "Street, there are several things I still don't understand about that case. Was that girl Dodson's daughter—or wasn't she?"

The rain drummed against the windows, and Street's smile was a trifle bitter. "I don't know why it is, Westing, that our society prefers disguising the love of elderly scientists as parenthood to regularizing it as marriage; but it does, and we must live and work in the world we find."

"May I ask one more question, Street?"

"I suppose so." My friend slouched wearily in his seat and pushed the deerstalker cap he always affected over his eyes. "Fire away, Westing."

"You told him to go down the escalator, but I don't see how that could help him—he would have ended up, well, goodness knows where."

"When," Street corrected me. "Goodness knows when. Actually I calculated it as July twenty-fourth, more or less."

"Well, I don't see how that could have helped him. And wouldn't we have seen him going down? I mean, when the top of his head reached the right level—"

"We could," Street answered sleepily. "I did. That was why I could speak so confidently. You didn't because you were all looking at me, and I didn't call your attention to it because I didn't want to frighten Miss Dodson."

"But I still don't see how his going down could have straightened out what you call his bend in orientation. He would just be downstairs sometime in July, and as helpless as ever."

"Downstairs," Street said, "but not helpless. He called himself —in his lab upstairs—on the Tri-D-phone and told himself not to do it. Fortunately a man of Dodson's age is generally wise enough to take his own advice. So you see, the bend was only a rubber bend after all; it was capable of being snapped back, and I snapped it."

"Street," I said a few minutes later, "are you asleep?"

"Not now I'm not."

"Street, is Wide's real name—I mean, is it really Wide?"

"I understand he is of Montenegrin manufacture, and it's actually something unpronounceable; but he's used Wide for years."

"The first time I was in his office—there was some correspondence on his desk, and one of the envelopes was addressed to Wolfe."

"That was intended for the author of this story," Street said sleepily. "Don't worry, Wide will forward it to him."

BUT AS A SOLDIER, FOR HIS COUNTRY

by Stephen Goldin

It may be that warfare is endemic to humanity, that our aggressions are an essential part of our urges for growth as individuals and as a race. Certainly we've always had wars, as far back as our histories can tell us or our prehistoric artifacts can suggest.

Stephen Goldin details some of the vast changes that the unfolding future may bring to us . . . but his story ends in a reductio ad absurdum *that isn't at all funny.*

HARKER awoke to dim lighting, to bells, to panic all around him. Fast, busy footsteps clacked down bunker corridors, scurrying to no visible result and no possible accomplishment. It was wartime. Naturally.

He was in the spacesuit he had worn last time, which meant that either this war was soon after that last one or else there had been no great improvements in spacesuits over the interval between. It fit him tightly, with an all-but-invisible bubble helmet close around his head. There was no need for oxygen tanks as there had been on the early models; somehow—the technology was beyond him—air was transmuted within the suit, allowing him to breathe.

There was a belt of diverse weapons around his waist. He knew instinctively how to use each of them.

A voice in front of him, the eternal sergeant, a role that persisted though its portrayers came and went. "Not much time for explanation, I'm afraid, men. We're in a bad hole. We're in a bunker, below some ruins. The enemy has fanned out upstairs, looking for us. We've got to hold this area for four more hours, until reinforcements get here. You're the best we've got, our only hope."

"Only hope" rang hollowly in Harker's ears. He wanted to laugh, but couldn't. There was no hope. Ever.

"At least with you now, we outnumber them about five to four. Remember, just four hours is all we need. Go on up there and keep them busy."

A mass of bodies moved toward the door to the elevator that would take them to the surface. A quiet, resigned shuffling. Death in the hundreds of haggard faces around him, probably in his own as well.

Harker moved with the group. He didn't even wonder who the "they" were that he was supposed to keep busy. It didn't matter. Perhaps it never had. He was alive again, and at war.

"We're asking you, Harker, for several reasons." The captain is going slowly, trying to make sure there are no misunderstandings. "For one thing, of course, you're a good soldier. For another, you're completely unattached—no wife, girlfriends or close relatives. Nothing binding you to the here and now."

Harker stands silently, still not precisely sure how to answer.

After an awkward pause, the captain continues. "Of course, we can't *order* you to do something like this. But we would like you to volunteer. We can make it worth your while to do so."

"I'd still like more time to think it over, sir."

"Of course. Take your time. We've got all the time in the world, haven't we?"

Later with Gary, as they walk across the deserted parade field together. "You bet I volunteered," Gary says. "It's not every day you get offered a two-month leave and a bonus, is it?"

"But what happens after that?"

Gary waves that aside. He is a live-for-the-moment type. "That's two months from now. Besides, how bad can it be, after what we've already been through? You read the booklet, didn't you? They had one hundred percent success thawing the monkeys out the last four times. It won't be any harder for us."

"But the world will be changed when we wake up."

"Who cares? The Army'll still be the same. The Army's always the same, ever since the beginning of time. Come on, join me. I'll bet if we ask them nice, they'll keep us together as a team. Don't let me go in there alone."

Harker volunteers the next day and gets his two-month leave, plus the bonus paid to the experimental subjects. He and Gary leave the post together to spend their last two months of freedom.

The first month they are together almost constantly. It is a riot of clashing colors and flashing girls, of endless movies and shows and drinks. It is largely cheerless, but it occupies their time and keeps their minds on *today*. The days sweep by like a brash brass carousel, and only by keeping careful track can it be noticed that the carousel goes around in a circle.

With a month to go, Harker suddenly leaves his friend and goes off on his own. He lets desolation sink in until it has invaded the roots of his soul. He often walks alone at night, and several times is stopped by police. Even when someone is with him, generally a streetgirl, he is alone.

He looks at things, ordinary things, with new strangeness. The cars going by on the street are suddenly vehicles of great marvels. The skyscrapers that reach above him, their defaced walls and smog-dirtied windows, all become symbols of a world that will not exist for him much longer. He stares for an hour at a penny on the sidewalk, until someone notices what he is staring at and picks the coin up for himself.

He talks but little and even his thoughts are shallow. He disengages his brain and lives on a primal level. When he is hungry, he eats; when his bladder or bowels are full, he relieves them. He takes whores to his hotel room for couplings that are merely the release of excess semen. During the last week, he is totally impotent.

He returns to the post when his leave is up and, as promised, is assigned to a room with Gary. The latter still seems to be in good spirits, undaunted by the prospects of the immediate future. The presence of his friend should brighten Harker up, but for some reason it only makes him more depressed.

For a week, they run him and the other volunteers—three hundred in all—through a battery of medical tests that are the most thorough Harker has ever experienced. Then they lead him, naked, to a white room filled with coffins, some of which are occupied and some of which are still empty.

There they freeze him against the time when they will need a good soldier again.

It was dark up on the surface, not a night-dark but a dreary, rainy, cloud-dark. A constant drizzle came from the sky, only to steam upward again when it touched the smoldering ruins of what had recently been a city. Buildings were mostly demol-

ished, but here and there a wall stood silhouetted against the dark sky, futilely defying the fearsomeness of war. The ground and wreckage were still boiling hot, but Harker's suit protected him from the temperature. The drizzle and steam combined to make the air misty, and to give objects a shadow quality that denied their reality.

Harker looked around on reflex, taking stock. All around him were his own people, who had also just emerged from the elevator. No sign yet of the mysterious "they" he was supposed to keep busy for four hours. "Spread out," somebody said, and ingrained instincts took over. Clustered together at the mouth of the elevator, they made too good a target. They scattered at random in groups of one, two or three.

Harker found himself with a woman—not a resurrectee, just another soldier. Neither of them spoke; they probably had little in common. One was rooted in time, the other drifted, anchorless and apart.

The clouds parted for a moment, revealing a green sun. *I wonder what planet it is this time,* Harker thought, *and even before the idea was completely formed, apathy had erased the desire to know. It didn't matter.* All that mattered was the fighting and killing. That was why he was here.

An unexpected movement off to the left. Harker whirled, gun at the ready. A wraithlike form was approaching out of the mists. Three meters tall, stick-man thin, it moved agonizingly, fighting what was, to it, impossibly heavy gravity. Memories flooded Harker's mind, memories of a planet with a red sun, gravity only a third of Earth's, of dust and sand and choking dryness. And tall thin forms like this one. The men at his side and an army advancing on him. The enemy. An enemy once more?

Harker fired. This gun fired pulses of blue that seemed to waft with dreamlike slowness to the alien being. They reached it with a crackling more felt than heard. Static electricity? The being crumpled lifeless to the ground.

The woman grabbed Harker's arm. "What'd you do that for?"

"It was a . . . a . . ." What had they been called? "A Bjorgn."
"Yes," said the soldier. "But they're on our side now."

    Resurrection is slow, the first time, and not a little painful.

Harker awakes to quiet and white. That is his first impression. Later, when he sorts it out, he knows there must have been heat too. A nurse in a crisp white blouse and shorts is standing beside him, welcoming him back to the land of the living. It's been seven years, she tells him, since he was frozen. There is a war in Africa now, and they need good fighting men like him. She tells him to rest, that nothing is expected of him just yet. He's been through an ordeal, and rest will be the best medicine. Accordingly, Harker sleeps.

The next day, there is a general briefing for all the resurrectees, piped in via TV to all their bedsides since they are still incapacitated. The briefing explains some of the background of the war, how the United States became involved, and which side they are fighting on. Then there is a review of the war to date and a quick, nondetailed discussion of strategy. The colonel in charge closes by thanking these men for volunteering for this most unusual and elite project, and by expressing confidence that they will be successful. Harker listens politely, then turns the set off and goes to sleep when the briefing is over.

Next day begins the calisthenics. Being in cold sleep for seven years has taken the tone out of the men's muscles, and they will have to get back into shape before going out onto the battlefield once again. In the exercise yard, Harker sees Gary and waves to him. They eat lunch together, congratulating one another on having survived the treatment. (Only five out of three hundred have not pulled through, and the project is considered a success.) Gary is as flamboyant as ever, and expresses optimism that this war will be over soon, and then they can return to civilian life.

They spend five days more in preparation, then go out into the field. War has not changed in seven years, Harker notices. The guns are a bit smaller and the artillery shoots a bit farther and with more accuracy, but the basic pattern is unchanged. The jungles of Africa are not greatly different from those of Asia where he learned his craft. The fears he had about being a stranger in the future when he awoke are proving pointless, and gradually his depression wears off. He fights with all the skill he learned in the last war, and learns a few new tricks besides.

The war continues for ten months, then finally breaks. Negotiations come through, the fighting ends. Celebrations are held all over the world at this latest outbreak of peace, but the joyousness is not completely echoed in the ranks of the soldiers. The resurrectees are used to war, and the thought of learning new peacetime skills makes them nervous. They know there is nothing out there in the world for them. They would be welcomed as veterans, but they would be strangers to this time. War is the only world they know.

Ninety-five percent of the surviving resurrectees, including Harker and Gary, sign up for another term of hibernation, to be awakened when needed to fight.

Harker took the other soldier down behind some rubble and talked with her. "On our side?"

The woman nodded. "Have been for the last, oh, hundred years or so. Where . . ." She cut off abruptly. She'd been about to ask, "Where have you been all that time?" then realized the answer. "It doesn't matter too much, I suppose," she continued. "They can always replay his tape if they need him."

"How much else don't I know?" Harker demanded.

"This is a civil war. Humans and aliens on both sides. You can't tell what side a person's on just by his race."

Like Asia and Africa, *Harker thought.*

"About the only way you can tell is by the armtag." She pointed at her own, and at Harker's. "We're green. They're red."

"What's to keep a red soldier from putting on a green armtag?"

The woman shrugged. "Nothing, I suppose. Except he'd likely get shot by his own side."

"Unless they knew him by sight."

The soldier shook her head. "No. They copied some of our tapes, which means they've been able to duplicate some of our personnel. Don't trust anyone just because you've seen them before. Look for the armtag."

Bolts of energy went hurtling by their temporary shelter. "Here comes the action," Harker said. "Let's move."

But before they could, the ground exploded in front of them.

The next resurrection is easier, the doctors having learned from experience. But it still is a shock.

Harker awakes to cold this time. He notices it even before the white of the hospital room. Not that the building isn't heated, but there is a chill in the atmosphere that pervades everything.

The nurse that stands beside him is older than the one he had last time. Her white blouse is not quite so crisp, and she wears a skirt that goes clear to the floor. It's a wonder she doesn't trip over it. The chill is a part of her, too; she is not as friendly as that previous nurse. She tells him brusquely that he has been hibernating for fifteen years, and that the war is now in Antarctica.

He takes the news with quiet astonishment. Of all the places in the world where he'd thought war would never be, Antarctica headed the list. But here he is, and here he will fight. He learns that the United States is fighting China here over a section of disputed territory. So he is back to fighting Orientals, though on new terrain.

Gary is here also, and they renew their friendship. There is a week of calisthenics, as they get in shape once more. The atmosphere, Harker notices, is less relaxed than it was the first time, as though people are impatient to get the resurrectees out and fighting again.

Antarctica, needless to say, has different physical conditions than most of them are used to. They bundle up in heavy boots and thin, electrically warmed coats and gloves. They wear goggles to protect their eyes. Their weapons now fire laser beams instead of projectiles; the lack of recoil takes some getting used to. So does the climate. Cold instead of hot, snow instead of rain, bare plains and snow fields instead of jungles and farms. The terrain under dispute seems no different to Harker than any of the rest that is free for the taking, but his superiors tell him that *this* is what they must have and so this is what he fights for.

After three months of fighting, Harker is wounded. A laser beam grazes his arm, burning flesh down to the bone. He is taken to a hospital, where they heal the wound quite efficiently—but while they do so, the war comes to an end. The decision arises again whether to reenlist or leave the service. Many resurrectees opt out before becoming too estranged from the world. But the slang of the contemporary soldiers is already becoming unrecognizable, and the few pictures Harker has received of the rest of the "modern" world seem strange and out of phase. After talking it over with Gary, they both decide on one more try aboard the resurrection express.

There is a new slant to it this time, though. A *very* experimental program, top-secret, is being worked out whereby, instead of putting a man in hibernation, they can record his mind as an individual and reconstruct him later when needed. This will make the system much more maneuverable, since they won't have the problem of transporting frozen bodies to and from battlegrounds. This method is a bit riskier, since it hasn't been fully tested yet, but it offers more advantages in the long run.

Gary and Harker sign up and are duly recorded.

Harker was thrown clear by the explosion, but the other soldier had not been so lucky. The left side of her torso had been blown away and guts were spilling onto the steaming ground. Harker shook his head to clear it from the shock, and rolled quickly behind a barely standing section of wall.

It was not nearly so dark now. Energy weapons were being fired, lighting up the countryside with their multicolored glows. The drizzle continued steadily, and the mists still steamed up from the ground. Like ghosts, Harker thought. But he didn't have much time for thinking. He had a job to do.

There could be no strategy in this type of combat—it was strictly man-to-man, a series of individual battles where the only winners were those who remained alive. Move cautiously, ever alert, looking for someone with the other color armtag. When you see him, shoot immediately, before he can shoot you. If he's too far out of range, hurl a grenade. Reduce the number of the enemy to increase your own odds. Stay alive. That was the law here on this nameless world beneath a green sun.

Harker emerged from one doorway after killing seven of the enemy, onto a main "street"—or what had been one—of this city. It was now clogged with heaps of rubble from the fallen buildings; stone, cement, steel, plastiglas jumbled every which way. Among the wreckage were strewn the bodies of thousands of the original inhabitants. They were not human, but it was impossible for Harker to reconstruct what they had looked like. Many of the bodies were in pieces, with an unusually short leg lying here, an oddly shaped arm over there, a limbless, headless torso further on. Some bodies were pinned beneath pieces of debris; others had been hideously mutilated by the latest advances in war technology.

Harker's stomach felt no unease at what his eyes were viewing. He had seen scenes like this before, many times, in countless places throughout the universe. It took him barely a second to absorb the silent tragedy before him, then he started moving on.

A bolt of energy hit his right calf. He whirled and fired instinctively at his attacker, even as he felt himself falling.

.　　　.　　　.

This new type of resurrection is a sudden, frightening thing, a lightning bolt summoning his soul from the depths of limbo.

Harker awakes to sterility, to a place of abnormal quiet. The air smells funny, antiseptic, even more so than most of the hospitals he's been in. His body feels funny too, as though he were floating in some strangely buoyant liquid; yet he can feel a firm couch underneath his back. His heart bangs away inside his chest, much too fast, much too hard.

He is in a room with other men, other resurrectees, all of whom feel equally strange and perplexed. Their number has almost tripled now from the original three hundred, and they have been crowded closely together to fit into one large hall. Harker lifts his head, and after much looking, manages to spot Gary a dozen rows away. The presence of his friend allays some of the alienness he feels here.

"Welcome to the Moon, men," blares a voice from a loudspeaker. There is a reverberation of gasps throughout the room at this revelation of their location. The Moon! Only astronauts and scientists got to go there. Are there wars on the Moon now? What year is this and who—and how—are they expected to fight?

The loudspeaker goes on to give further information. For one thing, they are no longer a part of the U.S. Army. The United States has been incorporated into the North American Union, which has inherited their tapes. The enemy is the South Americans, the Sammies, led largely by the Peruvian complex. The two powers are fighting for possession of the Mare Nectaris, which symbolizes the points of disagreement between them. Since the outlawing of war on Earth itself, aggressions have to be released here, on the Moon.

"The Moon!" Gary exclaims when they can finally talk together. "Can you believe it? I never thought I'd make it up here. Don't it knock you on your ass just thinking about it?"

Calisthenics are not necessary, since their bodies have been re-created in as good a shape as they were in when they were first recorded. But they do have to spend almost two weeks undergoing training to be able to deal with the lighter gravity of the Moon. There are also spacesuits they have to become accustomed to, and whole new instincts have to be drilled into the men to take care that nothing will rip their suits, the portable wombs they carry against Nature's hostility.

Projectile weapons are back, Harker notices, in use as antipersonnel armament. On the Moon, in spacesuits, a small sliver of shrapnel is just as deadly as a laser beam. Rifles that fire the lunar equivalent of buckshot are relied on heavily by the infantry in the field. Orbiting satellites cover their advances with wide-angle energy beams that Harker doesn't even begin to understand.

It is an entirely different style of fighting, he finds. Totally silent. There are radios in their spacesuits, but they are forbidden to use them because the enemy could triangulate their position. The soldiers make no noise, and on the airless surface of the Moon, the weapons make no noise. It is a battle in pantomime, with silent death ready to creep up at any time.

Gary is killed the third week out. It is during a battle at the open end of the crater Fracastorius, which proves to be the turning point of the war. Gary and Harker are part of a line advancing cautiously across the pockmarked plain, when suddenly Gary falls to the ground. Other men along the line fall too. Harker goes to the ground, feigning death so that the Sammie snipers will not waste any more ammunition on him. But Gary is not feigning it. Harker, otherwise motionless, can turn his head within the helmet and see the tiny tear in the right side of his friend's spacesuit. The wound would have been minuscule, but the explosive decompression has been fatal. Gary's eyes are bugged out, as though in horror at death, and blood is bubbling at his nostrils and mouth.

Harker cries for his friend. For the last time, he cries.

He lies there for three hours, motionless, until his air supply is almost exhausted. Then he is picked up by a Sammie sweep patrol and taken prisoner. He sits out the short remainder of the war in a

Sammie camp where he is treated decently enough, suffering only a few indignities. When the war ends, he is exchanged back to the N.A.U., where, still numbed from Gary's death, he allows himself to be retaped and rerecorded for future use.

Harker fell and hit his head against a block of stone rubble. The helmet withstood the blow—unlike the primitive ones he had worn at first, which would have cracked open—but it started a ringing in his ears which momentarily drowned out the pain impulses coming from his leg. He lay there stunned, waiting for death, in the form of the enemy soldier, to claim him. But nothing happened. After a while his head cleared, which only meant that he could feel the searing agony in his leg more deeply. It was hardly an improvement.

If the soldier had not delivered the killing blow, it could mean that Harker's reflex shot had killed or wounded him. He had to find out quickly; his life might depend on it. He twisted around painfully, his leg pulsing with agony. There, about thirty meters down the street, a spacesuited body lay flat on the ground. It wasn't moving, but was it dead? He had to know.

Harker crawled over the field of death, over the remains of shattered bodies. The front of his spacesuit became caked with mud and some not-quite-dried blood that had an inhuman, oily consistency. The drizzle was becoming harder, turning to rain, but still steaming up from the radioactively heated ground. Clouds of vapor fogged his way, hiding the object of his search. Still Harker crawled, keeping to the direction he knew to be the true one.

His leg was on fire, and every centimeter of the crawl was hell, a surrealist's nightmare of the world gone mad. Once he thought he heard a scream, and he looked around, but there was no one nearby. It must have been a hallucination. He'd had them before on the battlefield, under pain.

He reached his goal after an eternity of crawling. He could detect faint twitches; the enemy was still alive then, though barely. Harker turned him over on his back to deliver the death blow, then looked into the man's face.

It was Gary.

All the resurrections now seem to run together in his memory. The next one, he thinks, is Venus, the place of hot, stinking swamps, of nearly killing atmospheric pressure and protective bubble-pockets of life. These are the first aliens he's ever killed, the tiny creatures no more than twenty-five centimeters high who can swarm all over a man and kill him with a million tiny stabs. At first it is easier to kill nonhumans, less wearing on the scruples. But eventually it doesn't matter. Killing is killing, no matter whom it is done to. It becomes a clinical, mechanical process, to be done as efficiently as possible, not to be thought over.

Then back on the Moon again—or is it Mars?—fighting other humans. The spacesuits are improved this time, tougher, but the fighting is just as silent, just as deadly.

Then a war back on Earth again. (Apparently that outlawing of war on the mother planet has not worked out as well as expected.) Some of the fighting is even done under the oceans, in and around large domes that house cities with populations of millions. There are trained dolphins and porpoises fighting in this one. It doesn't matter. Harker kills them no matter what they look like.

This war is the last time Harker ever sets foot upon his native planet.

Then comes the big jump to an intersteller war. He is resurrected on a planet under a triple sun—Alpha Centauri, someone says—and the enemy is two-foot-long chitinous caterpillars with sharp pincers. They fight valiantly despite a much more primitive technology. By this time Harker is no longer sure whom he is working for. His side is the one that resurrects him and gives him an enemy to fight. They give him shelter, food, clothing, weapons and, occasionally, relaxation. They no longer bother to tell him *why* he is fighting. It no longer seems to matter to him.

Wake up and fight until there is no more killing to do; then retreat into purgatory until the next war, the next battle. The killing machine named Harker has trod the surfaces of a hundred planets, leaving nothing but destructon and death in his wake.

Gary stared up into Harker's eyes. He was in pain, near death, but was there some recognition there? Harker could not speak to him, their communicators were on different frequencies, but there was something in Gary's eyes . . . a plea. A plea for help. A plea for a quick and merciful death.

Harker obliged.

His mind was numb, his leg was burning. He did not think of the paradox of Gary still being alive though he had seen him die on the Moon years (centuries? millennia?) ago. He knew only that his leg hurt and that he was in an exposed position. He crawled on his side, with his left elbow pulling him forward, for ten meters to a piece of wall. He lifted himself over it and tumbled to the ground. If not completely safe, he was at least off the street, out of the open space.

He reached for the first-aid kid on his belt, to tend his leg. There was none there. That idea took a full minute to sink into his mind: THEY HADN'T GIVEN HIM A FIRST-AID KIT. He felt a moment of anger, but it subsided quickly. Why should they give him a kit? What was he to them? A pattern called out of the past, an anachronism—useful for fighting and, if necessary, dying. Nothing more. He was a ghost living far beyond his appointed hour, clinging to life in the midst of death. A carrion eater, feeding on death and destruction to survive, for he had no purpose except to kill. And when the killing was done, he was stored away until his time came round again.

He sat in the rubble with his back against the crumbling wall, and for the first time since Gary's death on the Moon, he cried.

.   .   .

Asia.

    Africa.

        Antarctica.

            Luna.

                Venus.

                    Pacifica.

                        Alpha Centauri 4.

                            The planet with the forests.

                                The world with oceans of ammonia.

                                Planets whose names he's never even bothered to learn.

The ghosts of billions of war dead assault his conscience. And Harker cries with them, for them, about them, over them, to them.

There was a movement. A man in a red armtag. A strangely familiar figure. He hadn't seen Harker yet. Without thinking, Harker's hand raised the gun to fire.

His motion attracted the other's attention. The soldier, with reflexes as fast as his own, whirled to face him. It was himself.

"They copied some of our tapes," he had been told. Exactly. Then they could make themselves a Harker, just as this side could. He wanted to laugh, but the pain in his leg prevented it. It would have been his first laugh in uncounted incarnations. This was the ultimate irony—fighting himself.

The two Harkers' eyes joined and locked. For one joyless instant, each read the other's soul. Then each fired at the other.

THE RAMPARTS

by Hilary Bailey

Here is a deceptively quiet story of a future Earth where mankind's ills of aggression and violence have been done away with, and a calm, near-pastoral utopia prevails. But it is a mysterious, ominous utopia of civilized townships surrounded by wild and dark forests—and the forests are once again encroaching.

Hilary Bailey's full name is Hilary Bailey Moorcock: her husband is the well-known writer and editor Michael Moorcock. She's the author of "The Fall of Frenchie Steiner" and "Dogman of Islington," among a number of other first-rank sf stories, and after you've read this understated but trenchant story, you'll want to watch for her byline in the future.

THIS afternoon, at last, I can put down my instruments, push aside my drawing board and watch the sunlight undulating over the long sweep of shadowed lawn in front of my house, see the waves of light playing over the grass right down to the first scattering of trees where the forest begins. From the glass-walled room at the top of the house the great curve of the lawn is like an ocean. And I can look up at the dark sky through the glass ceiling, gazing at the clouds which gather, part and move. When I turn my head I see the white city lying behind me—the straight, tree-lined avenues, the large houses with their pillared porticoes, the gardens brilliant with flowers and bushes. To right and left the lawns sweep down into the forest, darkening and lightening under the erratic sun. This house is a promontory of the city, an isthmus between it and the forest.

Below, the house is silent. Regan and Arthur are resting because Regan is playing tonight in our concert hall and Arthur is being allowed to stay up and hear her.

Tomorrow I shall be driving her along the Mendip Road to Juram, where she is to play for the citizens there. Our new car is ready, all but the batteries. If we decide to go. It would be pleasant to glide along the smooth paths through the forest—if, that is, we decide to go.

I must get ready soon for the council meeting where my plans are to be discussed. What a fuss over such a small, obvious project! But I think everything is settled at last and approval will be automatic.

I can remember going into the forest as a boy, on a dare, edging slowly through the trees and tangled brushwood, wondering if I had gone far enough to win the dare, with the darkness increasing as the trees grew thicker, bare legs scratched by fern and bramble, hearing the scutterings and flapping of wings in the gloom, tense with listening, forcing one foot in front of the other—oh, the tales that circulated about the Headless Man and the hunchbacked Monsterwoman of the Forest—but, good heavens, enough of this. It's quite time to get ready for the meeting. I must begin to lay the things out—but how dark it was in there. There were the terrifying little scratchings and scrapings in the undergrowth, no light, my feet cracking fallen branches at one moment and up to the ankles in mud the next. Day was like night in the forest. And at night—no, nothing could increase that blackness. No one could endure it. It is too dark.

I say hi, ho, but no one answers. The woman is by the fire with the babe. I crash down entangled and struggle up again. Why don't the bastards come? That on my leg is the dripping of blood from my sacks. Hi! Ho! No answer. Why don't the bastards come? I'll smash her hands, the bitch. Up again and stumble on. Move, move, move.

A note before we leave for the performance. The council has decided that the work is to begin next week. Keeney, the town clerk, continued to oppose but was overruled in the end. Why all this fuss about a simple, useful item? Regan says the children tell tales about how he traps rabbits from the forest—his house being on the outskirts on the other side of the town—and then eats them. One boy says he saw him burying the bones in his garden. But all this is nonsense. Goodness knows what makes children dream up these gruesome horrors to frighten each other. Keeney certainly has a gross and ruddy look. His eye is wild and distant too. He must be a throwback to more savage times. It makes you wonder how such a man could ever be elected to office by our citizens. Yet I do seem to remember a time when Keeney was quieter, paler, probably even a bit thinner. Is it my imagination?

I seem to be using these pages to gossip about fellow citizens, which would be much disapproved of if it were known. Looking through these pages, which I have kept since I gained my architectural qualifications at the town of London (and I must say I was thankful to gain them and leave that vast community, a dismal specter of history repeating itself), I notice that it is only in the past year that I have started to make comments not directly connected with my work. A sign of approaching oddity? I hope not. The city cannot afford eccentrics.

at last they come. I can see their fire. They need my sacks, old bloody sacks. Hi, ho, hee, hee. I'll hide the other sack. Let them roast hedgehogs while we feast in secret. Hallo, hallo, I'm here. Come on, you bastards, hurry.

The glide and hum of our cars through the streets did not sound over the birdsong, and as we went past the quiet, white houses with their colorful gardens, the birds were just settling for the night. The concert hall was full. Regan's playing was charming—some short pieces by Bach and Chopin and two of the delightfully intricate songs for the piano by our neighboring citizen, Jones of Piwelli. Nevertheless I wish Regan would take up writing music again. If only she had been more persistent, could have ironed out those roughnesses and unevennesses which she was so unprepared to work at. Nevertheless, as I sat in the concert hall I myself designed, surrounded by our friends and listening to the music rippling from the fingers of my wife at the piano, I wondered if any existence could be happier. We have our small lovely towns, interconnected but distant from each other. We have our beautiful homes; our children are reared according to the most humane principles, carefully guided into adulthood by all the citizens. Machines free us from drudgery so that we can all lead self-motivated lives. Our small numbers mean that creating and maintaining the machines occupies only a few of us, those who love the work, for a proportion of their time. And, of course, our simple dietary wants are easily met by a small number of dedicated men and women among the citizens.

No work, no want, no misery—as I sat in the hall with the sweet summer scents wafting through the open windows, I rejoiced. The past seems like a long horror story of grinding toil, men and women teeming like rodents—and, of course, the final self-inflicted end as the world went up in flames, roasting the men and women in it like the corpses of animals over one of their own spits.

Thank God we are now at peace.

As I write, men arrive with rules and markers and go down over the lawn to within a hundred and fifty yards of the forest's edge. The next few months, while the work continues, will be trying for those of us with houses on the city boundaries, but common sense must be served.

tug a spine from my soft mouth to hell with these hedgehogs and the lazy women cooking them while the music and dancing go on. Lie on my back with the child beside me playing some trick with beetles and ants. I can see some stars above through the branches. The sky's a fine thing if you're not afraid of it. There are places where it's all sky. Well, I'm not afraid of the sky. Thrum, thrum of the music. I'll go down and dance soon, oh, that tall, deep, wide sky, how mad it is.

It is raining this early morning. The sky is dark and cloudy as it moves over my head. The lawn down to the forest is dark and drenched. The men have not arrived to start their work. I feel annoyed that they should be discouraged by bad weather. Not that there is any need for haste, but such inefficiency and sloth gall me—we aim to lead a civilized life but must always strive to prevent cultivation and grace from deteriorating into laziness and enervation. What happens if it rains all summer? We all agreed the work should be completed by October, simply so that it should not drag on all through winter and into spring. As I say, there is no real need for haste, but if a job is being done it should be done swiftly. I shall go and speak to Keeney, who is, no doubt, partially responsible for the delay.

My irritability probably stems from the argument with my wife. At breakfast this morning she said we must make ready for the visit to Juram. I said that the weather was too bad, that the dripping of the trees over the road would penetrate the hood of the car. She demanded to know, if we could not travel in May, when could we travel? I said that the overcast sky, combined with overhanging trees, would make it too dark to drive. She responded by mentioning our car lights. Finally she called me irrational. Perhaps I am.

I do not want to take the forest road to Juram with my wife and child.

In the end she said that if I would not take her she would go alone or ask Keeney, whose business often takes him on visits to the Juram town officials, to take her with him. She began to toss her long hair about, a sign of determination. Eventually I gave in and said we would go. But I do not like it. I really do not like it at all. I like it less and less as the sky becomes more and more overcast and the rain heavier. It will be pitch-black on the Mendip Road and it is not altogether well maintained these days. Why Regan—but there, she must pursue her career. Although it is a pity she will not make herself concentrate and spend more time at home composing. Nevertheless, it would be a poor lookout for a concert pianist if she never played for anyone but audiences of her own townspeople. If you like, that is one of the few disadvantages of our social structure—we are somewhat cut off from each other. Our cars, although pleasant to drive in, travel scarcely any faster than one would on foot. Our journeys are lengthy, if pleasant and relaxing. We have no roar or stink or lung-clogging fumes, but our progress is slower than it was in the days of coaches drawn by horses. But we are not rovers who must go racing from place to place, nor speed-lunatics who will sacrifice all pleasantness for the excitement of crashing along.

Now the sky overhead looks truly black and threatening. I shall put my things together for the journey and hope that at the last moment my wife will see sense. And I shall go to see Keeney and inquire about why the work has not started.

A most alarming experience. I am still trembling.

Keeney was not there. I walked to his house, circumventing the town center, taking the broad and pleasant roads toward the edges of the forest. Even under rain and heavy skies our streets are still beautiful and the smell of the lovely gardens under rain is delicious.

Naturally I was shocked, although I tried not to be, when I reached Keeney's house. It is set on the edge of the town with streets on one side, and, on the other, the expanses of vegetable gardens and fruit trees which extend almost to the forest. What a spectacle met my eyes! To begin with, he has dug up his garden, so that the whole area, about an acre, I suppose, looks like a plowed field. And at the same time he has uprooted every paving stone from the path leading to his door and tossed them, higgledy-piggledy, to one side. To reach his front door I was obliged to trudge along the flattened earth where the stones had been, getting mud all over my shoes and the bottoms of my trousers. I considered it most careless and thoughtless of Keeney. Admittedly, sometimes the desire for change and alteration leads one to drastic action, but one has a duty to use a certain restraint and make sure that the changes are conducted with discretion so that they do not produce an unpleasant effect like that. It is surely unsuitable for a senior town official to reduce his home to such a filthy and depressing condition.

By the time I reached the door, I was in an understandable state of apprehension. I was not looking forward to my task of reproaching Keeney with his laxness over the question of the building work. And other things disconcerted me too, though I did not notice them consciously at the time.

When I got to the porch, the front door would not open—naturally I pushed it, and pushed again, but it would not yield. Can you imagine it? The man had, to all intents and purposes, locked his door, as if someone in the house were in the process of arriving or departing this earth. After my attempts to open the door I thought again and wondered if this were the case. But no one had visited us to tell us not to go to Keeney's house. Mrs. Keeney had certainly not informed the council that she wished to bear a child—in any case, at her age such a request would never have been granted. Keeney's daughter, Adela, was unmarried. The council had not been informed that any of the family were ill. The only possibility was that there had been an accident to one of them, or, unworthy thought, that Adela had defied the law again and committed the act which had nearly had such serious consequences for her before. I naturally pushed this thought from me. I reflected at that moment that the oddity which had struck me as I stood pushing the unyielding door was that the curtains in the upper rooms were drawn. But not in the lower—I had seen perfectly well into the living room as I squelched my way up to the house. As I stood on that step with the rain teeming down into Keeney's chaotic garden, I lost my temper and decided that, unannounced Arrival or Departure or not, I would gain entry. I first found the bell and rang it, and failing to get any result, began to knock and pound on the door. After I had been knocking for some time, I heard the bolts being drawn back . . .

clear out the bones I say to my wife and light a light. I can see nothing. She lies in a corner, not answering, so I beat her with my stick. She still says nothing. I beat her till the blood runs. She just groans and rolls over to face the wall. Of course, the child is weeping. I give him a kick, that'll teach him sobbing, not that he

*needs teaching, and walk off. I find Hodge, who smashed his
wife's head. We go hunting. Hey, ho, crashing through bush and
tree until we run it to earth near the mere and bash it to death.
Carry it back and they all come out and sing. All but my wife still
skulking in the home with the women. Feasting tonight, all thanks
to yours truly. Hurroo.*

. . . and Mrs. Keeney put her head out, looking worried.
Naturally it would be out of order to discuss a fellow citizen, but I
must say her pie and cake baking have fallen off significantly and
there is talk of giving her a lighter job. She looks thinner too.
Funnily enough, as Keeney increases in bulk, his wife seems to
diminish.

I stepped inside the house, although it seemed to me that Mrs.
Keeney was a second or two late in opening the door, so that I
almost felt I was elbowing my way in.

"I trust I have not come at any inconvenient moment," I said,
really expecting her to tell me that I had. Her depressed air and
the locked door all added up to an Arrival or a Departure taking
place.

But she said no, I had not come at such a moment. I walked
into the living room and asked if Keeney was at home. I observed
that he had moved all the furniture since I was last there,
somehow crowding it all over to one side of the room, which was
large, so that there was a huge space of blank floor (for he had also
rolled up the carpet) from the middle of the room to the window,
which looked out over the muddy garden. Once again there was
the same air of desolation, of changes about to be made, which I
had sensed when outside the house.

Mrs. Keeney told me her husband was out, with such a weary
air that I was surprised she offered me some refreshment. I
accepted her offer, and before she left the room, asked what her
husband had in mind for the house and garden. She shrugged, said
she did not know, was not certain, and left the room. As I sat in

that disordered room looking out at the rain over the garden, feeling profoundly uncomfortable and wishing I had never come, I heard an appalling sound—an eerie howling, followed by a heavy scratching and scrabbling at the door! I leaped to my feet and was retreating to the window, for I immediately recognized the sound for what it was, when, to my horror, the door opened. Mrs. Keeney entered with a tray, followed by—the beast!

"Come on," I called, raising the window. "Let's go out this way."

And I freely confess I vaulted out, landing up to my ankles in the mud of the garden. Once outside I immediately realized that this was a most cowardly action, to leave a fellow citizen, and a woman at that, to face the danger alone. So I raised one leg and put it back over the sill, getting some purchase on the floor with my muddy foot and trying to heave myself back into the room, calling out, "Come on. Come this way, Mrs. Keeney."

But the dog, a huge wolflike creature with feet as big as dinner plates, seemed to cause her no alarm. In fact they seemed on friendly terms. As the beast sniffed about her knees, she absent-mindedly broke off a portion of the cake she had on the tray and handed it to him. He snuffled it down and seemed to want more. I regained a certain calm, although I was still very reluctant to go into the room. I recalled hearing of a naughty child who had once apparently got hold of an abandoned infant from a dog pack and had illicitly reared it until she was detected. It seems she had made quite a friend of the animal, which she had hidden in a potting shed, to the extent that the animal would not harm her. Eventually, of course, the dog grew older, began to hunt, was detected and destroyed. They say she wept and swore she could feed it on milk and honey. A likely story.

However, as I say, I remained calm to a point. Theoretically, too, I knew that at one time the dog had been a domestic animal—loathsome thought. So I remained, half in and half out of the window, observing the animal sitting by Mrs. Keeney, pounding its tail on the floor with its huge red tongue hanging out and its yellow fangs exposed. I took a deep breath and said, "Does this animal belong to you?"

"Yes," she said. "It is my husband's."

I said with feeling, "I am very surprised."

Then I drew my foot and leg back over the sill into the garden, said goodbye through the open window, and went back through the mud into the road. Mrs. Keeney watched me and I should say she was on the verge of tears.

I do not know how I got home. I was shaking all the way. It was not so much the encounter with the dog. It was the dug-over garden, the pushed-about furniture and Mrs. Keeney's peculiar, nervous manner. It was the locked door. And halfway home it struck me forcibly that the boys' horror stories about the rabbit bones must be true. Keeney obviously was not eating the beasts himself, but he must be trapping them and feeding them to the dog. The thought of that great animal wolfing down raw flesh with its yellow fangs made me retch. And of Keeney setting the traps and extracting the results with bloody hands. Then digging pits for the bones to hide the existence of the dog. The implications of the matter were horrendous.

I was standing in my dripping clothes drinking a glass of wine when Regan came downstairs to greet me. I told her my story straightaway. Although at first she could hardly believe it, she then accepted it with strange calmness. She said, "Take off your wet clothes first. And on no account tell Arthur."

"As if I would," I said.

"Go on then," she ordered. "We'll have to report it to the town council immediately."

I nodded agreement. "Then he'll have to go to another town," she said matter-of-factly.

I turned in the doorway. "If they'll have him," I said.

She paused. "Yes, I suppose—"

"Do you remember Ritchie Callender?" I asked.

And neither of us spoke. Ritchie Callender had been one of our contemporaries. We had gone to school together, played together, robbed the orchards together. In his teens he had started doing a lot of gambling, neglected his work in the fields and finally got a girl pregnant and told her to say nothing to the council. When people eventually found out, the council tried to get another town to take him. But the councils of the towns he went to either rejected him outright or kept him a month or two and returned him to us. No town would accept him, he could not stay with us—so we had to exile him.

He came in again over our lawn one night, ragged, trembling and hungry. I went out to meet him. He stuttered out some horrible tale of what had happened to him—I forget it now, thank God—and at that moment the townspeople appeared in a mass. He gave me a despairing, hopeless look and ran back again over the lawn into the darkness. Try as I might, I've never forgotten his limping run over the grass, the way he ducked as he went into the trees. I left food on the grass for a week and it always went—packaging as well, so I know it was not taken by an animal. And then the food was left there, night after night, and after ten days I gave up putting it there. I've often wondered if he came back starving on the eleventh day, and the twelfth, and found nothing. But it was a big risk for me to leave it there. I doubt if I would do as much today.

Regan and I were staring at each other in horror. "Don't let's report him now," she said. "We've got to go to Juram. We can find him there and talk it over."

"It's wrong," I warned her.

"Perhaps he's ill," she told me. "Friends may be able to help."

We both knew there was no possible excuse for not going immediately to the council. In Juram we would be virtually unobserved talking to Keeney. It was secretive, furtive and uncitizenlike. Let all your conversations be open to scrutiny: that is one of our precepts.

But we packed up swiftly and the three of us set out along the forest road for Juram.

Recollection of that scene at Keeney's, the knowledge that we were acting in secret in defiance of the rights of our fellow citizens, apprehension about the trip—all these things troubled me deeply as we went. We were also sailing along in total darkness, apart from the light thrown by our headlamps. It was pouring rain and the road was unpleasantly potholed. I continually scanned the road and the verges of the forest as we went. Once or twice I imagined movements at the borders of the road, the shaking of bushes and grasses and so forth, but we glided on uneventfully, seeing and hearing nothing. Soon we were in Juram. It is a charming and well laid out city. The market square, with its colored dome and tropical plants, is particularly fine. The gardens have more flowers and the houses, in some cases, better proportions than in our own city. Nevertheless, I like ours better.

We went straight to the Town Hall when we arrived, to register our presence and to inquire after Keeney. We crossed the domed square, where the light was filtered through to provide a charming colored floor, and went straight up the marble steps into the Town Hall.

After giving our names and city of origin, we went to find Keeney. Imagine our surprise when we were told that our town clerk was not in Juram, had not been there since the week before and was not even expected at any time in the future. It was inconceivable. Where on earth could he be? The most alarming thoughts filled our minds. Nevertheless we naturally showed no surprise to the officials of Juram, not wishing to betray that there were any irregularities in our town arrangements. We merely said we must have mistaken the day.

Naturally, having tea in the Strangers' Restaurant, we chatted the matter over between ourselves in low voices until Arthur intruded in an objectionable way. "Ugh!" he said. "Old Keeney, flesh-eating Keeney."

We immediately silenced him, partly in case anyone at a nearby table should hear, partly because his exuberant rudeness did not suit us. But Arthur continued in the same vein. "He's got a *dog*. It lives in the *house*. They all pat it on the *head*. Ugh—it makes me feel sick. Keeney's *revolting*."

I told the boy he was making us feel sick, but I secretly thought that as things had turned out, we should have paid more attention to the children's fantastic tales. "I bet I could tell you where he is—the dirty old man," he added.

I pressed him to tell me, but he would not say. In fact he appeared afraid to tell me. Regan was now so upset that I urged her to go and relax in one of the rooms upstairs before the performance while I took Arthur on a sightseeing tour of the town.

As we went around the museum, examining the fused, charred and horrendous relics of the town's past, I again put pressure on Arthur to tell me where to find Keeney and he refused again to tell me. I decided he was just making childish mysteries and dropped the subject.

I was scarcely in the mood for Regan's recital after the hectic events of the day and she, I could tell, was almost equally disturbed. She played with an unwonted vigor and passion—the audience was perturbed by it and slightly displeased. The applause at the end was polite. In a way I had almost enjoyed her uncontrolled playing, but I did not expect anyone else to do the same.

She did not mention the performance at all over supper. She talked only of Keeney, about where he might be, about the dog. "We've got to find him, we've got to find him," she kept repeating.

Arthur was asleep in the Strangers' House, and I was for staying in Juram overnight and returning in the morning. But Regan, still speculating hysterically about Keeney, wanted to go home straightaway and was very distressed at the idea of not setting off immediately. It upset me so much to see her in this state that I gave in.

By the time we had woken Arthur and got him in the car, all I wanted to do was go home and get into bed. As we glided out of Juram, Arthur sat in the back crooning a tune he was making up and knocking together three round stones on a string which he had bought himself. Regan sat rigid in the seat next to me wearing on her face an expression of intensity I had not, I must say, seen since the days of our courtship and early marriage.

As we glided through the trees in the darkness, a memory came through my fatigue. I recalled—and it can only have been a deliberate forgetting—the name of the little girl who had hidden, and tried to rear, the little dog. It was, of course, Regan herself.

I can see her now, fat doe caught in the bush. Is she caught? She must be, for I see stars in a gap in the trees overhead, I see her. Creep up, creep up, singing my song in my head—catch, catchie, catcho, I'll kill you, dearie. And raise my club and leap. But she breaks, and runs on a broken leg. Follow swiftly, I'll tire her yet. Soft, catchie, catcho, I'll batter her head with my club, drag her back, her head, my club, all bloody. Run, panting, nearly there. The light, the sky, the open—I'll have to cross, I'll have to cross, I'll have to cross.

And I recalled that Regan had been an unorthodox child. Her mother feared for her.

We glided along the dark forest road. I pushed the car up to fifteen. Arthur crooned and knocked in the back. Regan sat in the same pose, pale and intent, as if listening to an important message from an invisible stranger. My headlights beamed along the forest edges. The weather was still—nothing stirred. I was half-asleep.

And suddenly Regan screamed and Arthur shouted, "Look—Dad!"

There was a shaking of bushes and the lower branches of the trees on one side of the road. Fifty feet ahead a deer broke from the trees and ran across the road.

I was about to speak when Regan screamed again.

The bushes parted and a man ran out in pursuit of the deer. He stopped short in the middle of the road, a club raised above his head, blinded by our lights. His eyes were tight shut against the glare. His mouth was open in a roar of pain, revealing blackened and broken teeth. He was short, thickset, his skin pasty and white, his eyes rimmed in red. He wore a torn shirt revealing blue tattoos in a geometric design all over his chest. His trousers were made of some animal skin. His feet were bare, toes splayed, ending in thick, curved nails. He wore a leather cap on which were sewn three or four hedgehog skins. His hair was long, black and matted. One short, very pale arm, covered in black hairs, was badly gashed and dripped blood onto the road.

He stood there roaring, with his eyes tight shut, as we drifted toward him.

I acted swiftly, stopping the car and switching off the lights at the same time, hoping desperately that he would go away. In the darkness, I guess, he and any others with him would be able to see us, although we could not see them. We sat there in the darkness on the forest road. Behind me Arthur moved a little.

Then I said, "I'm going to turn the lights on and start away quickly. If they're around us they may be dazed by the lights. Hold on to the handles of the doors."

I turned on the lights and the car leaped forward—down a perfectly empty road. In the darkness the man had run back into the forest.

After a pause Arthur said, rather shakily, "What was that? Who was that?"

Neither of us answered.

"It's what they say, isn't it?" Arthur demanded. "The forest's full of the misborn, isn't it?"

I said, "It's true that in the early days of the towns they used to put malformed babies just inside the forest edge—and they said they were picked up and reared there by the others. But my grandfather said that his father told him that they died."

He had said, in fact, that everyone knew they died. Their cries could be heard if you went too close. That must be one of the reasons why our houses have by tradition always been set so far back from the forest—so that people could not hear the cries of the dying babies.

I could hear Arthur retching in the back of the car.

"It was all a long, long time ago," Regan told him. "There are no malformed babies now."

"So you say," said Arthur. Regan did not reply. I wondered why not and then realized that I knew. The False Arrivals. A woman would take to her bed, bear a child, the council would visit, as usual, and she would declare the child Arrived and Departed. The women must know about all this. The men did not, said they did not, thought they did not—there are things people must forget, pretend not to know until they really do forget. I had forgotten that Regan was the girl with the small dog in the potting shed. She had forgotten the child who came before Arthur. City life relied on this forgetting. What else had we forgotten, eliminated, suppressed? For a second, there on the forest road, I was in a nightmare world where I was living my life beside a monster I never saw, a fiend which sat beside me as I ate, lay in bed with me at night, which I gazed over, around and through and never noticed at all.

Arthur's clear, plangent voice pierced this evil dream. "Well, if that man wasn't misborn, and he didnt look it, who was he, then? Where did he come from?"

Neither of us spoke. Then Regan said, "Arthur. You know very well what happens when someone in the city does things they shouldn't. Perhaps they steal or—whatever they do."

"There isn't anyone like that in the city," he said.

"Well, suppose there were?"

"The council asks them to go to another town," he said, remembering what he had learned.

"What happens if they go there and go on doing whatever they were doing in our town? What does the new town do?"

"They probably ask them to go to another town," he said.

"And suppose they do it again, and again, in every town they go to?"

He thought, then said, "I suppose you mean they put them in the forest."

"That's right," she said. "The man you saw was probably one of those. There are women too."

"It can't be very nice in there. Suppose they want to come back?"

"I think if they really wanted to live in the towns they would behave themselves," she said.

Probably, I thought, Regan did not know. Did not know. But a little girl such as she had been—showing signs of deviating, being an outsider? Her mother must have told her. She did not remember. I recalled Ritchie Callender. And I suddenly remembered someone else—Bennet, who had lived in twenty cities, who molested children, who had never been able to work. That moonlit night we were supposed to be asleep, my cousin and I, when we were woken up by the noise near our house. We leaned out of the window and saw the townspeople making rough music, beating on pots and pans and buckets, shouting. And there was Bennet, in the center of the crowd, being beaten back foot by foot into the forest, turning to them and shouting, turning back toward the forest, retreating under the full moon as they mobbed him over the lawn into the dark trees. We could not hear him above the din. We just saw his sagging mouth opening and closing as they pushed him on. My cousin, only five, had cried. I, being older, knew that Bennet, who had waited for us on the way home from school, had to be sent off somewhere. But the violence and fear frightened me. I could not see how the townsfolk could push him into the forest they were themselves so afraid of.

As we rode through the forest, those three scenes flashed in front of my eyes like photographs—the little girl laying her doll down to open the door of the shed where her dog was waiting to jump up and lick her face, my grandfather sitting behind his old carved desk telling me about the mutant babies, the moonlight falling on Bennet's upturned, grimacing face.

And now Arthur was silent too. From now on he would carry his own photograph with him. There would be a picture of the wild man caught in the headlights of the car. There would be his mother speaking and, I suppose, my back, my silence, as I steered the car forward.

I felt I had to say something. "It's very unpleasant, Arthur, but try not to think too much about it. These things have to happen. And don't tell any of the other children. It would only frighten them. There are very, very few people in the forests and they are only there because the towns cannot have them. We could not have people like that in the cities."

As I spoke I wondered how many people there really were in the forests. Three, four, five hundred years of antisocial men and women, abandoned babies, girls with unpermitted Arrivals. How many were there? How many? How had we in the cities let this happen? I felt my head was bursting. I didn't want to think these thoughts and yet they came crowding in, overwhelming me. And there was a perverse satisfaction in not being able to control them, like drinking too much wine, knowing it was unwise but not being able to stop. I wished Regan would speak so that I could reply and we could talk all the way home. But she had resumed her frozen, intent position. She was too engrossed in her thoughts to speak.

We thought they died, I told myself. At least, no one consciously thought that, but at the backs of our minds we assumed it was true. We never acknowledged it to ourselves, let alone to each other. Now, never mind how destructive the thought, we had— Why else were they building it—and I was the designer—and my mind seemed to collapse under the weight of it all. In my ears was the sound of someone groaning, groaning, groaning.

I am exhausted today. It is very early, and as I sit in my room at the top of the house, a few feathery wisps of cloud move in the blue sky above. There too is the long sweep of sunlit lawn down to the trees. Normally at this hour I can hear the birds singing. Today the men are working, digging the foundations for the ramparts. There is the sound of spades hitting the metal markers which show the course of the wall. The men call out to each other. Wheelbarrows full of bricks leave tracks on the dewy grass. Piles of bricks are dropped onto it from the barrows.

What did we say when the council confirmed the order for my plans? How did we put the proposal to each other? I seem to remember something about deer straying into the city in winter and spoiling the fields and gardens, small children straying out of the city into the forest. It all seemed very convincing at the time. I suppose, because it had to be convincing. We needed the ramparts. We needed to ignore the reasons why we needed them. But we must have known. We must have known.

at the feeding last night they sang of a wall of square stones outside the forest. I say, they want to keep us in, mates. I don't know why I say that. I had a flash in my brain, that's why. Outside there is light to glare and make you shut your eyes. You cannot open them or they burn. But those other men, they say, sleep on soft lying places, off the ground, under shelter. This place is hard. I'll fetch more leaves. The woman is sobbing in her sleep again. The child wails. Bloody noise. No, I'll sleep now.

.   .   .

The sun is up high now. I have put off my visit to the council for too long. I have so much to say. I must report my sighting of the man last night on the road. I must tell about Keeney's dog. I must ask the council to find out where he was yesterday when he should have been in Juram. I have an idea—it's absurd—that Keeney will harm me if I go to the council, the way Lesley used to when she was ten and I was seven. How disloyal to think this of a fellow citizen. I should report myself to the council as well. The sooner I make my report and return to get some sleep, the better I'll feel.

Regan comes in, ready to go out . . .

I asked her if she would prefer to stay at home and leave the council visit to me. She said she believed she ought to come, but when she picked up her handbag her hands were trembling. I thought: What are we all coming to?

I said, "Let's go straightaway, then, and get it over with. We can leave Arthur at the Children's Hall."

As we walked along our quiet streets, I sensed that the trees, pleasant gardens and fountains were all subtly different. I can't explain it. Contentment, pleasure in these things, had gone. I felt as I did the day Regan bore Arthur—upset, different, how to describe it? Disturbed? It took me back to those dreadful walks home from school when I knew Lesley was waiting down the road behind the big elm, ready to pounce on me, throw me on the ground and kick and punch me.

The Council House stood there in the center of the big square with its marble statues and twenty small fountains. There were people in the square buying and selling foodstuffs and material. All spoke in low voices, smiled at each other—there were more people walking to and fro on the long marble floor of the House. The smell of aromatic tea from the restaurant was strong, as it usually is in the mornings. All over the country the doors of the Houses had just swung open, the citizens had entered and were talking to each other, the scent of the tea was wafting through hall, offices and corridors.

As we mounted the stairs to the town officer's room, I felt quite easy and calm in my mind.

We went in. Hendricks, the town officer, sat in an easy chair by his big windows, which look out onto the square. The light flooded into the elegant room. Regan and I sat down. Hendricks poured tea for us. He is a big man, ruddy-skinned, round-headed, with a mane of golden hair. The sunlight caught it as we sat there, turning the top of his head into a cap of gold strands. I thought as he sat solidly in his chair that he must look very like a ship's captain of the old days.

He looked at us with his large, very bright blue eyes. He said, "You look—disturbed." There was a touch of mild dislike in his tone. Well, it is bad to have citizens walking about looking hard-pressed and upset.

"We have a reason," Regan said, somewhat defensively.

"I am sure you have," he replied. There was a pause as we drank our tea. Hendricks went on looking at us and said finally, "Perhaps you would like to tell me what is amiss with you."

I disliked the attitude implied in that "with you." It came to me that Hendricks scented disturbance in our manner and did not wish to have any part in it. But I was confident that once we had told our stories his attitude would alter.

"There are two stories we must tell you," I said briskly. I had worked often with Hendricks on building projects. I told myself he knew me as a sensible man and a reliable citizen. "In fact," I said, "these tales may disturb you very much. But they must be told. I will tell one, and Regan the other. Mine concerns Keeney."

I was studying his face. His eyes flickered at the mention of Keeney's name. He reminded me suddenly of a big, healthy child being accused of some misdeed which he has decided to deny.

I told him how I had gone to visit Keeney, of the disturbed look of the place, of the locked door, of Mrs. Keeney's peculiar air and, finally, of the dog. Then I told him that Keeney had not been in Juram when we went there.

Henricks said, "I am amazed. Tell me your story now, Regan."

And she told him about our drive from Juram and the wild man caught in the headlights of the car.

When she had finished, Hendricks looked at us with his bright-blue eyes and said, "Thank you. We will look into all this."

"What are we going to do?" I asked.

"It will be discussed in the council," he said. He sat stiffly in his chair and looked at me as if he were expecting me to go.

"That hardly satisfies me," I said. "These are not matters which can wait. Or be left to the council alone to decide—they are for all the citizens. Above all, I would like to know your thoughts."

He drank some tea and said, "It all needs sifting."

"Sifting!" I cried. "Do you imply there are errors in our reports?"

"We need to get to the bottom of it," he said slowly.

Regan sat up straight in her chair and said, "Come, come, Hendricks. You have accounts of disconcerting events from two responsible citizens. Either you believe that we are making up stories to mislead you, or that we are both deluded, or you must take us seriously and share your thoughts and ideas with us."

Hendricks gazed out of the window at the people in the square. He said, "I don't know."

We both stared at him. Then Regan stood up and said, "This will have been a great shock to you. Perhaps we should approach your deputy?"

"Leave it with me. Leave it with me," he muttered.

When we went out of the room, he was still sitting there staring from the window. The sun had gone in.

On the stairs Regan said decidedly, "We must approach someone else."

I stopped with my hand on the rail. "I wonder," I said, "if anyone will listen to us."

Standing on the stairs, she began to laugh. I looked at her in alarm, conscious that down in the hall people were beginning to look up at her.

"What—?" I said.

"You think anyone we tell about these events will behave like Hendricks?" she asked. She was still smiling.

"In most cases," I said.

She nodded, fairly accepting the situation, which I could not truly understand. "I knew it," she said. "I told my mother this would happen."

"What would happen?" said I.

"I said that one day she would wake up and"—she began to laugh again—"and she would be able to ignore the fact that it was raining and go for a walk without protective clothing and come home and catch pneumonia and die saying what a lovely day it had been."

I became impatient. "I don't know what you're talking about, Regan," I said. "But I do know that you're making a public spectacle of yourself. Come home."

She sobered down and said, "I suppose so. That's all there is to do, isn't it?"

the drum beater is beating tonight. He beat for many hours last night and the night before, drumming through the night while we kept fire alight with many logs. We did not sleep till morning. We love that wild drumming and our blood runs hot and fast.

Regan, Arthur and I ate our evening meal in my room at the top of the house this evening. We had never done it before. Through the glass walls we can see south, over the broad, white streets of the city and forward, north, down over the lawn to the forest. The building work lay abandoned. The men had downed tools in the afternoon. Bricks lay in small piles along its length; tools had been flung down on the grass. The deep trench lay like a gash across the lawn between the forest and my house. The foundations were almost ready. The real work should begin tomorrow.

A cool breeze shook the trees of the forest. The sky overhead was cloudy. We sat on as the evening grew darker.

drums beating, drums, beating, beating, beating . . .

Suddenly, in the dusk, a figure appeared, treading over the ramparts, straddling them, head down to examine them.

"Keeney," Regan said.

We sat watching him in silence.

In the gloom we could not make out his face. We could see his thickset figure walking heavily along the course of the foundations, bending over the bricks and tools.

Then, in the dusk, he stood athwart the trench, raised his big head, stood with his large hands hanging by his sides and laughed out loud, up at the sky. From where we sat we could catch the faint sound of his laughter.

Arthur said nothing at first. He looked at Keeney laughing in the dark. Then he said, "What the boys say is right."

"What do they say?" I asked.

But he only shook his head.

I looked at Regan. At last I had identified the uneasiness, uncertainty, I had felt this morning and wondered at. It was fear of the future. Regan shot a glance at Arthur.

Regan stood up suddenly and said, "I'm going down to talk to Keeney." She ran out of the room. I heard her feet on the stairs and saw her running over the lawn—and suddenly Keeney was gone. He had vanished in the darkness.

Regan came back and said, "Come on, Arthur—bed."

Arthur followed her out of the room. It was quite dark now. I could see the trees ahead and the dim lights of the town behind.

Later I said to Regan, "Shall we leave for another city?"

"It would be the same anywhere else," she said.

"Other cities may be more ready to defend themselves."

"After five hundred years of developing our kind of life," she said mildly. "Electing councils, planting gardens, living by the law, playing gentle music, writing gentle verse, creating beauty, pleasure and peaceful scenes everywhere, avoiding every kind of violence, even that of birth and death, as if it were a dreadful, contagious disease—"

"As it is," I said.

"Oh, certainly," Regan said. "The cities came out of the ruin created by violence, aggression and competitiveness. But our fear of violence may have been as destructive as the violence itself. Do you know what it's like to rear a child in constant terror of its rages, its hatreds, its inability to tell the difference between order and chaos? And then to know, and have to pretend not to know, that all these things were in us once—and probably still are? You men—hypocrites, all of you. Your Unexpected Arrivals—unexpected by you, perhaps, not by us. Your solemn conclaves, decisions that someone must leave the city for this crime or that. We women conceal the worst for you—we hide births and deaths, we deal with malformed babies as we've always done, we get sent away for conceiving, for giving birth without permission, we hide children who bite, whine and scream until we can eradicate enough of them to present them as citizens, we secretly threaten the older children until they abandon their uncontrolled way. And then we conceal from ourselves what we do."

"I'm going to bed," I said.

"Go to bed," she said. "But we still have to face the results of what we've done. And what about Arthur?"

"What about him?" I asked.

"What about him indeed," she said savagely. "When it happens—this thing we aren't talking about—what will happen to Arthur?"

"I'll think about that in the morning," I said.

"Goodnight," she said. "Goodnight."

.   .   .

the drums do not beat anymore. It is the Holy Time.

It is happening at last.

Night after night we have come up to my room here at the top of the house. We have eaten and sat in silence as the darkness came down, catching the scents and gentle sounds from the city on one side, seeing the trees of the forest waving ahead on the other. The ramparts creep up a little each day. They are three feet high now and go all around the town at that height, like a toy wall to stop little children from straying.

Almost every night Keeney comes at the same time and paces the length of the wall as far as we can see, with his short, heavy steps. Sometimes I think I can see him smiling.

The matters of the dog and his unexplained absence have never been raised. No one wants to know. So Keeney pads around his ramparts every night in peace.

But tonight everything is different. The city—men, women and children—have all come out in the soft, evening air. They are strolling about or sitting in groups all over the lawn behind the ramparts. The women are sewing, children playing ball, men chatting. We can hear laughter.

Arthur, sitting quietly with us, does not ask why they are there or want to go out and join them. His eyes have grown large over the weeks. We cannot tell him what is wrong. But I think he knows.

And, as we watch, it grows darker. Torches are brought out on stands and the stands are placed on the grass. There is a fire in the center of my smooth lawn. The women are heating food. Now we see people moving in and out of the light cast by the fire and the torches. An innocent and pleasant scene.

As they did not know why they wanted the wall, so they do not know why they are gathering behind its unfinished length.

Now it grows dark, really dark. There is a full moon which shines down when the cloud is not over it. It eclipses the light thrown by the torches. The children are laughing harder. The men talk more, the womens' voices grow shriller. Some children are tired and crying.

Regan and Arthur sit with their arms around each other, looking from the window. We three notice, from our vantage point, that the branches on the forest trees are beginning to shake, although there is no wind.

Our citizens begin to sing an old song, a high, clear song. They stand in the dark singing. Tears begin to run down Regan's cheeks.

And the first man comes out of the trees. He is very pale. He blinks, screws up his face against the light. He is a small man dressed in skins, with blue tattoos up his arms. He seems about to return to the safety of the trees and has taken a step back when the bushes part again and his woman, long-haired, tattered and very thin, comes out and stands beside him. She has only one eye. The other one is covered by a mass of scarred skin. She pulls and something, a child, comes out of the forest and stands in front of her. It is a small boy, barefoot and wearing a torn pair of shorts. He stands, head lowered, holding her hand. His head is scabby; patches of hair have fallen out completely.

Regan looks at the trio calmly. What does she think? That the woman might be her sister Jessica, who walked out into the forest when she became pregnant without authority for the second time? That the woman might have been she?

Quietly, the bushes part again and again. More and more of the forest people appear and stand together silently at the edge of the trees, getting used to the light falling into their eyes. There is a woman in a stocking cap. There is a fat man gnawing on a bloody bone. Strange how, even at this point, I find the sight of the blood running down the corners of his mouth so disgusting.

"Keeney," whispers Regan, incredulous.

Yes, of course the man in front of the wild men is Keeney. He stands there in a suit, gnawing his piece of meat, talking to a small man in front who carries a club.

Our citizens go on singing. They have not yet seen the men and women on the other side of the barrier. But now, over the song, I hear the drums inside the forest pounding out a strong, meaningless rhythm; and as the drums get louder, the singers, at last, hear them, and their song falters and dies away. They peer across the ramparts, trying to see what is happening.

Keeney whispers to his companion, the small man. The forest people seem to gather themselves together. The drums beat louder. Suddenly the wild men and women begin to scream. Yelling in high, weird voices, they run to the ramparts, scramble over them and hurl themselves at the citizens, clubbing and spearing. In one corner Keeney's dog fells a child and mauls it. The child's mother tries to pull it off but the animal is tearing at its prey. The child's face screams in the moonlight. Then the moon is covered by a cloud. In the darkness there are howls. Torches are overturned. In the light thrown by the fire I see the townspeople milling about, falling, crying out. They are like children. They do not know what is happening to them.

Arthur is asleep, asleep forever now. Our house is quiet as Regan and I watch the carnage below.

Yet I am not shocked by the scene, by the thought of our city in flames, as it will be, the pillars, the flower gardens, the fountains all destroyed. Our city turned its back on pain, violence and disorder. Now the accumulation of all that chaos over five hundred years is on us.

The horde pauses in its work. The moon reappears. Our men, women and children lie dead and wounded on the torn-up grass. The people of the forest look at the house and suddenly, like leaves driven by the wind, they begin to run toward us. Keeney, at their head, glances up at the window where I am sitting. He opens his mouth in a scream and leads them on and on in my direction. Soon we will hear their feet on the stairs.

Soon. Very soon.

ABOUT THE EDITOR

Terry Carr has been acclaimed as one of the major editors of modern science fiction. He has received six Nebula Award citations from the Science Fiction Writers of America. Born in Oregon and now living in California, he has received Hugo Award nominations both as author and editor in the field.